Disorders of Human Learning, Behavior, and Communication

Ronald L. Taylor and Les Sternberg
Series Editors

Nirbhay N. Singh   Ivan L. Beale
Editors

Learning Disabilities
Nature, Theory, and
Treatment

Springer-Verlag
New York Berlin Heidelberg London Paris
Tokyo Hong Kong Barcelona Budapest

Nirbhay N. Singh, Department of Psychiatry, Medical College of Virginia, Richmond, VA 23298, USA

Ivan L. Beale, Department of Psychology, University of Auckland, Auckland, NZ

Series Editors: Ronald L. Taylor and Les Sternberg, Exceptional Student Education, Florida Atlantic University, Boca Raton, FL 33431-0991, USA

Library of Congress Cataloging-in-Publication Data
Learning disabilities: nature, theory, and treatment/Nirbhay N.
Singh, Ivan L. Beale, editors.
    p.   cm.—(Disorders of human learning, behavior, and
communication)
    Includes bibliographical references and indexes.
    ISBN 0-387-97590-X (alk. paper)
    1. Learning disabilities—United States.   I. Singh, Nirbhay N
II. Beale, Ivan L.   III. Series.
LC4705.L37 1991
371.9—dc20   91-14587

With 8 illustrations.

Printed on acid-free paper.

Production managed by Ellen Seham; manufacturing supervised by Jacqui Ashri.
Typeset by Best-set Typesetter Ltd., Chai Wan, Hong Kong.
Printed and bound by Edwards Brothers, Inc., Ann Arbor, MI.
Printed in the United States of America.

9 8 7 6 5 4 3 2 1

ISBN 0-387-97590-X Springer-Verlag New York Berlin Heidelberg
ISBN 3-540-97590-X Springer-Verlag Berlin Heidelberg New York

We dedicate this book to the women in our lives
for their understanding and unconditional love

Preface

Our aim in editing this volume was to bring together a collection of chapters that adequately represented the contemporary field of learning disabilities, to serve as a useful guide to advanced students, and as a resource for practitioners and researchers. We saw the need for a book that not only presents the central concerns of the mainstream but also illustrates a variety of promising approaches to nature, theory, and treatment.

Just as learning disability is not a unitary disorder, neither is it a unitary field of study. From the outset, theory and clinical practice have been characterized by a wide diversity of approaches, many of which have waxed and waned throughout the decades over which the field has developed. Particular themes have fizzled out only to reemerge in new clothes further down the line. The modern result is a field full of conflicting viewpoints on almost every aspect, from definition and diagnosis to etiology and treatment. It has attracted on the one hand excellent scientists and clinicians, and on the other, the worst kind of charlatans and exploiters of those searching for a magic cure. The field is too broad and complex for complete coverage to be possible in just a single volume. Any attempt to do so would result in such an oversimplification of ideas that nothing useful would be achieved. Instead we have been selective, choosing according to our own biased views, what to include in this volume.

Both editors cut their teeth on the experimental psychology of learning, at a time when theoretical models of learning, with their associated methods of hypothesis testing, were giving way to the inductive methods of the experimental analysis of behavior. In the early 1960s the experimental psychology of learning was being applied to developmental learning problems, and strong efforts were made to characterize such problems as resulting from deficits or delays in underlying psychological processes. Even though the broad learning theories never fulfilled their promise, this general approach has continued to be applied in learning disabilities research, and is appropriately represented in some of the chapters of this book. Learning theory has continued to provide a basis both for ideas about the nature of learning disabilities and ideas about remediation.

The emergence of applied behavior analysis from the experimental analysis of behavior has largely overtaken traditional learning models in the field of learning disabilities, especially in the remedial area. A principal reason is that applied behavior analysis is about changing behavior rather than explaining it. A second reason is that behavior analysis emphasizes the role of single-subject design in the assessment and remediation of the individual. It is therefore consonant with the growing recognition of the uniqueness of each person's learning problems and responsiveness to particular remedial efforts. Some chapters in this book illustrate well both present fruits and the future promise of this approach.

A third general framework for understanding and remediating learning disabilities has been provided by cognitive psychology, broadly represented in this book in chapters on metacognitive processes, information processing, neuropsychology, and language. The physiological basis of learning disabilities is recognized in those chapters dealing with the genetic and pharmacological aspects, as well as the visual deficit hypothesis.

This particular selection of topics indicates our attempt to represent those areas of the whole field that we think the serious student should know about. No doubt we have neglected themes that others would have liked to see included, and probably included areas that others would consider not deserving of a place. We think we have selected themes that will endure the next decade of development of learning disabilities research, and will prepare the student for what is to come as well as placing it in an historical context. We hope that those new to the learning disabilities field, as well as those already conversant with some aspects of it, will find this book helpful.

We wish to thank those authors whose work we have brought together, for entrusting their efforts to us, and for their patience with the editorial process. Any success is theirs as much as ours. We thank all those others who have helped us with this project, especially those friends and families we have neglected in the process. We are grateful to the staff at Springer–Verlag for their support and encouragement, to Carol Adams, Christopher Lavach, Trudy McDaniel, Ashvind Singh, and Subhashni Singh for assistance in the preparation of the indexes, and to our diligent secretaries who make us look more efficient and productive than we really are. Finally, we thank those teachers, clients, and colleagues who got us interested in this field in the first place.

Nirbhay N. Singh
Ivan L. Beale

Contents

Contributors

Michael G. Aman, Ph.D., The Nisonger Center for Mental Retardation and Developmental Disabilities, and Department of Psychology, The Ohio State University, Columbus, Ohio 43210-1205 USA

Ivan L. Beale, Ph.D., Department of Psychology, University of Auckland, Auckland, New Zealand

Ennio Cipani, Ph.D., Department of Special Education, University of the Pacific, Stockton, California 95211 USA

Diane E. D. Deitz, Ph.D., Department of Counseling, Educational Psychology and Special Education, Northern Illinois University, DeKalb, Illinois 60115 USA

Steven R. Forness, Ph.D., UCLA Neuropsychiatric Hospital, Los Angeles, California 90024 USA

Sarah E. Friebert, Ph.D., School of Medicine, Case Western Reserve University, Cleveland, Ohio 44106 USA

Michael M. Gerber, Ph.D., Department of Education, University of California at Santa Barbara, Santa Barbara, California 93106 USA

Paul J. Gerber, Ph.D., School of Education, Program of Special Education, Virginia Commonwealth University, Richmond, Virginia 23284-2020 USA

Steve Graham, Ed.D., Department of Special Education, University of Maryland, College Park, Maryland 20742 USA

Karen R. Harris, Ed.D., Department of Special Education, University of Maryland, College Park, Maryland 20742 USA

Stephen R. Hooper, Ph.D., Clinical Center for the Study of Development and Learning, and Department of Psychiatry, University of North Carolina, School of Medicine, Chapel Hill, North Carolina 27599 USA

Charles Hulme, D.Phil., Department of Psychology, University of York, Heslington, York YO1 5DD, England

Kathryn G. Karsh, Ed.D., Educational Research and Services Center, Inc., DeKalb, Illinois 60115 USA

Kenneth A. Kavale, Ph.D., Division of Special Education, The University of Iowa, Iowa City, Iowa 52240 USA

Katherine A. Larson, Ph.D., Department of Education, University of California at Santa Barbara, Santa Barbara, California 93106 USA

John Wills Lloyd, Ph.D., Department of Curriculum, Instruction, and Special Education, Curry School of Education, University of Virginia, Charlottesville, Virginia 22903-2495 USA

William Lovegrove, Ph.D., Department of Psychology, University of Wollongong, Wollongong, Australia 2500

Jamie Metsala, Ph.D., Centre for Applied Cognitive Science, The Ontario Institute for Studies in Education, Toronto, Ontario M5S 1V6

Robert D. Morrow, Ed.D., Department of Special Education Studies, University of the Pacific, Stockton, California 95211 USA

Ruth Pearl, Ph.D., Department of Educational Psychology, University of Illinois at Chicago, Chicago, Illinois 60680 USA

Michael Pressley, Ph.D., Department of Special Education, University of Maryland, College Park, Maryland 20742 USA

Henry B. Reiff, Ph.D., Department of Education, Western Maryland College, Westminster, Maryland 21157 USA

Alan C. Repp, Ph.D., Educational Research and Services Center, Inc., DeKalb, Illinois 60115 USA

Johannes Rojahn, Ph.D., The Nisonger Center for Mental Retardation, and Department of Psychology, The Ohio State University, Columbus, Ohio 43210-1296 USA

Christopher W. Schatschneider, Ph.D., Department of Psychology, Case Western Reserve University, Cleveland, Ohio 44106 USA

Elizabeth J. Short, Ph.D., Department of Psychology, Case Western Reserve University, Cleveland, Ohio 44106 USA

Linda S. Siegel, Ph.D., Department of Instruction and Special Education, The Ontario Institute for Studies in Education, Toronto, Ontario M5S 1V6

Judy Singh, M.S., School of Education, Division of Educational Studies, Virginia Commonwealth University, Richmond, Virginia 23284 USA

Nirbhay N. Singh, Ph.D., Department of Psychiatry, Medical College of Virginia, Richmond, Virginia 23298-0489 USA

Margaret Snowling, Ph.D., National Hospital's College of Speech Sciences, London, England

Robert T. Solman, Ph.D., School of Education Studies, University of New South Wales, Kensington 2033, Australia

Keith E. Stanovich, Ph.D., Department of Psychology, Oakland University, Rochester, Michigan 48063 USA

Jim Stevenson, M.Sc., Department of Psychology, University of Surrey, Guildford, Surrey, England

Brenda H. Stone, Ph.D. candidate, Department of Psychology, University of Rhode Island, Kingston, Rhode Island 02881-0808 USA

Lynette J. Tippett, Ph.D., Department of Psychology, University of Auckland, Auckland, New Zealand

W. Grant Willis, Ph.D., Department of Psychology, University of Rhode Island, Kingston, Rhode Island 02881-0808 USA

Part 1
Nature

1
History, Definition, and Diagnosis

KENNETH A. KAVALE and STEVEN R. FORNESS

"You should say what you mean," the March Hare went on.
"I do," Alice hastily replied, "at least—at least I mean what I say—that's the
   same thing, you know."
"Not the same thing a bit!" said the Mad Hatter.

—Lewis Carroll

For a field that did not officially exist 25 years ago, learning disabilities
(LD) has experienced unprecedented growth and has had significant
impact on special education in particular, and education in general. The
growth and development, however, have not been without cost and LD,
besides being the largest category of special education, is also the most
problematic (Gallagher, 1986). It is a field marked by controversy, conflict, and crisis, which has placed LD at a critical juncture. There is a
continuing call for positive and rational answers to the question: What do
we do about learning disabilities? A first step in answering this question
is to examine the relationship between the LD category introduced 25
years ago and the LD category of today. The purpose of this chapter is
to examine that relationship by focusing on the history, definition, and
diagnosis of LD.

History of Learning Disabilities

Weiderholt (1974) conceptualized the history of LD along two dimensions: a developmental sequence delineating historical time periods and a
type of disorder analysis. The developmental phases included foundation
(circa 1800–1940), transition (circa 1940–1963), and integration (circa
1963–1980). The types of disorders included spoken language, written
language, and perceptual motor functioning. Each phase and disorder
was placed in a matrix where the work of significant individuals was described and their contributions noted to show how that thinking gradually
advanced toward the LD concept.

The foundation phase was marked by basic research on brain function and dysfunction. In the area of spoken language, the study of brain injured adults who lost expressive or receptive language was the focus. Efforts were directed at localizing the site of injury (e.g., Broca, 1988; Wernicke, 1908) or describing a more generalized theory of brain function (e.g., Head, 1926; Hughlings Jackson, 1932). For written language, the focus was on dyslexia and efforts were directed at describing congenital word blindness (Hinshelwood, 1917). Orton (1937) summarized the nature and characteristics of reading disability and coined the term "strephosymbolia" ("twisted symbols") to describe the role of confused cerebral dominance in causing reading difficulties. The work of Goldstein (1939) was primary in the perceptual–motor area. In studying brain injured soldiers, Goldstein (1942) found a common set of behavioral symptoms that included figure–ground confusion, perceptual difficulties, distractibility, perseveration, rigidity, concrete thinking, and a complex of emotional problems. This work was expanded to brain injured children by Heinz Werner and Alfred Strauss. Werner and Strauss (1939) first differentiated mentally retarded (MR) children into either exogenous, retardation resulting from neurological defects, or endogenous, retardation resulting from MR familial factors. In studying the exogenous group, Strauss and Werner (see Strauss and Lehtinen, 1947 for a summary) found evidence substantiating that all behavioral characteristics described by Goldstein in brain injured adults could be found in brain injured children.

The transition phase was marked by emphases on the clinical study of learning problems in children. For spoken language, the emphasis was on providing models of the communication process (Osgood, 1957). The most significant was the development of the Illinois Test of Psycholinguistic Abilities (Kirk, McCarthy, & Kirk, 1968), designed to describe intraindividual variation in language and communication. In the area of written language, emphasis was on describing the nature and characteristics of retarded readers (e.g., Fernald, 1943; Monroe, 1932; Robinson, 1946). Attention was also directed at the concept of specific reading disability and its relationship to maturational lags (Bender, 1957; deHirsch, 1952). The controversial concept of neurological organization was also introduced to explain reading problems and to treat reading disorders (Delacato, 1966). The perceptual–motor area focused on the development of theoretical positions relating perceptual–motor deficits to academic problems. The earlier work on brain injured MR children was extended to children with average intelligence manifesting problems in learning (Cruickshank, Bice, Wallen, & Lynch, 1957; Strauss & Kephart, 1955). Kephart (1960) postulated that all behavior is motor based, and that motor development precedes and is essential for perceptual development. The goal is to achieve a perceptual–motor match. A variety of other perceptual–motor theories were proposed and emphasized, for example, visual perception (Frostig & Horne, 1964; Getman, 1965), motor behavior (Barsch, 1967; Cratty, 1969), or the integration of perceptual information (Ayres, 1972; Birch & Belmont, 1964).

The integration phase saw the emergence of LD as a category of special education. In 1963, Kirk addressed a conference and stated that, "Recently, I have used the term learning disabilities to describe a group of children who have disorders in the development of language, speech, reading, and associated communication skills needed for social interaction" (Kirk, S. 1975, p. 9). This group immediately voted to organize itself as the Association for Children with Learning Disabilities (ACLD), and the LD field was born.

The attention directed at LD served to spur legislative action, most notably the Children with Specific Learning Disabilities Act (1969), which permitted the establishment of school programs for LD students. Later, Public Law 91-230 (PL 91-230) established a 5-year program of research, teacher training, and model centers for LD. In 1971, federal funding supported the development of Child Service Demonstration Centers to provide for innovation and experimentation. In 1978, the U.S. Office of Education sponsored five Learning Disabilities Research Institutes to conduct research on basic issues (see *Exceptional Education Quarterly*, 1983). Besides ACLD, primarily a parent advocacy organization, other professional organizations were organized, most notably in 1968 when the Division for Children with Learning Disabilities (DCLD) was founded within the Council for Exceptional Children (CEC). Later, DCLD became the independent Council for Learning Disabilities (CLD) while the new Division for Learning Disabilities (DLD) was reorganized within CEC. The LD field in 1967 also launched its first professional journal, the *Journal of Learning Disabilities*, which was followed by *Learning Disability Quarterly* and, most recently, *Learning Disabilities Research* and *Learning Disabilities Focus* (now called *Learning Disabilities Research and Practice*). Thus, the LD field grew rapidly and quickly established itself as an important category of special education.

This rapid growth suggests that there was a need for a LD field. Clearly, there were students in school experiencing academic difficulties who would not meet the requirements for MR or behavior disorders (BD). The school failure was the primary symptom even though it was not anticipated and might be associated with a variety of correlative problems. Although such students had always existed, special education did not have an appropriate classification for them. Thus, the forces that converged to create an LD category were justified and led to a classification that was differentiated from low achievement.

The form of the new LD field, however, created a number of problems still requiring resolution. Although three types of disorders formed the bases of LD, the perceptual–motor disabilities were primary in conceptualizations. Despite the fact that LD students most frequently have difficulties in reading (Lewis, 1983) and there was some emphasis on language problems (Kirk & Kirk, 1971; Johnson & Myklebust, 1968), the perceptual–motor strand predominated in LD thinking. Perceptual–motor models, however, were the weakest theoretically and most speculative about the nature of brain–behavior relationships (Kavale, 1987c). It was probably the case that this emphasis was necessary to differentiate the new LD field from already existing professional fields dealing with reading disabilities and speech–language pathology. Thus, to forge its own identity the LD field focused its efforts around perceptual–motor disabilities and their implications. To sec how the perceptual–motor strand was most influential in LD thinking, it would be instructive to review the evolution of LD definitions.

Definitions of Learning Disability

What is a learning disability? The question is reasonable but any response is likely to engender considerable controversy and contention. Definition is the "problem" in LD and has been almost from the outset. Although LD definitions, on the surface, are no better or worse than those found in MR or BD, the LD field has been plagued by definitional problems that have seriously undermined progress in the field (Gallagher, 1984).

It appears that four factors have exacerbated the definitional problem. The first is the propensity of the LD field itself to reinforce the perception that definition is its basic problem (see *Journal of Learning Disabilities*, 1983). This self-flagellation only serves to draw attention to the problem and leads to the conclusion that no resolution is possible. The second is the failure to recognize that definitions serve several purposes, including to serve as a guide for diagnostic criteria, to determine eligibility for special education funds and services, to describe standards for selection of research subjects, and to differentiate between LD and other similar conditions (Keogh, 1983). The third problem has been the expanded interest in LD by other professional disciplines. Although a multidisciplinary perspective of LD is appropriate, these disciplines have viewed LD from their narrow perspective, which has prevented these views from coalescing into a genuine interdisciplinary perspective (e.g., see the volumes edited by Ceci, 1986). The final problem is the internecine rancor that has characterized the relationship among LD professional organizations. Professionals have tended to factionalize into groups that represent polar opposites with respect to substantive, methodological, and ideological issues. The most egregious example was the split between the CLD and the CEC parent organization, with the subsequent reorganization of the DLD within CEC.

The definitional problem is best examined by seeing how definitions have evolved over time. Definitions of LD have reflected the different concepts in vogue at the time but also, over time, have tended to become less specific and more generalized.

The Brain Injury Stage

The initial emphasis grew out of the work of Strauss and Werner who defined the characteristics of the brain injured child and the consequent disturbances in learning ability. Strauss and Lehtinen (1947) defined a brain-injured child as:

the child who before, during or after birth has received an injury to or suffered an infection of the brain. As a result of such organic impairment, defects of the neuromotor system may be present or absent; however, such a child may show disturbances in perception, thinking, and emotional behavior, either separately or in combination. This disturbance can be demonstrated by specific tests. These disturbances prevent or impede a normal learning process. (p. 4)

Along with a definition, Strauss and Lehtinen (1947) also established criteria for delineating brain injury. These criteria fell into two broad classifications: behavioral and biological, but later Strauss (see Strauss & Kephart, 1955) suggested that brain injury could be diagnosed solely on the basis of behavioral criteria (i.e., perceptual difficulties, conceptual difficulties, and behavioral problems) without reference to biological criteria (i.e., neurological signs, history indicating central nervous system [CNS] injury and no MR).

Objection, however, was raised to the brain injured terminology (e.g., Birch, 1964; Stevens & Birch, 1957; Wortis, 1957). These objections were best summarized by Sarason (1949), who suggested that the Strauss and Lehtinen definition results in tautological reasoning since, "The logically minded may of course object to a reasoning which appears to go like this: Some individuals with known brain damage have certain behavioral characteristics, therefore individuals with these same behavioral characteristics must be presumed to be brain damaged" (p. 415).

The difficulties surrounding the definition of "brain injury" led Stevens and Birch (1957) to suggest the term "Strauss syndrome" to describe the symptom complex associated with presumed brain damage. The delineation of the "Strauss syndrome" (brain damage behavior syndrome) shifted the focus away from brain damage as an etiological concept to those behavioral characteristics defining the child with "brain injury." This shift extended the brain damage concept to relatively borderline disturbances only suggestive of brain damage wherein "behavior and learning . . . may be affected by minimal brain injuries without apparent lowering of the intelligence" (Strauss & Lehtinen, 1947, p. 128).

The Minimal Brain Injury Stage

The clinical psychiatric literature had long recognized a condition of minor brain impairment that affected academic and behavioral functioning (Strother, 1973). The precursor was found in Gessell's concept of "minimal cerebral injury" (Gessell & Amatruda, 1941), later elaborated by Pasamanick and Knobloch (1959), who also introduced the hypothesis of a "continuum of reproductive casualty" that, depending on the degree and location of the injury, ranged from severe abnormalities (e.g., cerebral palsy, mental deficiency) to mild abnormalities (e.g., learning disability, behavioral difficulty). The most important outcome of these descriptions was the renewed emphasis on minor brain injury by the addition of "minimal" as a modifying adjective (Paine, 1962). A problem remained, however, because "Regardless of any adjectives, we have the overriding obligation to demonstrate, in terms of replicable, valid, and clearly defined criteria, that the multiplicity of aberrant behaviors we now attribute to 'minimal brain damage' are, in fact the result of damage to the brain" (Birch, 1964, p. 5).

Since brain injury was difficult to infer from behavioral signs alone, there was a suggestion that "damage" should be replaced by "dysfunction" (Bax & MacKeith, 1963), which indicates that brain injury may be present even with "as yet unnamed subtle deviations of brain function" (Clements & Peters, 1962). The additional modification to "dysfunction" carried the implication that there was no structural change in the brain but rather only deviation of function.

In an attempt to refine the minimal brain dysfunction (MBD) concept, a task force was launched to interpret the concept and the results were reported by Clements (1966), who defined MBD as a state descriptive of:

Children of near average, average, or above average general intelligence with certain learning or behavioral disabilities ranging from mild to severe, which are associated with deviations of functions of the central nervous system.

These deviations may manifest themselves by various combinations of impairment in perception, conceptualization, language, memory, and control of attention, impulse, or motor function. The aberrations may arise from genetic variation, biochemical irregularities, perinatal brain insults, or other illnesses or injuries sustained during the years which are critical for the development and maturation of the CNS or from unknown causes . . . During the school years, a variety of learning disabilities is the most prominent manifestation of the condition which can be designated by this term. (pp. 9–10)

In reviewing the symptomatology associated with MBD, Clements (1966) listed the 10 most frequently cited characteristics, in order of frequency:

1. hyperactivity
2. perceptual–motor impairments

3. emotional lability
4. general coordination deficits
5. disorders of attention (short attention span, distractibility, perseveration)
6. impulsivity
7. disorders of memory and thinking
8. specific learning disabilities:
   a. reading
   b. arithmetic
   c. writing
   d. spelling
9. disorders of speech and hearing
10. equivocal neurological signs and EEG irregularities

With the publication of Clements' (1966) report, MBD achieved wide currency and became synonymous for the learning difficulties experienced by some children in school. Through the efforts of Clements (1966) and later by Wender (1971), the learning problems manifested by children in school were now linked to the MBD condition. Within the educational domain, the MBD concept was incorporated by Myklebust (1964) in the definition of "psychoneurological learning disability," a condition wherein the difficulty in learning is the "result of a dysfunction in the brain and the problem is one of altered processes, not of a generalized incapacity to learn" (Johnson & Myklebust, 1967, p. 8).

The MBD concept, however, was subject to criticism in the educational community because it reflected a medical–etiological perspective rather than an educational focus concerned with assessment and remedial techniques for learning problems (Gallagher, 1966).

The Educational Discrepancy Stage

Along with efforts in the medical community to define MBD were efforts in the educational community to provide an educational focus for LD. The educational focus was most clearly seen in an emphasis on poor academic achievement, especially as defined by a discrepancy.

Bateman (1965) emphasized discrepancy, a difference between expected and actual achievement, in the definition of learning disorders:

Children who have learning disorders are those who manifest an educationally significant discrepancy between their estimated intellectual potential and actual level of performance related to basic disorders in the learning process, which may or may not be accompanied by demonstrable central nervous system dysfunction, and which are not secondary to generalized mental retardation, educational or cultural deprivation, severe emotional disturbance, or sensory loss. (p. 220)

The emphasis on academic difficulties was echoed in a definition offered by Kirk (1962), which omitted reference to etiology and emphasized learning problems. The Institute for Advanced Study (Kass & Myklebust, 1969) proposed a definition behavioral in nature and advantageous for special education that stated that:

Learning disability refers to one or more significant deficits in essential learning processes requiring special education techniques for remediation. Children with learning disability generally demonstrate a discrepancy between expected and actual achievement in one or more areas, such as spoken, read, or written language, mathematics, and spatial orientation. The learning disability referred to is not primarily the result of sensory, motor, intellectual, or emotional handicap, or lack of opportunity to learn. (pp. 378–379)

Thus education shifted LD definitions away from an etiological focus to a behavioral focus emphasizing the primary difficulty, reduced learning performance manifested in academic achievement deficits.

The Legislative Stage

The need for a single definition was recognized when the Bureau of Education for Handicapped (BEH) was made responsible for funding services for LD children. The search for an acceptable definition became the responsibility of the *National Advisory Committee on Handicapped Children* (NACHC) headed by Samuel A. Kirk. The definition formulated by this group was incorporated into Public Law 91-230 Children with Specific Learning Disabilities Act (1969) and stated that:

Children with special (specific) learning disabilities exhibit a disorder in one or more of the basic psychological processes involved in understanding or using spoken or written language. These may be manifested in disorders of listening, thinking, talking, reading, writing, spelling, or arithmetic. They include conditions which have been referred to as perceptual handicaps, brain injury, minimal brain dysfunction, dyslexia, developmental aphasia, etc. They do not include learning problems which are due primarily to visual, hearing or motor handicaps, to mental retardation, emotional disturbance, or to environmental disadvantage. (NACHC, 1968, p. 34)

The NACHC definition established the LD field as a category of special education and provided a framework for establishing LD programs. Although these administrative concerns were important, the NACHC definition failed to provide a clear delineation of LD parameters, which was functional for educational classification and intervention (Hammill 1974; McIntosh & Dunn, 1973). Thus, the definitional problem had not been solved with the NACHC definition but it did aid the administrative considerations of funding, program development, and keeping areas of exceptionality mutually exclusive.

More Proposed Definitions

The contention surrounding available LD definitions led to a variety of proposed definitions attempting to remedy the perceived deficiencies in existing LD definitions (e.g., Kirk & Gallagher, 1989; McIntosh & Dunn, 1973). A different approach to definition focused on teaching rather than characteristics. The rationale was based on the view that the most significant variable is instruction and efforts should be directed at practical matters like teaching the LD child (e.g., Hewett & Forness, 1983; Reynolds & Birch, 1977). These ideas were incorporated into the suggestion (Hallahan & Kauffman, 1976) that the term "learning disabilities" be used as a concept rather than a specific category of special education.

Although none of these proposed definitions or modifications were widely accepted, discussion over the term "learning disability" was useful because it directed attention to a particular problem (Ross, 1976). Consequently, the search for a definition continued, with more emphasis placed on attempts to operationalize the parameters of LD.

The Operational Definition Stage

Operational definitions were assumed to possess the advantage of converting theoretical concepts into specific quantified terms meaningful for special education practitioners. Kerlinger (1973) suggested that an operational definition assigns meaning to a construct or a variable by specifying the activities or "operations" necessary to measure it.

Chalfant and King (1976) analyzed LD definitions and found five common components, including task failure, exclusion factors, physiological correlates, discrepancy, and psychological correlates. For each component, operational criteria were presented. For example, the psychological process of attention was defined as the selective narrowing or focusing on the relevant stimuli in a situation and assessed through asking a series of questions.

Additional operational definitions were proposed that focused on discrepancy (Brenton & Gilmore, 1976) or on academic achievement deficits (Schere, Richardson, & Bialer, 1980). In both cases, the goal was to quantify the level of academic deficit in relation to intellectual level and grade level. Operational approaches, however, were plagued by both conceptual and technical difficulties and Deese (1972) criticized them for substituting the appearance of rigor for explicit theoretical verification and concluded that, "At best, what our example may have accomplished is a low grade of psychometric engineering and at most a systematic fraud" (p. 10).

More Legislative Definitions

The *Project on the Classification of Exceptional Children* (Hobbs, 1975) proposed the following LD definition:

Specific learning disability refers to those children of any age who demonstrate a substantial deficiency in a particular aspect of academic achievement because of perceptual or perceptual-motor handicaps, regardless of etiology or other contributing factors. (Wepman, Cruickshank, Deutsch, Morency & Strother, 1975, p. 306)

The Hobbs task force definition never gained wide popularity, which left the NACHC definition (1968) as the standard and was incorporated into Public Law 94-142 The Education for All Handicapped Children Act (1975). This law defined LD as follows:

Specific learning disability means a disorder in one or more of the basic psychological processes involved in understanding or in using language, spoken or written, which may manifest itself in an imperfect ability to listen, think, speak, read, write, spell, or to do mathematical calculations. The term includes such conditions as perceptual handicaps, brain injury, minimal brain dysfunction, dyslexia, and developmental aphasia. The term does not include children who have learning problems which are primarily the result of visual, hearing, or motor handicaps, or mental retardation, or emotional disturbance, or of environmental, cultural, or economic disadvantage (Section 5B-4).

Comparisons with the NACHC (1968) definition finds no substantive differences in the PL 94-142 definition. The primary reason for this was found in the conflicting nature of the reported LD research. In the congressional testimony, a congressman indicated that since there are 53 basic learning disabilities and 99 minimal brain dysfunctions, "No one really knows what a learning disability is" (Congressional Record, 1975). Consequently, until research establishes more definitive parameters, it was recommended that no major legislative changes be made in LD definitions.

Although the "new" LD definition did not offer any real substantive changes, the U.S. Office of Education (USOE) attempted to clarify the law and to provide procedural guidelines for interpretation. The primary criterion for LD definition was a "major discrepancy between expected achievement and ability which is not the result of other known and generally accepted handicapping conditions or circumstances" (USOE, 1976, 52404). A discrepancy was presumed to exist when a child was achieving at or below the expected achievement level that was based on a formula for determining a severe discrepancy level (SDL).

Although there was some support for the USOE approach (e.g., Sulzbacher & Kenowitz, 1977), many questions were raised about the proposed federal guidelines (e.g., Lloyd, Sabatino, Miller, & Miller, 1977). When asked about the appropriateness of the formula-based approach, the LD field at large responded unfavorably. The overwhelmingly negative evaluation of the formula-based procedure led the USOE to drop the SDL formula (Danielson & Bauer, 1978).

With the deletion of the discrepancy formula, the revised federal rules suggested that LD classification be based on the notion of an already existing severe discrepancy between capacity and achievement:

(1) the child does not achieve commensurate with his or her age and ability when provided with appropriate educational experiences, and (2) the child has a severe discrepancy between achievement and intellectual ability in one or more of seven areas relating to communication skills and mathematics abilities. (USOE, 1977, 65083)

A child may not be identified as LD if the discrepancy is *primarily* the result of: (a) a visual, hearing, or motor handicap, (b) mental retardation, (c) emotional disturbance, or (d) environmental, cultural, or economic disadvantage (USOE, 1977, 65083). Thus, after 10 years of modification intended to improve the definition of LD, the final regulations endorsed a definition that left the NACHC (1968) definition essentially intact.

The next attempt at formulating an LD definition was attempted by the National Joint Committee for Learning Disabilities (NJCLD) comprising individuals from eight major organizations concerned with learning disabilities (see Abrams, 1987). The NJCLD believed that the PL 94-142 definition possessed inherent weaknesses that limited its usefulness (Hammill, Leigh, McNutt, & Larsen, 1981).

The definition issued by the NJCLD was basically a theoretical statement specifying the characteristics delineating the LD condition. The NJCLD (1981) definition is as follows:

Learning disabilities is a generic term that refers to a heterogeneous group of disorders manifested by significant difficulties in the acquisition and use of listening, speaking, reading, writing, reasoning, or mathematical abilities. These disorders are intrinsic to the individual and presumed to be due to central nervous dysfunction. Even though a learning disability may occur concomitantly with other handicapping conditions (e.g., sensory impairment, mental retardation, social and emotional disturbance) or environmental influences (e.g., cultural differences, insufficient/inappropriate instruction, psychological factors), it is not the direct result of those conditions or influences. (Hammill et al., 1981, p. 636)

The most recent foray into definition was by the Interagency Committee on Learning Disabilities (ICLD) formed by congressional action to review and to assess federal research priorities, activities, and funding regarding LD (Silver, 1988). Five special literature surveys were commissioned to provide a synthesis and overview of present knowledge (see Kavanagh & Truss, 1988). With this information and input from organizations and individuals in public hearings, four primary recommendations were made to Congress. These included further study of prevalence, increasing the effectiveness of research, improving research dissemination, and a uniform definition based on modifications in the NJCLD definition. The modified definition reads (changes italicized):

Learning disabilities is a generic term that refers to a heterogeneous group of disorders manifested by significant difficulties in the acquisition and use of listening, speaking, reading, writing, reasoning or mathematical abilities, *or of social skills*. These disorders are intrinsic to the individual and presumed to be due to central nervous *system* dysfunction. Even though a learning disability may occur concomitantly with other handicapping conditions (e.g., sensory impairment, mental retardation, social and emotional disturbance), *with socio-environmental* influences (e.g., cultural differences, insufficient or inappropriate instruction, psychogenic factors), *and especially with attention deficit disorder, all of which may cause learning problems, a learning disability* is not the direct result of those conditions or influences.

The changes in the NJCLD definition reflected recent trends, especially the belief that social skills deficits are a primary characteristic of LD (see Forness & Kavale, 1991). Furthermore, the relation between LD and attention deficit disorder-hyperactivity was addressed, including the assumption that several handicapping conditions might cause learning problems but not LD.

The Problem of Definition

The primary conclusion to be drawn about LD definitions is that the more they change the more they stay the same. The endemic nature of the definitional problem is evidenced by diversity found in federal practice (Mann, Davis, Boyer, Metz, & Wolford, 1983), state definitions (Mercer, Forgnone, & Wolking, 1976), local districts (Perlmutter & Parus, 1983), professional opinion (Tucker, Stevens, & Ysseldyke, 1983), and research implementation (Kavale & Nye, 1981; Torgesen & Dice, 1980). Despite negative implications, the LD field appears to have reached a status quo: definitional alternatives have appeared but no major substantive changes have occurred. Why has the LD field experienced so much difficulty in providing a definition acceptable to a broad constituency?

Kavale and Forness (1985b) provided an explanation based on concepts from the history and philosophy of science. Kuhn (1970) suggested that scientific descriptions follow a relatively predictable sequence based on the notion of "paradigm." When significant events in science cause the community to coalesce around a single interpretation (paradigm), the field moves from a preparadigmatic period with multiple explanations to a paradigmatic period with an integrative scheme. Paradigms define normal science that aims at theoretical development until too many exceptions (i.e., anomalies) to paradigm-based expectations are found. These anomalies are tolerated until the paradigm loses its capacity to account for these novel events. Then there is a period of extraordinary science until a paradigm shift occurs that provides a new conceptual framework better able to account for the anomalous data.

The presence of anomalous data alone does not necessarily provide a paradigmatic shift (Watkins, 1970). In fact, the history of science suggests that established paradigms are typically held tenaciously and challenges are vigorously rejected (Toulmin, 1970). An analogous situation seems to exist in the LD field. The prominence of the perceptual–motor paradigm is at least partially attributable to the seminal work of Alfred Strauss, Heinz Werner, and their colleagues at the Wayne County Training School. Their long-standing and widely disseminated program of basic research laid the foundation from which concepts used to describe the nature of the present-day LD field evolved.

Through experimental investigation and conceptual exposition (Strauss & Kephart, 1955; Strauss & Lehtinen, 1947), the Strauss and Werner "paradigm" includes (in varying degrees) the following postulates: (a) LD fits a medical model (implying something wrong with the child), (b) LD is associated with (or caused by) neurological dysfunction, (c) LD academic problems are related to process disturbance, most notably in perceptual–motor functioning, (d) LD is associated with academic failure as defined by discrepancy notions, and (e) LD cannot be due primarily to other handicapping conditions. Thus, the Strauss and Werner paradigm provided the foundation for normal science in LD, and the resulting fundamental postulates regarding the nature of LD were incorporated into LD definitions. The question arises: How valid are these postulates?

Validity of LD Definition Components

Locus of the Problem

The Strauss and Werner paradigm suggests that the locus of the problem is within the affected individual. The medical (disease) model assumes that the disorder emanates from some underlying physical cause. The medical model perspective has proved problematic from the LD field because:

1. it places too much emphasis on etiology (Ullman & Krasner, 1965)
2. data collected from a medical model perspective are of little value to education (MacMillan, 1973)
3. there is an increased possibility of a "self-fulfilling prophecy" because medical model categories are basically deficit-oriented (MacMillan, 1973)
4. scant evidence suggests that LD emanates from solely a biophysical basis (Owen, Adams, Forrest, Stolz, & Fisher, 1971)
5. the medical model does not consider the role of psychosocial forces in producing LD (Forness, 1982).

Physiological Correlates

The most prominent physiological correlate of LD is CNS dysfunction. Strauss and Werner's brain damage syndrome was extended to include children with relatively borderline disturbance and was reduced to a subclinical level that resulted in the MBD category.

The MBD concept is controversial for the LD field because:

1. the fact of brain damage (i.e., an anatomic or physiological alteration of the brain) must be differentiated from the concept of brain damage (i.e., a pattern of behavioral disturbance not necessarily applicable to all brain damaged children) (Benton, 1973; Birch, 1964)
2. the adjective "minimal" in MBD is problematic since minimal manifestations may stem from maximal damage or vice versa (Bax & MacKeith, 1963)
3. researchers have failed to find evidence for a homogeneous MBD syndrome (Crinella, 1973; Paine, Werry, & Quay, 1968; Routh & Roberts, 1972)
4. most MBD children fail to reveal "hard signs" (e.g., unequivocal evidence of underlying CNS impairment) (Cohn, 1964; Kenny & Clemmens, 1971)
5. "soft signs" (i.e., minimal, borderline, or equivocal indices of CNS impairment) are only presumptive of neurological dysfunction (Ingram, 1973; Touwen & Sporrel, 1979)
6. assessments of "brain damaged" children find an excess of "soft signs" but no major "hard signs" (Hertzig, Bortner, & Birch, 1969; Nichols & Chen, 1981)
7. there has been a failure to differentiate LD and normal children on the basis of "soft signs" (Adams, Kocsis, & Estes, 1974; Copple & Isom, 1968)
8. problems have been associated with diagnosing MBD on the basis of electroencephalographic (EEG) abnormalities (Freeman, 1967; Hughes, 1978)
9. psychological tests used to diagnose MBD have failed to meet acceptable psychometric standards (Herbert, 1964; Yates, 1954).

Psychological Process Deficiency

Most definitions of LD posit deficits in basic psychological processes. These process deficits are assumed to be primary manifestations of MBD and to underlie LD academic difficulties. Strauss and Werner laid the foundation for process concepts in LD, which were later refined and extended (see Chalfant & Scheffelin, 1969; Kephart, 1964). The current definition of LD in federal law even begins with the phrase, "specific learning disability means a *disorder in one or more of the basic psychological processes . . .*" (italics added, *Federal Register*, 1977, p. 65083).

The assumptions of psychological process deficiencies underlying LD have been subject to debate because:

1. measures of psychological processes assess hypothetical constructs and generally fail to demonstrate satisfactory construct validity (Cronbach & Meehl, 1955)

2. the limited empirical support for the constructs (abilities) makes it difficult to determine whether performance differences are the result of "real" ability difference or of the method of measurement (Mann, 1971)
3. it has been found that the relationship of perceptual abilities (visual and auditory) to academic achievement is of insufficient magnitude to validate the assumption that perceptual skills underlie academic learning (Hammill & Larsen, 1974; Kavale, 1981, 1982; Larsen & Hammill, 1975)
4. LD children do not exhibit greater difficulty than normal children in their ability to integrate one modality function with another modality function (intersensory integration, cross modal perception, intermodal transfer) (Freides, 1974; Kavale, 1980a)
5. evidence suggests that although LD children may exhibit perceptual deficiencies, reading ability is not related to the degree of perceptual deficiency (Black, 1974; Camp, 1973; Fisher & Frankfurter, 1977; Hare, 1977; Zach & Kaufman, 1972)
6. among subgroups of LD children, only a very small percentage exhibit perceptual difficulties as the major performance deficit (Mattis, 1978; Speece, 1987; Vellutino, Steger, Moyer, Harding, & Niles, 1977).

Academic Failure

Strauss and Lehtinen (1947) implied the presence of academic difficulties when they stated, "the response of the brain-injured child to the school situation is frequently inadequate, conspicuously disturbing, and persistently troublesome" (p. 27). Academic failure in the form of a discrepancy has become the most commonly accepted characteristic of LD. Definitions of discrepancy appear straightforward, but are fraught with complex issues and problems, among which are the following:

1. there have been difficulties in measuring "actual" achievement based on standardized achievement measures: tests with the same labels may not measure similar functions, scores have been found to be partially dependent in the test series used, and problems in norming and scoring (especially grade equivalents) have been found (Hopkins & Stanley, 1981; Jenkins & Pany, 1978; Kelley, 1927)
2. "expected" achievement is usually measured on the basis of intelligence tests, which include a variety of definitions of intelligence and which reveal a high correlation with achievement measures (Boring, 1923; Coleman & Cureton, 1954; Gallager & Moss, 1963; McNemar, 1964)
3. underachievement has been confused with low achievement; the contrast is further complicated by the less-than-perfect correlation between aptitude and achievement (Lavin, 1965; Thorndike, 1963)

4. unreliability in discrepancy formulations has been caused by the phenomenon of statistical regression (McLeod, 1979; Hoffman, 1980)
5. difficulties are inherent in the procedures for determining discrepancy regardless of the method used (Algozzine, Forgnone, Mercer, & Trifiletti, 1979; Shepard, 1980; Ullman, 1969)
6. all methods do not yield identical levels of expected achievement and reveal large standard errors of estimate (Epps, Ysseldyke, & Algozzine, 1983; Forness, Sinclair, & Guthrie, 1983; Sinclair & Alexson, 1986).

Exclusion Component

Most LD definitions state that LD must not be primarily the result of other handicapping conditions. The origins of this tradition are found in Strauss and Werner's diagnostic criteria for minor brain injury, wherein endogenous MR was excluded by the criterion that "the immediate family history indicates that the child comes from a normal family stock and that he is, in general, the only one of the sibship so affected" (Strauss & Lehtinen, 1947, p. 12).

The exclusion component has not isolated a unique and distinct LD category because:

1. when considered within a behavioral rather than a categorical framework, LD reveals more similarities than differences when compared with MR and BD (for a complete discussion of the issues see Hallahan & Kauffman, 1977; Hewett & Forness, 1983)
2. diagnostic test data have not reliably differentiated LD from MR and BD (Gajar, 1979, 1980; Webster & Schenck, 1978)
3. although average intelligence (IQ = 100) is a requisite for inclusion in the LD category, findings have shown that anywhere from 25% to 40% of labeled LD children are depressed in intellectual functioning (Ames, 1968; Belmont & Belmont, 1980; Koppitz, 1971; Smith, Coleman, Dokeck, & Davis, 1977) (even though this is a systemic problem, it nonetheless illustrates the problematic nature of exclusionary criteria)
4. although social–emotional problems represent the primary defining characteristics of BD, the LD group has been shown to manifest significant social–emotional difficulties that cannot be distinguished reliably from the behavioral profiles of BD children (Barr & McDowell, 1974; McCarthy & Paraskevopoulos, 1969; Wagonseller, 1973)
5. although academic underachievement is considered the primary criterion for LD, it is equally applicable to both MR and BD (Forness, Bennett, & Tose, 1983; Kavale, Alper, & Purcell, 1981; Schwarz & Cook, 1971)

6. although problems resulting primarily from environmental, cultural, or economic disadvantages (CD) are eliminated from LD consideration, conditions in CD environments place a child at high risk for academic failure and can result in learning impairments that are indistinguishable from the cognitive, perceptual, linguistic, and information processing behavior considered primary charcteristics of LD (Hallahan & Cruickshank, 1973; Herrick, 1973; Kavale, 1980b). As a result, any exclusionary criteria are determined by an arbitrary cut-off point within a continuum of causality
7. because most LD children exhibit reading problems as a primary deficit and receive remedial reading instruction, there is difficulty in reliably differentiating LD and reading disability (RD) with respect to etiology, identification procedures, or intervention techniques (Artley & Hardin, 1976; Gaskins, 1982; Kirk, W. 1975; Lerner, 1975; Stanovich, 1988).

A Victim of Its Own History

Evaluation of the primary definitional components of LD derived from the "paradigm" developed by Strauss and Werner finds that each is problematic and cannot be accepted unequivocally. Subsequent research has failed to demonstrate the manifest validity of the paradigmatic assumptions found in LD definitions. Consequently, the Strauss and Werner "paradigm" cannot be viewed as a universal framework for scientific development in LD.

The problematic nature of the LD definitional components suggests that they represent anomalies in the sense discussed by Kuhn (1970). The presence of anomalies (i.e., exceptions to paradigm-based expectations) should lead to a period of extraordinary science that results in a paradigm shift. This shift provides new formulations that are presumed better able to account for the anomalies. Yet, the LD field has not really experienced any major paradigm shift: The Strauss and Werner paradigmatic assumptions are still found (in varying degree) in almost all LD definitions including the most recent one proposed by the NJCLD. Why has the LD field not experienced a paradigm shift that would explain the anomalies and provide new theoretical perspectives?

A partial explanation is found in the fact that the prevailing paradigm (Strauss and Werner) biases the research process so that there is more often an attempt to prove rather than to modify a theory that results in an "unconscious" focus on supportive data (Scheffler, 1967). The consequences are reflected in an inability of the paradigm to solve basic problems (e.g., definition) that may result in an acute sense of failure. This sense of failure makes the LD field even more resistant to changing

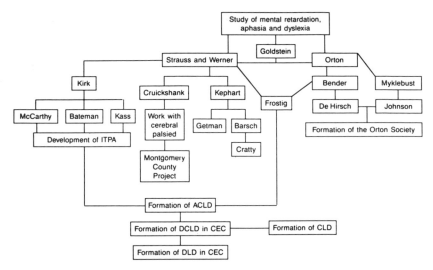

FIGURE 1.1. The "family tree" outlining the genealogical development of the LD field.

paradigms since there is a desire for closure on problems assumed to have been solved but that have not been really solved at all.

The history of the LD field reveals that the seminal work of Strauss and Werner evolved into the present-day LD field through the efforts of their colleagues and students who incorporated the paradigmatic assumptions of Strauss and Werner into basic conceptualizations about the nature of LD. The individuals involved represent key figures in shaping the fundamental thinking in both the emerging and present-day LD field. The historical linkages in the LD field have been outlined (Farnham–Diggory, 1978; Hallahan & Cruickshank, 1973; Hallahan & Kauffman, 1976; Haring & Bateman, 1977) and are illustrated in a "family tree" diagram shown in Figure 1.1.

The linkages shown are irrefutable in some instances, more tenuous in others, but everywhere they suggest the profound influence of Strauss and Werner on people and events in the evolution of LD. Consequently, there exists a bias toward the Strauss and Werner "paradigm" that is both profound and pervasive. Because proponents of competing paradigms operate in quite different spheres, the preeminent status of the Strauss and Werner group allows for the suppression of anomalies and the fitting of data into the prevailing paradigm. The tendency in normal science is to force empirical findings into the paradigm's conceptual structure. This can be accomplished by providing rationales for the lack of empirical support (anomalies), including methodological problems, inadequate instrumentation, and the presence of uncontrolled factors that conceal the expected effects. Paradigms necessarily reflect the assumptions, preconceptions, and models existing at the time of conception (Feigl, 1970). Unfortunately, the Strauss and Werner "paradigm" no longer appears to possess the explanatory power required to advance LD toward a mature scientific status.

Consequently, LD has become in essence a "victim of its own history" in the sense that its past continues to exert a strong influence and there has been a resistance to breaking the bonds of the past by reconceptualizing LD in light of new knowledge and new paradigms. A necessary step in resolving the problem of definition is to cease efforts at modifying available definitions. The LD field must be understood as really being in a preparadigmatic period where all conceptualizations are appropriate and justified for describing LD. Through constructive, cumulative, and co-operative endeavors, conceptualizations of LD can then coalesce into a common core that provides a critical description of LD (see Kavale & Forness, 1985a for a description of this process and the means by which it was accomplished in the MR field).

Diagnosis of Learning Disabilities

The problem of definitions is not just an academic one. The consequences of not having an acceptable definition has produced a number of negative influences. The problems created are not trivial and have called into question the very existence of LD (Algozzine & Ysseldyke, 1986). It is important first to reaffirm the reality of the LD phenomenon as a condition that imposes genuine constraints on a student's ability to function in school and not as some chimerical entity possessing only the reality imposed on it by an ever-changing political ideation (Kavale, 1987a). Then efforts can be directed at forging a consensus about the question: What is LD? In turn, an answer to that question will serve as a foundation for answering the equally important question: Who is LD? Answers to this later question are intimately related to diagnosis and a variety of issues that surround it.

Prevalence and Incidence

The lack of an acceptable LD definition has resulted in a failure to circumscribe parameters for the LD condition. The consequence is a vague and ill-defined set of boundary conditions and a failure to delimit the LD category. With the absence of standard practice, a student experiencing academic problems is said to be *like* an LD student. With no consensual basis for comparison, it becomes "fact" that the student *is* LD and simile becomes metaphor (Smith & Polloway, 1979). This situation multiplied many times over results in amoebalike growth for the LD field with no rational way to halt the increase.

Although it is virtually impossible to say with any precision how many LD students there should be, there seems to be agreement that currently there are too many students now identified as LD. Under the Public Law 94–142 guidelines, it was estimated that LD would represent 2% of the school-age population which, at the time (1975–1977), would be 17% of the handicapped population. To see the tremendous growth in LD, the PL 94-142 estimates should be compared with the *Ninth Annual Report to Congress* (1987), in which 5% of all school children were identified as LD, which represented 40% of all handicapped students. Analysis of the report reveals little rhyme or reason in LD identification by states. The percentages of LD in relation to the total handicapped population ranged from about 25% to 65%. The percentages of school enrollment for LD in the contiguous geographic regions of District of Columbia, Virginia, and Maryland were 3.5, 4.7, and 6.6, respectively (USOE, 1988). This variation also apparently has little relation to the total number of handicapped students in the state. For example, five states with more than 200,000 identified handicapped students classified, on average, 46% as LD whereas states with fewer than 50,000 identified handicapped students averaged 42% LD students. Thus, LD appears not to be a function of the total handicapped population.

To provide perspective, Table 1.1 shows the number of students served in four handicapping conditions over a 9-year period. Over that time period, LD established itself as the largest category of special education. Both speech impaired (the largest category in 1976–1977) and MR dropped in number while there was an increase in the number of students identified as emotionally disturbed (ED). Although the case can be made that ED was probably underrepresented (Forness, Sinclair, & Russell, 1984), no such case can be made for LD but it nevertheless revealed a 135% gain, indicating that, in absolute numbers, LD students more than doubled from about 800,000 to 1.9 million. This 135% gain is unprecedented

TABLE 1.1. Number of children served in four handicapping conditions in the United States and its territories over a nine-year period.[a]

Category	1976–77 year	1985–86 year	Differece	% of school enrollment	% in mainstream
Learning disabled	797,000	1,872,000	135% Gain	4.7%	77%
Speech impaired	1,303,000	1,128,000	14% Loss	2.9%	91%
Mentally retarded	907,000	686,000	29% Loss	1.7%	34%
Seriously emotionally disturbed	283,000	377,000	33% Gain	0.9%	46%

[a] Numbers rounded to the nearest thousand, and percents to the nearest hundreth.

especially when the number of individuals in all handicapping conditions incresed by only 16% since 1976–1977 (Edgar & Hayden, 1984–1985). Changes have thus occurred in other handicapping conditions but the absolute numbers remain rational and constrained in the sense of not showing wild and unabated increases. Undoubtedly, LD absorbed many of the losses experienced by the MR (see Forness & Kavale, 1984) and speech impaired categories but this still does not explain the LD increase and there is little justification for so many students being identified as LD (NJCLD, 1987).

Keogh (1988) provided perspective on the problem of LD numbers by differentiating between prevalence and incidence. Defining them in their epidemiological sense, incidence refers to the number of new cases of a disease in a population within a given time period whereas prevalence is the number of instances of a given disease in a given population at a given time. Prevalence thus includes the number of new cases in any given time period (incidence) plus cases already identified as exemplars of the condition. Most reports describing the number of students identified as LD (e.g., the *Annual Report to Congress*) are based on prevalence figures. Incidence figures are less frequently reported yet may be important in understanding changes in prevalence. Consequently, it should not be surprising then that prevalence increases annually.

As reflected in incidence figures, each year newly identified students are identified and provided services as LD. At the same time, many already identified pupils continue to be served as LD. What this means then is that the number entering programs is not balanced by the number leaving programs. As a consequence, the total number of identified LD cases (prevalence) increases. Further, it is likely that incidence numbers will increase. The notion of LD has been extended to younger and older age groups (preschool and adult populations), thereby enlarging the pool of possible cases, assessment techniques and screening programs are more refined and widely used, and advocacy programs for services are stronger. At the same time, interventions are only partially effective (Kavale & Glass, 1984) and many LD pupils continue to need services for many years (Kavale, 1988). In sum, both incidence and prevalence of LD will probably increase but will vary by state, given lack of agreed upon operational criteria for identification and given the still tenuous links between condition and intervention.

Identification Criteria

For the purposes of classifications, operational procedures are required to serve as the basis for any judgments. The confusion over the definition of LD, however, has led to controversy surrounding the most appropriate criteria (Epps, Ysseldyke, & Algozzine, 1985). Although many criteria have been suggested, consensus appears to have emerged only for discrepancy, that is, the difference between expected and actual achievement (Frankenberger & Harper, 1987; Mercer, Hughes, & Mercer, 1985). Because it is readily documented, discrepancy holds much appeal for LD identification but seems to have become a reified and deified concept. Discrepancy, however, is a hypothetical construct measured by other hypothetical constructs and really does not deserve its reified status (Kavale, 1987b).

Discrepancy possesses too many problems to be useful as the primary identification variable for LD (Algozzine & Ysseldyke, 1987). First are the many psychometric difficulties inherent in discrepancy. Cone and Wilson (1981) grouped discrepancy techniques into four categories: grade level deviation, expectancy formula, standard score comparison, and regression analysis. Evaluation of these methods (e.g., Berk, 1982; Reynolds, 1984–1985; Shepard, 1980) reveals that none of them is without limitations. Second is the adjective "significant," which is often attached to the notion of discrepancy. When is a discrepancy significant? One year, 2 years, 3 years, and are these the same across grade levels (see Algozzine, Ysseldyke, & Shinn, 1982)? Third is the influence of the measurement model on outcomes (Reynolds, 1985). Age-equivalent and grade-equivalent scores are inadequate because when used in discrepancy formulas, they overidentify pupils with below average IQ and pupils at the upper grade levels, and underidentify pupils with above average IQ.

The application of discrepancy formulas to real data reveals them to be less than satisfactory. Forness, Sinclair, and Guthrie (1983) demonstrated that the determination of severity can be affected simply by choosing from among eight available formulas. Similarly, Epps, Ysseldyke, and Algozzine (1983) found considerable variability in the number of identified LD pupils depending on the formula applied. It was concluded that discrepancy criteria result in LD identification being a function not only of pupil characteristics but the individual formula as well as the tests used to provide scores for the formula. When test data from a group of pupils identified as LD by an interdisciplinary formula were analyzed, Sinclair and Alexson (1986) found that 64% of that group were not identified by any discrepancy formula.

Perhaps the major difficulty with discrepancy is a conceptual one. Discrepancy has been linked to LD and practically defines LD but discrepancy is best linked theoretically to the concept of underachievement. Thorndike (1963) discussed the concept of discrepancy and demonstrated how it was legitimately associated with underachievement. The LD field, however, has elevated underachievement to the point where it is now the equivalent of LD. As Reynolds (1986) suggested, underachievement is a necessary condition for LD but it is not sufficient. The consequence of this reliance on discrepancy alone is a failure to differentiate LD and low achievement. It is probably the case that low achievement and underachievement are far closer conceptually to each other than either is to

LD. Yet, the work of Ysseldyke and his colleagues (e.g., Algozzine & Ysseldyke, 1983; Epps, Ysseldyke, & Algozzine, 1985; Ysseldyke, Algozzine, Shinn, & McGue, 1982) emphasizing the inability to distinguish between LD and low achievement is often cited to demonstrate the "LD problem." The problem, however, is not LD but the emphasis on a single criterion like discrepancy. Wilson (1985) argued that LD was a viable concept and rejected the idea that it should be eliminated in favor of more general concepts such as low achievement. Scruggs (1987) differentiated between expected and unexpected learning problems and showed how unexpected low achievement is really the precursor of LD. But the actual diagnosis of LD must transcend the unexpected school failure and include other factors that are intimately associated with LD.

The LD phenomenon is far more complex than that which is captured in the notion of discrepancy. Kavale and Nye (1985–1986) demonstrated how perceptual, memory, attention, linguistic, social, cognitive, and neuropsychological factors are an integral part of LD. In a meta-analysis of almost 1,100 studies that compared LD and normal comparison subjects along a variety of variables covering four major domains (linguistic, achievement, social/behavior, and neuropsychological), about 75% of LD subjects could be differentiated clearly but no area emerged as a primary source of LD, as shown in Figure 1.2.

When these domains were aggregated into individual variables, no differences emerged that would suggest that any single variable can be the focus for LD description. The LD subjects revealed about the same 75% level of differentiation across all variables. Because no single area emerged as a more significant descriptor, it was concluded that LD is a complex and multivariate problem involving a number of component deficits. With such a conclusion, it becomes necessary to acknowledge these variables in conceptualizations of LD and move away from the single criterion of discrepancy. The many variables influencing LD must be ordered and incorporated into identification models in addition to academic failure in order to operationalize fully the LD concept.

Classification

The inability to define LD has created significant problems in classification efforts. One major difficulty here is the negative influence it produces on research efforts. Without precision in sample definition, it is difficult to interpret research findings because of the limits it imposes on generalization and the possibilities for replication (Keogh, 1986). Although LD research is marked by many sources of variability, the major culprit is heterogeneity, which creates substantial differences in LD samples (Kavale, 1983). The nature and characteristics of LD samples vary so widely from one study to the next that it is virtually impossible to answer the question: Who are we talking about? (Olson & Mealor, 1981;

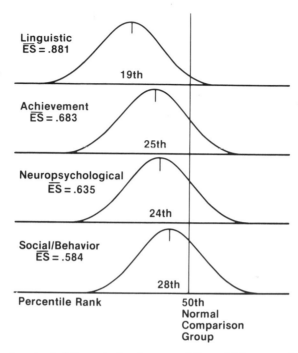

FIGURE 1.2. Level of differentiation between LD and N groups for the primary domains.

Torgesen & Dice, 1980). Kavale and Nye (1981) surveyed more than 300 research studies to determine the methods used to obtain LD samples. Although some attention was paid to sample selection, more than 50% defined their LD sample on the basis of previous diagnosis or classification. The use of these intact groups was compounded by the fact that neither the criteria nor the extent to which individual subjects met the criteria were reported.

The problem of heterogeneity has been acknowledged and, instead of simply decrying diversity, the LD field is attempting to organize the differences in a meaningful fashion (Keogh, 1988). The work on rationally defined subgroups (Torgesen, 1982), marker variables (Keogh, Major–Kingsley, Omori–Gordon, & Reid, 1982), and empirically derived subgroups (McKinney, 1984) represents a major step toward logically organizing the relationships among facets of LD.

McKinney (1984) reviewed the empirical subtyping efforts in LD and found them useful for providing a multiple syndrome paradigm for LD and reducing the overlap with other diagnostic groupings (e.g., MR, BD). Lyon and Risucci (1988) suggested that subtype research should be conducted within a developmental, longitudinal framework for maximum diagnostic utility. In this way, LD students could be differentiated from non-LD students at all age levels represented in the longitudinal design and then classified to identify homogeneous subgroups over time. Kavale and Forness (1987) offered a critical analysis of empirical subtyping research and, although viewing it positively, suggested that there be more commonality with respect to both methods and measures. In this way, a single classification scheme for LD might be developed that would aid diagnostic efforts by providing a taxonomy.

Assessment Practices

With LD becoming more and more an empirical phenomenon, assessment and testing itself becomes important. Psychometric data become all important and the LD field seems to possess a "diagnostic compulsion" where a student is tested and tested until qualified for LD services. This is because it is "known" that the student is LD. The position is similar to the Supreme Court's conception of pornography: they cannot define it but they know it when they see it. The diagnostic compulsion results in tremendous amounts of diagnostic data that never become translated into action for students (Ysseldyke, Algozzine, Richey & Graden, 1982).

The consequences are found in the nature of the Individual Education Plan (IEP) formulated. The IEP has become the cornerstone of PL 94-142 and was intended to ensure appropriate education and to guarantee the civil rights of handicapped children and their families (Forness, 1979). The intent was to involve parents fully as well as outside professionals in designing educational provisions. It should be noted, however, that the only persons actually required by federal law to participate in IEP development are the parent or guardian, the child's teacher, and a special education representative (Turnbull, Strickland, & Hammer, 1978). Although three parties must participate, other professionals could be, and in fact routinely are, involved. Examination of the IEP process reveals, however, that parents are not as influential in its outcome as the law might have intended (Gilliam & Coleman, 1981; Goldstein, Strickland, Turnbull & Curry, 1980). Much of the diagnostic assessment data seem actually to be ignored in determining need for programs and services (Ysseldyke, Algozzine, Richey, & Graden, 1982).

It has been suggested that the need to produce quantifiable data to satisfy rigid eligibility criteria has, in fact, forced school personnel not only to rely more heavily than necessary on psychometric tests but also unwittingly to favor the influence of the school psychologist or other evaluation personnel in determining outcome of IEP meetings, even though such professionals are relatively less involved or less familiar with the day-to-day process of a child's schooling (Forness & Kavale, 1987; Ysseldyke, Algozzine & Allen, 1981).

Problems exist with respect to what psychologists do but also with what they do it with. Here the issue is tests. For LD identification, the entire battery of tests used for diagnosis has come under attack in the past (Coles, 1978) and continues to be assailed currently (Shepard, 1989). Ysseldyke and Thurlow (1984) found that the tests used in LD diagnosis were often psychometrically inadequate in terms of the American Psychological Association (APA) (1974) technical standards for reliability, validity, and norms. In an earlier analysis of the tests used in LD model centers, Thurlow and Ysseldyke (1979) found that only 9 of the 30 most commonly used instruments (23%) met the three APA criteria. Later, Ysseldyke, Algozzine, Regan, and Potter (1980) found that the choice of technically adequate tests varied during the decision process, the earlier choices being more adequate than later choices. LaGrow and Prochnow–LaGrow (1982) applied the same three criteria to the 11 tests most commonly used for LD diagnosis in the state of Illinois, finding that only 2 (WISC–R and the PPVT) met all three technical requirements. It appears then that LD specialists are far more likely to use inadequate tests when compared, for example, to reading specialists whose emphasis on instruction leads them to use poor tests relatively infrequently (German, Johnson, & Schneider, 1985).

The use of inadequate tests is fostered because many states require a determination that an underlying process deficit is actually in evidence, principally because of the federal definitions emphasis on LD as first and foremost a disorder in basic psychologic processing. This requires administration of certain tests to assess visual perception, visual–motor ability, auditory perception, aspects of psycholinguistic functioning, or analysis of subtest clusters on the WISC–R. These tests and practices are most troublesome because of their dubious psychometric validity (Coles, 1978; Kavale & Forness, 1984, 1987b).

An example of problems inherent in the entire battery of psychoeducational tests is depicted in Table 1.2. This table summarizes findings on technical adequacy of three selected tests from among the three types of instruments comprising a typical test battery (Berk, 1984). Actually, there were 17 intellectual tests in this review, of which only 7 met adequate psychometric criteria in each area. There were 19 achievement tests reviewed, of which only 8 met such criteria. Results for the processing tests are quite typical in that virtually none of the 11 process tests reviewed met the criteria.

These findings were supported by Davis and Shepard's (1983) study of Colorado specialists' use of tests. Their sample was made up of LD teachers, school psychologists, and speech and language teachers. Overall they found that professionals "preferred" technically better tests, but frequently used those whose reliability and validity were inadequate. Tests were overrated by all three groups, and in general there was a notable lack of understanding of their psychometric limitations. Inter-

TABLE 1.2. Technical adequacy of selected tests.[a]

Type of test: test name	Norms	Validity	Reliability
Intellectual			
WISC–R	+	+	+
Stanford Binet	+	−	−
PPVT	−	+	+
Achievement			
PIAT	+	+	+
Woodcock Reading	+	+	+
WRAT	−	−	−
Psychologic processes			
Bender	−	−	−
ITPA	−	−	−
VMI	−	−	−

[a] Adapted from tabular data appearing in Berk (1984, p. 58–59).
Plus sign indicates minimum standards have been met in the area, minus sign indicates standards not met.

pretation was also problematic. More than one third of the professionals sampled could not correctly identify a significant discrepancy presented in percentiles, many overestimating the significance of lesser discrepancies. In this regard, McDermott (1981) suggested that errors of diagnostic decision making include inconsistent decision rules, inconsistent theoretical orientations, inconsistent weighting of diagnostic cues, and inconsistency of diagnostic style.

Clearly, there are problems on two levels: the actual psychometric properties of the tests and the level of knowledge of the practitioners who use them. Both are likely contributors to the inconsistencies in LD prevalence rates. Further, as noted by Shepard (1983), an additional problem in LD identification relates to specialists' limited understanding of normal variability. Because of the focus on referred pupils, many professionals do not have a frame of reference grounded in normal development. There is thus a tendency to interpret particular behaviors as deviant when in fact they fall well within the range of individual differences expected in normal variation. This may be an additional factor that contributes to the high number of pupils identified as LD.

Institutional Constraints and Perspectives

A number of recent analyses of LD programs (Christenson, Ysseldyke, & Algozzine, 1982; Mehan, Meihls, Hertweck, & Crowdes, 1981; Smith, 1982) have suggested that referral, identification, and placement of pupils was influenced, even determined in part, by "institutional constraints," that is, by federal and state legislation, by local school district policy, and by organizational arrangements within school districts.

Based on a microethnographic study of a school district, Mehan et al. (1981) identified powerful institutional constraints that affected the referral and placement process and, thus, the nature of educational decisions about individual pupils. These institutional constraints also determined in part the number of pupils identified as LD. In the district studied, 141 new referrals (5% of the total 2,781 pupils enrolled) were processed in a given calendar year. Thirty six (25.7%) of those referred were placed in LD programs; 28 pupils (20%) were reviewed by the school appraisal team but were retained in regular classes; another 29 pupils (20%) remained in regular classes because of interruptions in the review process—in a sense, a placement by default. Progress through the system was thus not primarily a function of pupil characteristics but rather was based on a number of decisions related directly to institutional constraints.

Differences in definitions of LD and in formal and informal screening practices across schools lead to differences in formal referral rates. In the school district studied by Mehan et al. (1981), formal referral rates varied because some building principals were actively involved in school-level informal screening and review. In such cases, students were expedited through the system, which led to faster placement decisions and higher placement rates. Time of year was also found to influence referral rates, with few referrals occurring in the last months of the school year (May and June) and the highest referral rates occurring in mid-fall (October) and mid-winter (February and March). These peaks and valleys in referrals reflected in part teachers' awareness of children's problems and their feelings that referral would lead to services. They also may have reflected the school psychologists' caseloads, the backlog of accumulated cases in the spring, or the availability of space in particular programs.

The effect of policy on prevalence may also be seen in the adoption of a 50% discrepancy formula as a criterion for identification as LD in New York State. As noted by Stark (1982), in the 12 months that followed adoption of the 50% discrepancy criterion, the number of pupils identified as LD dropped from 28,000 to 12,167. In essence, the 50% discrepancy criterion made the LD category available primarily to severely impaired pupils. This policy was challenged by 18 LD pupils and their parents on the basis that it exclusively affected one disability group (LD) and that it disfavored children with mild handicaps. The U.S. District Court ruled in their favor but was reversed by the U.S. Court of Appeals. In arriving at this decision, the Court acknowledged that the 50% discrepancy rule might deny special education opportunities to children but noted that federal regulations did not prohibit such a formula. Apparently, the number of children identified as LD in New York may vary as a function of particular court decisions.

Finally, Christenson et al. (1982) studied the influences on teachers' decisions to refer children for evaluation and possible placement. These investigators suggested that factors influencing referral could be grouped into two general categories. The first, institutional constraints, included three factors: organizational factors (e.g., district procedures), availability of services, and "hassle" (e.g., amount of paperwork, scheduling of meetings). The second, external pressures, included external agencies (advocacy groups), federal and state guidelines and regulations, parents, and the sociopolitical climate. The institutional and external pressures as perceived by teachers were consistent with the findings of other investigators, thus lending support to the importance of system variables in decision making (Morrison, MacMillan, & Kavale, 1985). It is likely that a range of system-related variables also influences decisions of placement teams, as it has been shown that team decisions are often not data based (Ysseldyke, Algozzine, & Mitchell, 1982).

The evidence, then, supports Mehan et al.'s (1981) contention that most LD classification decisions are "rarely developed in the manner implied by law" (p. 147), as the force of the many institutional constraints practically negates this possibility. This is not to imply anything negative about school district personnel, but rather to emphasize that classifications are not only functions of child characteristics but also involve powerful organization influences. Number of programs, availability of space, incentives for identification, range and kind of competing programs and services, number of professionals, and federal, state, and community pressures all affect classification decision about LD.

Conclusion

The problems imposed by the history, definition, and diagnosis of LD are not trivial. The consequences are significant and best illustrated when LD is compared and contrasted with its partners in the mildly handicapped. It appears that as a consequence of legislation and litigation, the MR and BD fields have changed their basic character. The mild MR population reveals a lower IQ level and less ability whereas the BD population includes more seriously disturbed students with significant social/emotional difficulties. The result is less equivocation about diagnosis and greater confidence in the reality of the designated population but also the exclusion of students who at another time and place might be eligible for mild MR or BD classification and consequent special services.

What is to become of these mild MR and BD students? If they need special education, the only alternative is LD classification. The declining IQ scores and increased emphasis on social/emotional deficits in LD students indicates that the LD field is incorporating students previously eligible under the MR and BD designations. The difficulties in differential diagnosis among mildly handicapping conditions has led the MR and BD fields to lower the level at which they will accept a student. The LD field cannot simply lower its acceptance level because the difficulties in defining LD have resulted in it being solely a quantitative phenomenon. But as MR and BD become more severe, they are qualitatively as well as quantitatively different. Although the nature of MR and BD change with greater severity, LD does not since it is only more of the same, such as a greater discrepancy or lower process test score. The MR and BD fields are thus no longer in a position to qualify students who do not manifest the qualitative characteristics associated with greater severity. This adjustment is not possible in the LD field and hence diagnosis is not as precise or unequivocal. The inherent flexibility in LD diagnosis leads to LD classification, in essence, because of the need for special education despite being abandoned by the MR and BD fields.

The LD category has thus become a catch-all classification. The situation is critical and the LD field must seek to regain its integrity (Kavale, 1987a). The LD field can no longer afford to accommodate the residual members of the MR and BD categories. These areas have maintained their integrity by modifying eligibility criteria and the LD field can do no less if the numbers problem is to be resolved. Any political, ideological, or philosophical pressures must be cast aside and attempts to regain control must be initiated. The LD field cannot afford the status quo and must define itself as something more than the designation for mildly handicapped students who do not qualify under any other category. Positive and productive efforts must be undertaken to define the boundaries of LD with enough precision to make LD an integral and legitimate part of special education.

References

Abrams, J. C. (1987). The National Joint Committee on Learning Disabilities: History, mission, process. *Journal of Learning Disabilities, 20,* 102–106.

Adams, R. M., Kocsis, J. J., & Estes, R. E. (1974). Soft neurological signs in learning-disabled children and controls. *American Journal of Diseases of Children, 128,* 614–618.

Algozzine, B., & Ysseldyke, J. (1983). Learning disabilities as a subset of school failure: The oversophistication of a concept. *Exceptional Children, 50,* 242–246.

Algozzine, R., Forgnone, C., Mercer, C., & Trifiletti, J. (1979). Toward defining discrepancies for specific learning disabilities: An analysis and alternatives. *Learning Disability Quarterly, 2,* 25–31.

Algozzine, R., & Ysseldyke, J. (1986). The future of the LD field: Screening and diagnosis. *Journal of Learning Disabilities, 19,* 394–398.

Algozzine, R., & Ysseldyke, J. (1987). Questioning discrepancies: Retaking the first step 20 years later. *Learning Disability Quarterly, 10,* 301–312.

Algozzine, B., Ysseldyke, J. E., & Shinn, M. (1982). Identifying children with learning disabilities: When is a discrepancy severe? *Journal of School Psychology, 20,* 298–305.

American Psychological Association. (1974). *Standards for educational and psychological tests.* Washington, DC: American Psychological Association.

Ames, L. B. (1968). A low intelligence quotient often not recognized as the chief cause of many learning difficulties. *Journal of Learning Disabilities*, *1*, 735–739.

Artley, A., & Hardin, V. (1976). A current dilemma: Reading disability or learning disability? *The Reading Teacher*, *29*, 361–366.

Ayres, A. J. (1972). *Sensory integration and learning disorders*. Los Angeles: Western Psychological Services.

Barr, K., & McDowell, R. (1974). Comparison of learning disabled and emotionally disturbed children on three deviant classroom behaviors. *Exceptional Children*, *39*, 60–62.

Barsch, R. H. (1967). *Achieving perceptual-motor efficiency: A space-oriented approach to learning*. (Vol. 1: Perceptual-motor curriculum). Seattle, WA: Special Child Publications.

Bateman, B. (1965). An educator's view of a diagnostic approach to learning disorders. In J. Hellmuth (Ed.), *Learning disorders*, (Vol. 1, pp. 219–239). Seattle, WA: Special Child Publications.

Bax, M., & MacKeith, R. (Eds.). (1963). *Minimal cerebral dysfunction*. Little Club Clinics in Developmental Medicine (No. 10). London: Heinemann.

Belmont, I., & Belmont, L. (1980). Is the slow learner in the classroom learning disabled? *Journal of Learning Disabilities*, *13*, 496–499.

Bender, L. (1957). Specific reading disability as a maturational lag. *Bulletin of the Orton Society*, *7*, 9–18.

Benton, A. L. (1973). Minimal brain dysfunction from a neuropsychological point of view. *Annals of the New York Academy of Sciences*, *205*, 29–37.

Berk, R. A. (1982). An evaluation of procedures for computing an ability achievement discrepancy score. *Journal of Learning Disabilities*, *17*, 262–265.

Berk, R. A. (1984). *Screening and diagnosis of children with learning disabilities*. Springfield, IL: Charles C. Thomas.

Birch, H. G. (1964). The problem of "brain damage" in children. In H. Birch (Ed.), *Brain damage in children: The biological and social aspects* (pp. 3–12). Baltimore: Williams & Wilkins.

Birch, H. G., & Belmont, L. (1964). Auditory-visual integration in normal and retarded readers. *American Journal of Orthopsychiatry*, *34*, 852–861.

Black, W. F. (1974). Achievement test performance of high and low perceiving learning disabled children. *Journal of Learning Disabilities*, *7*, 178–182.

Boring, E. G. (1923, June 6). Intelligence as the tests test it. *The New Republic*, pp. 35–37.

Brenton, B. W., & Gilmore, D. (1976). An operational definition of learning disabilities (cognitive domain) using WISC Full Scale IQ and Peabody Individual Achievement Test scores. *Psychology in the Schools*, *13*, 427–432.

Broca, P. (1888). *Memoires sur le cerveau de l'homme*. (Introduction by S. Pozzi). Paris: C. Reinwald.

Camp, B. W. (1973). Psychometric tests and learning in severely disabled readers. *Journal of Learning Disabilities*, *6*, 512–517.

Ceci, S. (Ed.). (1986). *Handbook of cognitive, social and neuropsychological aspects of learning disabilities* (Vols. I & II). Hillsdale, NJ: Lawrence Erlbaum.

Chalfant, J. C., & King, F. S. (1976). An approach to operationalizing the definition of learning disabilities. *Journal of Learning Disabilities*, *9*, 228–243.

Chalfant, J. C., & Scheffelin, M. A. (1969). *Central processing dysfunctions in children: A review of research* (NINDS Monograph No. 9). Washington, DC: U.S. Department of Health, Education, and Welfare.

Children with Specific Learning Disabilities Act (1969). Public Law 91–230. 91st Congress.

Christenson, S., Ysseldyke, J., & Algozzine, B. (1982). Institutional constraints and external pressures influencing referral decision. *Psychology in the Schools, 19*, 341–345.

Clements, S. D. (1966). *Minimal brain dysfunction in children. Terminology and identification* (NINDS Monograph No. 3, U.S. Public Health Service Publication No. 1415). Washington, DC: U.S. Department of Health, Education, and Welfare.

Clements, S. D., & Peters, J. E. (1962). Minimal brain dysfunction in the school-age child. *Archives of General Psychiatry, 6*, 185–197.

Cohn, R. (1964). The neurological study of children with learning disabilities. *Exceptional Children, 31*, 179–185.

Coleman, W., & Cureton, E. E. (1954). Intelligence and achievement: The jangle fallacy again. *Educational and Psychological Measurement, 14*, 347–351.

Coles, G. S. (1978). The learning disability test battery: Empirical and social issues. *Harvard Educational Review, 48*, 313–340.

Cone, T. E., & Wilson, L. R. (1981). Quantifying a severe discrepancy: A critical analysis. *Learning Disability Quarterly, 4*, 359–371.

Congressional Record Daily Edition. (July 29, 1975). H 7755.

Copple, P. J., & Isom, J. B. (1968). Soft signs and scholastic success. *Neurology, 18*, 304–308.

Cratty, B. J. (1969). *Perceptual-motor behavior and educational processes.* Springfield, IL: Charles C. Thomas.

Crinella, F. M. (1973). Indentification of brain dysfunction syndromes in children through profile analysis: Patterns associated with so-called "minimal brain dysfunction." *Journal of Abnormal Psychology, 82*, 33–45.

Cronbach, L. J., & Meehl, P. E. (1955). Construct validity in psychological tests. *Psychological Bulletin, 52*, 281–301.

Cruickshank, W. M., Bice, H. V., Wallen, N. E., & Lynch, K. S. (1975). *Perception and cerebral palsy: A study of figure-background relationship.* Syracuse, NY: Syracuse University Press.

Danielson, L. C., & Bauer, J. N. (1978). A formula-based classification of learning disabled children: An examination of the issues. *Journal of Learning Disabilities, 11*, 163–176.

Davis, W. A., & Shepard, L. A. (1983). Specialists' use of tests and clinical judgment in the diagnosis of learning disabilities. *Learning Disability Quarterly, 6*, 128–138.

Deese, J. (1972). *Psychology as science and art.* New York: Harcourt Brace Jovanovich.

deHirsch, K. (1952). Specific dyslexia or strephosymbolia. *Folia Phoniatrica, 4*, 231–248.

Delacato, C. H. (1966). *Neurological organization and reading.* Springfield, IL: Charles C. Thomas.

Edgar, E., & Hayden, A. H. (1984–1985). Who are the children special education should serve and how many children are there? *The Journal of Special Education, 18*, 523–539.

Epps, S., Ysseldyke, J. E., & Algozzine, B. (1983). Impact of different definitions of learning disabilities on the number of students identified. *Journal of Psychoeducational Assessment, 1*, 341–352.

Epps, S., Ysseldyke, J. E., & Algozzine, B. (1985). An analysis of the conceptual framework underlying definitions of learning disabilities. *Journal of School Psychology, 23*, 133–144.

Exceptional Education Quarterly. (1983). Summary of the Institutes for Research in Learning Disabilities, *4*, 1–144.

Farnham–Diggory, S. (1978). *Learning disabilities.* Cambridge, MA: Harvard University Press.

Federal Register. (1977, December 29, pp. 65082–65085). Washington, DC: Government Printing Office.

Feigl, H. (1970). The "orthodox" view of theories: Remarks in defense as well as critique. In M. Radner & S. Winokur (Eds.), *Minnesota studies in the philosophy of science, Vol. IV: Analyses of theories and methods of physics and psychology* (pp. 3–16). Minneapolis: University of Minnesota Press.

Fernald, G. M. (1943). *Remedial techniques in basic skill subjects.* New York: McGraw-Hill.

Fisher, D. F., & Frankfurter, A. (1977). Normal and disabled readers can locate and identify letters: Where's the perceptual deficit? *Journal of Reading Behavior, 9*, 31–43.

Forness, S. R. (1979). Developing the individual educational plan: Process and perspectives. *Education and Treatment of Children, 2*, 43–54.

Forness, S. (1982). Diagnosing dyslexia: A note on the need for ecologic assessment. *American Journal of Diseases of Children, 136*, 794–799.

Forness, S., Bennet, L., & Tose, J. (1983). Academic deficits in emotionally disturbed children revisited. *Journal of Child Psychiatry, 22*, 140–144.

Forness, S. R., & Kavale, K. (1984). Education of the mentally retarded: A note on policy. *Education and Training of the Mentally Retarded, 19*, 239–245.

Forness, S. R., & Kavale, K. (1987). De-psychologizing special education. In R. B. Rutherford, C. M. Nelson, & S. R. Forness (Eds.), *Severe behavior disorders of children and youth* (pp. 2–14). San Diego: College-Hill Press.

Forness, S. R., & Kavale, K. (1991). Social skills deficit as primary learning disabilities: A note on problems with ICLD diagnostic criteria. *Learning Disabilities, Research and Practice, 6*, 44–49.

Forness, S. R., Sinclair, E., & Guthrie, D. (1983). Learning Disability discrepancy formulas: Their use in actual practice. *Learning Disability Quarterly, 6*, 107–114.

Forness, S. R., Sinclair, E., & Russell, D. (1984). Serving children with emotional or behavioral disorders: Implications for educational policy. *American Journal of Orthopsychiatry, 544*, 22–32.

Frankenberger, W., & Harper, J. (1987). States' criteria and procedures for identifying learning disabled children: A comparison of 1981/82 and 1985/86 guidelines. *Journal of Learning Disabilities, 20*, 118–121.

Freeman, R. D. (1967). Special education and the electroencephalogram: Marriage of convenience. *Journal of Special Education, 2*, 61–73.

Freides, D. (1974). Human information processing and sensory modality: Cross-modal functions, information complexity, memory, and deficit. *Psychological Bulletin, 81*, 284–310.

Frostig, M., & Horne, D. (1964). *The Frosting Program for the development of visual perception. Teacher's guide.* Chicago: Follett.

Gajar, A. H. (1979). Educable mentally retarded, learning disabled, emotionally disturbed: Similarities and differences. *Exceptional Children, 45*, 470–472.

Gajar, A. H. (1980). Characteristics across exceptional categories: EMR, LD, and ED. *Journal of Special Education*, *14*, 165–173.

Gallagher, J. J. (1966). Children with developmental imbalances: A psycho-educational definition. In W. Cruickshank (Ed.), *The teacher of brain-injured children* (pp. 23–43). Syracuse, NY: Syracuse University Press.

Gallagher, J. J. (1984). Learning disabilities and the near future. *Journal of Learning Disabilities*, *11*, 120–123.

Gallagher, J. J. (1986). Learning disabilities and special education: A critique. *Journal of Learning Disabilities*, *19*, 595–601.

Gallagher, J. J., & Moss, J. (1963). New concepts of intelligence and their effect on exceptional children. *Exceptional Children*, *30*, 1–5.

Gaskins, I. W. (1982). Let's end the reading disabilities/learning disabilities debate. *Journal of Learning Disabilities*, *15*, 81–83.

German, D., Johnson, B., & Schneider, M. (1985). Learning Disability versus reading disability: A survey of practitioners diagnostic populations and test instruments. *Learning Disability Quarterly*, *8*, 141–157.

Gessell, A. L., & Amatruda, C. S. (1941). *Developmental diagnosis*. New York: Hoeber.

Getman, G. N. (1965). The visuomotor complex in the acquisition of learning skills. In J. Hellmuth (Ed.), *Learning disorders* (Vol. 1, pp. 49–76). Seattle, WA: Special Child Publications.

Gilliam, J. E., & Coleman, M. C. (1981). Who influences IEP committee decisions? *Exceptional Children*, *47*, 642–644.

Goldstein, K. (1939). *The organism*. New York: American Book Co.

Goldstein, K. (1942). *After-effects of brain injuries in war: Their evaluation and treatment*. New York: Grune & Stratton.

Goldstein, S., Strickland, B., Turnbull, A., & Gurry, L. (1980). An observation analysis of the IEP conference. *Exceptional Children*, *46*, 278–286.

Hallahan, D. P., & Cruickshank, W. M. (1973). *Psychoeducational foundations of learning disabilities*. Englewood Cliffs, NJ: Prentice-Hall.

Hallahan, D. P., & Kauffman, J. M. (1976). *Introduction to learning disabilities: A psycho-behavioral approach*. Englewood Cliffs, NJ: Prentice-Hall.

Hallahan, D. P., & Kauffman, J. M. (1977). Labels, categories, behaviors: ED, LD, and EMR reconsidered. *Journal of Special Education*, *11*, 139–149.

Hammill, D. D. (1974). Learning disabilities: A problem in definition. *Division for Children with Learning Disabilities Newsletter*, *4*, 28–31.

Hammill, D., & Larsen, S. (1974). The relationship of selected auditory perceptual skills to reading ability. *Journal of Learning Disabilities*, *7*, 429–436.

Hammill, D. D., Leigh, J., McNutt, G., & Larsen, S. (1981). A new definition of learning disabilities. *Learning Disability Quarterly*, *4*, 836–842.

Hare, B. (1977). Perceptual deficits are not a cue to reading problems in second grade. *Reading Teacher*, *30*, 624–627.

Haring, N., & Bateman, B. (1977). *Teaching the learning disabled child*. Englewood Cliffs, NJ: Prentice-Hall.

Head, H. (1926). *Aphasia andd kindred disorders of speech* (Vols. I & II). London: Cambridge University Press.

Herbert, M. (1964). The concept and testing of brain-damage in children: A review. *Journal of Child Psychology and Psychiatry*, *5*, 197–216.

Herrick, M. J. (1973). Disabled or disadvantaged: What's the difference? *Journal of Special Education*, *7*, 381–386.

Hertzig, M. E., Bortner, M., & Birch, H. G. (1969). Neurologic findings in children educationally designated as "brain-damaged." *American Journal of Orthopsychiatry*, *39*, 473–446.

Hewett, F. M., & Forness, S. R. (1983). *Education of exceptional learners* (3rd ed.). Boston: Allyn & Bacon.

Hinshelwood, J. (1917). *Congenital word blindness*. London: Lewis.

Hobbs, N. (Ed.). (1975). *The futures of children: Categories, labels, and their consequences*. San Francisco: Jossey-Bass.

Hoffman, J. V. (1980). The disabled reader: Forgive us our regressions and lead us not into expectations. *Journal of Learning Disabilities*, *13*, 7–11.

Hopkins, K. D., & Stanley, J. C. (1981). *Educational and psychological measurement and evaluation* (6th ed.). Englewood Cliffs, NJ: Prentice-Hall.

Hughes, J. R. (1978). Electroencephalographic and neurophysiological studies in dyslexia. In A. L. Benton & D. Pearl (Eds.), *Dyslexia: An appraisal of current knowledge* (pp. 205–249). New York: Oxford University Press.

Ingram, T. T. S. (1973). Soft signs. *Development Medicine and Child Neurology*, *15*, 527–529.

Jackson, J. H. (1932). On the nature and duality of the brain (1874). In J. Taylor (Ed.), *Selected writings of John Hughlings Jackson* (Vol. 2, pp. 129–145). London: Hodder-Stoughton.

Jenkins, J. R., & Pany, D. (1978). Standardized achievement tests: How useful for special education? *Exceptional Children*, *44*, 448–453.

Johnson, D., & Myklebust, H. R. (1967). *learning disabilities: Educational principles and practices*. New York: Grune & Stratton.

Journal of Learning Disabilities. (1983). Feature: LD definition. *16*, 6–31.

Kass, C. E., & Myklebust, H. R. (1969). Learning disability: An educational definition. *Journal of Learning Disabilities*, *2*, 377–379.

Kavale, K. A. (1980a). Auditory-visual integration and its relationship to reading achievement: A meta-analysis. *Perceptual and Motor Skills*, *51*, 947–955.

Kavale, K. A. (1980b). Learning disability and cultural-economic disadvantage: The case for a relationship. *Learning Disability Quarterly*, *3*, 97–112.

Kavale, K. A. (1981). The relationship between auditory perceptual skills and reading ability: A meta-analysis. *Journal of Learning Disabilities*, *14*, 539–546.

Kavale, K. A. (1982). Meta-analysis of the relationship between visual perceptual skills and reading achievement. *Journal of Learning Disabilities*, *15*, 42–51.

Kavale, K. A. (1983). Fragile findings, complex conclusions, and meta-analysis in special education. *Exceptional Education Quarterly*, *4*, 97–106.

Kavale, K. A. (1987a). On regaining integrity in the LD field. *Learning Disabilities Research*, *2*, 60–61.

Kavale, K. A. (1987b). Theoretical issues surrounding severe discrepancy. *Learning Disabilities Research*, *3*, 12–20.

Kavale, K. A. (1987c). Theoretical quandries in learning disabilities. In S. Vaughn & C. Bos (Eds.), *Research in learning disabilities: Issues and future directions* (pp. 111–131). Boston: Little, Brown/College Hill.

Kavale, K. A. (1988). The long-term consequences of learning disabilities. In M. Wang, M. Reynolds, & H. Walberg (Eds.), *Handbook of special education: Research and practice* (Vol. 2, pp. 303–344). Oxford: Pergamon Press.

Kavale, K. A., Alper, A. E., & Purcell, L. L. (1981). Behavior disorders, reading disorders, and teacher perceptions. *The Exceptional Child*, *28*, 114–118.

Kavale, K. A., & Forness, S. R. (1984). A meta-analysis assessing the validity of

Wechsler Scale profiles and recategorization: Patterns or parodies? *Learning Disability Quarterly*, 7, 136–156.

Kavale, K. A., & Forness, S. R. (1985a). Learning disability and the history of science: Paradigm or paradox? *Remedial and Special Education*, 6 (4), 12–24.

Kavale, K. A., & Forness, S. R. (1985b). *The science of learning disabilities*. San Diego: College-Hill Press.

Kavale, K. A., & Forness, S. R. (1987). The far side of heterogeneity: A critical analysis of empirical subtyping research in learning disabilities. *Journal of Learning Disabilities*, 20, 374–382.

Kavale, K. A., & Glass, G. V. (1984). Meta-analysis and policy decisions in special education. In B. K. Keogh (Ed.), *Advances in special education: Vol. IV: Documenting program impact* (pp. 195–247). Greenwich, CT: JAI Press.

Kavale, K. A., & Nye, C. (1981). Identification criteria for learning disabilities: A survey of the research literature. *Learning Disability Quarterly*, 4(4), 383–388.

Kavale, K. A., & Nye, C. (1986). Parameters of learning disabilities in achievement, linguistics, neuropsychological, and social/behavior domains. *The Journal of Special Education*, 19(3), 443–458.

Kavanagh, J. F., & Truss, T. J. (1988). *Learning diabilities: Proceedings of the national conference*. Parkton, MD: York Press.

Kelley, T. L. (1927). *Interpretation of educational measurements*. New York: World Book.

Kenny, T. J., & Clemens, R. C. (1971). Medical and psychological correlates in children with learning disabilities. *Journal of Pediatrics*, 78, 273–277.

Keogh, B. K. (1983). Classification, compliance, and confusion. *Journal of Learning Disabilities*, 16, 25.

Keogh, B. K. (1986). Future of the LD field: Research and practice. *Journal of Learning Disabilities*, 19, 455–460.

Keogh, B. K. (1988). Learning disabilities: Diversity in search of order. In M. C. Wang, M. C. Reynolds, & H. J. Walberg (Eds.), *The handbook of special education: Research and practice* (Vol. 2, p. 4). Oxford: Pergamon Press.

Keogh, B. K., Major–Kingsley, S., Omori–Gordon, H., & Reid, H. P. (1982). *A system of marker variables for the field of learning disabilities*. Syracuse, NY: Syracuse University Press.

Kephart, N. C. (1960). *The slow learner in the classroom*. Columbus, OH: Charles E. Merrill.

Kephart, N. C. (1964). Perceptual-motor aspects of learning disabilities. *Exceptional Children*, 31, 201–206.

Kerlinger, F. N. (1973). *Foundations of behavioral research* (2nd ed.). New York: Holt, Rinehart & Winston.

Kirk, S. A. (1962). *Educating exceptional children*. Boston: Houghton-Mifflin.

Kirk, S. A. (1975). Behavioral diagnosis and remediation of learning disabilities. In S. A. Kirk & J. M. McCarthy (Eds.), *Learning disabilities: Selected ACLD papers* (pp. 7–10). Boston: Houghton-Mifflin.

Kirk, S. A., & Gallagher, J. J. (1989). *Educating exceptional children* (6th ed.). Boston: Houghton-Mifflin.

Kirk, S. A., & Kirk, W. D. (1971). *Psycholinguistic learning disabilities: Diagnosis and remediation*. Urbana, IL: University of Illinois Press.

Kirk, S. A., McCarthy, J., & Kirk, W. D. (1968). *Illinois test of psycholinguistic abilities*. Urbana, IL: University of Illinois Press.

Kirk, W. D. (1975). The relationship of reading disabilities to learning disabilities. *Journal of Special Education*, 9, 132–137.

Koppitz, E. M. (1971). *Children with learning disabilities: A five year follow-up study*. New York: Grune & Stratton.

Kuhn, T. S. (1970). *The structure of scientific revolutions* (2nd ed.). Chicago: University of Chicago Press.

LaGrow, S. J., & Prochnow–LaGrow, J. E. (1982). Technical adequacy of the most popular tests selected by responding school psychologists in Illinois. *Psychology in the Schools*, 19, 186–189.

Larsen, S., & Hammill, D. (1975). The relationship of selected visual perceptual skills to academic abilities. *Journal of Special Education*, 9, 281–291.

Lavin, D. E. (1965). *The prediction of academic performance*. New York: Russell Sage Foundation.

Lerner, J. W. (1975). Remedial reading and learning disabilities: Are they the same or different? *Journal of Special Education*, 9, 119–131.

Lewis, R. B. (1983). Learning disabilities and reading: Instructional recommendations from current research. *Exceptional Children*, 50, 230–240.

Lloyd, J., Sabatino, D., Miller, T. & Miller, S. (1977). Proposed federal guidelines: Some open questions. *Journal of Learning Disabilities*, 10, 69–71.

Lyon, G. R., & Risucci, D. (1988). Classification of learning disabilities. In K. A. Kavale (Ed.), *Learning disabilities: State of the art and practice* (pp. 44–70). Boston: Little, Brown/College Hill.

MacMillan, D. L. (1973). *Behavior modification in education*. New York: Macmillan.

Mann, L. (1971). Psychometric phrenology and the new faculty psychology: The case against ability assessment and training. *Journal of Special Education*, 5, 3–14.

Mann, L., Davis, C. H., Boyer, C. W., Metz, C. M., & Wolford, B. (1983). LD or not LD, that was the question: A retrospective analysis of Child Service Demonstration Center's compliance with the federal definition of learning disabilities. *Journal of Learning disabilities*, 16, 14–17.

Mattis, S. (1978). Dyslexia syndromes: A working hypothesis that works. In A. L. Benton & D. Pearl (Eds.), *Dyslexia: An appraisal of current knowledge* (pp. 43–58). New York: Oxford University Press.

McCarthy, J. M., & Paraskevopoulos, J. (1969). Behavior patterns of learning disabled, emotionally disturbed, and average children. *Exceptional Children*, 35, 69–74.

McDermoff, P. A. (1981). Sources of error in the psychoeducational diagnosis of children. *Journal of School Psychology*, 19, 31–34.

McIntosh, D., & Dunn, L. (1973). Children with major specific learning disabilities. In L. Dunn (Ed.), *Exceptional children in the schools: Special education in transition* (2nd ed., p. x). New York: Holt, Rinehart & Winston.

McKinney, J. D. (1984). The search for subtypes of specific learning disability. *Journal of Learning Disabilities*, 17, 43–50.

McLeod, J. (1979). Educational underachievement: Toward a defensible psychometric definition. *Journal of Learning Disabilities*, 12, 322–330.

McNemar, Q. (1964). Lost: Our intelligence? Why *American Psychologist*, 19, 871–882.

Mehan, H., Meihls, J. L., Hertweck, A., & Crowdes, M. (1981). Identifying handicapped students. In S. B. Bacharach (Ed.), *Organizational behavior in school and school districts* (pp. 381–428). New York: Praeger.

Mercer, C. D., Forgnone, C., & Wolking, W. D. (1976). Definitions of learning disabilities used in the United States. *Journal of Learning Disabilities, 9*, 376–386.

Mercer, C., Hughes, C., & Mercer, A. (1985). Learning Disabilities definitions used by state education departments. *Learning Disability Quarterly, 8*, 45–55.

Monroe, M. (1932). *Children who cannot read*. Chicago: University of Chicago Press.

Morrison, G. M., MacMillan, D. L., & Kavale, K. A. (1985). System identification of learning disabled children: Implications for research sample. *Learning Disability Quarterly, 8*, 2–10.

Myklebust, H. R. (1964). Learning disorders: Psychoneurological disturbances in childhood. *Rehabilitation Literature, 25*, 354–359.

National Advisory Committee on Handicapped Children. (1968). *First Annual Report, Special Education for Handicapped Children*. Washington, DC: U.S. Office of Education, Department of Health, Education, & Welfare.

National Joint Committee on Learning Disabilities. (1981, January 30). *Learning Disabilities: Issues on definition*. A position paper of the National Joint Committee on Learning Disabilities.

National Joint Committee on Learning Disabilities. (1987). Issues in the delivery of educational services to individuals with learning disabilities. *Journal of Learning Disabilities, 20*, 286–288.

Nichols, P. L., & Chen, T. C. (1981). *Minimal brain dysfunction: A prospective study*. Hillsdale, NJ: Erlbaum.

Olson, J. L., & Mealor, D. J. (1981). Learning Disabilities identification: Do researchers have the answer? *Learning Disability Quarterly, 4*, 389–392.

Orton, S. T. (1937). *Reading, writing, and speech problems in children*. New York: Norton.

Osgood, C. E. (1957). Motivational dynamics of language behavior. In M. R. Jones (Ed.), *Nebraska symposium on motivation* (p. 4). Lincoln: University of Nebraska Press.

Owen, F. W., Adams, P. A., Forrest, T., Stolz, L. M., & Fisher, S. (1971). Learning disorders in children: Sibling studies. *Monographs of the Society for Research in Child Development, 36* (Serial No. 144).

Paine, R. S. (1962). Minimal chronic brain syndromes in children. *Developmental Medicine and Child Neurology, 4*, 21–27.

Paine, R. S., Werry, J. S., & Quay, H. C. (1968). A study of "minimal brain dysfunction." *Developmental Medicine and Child Neurology, 10*, 505–529.

Pasamanick, B. & Knoblooh, H. (1959). Syndrome of minimal cerebral damage in infancy. *Journal of the American Medical Association, 170*, 1384–1387.

Perlmutter, B. F., & Parus, M. V. (1983). Identifying children with learning disabilities: A comparison of diagnostic procedures across school districts. *Learning Disability Quarterly, 6*, 321–328.

Public Law 94–142. (November 29, 1975). *Education for All Handicapped Children Act*. U.S. Congress.

Reynolds, C. R. (1984–1985). Critical measurement issues in learning disabilities. *Journal of Special Education, 18*, 451–475.

Reynolds, C. R. (1985). Measuring the aptitude-achievement discrepancy in learning disability diagnosis. *Remedial and Special Education*, *6*, 37–55.

Reynolds, C. R. (1986). Toward objective diagnosis of learning disabilities. *Special Services in the Schools*, *2*, 161–176.

Reynolds, M. C., & Brich, J. W. (1977). *Teaching exceptional children in all America's schools: A first course for teachers and principals*. Reston, VA: Council for Exceptional Children.

Robinson, H. M. (1946). *Why pupils fail in reading*. Chicago: University of Chicago Press.

Ross, A. O. (1976). *Psychological aspects of learning disabilities and reading disorders*. New York: McGraw-Hill.

Routh, D. K., & Roberts, R. D. (1972). Minimal brain dysfunction in children: Failure to find evidence for a behavioral syndrome. *Psychological Reports*, *31*,307–314.

Sarason, S. B. (1949). *Psychological problems in mental deficiency*. New York: Harper & Row.

Scheffler, I. (1967). *Science and subjectivity*. Indianapolis: Bobbs-Merrill.

Schere, R. A., Richardson, E., & Bialer, I. (1980). Toward operationalizing a psychoeducational definition of learning disabilities. *Journal of Abnormal Child Psychology*, *8*, 5–20.

Schwarz, R. H., & Cook, J. J. (1971). Mental age as a predictor of academic achievement. *Education and Training of the Mentally Retarded*, *6*, 12–15.

Scruggs, T. E. (1987). Theoretical issues surrounding severe discrepancy: A discussion. *Learning Disabilities Research*, *3*, 21–23.

Shepard, L. A. (1980). An evaluation of the regression discrepancy method for identifying children with learning disabilities. *Journal of Special Education*, *14*, 80–91.

Shepard, L. A. (1983). The role of measurement in educational policy: Lessons from the identification of learning disabilities. *Educational Measurement: Issues and Practice*, *2*, 4–8.

Shepard, L. A. (1989). Identification of mild handicaps. In R. L. Linn (Ed.), *Educational measurement* (3rd ed.) (pp. 545–572). New York: Macmillan.

Silver, L. B. (1988). A review of the federal government's Interagency Committee on Learning Disabilities report to Congress. *Learning Disabilities Focus*, *3*, 73–80.

Sinclair, E., & Alexson, J. (1986). Learning disability discrepancy formulas: Similarities and differences among them. *Learning Disability Research*, *1*, 112–118.

Smith, J. D. & Polloway, E. A. (1979). Learning disabilities: Individual needs or categorical concerns? *Journal of Learning Disabilities*, *12*, 525–528.

Smith, M. L. (1982). *How educators decide who is learning disabled: Challenge to psychology and public policy in the schools*. Springfield, IL: Charles C. Thomas.

Smith, M. D., Coleman, J. C., Dokeck, P. R., & Davis, E. E. (1977). Intellectual characteristics of school labeled learning disabled children. *Exceptional Children*, *43*, 352–357.

Speece, D. L. (1987). Information processing subtypes of learning-disabled readers. *Learning Disabilities Research*, *2*, 91–102.

Stanovich, K. E. (1988). Explaining the differences between the dyslexic and the garden-variety poor reader: The phonological-core variable-difference model. *Journal of Learning Disabilities*, *21*, 590–604.

Stark, J. H. (1982). Tragic choices in special education: The effects of scarce resources on the implementation of P.L. 94–142. *Connecticut Law Review*, *14*, 477–493.

Stevens, G. D., & Birch, J. W. (1957). A proposal for clarification of the terminology used to describe brain-injured children. *Exceptional Children*, *23*, 346–349.

Strauss, A. A., & Kephart, N. C. (1955). *Psychopathology and education of the brain-injured child, Vol. II: Progress in theory and clinic*. New York: Grune & Stratton.

Strauss, A. A., & Lehtinen, L. E. (1977). (1947).*Psychopathology and education of the brain-injured child*. New York: Grune & Stratton.

Strother, C. R. (1973). Minimal cerebral dysfunction: An historical overview. *Annals of the New York Academy of Sciences*, *205*, 6–17.

Sulzbacher, S., & Kenowitz, L. A. (1977). At last, a definition of learning disabilities we can live with? *Journal of Learning Disabilities*, *10*, 67–69.

Thorndike, R. L. (1963). *The concepts of over- and under-achievement*. New York: Columbia University, Teachers College Press.

Thurlow, M. L., Ysseldyke, J. E. (1979). Current assessment and decision-making practices in model LD programs. *Learning Disability Quarterly*, *2*, 15–24.

Torgesen, J. K. (1982). The use of rationally defined subgroups in research on learning disabilities. In J. P. Das, R. F. Mulcahy, & A. F. Wall (Eds.), *Theory and research in learning disabilities* (pp. 111–131). New York: Plenum.

Torgesen, J. K., & Dice, C. (1980). Characteristics of research on learning disabilities. *Journal of Learning Disabilities*, *13*, 531–535.

Toulmin, S. (1970). Does the distinction between normal and revolutionary science hold water? In I. Lakatos & A. Musgrave (Eds.), *Criticism and the growth of knowledge* (pp. 39–47). Cambridge: Cambridge University Press.

Touwen, B. C. L., & Sporrel, T. (1979). Soft signs ans MBD. *Developmental Medicine and Child Neurology*, *21*, 528–538.

Tucker, J., Stevens, L., & Ysseldyke, J. (1983). Learning disabilities: The experts speak out. *Journal of Learning Disabilities*, *16*, 6–14.

Turnbull, A. P., Strickland, B., & Hammer, S. E. (1978). The individualized education program—Part 1: Procedural guidelines. *Journal of Learning Disabilities*, *11*, 40–46.

Ullman, C. A. (1969). Prevalence of reading disabilities as a function of the measure used. *Journal of Reading Disabilities*, *2*, 556–558.

Ullman, L. P., & Krasner, L. (1965). *Case studies in behavior modification*. New York: Holt, Rinehart & Winston.

U.S. Office of Education. (1976). Public Law 94–142 regulations: Proposed rulemaking. *Federal Register*, *41*, 52404–52407.

U.S. Office of Education. (1977). Public Law 94–142 regulations: Procedures for evaluating specific learning disabilities. *Federal Register*, *42*, 65082–65085.

U.S. Department of Education. (1987). *Ninth annual report to Congress on the implementation of the education of the handicapped act*. Washington, DC: Office of Special Education.

U.S. Department of Education. (1988). *Tenth annual report to Congress on the implementation of the education of the handicapped act*. Washington, DC: Office of Special Education.

Vellutino, F. R., Steger, B. M., Moyer, S. C., Harding, C. J., & Niles, J. A. (1977). Has the perceptual deficit hypothesis led us astray? *Journal of Learning Disabilities, 10*, 375–385.

Wagonseller, B. R. (1973). Learning disability and emotional disturbance: Factors relating to differential diagnosis.*Exceptional Children, 40*, 205–206.

Weiderholt, J. L. (1974). Historical perspectives on the education of the learning disabled. In L. Mann & D. Sabatino (Eds.). *The second review of special education* (pp. 103–152). Philadelphia: JSE Press.

Wender, P. H. (1971). *Minimal brain dysfunction in children*. New York: John Wiley.

Wepman, J. M., Cruickshank, W. M., Deutsch, C. P., Morency, A., & Strother, C. R. (1975). Learning disabilities. In N. Hobbs (Ed.). *Issues in the classification of children* (Vol. 1, pp. 300–317). San Francisco: Jossey-Bass.

Werner, H., & Strauss, A. (1939). Problems and methods of functional analysis in mentally deficient children. *Journal of Abnormal and Social Psychology, 34*, 37–62.

Wernicke, C. (1908). The symptom-complex of aphasia. In A. Church (Ed.), *Diseases of the nervous system* (pp. 265–324). New York: Appleton.

Wilson, L. R. (1985). Large-scale learning disability identification: The reprieve of a concept. *Exceptional Children, 52*, 44–51.

Wortis, J. (1957). A note on the concept of the "brain-injured" child. *American Journal of Mental Deficiency, 61*, 204–206.

Yates, A. J. (1954). The validity of some psychological tests of brain damage. *Psychological Bulletin, 51*, 359–379.

Ysseldyke, J. E., Algozzine, B., & Allen, D. (1981). Participation of regular education teachers in special education team decision making: A naturalistic investigation. *Elementary School Journal, 82*, 160–165.

Ysseldyke, J. E., Algozzine, B., & Mitchell, J. (1982). Special education team decision-making: An analysis of corrent practice. *Personnel and Guidance Journal, 60*, 308–313.

Ysseldyke, J. E., Algozzine, B., Regan, R., & Potter, M. (1980). Technical adequacy of tests used by professionals in simulated decision making. *Psychology in the Schools, 17*, 202–209.

Ysseldyke, J. E., Algozzine, B., Richey, L., & Graden, J. (1982). Declaring students eligible for learning disability services: Why bother with the data? *Learning Disability Quarterly, 5*, 37–43.

Ysseldyke, J. E., Algozzine, B., Shinn, M. R., & McGue, M. (1982). Similarities and differences between low achievers and students classified learning disabled. *Journal of Speical Education, 16*, 73–85.

Ysseldyke, J. E., & Thurlow, M. L. (1984). Assessment practices in special education: Adequacy and appropriateness. *Educational Psychologist, 9*, 123–136.

Zach, L., & Kaufman, J. (1972). How adequate is the concept of perceptual deficit for education? *Journal of Learning Disabilities, 5*, 351–356.

2
An Alternative to the Food Processor Approach to Subtypes of Learning Disabilities

Linda S. Siegel and Jamie Metsala

Individuals who are called learning disabled are a heterogeneous group. Most investigators and educators would agree with this statement. While there is recognition of the reality of this heterogeneity, awareness of it does not seem to have had any impact on research or educational management of these children. Most articles on learning disabled children do not categorize them into subtypes but treat them as one unitary group. Educational placements and discussions of children with learning disabilities also do not attempt to categorize individuals on the basis of their type of learning disability.

At least part of the reason for the disregard of subtypes has been a lack of agreement as to what these subtypes actually are or even whether they exist at all. There are several reasons why the existence of subtypes has been ignored. These reasons include problems with the definition of who is learning disabled and difficulties with the statistical procedures used to delineate the subtypes.

In this chapter we review these issues and consider what is actually known about the issue of subtypes of learning disabilities. We also suggest a way of conceptualizing subtypes that is consistent with empirical evidence and theoretical formulations.

Definitional Issues

A complication that makes most of the studies of subtypes difficult or impossible to interpret is the lack of a precise definition of a learning disability. Before we explore the question of subtypes, there are some definitional issues that need to be clarified. These issues include the role of intelligence (IQ test scores) in the assessment of learning disabilities, the discrepancy definition, the actual manner in which achievement is measured, and the arbitrary nature of any definition.

Discrepancy Definition

Siegel (1988a, 1988b) has argued that conceptualizations of learning disability should ignore both the concept of IQ and the discrepancy definition of learning disabilities. The discrepancy concept means that an individual is considered learning disabled only if achievement is considerably lower than that predicted by the IQ test score. The reasons for this opposition to the discrepancy definition are outlined in detail in those articles but some of the important ones are identified here.

One of the problems with IQ tests is that they measure specific knowledge, vocabulary, expressive language skills, and short- and long-term memory, all of which may be deficient in the individual with a learning disability. Therefore, the IQ score may not be a measure of "potential" in the learning disabled individual and the IQ may be an underestimate of their actual ability. Consider the case of an individual with an IQ of 90 and a standard score of 85 on a reading test. With a traditional discrepancy formula, this child would not be considered learning disabled although his profile of reading and/or arithmetic-related skills may actually resemble that of a child who does show a discrepancy between IQ and reading achievement. In fact, Siegel (1989) has shown that when children who have a discrepancy between reading and IQ are compared to those who do not, there are no statistically significant differences in phonological processing, language, and short-term and working memory skills between these two groups, although both these reading disabled groups have scores that are significantly below normal readers.

Another assumption of the discrepancy definition is that the IQ score should predict reading, so that if you have a low IQ score you should be a poor reader and that poor reading is an *expected consequence* of low IQ. However, there are individuals who have low IQ scores and are good readers, so low IQ scores are not sufficient to cause poor reading (e.g., Siegel, 1984, 1988b).

Use of the discrepancy definition assumes that children who are poor readers and have low IQ scores should display different patterns of cognitive functioning from children who are poor readers and have higher IQ scores. This assumption is the basis of the calculation of discrepancy between IQ and achievement. However, Siegel (1988b) has found that reading disabled children of different IQ levels do not display different reading, spelling, language, and memory skills and all of the reading disabled children at any IQ level performed on these tests at a level below that of normally achieving children. These findings lead to the conclusion that IQ scores do not predict differences in cognitive functioning within the learning disabled population and do not appear to be important in the definition.

Measurement of Achievement

In addition to the issue of the role of IQ in the definition, the actual definition used can make a difference in conclusions about subtypes. Siegel and Ryan (1989) have shown that the way a reading disability is defined can influence the conclusions that will be drawn about the information processing characteristics and whether there are subtypes. This study compared poor readers, defined in one of four ways: (1) inadequate phonics skills based on the reading of pseudowords significantly below the expected level for age (Phonics Deficit), (2) inadequate word recognition skills based on performance significantly below the expected level for age on the Reading Subtest of the Wide Range Achievement Test (Word Recognition Deficit), (3) inadequate reading comprehension skills but adequate word recognition skills (Comprehension-Only Deficit), and (4) slow reading speed but adequate word recognition skills (Rate-Only Deficit).

The first two groups, the Phonics Deficit group and the Word Recognition Deficit group, were almost totally overlapping groups, as the correlation between word reading and pseudoword reading is quite high (e.g., Siegel & Ryan, 1988). There was approximately a 25% overlap between the poor comprehenders and poor readers. Because of this overlap, the groups could not be compared within the same statistical analyses. Each of these groups was compared with age-matched children who had average or above average scores on the reading task in question. These groups were compared with normally achieving children on tasks measuring grammatical, short-term memory, reading, spelling, arithmetic, and visual–spatial skills.

The results were quite clear and indicated that children with a Phonics Deficit or a Word Recognition Deficit had significantly below normal scores on all of the cognitive tasks except for the visual–spatial ones. Children with the Comprehension-Only Deficit had significantly lower than normal scores on the short-term memory tasks but scores that were not significantly different from normal readers on the language tasks. Slow readers (Rate-Only Deficit) had cognitive profiles similar to normal children. Therefore, the type of reading test used to define the reading problem will have a significant impact on the conclusions that are reached about a reading disabled child. Obviously, if a reading comprehension test is used to define the group and word recognition problems are not taken into account, some of the so-called reading disabled children will have word recognition problems and others will not. Therefore, the group will appear to be heterogeneous and subtypes may be found, including a non–language-impaired group. The ones with word recognition problems are probably the ones with language problems and those with only a reading comprehension problem probably do not have language deficits. However, with the use of a reading comprehension measure to define the reading disabled group, it is impossible to know. Children with deficits in phonics and/or word recognition all have problems with language and there does not seem to be evidence for a non–language-impaired subtype within this disability. Children who are slow readers and/or have problems with comprehension but not word recognition do not have language problems but do have memory problems.

Using a reading comprehension test, as opposed to a word recognition or pseudoword test of reading, creates the illusion of "heterogeneity" in a number of studies. For example, Bialystok and Mitterer (1987) examined the performance of poor readers on measures of metalinguistic knowledge. The two types of poor readers were identified: "Recoders," who appeared to be sounding out words but lacked a sight word vocabulary, and "whole worders," who appeared to be reading on the basis of whole words, but lacked phonetic analysis skills. However, these "poor readers" were selected on the basis of a reading comprehension test so they were probably a heterogeneous group and these two types of readers do not necessarily constitute subtypes of poor readers.

Prior, Frye, and Fletcher (1987) developed a chassification scheme for poor readers. "Chinese" readers were classified as those who appeared to read by whole words and "Phonecians" were those who appeared to read by sounding out. Young high school students were referred who had a history of reading difficulties, but were not receiving any special remediation. The fact that none of these children were receiving remediation raises questions as to the severity of their reading problems. These was no objective measure of their reading skills so it is difficult to know whether or not they were reading disabled. Only one third of this "reading disabled" sample could be classified as either "Chinese" or "Phonecian" readers. Further, these two subtypes had equal scores on a pretest requiring recognition of exception words and only really differed in their ability to decode pseudowords. Thus, it is perhaps more appropriate to differentiate these two groups with respect to their ability to apply a phonetic code than on the basis of differential methods of lexical access. Both subtypes had some skill in the use of visual or whole-word recognition, but "Phonecians" also had the use of phonological access. It may be that the "Chinese" readers were reading disabled in terms of poor word decoding and phonetic skill use; "Phonecian" readers appear to have been higher functioning and may not have been reading disabled at all.

Wood, Richman, and Eliason (1989) defined three subtypes of disabled readers on the basis of neuropsychological strengths and weaknesses. All reading disabled children were at least one grade below their current placement on a word recognition test (WRAT or Stanford Reading Inventory) and on an oral reading comprehension test (Stanford Reading Inventory), had a WISC–R Verbal or Performance IQ of at least 85, and had no primary behavior or emotional disorder. Subtype 1 demonstrated adequate verbal skills, but a perceptual–motor deficit; subtype 2, a general verbal deficit group showed below average performance on tasks of verbal learning and language association; subtype 3, a specific memory–verbal disordered group showed below average performance on two out of three verbal memory tests, but average performance on a verbal reasoning task. The definition of reading disabled children used by Wood et al. suffers from problems similar to those found in many subtyping studies. Namely, a 1-year grade level reading retardation criterion was used. Grade levels are not a good measure of reading retardation because they are not interval units of measurement (Siegel & Heaven, 1986). Grade level discrepancies mean different degrees of disability at different developmental stages. Wood et al. also used a measure of reading comprehension to define their sample. Therefore, the sample was probably heterogeneous, thus accounting for the non–language-impaired group.

In an investigation of the relationship between lexical naming tasks and reading, Wolf and Goodglass (1986) and Wolf (1986) (see also Wolf, Bally, & Morris, 1986) proposed that subtypes of reading disabilities could be predicted from early naming performance. Dyslexic children were selected on the basis of a 1.5 grade level reading retardation by the end of grade 2 on a word recognition or a reading comprehension test. Performance measures were collected from 15 dyslexic children over 3 years. Three subtypes of poor readers were defined. Group 1 showed a rate deficit in lexical retrieval in kindergarten and a word decoding deficit (but average reading comprehension) at the end of grade 2. Group 2 presented with early naming accuracy deficits and subsequent poor comprehension (but average decoding skills). The third group was initially deficient in both their rate and accuracy for word retrieval and showed poor decoding and comprehension skills at the end of grade 2.

The investigators of these studies caution that results are preliminary as dyslexic subtypes comprised so few children (n = 3, n = 2, n = 6–9 for subtype 1, 2, and 3, respectively). In addition, initial selection of the 15 dyslexic readers was based on poor decoding or poor comprehension. Therefore, the group is quite probably heterogeneous.

Harness, Epstein, and Gordon (1984) studied subtypes of dyslexic children to determine if they differed in their hemispheric functioning. Children who were referred to a reading disabilities clinic were given a test consisting of word recognition, oral reading, and reading comprehension subtests (in Hebrew). These investigators attempted to find evidence for the existence of Boder's subtypes of dyslexia (dyseidetic, dysphonetic, and mixed) based on a factor analysis of hemispheric laterality measures. Boder's approach suggests that dyseidetics should show a left hemisphere advantage and dysphonetics a right hemisphere advantage. However, the group of reading disabled children formed a homogeneous group with a right hemisphere cognitive processing advantage. This result was partly due to the dyslexic's poorer than normal left hemisphere functioning. These results suggest that there are not meaningful subtypes within the reading disabled group.

Breen (1986) identified subtypes of learning disabilities based on patterns of academic achievement (as measured by the Woodstock–Johnson Academic subtests). Children were referred who met the Colorado state criteria for learning disabilities (average intelligence with a significant discrepancy between intelligence and achievement). Three subtypes were identified: group 1 showed higher math than reading scores (standard score [s.s.] means = 91 and 75), group 2 presented with higher reading than math scores (s.s. mean = 92 and 73), and group 3 showed equally low math and reading scores (s.s. mean = 67 and 67). Patterns of cognitive functioning were examined on the 12 subtests of the Woodcock–Johnson Psychoeducational battery. Although factors most contributing to the overall index of each group did differ, multivariate tests revealed that groups 1 and 2 performed in a similar manner and tended to score higher than group 3. This finding is not consistent with other academic subtyping studies of neuropsychological functioning in which groups 1 and 2 have shown opposite strengths and weaknesses (e.g., Rourke & Finlayson, 1978; Rourke & Strang, 1983; Share, Moffitt, & Silva, 1988). However, the inclusion of children on the basis of school selection is problematic (Keogh, 1983; Siegel & Heaven, 1986). Further, the inclusion of a reading comprehension test for subtype selection presents the methodological problems discussed earlier.

Other definitional issues can prove a threat to the validity of the findings. Freebody and Byrne (1988) cluster analyzed z scores on irregular and pseudoword recognition lists for a sample of grades 2 and 3 children with a wide range of reading abilities. Four groups of readers were obtained: those scoring well above average on both lists; those scoring substantially below average on both lists; a group showing adequate performance on irregular words, but below average on pseudowords ("Chinese" readers); and a group showing adequate recognition of pseudowords, but below average on irregular word recognition ("Phonecian" readers). Individual groups were formed based on similarity to cluster means; however; the absolute word decoding level of subjects, and thus the degree of disability for the latter three groups, is not known. Indeed, the investigators conclude that Phonecian readers appear to develop normal reading comprehension from grade 2 to grade 3. Thus, at this young age, identification of preferred word decoding strategies is not synonomous with identification of reading disability subtypes. That is, dependence on a particular method of decoding does not automatically indicate a reading disability. This case is an illustration of how definitional issues can present a threat to the interpretation of the findings.

There are other definitional issues. Different achievement tests may identify different children as being reading disabled. Caskey (1986) has shown that the Peabody Individual Achievement Test (PIAT) and the

Woodcock Reading Mastery Tests identify different children as being reading disabled. The Woodcock Word Identification identified more children than the PIAT as being reading disabled.

As Adelman and Taylor (1986) have noted, the tests used to define constructs such as language, visual perception, and memory are quite varied and often of questionable validity. This problem has been discussed in relation to reading tests (e.g., Siegel & Heaven, 1986) and intelligence tests (e.g., Siegel, 1989) but similar issues could be raised with all these concepts. For example, language tasks may measure syntax, morphology, expressive fluency, pragmatics, and/or phonology. A child might have a problem in one of these areas and not another. Unfortunately, in discussions of subtypes of learning disabilities, these subtleties are ignored.

Definitional issues plague many studies of subtypes, for example, Watson and Goldgar (1988), who used a sample of "reading disabled" individuals. Their calculation of reading disability has a number of methodological problems. First, reading was calculated from a score on three different tests: word identification, word attack, and passage comprehension. As Siegel and Ryan (1989) have shown, a group that is defined on the basis of problems with reading comprehension is quite heterogeneous. Therefore, it is not clear that all of these individuals were reading disabled so that when subtypes are produced, these subtypes may include individuals who are not reading disabled. In addition, a mental age is calculated from the full scale IQ, which is a questionable statistical procedure. Four clusters among these reading disabled were described. The scores of all of the children appear to be quite similar, except that one group had higher scores on sound blending and on the Peabody Picture Vocabulary Test and another group had average (rather than below average) scores on the visual motor integration test. In reality, it appears as if there are several small differences among the groups, but basically there is a continuum with many of the children having problems, although not all of them, because an indeterminate number of them were probably not reading disabled. They may have had other learning disabilities because of the strange calculation of adjusting the scores for MA or grade level; it is impossible to tell how many of these children were below average. Most importantly, when presented with the scores of an individual child, it would be impossible to place them into categories. It is not clear whether these are not just normal individual differences in any group. In addition, no information is presented about the reading performance of these groups and we do not know whether or not these subtypes differed in reading performance or whether there are any educational implications of these "subtypes."

Morris, Blashfield, and Satz (1986) have shown that there is variation within the group of poor readers. However, all of these groups had difficulties with verbal skills. One of the subtypes had greater skills in the visual–spatial and perceptual motor areas, but there was no evidence that the reading, language, and memory skills of the subtypes were different.

One of the subtypes that has been proposed is that of Boder (1973): dysphonetics, dysiedetics, and nonspecific. It is important to note this distinction is not based on reading but based on performance on spelling and the difficulties of this have been discussed previously. Aylward (1984) studied hemispheric dominance in dyslexics defined this way and did not find significant differences among these three groups.

It appears that the study of subtypes has been plagued by serious definitional issues and that there does not appear to be any evidence of reliable subtypes within the reading disabled population.

Statistical Considerations

The difficulties in subtype identification are compounded further by the fact that most of the studies of subtypes have used elaborate statistical procedures that sort individuals, called learning disabled, into groups but use methods that make it impossible to determine, on a clinical basis, what the subtype is for an individual child.

These statistical procedures and methodology is what we call the "food processor approach." A group of tests are administered to children, the scores are incorporated into some statistical procedure such as factor analysis, cluster analysis, or a Q-sort, and analyzed in the computer in the manner of a chef blending ingredients in the food processor. Magically, subtypes emerge. However, there is no a priori rationale for these subtypes and what emerges depends on the tests that were included in the analysis, in the manner of the results produced by the food processor, being related, obviously, to the ingredients placed into it. The most important problem is the lack of application to the individual case. Cut-off scores are not used, that is, defining a subtype as having a score below x on test A, below y on test B, and below z on test C and another subtype as having a sore below x on test A, above y on test B, and z+5 on test C. Although the statistical analysis of test scores yields subtypes, these subtypes are a statistical abstraction. When confronted with an individual child, we do not know the subtype. Investigations of subtypes of learning disabilities that use elaborate statistical procedures lend an apparently scientific basis to the classification system. However, they make it impossible to decide about classification of an individual case.

McKinney (1984) has noted a number of problems with the use of multivariate statistical procedures. Often there is the confusion between reading disability and learning disability in general. Often the study does not include normal achievers so that it is not clear what normal patterns would be. Often the clusters are not meaningful in terms of specific achievement difficulties.

Achievement-Based Definition

In contrast to the work on subtypes within the reading disabled population, there do appear to be subtypes within the learning disabled population. Rourke and his colleagues have defined subtypes of learning disabled children based on patterns of academic performance (Ozlos & Rourke, 1988; Petrauskas & Rourke, 1979; Rourke, 1988a, 1988b; Rourke & Finlayson, 1978; Rourke & Strang, 1983). Based on three patterns of academic achievement, differences in neuropsychological functioning have been identified for older learning disabled children (9- to 14-year-old). Subtype 1 presented with uniformly depressed WRAT scores; subtype 2 with higher WRAT arithmetic relative to reading and spelling scores, but still deficient in all three areas; Subtype 3, a specific arithmetic disabled group presented with WRAT reading and spelling scores in the normal range, but impaired arithmetic scores.

On measures of neuropsychological functioning, the specific arithmetic disabled group (subtype 3) had higher verbal than performance IQ test scores. In comparison to the other two subtypes, these children showed poorer psychomotor and tactile–perceptual skills and superior auditory–perceptual and verbal skills. Subtype 2 showed the reverse pattern of strengths and weaknesses than the specific arithmetic group. The group with uniformly deficient WRAT scores showed only small verbal–performance IQ discrepancies and had similar psycholinguistic skills as subtype 2. These studies have served to delineate neuropsychological strengths and weaknesses in subtypes of learning disabled children based on academic patterns. Without appropriate control groups, questions might be raised as to the discriminant validity of patterns of neuropsychological functioning to differentiate between normal and learning disabled children.

Share, Moffitt, and Silva (1988) attempted to replicate the above findings with respect to neuropsychological patterns and compared learning disabled groups with a normal control group, as well as girls' performance with boys'. These investigators used a cut-off score on the Progressive Achievement Test (PAT) below the 30th percentile to identify deficient academic skills and above the 40th percentile to identify areas of average academic skills. Although these authors make direct comparisons between the subtypes in their study and those in Rourke and Strang (1983), there may be differences. Share et al. used a reading comprehension test as opposed to a word recognition test (WRAT) to define levels of reading achievement. Further, Share et al. did not survey and include spelling skills in the profile in their groups.

The two disabled groups in Share et al. (1988) were an arithmetic-and-reading disabled group and a specific arithmetic disabled group. Measures on neuropsychological tests were collected on a cohort of children between their 9th and 13th years+. Results indicated that for boys, Rourke's previous findings were replicated. That is, arithmetic-and-reading disabled boys showed the opposite strengths and weaknesses from those of the specific arithmetic disabled boys. An additional finding was that the specific arithmetic disabled boys performed lower on measures of non-verbal skills than same-age boys with equal reading ability and normal levels of arithmetic ability. Girls with arithmetic-and-reading disability showed a similar pattern of neuropsychological functioning as their male counterparts. They were significantly below controls in terms of verbal and performance IQ test scores and on a language-based composite. Girls with specific arithmetic disability, however, did not differ from controls and did not show the opposite pattern of strengths and weaknesses than the arithmetic and reading disabled girls.

The investigators suggest that nonverbal deficits may play a role in accounting for specific arithmetic disabilities in boys, but factors other than neuropsychological functioning (such as motivation and expectations) may account for specific arithmetic disability in girls. They further propose that poor verbal abilities alone may not account for depressed arithmetic scores in arithmetic-and-reading disabled boys and girls, as they also showed lower performance IQ scores than the nondisabled controls. However, lowered performance IQ scores were not found in a reading-and-spelling disabled group (who also presented with impaired arithmetic achievement scores) in a study reported by Share, Silva, and Adler (1987). Thus, for children with disabilities in reading and arithmetic the relative contribution of deficits in psycholinguistic versus visual–spatial/visual–perceptual skills remains unanswered. It may be that poor verbal abilities affect arithmetic performance to such a degree that intact nonverbal skills cannot compensate for this deficit. However, it may be that such groups also show depressed visual–spatial skills that further impede arithmetic learning.

Ozols and Rourke (1988) attempted to find evidence for similar patterns of neuropsychological functioning in academic subtypes of younger learning disabled children (7–8 years). Subtypes were defined in a manner similar to that of Rourke and Strang (1983). Young learning disabled children with uniformly depressed WRAT arithmetic, spelling, and reading scores and those with higher arithmetic relative to reading and spelling scores were inferior to a specific arithmetic disabled group (and to norms) on tests of auditory–perceptual and psycholinguistic functioning. It is suggested that these subtypes of learning disabled children may have a left hemisphere dysfunction and that it is their verbal deficits that depress their arithmetic learning. Evidence suggested that the specific arithmetic disabled group may have deficits in visual–spatial and nonverbal skills. This subgroup was within the normal range, however, on most dependent measures. Ozols and Rourke suggest that these children may suffer from a dysfunctional right hemispherical system.

Rourke and his colleagues have discussed specific patterns of central processing deficits as causes of specific forms of socioemotional disturbances as well as causes of academic learning disabilities (Porter & Rourke, 1985; Rourke, 1988a, 1988b; Strang & Rourke, 1978, 1985). Studies using both a priori subtyping and Q-factor analysis have supported the hypothesis that children with specific arithmetic disability (or nonverbal learning disabilities) are most likely to be described by parents as emotionally and behaviorally disturbed. On the other hand, psycholinguistic and auditory–perceptual dysfunctions do not appear to be sufficient to cause disturbed socioemotional functioning. Thus, Rourke et al. suggest that one type of central processing profile appears to lead to specific learning problems and to a specific form of socioemotional disturbance.

A related conceptualization of subtypes based on achievement has been proposed by Denckla (1972) and Siegel and Heaven (1986). There appear to be three subtypes based on achievement and behavior: (a) a reading disability, (b) an arithmetic writing disability, and (c) an attentional deficit disorder called the "dyscontrol syndrome" by Denckla. The reading disorder, called "specific language disability" by Denckla, is characterized by poor decoding and word recognition skills and problems with phonological processing, language, and short-term and working memory (Siegel, 1986; Siegel & Faux, 1989; Siegel & Linder, 1984; Siegel & Ryan, 1988, 1989). Those with arithmetic disability, called "Gerstmann syndrome" by Denckla, are deficient in computational arithmetic, fine motor, and visual–spatial abilities but have age-appropriate language and auditory–perceptual abilities (Fletcher, 1985; Rourke & Finlayson, 1978; Share, Moffitt, & Silva, 1988; Siegel & Feldman, 1983; Spellacy & Peter, 1978). They also have problems in tasks that measure visual–spatial analyses, visual perceptual organization, and psychomotor abilities (e.g., Rourke & Strang, 1978; Siegel & Feldman, 1983; Strang & Rourke, 1983; Spellacy & Peter, 1978). Rourke and Strang (1978) claim that these arithmetic disabled individuals have normal right hand performance but impaired left hand performance. Strang and Rourke claim that this group has problems with nonverbal concept formation, make more errors, and do not use efficient and effective strategies in these types of problems.

These results have led Rourke (1978, 1982, 1985, 1987, 1988a, 1988b; Strang & Rourke, 1985) to suggest that children with an arithmetic disability who have normal reading scores have a nonverbal learning disability with problems in information processing related to right hemisphere functioning whereas individuals with a reading disability have a language-based learning disability with problems related to nonoptimal right hemisphere functioning. There are some problems with this conceptualization. For a detailed discussion see Morrison and Siegel (1991). Fletcher (1985) found that children with an arithmetic disability had significantly lower scores than normally achieving children on a memory task that involved visual–spatial stimuli but not on a task involving verbal stimuli, whereas those with a reading disability but not an arithmetic disability had received lower scores on the verbal memory task but on the visual–spatial memory task.

Siegel and Linder (1984) have provided evidence that although the reading disabled and specifically arithmetic disabled groups had significantly poorer performance than normally achieving children in a visual short-term memory task, these two subtypes were different in an auditory short-term memory task. On the auditory short-term memory task the arithmetic disabled children had scores that were in the normal range. Similarily, in a working memory task involving language, the reading disabled children had scores below the normal achieving children while the arithmetic disabled did not (Siegel & Ryan, 1989). In a task involving working memory for numbers, both arithmetic and reading disabled groups had scores that were lower than those of normally achieving children.

Attention Deficit Disorder with or without hyperactivity (ADD) seems to exist in many children with learning disorders although it can occur by itself (e.g., Holborow & Berry, 1986). Children with a learning disability (of either variety) and with ADD do not differ from children with a learning disability but no ADD, except on the most difficult tasks. Felton, Wood, Brown, Campbell, and Harter (1987) have also shown memory deficits in children with ADD, suggesting that the learning disability rather than the attention deficit is what contributes to their problems with information processing.

Siegel and Ryan (1988) compared children with a specific learning disability in arithmetic and those with a disability in reading to normally achieving children. The reading disabled children had significantly lower scores than normally achieving children on phonological processing tasks and tasks that involved the understanding of the syntactic and morphological aspects of language whereas the arithmetic disabled children had scores on these tests that were not significantly different from normally achieving children. Therefore, there was a significant difference between the subtypes in that the reading disabled children had problems related to language and phonological processing whereas those children with a specific arithmetic disability did not. It is also interesting to note that children with an ADD but who had no other learning disability had scores that were not significantly lower than normally achieving children except on a reading comprehension task that has significant memory and attention components (Siegel & Ryan, 1988).

A study by Shafrir, Siegel, and Chee (1989) has shown the validity of subtyping. In this study, problem-solving behavior and metacognitive strategies of groups of children with learning disabilities were examined. When the learning disabled group was considered as a whole without subtyping, children with learning disabilities made more errors and showed less attention to errors than normally achieving children. However, when the learning disabled children were separated into those with a reading disability and those with normal reading but with an arithmetic disability, the latter group had scores that were not significantly different from normally achieving children. On the other hand, the children with a reading disability, all of whom also had problems with arithmetic, had significantly lower scores than the normally achieving children.

Rourke (1988a) has argued that these subtypes differ in social emotional characteristics. The arithmetic learning disabled group, as opposed to the group with reading problems, performed more poorly on nonverbal tests and he has suggested that social awareness and responsiveness may be impaired in this group. These arithmetic disabled children are more likely to be perceived by their parents as disturbed.

Strawser and Weller (1985) appear to have found subtypes that are somewhat consistent wtih the achievement subtypes outlined above. They found one reading disabled subtype with problems in language and auditory processing, one arithmetic disabled subtype with problems in fine motor skills and visual–spatial functioning, and one subtype with problems in all academic areas similar to the reading disabled children who also have problems in computational arithmetic. It is interesting to note that the arithmetic disabled group had the most severe behavior problems, a finding reported by Ozols and Rourke.

The Solution

Conceptualizing learning disability subtypes as being based on differences in achievement profiles seems to be the most meaningful approach, with considerable empirical verification. There appear to be at least three subtypes: reading disabled, arithmetic disabled, attentional deficit. The following criteria are recommended for the definition of these learning disabilities: reading disability, a score on a pseudoword reading or word reading test ≤ 25 percentile; arithmetic disability, a score on a computational arithmetic test ≤ 25 percentile; attentional deficit disorder, a score ≥ 1.5 (or 2) standard deviations above the mean on a behavior rating scale such as the Conners Parent Questionnaire (Goyette, Conners, & Ulrich, 1978). Discrepancy scores based on IQ and achievement are not necessary. IQ scores appear to be irrelevant but if this solution is too uncomfortable, a minimum score of 80 (admittedly arbitrary) seems to be the most appropriate. However, there are some difficulties with this approach. One of the major difficulties faced in the definition of learning disability is that we are, in fact, dealing with a continuum. At some point we make the choice to use a particular cut-off score but, in reality, the distribution is continuous. We decide in an arbitrary manner that the individual has a severe enough problem to be considered learning disabled. There will always be a borderline group that we are not sure about. This type of distribution should be kept in mind when studying learning disabilities.

In summary, the most important aspect of the study of learning disabilities is to use objective and meaningful operational definitions that can be applied to an individual case. When the field achieves that goal, then we will be able to ascertain the nature of subtypes.

References

Adelman, H. S., & Taylor, L. (1986). The problems of differentiation and the need for a classification schema. *Journal of Learning Disabilities*, *19*, 514–520.

Aylward, E. H. (1984). Lateral asymmetry in subgroups of dyslexic children. *Brain and Language*, *22*, 221–231.

Bialystok, E., & Mitterer, J. (1987). Metalinguistic differences among three kinds of readers. *Journal of Educational Psychology*, *79*, 147–153.

Boder, E. (1973). Developmental dyslexia: A diagnostic approach based on three atypical reading-spelling patterns. *Developmental Medicine and Child Neurology*, *15*, 663–687.

Breen, M. J. (1986). Cognitive patterns of learning disability subtypes as measured by the Woodcock–Johnson Psycho-Educational Battery. *Journal of Learning Disabilities*, *19*, 86–90.

Caskey, W. E., (1986). The use of the Peabody Individual Achievement Test and the Woodcock Reading Mastery Tests in the diagnosis of a learning disability in reading: A caveat. *Journal of Learning Disabilities*, *19*, 336–337.

Denckla, M. (1972). Clinical syndromes in learning disabilities: The case for "splitting" vs. "lumping." *Journal of Learning Disabilities*, *7*, 401–406.

Felton, R. H., Wood, F. B., Brown, I. S., Campbell, S. K., & Harter, M. R. (1987). Separate verbal memory and naming deficits in attention deficit disorder and reading disability. *Brain and Language*, *31*, 171–184.

Fletcher, J. M. (1985). External validation of learning disability typologies. In B. P. Rourkes (Ed.), *Neuropsychology of learning disabilities: Essentials of subtype analysis* (pp. 187–211). New York: Guilford Press.

Freebody, P., & Byrne, B. (1988) Word-reading strategies in elementary school children: Relations to comprehension, reading and phonemic awareness. *Reading Research Quarterly*, *23*, 441–453.

Goyette, C. H., Conners, C. K., & Ulrich, R. F. (1978). Normative data on revised Conners parent and teacher ratings scales. *Journal of Abnormal Child Psychology*, *6*, 221–236.

Harness, B. Z., Epstein, R., & Gordon, H. W. (1984). Cognitive profile of children referred to a clinic for reading disabilities. *Journal of Learning Disabilities*, *17*, 346–351.

Holborow, P. L., & Berry, P. S. (1986). Hyperactivity and learning difficulties. *Journal of Learning Disabilities*, *19*, 426–431.

Keogh, B. (1983). Classification, compliance and confusion. *Journal of Learning Disabilities*, *16*, 25.

McKinney, J. D. (1984). The search for subtypes of specific learning disability. *Journal of Learning Disabilities*, *17*, 43–50.

Morris, R., Blashfield, R., & Satz, P. (1986). Developmental classification of reading-disabled children. *Journal of Clinical and Experimental Neuropsychology*, *8*, 371–392.

Morrison, S. R., & Siegel, L. S. (1991). Arithmetic disability: Theoretical considerations and empirical evidence for this subtype. In L. V. Feagans, E. J. Short, & L. J. Meltzer (Eds.), *Subtypes of Learning Disabilities*. Hillsdale, NJ: Erlbaum.

Ozols, E. J., & Rourke, B. P. (1988). Characteristics of young learning-disabled children classified according to patterns of academic achievement: Auditory-perceptual and visual-perceptual abilities. *Journal of Clinical Child Psychology*, *17*, 44–52.

Petrauskas, R. J., & Rourke, B. P. (1979). Identification of subtypes of retarded readers. A neuropsychological multi-variate approach. *Journal of Clinical Neuropsychology*, *1*, 17–37.

Porter, J., & Rourke, B. P. (1985). Socio-emotional functioning of learning disabled children: A subtypal analysis of personality patterns. In B. P. Rourke (Ed.), *Neuropsychology of learning disabilities: Essentials of subtype analysis* (pp. 257–279). New York: Guilford Press.

Prior, M., Frye, S., & Fletcher, C. (1987). Remediation for subgroups of retarded readers using a modified oral spelling procedure. *Developmental Medicine and Child Neurology*, *29*, 64–71.

Rourke, B. P. (1978). Reading, spelling, arithmetic disabilities: A neuropsychologic perspective. In H. R. Myklebust (Ed.), *Progress in learning disabilities* (Vol. 4, pp. 97–120). New York: Grune & Stratton.

Rourke, B. P. (1982). Central processing deficiencies in children: Toward a developmental neuropsychological model. *Journal of Clinical Neuropsychology*, *4*, 1–18.

Rourke, B. P. (1985). An overview to learning disability subtypes. In B. P. Rourke (Ed.), *Neuropsychology of learning disabilities: Essentials of subtype analysis* (pp. 3–17). New York: Guilford Press.

Rourke, B. P. (1987). Syndrome of nonverbal learning disabilities: The final common pathway of white matter disease/dysfunction? *Clinical Neuropsychologist*, *1*, 209–234.

Rourke, B. P. (1988a). Socioemotional disturbances of learning disabled children. *Journal of Consulting and Clinical Psychology*, *56*, 801–810.

Rourke, B. P. (1988b). The syndrome of nonverbal learning disabilities: Developmental manifestations in neurological disease, disorder, and dysfunction. *The Clinical Neuropsychologist*, *2*, 293–330.

Rourke, B. P., & Finlayson, M. A. (1978). Neuropsychological significance of variations in patterns of academic performance: Verbal and visual-spatial abilities. *Journal of Abnormal Child Psychology*, *6*, 121–133.

Rourke, B. P., & Strang, J. D. (1978). Neuropsychological significance of variations in the patterns of academic performance: Motor, psychomotor, and tactile-perceptual abilities. *Journal of Pediatric Psychology*, *3*, 62–66.

Rourke, B. P., & Strang, J. D. (1983). Subtypes of reading and arithmetic disabilities: A neuropsychological analysis. In M. Rutter (Ed.), *Developmental neuropsychiatry* (pp. 473–488). New York: Guilford Presse.

Shafrir, U., Siegel, S. L., & Chee, M. (1990). *Learning disability, inferential skills and post-failure reflectivity. Journal of Learning Disabilities*, *23*, 506–517.

Share, D. L., Moffitt, T. E., & Silva, P. A. (1988). Factors associated with arithmetic-and-reading disability and specific arithmetic disability. *Journal of Learning Disabilities, 21*, 313–320.

Share, D. L., Silva, P. A., & Adler, C. J. (1987). Factors associated with reading-plus-spelling retardation and specific spelling retardation. *Developmental Medicine and Child Neurology, 29*, 64–71.

Siegel, L. S. (1984). A longitudinal study of a hyperlexic child: Hyperlexia as a language disorder. *Neuropsychologia, 22*, 577–585.

Siegel, L. S. (1986). Phonological deficits in children with a reading disability. *Canadian Journal of Special Education, 2*, 45–54.

Siegel, L. S. (1988a). Definitional and theoretical issues and research on learning disabilities. *Journal of Learning Disabilities, 21*, 264–266.

Siegel, L. S. (1988b). Evidence that IQ Scores are irrelevant to the definition and analysis of reading disability. *Canadian Journal of Psychology, 42*, 201–215.

Siegel, L. S. (1989). A reconceptualization of prediction from infant test scores. In M. Bornstein & N. Krasnegor (Eds.), *Stability and continuity in mental development*. Hillsdale, NJ: Erlbaum.

Siegel, L. S. (1989). IQ is irrelevant to the definition of learning disabilities. *Journal of Learning Disabilities, 22*, 514–518.

Siegel, L. S. (1990). IQ and learning disabilities: R.I.P. In H. L. Swanson and B. Keogh (Eds.), *Learning disabilities: Theoretical and research issues*. Hillsdale, NJ: Erlbaum.

Siegel, L. S., & Faux, D. (1989). Acquisition of certain graphemephoneme correspondences in normally achieving and disabled readers. *Reading and Writing: An Interdisciplinary Journal, 1*, 37–52.

Siegel. L. S., & Feldman, W. (1983). Non-dyslexic children with combined wirting and arithmetic difficulties. *Clinical Pediatrics, 22*, 241–244.

Siegel, L. S., & Heaven, R. (1986). Categorization of learning disabilities. In S. J. Ceci (Ed.), *Handbook of cognitive, social, and neuropsychological aspects of learning disabilities* (Vol. 1, pp. 95–121). Hillsdale, NJ: Erlbaum.

Siegel, L. S., & Linder, B. (1984). Short-term memory processes in children with reading and arithmetic learning disabilities. *Developmental Psychology, 20*, 200–207.

Siegel, L. S., & Ryan, E. B. (1988). Development of grammatical-sensitivity, phonological, and short-term memory skills in normally achieving and learning disabled children. *Developmental Psychology, 24*, 28–37.

Siegel, L. S., & Ryan, E. B. (1989). The development of working memory in normally achieving and subtypes of learning disabled children. *Child Development, 60*, 973–980.

Spellacy, F., & Peter, B. (1978). Dyscalculia and elements of the developmental Gerstmenn Syndrome in school children. *Cortex, 14*, 197–206.

Strang, J. D., & Rourke, B. P. (1983). Concept formation/non-verbal reasoning abilities of children who exhibit specific academic problems with arithmetic. *Journal of Clinical Child Psychology, 12*, 33–39.

Strang, J. D., & Rourke, B. P. (1985).Adaptive behavior of children with specific arithmetic disabilities and associated neturopsychological abilities and deficits. In B. P. Rourke (Ed.), *Neuropsychology of learning disabilities: Essentials of subtype analysis* (pp. 167–183). New York: Guilford Press.

Strawser, S., & Weller, C. (1985). Use of adaptive and discrepancy criteria to determine learning disabilities severity subtypes. *Journal of Learning Disabilities*, *18*, 205–211.

Watson, B. U., & Goldgar, D. E. (1988). Evaluation of a typology of reading disability. *Journal of Clinical and Experimental Neuropsychology*, *10*, 432–450.

Wolf, M. (1986). Rapid alternating stimulus naming in the developmental dyslexias. *Brain and Language*, *27*, 360–369.

Wolf, M., Bally, H., & Morris, R. (1986). Automaticity, retrieval processes, and reading: A longitudinal study in average and impaired readers. *Child Development*, *57*, 988–1000.

Wolf, M., & Goodglass, H. (1986). Dyslexia, dysnomia, and lexical retrieval: A longitudinal investigation. *Brain and Language*, *28*, 154–168.

Wood, K. M., Richman, L. C., & Eliason, M. J. (1989). Immediate memory functions in reading disability subtypes. *Brain and Language*, *36*, 181–192.

3
Educational Assessment

ENNIO CIPANI and ROBERT MORROW

Assessment has been defined broadly as the process of collecting information (Salvia & Ysseldyke, 1988). In the educational delivery system, assessment information can be used for three related, but somewhat different, purposes: (a) referral and screening, (b) diagnosis and placement, and (c) instructional planning and evaluation of student progress. This chapter examines assessment methods and procedures as regards the three purposes stated above. First, assessment from a referral and screening standpoint is discussed. Assessment from a diagnostic/placement concern follows. Once an individual is diagnosed as learning disabled and placed in the continuum of special education services, instructional and behavioral programming needs have to be determined. Assessment from this perspective, both in terms of instructional and behavioral deficits, is also addressed.

Referral and Screening

Referral

Referral, according to McLoughlin and Lewis (1986), is the process of referring the student to special education for assessment and informing the child's parent(s). Once referred, an overwhelming majority of the students are assessed (92%), and a large percentage of those tested (73%) are then placed in special education (Algozzine, Christenson, & Ysseldyke, 1982). For example, a hypothetical 2nd grade regular education teacher has identified Johnny as a "troublemaker" who always appears to be off-task. After repeated attempts to get him on-task, she refers him to the school psychologist for assessment. Research suggests that regardless of the results of Johnny's assessment, the odds are highly in favor of his qualifying for, or being placed in, a special education program. This scenario is played out across the country every year. The data gathered by Algozinne et al. (1982) illustrate the power that teacher referrals have on subsequent assessment and placement decisions.

It is certainly understandable that teachers may not be able to identify children with learning disabilities. The learning disabled category is often referred to as "exclusionary" rather than "inclusionary." A major emphasis of the identification process stresses the types of conditions that are *excluded* rather than those that signify inclusion. According to Salvia and Ysseldyke (1988), the areas that must be excluded from the learning disabled category include mental retardation, blindness or partial sightedness, deafness or hearing impairment, physical handicaps, emotional disturbance (severe enough to require therapy), and environmental and/or cultural factors. This list of categories to be excluded can lead to confusion on the part of teachers, who may tend to refer students either having no need for special education services or having needs in another handicapping category.

As the regular education teacher begins to identify a student with problems, she *must* schedule a parent conference to identify workable solutions in the current regular education class placement. If the problem persists, the teacher then proceeds to the next level: a referral to other school professionals for further study of the problem. Paul and Epanchin (1982) stressed that regular education teachers should meet the following five requirements when proceeding to student referral:

1. keep records
2. know the referral process
3. try to solve the problem first
4. participate actively in screening
5. participate actively in writing the Individualized Educational Program (IEP).

Graden, Casey, and Bronstrom (1983) describe a prereferral assessment process that has five stages, including: (a) request for consultation from a resource teacher or some other specialist, (b) consultation from a resource teacher or other specialist to verify the existence and the nature of the problem, (c) conference with appropriate school personnel to review the student's progress, and (if none of the above procedures alleviate the problem) (d) formal referral for psychoeducational assessment and intervention. Should these steps be followed, the high percentages reflected in the data of Algozzine et al. (1982) might be reduced dramatically (Graden et al., 1983).

Another variation of the prereferral process (as mentioned earlier) is the use of a Student Study Team (SST), a preventive approach that is primarily a regular education function. The purpose of the SST is to try to resolve the problem before a formal referral. The referring teacher is always a member of the SST, while the school principal or designee chairs the meeting.

The SST reviews the problem and examines strategies or interventions tried. The team then attempts to identify intervention alternatives and, subsequently, recommends the most promising of those to the regular class teacher. Meetings are often scheduled as a follow-up to review the student's progress in light of the suggested intervention strategies. However, if the problem is not resolved by the SST, a formal referral for consideration of special education placement can by made by the regular class teacher or by any member of the SST. At this point, the referral ceases to be a regular education function and comes under the jurisdiction of special education.

Common assessment methods used during the referral process included both standardized and informal measures of student behavior and performance. Among such assessment methods are various types of observation checklists, anecdotal observational data, rating scales, and other types of standardized, as well as teacher-made instruments. Some of the more popular behavioral scales are the Walker Problem Identification Behavior Checklist (Walker, 1983), Behavior Rating Profile (Brown & Hammill, 1983a), and the Coopersmith Self-Esteem Inventories (Coopersmith, 1981).

Screening

Screening is another important assessment function when identifying children in need of special services (Salvia & Ysseldyke, 1988). The purpose of screening is to provide a brief check of a child's skills in order to "sort out" those children who may need further assessment and may fall into an at-risk category. Salvia and Ysseldyke (1988) describe the sole purpose of screening as "an initial stage during which those who may evidence a particular problem, disorder, disability or disease are sorted out from among the general population" (p. 6). Thus, screening is used to decide whether a child should be assessed further to diagnose his specific skill strengths and weaknesses. Screening programs are put into operation on the assumption that early identification and treatment is an efficient, effective, and humane method of identifying handicapped children. Screening procedures function to identify early on those children with potential problems, contrasting with the alternative of waiting until a child is primary school aged to identify and treat the problem, thus letting the problem increase in magnitude (Kaufman, 1989).

Screening measures are used in an attempt to identify children at risk (Salvia & Ysseldyke, 1988). Tjossen (1976) identified the three categories of risk status as established risk, biological risk, and environmental risk. Established-risk children are perhaps the most easily identifiable group as their disorders result from medically diagnosed conditions and may include physical defects and marked mental retardation. Children identified as being at risk biologically are those who have suffered head trauma, toxic exposure, diseases, and/or infection. The third category, environmental risk, includes children who may appear to be stable from a neurophysiological standpoint but have impoverished environments that might limit their ability to learn.

The screening procedures used for preschool children can be different markedly from those used for school-aged children. Therefore, each of these two populations will be treated in separate sections below.

Preschool Screening

There are many issues surrounding the screening of preschool children that make it a difficult task and often lead to disagreement as to its efficacy. One of the major problems in screening preschool children is the poor predictive validity of most screening measures designed for children of this age. The validity of any screening measure can be determined by the rate of "false positives" (the number of children who perform poorly on the measure but succeed later in school) and the number of "false negatives" (those who are successful on the screening measure, and yet in later years do poorly in school). Predictive validity is the measure's ability to predict a child's success or failure in future years. A screening test conceivably may result in a large number of false positives, as well as false negatives, due to poor predictive validity.

TABLE 3.1. Screening instruments.

Test name	Age/grade	Behavior sampled
Denver Developmental Screening Test (Frankenburg et al., 1975)	0–6 years	Personal–social, fine motor; gross motor, language
Boehm Test of Basic Concepts— Revised (Boehm, 1986)	K–Grade 2	Knowledge of concepts
Lee–Clark Reading Readiness Test (Lee & Clark, 1962)	K–Grade 1	Letter matching, letter discrimination, vocabulary, letter & word recognition
Test of Basic Experience 2 (Moss, 1979)	Level K– Preschool	Mathematics, language, science, social studies
Developmental Indication for the Assessment of Learning— Revised (Mardell–Czudnowski & Goldenberg, 1983)	Ages 2–6	Motor, conceptual, language
Metropolitan Readiness Test (Nurss & McGauvran, 1986)	Level 1– Preschool through mid-K through beginning Grade 1	Basic skills (e.g., memory matching, language, premath, etc.)
Comprehensive Development Scale (Quick, Little, & Campbell, 1974)	3 months–6 years	Personal–social, gross motor, fine motor, language, perceptual– cognitive

A second set of problems in identifying at-risk preschool children includes the reliability of the screening measure, the integrity of the parental report of child behavior, and the subsequent variability in measuring such behavior. According to Kaufman (1989), problems with parental reports often are due to different tolerance levels of parents for certain behaviors. What may be considered a "problem behavior" by one parent may not be for another parent, even if the problem behavior is performed with the same frequency and severity across parents (Salvia & Ysseldyke, 1988). Other issues surrounding preschool screening include the labeling of young children and disagreement as to what assessment approach to use (e.g., developmental versus functional skills methods).

Some of the instruments more commonly used for screening preschool children include the Developmental Indicators for the Assessment of Learning—Revised (DIAL–R), Boehm Test of Basic Concepts—Revised (BTBC–R), and Denver Developmental Screening Test (DDST). See Table 3.1 for an analysis of these instruments.

School Screening

Typically, the classroom teacher conducts the screening of those children suspected of being at risk for school failure. Global judgments of classroom teachers appear to be a reliable and valid method of identifying such students (Bryan & Wheeler, 1972).

Methods for screening school-aged children include those mentioned in the previous section on referral. Although sometimes time-consuming, the repetitive, direct observation method can be reliable in screening children, particularly when used with a social-comparison methodology (Kazdin, 1977; Kazdin & Matson, 1981; Minkin, Braukmann, Minkin, Timbers, Fixsen, Phillips, & Wolf, 1976). Direct observational data collection identifies rates of specific problematic behaviors in a particular child, but fails to provide a standard reference point when judging the behavior as acceptable or unacceptable. However, by collecting data on a child's peers, whose behavior would be considered nonproblematic given the same social situation, the at-risk child's problematic behavior can be compared to his peers' behavior, and judgments then can be made about the child's level of problematic behavioral excesses and deficits.

Diagnosis and Placement

After referral and screening, the next step in the assessment sequence is diagnosis. As noted, the major purpose of assessment is to gather information and data about an individual to (a) determine the individual's eligibility for special education services and (b) develop a relevant program plan for the individual once eligibility has been established. Diagnostic information can be gathered through formal or informal means.

Formal Diagnostic Instruments

Formal diagnostic instruments also are known as norm-referenced assessment instruments. By definition, such instruments have been standardized on a large sample population for a specific purpose, a set of directions is included for implementation that must be followed as stated in the assessment manual, and also included is a set of specific directions for interpreting and reporting the assessment results.

Over the years, literally hundreds of norm-referenced tests have been developed in all areas of development, including the cognitive, achievement, social, physical, and language areas. There are a number of commonly used assessment devices: Wechsler Intelligence Scales for Children—Revised, Illinois Test of Psycholingustic Abilities, Stanford–Binet Intelligence Test, Kaufman Assessment for Children, Peabody Picture Vocabulary Test—Revised, Peabody Individual Achievement Test—Revised, Wide Range Achievement Test—Revised, and the Woodcock–Johnson Psychoeducational Battery—Revised.

All norm-referenced assessments share several common characteristics, including the following:

1. The tests sample behaviors of the total array of possible skills, knowledge, or adaptive behaviors that potentially could be assessed.
2. General information about the individual being assessed is provided. The assessment may provide specific diagnostic information that then can be used as a basis for an IEP.
3. Comparisons can be made between individuals in the same program. Each individual assessed can be compared to all others who have been assessed as each is compared to a standard (normative) sample.
4. Comparisons can be made between or among groups in different programs. By using the same standard, it is feasible to compare students who are in one program to students in a different program.
5. Adminstration procedures are standardized to help eliminate invalid results due to faulty administration of an assessment instrument.
6. Both the scoring and interpretation of test results are standardized so that the margin of error is minimal when evaluating the individual's score on any specific test.
7. A degree of confidence regarding obtained data is gained through a standardized assessment of an individual. Most standardized tests furnish both validity and reliability data, thereby providing the tester with a measure of confidence when administering a particular assessment device.
8. Some formal assessment tests often are required by law (state or federal) or local policy for purposes of program placement. PL 94-142 requires that an individual be placed in a special education setting only after the individual has been thoroughly assessed, using the assessment sequence outlined earlier.

9. Specialized training is required for both test administration and interpretation. Some formal instruments can be administered only by certified examiners (e.g., WISC–R, Stanford–Binet, KABC), whereas others, such as the ITPA and Woodcock–Johnson Battery, require minimal training. Who can or cannot administer certain formal tests may vary from state to state.

10. Tests often are expensive. The expense in using formal tests is two-fold: (a) initial cost of the assessment instrument and (b) the cost in tester's time, as many formal tests are lengthy and are administered on an individual basis.

11. Various administrative needs may be met by formal tests. When evaluating the effectiveness of a program curriculum, reviewing students' progress, or evaluating a teacher's performance, formal assessment data often are used as a basis for such determination.

Table 3.2 provides a detailed breakdown of norm-referenced and criterion-referenced tests that are commonly used to assess handicapped students. The areas assessed include intelligence, general school achievement, reading (comprehension, word attack, and recognition), spelling, mathematics, and general information as well as specific subject areas such as science, humanities, and social studies. In addition, several perceptual–motor tests are included. The table provides a comprehensive look at test age range, normative sample, validity, reliability data, and a general description of what each test measures. This list reflects the norm-referenced and criterion-referenced tests most often used in the field today.

Appropriate and Inappropriate Uses

According to Salvia and Ysseldyke (1988), caution must be used when selecting and administering norm-referenced tests. Careful attention must be paid to selecting valid and reliable tests that have been normed on a population identical (or at least similar) to the one being tested. Such questions as, "Who is to be tested?", "What behaviors are to be tested?", and "What interpretative data are desired?" must be asked before choosing.

In addition, the limitations of each test must be considered when interpreting test results. For example, the WRAT–R test has been criticized severely for use as a diagnostic instrument. According to Witt (1986), the WRAT–R is found to be lacking from the standpoint of (a) assessing too few behviors to be used as a measure of a student's specific learning problems, (b) having poor content and criterion-related validity, and (c) having a "suspiciously high" reliability figure (p. 88). Yet, both the WRAT and the WRAT–R are used widely not only for determining eligibility but for diagnosing learning problems as well.

TABLE 3.2. Characteristics of tests for use with the learning disabled.

Intelligence

Test	Age range	Normative sample	Validity	Reliability	Measures
Wechsler Intelligence Scale for Children— Revised (Wechsler 1974)	Ages 6–0 to 15–11	Normal children (stratified sample: age, sex, race, etc.)	Acceptable (Sattler, 1982)	Acceptable (McLoughlin & Lewis, 1986)	Measures general intellectual performance
Wechsler Intelligence Scale for Adults (Wechsler, 1981)	Ages 16 to 74	Normed on both white and nonwhite	Acceptable (Simeonsson, 1986)	Acceptable (Simeonsson, 1986)	Measures general intellectual function
Stanford–Binet (Thorndike et al., 1985)	Ages 2–0 to adulthood	Normed on white and nonwhite	Very good (Swanson & Watson, 1982)	Very good (Sattler, 1982)	Measures general intellectual function
Kaufman Assessment Battery for Children (Kaufman & Kaufman, 1983)	Ages 2–5 to 12–5	National norms (stratified sample: sex, education of parent, ethnic and geographic considerations and school placement)	Not established (Salvia & Ysseldyke, 1988)	General scales; generally reliable, subtests are not (Salvia & Ysseldyke, 1988)	Assesses the way children process information and amount of information obtained for age level
Woodcock–Johnson Psychoeducational Battery, Part 1: Tests of Cognitive Ability (Woodcock, 1978)	Ages 3 to 80	Normal subjects (stratified sample: sex, race, occupational status, geographic area, and type of community)	Excellent (McLoughlin & Lewis, 1986 Salvia & Ysseldyke, 1988)	Excellent (McLoughlin & Lewis, 1986; Salvia & Ysseldyke, 1988)	Measures general cognitive function, specific cognitive abilities, and academic aptitudes
McCarthy Scales of Children's Abilities (McCarthy, 1972)	Ages 2–5 to 8–5	National norms (stratified sample: sex, age, "color," geographic region, father's occupation, urban–rural residence)	Excellent (Salvia & Ysseldyke, 1988)	Varies from poor to high (Salvia & Ysseldyke, 1988)	Wide range of skills (e.g., memory, reasoning, concepts, etc.)

Test	Range	Standardization sample	Predictive validity	Reliability	Skills measured
Key Math—Revised (Connolly, 1988)	Grades K–9	Nationally representative sample	Moderately predictive (Taylor, 1988)	Relatively low (Taylor, 1988)	Basic concepts, operations, and application (13 subtests)
Diagnostic Math Inventory/ Mathematics Systems (Gessell, 1983)	Grades K–8 9 and up	Criterion—referenced	Not included in manual (Salvia & Ysseldyke, 1988)	Not included in manual (Salvia & Ysseldyke, 1988)	Whole numbers, fractions, decimals, measurement and geometry, problem solving, and special topics
Stanford Achievement Test Series (Madden et al., 1983)	K–Grade 12	Exceptional standardization (Salvia & Ysseldyke, 1988)	Exceptionally good (Salvia & Ysseldyke, 1988)	Exceptionally good (Salvia & Ysseldyke, 1988)	Counting, shapes and forms, number concept: addition and subtraction
Physical development					
Bender Visual Motor, Gestalt Test (Bender, 1938)	Ages 5–0 to 11–0	Normal children (stratified on race)	Not established (Salvia & Ysseldyke, 1988) Questionable (Luftig, 1989)	Relatively low (Salvia & Ysseldyke, 1988) Questionable (Bush & Waugh, 1988)	Skill development in copying geometric designs (eye–hand coordination)
Developmental Test of Visual Perception (Frostig, et al., 1966)	Ages 4–0 to 7–11	Southern California (mostly middle class)	Lacking (Salvia & Ysseldyke, 1988) Little evidence (Luftig, 1989) Very low (Swanson & Watson, 1989)	Lacking (Salvia & Ysseldyke, 1988) Unacceptable (Luftig 1989) Inadequate (Swanson & Watson, 1989)	Eye–hand coordination, Figure–ground perception. Form consistency, position in space and spatial relations
Developmental Test of Visual–Motor Integration (Beery, 1982)	Ages 2–0 to 19–0	Normal children (stratified on sex, ethnicty, income, levels, and residence areas—urban rural, suburban)	Relatively high (Salvia & Ysseldyke, 1989)	Relatively high (Salvia & Ysseldyke, 1988)	Motor coordination and visual perception

TABLE 3.2. Continued

			Intelligence			
Test	Age range	Normative sample	Validity	Reliability	Measures
Purdue Perceptual Motor Survey (Roach & Kephart 1966)	Grades 1 to 4	Normal children (stratified on sex and socioeconomic status)	Questionable (Luftig, 1989)	Good (Salvia & Ysseldyke, 1988) Suspect (Luftig, 1989)	Perceptual motor abilities, including balance and posture, body image, and differentiation. Perceptual—motor match, ocular control, and form perception
Motor-Free Visual Perception Test (Colarusso & Hammill, 1972)	Ages 4–0 to 8–0	Normal children (stratified on race, economic levels, residence areas—urban, suburban, and rural)	Good (Swanson & Watson, 1989)	Reliable except for 4-year-olds (Swanson & Watson, 1989)	Spatial relationships visual discriminatory figure closure, and visual memory
			Reading			
Woodcock Reading Mastery Tests (Woodcock, 1987)	Grade 1 to 12 Ages 6 to 18	Normal subjects (stratified sample: race, community size, years of schooling, occupation, and income)	Highly variant (Salvia & Ysseldyke, 1988)	Low (Salvia & Ysseldyke, 1988)	Letter identification, word attack, word comprehension, and passage comprehension
Stanford Diagnostic Reading Test (Karlsen & Gardner, 1985)	Grades 1 to college	Stratified sample Exceptionally well done (Salvia & Ysseldyke, 1988)	Local judgment required (Salvia & Ysseldyke, 1988)	Very reliable (Salvia & Ysseldyke, 1988)	Wide range of reading skills
Test of Reading Comprehension (Brown & Hammill, 1985)	Ages 7–0 to 17–11	Questionable (Salvia & Ysseldyke, 1988)	Not convincing (Salvia & Ysseldyke, 1988)	Exceptionally good (Salvia & Ysseldyke, 1988)	Wide range of reading skills

Test	Age/Grade	Sample / Type	Validity	Reliability	Content
Standardized Reading Inventory (Newcomer, 1986)	Up to grade 8	Criterion referenced	Good (Salvia & Ysseldyke, 1988)	High (Salvia & Ysseldyke, 1988)	Oral plus silent skills
Prescriptive Reading Inventory/Reading System (CTB/McGraw-Hill, 1980)	Grades K–9	Criterion referenced	Expert opinion (Salvia & Ysseldyke, 1988)	No data in manual (Salvia & Ysseldyke, 1988)	
School achievement					
Peabody Individual Achievement Test, (Dunn & Markwardt, 1970)	Ages 5–3 to 18–3	Normal children (stratified on geographic region and community size)	Low (McLoughlin & Lewis, 1986; Salvia & Ysseldyke, 1988)	Low (McLoughlin & Lewis, 1986; Salvia & Ysseldyke, 1988)	Content areas: reading (recognition and comprehension), spelling, mathematics, and general information
Wide Range Achievement Test—Revised (Jastak & Wilkinson, 1984)	Ages 5–0 to 74 11	No information available on type of sample	Low (McLoughlin & Lewis, 1986; Salvia & Ysseldyke, 1988)	Low (McLoughlin & Lewis, 1986; Salvia & Ysseldyke, 1988)	Content areas: reading math, written language, and knowledge (science, social studies, and humanities)
Woodcock–Johnson Psycho-educational Battery, Part 2, Tests of Achievement (Woodcock, 1978)	Ages 3–0 to 8–0	Normal subjects (stratified sample: sex, race, occupational status, geographic area)	Excellent (McLoughlin & Lewis, 1986; Salvia & Ysseldyke, 1988)	Excellent (McLoughlin & Lewis, 1986; Salvia & Ysseldyke, 1988)	Content areas: reading, math, written language, and knowledge (science, social studies, and humanities)

TABLE 3.2. Continued

Intelligence

Spelling

Test	Age range	Normative sample	Validity	Reliability	Measures
Test of Written Language and Spelling (Hammill & Larsen, 1983)	Ages 7–0 to 18–11	Parallels 1980 census (no data on SES or ethnic composition)	Modest (Salvia & Ysseldyke, 1988)	Low (Salvia & Ysseldyke, 1988)	Word usage, punctuation and capitalization, spelling, handwriting, vocabulary, and sentence production
Test of Written Spelling, 2 (Larsen & Hammill, 1986)	Ages 6–0 to 18–5	Close to 1985 census	Excellent (Salvia & Ysseldyke, 1988)	Unusually good (Salvia & Ysseldyke, 1988) Good (Taylor, 1989)	Predictable and unpredictable words

In summary, those responsible for selecting norm-referenced tests must develop a "show-me" attitude when evaluating a test's suitability for use with an individual or a group of individuals. The technical aspects of the test, including the normative sample, validity, and reliablity as well as the age range addressed by the test, must by scrutinized carefully before administering the test. Responsibility for proving the test's suitability lies with the test's author(s), and such information must be stated clearly in accompanying test manuals.

For a comprehensive review of normative tests, readers should consult *Tests in Print—3* (Buros, 1983). This reference work contains a listing of every test registered with the Buros Institute of Mental Measurement, founded by Oscar Buros. The register contains the most comprehensive sources of test data in the world (Salvia & Ysseldyke, 1988).

Requirements of Assessment for Placement Purposes

PL 94-142 serves as a federal mandate for a free, appropriate public education for all handicapped children. This education is to be provided in the least restrictive environment, with the environment being specified and justified for each particular child. A comprehensive assessment should lead to data-based identification of each child's least restrictive educational setting(s). Because of the importance of assessment, a number of assessment criteria are stipulated in PL 94-142, and these criteria are as follows:

1. The assessment must be in the child's primary language or mode of communication.
2. The assessment should be culturally nonbiased.
3. The assessment must be multifaceted, with no reliance on a single measure. Rather, a battery of assessments must be given.
4. The test must be used for the purpose intended.
5. The assessment process must include relevant professionals within an interdisciplinary team.
6. Tests should be administered by personnel qualified to administer such tests.
7. The standardization sample used for the test must be similar to the child being tested.

Because the assessment must be administered in the child's native language, the primary language must be established before assessment. For example, a child whose native language is Spanish cannot be tested with instructions written in English. As an alternative, a Spanish-speaking, fully qualified/certified examiner may administer the test(s). This is the most preferable situation, but an acceptable alternative may include the use of an interpreter to translate the instructions for the child and the child's responses for the examiner. A word of caution, however, should be given in the use of interpreters. Often the translation of either instructions or responses may lead to some lost or changed meaning and, consequently, affect the obtained score or data. If a child's primary mode of communication is manual signing, an assessment must be given by an examiner who is trained in the same signing system. Another alternative, the use of culture-free tests, is not viable due to the lack of availability of such valid and reliable instructions for administration of the tests in the field.

When determining the child's eligibility for special education services, a battery of tests must be given. This requires the involvement of many professionals in the assessment process, each assessing the skills relevant to his area of specilization. For example, a psychiatrist or psychologist often is involved in assessing children who exhibit behavior problems. A speech and language pathologist may be part of an assessment team when the child's deficit area is speech, language, and/or hearing. The classroom teacher's role in the assessment process should be the providion of data in the area of academic achievement. Other professionals who may be involved in the process include physicians, social workers, and so forth. Only those who have been trained and earned certification in assessment of specialty areas may administer certain instruments, for example, the psychologist who is trained and certified to administer intelligence tests.

Regardless of the test to be used, it must be both valid and reliable. Additionally, the normative sample upon which the test was standardized must match the child's own background (e.g., socioeconomic status, geographic location, sex, age, etc.). Further, a test should be used only for its intended purpose. A reading test, for example, connot be used as a measure of intelligence, nor should inference about intelligence be made based on the reading test results. These results should be used only for the purposes of assessing reading skills and planning instructional strategies. Should a test not be valid, reliable, or match the child's background, the test results will be invalid. When assessing any child, written consent must be obtained before the assessment takes place.

Placement Process

When the assessment are completed, the parents should be notified that an IEP meeting will be held. This meeting must be held within 50 days of the receipt of the referral. The members of an IEP team include relevant school personnel, such as regular classroom teachers of the student, special education teacher(s) from current and target settings, a special education administrator, school psychologists, and specialists as well as parents or guardians of the student and the student, if appropriate. Parents particularly should be encouraged to attend the IEP meeting and the school must take the following steps to promote parent participation (McLoughlin & Lewis, 1986):

parent must be notified in advance of meetings, purpose, times, locations, and participants

there must be mutual agreement on time and place

conference call should be used if the parents cannot attend

school must document all attempts to encourage parents' attendance

interpreters are to be used, if needed, so parents can fully understand proceedings of IEP meeting.

The overriding concern in placement decisions is in attempting to meet the needs of the child in an educational setting that is as close to the educational mainstream as possible. Changing placements (i.e., mobility in the educational continuum of services) must be an option available to each child at all times and must be considered in decision making. Adapted from Mercer and Mercer's (1989) description of placement options, the following model describes the range of educational placements.

Regular Classroom

The optimal placement for a learning disabled child is in the regular classroom where the student remains all day. The normalization principle is best exemplified by this placement, as the regular class is the least restrictive environment of all levels described by many models (Mercer & Mercer, 1989). Careful consideration of each child's needs on a student-by-student basis must be made before recommending the regular classroom placement. Two of the advantages are: (a) provision of interaction between handicapped and nonhandicapped peers and (b) reduction of the problem of labeling the handicapped child. Some of the disadvantages include: (a) handicapped student is included in a large class population, (b) regular classroom teacher may not be specifically trained to work with handicapped students, and (c) teacher may not provide small group or individual instruction (Mercer & Mercer, 1989).

Consultant Model

When a handicapped student's needs can be met in the regular classroom by using additional materials and equipment, this model may be appropriate. Idol–Maestas (1983) defines consultation as support provided to regular classroom teachers to assist them with the academic and social behavior problems of handicapped learners. Graden, Casey, and Christenson (1985) note that the consultation model helps in identifying areas of concern, exploring alternative interventions, and implementing and evaluating intervention strategies. Advantages of this model, according to Mercer and Mercer (1989), include the consultant's being able to (a) reach more teachers, (b) serve more children, (c) supply specific instructional methods, programs, and materials to teachers, (d) influence environmental learning variables, and (e) coordinating comprehensive services for children. Disadvantages are (a) not possessing the firsthand knowledge of students that comes from teaching them and (b) separating assessment from instruction.

Itinerant Services

Mercer and Mercer (1989) define "itinerant services" as those provided by a special education teacher to regular education teachers in various schools. Children served by this model are those whose difficulties are not severe enough to warrant resource room instruction or special class placement. The itinerant teacher serves as a facilitator who assists regular education teachers by demonstrating "best practice" skills. The services may range from daily to biweekly visits, with the basic responsiblity for the child remaining with the regular classroom teacher. Mercer and Mercer (1989) claim the advantages as (a) aiding in the screening and diagnosing of handicapped students, (b) offering part-time services to regular education teachers, (c) covering needs of children in different schools, and (d) providing an economical way of addressing mild learning problems. Disadvantages include (a) the inability to provide consistent support to more involved students, (b) the difficulty of transporting materials from one school to another, (c) the lack of program continuity, and (d) the lack of regular follow-up.

Resource Room

Many students with learning difficulties spend a large portion of the day in a regular classroom and are "pulled out" to go to a resource room. The specified amount of time may varies according to the individual child's needs. The resource teacher is located on the school site and works closely with the handicapped students' teachers in coordinating the students' instructional programs.

Several service options are available to the resource teacher who may, in a separate classroom (resource room), teach small groups of children or a child individually on a weekly basis, or teach children either one-to-one or in small groups on a daily basis. When working with the regular education teacher, the resource teacher may provide consultation services or teach the learning disabled child in the regular class. In addition, the resource teacher may refer the child for outside help or recommend special class placement.

Many researchers claim major advantages to the resource teacher model (Mercer & Mercer, 1989; Sargent, 1981; Speece & Mandell, 1980; Wiederholt, Hammill, & Brown, 1983). The advantages include better use of resources, serving learning disabled students while they are being mainstreamed, provision of individualized instruction, prevention of needless labeling, and supplementing regular classroom instruction.

Disadvantages to this model, according to Mercer and Mercer (1989), include not being well suited to serve severely learning disabled students, tendency toward overenrollment, provision of no time to observe students or consult with regular education teachers, provision of little time to assess and plan, and creation of scheduling problems.

Assessment for Instructional Planning and Evaluation

The previous sections of this chapter dealt with the utilization of assessment instruments and materials for the purposes of (a) referral and screening and (b) diagnosis and placement. This section will examine assessment methods relevant for planning instructional programs and evaluating instruction. If the purpose of assessment is instructional planning, then assessment should lead directly to instructional intervention. Therefore, assessment in academic areas should be directly related to current and future instructional programming efforts (Brown, 1987; Gickling & Thompson, 1985; Tucker, 1985). One should be able to assess sequenced skills that, when found deficient, are targeted for intervention. Furthermore, evaluation of student progress should be related directly to the skills being targeted.

Such is not the case with commonly used norm-referenced assessment instruments. The utilization of norm-referenced materials for instructional planning has been criticized as being either inappropriate and/or unrelated (Jenkins & Pany, 1978; Salvia & Ysseldyke, 1988). In using standardized norm-referenced tests, the teacher is unable to identify a hierarchy or sequence of skills assessed and, therefore, cannot identify which skills are deficient and which skills have been mastered.

Testing that is administered primarily to determine that a student has a learning disability for the purpose of eligibility for special services usually does not provide any specific program recommendations (Tucker, 1985). The traditional assumption that such a diagnosis is important in programming curriculum or treatment is to imply that education has a very specific technology that works for all children with learning disabilities. Therefore, a related assumption is that identifying a particular student as learning disabled allows us to treat him effectively in the same fashion as other students diagnosed with learning disabilities. In point of fact, the exact opposite can be contended! More commonly, children with deficits diagnosed as learning disabilites have different skill deficits, different rates of acquisition of new skills, and probably respond differently to a variety of academic interventions. Therefore, the usefulness of such a diagnosis seems to be rather limited in providing specific recommendations to teaching personnel as to what specific curriculum content and what methods of instruction should be provided for any given student diagnosed as learning disabled.

Currently, there is movement away from norm-referenced assessment, with a preference for curriculum-based assessment (CBA), to allow for a more direct relationship between assessment and programmatic and curriculum prescription (Tucker, 1985). Curriculum-based assessment, broadly defined, is any procedure that directly assesses student performance within the course content of the local school for the purpose of determining that student's instructional needs (Tucker, 1985).

The characteristics of CBA vary across applications, but in general involve the following:

1. a direct relationship between assessment and instruction
2. direct frequent measurement of student performance
3. a way of matching student ability to instruction.

The relationship between curriculum-based assessment and instruction is direct and straightforward. The assessment of student performance is conducted using current curriculum materials already in use, thereby providing a direct measure of the target behaviors. Therefore, the utilization of CBA can enhance instructional planning and subsequent evaluation of student progress (Fuchs, Deno, & Mirkin, 1984; Fuchs, Fuchs, & Hamlett, 1989; Fuchs, Fuchs, Hamlett, & Hasselbring, 1987; Fuchs, Fuchs, & Stecker, 1989). By measuring student performance directly, the teacher can use such data to evaluate current student progress and plan future instruction more effectively for each individual student.

Research has substantiated the relationship between CBA and student progress (Bigge, 1988; Deno & Fuchs, 1987; Fuchs, Fuchs, & Maxwell, 1988; Marston & Magnusson, 1985). Teachers who use CBA with frequent measurement of student performance cite more objective and frequent data sources for determining the adequacy of student progress (Fuchs, Fuchs, & Stecker, 1989). Also, positive results of using CBA have been found with respect to teacher satisfaction and efficiency (Fuchs, Fuchs, et al., 1987) as well as students' knowledge of their performance (Fuchs, Butterworth, & Fuchs, in press). In the latter study, the teachers systematically monitored and graphed students' progress toward goals for 3 months. Students reported that they received more teacher feedback than students in a control group, in which the teachers did not use such systematic monitoring of performance.

For the purposes of this chapter, CBA will be delineated in regard to two specific applications: (a) CBA applications to existing (commercially available) curricula and (b) CBA applications to specifically designed curricula that a priori designate a set of assessments within the curriculum (assessment is an inherent feature).

CBA for Existing Curriculum

One of the goals of CBA is to make data on student achievement available to teachers on a daily basis, thus allowing them to use such data in decision-making procedures (Deno, 1985). According to Deno (1985), a useful curriculum-based measurement system should have the following characteristics:

1. reliable and valid in terms of assessing student achievement and "should provide data for making instructional decisions"
2. simple and efficient to implement so that it encourages teachers to use it
3. easily understood so that results can be communicated to others
4. inexpensive since multiple forms are required to conduct repeated measurement of student performance.

The importance of establishing the above criteria and using such in the development of a CBA measure is strikingly apparent when one deals with a curriculum area such as reading. The best measurement of student performance would be achieved by the teacher designing questions around the reading text material. Although the development of questions on specific reading materials certainly would be reliable and valid (meeting the first criterion), it would not be efficient for teachers to invest that much time for all curriculum text materials. Thus, such a measure does not meet the second criterion and probably would not develop widespread appeal.

There are other measurement methods that meet all of the above criteria in assessing skill performance in the reading content area. Four measures that Deno (1985) identified as meeting the above criterial are the following:

1. cloze procedures—supplying words deleted from text
2. saying the meaning of words underlined in the text
3. reading aloud from isolated word lists
4. reading aloud from text passages.

The above methods do not possess the same degree of validity as responding to questions designed to measure the student's comprehension of text material, but they do meet the other criteria (e.g., simple and efficient system, easily understood). Some of these measures of reading performance have proven to be more valid than the others in assessing reading skill.

The most efficient and valid CBA measure of reading skill supported by research studies is to measure the student's rate of correct responses when reading aloud from text passages (Deno, Marston, Shinn, & Tindall, 1983; Fuchs et al., 1988). Correct rate of response when reading aloud from a text has correlated highly with comprehension scores on standardized tests (Deno et al., 1983, Fuchs et al., 1988). For example, Fuchs and Deno (1981) found a .93 correlation between reading aloud from text and word identification subtest and a .93 correlation between reading aloud from text and the passage change subtest on the Woodcock Reading Mastery Test. Similar correlations have been found between "reading aloud from text" and word-study skills subtests of the Stanford Achievement Test (Fuchs et al., 1988). Other CBA measures (e.g., saying the meaning of words) demonstrated a lower validity coefficient with the Stanford Achievement Test (Fuchs et al., 1988). "One-minute samples of number of words read correctly" have demonstrated high correspondence with reading proficiency across all elementary grade levels (Deno, 1985). Final evidence for the validity of reading aloud from text as a measure of reading skill is its ability to discriminate students who are in special education programs from students not in special education (Deno, 1985).

The cloze procedure is designed as an alternative to reading aloud from text in measuring reading comprehension (Salvia & Hughes, 1990). In the cloze procedure, the teacher selects a passage of about 250 words from several stages in the reading curriculum. The teacher types the passage, omitting every fifth word, leaving intact the first and last sentence (Salvia & Hughes, 1990). The students then write the missing words in the blank spaces.

Curriculum-based measures also can be developed for written expression and spelling (Deno, Marston, & Mirkin, 1982; Deno, Mirkin, Lowry, & Kuehnle, 1980; Fuchs, Fuchs, Hamlett, & Allinder, 1989), with similar levels of criterion validity found for such CBA measures. When an assessment was made of students using CBA and an error analysis in spelling and achievement levels were compared with those of a control group of students not using CBA and a phonetic error analysis in spelling, it was found that the experimental students had significantly greater achievement levels (Fuchs et al., 1989). Developmental trends obtained in the reading research on CBA are paralleled in both of these areas as well. The use of CBA, with written expression and spelling, requires the teacher to obtain repeated samplings of student performance in the curriculum. Again, brief measurement samples within the curriculum provide a valid and efficient method of determining a student's progress.

Curriculum Materials Designed for CBA

The advantages of using a CBA measurement system with existing curricula are obvious. However, a major flaw in designing a CBA system based on existing curriculum is the inherent assumption that the current curriculum contains a hierarchical, well designed sequence of objectives. A second assumption is that the current, commercially available curriculum is designed in such a manner that mastery performance of one skill is required before advancement to the next skill or objective. In many cases, these two assumptions are false. Designing a CBA system for an existing curriculum certainly will allow the teacher to monitor student performance more readily and frequently. However, CBA is less effective as an ongoing intervention technique if the curriculum is poorly designed. Subsequently, students may not acquire skills in a timely and efficient manner. Further, the ability to pinpoint precisely the deficient skill or subskill areas may not be available with curriculum that is not designed in a task-analyzed hierarchical manner.

A more preferred approach to curriculum design and CBA would be to design materials that provide CBA as an inherent component of the curriculum using an instructional systems approach. In this manner, one would be sure that the assessment of valid relevant measures is inherent in the curriculum materials. This would require curriculum designers to focus on developing a sequence of hierarchically ordered objectives, with multiple test items available for each objective. Such items would be used to probe learner acquisition and to determine the current and future instructional programs.

The following steps, or instructional design components, have been advanced (Cipani, 1987; Dick & Carey, 1985) in developing curriculum materials that provide for functional assessment within the materials.

1. Identify the terminal objective(s) with the content area.
2. Sequence subordinate objectives for each terminal objective within the content area by conducting an instructional analysis.
3. Design criterion-referenced tests to measure each subordinate objective.
4. Design a pretest to measure student performance before entrance on instructional material for each subordinate objective.
5. Develop decision rules as they relate to student progression on curriculum materials/objectives.
6. Design the instructional units for each subordinate objective.
7. Ensure that the amount of new behavior to be presented in drill or rehearsal format is small and that student practice provides for a greater proportion of new material to material already acquired.
8. Assess frequently, through probes, newly acquired material along with previously acquired material.

Examples of curricula materials that feature inherent CBA systems include a set of materials in basic math called Number Facts Mastery Program (Henderson & Erken, 1989a) and another called Reading Mastery Program (Henderson & Erken, 1989b). The performance criterial involves three components: (a) accuracy, (b) rate, and (c) maintenance. The student's performance must be accurate as well as occurring at a designated rate (approximating one response per second). Henderson and Erken (1989a, 1989b) contend that a fluent (rate/time) response is needed, in addition to accuracy, in order to facilitate maintenance across time and transfer to new skills. Additionally, probe assessments always involve evaluation of previously acquired skills in addition to the current target skill. Sets of math and reading program materials both incorporate the same format in design and measurement of student progress in the curriculum. The assessment format is the following:

1. The terminal objective is identified.
2. Sequence of objectives/skills is designed from that terminal objective.
3. A pretest is given to determine if the child is deficient in the terminal skill.
4. A prerequisite test for the target skill is given to determine if such skills are at mastery level.

Given the above assessment information, the instructional program provided is relevant for the current specific objective. Using direct instruction and independent practice, the student is trained on each new skill to criterion. The probe test, called a "timed drill," is given by the teacher, with the items/material on the practice sheet. Mastery criteria are usually set (at one response per second, 100% accuracy over items, with a brief probe of 6–10 items). Achievement of mastery criteria allows the student to progress to the next objective, with the new instructional program geared specifically to the development of that objective.

In summary, curriculum-based assessment procedures are best suited for linking the program of assessment to the planning and evaluation of instruction. The design of a CBA instrument, with existing or adopted curriculum materials, is usually done by the teacher or a team of school district personnel. However, future trends in curriculum design should lead to curriculum-based measures as an inherent part of the curriculum program.

Assessment of Problem Behaviors in Learning Disabled Students

Authors of a chapter on educational assessment of children, adolescents, and young adults with learning disabilities would be remiss if they did not include a section on the assessment of problem behavior. The types of problems encountered in working with students who have learning and behavior problems vary. Research has indicated that such children tend to be off-task and less attentive than their classmates (Bryan & Wheeler, 1972; Forness & Esveldt, 1971; Richy & McKinney, 1978). Boys with learning disabilities repeatedly show more verbal aggression than their classmates and exhibit other social interaction problems (Bryan & Bryan, 1983). Quite often, classroom teachers must deal with social behavior as well as academic deficits when working with children with learning disabilities.

A functional assessment for problem behaviors should serve the primary purpose of allowing the consumer of the assessment report to prescribe a potentially successful intervention. Such an assessment should include an analysis of the problem behavior in the context of the classroom and/or other relevant settings or conditions. Therefore, the environmental context (or contexts) that occasions and maintains the problem behavior is of utmost relevance in determining the possible solution(s) to such a problem behavior (Bailey & Pyles, 1989; Danforth & Drabman, 1989). Given this premise, data collection efforts must be related to the characteristics of the behavior problem and not the individual person.

Most assessments of problem behavior focus heavily on defining the topography (or response form) of the specific behavior(s) and quantifying the rate of occurrence. Observational systems designed for classroom use often measure the rate of target behaviors (e.g., frequency, duration, percentage of occurrence), but do not provide an analysis of antecedent conditions or setting events that occasion higher rates of target behavior, nor do they provide for an analysis of current maintaining contingencies. In contrast, a growing body of Literature is identifying the need to assess response–consequence relationships (Carr & Durand, 1985; Repp, Felce, & Barton, 1988; Steege, Wacker, Berg, Cigrand, & Cooper, 1989) as well as the role of antecedent conditions and stimuli (Bailey & Pyles, 1989; Mace, Hock, Lalli, West, Belfiore, Pinter, & Brown, 1988; Singh & Repp, 1988; Touchette, MacDonald, & Langer, 1985; Weeks & Gaylord–Ross, 1981) in providing a usedul behavioral analysis of problem behavior. The need to incorporate assessment procedures that would allow one to collect data about the relationships between the controlling environmental and/or physiological variables (Bailey & Pyles, 1989) and the student's behavior requires a shift in emphasis from a response driven topographic assessment to one that focuses on an anlysis of the environmental function(s) of the problem behaviors.

A functional analysis involves collecting assessment data that aid in identifying the environmental function that a behavior problem (or problems) serves. This type of assessment is in contrast to the traditional assessment focus on the characteristics of the student, with environmental variables playing a much lesser role in the analysis and treatment of the problem behavior.

Assumptions and Characteristics of a Functional Analysis

The assumptions and characteristics delineated below exemplify a functional analysis:

1. The primary purpose of a functional analysis is to identify the function that the problem behavior serves.
2. Identifying the function of a behavior problem will lead directly to the selection of a relevant intervention (Repp et al., 1988; Steege et al., 1989).

3. The cause(s) and maintenance of the problem behavior are derived primarily from the environmental contingencies supporting such a behavior (Repp et al., 1988).
4. Behavior problems are analyzed in the context of the environmental ecology (LaVigna, Willis, & Donnellan, 1989).
5. A focus on the topography of the problem behavior alone is inadequate.
6. One problem behavior can serve multiple functions under different antecedent conditions.
7. One environmental function can be produced by multiple topographically dissimilar behaviors.

A major assumption of a functional analysis is that the cause and/or maintenance of the problem behavior(s) can be found by examining the environmental conditions under which the behavior occurs. This is not to say that all behavior problems are caused by "faulty" environmental contingencies. The potential for inherited characteristics as the cause of certain behavior problems is not discounted. For example, an organic basis for learning disabilities necessarily would not be ruled out. Nevertheless, the rate and/or maintenance of behavior, however caused, can be altered by the environmental contingencies that follow it under identified antecedent conditions. A related tenet is that identification of controlling variables will lead directly to a treatment strategy that is functionally related to such variables (Durand, 1987).

As an example of the use of a functional analysis of behavior to determine the controlling variables, Repp et al. (1988) identified three possible hypotheses for the maintenance of target problem behaviors for three students with severe mental retardation who were enrolled in special education classes. The three hypotheses were: (a) behaviors may be maintained by positive reinforcement, (b) behaviors may be maintained by negative reinforcement, and (c) behaviors may be maintained by self-stimulation. Baseline date were collected to identify which hypothesis was more likely. Data were collected on the consequence of each behavior. For example, if the teacher was close to the child, if the child was touched, or if the child was given verbal attention, positive reinforcement was presumed to be operable. To determine if negative reinforcement was operable, the observers noted if any events were removed contingent upon the occurrence of the behavior. To determine if the behavior was occurring due to a lack of stimulation (Reep, Karsh, & VanAcker, 1987), the observers noted if the child was held or addressed by another person or if the child engaged in an activity in the 10-sec period before the behavior.

If positive reinforcement was responsible for maintaining the problem behavior, extinction was programmed (i.e., removal of staff attention). If negative reinforcement was hypothesized as responsible for maintaining the behavior, a general compliance training procedure was the intervention of choice. If self-stimulation was identified as the most likely hypothesis, then increased contact between child and the environment was programmed. Results indicated that when the intervention was selected on the basis of the hypothesis generated from the initial baseline data, the child's level of problem behavior was reduced drastically. However, when the intervention was not relevant for the hypothesis regarding the function of behavior, the level of behavior change was not substantial.

The third characteristic enumerated is that problems are analyzed in the context of their environmental ecologies. The roles of antecedent and consequent stimuli are analyzed to determine their relationship to the level of the behavior problem. Given this tenet, a sole focus on the topography or form of the behavior (e.g., aggression) presents an inadequate analysis and data base to solve the problem. Behavior problems should be analyzed and subsequently treated according to their environmental function, not their topography (Repp et al., 1988).

Another assumption is that one problem behavior can serve multiple functions. For example, a child's aggression during math period may serve a completely different environmental function than similar aggression exhibited during free play on the playground. These two instances of aggression can serve two different functions and, therefore, should be treated differently. Also, one environmental function can be produced by multiple, topographically dissimilar behaviors. For example, different topographical behaviors, such as aggression, having tantrums, and noncompliance, may serve the same environmental function for one child or several different children within the same class. These latter two assumptions will be explained in more detail in a later section.

In conducting a functional analysis, two sets of relations essentially must be examined: (a) type of reinforcement contingency, and (b) type of access to reinforcers.

Reinforcement Contingencies

There are two types of reinforcement contingencies. Positive reinforcement contingencies are defined as those in which an environmental event is presented contingent on the behavior and, as a result, the behavior increases or maintains in frequency across time (Foxx, 1982a; Repp, 1983). As an example, a child in the classroom throws a pencil in an attempt to hit the trash can, causing a peer to giggle upon observing such a behavior. If the consequence of the behavior (i.e., giggling by a peer) is reinforcing, and throwing a pencil reliably produces peer attention, then such a relationship between behavior and consequence will result in an increase and/or maintenance of that behavior. From this hypothetical example one would deduce that inappropriate or problem behavior is maintained by positive reinforcement.

Negative reinforcement contingencies are those in which an environmental event is terminated as a function of the occurrence of a specified behavior, with a subsequent increase or maintenance in the level of that behavior, given the presence of those antecedent conditions (Foxx, 1982b; Repp, 1983). For example, a child fails to comply with a teacher's request to turn in his seat work. The teacher makes several requests, and each request is met by noncompliance on the child's part. After the third request, the teacher withdraws her request. This teacher's behavior negatively reinforces (by removal of task demands) a chain of noncompliance on the part of the child. For further delineation of these paradigms and examples illustrative of such operants, the reader should consult any number of texts in applied behavior analysis, including those reference above (Foxx, 1982a, 1982b; Repp, 1983).

Different contingencies could be operable, under different antecedent conditions or stimuli, for the same problem behavior. For example, a young child's tantrum behavior during reading could be maintained by negative reinforcement contingencies (via removal of instructional demands), whereas the same type of behavior, tantrums, could be positively reinforced during lunch (via access to desired items). It is therefore important to identify the antecedents (including setting events), discriminative stimuli, and/or establishing operations (Sundberg, 1983) that have stimulus control over the occurrence of problem behaviors. Noncompliance, for example, as identified in the previous illustration, may occur more frequently with certain tasks, certain settings, or certain people. Identifying these antecedents allows one to use these data in setting up alternate contingencies in keeping with the prevailing antecedents.

Types of Access

Within the contingencies, Skinner (1957) identified two types of access to consequent events, which define two different classes of operant behavior. One class of operant behavior is termed *verbal behavior*. Skinner (1957) operationally defines verbal behavior as any behavior that achieves its effect on the environment through the behavior of some other person(s). In simpler terms, verbal behavior is behavior that is reinforced through the mediation of another person (Cipani, 1988; Michael, 1988; Sundberg, 1983). The speaker's behavior contacts the mediating agent who, in turn, contacts the environment. The result of such contact is the delivery of an event that reinforces the behavior of the speaker (Vargas, 1988). Requesting someone to unlock a locked door is an example of a behavior (requesting) that achieves its effect through the mediation of another person.

Verbal behavior need not be vocal (Cipani, 1988; Sundberg, 1983). In the above example, if the same effect of someone unlocking the door is achieved by pointing to the door, that behavior (pointing) is verbal behavior. Under this definitive example, many aberrant behaviors that are displayed by persons with severe handicaps (e.g., self-abuse) that are maintained by indirect access to desired events (Carr & Durand, 1985; Donnellan, Mirenda, Mesaros, & Fassbender, 1984; Repp et al., 1988) would be classified as verbal behaviors. As an illustration, a child hits himself, which then serves to bring an adult to him, thereby resulting in the provision of attention and reassurance to the child. An analysis of these contingencies reveals that this result maintains the self-abusive behavior, particularly when access to attention is either absent or minimal for other behaviors. Self-abuse serves the same function in this particular case as more common requesting forms such as "Come here, I want to be with you" or "Pay attention to me" would serve. Because self-abuse in this context serves the same function (i.e., accessing adult attention) as alternate vocal communicative behaviors, it is a verbal behavior, given this analysis.

Another type of operant behavior is *nonverbal behavior*. Nonverbal behavior involves behavior that directly contacts the physical environment, directly accessing the reinforcer. For example, a person wants to open a locked door. Instead of requesting a key from someone, he gets the key off the key rack and unlocks the door. The behavioral chain of getting the key, then inserting and turning the key constitutes nonverbal behavior, in that the reinforcer (gaining access) is directly produced by the occurrence of the chain of behaviors. Note that both types of behaviors, verbal and nonverbal, produce the same environmental outcome.

Environmental Function

There are four possible environmental functions, given the two types of contingencies and two types of access (indirect and direct). In assessment of problem behavior, one needs to identify which environmental function(s) the problem behavior is serving. This analysis allows one to determine why a problem behavior is maintained at high levels. An example of this analysis is given below with a child's aggression during morning math as the referral problem. Assume that aggression is operationally defined as "hits the teacher or other children in the class." The behavior analyst has observed that the result of aggressive behavior is that the child usually is sent to the corner of the room or outside of the classroom. Examination of this contingent relation reveals that aggressive behavior serves to remove or postpone math seat work. One can see a negative reinforcement paradigm operating and that access to task removal is indirect, in that the teacher mediates such a relationship by terminating math seat work contingent upon the occurrence of aggression. Therefore, a functional analysis reveals that this problem, given the presence of math seat work, serves a negative reinforcement, indirect access, function.

To illustrate a different environmental function, the same aggressive behavior of the same child, in a different setting (recess on playground), can be used. Observation of the child's behavior in this context reveals that the aggression occurs when a peer has a toy that the child wants. As a result of being aggressed upon repeatedly, the victim eventually leaves the toy and moves away from the aggressive child. The child then picks up the toy he wanted. One can recognize positive reinforcement contingencies in effect, in that access to the toy is mediated by the child who relinquishes the toy by dropping it. Therefore, a different environmental function is operable during this time, that is, indirect access to positive reinforcement. Note that the same aggressive behavior can serve two different functions in two different contexts. Therefore, a functional analysis must identify the specific function of the problem behavior for specific contexts.

Antecedent variables need to be identified as well for each function. To assist in identifying the antecedents to problem behaviors, Touchette et al. (1985) have identified a method called *scatter plotting*. In scatter plotting, the occurrence of the target behavior is plotted as a function of time. Using scatter plot data, one can determine specific time periods that seem to occasion higher rates of behavior and the motivation for such behaviors can then be assessed.

Identifying "Replacement" Behavior

In order for assessment to truly be functional, it should link assessment results with prescriptive intervention. After the analysis of the environmental function of the problematic behavior has been conducted, one needs to identify potential alternative behaviors that are appropriate and serve the same function. These are termed *replacement* behaviors or functionally equivalent behaviors (LaVigna et al., 1989). Replacement behaviors are behaviors that result in reinforcement and serve the same environmental function for same-aged peers under similar antecedent conditions (Cipani, 1990). The use of a social comparison method (Kazdin & Matson, 1981) allows one to identify what behaviors result in natural reinforcement contingencies in specified settings and/or natural contexts. This approach is consistent with the emphasis placed on serving students in less restrictive environments.

When conducting an assessment of the strength of alternate replacement behaviors that serve the same function, one would want to include the following information:

1. rate of both sets of alternate replacement behaviors
2. operable natural contingencies for both replacement behaviors
3. antecedent events or stimuli that should occasion either or both replacement behaviors.

This will allow the professional who is conducting the assessment to determine if selected replacement behaviors result in reinforcement in the natural environment and also the antecedent conditions for their occurrence.

One should be able to identify two types of alternative behaviors that could "replace" the problem behavior in terms of its current environmental function. One alternate replacement behavior can serve a direct access function and the other can serve an indirect access function.

An example of two sets of replacement behaviors can be illustrated in a hypothetical example of a child stealing food from other children during lunch. The environmental function of such a behavior might reveal a direct access, positive reinforcement function, that is, the child directly accesses desired food items. Two sets of alternate behaviors can be identified for differential reinforcement:

1. allow child to take a second lunch tray (after getting in line again, etc.), which results in direct access to reinforcement
2. have child request an additional helping from cafeteria staff, which results in indirect access to reinforcement.

Prescriptive Treatment for Environmental Functions

The selection of a treatment strategy is a direct result of an environmental functional analysis of the problem behavior. Behavior problems exhibited by students with learning disabilities would be addressed by treatments that directly relate to the environmental function that such a behavior serves. For example, a treatment strategy for a behavior serving an indirect access to positive reinforcement function would involve the shaping and reinforcement of an alternate behavior, or behaviors, that could serve the same function. Concurrently, contingencies that reinforce and maintain the target problem behavior should be removed. Problems that serve an indirect access to negative reinforcement function can be analyzed in the same fashion, using a prescriptive treatment model.

In conclusion, the assessment of problem behaviors in children, adolescents, and young adults with learning disabilities cannot focus exclusively on the topography of the behavior. Rather, the analysis of the behavior's environmental function must be conducted. A model for assessing problem behavior through an environmental functional analysis was provided. The environmental function is viewed for each behavior within each antecedent context. Prospective treatment is based on the identified environmental function(s) for each problem behavior. The selection of replacement behavior is made on the basis of those behaviors serving the same function as the problem behavior in the specific environment(s).

Summary

This chapter has delineated assessment methods relevant for three aspects of assessment: (a) referral and screening, (b) diagnosis and placement, and (c) instructional planning and evaluation of student progress. Additionally, a behavioral functional analysis has been identified as a useful method for assessing and analyzing the environmental context of problem behavior.

References

Algozzine, B., Christenson, S., & Ysseldyke, J. E. (1982). "Probabilities" associated with the referral to placement process. *Teacher Education and Special Education, 5*, 19–23.

Bailey, J. S., & Pyles, D. A. M. (1989). Behavioral diagnostic. In E. Cipani (Ed.), *The treatment of severe behavior disorders: Behavior analysis approaches* (pp. 85–110). Washington, DC: American Association on Mental Retardation.

Beery, K. E. (1982). *Revised administration, scoring, and teaching manual for the developmental test of visual-motor integration.* Cleveland, OH: Modern Curriculum Press.

Bender, L. (1938). *A visual motor gestalt test and its clinical use* (Research Monograph No. 3). New York: American Orthopsychiatric Association.

Bigge, J. (1988). *Curriculum-based instruction for special education students.* Mountain View, CA: Mayfield Publishing.

Boehm, A. E. (1986). *Boehm Test of Basic Concepts—Revised.* San Antonio, TX: The Psychological Corporation.

Brown, F. (1987). Meaningful assessment of people with severe and profound handicaps. In M. E. Snell (Ed.), *Systematic instruction of persons with severe handicaps*, (3rd ed., pp. 39–63). Columbus, OH: Merrill Publishing.

Brown, L. L., & Hammill, D. D. (1983a). *Behavior rating profile.* Austin, TX: Pro-Ed.

Brown, V. L., Hammill, D. D., & Wiederholt, H. L. (1986). *Test of reading comprehension: Revised.* Austin, TX: Pro-Ed.

Bryan, J. H., & Bryan, T. (1983). The social life of LD youngsters. In J. D. McKinney & L. Feagan (Eds.), *Current topics in learning disabilities* (Vol. 1). Norwood, NJ: Ablex.

Bryan, T., & Wheeler, R. (1972). Perceptions of children with learning disabilities: The eye of the observer. *Journal of Learning Disabilities, 5*, 484–488.

Buros, O. K. (1983). *Tests in print—3.* Lincoln, NE: Buros Institute of Mental Measurements.

Bush, W. J., & Waugh, K. W. (1982). *Diagnosing learning problems* (3rd ed.). Columbus, OH: Charles E. Merrill.

Carr, E., & Durand, V. M. (1985). Reducing behavioural problems through functional communication training. *Journal of Applied Behavior Analysis, 18*, 111–126.

Cipani, E. (1987). Errorless learning technology: Theory, research and practice. In J. L. Matson & R. P. Barrett (Eds.), *Advances in developmental disorders* (Vol. 1, pp. 237–275). Greenwich, CT., JAI Press.

Cipani, E. (1988). *Behavior analysis language program: Theory, assessment and training practices for personnel working with people with severe handicaps.* Bellevue, WA: Edmark Publishers.

Cipani, E. (1990). The communicative function hypothesis: An operant behavior perspective. *Joural of Behavior Theory and Experimental Psychiatry, 21,* 239–247.

Colarusso, R., & Hammill, D. (1972). The motor-free test of visual perception. San Rafael, CA: Academic Therapy Publications.

Connolly, A. J. (1988). *Key Math—Revised: A diagnostic inventory of essential mathematics.* Circle Pines, MN: American Guidance Service.

Coopersmith, S. (1981). *Coopersmith self-esteem inventories.* Palo Alto, CA: Consulting Psychologists Press.

CTB/McGraw-Hill. (1980). *Prescriptive reading inventory/reading system.* Monterey, CA:

Danforth, J. S., & Drabman, R. S. (1989). Aggressive and disruptive behavior. In E. Cipani (Ed.), *The treatment of severe behavior disorders: Behavior analysis approaches* (pp. 111–128). Washington, DC: American Association on Mental Retardation.

Deno, S. L. (1985). Curriculum-based measurement: The emerging alternative. *Exceptional Children, 52,* 219–238.

Deno, S. L., & Fuchs, L. (1987). Developing curriculum-based measurement systems for data-based special education problem solving. *Focus on Exceptional Children, 19,* 1–16.

Deno, S. L., Marston, D., & Mirkin, P. (1982). Valid measurement procedures for continuous evaluation of written expression. *Exceptional Children, 48*(4), 368–371.

Deno, S. L., Marston, D., Shinn, M., & Tindall, G. (1983). Oral reading fluency: A simple datum for scaling reading disability. *Topics in Learning and Learning Disabilities, 2*(4), 53–59.

Deno, S., Mirkin, P., Lowry, L., & Kuehnle, K. (1980). *Relationships among simple measures of spelling and performance on standardized achievement tests (Research Report No. 21).* Minneapolis: University of Minnesota. Institute for Research on Learning Disabilities (ERIC Document Reproduction Service No. ED 197 508).

Dick, W., & Carey, L. (1985). *The systematic design of instruction* (2nd ed.). Glenview, IL: Scott, Foresman & Company.

Donnellan, A. M., Mirenda, P. L., Mesaros, R. A., & Fassbender, L. L. (1984). Analyzing the communicative function of aberrant behavior. *Journal of the Association for Persons with Severe Handicaps, 9,* 201–212.

Dunn, L. M., & Markwardt, F. C. (1970). *Peabody individual achievement test.* Circle Pines, MN: American Guidance Service.

Durand, V. M. (1987). "Look homeward angel": A call to return to our (functional) roots. *The Behavior Analyst, 10,* 299–302.

Forness, S. R., & Esveldt, K. C. (1971). *Classroom observation of learning and behavior problem children.* Graduate School of Education, University of California at Los Angeles, CA.

Foxx, R. M. (1982a). *Increasing behaviors of severely handicapped and autistic persons*. Champaign, IL: Research Press.

Foxx, R. M. (1982b). *Increasing behaviors of severely handicapped and autistic persons*. Champaign, IL: Research Press.

Frankenburg, W., Dodds, J., Fandal, A., Kazuk, E. & Cohrs, M. (1975). *Denver Developmental Screening Test, Reference Manual* (Revised 1975 edition). Denver, CO: LA-DOCA Project and Publishing Foundation.

Frostig, M., Lefever, W., & Whittlesey, J. (1966). *Administration and scoring manual: Marianne frostig developmental test of visual perception*. Palo Alto, CA: Consulting Psychologists Press.

Fuchs, L. S., Butterworth, J., & Fuchs, D. (in press). Effects of curriculum-based progress monitoring on student knowledge of performance. *Education and Treatment of Children*.

Fuchs, L., & Deno, S. (1981). *A comparison of reading placements based on teacher judgment, standardized testing and curriculum-based assessment* (Research Report No. 56). Minneapolis: University of Minnesota, Institute for Research on Learning Disabilities.

Fuchs, L., Deno, S. L., & Mirkin, P. K. (1984). The effects of frequent curriculum-based measurement and evaluation on pedagogy, student achievement and student awareness of learning. *American Educational Research Journal, 21*(2), 449–460.

Fuchs, L. S., Fuchs, D., & Hamlett, C. L. (1989). Effects of alternative goal structures on teacher's instructional planning and student achievement. *Exceptional Children, 55*, 229–238.

Fuchs, L. S., Fuchs, D., Hamlett, C. L., & Allinder, R. (1989). *Importance of skills analysis to curriculum-based measurement in spelling instruction*. (Research Report No. 414–415). Nashville, TN: Peabody College of Vanderbilt University.

Fuchs, L. S., Fuchs, D., Hamlett, C., & Hasselbring, T. S. (1987). Using computers with curriculum-based progress monitoring: Effects on teacher efficiency and satisfaction. *Journal of Special Education Technology, 8*(4), 14–27.

Fuchs, L. S., Fuchs, D., & Maxwell, L. (1988). The validity of informal reading comprehension measures. *Remedial and Special Education, 8*(2), 20–28.

Fuchs, L. S., Fuchs, D., & Stecker, P. M. (1989). Effects of curriculum-based measurement on teacher's instructional planning. *Journal of Learning Disabilities, 22*, 51–59.

Gessell, J. K. (1983). *Diagnostic mathematics inventory/mathematics system*. Monterey, CA: CTB/McGraw-Hill.

Gickling, E. E., & Thompson, V. P. (1985). A personal view of curriculum-based assessment. *Exceptional Children, 52*, 205–218.

Graden, J., Casey, A., & Bronstrom, O. (1983). *Prereferral interventions: Effects on referral rates and teacher attitudes* (Research Report No. 140). Minneapolis: University of Minnesota, Institute for Research on Learning Disabilities.

Graden, J. L., Casey, A., & Christenson, S. L. (1985). Implementing a prereferral intervention system. Part I: The model. *Exceptional Children, 48*, 422–433.

Hammill, D., & Larsen, S. (1983). *Test of written language*. Austin, TX: Pro-Ed.

Henderson, H. S., & Erken, N. F. (1989a). *Number Facts Mastery Program*. Bellevue, WA: Edmark.

Henderson, H. S., & Erken, N. F. (1989b). *Reading Mastery Program*. Bellevue, WA: Edmark.

Idol-Maestas, L. (1983). *Special Educator's Consultation Handbook*. Aspen Systems: Rockville, MD.

Jastak, S., & Wilkinson, G. S. (1984). *Wide range achievement test—revised*. Wilmington, DE: Jastak Associates.

Jenkins, J. R., & Pany, D. (1978). Standardized achievement tests: How useful for special education? *Exceptional Children, 44*, 448–453.

Karlsen, B., & Gardner, E. (1985). *Stanford diagnostic reading test* (3rd ed.). San Antonio, TX: The Psychological Corporation.

Kaufman, A., & Kaufman, J. (1983). *Kaufman Assessment Battery for Children, interpretive manual*. Circle Pines, MN: American Guidance Service.

Kaufman, J. M. (1989). *Characteristics of behavior disorders of children and youth* (4th ed.). Columbus, OH: Merrill Publishing.

Kazdin, A. E. (1977). Assessing the clinical or applied importance of behavior change through social validation. *Behavior Modification, 1*, 427–452.

Kazdin, A. E., & Matson, J. L. (1981). Social validation in mental retardation. *Applied Research in Mental Retardation, 2*, 39–53.

Larsen, S., & Hammill, D. (1986). *Test of written spelling 2*. Austin, TX: Pro-Ed.

LaVigna, G. W., Willis, T. J., & Donnellan, A. M. (1989). The role of positive programming in behavioral treatment. In E. Cipani (Ed.), *The treatment of severe behavior disorders: Behavior analysis approaches* (pp. 55–84). Washington, DC: American Association on Mental Retardation.

Lee, J., & Clark, W. (1962). *Manual Lee–Clark Reading Readiness Test*. Monterey, CA: CTB/McGraw-Hill.

Luftig, R. L. (1989). *Assessment of learners with special needs*. Boston: Allyn and Bacon.

Mace, F. C., Hock, M. L., Lalli, J. S., West, B. J., Belfiore, P., Pinter, E., and Brown, K. D. (1988). Behavioral mountain in the treatment of non-compliance. *Journal of Applied Behavior Analysis, 21*, 123–141.

Madden, R., Gardner, E. F., & Collins, C. S. (1983). Stanford early school achievement test (2nd ed.). Cleveland, OH: The Psychological Corporation.

Mardell–Czudnowki, C., & Goldenberg, D. (1983). *Developmental indicators for the assessment of learning—Revised*. Edison, NJ: Childcraft Education Corp.

Marston, D., & Magnusson, D. (1985). Implementing curriculum-based measurement in special and regular education settings. *Exceptional Children, 52*, 226–276.

McCarthy, D. (1972). *Manual for the McCarthy scales of childrens abilities*. San Antonio, TX: The Psychological Corporation.

McLoughlin, J. A., & Lewis, R. B. (1986). *Assessing special students* (2nd ed.). Columbus, OH: Merrill Publishing Company.

Mercer, C. D., & Mercer, A. R. (1989). Teaching students with learning problems (3rd ed.). Columbus, OH: Merrill Publishing Co.

Michael, J. (1988). Establishing operations and the mand. *The Analysis of Verbal Behavior, 6*, 3–9.

Minkin, N., Braukman, C. J., Minkin, B. L., Timbers, B. J., Fixsen, D. L., Phillips, E. L., & Wolf, M. M. (1976). The social validation and training of conversational skills. *Journal of Applied Behavior Analysis, 9*, 127–139.

Moss, M. (1979). *Test of basic experiences 2: Norms and technical data book*. Monterey, CA: CTB/McGraw-Hill.

Newcomer, P. (1986). *Standardized reading inventory*. Austin, TX: Pro-Ed.

Nurss, J. R., & McGauvran, M. E. (1986). *Metropolitan Readiness Tests*. San Antonio, TX: The Psychological Corporation.

Paul, J. L., & Epanchin, B. C. (1982). *Emotional disturbance in children*. Columbus, OH: Merrill Publishing.

Quick, A., Little, T., & Campbell, A. (1974). *Project Memphis: Enhancing developmental progress in preschool exceptional Children*. Belmont, CA: Fearon.

Repp, A. C. (1983). *Teaching the mentally retarded*. Englewood Cliffs, NJ: Prentice-Hall, Inc.

Repp, A. C., Felce, D., & Barton, L. E. (1988). Basing the treatment of stereotypic and self-injurious behavior on hypotheses of their causes. *Journal of Applied Behavior Analysis*, *21*, 281–289.

Repp, A. C., Karsh, K., & VanAcker, R. (1987). Arousal states: The relationship between stereotype and activity level. Paper presented at the annual meeting of the Association for Persons with Severe Handicaps, Chicago, IL.

Richy, D. D., & McKinney, J. D. (1978). Classroom behavioral styles of learning disabled children. *Journal of Learning Disabilities*, *11*, 297–302.

Roach, E. F., & Kephart, N. C. (1966). *The Purdue perceptual-motor survey*. Columbus, OH: Merrill.

Salvia, J., & Hughes, C. (1990). *Curriculum-based assessment: Testing what is taught*. New York: MacMillan.

Salvia, J., & Ysseldyke, J. E. (1988). *Assessment in remedial and special education* (4th ed.). Boston: Houghton-Mifflin Company.

Sargent, L. R. (1981). Resource teacher time utilization: An observational study. *Exceptional Children*. *47*, 420–425.

Sattler, J. M. (1982). *Assessment of children's intelligence and special abilities* (2nd ed.). Boston: Allyn and Bacon, Inc.

Simeonsson, R. J. (1986). *Psychological and developmental assessment of special education*. Boston: Allyn and Bacon, Inc.

Singh, N. N., & Repp, A. C. (1988). Current trends in the behavioral and psychopharmacelogical management of problem behaviors of mentally retarded persons. *Irish Journal of Psychology*, *9*, 362–384.

Skinner, B. F. (1957). *Verbal behavior*. New York: Appleton-Century-Crofts.

Speece, K. L., & Mandell, C. J. (1980). Resource room support services for regular teachers. *Learning Disability Quarterly*, *3*(1), 49–53.

Steege, M. W., Wacker, D. P., Berg, W. K., Cigrand, K. K., & Cooper, L. J. (1989). The use of behavioral assessment to prescribe and evaluate treatments for severely handicapped children. *Journal of Behavior Analysis*, *22*, 23–33.

Sundberg, M. (1983). Language. In J. L. Matson & S. E. Breuning (Eds.), *Assessing the mentally retarded* (pp. 285–310). New York: Grune & Stratton.

Swanson, H. L., & Watson, B. L. (1982). *Educational and psychological assessment of exceptional children: Theories, strategies and applications*. St. Louis, MO: The C. V. Mosby Company.

Taylor, R. L. (1989). *Assessment of exceptional students: Educational and psychological procedures* (2nd ed.). Englewood Cliffs, NJ: Prentice-Hall.

Thorndike, R. L., Hagen, E., & Sattler, J. (1985). *Stanford–Binet Intelligence Scale*. Chicago, IL: The Riverside Publishing Company.

Tjossen, T. D. (Ed.). (1976). *Intervention strategies for high risk infants and young children*. Baltimore: University Park Press.

Touchette, P. E., MacDonald, R. F., & Langer, S. N. (1985). A scatter plot for identifying stimulus control of problem behavior. *Journal of Applied Behavior Analysis*, *18*, 343–351.

Tucker, J. A. (1985). Curriculum-based assessment: An introduction. *Exceptional Children*, *52*, 199–204.

Vargas, E. A. (1988). Event-governed and verbally-governed behavior. *The Analysis of Verbal Behavior*, *6*, 11–22.

Walker, H. M. (1983). *Walker problem behavior identification checklist*. Los Angeles: Western Psychological Services.

Wechsler, D. (1974). *Manual for the Wechsler intelligence scale for children— revised*. Cleveland: The Psychological Corporation.

Wechsler, D. (1981). *Manual for the Wechsler adult intelligence scale—revised*. New York: The Psychological Corporation.

Weeks, M., & Gaylord-Ross, R. (1981). Task difficulty and aberrant behavior in severely handicapped students. *Journal of Applied Behavior*, *14*, 449–463.

Wiedholt, J. L., Hammill, D. D., & Brown, V. (1983). *The resource teacher: A guide to effective practices* (2nd ed.). Austin, TX: Pro:Ed.

Witt, J. C. (1986). Review of the Wide Range Achievement Test—Revised. *Journal of Psychoeducational Assessment*, *4*, 87–90.

Woodcock, R. (1978). *Woodcock–Johnson psychoeducational battery*. Hingham, MA: Teaching Resources Corporation.

Woodcock, R. (1987). *Woodcock reading mastery tests—revised*. Circle Pines, MN: American Guidance Service.

4
Psychosocial Characteristics of Learning Disabled Students

RUTH PEARL

The scope of research on learning disabilities has broadened over the past 15 years to include the examination of psychosocial characteristics of individuals with learning disabilities. This attention to the social characteristics of students whose presenting problem is presumably in the academic domain is not surprising. It is now generally accepted that students' self-perceptions, the quality and quantity of their social experiences, and other psychosocial concerns in some way may be significant among the complex set of factors that are involved in the manifestation of a learning disability.

How they are significant has been a matter of conjecture. Does the underlying disability manifest itself in the social realm as well as in the students' academic performance? Alternatively, are psychosocial problems likely to be characteristic of any student with learning difficulties, not just of those who have been identified as learning disabled? Or do these characteristics in some way cause the learning disability, or at least increase the likelihood that individuals will be considered to be learning disabled?

Research is just beginning to sort out these different possibilities. Nonetheless, at this point a review of research on psychosocial characteristics of students with learning disabilities does allow one to draw two broad conclusions. First, as a group, these individuals are more likely than nondisabled students to have what most would consider to be less than optimal psychosocial characteristics. But second, not all of the individuals with learning disabilities, perhaps not even the majority, actually develop these problems.

As a result of the increasing acknowledgment of the heterogeneity of the category of learning disabilities, investigations are starting to examine which learning disabled students may be at greatest risk for psychosocial problems. Because these studies subdivide this population in different ways—by sex, by behavioral subgroup, by educational placement, for instance—few studies are cumulative, and so at this point conclusions are at best tenuous. Nevertheless, these studies provide some preliminary suggestions of which learning disabled students may be most likely to develop problems in the psychosocial domain.

This chapter reviews research on four interrelated areas. One important indicator of the quality of a social environment is the degree to which one is accepted or rejected by one's peers. Accordingly, the chapter begins with an examination of research on learning disabled students' social status. To provide a more complete view of these students' social world, the next section reviews studies focusing on their behavior, as indicated both through actual observations and through assessments made by teachers and parents. Studies that examine different areas of competence that may contribute to behavioral and social status differences are examined next. Finally, studies of the self-perceptions of students with learning disabilities are reviewed to examine these students' assessments of their academic and social competence as well as their general self-esteem. Because most research on these topics has been aimed at delineating ways in which learning disabled students, as a group, tend to differ from nondisabled students, this chapter necessarily concentrates on these findings. However, whenever possible, findings indicating which students within the learning disabled population are most at risk will be described.

Peer Attitudes

One way to estimate the social climate experienced by learning disabled students is to evaluate whether they are liked by classmates as much as students without disabilites, or are disproportionately ignored or rejected. This issue has been studied by using sociometric measures, a technique developed more than 50 years ago (Moreno, 1934), which, in essence, simply asks students about their views of their peers. There are two major sociometric techniques, both of which have been used in studies with learning disabled students. In the first, students are asked to nominate classmates whom they feel exhibit certain specified characteristics. For instance, students may be asked to name their three best friends. Some studies attempt to identify the status of students in a less direct way, by asking, for example, which students the respondents would like to invite to their birthday party, or which student would make a good class president. Often, negative nominations are solicited as well; for instance, students may be asked to name three classmates they do not like.

By examining the pattern of nominations received by individual students, it is possible to get some idea of their status within their classroom. Researchers have used the results of nomination sociometrics in different ways, some adding positive and negative nominations together to derive a composite score, others using both measures to develop discrete categories indicating more specifically classmates' level of regard. These typically include the category of *popular* or *star*, made up of children who receive many positive and few negative nominations; the category of *rejected*, used for children who receive many negative and few positive nominations; and the category of *neglected* or *isolated* for children who are seldom mentioned in either a positive or negative way.

While the first type of sociometric technique asks students to nominate a few students from among their classmates, the second sociometric technique asks students to rate every child in their class. Most frequently, students are asked to rate on either a three-point or five-point scale how much they like to play with each of their classmates, or alternatively, how much they like to work with them. This measure gives a somewhat different picture of a student's status within the group, revealing the student's relative likeability or acceptance by the class as a whole.

Bryan (1974a) conducted the first study examining the sociometric status of learning disabled students. Students in the 3rd, 4th, and 5th grades were asked to nominate classmates who were and were not desired as friends, classroom neighbors, and guests at a party. The children were also asked questions like, "Who is handsome or pretty?" and "Who finds it hard to sit still in class?" The results indicated that the learning disabled students received both fewer positive nominations and more negative nominations than did nondisabled students. A follow-up study (Bryan, 1976) indicated that these students' low status was not ephemeral. When they were in new classes and, for the most part, with different classmates a year later, the students continued to receive fewer positive and more negative nominations.

Studies that followed using both nomination measures and rating scales confirm that many learning disabled students experience low status compared to peers in elementary school and high school (Bruininks, 1978a, 1978b; Coben & Zigmond, 1986; Donahue & Prescott, 1988; Garrett & Crump, 1980; Gottlieb, Gottlieb, Berkell, & Levy, 1986; Horowitz, 1981; Kistner & Gatlin, 1989; Levy & Gottlieb, 1984; Perlmutter, Crocker, Cordray, & Garstecki, 1983; Scranton & Ryckman, 1979; Sheare, 1978; Siperstein, Bopp, & Bak, 1978; Siperstein & Goding, 1983). One of these studies (Horowitz, 1981), however, found that the group differences disappeared when analyses controlled for the effects of intelligence. This suggests the possibility that the low status found for students with learning disabilities is simply a function of their intelligence or achievement level, and only coincidentally related to the fact that they have learning disabilities.

This issue has been examined by comparing learning disabled students to other low achievers rather than to a random or sex/race matched group of nondisabled students, as has typically been the case. One study that compared 3rd and 4th grade learning disabled boys with boys matched on reading achievement found no sociometric differences between groups on either a "play with" rating scale or a measure asking for nominations of especially liked classmates (Bursuck, 1983). Similar results were found in another study (Sater & French, 1989) that examined play ratings of 4th, 5th, and 6th graders. Both learning disabled and low achieving students received lower ratings than did normal achievers, but these two groups did not differ from each other.

In contrast, several other studies have found that even in comparison with low achievers, learning disabled students experience less acceptance (Bursuck, 1989; LaGreca, Stone, & Halpern, 1988; Perlmutter et al., 1983), lower popularity (LaGreca et al., 1988), more rejection (LaGreca et al., 1988), and more neglect (LaGreca et al., 1988). Another study (Flicek & Landau, 1985), noting that peer relationship problems have been found to be common among hyperactive children (Milich & Landau, 1982), examined the possibility that hyperactive students among the learning disabled population might be responsible for the low status found in previous studies. This study, which included only boys, found that although hyperactive learning disabled boys were even less popular and more rejected than learning disabled boys who were not hyperactive, nonhyperactive learning disabled boys were nevertheless less popular and more rejected than nondisabled classmates.

The findings suggest that learning disabled students, as a group, are at risk for lower status than are students without learning disabilities. Nevertheless, it is not the case that all, or maybe even most, learning disabled students are poorly regarded by their peers. A few studies have in fact found no differences in acceptance levels between learning disabled and nondisabled samples (e.g., Prilliman, 1981; Sabornie & Kauffman, 1986; Sainato, Zigmond, & Strain, 1983). Some investigators have suggested that even when group differences in sociometric status are found, many students with learning disabilities are of average status, and some are even well liked (Dudley–Marling & Edmiaston, 1985; Perlmutter et al., 1983; Sater & French, 1989).

If not all students with learning disabilities experience problems in their peer relations, then, is there any evidence suggesting which learning disabled students are most at risk? Landau, Milich, and McFarland (1987) hypothesized that the performance and verbal scales of the Weshsler Intelligence Scale for Children—Revised (WISC–R) might differentiate groups of learning disabled boys varying in peer relations. These boys were divided into three groups: those who performed equally well on the performance and verbal scales, those who scored higher on the performance scale, and those who scored higher on the verbal scale. The results indicated that boys who performed equally on the two scales were the most rejected and were perceived by their peers to be most aggressive. In addition, boys in this group, as well as boys in the group with higher scores on the performance than on the verbal scale, were less popular than classmates. The boys who scored higher on the performance scale were considered by peers to be more withdrawn than were a comparison nondisabled sample. All three groups of learning disabled students were considered less likeable by peers than the comparison sample. Thus, although all groups were viewed by peers more negatively than were nondisabled students, there is some suggestion that learning disabled boys with strengths in verbal skills may not receive the same degree of rejection as other learning disabled students.

Weiner (1980) differentiated children attending a camp for learning disabled students according to whether the discrepancy between their age and achievement level was more or less than two grades. She found that the more severely disabled children received more negative and fewer positive nominations from their fellow campmates. Several other studies have suggested that learning disabled girls may be at particular risk for peer relationship problems (Bryan, 1974a; Hutton & Polo, 1976; LaGreca et al., 1988; Scranton & Ryckman, 1979), with one study finding greater rejection for white learning disabled girls but not for black learning disabled girls (Kistner & Gatlin, 1989).

The question of what behaviors and skills may lie behind the low status so many learning disabled students experience has most often been studied indirectly by examining group differences in behaviors or social skills that seem likely to influence peers' attitudes (see the following sections of this chapter). Few published studies have directly assessed the characteristics of learning disabled students varying in sociometric status. Siperstein et al. (1978) and Siperstein and Goding (1983) found that learning disabled students who were nominated as having various positive attributes (e.g., best looking, best athlete) tended to receive higher sociometric scores. Sater and French (1989) found that teachers and parents considered rejected learning disabled and low achieving students to have less social competence and more behavior problems than accepted learning disabled and low achieving students. Popular learning disabled adolescents in a study by Perlmutter et al. (1983) were viewed by peers as more independent and withdrawn than were disliked students with learning disabilities. Popular learning disabled students were also rated by their teachers as less anxious, and were better able to predict the extent to which individual classmates liked them.

Although Perlmutter et al. (1983) found that popular learning disabled adolescents were rated as more withdrawn than unpopular learning disabled students, studies with younger children suggest that learning disabled students with high status are likely to engage in more informal social interactions with classmates than are lower status learning disabled students. Gottlieb et al. (1986) examined the playground behavior of mainstreamed learning disabled elementary school students. Learning disabled students who, according to sociometric ratings, were considered to be relatively undesirable playmates, spent more time on the playground in solitary free play. Ackerman and Howes (1986) examined the relations between sociometric status and self-reported after-school activities among learning disabled boys attending a private school for children with learning disabilites. They found a positive correlation between popularity and participation in informal after-school activities, for instance, playing together with friends after school. Whether the learning disabled students in these studies were less popular because they interacted less with peers or whether the lower rates of interaction were the result of their being less welcomed by their classmates, is of course not known from these results.

One interesting finding from the Ackerman and Howes (1986) study was that although popularity was positively related to participation in informal after-school activity, peer acceptance was negatively correlated with the number of structured after-school activities attended, for instance, sports programs or religious school. The authors suggest that these more formal settings may provide an alternative setting for low-accepted children to be with their peers, although they speculate that the children might not be any more accepted in these settings than they are in the classroom. Children in this study who received no nominations as a best friend may be the most isolated after school: these children reported participating both in fewer formal and fewer informal after-school activities. These children, however, did not report having fewer friends than other children.

In summary, a large body of research indicates that learning disabled students are more likely than their nondisabled classmates to be of low sociometric status. However, not all learning disabled students are of low status. Although a few studies provide some tentative suggestions of which learning disabled students are most at risk, more research on this issue is clearly needed.

Behavior of Learning Disabled Students

Concern about learning disabled students' functioning in academic and social domains has led to an interest in whether behaviors can be identified that may be the source of learning disabled students' difficulties in these areas. McKinney (1989), for instance, has hypothesized that many learning disabled students exhibit classroom behaviors that undermine their achievement. Other investigations have focused more on social conduct in an attempt to find behaviors that might contribute to the social difficulties that many learning disabled students experience.

Observational studies conducted in classroom settings have consistently found learning disabled students to be more distractible and off-task than nondisabled students (Bender, 1985; Bryan, 1974b; Bryan & Wheeler, 1972; Dorval, McKinney, & Feagans, 1982; Feagans & McKinney, 1981, 1982; Forness & Esveldt, 1975; Gettinger & Fayne, 1982; McKinney, McClure, & Feagans, 1982; Richey & McKinney, 1978). More frequent interactions with teachers have been found in some studies (Chapman,

Larsen, & Parker, 1979; Dorval et al., 1982; Feagans & McKinney, 1981, 1982; McKinney et al., 1982; Siperstein & Goding, 1983); but not all (Bryan, 1974b; Bryan & Wheeler, 1972; Fellers & Saudargas, 1987; Richey & McKinney, 1978; Slate & Saudargas, 1986).

When teachers interact more with learning disabled students, it apparently is a reaction to perceived deficits in these students. Dorval et al. (1982), for instance, reported a greater frequency of teacher initiations directed at behavior management with learning disabled children. Teachers in another study directed more corrective and less supportive behavior to learning disabled students, even though in this sample the learning disabled and nondisabled students did not differ in their frequency of negative initiations or inappropriate responses (Siperstein & Goding, 1983). Similar results were reported by Slate and Saudargas (1986), who found that although learning disabled and nondisabled students did not differ in the degree to which they were engaged in an activity other than their assigned academic work, the learning disabled students received more teacher contacts and directions. Teachers also may be at times less responsive to students with learning disabilities. In one study, they responded less frequently to verbal initiations of learning disabled students (Bryan, 1974b), and in another study using only girls as subjects, teachers responded less to the "call outs" of the learning disabled students (Fellers & Saudargas, 1987).

Few observational studies have focused on learning disabled children's peer interactions in regular school classrooms. However, those that have included measures of peer interaction have not found that learning disabled and nondisabled children differ in the amount of time spent in interaction with classmates. Although Bryan (1974b) found that the initiations of 3rd grade learning disabled children were more likely to be ignored than were those of other children, most classroom studies have not detected differences in peer interaction. This may be because the range of possible interpersonal behaviors was constrained by the situations in which the students were observed or because observational systems used to code classroom behavior are relatively insensitive to subtle behavioral differences.

Research more closely examining the verbal content of children's interactions during nonacademic periods or summer school classes has found some significant differences in the affective tone of learning disabled students' conversations with peers and those between nondisabled students. Learning disabled 4th and 5th graders made more "very nasty" statements and received more rejection statements than nondisabled classmates during art and physical education classes (Bryan & Bryan, 1978). Third, 4th, and 5th grade learning disabled students in summer school classes made more competitive statements and received fewer "consideration" statements than other children (Bryan, Wheeler, Felcan, & Henek, 1976)

Other descriptions of learning disabled students' behavior come from studies that used questionnaire measures of teachers' assessments to substitute for or supplement observational measures. These measures are enlightening not only because they presumably reflect the students' behavior, but also because teacher perceptions are themselves important in that they are likely to influence the teachers' responses to these children.

These studies confirm and extend the depiction of learning disabled students' classroom behavior provided by observational studies. Consistent with observational studies, teachers report differences in task-related behavior and distractability (Bender, 1985; Bender & Golden 1988; Cartledge, Stupay, & Kaczala, 1986; Gresham & Reschly, 1986; LaGreca et al., 1988; McKinney & Feagans, 1984). Questionnaires that included assessments of social behavior have found teachers to rate learning disabled students as deficient on a variety of social skills. Bender and Golden (1988) found that mainstream teachers rated learning disabled students lower than nondisabled students on scales indicating social coping, relationships, pragmatic language, and work production. These students were also rated higher than other children on scales indicating disturbed peer relationships and acting out, replicating an earlier finding (Bender, 1985). Gresham and Reschly (1986) found teachers of elementary school children gave learning disabled students lower ratings than comparison children on scales indicating environmental behaviors (e.g., "follows rules for emergencies"), self-related behaviors (e.g., "accepts consequences for wrongdoing"), and interpersonal behaviors (e.g., "pays attention in a conversation to the person speaking").

In other studies, mainstream teachers indicated that, compared to nondisabled students, learning disabled students are lacking in cooperation, attention, ability to organize, ability to cope with new situations, social acceptance, acceptance of responsibility, completion of assignments, and tact (Bryan & McGrady, 1972); are more anxious, withdrawn (LaGreca et al., 1988), and immature; and have more conduct problems (Bursuck, 1989; Touliatos & Lindholm, 1980). Although Pullis (1985) found that special education teachers viewed their learning disabled students more positively than did mainstream teachers, many special education teachers apparently detect deficiencies in learning disabled students as well. In a study by Center and Wascom (1986), special education teachers perceived their learning disabled students to behave less prosocially and more antisocially than other teachers rated students whom they considered "socially normal." A survey of 500 resource room teachers found that these teachers felt that 38% of their learning disabled students were in need of social skills intervention (Baum, Duffelmeyer, & Geelan, 1988).

These studies, then, indicate that learning disabled students' behavior in classrooms is likely to be viewed by teachers to be less desirable in a variety of ways than the behavior of nondisabled students. Studies that compared the assessments made by parents of learning disabled children with either the assessments made by these same parents about their nondisabled children, the assessments made by other parents of non-disabled children, or questionnaire norms, found that parents also view their learning disabled students as exhibiting comparatively undesir-able behavior (e.g., Gresham & Reschly, 1986; McConaughy, 1986; McConaughy & Ritter, 1986; Owen, Adams, Forrest, Stolz, & Fisher, 1971; Ritter, 1989).

However, it clearly does not appear to be the case that all learning disabled students exhibit undesirable behavior, or even that all learning disabled students who show behavioral deficiencies are alike. Important data addressing this issue come from a study that used teacher ratings of classroom behaviors to identify subtypes of 1st and 2nd grade learning disabled students (Speece, McKinney, & Appelbaum, 1985). Two sub-types exhibited essentially normal behavior; one was somewhat high in considerateness and introversion, the other in hostility, although both were within the normal range. Together these subtypes comprised 34.9% of the sample. An attention deficit subtype, consisting of 28.6% of the sample, was deficient in task orientation and independence, but not in personal–social behavior. Another subtype consisted of withdrawn chil-dren who were rated as overly dependent and introverted. This subtype described 11% of the sample, and was mainly made up of girls. The final three subtypes described children with different classroom management problems, and represented 25.4% of the sample.

Longitudinal data indicated that despite the fact that approximately 50% of the children changed subgroups over the subsequent 2 years, their initial subgroup did predict future achievement test scores. Children who had classroom management problems and those with attention deficits performed more poorly than the children in the normal and withdrawn subgroups (McKinney & Speece, 1986).

Causes of Social Relationship Problems

The research described thus far indicates that many learning disabled students differ from classmates in sociometric status and behavior. The issue of whether learning disabled students differ on skills that are likely to underlie performance in these areas has also received a consider-able amount of research attention. Most of these studies have examined whether learning disabled students differ from nondisabled students on the measures of interest; for the most part, these studies have not assessed differences among subgroups of learning disabled students or evaluated whether variations on their measures are systematically related to variations in the students' behavior or degree of peer acceptance.

Hence, there is little direct evidence of these skills' relationship to behavior and status, and there are virtually no studies manipulating these skills and measuring consequent changes in behavior and status. Therefore, these studies do not provide the "smoking gun" needed to pinpoint unequivocally the cause or causes of learning disabled students' social functioning. Nevertheless, they do suggest a number of factors that might be important contributors.

Behavioral Deficits

Behavioral deficits have been suggested as one factor that might be responsible for learning disabled students' social problems. For instance, many learning disabled students appear to have deficits in vocabulary and syntactic structure (Donahue, Pearl, & Bryan, 1983; Wiig & Semel, 1980). These could interfere with these students' ability to communicate clearly, thereby making their interactions with others more awkward. Learning disabled students have also been found to be deficient on tests of motor skills (Bryan & Smiley, 1983). Since athletic skills are highly valued, particularly by boys (Schofield, 1981), limitations in this area might contribute to others' low regard. Other studies suggest that learning disabled students' nonverbal behavior may elicit negative reactions from others (Bryan & Perlmutter, 1979; Bryan & Sherman, 1980).

Social Cognitive Deficits and Biases

Another possibility is that learning disabled students have deficits or biases in various aspects of social cognition, and thus are more likely than other students to misread social cues and respond inappropriately in social situations (Pearl, 1987). Several aspects of social cognition have been examined. Some studies have evaluated whether learning disabled students differ from others in their knowlege base about typical social situations. For example, Bachara (1976) examined boys' assumptions about the emotions experienced by children in different situations. Learning disabled boys were found to be less accurate than nondisabled boys in identifying the children's emotions. Pearl, Bryan, and Herzog (1990) found that learning disabled adolescents differed from nondisabled teenagers in their beliefs about how teenagers would be likely to try to influence a peer to join in an undesirable activity. If, as these studies suggest, learning disabled students differ from nondisabled students in their expectations about different situations, it is understandable why they would be likely to behave differently in these circumstances.

However, learning disabled students do not appear to have deficient or different social knowledge bases in all areas since some studies have not found differences in social knowledge (Bryan & Sonnefeld, 1981; Bursuck, 1983; Stone & LaGreca, 1984). Even so, how well this knowledge is actually applied may distinguish many learning disabled students from their peers. For instance, Stone and LaGreca (1984) found that despite the fact that learning disabled and nondisabled children did not differ on role-playing how to make friends, adults observing their performance rated them as being less socially skilled. Similarly, Bryan, Sonnefeld, and Greenberg (1981) found that despite evidence that learning disabled students were as aware as nondisabled students of the effectiveness of different ingratiation strategies, when asked which strategies they would use, they chose ones that were relatively socially undesirable.

Shortcomings in social perception skills have also been hypothesized to be a possible reason for learning disabled students' social difficulties. Researchers have examined learning disabled students' understanding of nonverbal emotional expressions, social situations depicted in drawings, and complex social interactions. Lower skillfulness in interpreting social displays has been found both in elementary school age and adolescent learning disabled students (Axelrod, 1982; Bruno, 1981; Bryan, 1977; Gerber & Zinkgraf, 1982; Jackson, Enright, & Murdock, 1987; Pearl & Cosden, 1982; Saloner & Gettinger, 1985; Wiig & Harris, 1974). Nevertheless, other studies indicate that if redundant cues are available, or if the children are highly motivated to pay attention, learning disabled students may not differ from nondisabled students in their performance on social perception tasks (Maheady & Maitland, 1982; Stone & LaGreca, 1984). Research by Weiss (1984) suggests that some learning disabled boys may view interactions with a negative bias. After observing videotapes or hearing descriptions of boys interacting, the learning disabled boys rated the interactions as more unfriendly than did nondisabled boys.

Other research has evaluated learning disabled students' role-taking skills. Role-taking studies examine whether individuals are able to ignore their own experience in making inferences about the experience of another person. Although not all studies have detected less skilled role-taking in learning disabled students (Ackerman, Elardo, & Dykman, 1979; Fincham, 1979), a number have found learning disabled students to have more difficulty than nondisabled students in understanding another's perspective (Bruck & Hebert, 1982; Dickstein & Warren, 1980; Horowitz, 1981; Wong & Wong, 1980). Several studies indicate how the lack of role-taking skill might be manifested in the children's behavior. One found that although learning disabled students were as able as other students to recognize that deceptive statements were untrue, they were less able to recognize the speaker's deceptive intent (Pearl, Bryan, Fallon, & Herzog, 1991). In another study, children were asked what they would say to a peer in hypothetical situations in which they had to communicate bad news, for example, that the other child was not chosen for the starring role in the class play. The learning disabled students were less tactful than the nondisabled students in that they were less likely to communicate the news in a way that would allow the listener to save face (Pearl, Donahue, & Bryan, 1985).

Pragmatics

Because of evidence suggesting that many learning disabled students may have both linguistic and social cognitive deficits, it seems likely that these students' actual use of language in context may differ from that of class-mates. Effective communication, after all, generally requires both linguistic facility and skilled social cognition. This possibility has been investigated in a number of studies.

Learning disabled 3rd through 8th graders were asked to rank order with two of their classmates a list of potential presents for their class (Bryan, Donahue & Pearl, 1981). Although the learning disabled students participated in the group's discussion as much as nondisabled students, they were more unassertive and deferential. To examine whether learning disabled students would be more assertive and active in maintaining a conversation if placed in a leadership role, a second study asked students to play the role of a talk show host and interview a classmate "guest" about television programs and movies (Bryan, Donahue, Pearl, & Sturm, 1981). Analyses indicated that learning disabled students were less skillful in sustaining a conversation, even though they had been assigned the responsibility to do so.

Other studies have attempted to identify specific aspects of communication that pose difficulties for learning disabled students. Several studies have found differences in the way learning disabled students adapt their speech according to the characteristics of the listener (Bryan & Pflaum, 1978; Donahue, 1981; Soenksen, Flagg, & Schmits, 1981). Other studies have found that learning disabled students are less successful than other students in clearly communicating information (Feagans & Short, 1986; Knight–Arest, 1984; Mathinos, 1988; Noel, 1980; Spekman, 1981) Studies examining learning disabled students in the role of a listener have found them to have more difficulty comprehending instructions than do non-disabled peers (Feagans & Short, 1986), but at the same time to be less likely to request more information when they do not understand a communication (Donahue, Pearl, & Bryan, 1980). Thus, the communication style of many learning disabled students appears to distinguish them from their peers.

Social Motivation

It is also possible that students with learning disabilities interact differently and are less accepted because they simply do not care as much as other students about social acceptance. However, this does not seem to be the case. If they were not interested in their peers, it is unlikely that learning disabled students would interact with them as much as they do; in virtually every study examining this issue, learning disabled students' involvement in social interaction was equal to that of nondisabled class-mates. This eagerness to be part of a social group is also evident in studies that examined conformity in junior high school students (Bryan, Werner, & Pearl, 1982; Bryan, Pearl, & Fallon, 1989). Compared to nondisabled students, learning disabled students indicated that they would be as willing to participate with peers in prosocial actions and more willing to partipate with peers in antisocial actions.

Although learning disabled students do not seem less interested in their peers than other children, they may have different goals for their inter-actions with peers. This was examined in two studies that assessed the goals and strategies adopted by boys in response to four hypothetical situations involving the establishment or maintenance of peer relation-ships. Oliva and LaGreca (1988) found that the goals of learning disabled boys were less sophisticated and specific than were those of other boys. Carlson (1987) found differences in response to a story involving conflict, with nondisabled boys more likely to have compromise as a goal, and learning disabled boys more likely to have the goal of accommodation, avoidance, or following rules. The strategies selected by many of the learning disabled boys in response to this situation were more unilateral in approach in that only one of the disputing peers could win. Learning disabled boys were also less likely in the Carlson (1987) study to produce alternative strategies, and those that were produced were rated of lower quality.

Thus, although learning disabled students appear to have an interest in their peers equivalent to that of nondisabled students, their specific goals in interactions may not be the same, and the strategies adopted may differ. This could be due to a number of reasons (Pearl, Donahue, & Bryan, 1986), for example, because of social cognitive deficits or because their self-perceptions lead them to believe that different goals or strategies are appropriate.

Environmental Context

Finally, the context in which learning disabled students interact with peers may be an important determinant of the students' behavior and acceptance. Studies have found that children are likely to assume that students with learning disabilities compare unfavorably to nondisabled students (Cartledge, Frew, & Zaharias, 1985; Miller, 1984). This suggests that at least to some degree, learning disabled students' social problems may be due as much to the biases of other children as to their own behavior. Situations that minimize or counteract these biases, then, could be expected to be more conductive to the development of positive rela-tions among students. This has been found to be the case in studies that examine students' interaction under goal structures that motivate students to cooperate (Bryan, Cosden, & Pearl, 1982; Cosden, Pearl, & Bryan, 1985).

Similarly, situations that are accepting and comfortable for learning disabled students may be more likely to encourage positive, appropriate behavior. Mathinos (1988) found, for instance, that learning disabled students with familiar rather than unfamiliar partners were more successful in their communicative interactions. Another study found that learning disabled students' sociometric status was higher in classrooms that had a relatively high proportion (more than 25%) of learning disabled students in the class (Perlmutter et al., 1983). Thus, situations appear to vary in the type of social behavior and the degree of peer acceptance they promote.

Summary

Although each of the factors discussed above may be responsible for behavior and acceptance of some learning disabled students, it clearly is not the case that all of these factors constitute problems for all learning disabled students. It remains for future research to identify links between different social relationship problems and different underlying causes.

Self-Perceptions

Because many learning disabled students experience social and academic difficulties, it would not be surprising if their self-perceptions were more negative than those of their nondisabled classmates. Concern about this issue has also emerged because of research showing that self-perceptions can be the cause, not only a result, of social and academic problems. Considerable research has now examined how individuals with learning disabilities feel about their intellectual and interpersonal competence, and even their general self-esteem.

Self-Perceptions of Academic Competence

Since low academic performance is one of the few attributes most students with learning disabilities have in common, one might predict that this would be the domain in which differences in the self-perceptions of learning disabled and nondisabled students would be most evident. That, in fact, is the case. Consistent differences between the academic self-perceptions of students with and without learning disabilities have been found. These differences show that many learning disabled individuals perceive their academic performance to be lower than that perceived by their typical nondisabled classmate.

Studies investigating academic self-concept have generally used one of three measures. The Piers Harris Children's Self-Perception Scale (1964) requires respondents to indicate whether each of 80 statements accurately describes them. Factor analyses of these statements have identified an Intellectual and School Status subscale, which focuses on self-perceptions of academic performance. Typical of the results found with this measure (e.g., Coleman, 1985; Jones, 1985) are those of Cooley and Ayres (1988), who found 10- to 14-year-old students with learning disabilities to score lower on this scale than did nondisabled students.

More frequently used is the Student's Perception of Ability Scale (Boersma & Chapman, 1977), now called the Perception of Ability Scale for Students (Boersma & Chapman, in press). This scale contains items relating to performance in specific academic areas as well as to school in general. Again, the results of studies using this scale found lower academic self-perceptions in learning disabled samples than in non-disabled samples (e.g., Chapman, 1988a; Chapman & Boersma, 1979; Cullen, Boersma, & Chapman, 1981; Rogers & Saklofske, 1985).

A newer scale is the Perceived Competence Scale for Children (Harter, 1982). This scale is divided into four subscales, one of which refers to academic abilities. This subscale consists of six pairs of contrasting statements, for instance, "Some kids do very well at their classwork but other kids don't do well at their classwork." Students are asked to decide which statement in the pair is more like them, and then to indicate whether that statement is "really true for me" or only "sort of true for me." Kistner and Osborne (1987) and Kistner, Haskett, White, and Robbins (1987) reported that learning disabled students expressed lower self-perceptions on this scale than did nondisabled students.

The issue of whether learning disabled students' assessments of their academic competence change over time has been the subject of several investigations. Age-related changes have not been detected either in cross-sectional studies (Chapman & Boersma, 1979; Kistner et al., 1987) or longitudinal studies with labeled (Kistner & Osborne, 1987) or un-labeled (Chapman, 1988b) learning disabled students. Thus, the low assessments these students make about their academic attainment appear to be maintained over time. Other studies examined whether students with learning disabilities differ from their classmates in their expectations about future performance. These suggest that learning disabled students are more pessimistic about the likelihood of future success (e.g., Chapman, 1988b; Hiebert, Wong, & Hunter, 1982; Rogers & Saklofske, 1985).

Studies examining the academic self-perceptions of students with learning disabilities, then, show virtual unanimity in indicating that many of these students believe they are less competent, and are likely to remain less competent, than believe students without learning disabilities. A related question is whether learning disabled students view their academic *experiences* in a different way than do nondisabled students. When learning disabled students are successful on an academic task, do they credit themselves in the same way as other students? When students with learning disabilities encounter difficulty, do they differ in their assumptions about why they are having trouble? These issues are examined in research investigating students' attributions for success and failure, a topic that first received attention as a result of the conceptualization of locus of control (Rotter, 1966), with subsequent interest bolstered considerably by Weiner's observations that differences in attributions result in differences in perseverance, expectations for the future, and affect (Weiner, 1979).

Although findings are not entirely consistent, the research indicates that learning disabled students frequently differ from other students in their explanations for different outcomes. Differences in the interpretation of success between learning disabled and nondisabled groups have been found in a number of studies. Learning disabled students appear to take less personal credit for success (Chapman, 1988b; Pearl, Bryan, & Donahue, 1980; Rogers & Saklofske, 1985), attributing their success less to ability (Aponik & Dembo, 1983; Jacobsen, Lowery, & DuCette, 1986; Pearl, 1982) and more to luck (Aponik & Dembo, 1983; Jacobsen et al., 1986) and the easiness of the task (Jacobsen et al., 1986) than do their nondisabled peers.

Students with learning disabilities have also been found to differ from other students in their attributions for failure. Learning disabled students appear to be more likely than classmates to attribute their failures to a lack of ability (Kistner, Osborne, & LeVerrier, 1988; Kistner, White, Haskett, & Robbins, 1985; Jacobsen et al., 1986; Palmer, Drummond, Tollison, & Zinkgraff, 1982), and less likely to attribute them to a lack of effort (Kistner et al., 1985, 1987; Licht, Kistner, Ozkaragoz, Shapiro, & Clausen, 1985; Pearl, 1982; Pearl et al., 1980). An exception to this latter finding was reported by Jacobsen et al. (1986), who found that learning disabled students felt that a lack of effort was *more* of a reason for their failures than did nondisabled students.

A possible reason for this discrepant result has to do with variations over different studies in the description of the event for which an attribution was solicited. In the Jacobsen et al. (1986) study, students were questioned about a situation where there was a clear opportunity for prior effort to alter the outcome ("Imagine your English teacher assigned a story for you to read for homework. She tells you that there will be a quiz on the story the next day. You receive an 'F' on this quiz. Why do you think that happened?"), whereas in most other investigations, students are questioned only about the outcome (e.g., "If your teacher asks you about a story and you can't answer the question, is it because . . ."). Thus, the differences in results may be due to the fact that the learning disabled students in Jacobsen et al. (1986) felt that since they had sufficient opportunity for adequately studying the story their English teacher assigned, a failure must be due to a lack of effort. The content of the academic task may play a role, too; although the learning disabled students may feel that given time, they might be able to learn a story, they might not feel that time will make much difference in their preparation for a social studies test. Differences and ambiguities in the use of the term *effort* (meaning in some cases, prior effort and in other cases, effort in figuring out a task) also complicate the interpretation of the results of differing studies.

Sex differences in attributions for failure were found in a study by Licht et al. (1985). Both boys and girls with learning disabilities were less likely than their nondisabled counterparts to attribute failure to a lack of effort. However, compared with nondisabled children of the same sex, learning disabled boys were more likely to attribute failures to external factors, and learning disabled girls were more likely to attribute failures to insufficient ability. In another study (Kistner et al., 1987), learning disabled students of both sexes attributed failures more to ability and less to effort than did nondisabled students. However, cross-sectional data indicated that although learning disabled boys increased their attributions of failure to insufficient effort from the elementary school to middle-school period, learning disabled girls did not. These sex differences have not been found in all studies, however. For instance, a longitudinal study (Kistner et al., 1988) found that learning disabled girls as well as boys increased in effort attributions for failure over time. Nevertheless, at each measurement the learning disabled students attributed failures less to effort than did nondisabled students.

Thus, the research presents a fairly consistent portrait of students with learning disabilities being less likely than nondisabled students to feel responsible for their successes, and less likely to assume that their failures are caused simply by a lack of effort. These perceptions have been found in other studies to be often accompanied by negative affect, low expectations for future success, and the abandonment of concerted attempts to achieve mastery on a task (Weiner, 1979). A particularly vivid demonstration of the importance of attributions for failure was found in a recent study by Kistner et al. (1988). Learning disabled students who tended to attribute failures to insufficient effort made greater gains in achievement test scores over a 2-year period than students who believed a lack of effort was a less important reason for their failures. At the same time, the tendency to attribute failure to a lack of ability was negatively related to achievement gains.

Because of these kinds of findings, several studies (Borkowski, Weyhing, & Carr, 1988; Schunk & Cox, 1986; Shelton, Anastopoulos, & Linden, 1985; Tollefson, Tracy, Johnsen, Farmer, & Buenning, 1984) have attempted to alter learning disabled students' maladaptive attributions through variations of a procedure called *attribution retraining*. For instance, Shelton et al. (1985) encouraged children to say to themselves when they succeeded, "I got that right. I tried hard and did a good job." When these children failed, they were told to tell themselves, "No, I didn't get that quite right, but that's okay. Even if I make a mistake, I can go back and try a little harder to get it right." These studies have reported some success in increasing task persistence and in changing the maladaptive attributions made by these children. This intervention can be a helpful technique for improving learning disabled students' achievement behavior, but it must be used with discretion (Pearl, 1985); for example, it is not likely to be useful to implore a child to try harder when that child lacks the strategies needed to succeed in the task.

One other trend that has surfaced in a number of studies is worth mentioning. That is, that attributions to external factors have been found in some samples of learning disabled students to be related (albeit, in most cases, nonsignificantly) to persistence (Licht et al., 1985), achievement test gains (Kistner et al., 1988), grades (Luchow, Crowl, & Kahn, 1985), and teacher-rated academic success (Rogers & Safloske, 1985). Other studies have found children who tend to make external attributions do better than other children when teachers are highly directive (Bendell, Tollefson, & Fine, 1980; Pascarella, Pflaum, Bryan, & Pearl, 1983). It may be, then, that an external orientation is compatible with the type of instruction some learning disabled students receive (Kistner et al., 1988; Rogers & Safloske, 1985). However, since findings showing the adaptiveness of external attributions have been for the most part of only marginal statistical significance, at this point this should be considered only an intriguing finding worthy of further research.

Self-Perceptions of Social Competence

Consonant with research suggesting that social problems are less universal among learning disabled students than academic problems, studies less consistently find negative self-perceptions in the social domain than in the academic domain. However, learning disabled students' assessments of their social competence have been measured in different ways, and some of the inconsistency appears to be due to the assessment approach used.

One approach to investigating this issue has been to ask students to indicate on a questionnaire whether items describing different behaviors are typical for them. These studies then evaluate whether learning disabled students view their own behavior differently from how other students view theirs. Bender and Golden (1988) examined elementary school students' responses on a subscale of the Piers–Harris Children's Self-Concept Scale that assesses self-perceptions of behavior. Bursuck (1989) had elementary students rate themselves on an instrument measuring inappropriate social skills, inappropriate assertiveness, impulsive/recalcitrant behavior, and overconfidence. Perlmutter et al. (1983) asked students to indicate items they felt described themselves on a measure that included subscales assessing aggression–disruptiveness, withdrawal, anxiety, social competence, independence, and influence over others. None of these studies found differences between the self-assessments of the learning disabled and nondisabled students.

Other studies have attempted to assess students' views of others' attitudes by asking them how they think classmates would rate them on sociometric measures. This type of assessment yields two measures of interest: first, whether the learning disabled and nondisabled students differ in the accuracy of their assessments, and second, whether they differ in their predicted social status. Although two studies found that learning disabled students were less accurate than nondisabled students in assessing their status (Bruininks, 1978a, 1978b), these studies compared only students' mean sociometric score with their mean self-assessment score. Studies that used the more precise measure of comparing each classmate's rating with the students' expected rating from that classmate found no difference in accuracy of students' perceptions (Garrett & Crump, 1980; Perlmutter et al., 1983). Despite the fact that all of these studies found that the learning disabled students' actual status was lower than that of the nondisabled students, there was no difference in their predicted status (Bruininks, 1978a, 1978b; Garrett & Crump, 1980). However, Garrett and Crump (1980) found that this was because a significant number of nondisabled students underestimated their status, rather than because of overestimates on the part of the learning disabled students.

Finally, a number of studies have directly asked students about their perceived acceptance. Several of these have used Harter's Self-Perception Profile for Children (1985) or its predecessor, the Perceived Competence Profile for Children (1982). These measures contain a subscale assessing perceptions of social acceptance. For instance, items include, "Some kids find it hard to make friends but other kids find it's pretty easy to make friends," and "Some kids are popular with others their age but other kids are not very popular." Although one study found no differences between learning disabled and nondisabled students on this scale (Kistner et al., 1987), two other studies found learning disabled students to rate themselves more negatively (Kistner & Osborne, 1987; LaGreca et al., 1988). Similarly, Sobol, Earn, Bennett, and Humphries (1983) found that learning disabled students scored lower than either low- or high-accepted nondisabled students on a measure of expectancy of social success. In addition, both the learning disabled and low-accepted nondisabled students rated themselves lower on a scale indicating peer-related self-esteem than did the nondisabled students with higher social acceptance. Thus, although studies of students' perceptions of their social behavior and sociometric status have generally revealed no differences between learning disabled students and nondisabled students, differences have been found in studies that used questionnaires to assess these students' feeling of peer acceptance.

General Self-Esteem

A common expectation has been that the difficulties faced by many learning disabled students would take their toll on the students' general self-esteem. Certainly, a loss of self-esteem does not seem an unlikely consequence when individuals find they have significantly more difficulty than most peers in their academic work, and even, for many, in their social encounters. Although the results of studies examining self-esteem do not show the consistent differences found in learning disabled and nondisabled students' academic self-concepts, a number of studies have found that many learning disabled students seem to have lower self-estimations than do their nondisabled classmates (e.g., Bruininks, 1978b; Margalit & Zak, 1984; Omizo, Amerikaner, & Michael, 1985; Rogers & Saklofske, 1985). Nevertheless, studies on this topic also suggest that students' feelings about themselves do not necessarily suffer as a result of a learning disability, and that, even for those learning disabled students whose self-esteem is lower than that of their nondisabled peers, it is still not necessarily low.

Variations in the results of research on this topic again to some degree may be due to the different instruments that are used over studies. Some studies have attempted to examine this issue by using scales that contain items referring to the students' self-evaluation about a variety of areas. The Piers–Harris Children's Self-Concept Scale (1969), for instance, examines students' feelings about their behavior, intellectual and school status, physical appearance, anxiety, popularity, and happiness. Similarly, the Coopersmith Self-Esteem Inventory assesses self-perceptions about a range of topics. In some cases, then, differences that are found on the total scale scores of these measures could be due to differences in self-perceptions in only some of the areas probed. Since it is clear that many learning disabled students have lower academic self-concepts than non-disabled peers, items tapping this area may be largely responsible for differences in total scale scores (Cooley & Ayres, 1988).

Even when learning disabled students score lower on these measures than nondisabled students, their assessments may not necessarily be excessively negative. Chapman (1988) observed that in most studies using the Piers–Harris Self-Concept Scale, the scores of learning disabled students were near or even above the norms reported in the Piers–Harris manual.

Fewer studies have used measures that tap individuals' feelings of self-worth without referring to particular areas of competence. For example, the Rosenberg Self-Esteem Scale (1965) contains items such as, "I feel that I have a number of good qualities." Similarly, Harter's Perceived Competence Scale for Children (1982) contains a subscale measuring general self-esteem.

Results of studies using these types of scales have less frequently found differences between students with and without learning disabilities (Kistner et al., 1987; Lincoln & Chazan, 1979; Tollefson, Tracey, Johnsen, Farmer, Beunning, & Barke, 1982). These findings suggest that many learning disabled students are able to maintain a generally positive attitude about themselves despite their difficulties. Kistner and Osborne (1987), while finding lower general self-esteem among students with learning disabilities, also found that these students' general self-esteem scores were unrelated to their perceptions of cognitive competence. Thus, for many learning disabled students, awareness of academic difficulties does not necessarily result in generally negative self-perceptions. However, general self-esteem scores were related in Kistner and Osborne (1987) to the students' beliefs about their social and physical competence.

One factor that appears to be related to learning disabled students' general self-esteem is whether they are receiving some sort of remedial help. A recent review of studies investigating this issue concluded that students who attended regular classes and received no additional help had lower general self-concepts than did other learning disabled students; however, there were no consistent differences between students who attended mainstream versus self-contained classes (Chapman, 1988). Perceived social support, particularly from classmates, was also found to be related to learning disabled students' feelings of self-worth (Forman, 1988). Studies of students' general self-esteem, then, indicate that although some learning disabled students' self-esteem is lower than that of their peers, this is by no means an inevitable consequence of a learning disability.

Conclusion

Clearly, a disproportionate number of students with learning disabilities experience difficulties in the psychosocial domain. Many learning disabled students must cope with academic problems, peer rejection, low self-esteem, and even depression (Maag & Behrens, 1989; Stevenson & Romney, 1984). However, just as clearly, many students with learning disabilities are indistinguishable in psychosocial characteristics from their nondisabled peers. Identifying the factors that put some learning disabled students at risk for psychosocial problems, and just as important, the factors that make other learning disabled students less vulnerable to these problems, are crucial topics for future research.

References

Ackerman, D., & Howes, C. (1986). Sociometric status and after-school social activity of children with learning disabilities. *Journal of Learning Disabilities*, *19*, 416–419.

Ackerman, P. T., Elardo, P. T., & Dykman, R. A. (1979). A psychosocial study of hyperactive and learning disabled boys. *Journal of Abnormal Child Psychology*, *7*, 91–99.

Aponik, D. A., & Dembo, M. H. (1983). LD and normal adolescents' causal attributions of success and failure at different levels of task difficulty. *Learning Disability Quarterly*, *6*, 31–39.

Axelrod, L. (1982). Social perception in learning disabled adolescents. *Journal of Learning Disabilities*, *15*, 610–613.

Bachara, G. H. (1976). Empathy in learning disabled children. *Perceptual and Motor skills*, *43*, 541–542.

Baum, D. D., Duffelmeyer, F., & Geelan, M. (1988). Resource teacher perceptions of the prevalence of social dysfunction among students with learning disabilities. *Journal of Learning Disabilities*, *21*, 380–381.

Bendell, D., Tollefson, N., & Fine, M. (1980). Interaction of locus-of-control orientation and the performance of learning disabled adolescents. *Journal of Learning Disabilities*, *13*, 32–35.

Bender, W. N. (1985). Differences between learning disabled and non-learning disabled children in temperament and behavior. *Learning Disability Quarterly*, *8*, 11–18.

Bender, W. N., & Golden, L. B. (1988). Adaptive behavior of learning disabled and non-learning disabled children. *Learning Disability Quarterly*, *11*, 55–61.

Boersma, F. J., & Chapman, J. W. (1977). *Student's perception of ability scale*. Edmonton, Alberta, Canada: University of Alberta.

Boersma, F. J., & Chapman, J. W. (in press). *The perception of ability scale for students*. Los Angeles: Western Psychological Services.

Borkowski, J. G., Weyhing, R. S., & Carr, M. (1988). Effects of attribution retraining on strategy-based reading comprehension in learning disabled students. *Journal of Educational Psychology*, *80*, 46–53.

Bruck, M., & Hebert, M. (1982). Correlates of learning disabled students' peer interaction patterns. *Learning Disability Quarterly*, *5*, 353–362.

Bruininks, V. L. (1978a). Actual and perceived peer status of learning disabled students in mainstream programs. *Journal of Special Education*, *12*, 51–58.

Bruininks, V. L. (1978b). Peer status and personality of learning disabled and nondisabled students. *Journal of Learning Disabilities*, *11*, 29–34.

Bruno, R. M. (1981). Interpretation of pictorially presented social situations by learning disabled and normal children. *Journal of Learning Disabilities*, *14*, 350–352.

Bryan, J. H., & Perlmutter, B. (1979). Female adults' immediate impressions of learning disabled children. *Learning Disability Quarterly*, *2*, 80–88.

Bryan, J. H., & Sherman, R. (1980). Immediate impressions of nonverbal ingratiation attempts by learning disabled boys. *Learning Disability Quarterly*, *3*, 19–28.

Bryan, J. H., & Sonnefeld, L. J. (1981). Children's social desirability ratings of ingratiation tactics. *Learning Disability Quarterly*, *4*, 287–293.

Bryan, J. H., Sonnefeld, L. J., & Greenberg, F. Z. (1981). Ingratiation preferences of learning disabled children. *Learning Disability Quarterly*, *4*, 170–179.

Bryan, T. H. (1974a). Peer popularity of learning disabled children. *Journal of Learning Disabilities*, *7*, 621–625.

Bryan, T. H. (1974b). An observational analysis of classroom behaviors of children with learning disabilities. *Journal of Learning Disabilities*, *7*, 26–34.

Bryan, T. H. (1976). Peer popularity of learning disabled children: A replication. *Journal of Learning Disabilities*, *9*, 307–311.

Bryan, T. H. (1977). Children's comprehension of non-verbal communication. *Journal of Learning Disabilities*, *10*, 501–506.

Bryan, T. H., & Bryan, J. H. (1978). Social interactions of learning disabled children. *Learning Disability Quarterly*, *1*, 33–39.

Bryan, T., Cosden, M., & Pearl, R. (1982). The effects of cooperative goal structures and cooperative models on learning disabled and nondisabled students. *Learning Disability Quarterly*, *5*, 415–421.

Bryan, T., Donahue, M., & Pearl, R. (1981). Learning disabled children's peer interactions during a small-group problem solving task. *Learning Disability Quarterly*, *4*, 13–22.

Bryan, T., Donahue, M., Pearl, R., & Sturm, C. (1981). Learning disabled children's conversational skills: The "TV Talk Show." *Learning Disability Quarterly*, *4*, 260–270.

Bryan, T., & McGrady, H. (1972). Use of a teacher rating scale. *Journal of Learning Disabilities*, *5*, 199–206.

Bryan, T., Pearl, R., & Fallon, P. (1989). Conformity to peer pressure by students with learning disabilities: A replication. *Journal of Learning Disabilities*, *22*, 458–459.

Bryan, T., & Pflaum, S. (1978). Social interactions of learning disabled children: A linguistic, social, and cognitive analysis. *Learning Disability Quarterly*, *1*, 70–79.

Bryan, T., & Smiley, A. (1983). Learning disabled boys' performance and self-assessments on physical fitness tests. *Perceptual and Motor Skills*, *56*, 443–450.

Bryan, T., Werner, M. A., & Pearl, R. (1982). Learning disabled students' conformity responses to prosocial and antisocial situations. *Learning Disability Quarterly*, *5*, 344–352.

Bryan, T., & Wheeler, R. (1972). Perception of learning disabled children: The eye of the observer. *Journal of Learning Disabilities*, *5*, 484–488.

Bryan, T. H., Wheeler, R., Felcan, J., & Henek, T. (1976). "Come on dummy": An observational study of children's communications. *Journal of Learning Disabilities*, *9*, 661–669.

Bursuck, W. D. (1983). Sociometric status, behavior ratings, and social knowledge of learning disabled and low-achieving students. *Learning Disability Quarterly*, *6*, 329–338.

Bursuck, W. (1989). A comparison of students with learning disabilities to low achieving and higher achieving students on three dimensions of social competence. *Journal of Learning Disabilities*, *22*, 188–194.

Carlson, C. I. (1987). Social interaction goals and strategies of children with learning disabilities. *Journal of Learning Disabilities*, *20*, 306–311.

Cartledge, G., Frew, T., & Zaharias, J. (1985). Social skill needs of mainstreamed students: Peer and teacher perceptions. *Learning Disability Quarterly*, *8*, 132–140.

Cartledge, G., Stupay, D., & Kaczala, C. (1986). Social skills and social perception of LD and nonhandicapped elementary-school students. *Learning Disability Quarterly*, *9*, 226–234.

Center, D. B., & Wascom, A. M. (1986). Teacher perceptions of social behavior in learning disabled and socially normal children and youth. *Journal of Learning Disabilities*, *7*, 420–425.

Chapman, R. B., Larsen, S. C., & Parker, R. M. (1979). Interactions of first-grade teachers with learning disordered children. *Journal of Learning Disabilities*, *12*, 225–230.

Chapman, J. W. (1988a). Learning disabled children's self-concepts. *Review of Educational Research*, *58*, 347–371.

Chapman, J. W. (1988b). Cognitive-motivational characteristics and academic achievement of learning disabled children: A longitudinal study. *Journal of Educational Psychology*, *80*, 357–365.

Chapman, J. W., & Boersma, F. J. (1979). Academic self-concept in elementary learning disabled children: A study with the student's perception of ability scale. *Psychology in the Schools*, *16*, 201–206.

Coben, S. S., & Zigmond, N. (1986). The social integration of learning disabled students from self-contained to mainstream elementary school settings. *Journal of Learning Disabilities*, *19*, 614–618.

Coleman, J. M. (1985). Achievement level, social class and the self-concepts of mildly handicapped children. *Journal of Learning Disabilities*, *18*, 26–30.

Cooley, E. J., & Ayres, R. R. (1988). Self-concept and success–failure attributions of nonhandicapped students and students with learning disabilities. *Journal of Learning Disabilities*, *21*, 174–178.

Cosden, M., Pearl, R., & Bryan, T. (1985). The effects of cooperative versus individual goal structures on learning disabled and nondisabled students. *Exceptional Children*, *52*, 103–114.

Cullen, J. L., Boersma, F. J., & Chapman, J. W. (1981). Characteristics of third grade learning disabled children. *Learning Disability Quarterly*, *4*, 224–230.

Dickstein, E. B., & Warren, D. R. (1980). Role taking deficits in learning disabled children. *Journal of Learning Disabilities*, *13*, 378–382.

Donahue, M. L. (1981). Requesting strategies of learning disabled children. *Applied Psycholinguistics*, *2*, 213–234.

Donahue, M., Pearl, R., & Bryan, T. (1980). Learning disabled children's conversational competence: Responses to inadequate messages. *Applied Psycholinguistics*, *1*, 387–403.

Donahue, M., Pearl, R., & Bryan, T. (1983). Communicative competence in learning disabled children. In I. Bialer & K. Gadow (Eds.), *Advances in Learning and Behavioral Disabilities* (Vol. II, pp. 49–84). Greenwich; CT: JAI Press.

Donahue, M., & Prescott, B. (1988). Reading disabled children's conversational participation in dispute episodes with peers. *First Language*, *8*, 247–258.

Dorval, B., McKinney, J. D., & Feagans, L. (1982). Teachers' interaction with learning disabled children and average achievers. *Journal of Pediatric Psychology*, *17*, 317–330.

Dudley-Marling, C. C., & Edmiaston, R. (1985). Social status of learning

120   Ruth Pearl

disabled children and adolescents: A review. *Learning Disability Quarterly*, *8*, 189–204.

Feagans, L., & McKinney, J. D. (1981). The pattern of exceptionality across domains in learning disabled children. *Journal of Applied Developmental Psychology*, *1*, 313–328.

Feagans, L., & McKinney, J. D. (1982). *Longitudinal studies of learning disabled children*. Paper presented at the Association for Children and Adults with Learning Disabilities, Chicago, IL.

Feagans, L., & Short, E. J. (1986). Referential communication and reading performance in learning disabled children over a 3-year period. *Developmental Psychology*, *22*, 177–183.

Fellers, G., & Saudargas, R. A. (1987). Classroom behaviors of LD and nonhandicapped girls. *Learning Disability Quarterly*, *10*, 231–236.

Fincham, F. (1979). Conservation and cognitive role-taking ability in learning disabled boys. *Journal of Learning Disabilities*, *12*, 34–40.

Flicek, M., & Landau, S. (1985). Social status problems of learning disabled and hyperactive/learning disabled boys. *Journal of Clinical Child Psychology*, *14*, 340–344.

Forman, E. A. (1988). The effects of social support and school placement on the self-concept of LD students. *Learning Disability Quarterly*, *11*, 115–124.

Forness, S. R., & Esveldt, K. C. (1975). Classroom observations of children with learning and behavior problems. *Journal of Learning Disabilities*, *8*, 382–385.

Garrett, M. K., & Crump, W. D. (1980). Peer acceptance, teacher references, and self-appraisal of social status among learning disabled students. *Learning Disability Quarterly*, *3*, 42–48.

Gerber, P. J., & Zinkgraf, S. A. (1982). A comparative study of social-perceptual ability in learning disabled and nonhandicapped students. *Learning Disability Quarterly*, *5*, 374–378.

Gettinger, M., & Fayne, H. R. (1982). Classroom behaviors during small group instruction and learning performance in learning disabled and nondisabled children. *Journal of Educational Research*, *75*, 182–187.

Gottlieb, B. W., Gottlieb, J., Berkell, D., & Levy, L. (1986). Sociometric status and solitary play of LD boys and girls. *Journal of Learning Disabilities*, *19*, 619–622.

Gresham, F. M., & Reschly, D. J. (1986). Social skill deficits and low peer acceptance of mainstreamed learning disabled children. *Learning Disability Quarterly*, *9*, 23–32.

Harter, S. (1982). The perceived competence scale for children. *Child Development*, *53*, 87–97.

Harter, S. (1985). *Manual for the self-perception profile for children*. Denven: University of Denver.

Hiebert, B., Wong, B., & Hunter, M. (1982). Affective influences on learning disabled adolescents. *Learning Disability Quarterly*, *5*, 334–343.

Horowitz, E. C. (1981). Popularity, decentering ability, and roletaking skills in learning disabled and normal children. *Learning Disability Quarterly*, *4*, 23–30.

Hutton, J., & Polo, L. (1976). A sociometric study of learning disability children and types of teaching strategy. *Group Psychotherapy and Psychodrama*, *29*, 113–120.

Jackson, S. C., Enright, R. D., & Murdock, J. Y. (1987). Social perception problems in learning disabled youth: Developmental lag versus perceptual deficit. *Journal of Learning Disabilities, 20*, 361–364.

Jacobsen, B., Lowery, B., & DuCette, J. (1986). Attributions of learning disabled children. *Journal of Educational Psychology, 78*, 57–64.

Jones, C. J. (1985). Analysis of the self-concept of handicapped students. *Remedial and Special Education, 6*, 32–36.

Kistner, J., Haskett, M., White, K., & Robbins, F. (1987). Perceived competence and self-worth of LD and normally achieving students. *Learning Disability Quarterly, 10*, 37–44.

Kistner, J., & Osborne, M. (1987). A longitudinal study of LD children's self-evaluations. *Learning Disability Quarterly, 10*, 258–266.

Kistner, J. A., & Gatlin, D. F. (1989). Sociometric differences between learning-disabled and nonhandicapped students: Effects of sex and race. *Journal of Educational Psychology, 81*, 118–120.

Kistner, J., White, K., Haskett, M., & Robbins, F. (1985). Development of learning-disabled and normally achieving children's causal attributions. *Journal of Abnormal Child Psychology, 13*, 639–647.

Kistner, J. A., Osborne, M., & LeVerrier, L. (1988). Causal attributions of learning-disabled children: Developmental patterns and relation to academic progress. *Journal of Educational Psychology, 80*, 82–89.

Knight-Arest, I. (1984). Communicative effectiveness of learning disabled and normally achieving 10- to 13-year-old boys. *Learning Disability Quarterly, 7*, 237–245.

LaGreca, A. M., Stone, W. L., & Halpern, D. A. (1988, February). *LD status and achievement: Confounding variables in the study of children's social and behavioral functioning?* Paper presented at the annual meeting of the International Academy for Research in Learning Disabilities (IARLD). Los Angeles, CA.

Landau, S., Milich, R., & McFarland, M. (1987). Social status differences among subgroups of LD boys. *Learning Disability Quarterly, 10*, 277–282.

Levy, L., & Gottlieb, J. (1984). Learning disabled and non-LD children at play. *Remedial and Special Education, 5*, 43–50.

Licht, B. G., Kistner, J. A., Ozkaragoz, T., Shapiro, S., & Clausen, L. (1985). Causal attributions of learning disabled children: Individual differences and their implications for persistence. *Journal of Educational Psychology, 77*, 208–216.

Lincoln, A., & Chazan, S. (1979). Perceived competence and intrinsic motivation in learning disabled children. *Journal of Clinical Child Psychology, 8*, 213–216.

Luchow, J. P., Crowl, T. K., & Kahn, J. P. (1985). Learned helplessness: Perceived effects of ability and effort on academic performance among EH and LD/EH children. *Journal of Learning Disabilities, 18*, 470–474.

Maag, J. W., & Behrens, J. T. (1989). Depression and cognitive self-statements of learning disabled and seriously emotionally disturbed adolescents. *Journal of Special Education, 23*, 17–27.

Maheady, L., & Maitland, G. (1982). Assessing social perception abilities in learning disabled students. *Learning Disability Quarterly, 5*, 363–370.

Margalit, M. & Zak, I. (1984). Anxiety and self-concept of learning disabled children. *Journal of Learning Disabilities, 17*, 537–539.

Mathinos, D. A. (1988). Communicative competence of children with learning disabilities. *Journal of Learning Disabilities, 21*, 437–443.

McConaughy, S. H. (1986). Social competence and behavioral problems of learning disabled boys aged 12–16. *Journal of Learning Disabilities, 19*, 101–106.

McConaughy, S. H., & Ritter, D. R. (1986). Social competence and behavioral problems of learning disabled boys aged 6–11. *Journal of Learning Disabilities, 19*, 39–45.

McKinney, J. D. (1989). Longitudinal research on the behavioral characteristics of children with learning disabilities. *Journal of Learning Disabilities, 22*, 141–150.

McKinney, J. D., & Feagans, L. (1984). Academic and behavioral characteristics: Longitudinal studies of learning disabled children and average achievers. *Learning Disability Quarterly, 7*, 251–265.

McKinney, J. D., McClure, S., & Feagans, L. (1982). Classroom behavior of learning disabled children. *Learning Disability Quarterly, 5*, 45–52.

McKinney, J. D., & Speece, D. L. (1986). Academic consequences and longitudinal stability of behavioral subtypes of learning disabled children. *Journal of Educational Psychology, 78*, 365–372.

Milich, R., & Landua, S. (1982). Socialization and peer relations in hyperactive children. In K. Gadow & I. Bialer (Eds.), *Advances in Learning and Behavior Disabilities* (Vol. 1, pp. 283–339). Greenwich, CT: JAI Press.

Miller, M. (1984). Social acceptability characteristics of learning disabled students. *Journal of Learning Disabilities, 17*, 619–621.

Moreno, J. L. (1934). *Who shall survive? A new approach to the problem of human interrelations*. Washington, DC: Nervous and Mental Disease Publishing Co.

Noel, N. M. (1980). Referential communication abilities of learning disabled children. *Learning Disability Quarterly, 3*, 70–75.

Oliva, A. H., & LaGreca, A. M. (1988). Children with learning disabilities: Social goals and Strategies. *Journal of Learning Disabilities, 21*, 301–306.

Omizo, M. M., Amerikaner, M. J., & Michael, W. B. (1985). The Coopersmith self-esteem inventroy as a predictor of feelings and communication satisfaction toward parents among learning disabled, emotionally disturbed, and normal adolescents. *Educational and Psychological Measurement, 45*, 389–395.

Owen, R. W., Adams, P. A., Forrest, T., Stolz, L. M. & Fisher, S. (1971). Learning disorders in children: Sibling studies. *Monographs of the Society for Research in Child Development, 36*, No. 144.

Palmer, D. J., Drummond, F., Tollison, P., & Zinkgraff, S. (1982). An attributional investigation of performance outcomes for learning-disabled and normal-achieving pupils. *Journal of Special Education, 16*, 207–217.

Pascarella, E. T., Pflaum, S. W., Bryan, T. H., & Pearl, R. A. (1983). Interaction of internal attribution for effort and teacher response mode in reading instruction: A replication note. *American Educational Research Journal, 20*, 269–276.

Pearl, R. (1982). Learning disabled children's attributions for success and failure: A replication with a labeled learning disabled sample. *Learning Disability Quarterly, 5*, 173–176.

Pearl, R. (1985). Cognitive-behavioral interventions for increasing motivation. *Journal of Abnormal Child Psychology*, *13*, 443–454.

Pearl, R. (1987). Social cognitive factors in learning-disabled children's social problems. In S. J. Ceci (Ed.), *Handbook of cognitive, social, and neuropsychological aspects of learning disabilities* (pp. 273–294). Hillsdale, NJ: Lawrence Erlbaum.

Pearl, R., Bryan, T. H., & Donahue, M. (1980). Learning disabled children's attributions for success and failure. *Learning Disability Quarterly*, *3*, 3–9.

Pearl, R., Bryan, T., Fallon, P., & Herzog, A. (1991). Learning disabled students' detection of deception. *Learning Disabilities Research & Practice*, *6*, 12–16.

Pearl, R., Bryan, T., & Herzog, A. (1990). Resisting or acquiescing to peer pressure to engage in misconduct: Adolescents' expectations of probable consequences. *Journal of Youth and Adolescence*, *19*, 43–55.

Pearl, R., & Cosden, M. (1982). Sizing up a situation: Learning disabled children's understanding of social interactions. *Learning Disability Quarterly*, *5*, 371–373.

Pearl, R., Donahue, M., & Bryan, T. (1985). The development of tact: Children's strategies for delivering bad news. *Journal of Applied Developmental Psychology*, *6*, 141–149.

Pearl, R., Donahue, M., & Bryan, T. (1986). Social relationships of learning disabled children. In J. K. Torgesen & B. Y. L. Wong (Eds.), *Psychological and educational perspectives on learning disabilities* (pp. 193–224). Orlando, FL: Academic Press.

Perlmutter, B. F., Crocker, J., Cordray, D., & Garstecki, D. (1983). Sociometric status and related personality characteristics of mainstreamed learning disabled adolescents. *Learning Disability Quarterly*, *6*, 21–31.

Piers, E. V. (1969). *Manual for the Piers–Harris Children's Self-Concept Scale*. Nashville, TN: Counselor Recordings and Tests.

Prilliman, D. (1981). Acceptance of learning disabled students in the mainstream environment: A failure to replicate. *Journal of Learning Disabilities*, *14*, 344–346.

Pullis, M. (1985). LD students' temperament characteristics and their impact on decisions by resource and mainstream teachers. *Learning Disability Quarterly*, *8*, 109–122.

Richey, D. D., & McKinney, J. D. (1978). Classroom behavioral styles of learning disabled children. *Journal of Learning Disabilities*, *11*, 297–302.

Ritter, D. R. (1989). Social competence and problem behavior of adolescent girls with learning disabilities. *Journal of Learning Disabilities*, *22*, 460–461.

Rogers, H., & Saklofske, D. H. (1985). Self-concepts, locus of control and performance expectations of learning disabled children. *Journal of Learning Disabilities*, *18*, 273–278.

Rosenberg, M. (1965) *Society and the Adolescent Self-Image*. Princeton: Princeton University Press.

Rotter, J. B. (1966). Generalized expectancies for internal versus external control of reinforcement. *Psychological Monographs*, *80*.

Sabornie, E. J., & Kauffman, J. M. (1986). Social acceptance of learning disabled adolescents. *Learning Disability Quarterly*, *9*, 55–60.

Sainato, D. M., Zigmond, N., & Strain, P. (1983). Social status and initiations of interaction by learning disabled students in a regular education setting. *Analysis and Intervention in Developmental Disabilities, 3*, 71–87.

Saloner, M. R., & Gettinger, M. (1985). Social inference skills in learning disabled and nondisabled children. *Psychology in the Schools, 22*, 201–207.

Sater, G. M., & French, D. C. (1989). A comparison of the social competencies of learning disabled and low achieving elementary-aged children. *Journal of Special Education, 23*, 17–27.

Schofield, J. (1981). Complementary and conflicting identities: Images and interactions in an interracial school. In S. R. Asher & J. M. Gottman (Eds.) *The Development of Children's Friendships* (pp. 53–90), England: Cambridge University Press.

Schunk, D.H., & Cox, P. D. (1986). Strategy training and attributional feedback with learning disabled students. *Journal of Educational Psychology, 78*, 201–209.

Scranton, T., & Ryckman, D. (1979). Sociometric status of learning disabled children in an integrative program. *Journal of Learning Disabilities, 12*, 402–407.

Sheare, J.B. (1978). The impact of resource programs upon the self-concept and peer acceptance of learning disabled children. *Psychology in the Schools, 1978, 15*, 406–412.

Shelton, T. L., Anastopoulos, A. D., & Linden, J. D. (1985). An attribution training program with learning disabled children. *Journal of Learning Disabilities, 18*, 261–265.

Siperstein, G. N., Bopp, M. J., & Bak, J. J. (1978). Social status of learning disabled children. *Journal of Learning Disabilities, 11*, 98–102.

Siperstein, G. N., & Goding, M. J. (1983). *Social integration of learning disabled children in regular classrooms*. Greenwich, CT: JAI Press.

Slate, J. R., & Saudargas, R. A. (1986). Differences in learning disabled and average students' classroom behaviors. *Learning Disability Quarterly, 9*, 61–67.

Sobol, M. P., Earn, B. M., Bennett, D., & Humphries, T. (1983). A categorical analysis of the social attributions of learning-disabled children. *Journal of Abnormal Child Psychology, 11*, 217–228.

Soenksen, P. A., Flagg, C. L., & Schmits, D. W. (1981). Social communication in learning disabled students: A pragmatic analysis. *Journal of Learning Disabilities, 14*, 283–286.

Speece, D. L., McKinney, J. D., & Appelbaum, M. I. (1985). Classification and validation of behavioral subtypes of learning disabled children. *Journal of Educational Psychology, 77*, 67–77.

Spekman, N. (1981). A study of the dyadic verbal communication abilities of learning disabled and normally achieving fourth- and fifth-grade boys. *Learning Disability Quarterly, 4*, 139–151.

Stevenson, D. T. & Romney, D. M. (1984). Depression in learning disabled children. *Journal of Learning Disabilities, 17*, 579–582.

Stone, W. L. & LaGreca, A. M. (1984). Comprehension of nonverbal communication: A reexamination of the social competencies of learning disabled children. *Journal of Abnormal Child Psychology, 12*, 505–518.

Tollefson, N., Tracy, D. B., Johnsen, E. P., Farmer, A. W., & Buenning, M. (1984). Goal setting and personal responsibility training for LD adolescents. *Psychology in the Schools, 21*, 224–233.

Tollefson, N., Tracy, D. B., Johnsen, E. P., Farmer, A. W., Buenning, M., & Barke, C. R. (1982). Attribution patterns of learning disabled adolescents. *Learning Disability Quarterly, 5*, 14–20.

Touliatos, J., & Lindholm, B. W. (1980). Dimensions of problem behavior in learning disabled and normal children. *Perceptual and Motor Skills, 50*, 145–146.

Weiner, B. (1979). A theory of motivation for some classroom experiences. *Journal of Educational Psychology, 71*, 3–25.

Weiner, J. (1980). A theoretical model of the acquisition of peer relationships of learning disabled children. *Journal of Learning Disabilities, 13*, 506–511.

Weiss, E. (1984). Learning disabled children's understanding of social interactions of peers. *Journal of Learning Disabilities, 17*, 612–615.

Wiig, E. H., & Harris, S. P. (1974). Perception and interpretation of nonverbally expressed emotions by adolescents with learning disabilities. *Perceptual and Motor Skills, 38*, 239–245.

Wiig, E., & Semel, E. (1980). *Language assessment and intervention for the learning disabled*. Columbus, Ohio: Charles E. Merrill.

Wong, B. Y., & Wong, R. (1980). Role-taking skills in normal achieving and learning disabled children. *Learning Disability Quarterly, 3*, 11–18.

5
Metacognition

KATHERINE A. LARSON and MICHAEL M. GERBER

Joe, a 5th grade student, picks up a pencil and immediately begins to compute the math test problems his teacher just passed out. A few minutes later, Mrs. Brown points out to Joe that for every problem he has completed he has performed addition when, in fact, the worksheet is an assortment of addition, subtraction, and multiplication problems. Mrs. Brown also reminds Joe that he doesn't have to rush because the test is not timed and the goal of the task is accuracy. Joe nods, erases his work (including the addition problems) and begins from the beginning. Joe has mastered all levels of addition, subtraction without regrouping, and single digit multiplication. He is still struggling but approaching mastery of subtraction with regrouping. The first problem on the test is addition, and so are the fourth and fifth problems. Joe is now beginning the subtraction. He struggles with the first part of the regrouping and marks his paper incorrectly. As he continues to complete the first subtraction problem, obviously with frustration, he begins to hum quietly and keep body rhythm of a popular song. As Joe works he fails to use the strategy of crossing out and rewriting minuend digits. Instead, he tries to keep mental track of changed values. Before he's finished with the subtraction calculation he has let his attention wander several times to other things in the classroom. This is unfortunate because attention to task is just what this particular problem requires. By the time Joe finishes the first subtraction problem, he is quite frustrated. And, Joe's answer is not only incorrect, but really outlandish, with the remainder three times the value of the minuend. Joe takes a second to glance at his answer and then moves on to the next problem. If Joe had thought to check his work, even by just simply reading the problem and his answer back to himself, he would have readily recognized that he had miscalculated. However, he fails to recognize his error and leaves his answer as written. When Joe sees that the next problem is also subtraction with regrouping, he says something like "I'm just stupid" under his breath, frowns, drops his pencil on the test paper, and then puts his head down on the desk. After a few moments, Joe begins again to work on the test. He shows visible signs of consternation and frustration, signs that characteristically precede his giving-up; yet, Joe does not attempt to modulate his negative feelings and increase his motivation by selecting test problems that he knows how to compute easily. Instead, Joe begins again to try to calculate the second subtraction problem. A few minutes later, Joe gives up and withdraws from the task by pulling his jacket over his head.

What happened to Joe?

Obviously, Joe did not perform successfully on this task. His failure, however, cannot be attributed to lack of skills. Indeed, during guided practice, Joe has completed similar problems accurately. Joe, typical of many learning disabled students, failed this task because he did not spontaneously employ metacognitive problem-solving skills—skills that would have helped Joe approach and manage the task successfully. For example, Joe *failed* (a) to approach the task planfully (he did all the problems in order and started completely over when he erased), (b) to clarify the task goal (accuracy, not speed, was required), (c) to identify task parameters (a test, unlimited time, some problems more difficult than others), (d) to identify relevant variables (different kinds of problems, subtraction is hard, "I give up when its hard"), (e) to employ effective strategies (carried and manipulated minuend in his head), and (f) to engage in self-monitoring (did not correct error, did not allocate attention as needed, and did not self-manage motivation and persistence). This kind of ineffective problem solving, characteristic of the Joes and Joannas in classes for the learning disabled, has propelled special education's intensive efforts during the last decade in designing and evaluating instructional programs that train domain-specific as well as general metacognitive skills.

Defining Metacognition

Metacognition is the ability to select and manage cognitive strategies effectively. The key and critical concern over metacognition is that it will promote generalized improvements in learning. Most models of metacognition speculate that it is a highly specialized and involuted form of cognition that oversees, manages, and orchestrates cognitive activity, especially when problem solving, effortful learning, or other attention-demanding cognitive activity is required. Normally developing children as well as educators and psychologists come to know something about human thought processes and find that they can both express and use this knowledge to facilitate successful adaptation. That is, children come to know that mental activity accompanies making choices, decisions, judgments, or plans before acting, they know that they know it, and can often discuss it. This self-knowledge is generalized by inference to explain how or why other people behave as they do. That is, we "know" that we engage in various cognitive processes, and we infer that others do too. In fact, in social transaction of any type we rely on our belief that others engage in cognitive activity much as we do.

Historically, theoretical models have divided metacognition into two general types of skills: (a) skills for knowing when and how to be planful and for selecting effective strategies and (b) skills for monitoring and managing ongoing strategy behavior. More recently, metacognitive theory has elaborated these two subdivisions of metacognition to include complex interactive components (see next section, Borkowski and Sternberg).

The first type of metacognitive skills, that is, planning to have a plan and selecting effective strategies, have been variously described as knowing about knowing (Brown, 1975); awareness of person, task, and strategy variables (Flavell, 1978); shared awareness of what you know about how you know (Paris, 1978); cognitive self-appraisal (Paris, Wasik, & Van der Westhuizen, 1988); stable and statable information about one's own cognitive processes (Slife, Weiss, & Bell, 1985); and general strategy knowledge (Borkowski, Carr, Rellinger, & Pressley, 1990).

Monitoring ongoing strategy behavior has been variously referred to as regulation of cognition (Brown, 1978); executive functioning (Butterfield & Belmont, 1977); metacontrol skills (Larson & Gerber, 1987); and monitoring strategy knowledge (Borkowski et al.,1990).

Metacognition and Learning Disabilities

Since the early 1980s, researchers and practitioners in the field of learning disabilities have increasingly adopted the hypothesis that learning disabled children perform academic tasks poorly because they fail spontaneously and effectively to select and manage task-appropriate strategies. Metacognitive deficits have been found consistently to characterize learning disabled students as well as other underachieving populations such as slow learners, poor readers, mildly retarded, and impulsive children.

Metacognitive deficits are found to be directly related to specific academic tasks. In the area of *reading*, poor readers are found to be less aware of the purpose of reading as meaning-getting, less knowledgeable about strategies for decoding, comprehending, and reading for a specific purpose, less sensitive to important parts of text, and less aware of text inconsistencies (Forrest & Waller, 1980; Garner, 1981; Garner & Kraus, 1982; Kurtz & Borkowski, 1984; Winograd, 1984; Wong & Jones, 1982). In the area of *spelling*, learning disabled students are found to be inefficient problem solvers. They have difficulty with spontaneously generating appropriate and effective spelling study strategies, error monitoring, and efficient search and retrieval of spelling relevant information (Gerber & Hall, 1987, 1989; Graham & Freeman, 1986; Harris, Graham, & Freeman, 1988; Wong, 1986). In the area of *math*, learning disabled students have been described as having significant difficulties selecting correct algorithms, applying rote-learned algorithms in a strategic manner, using strategies correctly, applying debugging, and monitoring procedures (Cawley, 1985; DeCorte & Verschaffel, 1981; Lloyd, Saltzman, & Kauffman, 1981; Russell & Ginsburg, 1984).

Although metacognitive theory has been generated outside the field of special education, Wong (1986) notes that the field of learning disabilities has nevertheless benefited in two ways. According to Wong, metacognitive theory and its support research have provided special educators with (a) specific things to teach—the cognitive content of remediation programs, and (b) specific prescriptive approaches—how to teach academic skills effectively.

Wong also advises special educators, we think correctly, to be wary of "unbridled, extravagant, or faddish impact by (the metacognitive) theoretical construct" (1986, p. 22). We concur fully with Wong's concern that the field of learning disabilities has essentially adopted without modification the metacognitive constructs and paradigms generated by developmental and cognitive psychologists. That is, what we know about metacognition of learning disabled children has emanated from research on the construct of metacognition and not from research on the construct of learning disabilities. Thus far, special education's major contribution has been to replicate and apply methods and constructs developed in laboratory analog research outside the field. The key issue for future research directions, as we see it, is to develop a theoretical orientation to metacognition that is founded on a description of learning disabled children in the context of natural classroom environments.

We suggest in this chapter how metacognitive theory might be reformulated to address issues in the field of learning disabilities. We propose that the general metacognitive construct be reformulated as a construct with a social dimension. Such a model of metacognition would include a bidirectional interactive relationship between mainstream teaching constraints, classroom social–cognitive milieus, and the metacognitive make-up and histories of both the teacher and learning disabled student.

We are committed to the belief that our special education friends and colleagues are currently the best sources for increasing the utility of metacognitive theory to enhance learning opportunities of learning disabled students. One goal of this chapter is to stimulate future discussion, speculation, and research within special education for discerning how to apply adopted metacognitive constructs effectively to the complex phenomenon of learning disability which is, we think by definition, an interaction phenomenon.

Chapter Organization

In presenting our ideas on the significance of the concept of metacognition for understanding and teaching learning disabled students, we have not attempted to summarize what already has become a vast literature. There already are numerous excellent reviews and commentaries on research on metacognition, many that will be cited in this chapter, that we invite the reader to consider. Instead, we have chosen to compress the main aspects of this large literature by discussing a few of its most influential theorists and how their contributions have impacted the field of learning disabilities. We have hoped to accomplish this aim by discussing the work of six researchers—John Flavell, Ann Brown, John Borkowski, Michael Pressley, Robert Sternberg, and Bernice Wong—whose individual and collective contributions to current understanding of metacognition are widely acknowledged. These six, in their unusually long and influential programs of productive research on cognitive strategy instruction and metacognition, represent intellectual positions and research paradigms that illustrate well the critical features of metacognitive theory as it has come to be applied to learning disabilities. In selecting for discussion these six individuals, we in no way wish to denigrate the contributions of others.

In the remainder of the chapter we present our ideas for broadening perspectives on metacognition to include, not only as Borkowski and others have suggested, the child's self-system, but also the classroom and teaching as a social metacognitive context. Also included are the importance of a teacher's own metacognitive awareness and control skills for both the academic content and for teaching as problem solving.

Theorists and Theories

John Flavell

Background

John Flavell, a developmental psychologist, is considered by many to be the "father" of the concept *metacognition*. Studying the development of memory, in 1970 Flavell reported empirical data showing that young children are quite limited in their knowledge about memory phenomena, and that their awareness and monitoring of memory increases with age (Flavell, Friedrichs, & Hoyt, 1970). In 1971, Flavell coined the term *metamemory* to describe an individual's knowledge or awareness of anything pertinent to information storage. As a developmental psychologist interested in memory phenomena, Flavell's research program can be seen as an attempt to answer the question "What might a person conceivably come to know, or know how to find out, concerning memory as a function of cognitive growth and learning experience?" (Flavell & Wellman, 1977, p. 5). What individuals learn about memory Flavell referred to as *metacognitive knowledge*.

During the 1970s, Flavell's contribution to the study of metacognition, both theoretically and empirically, was specification and elaboration of the concept metacognitive knowledge. The long-standing usefulness and perceived validity of this concept is demonstrated by the fact that during the last 15 years a variety of researchers and theorists have felt compelled to incorporate the concept into their own models and constructions of metacognition. Although Flavell's term metacognitive knowledge has been repeatedly relabeled over the years with terms such as *knowledge about cognition* (Brown, 1975), *knowing about knowing* (Brown, 1975), *knowing that* (Bobrow, 1975), and *cognitive self-appraisal* (Paris et al., 1988), there seems to be consensus in the field that the concept of metacognitive knowledge as Flavell first described it has had, and continues to have, significant impact on both basic and instructional research. It has significant validity as a central component of hypothesized metacognitive models.

Theoretical Contribution

Flavell published extensively from the late 1960s through the late 1970s; however, it is in two papers (Flavell, 1979; Flavell & Wellman, 1977) that he specified and elaborated most completely his ideas regarding the concept metacognitive knowledge. Although Flavell discusses concepts in reference to memory tasks and phenomena, he believed (Flavell, 1970) that metacognitive concepts are generic to all cognitive or problem-solving tasks. We present his ideas in the more general context of cognition. Flavell posited that because cognitive performance is influenced by three factors (relevant attributes of the person, the task, and the potential strategies), these would be part of the *meta knowledge* an individual acquires as a result of experience and development. Flavell also believed that metacognitive knowledge includes the recognition and differentiation by an individual that some cognitive tasks require planful and goal-directed behavior whereas other cognitive tasks do not.

Flavell contended that an individual's metacognitive knowledge of person variables includes a general understanding of the human cognitive learning system and its limitations, capacities, and idiosyncrasies as well as knowledge of one's own temporary and enduring personal attributes and states as a thinking organism. Flavell demonstrated that children form self-schemata concerning their cognitive and social capabilities and limitations (Flavell et al., 1970; Kreutzer, Leonard, & Flavell, 1975). Flavell and Wellman (1977) referred to the development of a *mnemonic self-concept*. They argued that the developing child gradually learns to read accurately his own knowing states as reflected in, for example, *mnemonic sensations*, and the child comes to understand the behavioral implications of these knowing states.

Flavell, colleagues, and others accumulated a substantial body of evidence supporting both the concept and the developmental nature of metacognitive knowledge of person variables. For example, awareness of what one has forgotten, or tip-of-the-tongue awareness, was found to increase with age (Wellman, 1978). Younger children were found less able than older children to assess or predict their readiness to retrieve (Flavell et al., 1970). Accuracy in predicting recall ability was found to be very poor in young children but to increase with age (Markman, 1973; Yussen & Levy, 1975).

Every problem provides task information, abundant or meager, familiar or unfamiliar, trustworthy or untrustworthy. Flavell posited that metacognitive knowledge of task variables was understanding, for a given task, what the task demands or goals were, which problem information was relevant, what the information portended for likelihood and difficulty of goal achievement, and what the information implied for how the task could most effectively and efficiently be managed, including which strategies would be most appropriate employ.

Empirical evidence supports the concept and developmental nature of metacognitive knowledge of task variables as posited by Flavell. Several studies found that ability to judge accurately the relative difficulty of different memory tasks increased with age, as did ability to identify task variables and strategies relevant to ease of goal attainment (Danner, 1976; Kreutzer et al., 1975; Moynahan, 1973; Salatas & Flavell, 1976; Tenney, 1975).

Flavell states (Flavell & Wellman, 1977) that individuals acquire both metacognitive and cognitive strategies. He defined cognitive strategies as tactics used for the purpose of accomplishing the task goal and metacognitive strategies as tactics used for monitoring one's progress toward goal attainment. According to Flavell, storage of *both* cognitive and metacognitive strategies is a metacognitive function and part of one's repertoire of metacognitive knowledge. Indeed, according to Flavell, cognitive and metacognitive strategies can actually be identical behavior. It is the purpose to which the strategy or tactic is subordinated that distinguishes it as a cognitive or metacognitive act. Flavell also introduced the term *production deficiency* to describe performance of an individual who failed to employ spontaneously a cognitive strategy even though the strategy is known. Flavell used the term *mediational deficiency* to describe performance of an individual who does employ an appropriate cognitive strategy but the strategy fails to enhance performance.

Instructional Implications

Flavell believed that metacognitive skills could be trained (Flavell, 1979), although he did not himself directly apply his theoretical constructs to academic and social learning activities. Nevertheless, his notion of meta-cognitive knowledge has had and continues to have broad and significant impact on special educators who have designed cognitive instructional programs in reading, writing, math, and social behavior. In conjunction with other theorists, Flavell's theoretical concepts have influenced cognitive instructional design in three areas: addressing attribution/motivation, teaching planful intent, and transfer of knowledge as socialization.

Flavell and Wellman (1977) wrote that much of what they posited about person variables and the interaction among task, person, and strategy variables "has obvious overlaps with social cognition in its attri-bution theory and self-attribution forms" (p. 25). Flavell and Wellman postulated that intentions, attributions, expectancies, and beliefs about one's own competence and learning abilities affect cognitive efficiency. This notion of a metacognitive self-concept is seen in instructional designs that include attribution retraining as a central component of cognitive instruction (e.g., Borkowski 1990; Borkowski, Johnston, & Reid, 1986).

Flavell also noted that one of the most basic metacognitive knowledges is for an individual to recognize that some tasks require strategic and planful behavior in order to be solved effectively and that a child must come to recognize the importance of strategic approaches to problem solving. This concept is reflected in research and instructional designs using informed strategy training (e.g., Day, 1980; Duffy, Roehler, Meloth, Putnam, Wesselman, 1986; Palincsar, 1986a, 1986b; Paris, Cross, & Lipson, 1984), which explicitly explains to students why the strategy is needed, how the strategy works, and what task-related rewards will be gained for using the strategy (e.g., Hansen, 1981; Paris et al., 1984).

Flavell's third influence, although it was more of an idea he cited in passing than a concept he elaborated, was his hypothesis that much of metacognitive development was "something analogous to Piaget's reflec-tive abstraction process" and that according to what he referred to as "the Russian point of view" (Flavell & Wellman, 1977, p. 29), a child's abstractions about his own cognitive behavior is a social phenomenon and greatly influenced by parents, teachers, and other adults who set various cognitive tasks and model cognitive behavior for the child. This notion of how a child comes to acquire metacognitive knowledge is implied in instructional designs such as scaffolding (e.g., Wood, Bruner, & Ross, 1976), which is characterized by maintaining the difficulty of the task but providing just enough cues and help to the student so that the student experiences performance success and learning is extended. Reciprocal teaching (e.g., Palincsar, 1986a, 1986b; Palincsar & Brown, 1984) also reflects this notion of learning and provides for the gradual transfer of the cognitive strategy to the student through dialogue and modeling by a significant adult.

Ann Brown

Background

During the last decade and a half, Ann Brown has been a significant force in the production of metacognitive theory and knowledge. She has consistently led and at times pushed the field to better understanding by generating new insights, by setting superlative standards for programmatic research, and by critical review of ongoing research practices.

A developmental psychologist, Brown entered into the study of cognitive development in the early to mid-1970s—a time when memory development research dominated the field. Her work helped merge memory development and problem-solving research and, as a consequence, the pace and depth of metacognitive knowledge was significantly increased.

Theoretical Contribution

As a way of discussing Ann Brown's many contributions during the last 15 years, we have divided our discussion to highlight both her conceptual and her research practice ideas most directly impacting the field of special education.

Throughout her career, Brown has contributed important ideas in terms of *how* cognitive theory and knowledge might best be generated. She was critical early on of cognitive development research practices (Brown & DeLoache, 1977). Essentially, Brown criticized memory research for (a) having "little practical utility" (p. 14) for meaningful learning and for (b) investigating research tasks in such a way "that we cannot say anything about nonproducers" (p. 8). By urging cognitive researchers to apply the instructional research method to school-related learning tasks, Brown helped focus cognitive research implications on the education of disabled students.

Also early on, Brown cautioned researchers to be aware that cognitive and metacognitive skills and capacities are unrealistically influenced by the artificiality of laboratory experiments (Brown & DeLoache, 1977; Murphy & Brown, 1975). She was concerned that a child's motivations and task meaningfulness were not sufficiently taken into account by laboratory research pratices. She also noted the influence the researcher's interaction with the child would have on the child's performance. Years later these concerns for how a child responds to instruction and learns to generalize, and consequently, how children must be instructed to perform cognitive training tasks effectively emerged as one rationale for her reciprocal instruction approach to academic training of learning disabled students.

Brown most recently suggests the use of a three-pronged convergent evidence approach to determining causal relationships between specific cognitive processes and performance. She advises researchers first to generate a theory about the underlying processes involved, then correlate task performance with spontaneous and effective use of the underlying processes, and finally, train poor performers to use and monitor the underlying processes and test their after-training performance. If the theory is correct, trained performance should become more like that of spontaneous user's performance (Brown & Campione, 1984; Brown, Palincsar, & Armbruster, 1984).

On the conceptual side, one of Brown's major theoretical contributions was development of the concept that has been termed variously *executive control, metacognitive monitoring*, or *cognitive self-regulation*. In her early writings, Brown noted that poor self-regulation is not necessarily age-related but more a function of familiarity with the problem-solving task. Thus, adults facing novel problems are, according to Brown, also deficient in self-conscious, intelligent, self-regulation of their actions. Brown noted that developmental trends in this phenomenon are accounted for by the fact that children, and especially young children, are usually neophytes at most problem solving tasks. As children grow older they learn to apply more conscious control and regulation of these natural strategies:

... what develops in a variety of problem-solving situations is the increasing conscious control and regulation of goal-oriented strategies. (Brown & DeLoache, 1977, p. 22)

Brown and colleagues (e.g., Brown, 1974; Brown & Barclay, 1976; Campione & Brown, 1977) emphasize the importance of executive control processes for development of memory skills in retarded children and youth. She was the first to propose that retarded children did poorly on memory and problem-solving tasks because, just as young children, the retarded lacked awareness of their own cognitive abilities and they lacked awareness of the need to be strategic. Brown argued that in order for retarded individuals to produce effective memorizing strategies they would need what Flavell termed *self-awareness* and, additionally, what she referred to as self-regulation and *monitoring processes* or the ability to select, modify, and abandon strategies as needed during ongoing problem solving. Brown supported her speculations by (a) noting that with tasks that did not require strategic behavior their were no developmental trends in the normal population, (b) showing that retarded children performed well on nonstrategic cognitive tasks (Brown, 1972; 1973), and (c) showing that strategy training significantly improved memory performance in retarded subjects (e.g., Brown, Campione, & Murphy, 1974; Brown, Campione, Bray, & Wilcox, 1973).

Before Brown's theory of metacognitive control process deficits in the retarded, the dominating theory of retardation was one proposing structural deficits that were stable and unmodifiable features of intelligence (e.g., Fisher & Zeaman, 1973). The essential difference between the structural and "control" theories of intelligence is susceptibility to training. Brown's "metacognitive control process hypothesis" was instrumental in propelling research efforts in the direction of designing effective training regimens to help disabled learners overcome ineffective performance due to control process deficits.

In the late 1970s, Brown focused her efforts on skill generalization. After considerable work in strategy training with retarded populations, Brown (Campione & Brown, 1977) noted that generalization of training in retarded individuals is extremely difficult if not impossible to achieve if only strategies are trained. She speculated that disabled learners would have to be trained to generalize learned strategies through development of conscious control of their cognitive activity. She also suggested that explicit instructions to generalize are necessary.

Brown (Reeve & Brown, 1985) has recently argued that in order to enhance the problem-solving performance of youth with learning difficulties, more attention needs to be directed toward determining how metacognitive abilities are acquired. In speculating on the acquisition of metacognition, Brown agrees with Luria (1976) and Vygotsky (1978) that development of conscious control of thinking activities occurs in social interaction with others. According to this view, others initially take responsibility for articulating metacognitive processes by scaffolding, prompting, and modeling and, with time, the child gradually learns to take charge and internalize his thought processes and problem-solving behavior. Brown also suggests that children are not likely to develop metacognitive skills at an even level across different problem-solving domains. Last, in agreement with Borkowski, Brown believes that self-concept for learning is another critical factor influencing metacognitive development. Brown (Reeve & Brown, 1985) postulates that a negative self-concept for learning is acquired through repeated academic learning failures. In turn, negative self-concepts hamper students from learning and applying effective and proactive learning strategies.

Instructional Implications

In the early 1980s, in conjunction with Palincsar, Brown began concentrated research on teaching reading comprehension to low-achieving and learning disabled youth. Their approach to overcoming "the generalization and transfer problem" was based on the hypothesis that generalization was impeded by the learner's (a) lack of understanding of the need for and benefits of strategic behavior and lack of self-awareness of cognitive capacities and abilities, (b) passive participation in the learning process, (c) lack of effective strategies for solving the task, and (d) lack of metacognitive control strategies for selecting cognitive strategies and monitoring performance:

We needed, then, a mode of instruction that would ensure that the students would participate at whatever level they were capable, that would enable them to witness the success of such activities, and that would situate the strategies in an actual reading context where the goal of the activities would be transparent. (Palincsar & Brown, 1984, p. 122)

In designing a mode of training, Brown and Palincsar were influenced by the belief that average and above average achieving children, unlike most underachievers, are exposed to better and more cognitive scaffolding and interactive teaching during parent–child storybook experiences and "good" reading group experiences. Consequently, they attempted to:

... mimic, as closely as possible, naturally occurring guided learning interactions in which the teacher could both model appropriate comprehension-fostering activities and at the same time guide the child to participate at an ever-increasing level of competence. (Palincsar & Brown, 1984, p. 124)

Brown and Palincsar term this approach to strategy training *reciprocal teaching*. In piloting their method, poor comprehenders moved from 15% comprehension accuracy to 85% comprehension accuracy of independently read novel passages (Brown & Palincsar, 1982). Subsequent research has demonstrated the efficacy of this approach for improving skills in recognizing main ideas, summarizing, predicting, and detecting incongruities (Palincsar & Brown, 1984). Most importantly, data from these studies show that students' comprehension monitoring skills transferred to texts other than the training materials, generalized to the classroom context, and that effects were durable at least 8 weeks after training was terminated.

As a consequence of her perspectives on how metacognition is acquired, Brown articulates three instructional implications that are applicable for learning disabled and other poor achieving youth: (a) remedial training programs should be interactive and emphasize the social context of learning, (b) the child should be regarded as an active agent in gaining insight into his own metacognitive processes and should, therefore, be kept fully informed of the purposes of the teaching interactions, and (c) metacognitive skills do not necessarily develop evenly within each child and, therefore, metacognitive training cannot necessarily be of a similar level across different academic domains for the same child.

John Borkowski

Background

Borkowski began his programmatic research at a time when cognitive researchers were experiencing disappointing results and expressing grave doubts as to the possibility of training retarded children to generalize cognitive strategies. Borkowski, on the other hand, seems to have had grave doubts about the teaching competence of researchers. Indeed, early on, he challenged the field by contending that "Given optimal training, acquired skills and strategic behaviors of retarded persons are persistent and generalizable" (Borkowski & Cavanaugh, 1979, p. 569).

Although Borkowski has most certainly been interested in cognition as a phenomenon per se, his writings indicate that from the outset he has also been interested in developing methods to enhance achievement in disabled youth. Metacognition seems to have been a means to an end and not the other way around. It is not surprising then that he adopted the instructional approach as his research methodology—a method he felt was most suitable for studying the performance of learning handicapped individuals. Borkowski believed that instructional research using task analysis, well formulated strategy instructions, direct measurement of performance, and high standards for measuring success was most optimal for elevating and remediating the performance of learning handicapped individuals.

Additionally, instead of bemoaning the confounding effects of individual differences, which are part of the special educator's research reality, Borkowski has actively sought to use the individual difference phenomenon to his advantage for constructing theory and designing instructional programs:

Our view is that a detailed understanding of consistencies within and between retarded and nonretarded individuals is a prerequisite for any satisfactory account of how instructions can change cognitions, permanently and with generality. (Borkowski & Cavanaugh, 1979, p. 573)

After his entry into the cognitive arena, Borkowski eventually expanded his focus on exceptional populations to include the learning disabled. As a consequence of his interest in learning disabled youth, Borkowski began to address the problem of training strategies for learning academic content such as reading and writing. After working on this problem for several years, he noted that generalization of strategies and skills is not readily achieved by learning disabled youth (Borkowski, Johnston, & Reid, 1987).

Theoretical Contribution

Over the years Borkowski has contributed an impressive and significant body of knowledge to the field of special education and cognitive psychology. Of the many theoretical and instructional insights Borkowski has contributed to the field of learning disabilities, it is at least arguable that one of his most important contributions is the specification of a meta-cognitive model positing a dynamic, interactional, and bidirectional link between causal attributions, motivation, cognitive performance, and cognitive strategy generalization. We will limit our discussion of his research efforts to describing the metacognitive model he proposes.

Borkowski's metacognitive model (Borkowski et al., 1990; Borkowski et al., 1987; Borkowski, Reid, & Kurtz, 1984; Pressley, Borkowski, & O'Sullivan, 1985) finds roots in his longstanding search for generalization effects and from his interest in explaining individual differences in per-formance. Borkowski conceptualizes metacognition in terms of several interactive components: specific strategy knowledge, general strategy knowledge, relational strategy knowledge, and metamemory acquisition procedures.

Specific strategy knowledge (SSK) is the core of the model. Cognitive strategies are assumed to be implemented when certain conditions are met. One function of SSK is the encoding of strategy use conditions. Borkowski contends that strategies are almost always potentially con-scious and controllable by SSK, although individuals are unlikely to refer consciously to SSK when facing familiar or easy tasks and will, in these cases, apply strategies automatically. Specific strategy knowledge includes the individual's understanding of (a) a strategy's goals and objectives, (b) the tasks for which the strategy is most appropriate, (c) the range of the strategy's applicability, (d) the learning gains expected from implementa-tion of the strategy, (e) amount of effort needed to use the strategy, and (f) how enjoyable or burdensome the strategy is to use. Thus, without SSK an individual could not recognize when to apply a strategy. Not only does SSK direct use of strategies, but use of strategies can result in the growth of SSK. According to Borkowski, individuals learn about specific strategies as they use them; however, some learners do not automatically abstract information about strategies and therefore external agents must provide the specific strategy knowledge. Borkowski (Borkowski & Kurtz, 1984) contends that poor strategic behavior reported in learning disabled populations is due in part to inadequate SSK.

Borkowski delineates three categories of specific strategies: goal-specific strategies, monitoring strategies, and higher order sequencing strategies. According to Borkowski, there are many kinds of goal-specific strategies (GSS) and Borkowski contends that most GSS are domain-specific, such as rehearsal and clustering for memorizing, summarizing and underlining for reading, and brainstorming and reasoning by analogy for solution generation. Monitoring strategies permit on-line decision making in terms of continuing, terminating, or modifying current behavior. Borkowski notes that monitoring strategies also increase specific strategy knowl-edge by providing feedback on how better to use a particular GSS and the benefits gained from doing so. Higher order strategies are planned sequences of goal-specific monitoring strategies. Sequencing of strategies is the most typical application of strategic behavior. Thus, by definition, higher order sequencing strategies integrate lower order specific-goal and monitoring strategies.

General strategy knowledge (GSK) reflects an individual's understanding of the purpose of behaving strategically. General strategy knowledge includes understanding that effort is required to execute strategies, that effort and appropriate strategy use often produce success, that preliminary plans should be made before attempting to solve a problem, and that initial plans and efforts may need to be modified as the problem solving proceeds. Another important GSK is understanding that to behave strategically, actions must be shielded from competing behavior such as inattention, environmental distractions, and negative emotions. A central feature of GSK is its potential motivational character. In 1987, Borkowski (Borkowski et al., 1987) noted the relationship between metacognition and motivation by proposing that GSK has "energizing components" that can motivate the child to confront difficult learning tasks because self-efficacy and expectations can be enhanced by knowing and experiencing the value of behaving strategically. More recently, Borkowski (Borkowski, Carr, Rellinger, & Pressley, 1990), as an extension of his metacognitive model, delineated a more complex relationship between motivation and metacognition.

Borkowski notes that his ideas about the relationship between motivation, attribution, and cognitive performance are based on the earlier work of researchers and theorists such as Sears (1940), who was able to demonstrate the link between a child's self-judgment about his competence and that child's actual performance on school-related tasks; Weiner (1972, 1979), who theorized that causal attributions are critical determinants of a child's future expectancies, task persistence, and affective responses; Dweck (Dweck & Goetz, 1978; Dweck & Licht, 1980), who examined the relationship between learned helplessness and efforts at problem-solving behavior; Licht (1983), who suggested that learning disabled students be taught that failure is in part due to ineffective task strategies as well as lack of effort; and others who demonstrated the positive effects of "attribution retraining" (e.g., Andrews & Debus, 1978; Dweck, 1975; Fowler & Peterson, 1981).

The self-system includes a variety of psychological phenomena such as a child's self-esteem, self-confidence, feelings of self-determination, attributional beliefs, and affective responses that interact dynamically with metacognitive development. Borkowski argues that attributional beliefs are the most powerful component of the self-system in terms of impacting self-esteem, learning, and performance. In his most recent research (Borkowski et al., 1990), Borkowski uses a path analysis approach and concludes that attribution beliefs are the most significant factor distinguishing underachieving students from average-achieving peers. According to Borkowski, an individual's self-system underlies the development of metacognition and helps to determine how a child will respond to academic experiences. In Borkowski's view, children develop self-systems from their family and early school experiences and, because learning disabled children are not diagnosed until after a period of school failure, learning disabled children often develop a negative self-system. This in turn impedes development of metacognition, leading to increased probability of school failure; unless interrupted, the cycle continues.

Relational strategy knowledge provides the individual with a system for comparing strategies. Relational strategy knowledge is useful for strategy selection and for strategy revision. Borkowski does not elaborate this construct further.

Metacognitive acquisition procedures (MAP) allow an individual to learn more information about new or underdeveloped strategies. Metacognitive acquisition procedures are a higher order metacognitive component and a central factor in producing self-controlled behavior in young and developmentally delayed children. Borkowski postulates that MAP's are the "hallmarks of human intelligence" (Borkowski et al., 1987, p. 153). Because monitoring strategies can increase understanding of how to use a strategy, they are also, in this sense, metacognitive acquisition procedures. According to Borkowski, SSK develops spontaneously in most individuals as a function of metacognitive acquisition procedures. Metacognitive acquisition procedures are critical for school success because they help the learner fill in the gaps of instruction when teachers are not explicit or detailed in providing strategy instructions. One implication of this model is that if a child has poor metacognitive acquisition skills, he will not increase SSK without external and explicit instruction.

Borkowski's model predicts that generalization failures in learning disabled individuals are due to deficits in one or more of these metacognitive components. Additionally, in Borkowski's view, individual differences in learning disabled children's generalization performances are best understood as a function of the dynamic interplay between metacognitive components, cognitive strategies, automatic processes, and self-systems. That is, some learning disabled youth may know less than other learning disabled children about the to-be-learned strategy before its instruction. Hence, they may fail to transfer the strategy even though they can produce it in a rote fashion because they lack sufficient SSK. Some learning disabled youth may not understand the value of a planful and strategic approach to tasks and may ascribe success to external factors. Hence, these children will be less motivated to learn and apply strategic behavior. Other learning disabled youth may not know how to select, monitor, and modify strategies. Hence, they may fail to complete novel tasks successfully. And finally, some learning disabled youth may perform poorly and fail to generalize because they lack metacognitive acquisition procedures. These youth are not likely to increase their strategic development if left to their own resources.

Instructional Implications

One of Borkowski's great strengths and significant contributions to special education is his consistent ability to infer and specify concrete instructional methods from abstract theoretical concepts. Indeed, the major portion of his research has been devoted to systematically testing various cognitive instructional methods.

Borkowski's most recent instructional suggestion (Borkowski et al., 1990) is to provide *attribution retraining* in conjunction with highly explicit, direct instruction of strategies and strategy use. The method of strategy teaching he recommends can be described as making the implicit explicit. For example, students should be informed about the existence and effectiveness of metacognitive knowledge in the subject area under consideration. Students then observe the teacher model the strategy while verbalizing the strategy steps explicitly. The teacher should tell and show how the steps should and should not be applied. Students should then be allowed guided practice by going through each step of the strategy verbally and then gradually shifting to covert processing. Students must be required to master each step before advancing to the next stage of training. Underachieving and learning disabled students should also be provided with attribution retraining. This is accomplished in part by having the teacher inform students about the relationship of effort, appropriate strategy use, and successful performance. Students should be taught to verbalize self-statements such as "try harder," "you'll enjoy this story," and "you'll feel good if you do well." Additionally, when the child or teacher makes a mistake during practice or instruction, the teacher should use this occasion for stressing the importance of internal controllable factors. Borkowski also recommends that teachers provide the student with an opportunity to complete successfully a previously failed task and then engage the student to reflect on his beliefs about the causes of success and failure.

Borkowski reports empirical support for this method of cognitive training (Borkowski et al., 1990; Reid & Borkowski, 1984; Short & Ryan, 1984). In these studies, learning disabled students significantly enhanced their performance and, most importantly, the students both maintained and generalized trained skills.

Michael Pressley

Background

Michael Pressley and his colleagues are perhaps best known for their long and highly influential series of studies on the development and effectiveness of mnemonic strategies in children and adolescents. Pressley and his colleagues have tirelessly pursued fuller understanding of how children develop and use specific mnemonic strategies, such as imagery (e.g., the keyword method) and elaboration. Pressley's body of work illustrates how strategy research by psychologists has moved gradually from narrow, laboratory-based questions about mnemonic strategy deficit (Pressley, Levin, & Delaney, 1982) to more applied questions that concern complex interactions among domain knowledge, strategy knowledge, and processes for dynamic and flexible selection, use, and monitoring of appropriate strategies in natural learning situations (Pressley, Goodchild, Fleet, Zajchowski, & Evans, 1989; Pressley, Symons, Snyder, & Cariglia-Bull, 1989).

The systematic nature of the better exemplars of this type of research inevitably leads to questions about maintenance, transfer, generalization, and utility of laboratory-researched strategies for applied learning tasks and contexts. That is, once reliable experimental effects are established, it is logical to question the range or limits of such effects. Thus, for example, once Pressley et al. carefully documented utility of the keyword method for recalling paired information with an "associative component," they addressed questions concerning most effective components of training, developmental differences in acquisition and use, aptitude–treatment interaction, range of applicable tasks, and maintenance over time (Pressley et al., 1982, p. 61).

Theoretical Contribution

From this prodigious body of experimental work has come a model that Pressley calls "the good strategy user" (Pressley et al., 1985; Pressley, Goodchild, et al., 1989; Pressley, Symons, et al., 1989). The good strategy user (GSU) is an abstracted learner and problem solver with an idealized level of learning competence. In many ways, Pressley's GSU is an "expert" learner in the same cognitive psychology tradition that differentiates experts from novices in specific domains of skilled performance.

According to Pressley, Goodchild, et al. (1989), the GSU possesses substantial factual knowledge in a number of academic domains, equally substantial knowledge about specific strategies, and, most importantly, a powerful array of metacognitive abilities, including ability to select and schedule appropriate strategies, smoothly monitor unfolding task performance, recognize need for changing or shifting cognitive effort, and activate such changes when necessary. Moreover, these metacognitive abilities are founded on a base of specialized knowledge concerning when, why, and how strategies can or should be used.

In short, Pressley, whose views on metamemory specifically, and metacognition in general, are compatible with Borkowski's, sees metacognition acting as both executive monitor and agent responsible for arranging the most task-appropriate and efficient transactions between two types of knowledge—what fact knowledge students possess and what they know about behaving strategically—when they are required to engage in different types of learning tasks. Such a system is componential, much like Sternberg's (see next section), because identifiably different functions (i.e., component processes) must operate (i.e., interact) in concert or else "poor" strategy use can occur (Pressley, Goodchild, et al., 1989, p. 302).

Instructional Implications

Pressley et al. believe that there are short-term and long-term goals that should be pursued in reaching the instructional potential of the GSU model. In the short term, teachers should teach a few, facilitating strategies. Pressley et al. urge that, at least initially, teachers should select "across-domain, goal-limited" strategies, by which he means techniques or tactics that have applicability in more than one content domain, but that function in a limited way within a particular task (e.g., remembering strategies, comprehending strategies, problem-solving strategies, etc.).

In the long term, teachers should aim to teach not only a very large set of strategies applicable specifically and generally to different areas of the curriculum, but also to facilitate automaticity of strategy selection, monitoring, and use. Pressley and his colleagues recognize that achieving this goal will require considerable effort, new knowledge, improved research, sizable investment of resources (e.g., teaching time), and probably occupy years within the curriculum. They have discussed specific obstacles to instruction of "good strategy use."

First, according to Pressley, teacher training programs are said not to provide much exposure to methods or rationales for teaching strategies. This problem results from more than lack of coursework, according to Pressley, Goodchild, et al. (1989a). Current work aimed at translating strategy research into classroom practice is based on information-processing models of cognitive development and functioning. This approach is but one of many orientations to students' learning and educationally relevant behavior. Moreover, as Pressley et al. note, many strategy-instruction packages are quite complex, even for those familiar with information processing models and strategy research. Pressley et al. are cautiously confident that reforms in teacher training and improvements in instructional guides accompanying curriculum materials will remove these obstacles.

One obstacle identified by Pressley et al. that is perhaps less tractable concerns the greater responsibility and effort strategy-instruction requires from classroom teachers. It is not merely the case that effective strategy instruction must be predicated on the belief that much student failure is *teaching*, rather than *learner*, failure. In the words of Pressley et al.:

Even if the teacher succeeds in figuring out where the students are and manages to organize that information, there is the additional challenge of providing instruction that is adjusted to each child's level and particular problems. (Pressley, Goodchild, et al., 1989, p. 313)

What is more, according to Pressley, teachers need to be able to do this more or less automatically. Other potential obstacles identified by Pressley and his colleagues include the fact that the relatively large number of strategies that have been studied thus far would require "considerable" instructional time to teach. Also, Pressley et al. recognize that individual strategies are likely to achieve only limited learning goals. Moreover, durable strategy use often does not follow automatically from instruction in strategy use.

Other implications for instruction emerge from Pressley's work. Acquisition of parallel, metacognitive knowledge is deemed critical to the success of strategy instruction. Pressley contends that maintenance and transfer of learned strategies are obtained only if there is accompanying instruction in metacognitive knowledge about how the strategy should be used. This allows the GSU to guide overall strategic behavior during learning.

In support of this latter point, Pressley and his colleagues, specifically Elizabeth Ghatala, have conducted some of the only systematic research to examine the separability of strategy and metacognitive learning effects (Ghatala, Levin, Pressley, & Goodwin, 1986; Ghatala, Levin, Pressley, & Lodico, 1985; Lodico, Ghatala, Levin, Pressley, & Bell, 1983; Pressley, Ross, Levin, & Ghatala, 1984). In a series of careful studies, Ghatala and her colleagues were able to demonstrate that as a consequence of being specifically taught about strategy utility and how and when to monitor strategy effectiveness, even very young children could be taught to discriminate the differential efficacy (i.e., metacognitive knowing) of mnemonic strategies in relationship to task demands and shift strategies (i.e., metacognitive control) when necessary, and maintain learned strategies longer. Ghatala et al. (1986) found that more effective metacognitive training required that students not only learn about assessing strategy utility but also that they receive

... practice in attributing changes in performance to strategies *in order to select the more effective strategy* .... (p. 90, emphasis in original)

Nevertheless, the generality of Pressley, Ghatala, and colleagues' finding for learning disabled students remains unclear. Do learning disabled students acquire metacognitive awareness and self-regulation as a function of strategy training and experience in strategy use, or do learning disabled students require separate, specific metacognitive training? A further issue is whether metacognitive training is needed to enhance the likelihood of specific strategy learning. A similar issue was raised by Brown, Campione, and Day (1981) when they argued for "informed" strategy training, or by Borkowski and Cavanaugh (1979) when they argued for more complex, multifaceted strategy training that included explicit training in metacognitive, or executive, processes.

In light of the complexity of strategy acquisition and maintenance under experimentally controlled situations, Pressley, Goodchild, et al. (1989) recommend that teachers be selective, choosing well researched strategies that "confer large gains in achievement arenas important to students (p. 314)." However, they concede that following this recommendation may not be easy. One important reason is that adequate evaluation of strategy instruction packages and materials is often not available. Even when evaluation is adequate, it may be the case that teachers have only limited access to pertinent sources of information. Pressley, Goodchild, et al. (1989) recommend that validity of strategy instruction procedures be fully documented in nontechnical terminology, periodically updated, and then disseminated in catalogue form to educators.

Robert Sternberg

Background

Unlike other researchers reviewed in this chapter who have pursued metacognition in terms of memory development or strategic functioning in retarded and learning disabled children, Robert J. Sternberg's focus has been on the nature of human intelligence. Sternberg argues that his is a "subtheory," in part because he does not attempt to incorporate explicitly issues of motivation, initiative, social competence, or creativity. Intelligence, in Sternberg's subtheory, pertains to acquisition and application of reasoning and problem-solving abilities. In particular, it refers to display of intelligent behavior in problem situations.

Theoretical Contribution

In 1980, Sternberg presented a "subtheory" of intelligence (Sternberg, 1980) that described a "component" as an *"elementary information process that operates upon internal representations of objects or symbols"* (p. 574). Components vary in terms of duration, difficulty, and probability of execution. According to Sternberg's formulation, components also perform five kinds of functions, four of which are described as related to performance, acquisition, retention, and transfer. Sternberg calls the components that perform the fifth function *metacomponents*. Metacomponents are "higher order" control processes *"used for executive planning and decision-making in problem solving"* (p. 575).

Sternberg believes that there are six metacomponents that commonly emerge as part of intellectual functioning. Two of these metacomponents involve some level of "decision," three metacomponents involve "selection" processes, and one is devoted to "monitoring" functions. For purposes of discussion, we will simplify the description of how these various metacomponents operate in Sternberg's subtheory by thinking of them as questions, posed and answered by the problem solver, about the particular problem-solving situation.

The specific metacomponents proposed by Sternberg are as follows.

Decision:

1. What problem needs to be solved?
2. What (tradeoff) is needed, speed or accuracy?

Selection:

1. What lower order components (performance, acquisition, retention, transfer) should be used?
2. What representation or organization of information is needed?
3. What strategy is needed to combine lower order components?

Monitoring:

1. What has been done, what is being done currently, and what needs to be done to solve the problem?

For example, the first decision metacomponent asks and answers the question, "What is the problem?" Clearly, one of the most obvious hallmarks of intelligent behavior is the ability not only to recognize that a problem exists, but also to depict mentally or represent the problem in a way that promotes and facilitates problem solving. Most research on problem solving has been concerned with older, competent individuals attempting to solve problems in complex knowledge domains. Gerber and Hall (1987), however, have proposed that basic academic skills (e.g., word reading, letter writing, simple arithmetic, spelling) constitute a more relevant class of "problems" for young or less competent learners, and acquisition of these skills can be usefully construed as specific cases of general problem solving. For example, research on early acquisition of spelling has been interpreted to show that learning handicapped students, similar to younger, normally achieving students, attempt to apply their limited orthographic knowledge to produce spellings in response to demand situations, like list dictation or story writing. This situation is problematic in a general sense and not merely a problem of memory since the correct spelling is not yet known. Although recall of relevant information is critical, it is *how* adequately children access and orchestrate available information that determines the quality of their ultimate spelling attempt. In Sternberg's terms, students will progress satisfactorily toward correct (i.e., conventional) orthography and generalized spelling ability if they can recognize when spelling will be uncertain, and therefore, difficult; that is, that a problem exists.

In 1984, Sternberg revised and expanded his basic model (Sternberg, 1984) as part of a *triarchic theory of intelligence*. In this revision, Sternberg redefined the decision metacomponent concerned with speed–accuracy tradeoff. The new version of this metacomponent incorporated the need to decide between speed and accuracy by emphasizing attention alloca-tion decisions. In this formulation, each component requires an allocation of limited attentional resources. Allocational decisions, therefore, impact directly on the speed and ultimate accuracy of problem solution.

Sternberg also added a seventh metacomponent that might be con-sidered in the category of monitoring. Sternberg describes this mcta-component as *sensitivity to external feedback*, or the self-selected degree to which an individual is prepared to modify problem solving to conform with changes in the environment resulting from problem-solving behavior.

In both versions, metacomponents are critical in Sternberg's under-standing of individual differences in "general intelligence," or Spearman's elusive "g." In Sternberg's words,

In componential analysis, individual differences in general intelligence are attri-buted to individual differences in the effectiveness with which general components are used. (Sternberg, 1980, pp. 580–581)

That is, the common component of intelligent behavior across a range of tasks, problems, and contexts is the ability to manage one's own cognition effectively. Therefore, Sternberg argued, it is how individuals differ in metacomponential functioning that mostly accounts for the "persistent appearance of a general factor" (p. 581). However, Sternberg acknowl-edges that "g" results in part from learning, which, in turn, implicates an important role for other components, especially the *acquisition* com-ponent, in behaviors exhibited on intelligence tests. But, since in his theoretical view use of all of these components is controlled and con-strained by ability to use metacomponents, metacomponent functioning is still critical for explaining individual differences in intelligent behavior.

Instructional Implications

Sternberg's theoretical work was not intended to address developmental or educational questions. Rather, his model alludes to a "normal," mature, and somewhat idealized person. Its instructional implications for teaching children, particularly learning handicapped children, must be inferred.

Sternberg's depiction of metacomponents (i.e., elemental meta-cognitive processes) in terms related to problem-solving functions such as decision, selection, and monitoring may be particularly useful for design-ing instructional interventions. As we suggested earlier, the function of each component can be accessed as part of a series of self-questions that, when answered, link and function together as a generic, strategic, and self-regulated routine for solving problems. For example, if simple academic skill acquisition can be construed as a form of problem solving, its cognitive self-regulation schema might also constitute an instructional goal worthy of elaboration and empirical experiment.

Although Sternberg's notion of metacomponents does not suggest any particular technique for teaching such a problem-solving routine, it does provide an explicit set of general targets. If we set out to teach children to recognize when something is a "problem" (one of Sternberg's "decision" metacomponents), we are led to pose a host of necessarily related instructional objectives. For example, how shall we define the problem domain? What are its contents? How shall they be articulated and their presentation instructionally sequenced? Each of these questions, in turn, implies a series of related operational questions regarding time allocation, materials, evaluative criteria, and so on. Or, consider how self-questions relevant to metacomponents related to "selection" might be posed in relationship to the instructional goals, sequences, and techniques resulting from analysis of problem domain? Specifically, how shall we operationalize and materially represent for students the selection of lower order components, representation or organization of information, coordinative or combinatory strategies? Pursued in this manner, Sternberg's metacomponents constitute a potentially valuable *metainstructional* schema for educators to ponder.

Bernice Wong

Background

Bernice Wong, more than most investigators interested in learning disabilities, has persistently modeled the importance of theoretical analysis and theoretically guided research. Not only has her own empirical work on the use of self-questioning pursued an important line of investigation on a potentially critical aspect of metacognitive self-regulation, but she has also acted in the role of theoretical critic and commentator for the field at large.

In particular, she suggests that there are three areas of research on metacognition and learning disabilities that have been fruitful. The first of these is represented by a body of research concerned with the role of "phonemic awareness" in acquisition of reading and reading-related skills. The second area focuses on the role of metacognition in fostering acquisition and use of higher level reading comprehension skills, including skills needed for studying content material for later recall or testing. The third area that Wong feels shows evidence of useful application involves maintenance and generalization of skills and strategies once they are learned. However, she also cautions against wholesale adoption of metacognitive constructs to explain all problems associated with learning disabilities. For example, she argues that metacognition cannot explain certain learning difficulties, such as slow or inaccurate decoding, frequently associated with learning disabilities. Also, Wong indicates that exclusive focus on metacognitive mechanisms distracts from the equally important role played by a child's accumulating knowledge base and the necessary interdependence of the two. Finally, and somewhat in contrast to Borkowski's view, Wong insists that metacognition may not contribute to understanding of the role of noncognitive variables, such as motivation, attribution, and self-esteem, variables frequently associated with learning difficulties of learning disabled students.

Theoretical Contribution

Wong's major empirical contribution to theories of metacognition has come from her analysis of the effects of self-questioning routines taught to learning disabled students to prepare them for later recall or testing of reading comprehension (Wong, 1979; Wong & Jones, 1982; Wong & Wong, 1986). The general thrust of this work has been to examine the way in which task-relevant questions, once taught to learning disabled students, are applied so that they appropriately activate and regulate reading comprehension performance. In a narrow sense, Wong's interest in the relationship between self-questioning as a learned strategy and self-questioning as a form of metacognitive self-regulation relates to the instructional implications of Sternberg's theory of metacognitive components discussed above.

In her review of self-questioning experiments on prose learning, Wong (1985) hunted beyond learning disabilities and metacognition literature to map elegantly three possible theoretical positions that might account for positive effects on reading comprehension performance indicators. The majority of studies she reviewed emanated from what she termed an *active processing* perspective. That is, self-questioning can be viewed as a natural and necessary part of the reading comprehension process for successful readers. In this view, the nature of thinking about what has been read is shaped, focused, and guided by self-generated, "higher order" questions (i.e., evaluative, comparative, problem-solving oriented, cause–effect relating).

However, Wong criticized the general notion of activation or active processing around which this literature is organized, saying that it lacked conceptual clarity about which of a number of potential processing mechanisms are activated by self-generated questions at different points in prose processing. In other words, how self-questioning worked to select, sequence, and organize appropriate information processing components needed theoretical clarification. She also noted that there is lack of consistent evidence about whether it is the "quality" of higher order question or the quantity of questions self-generated that most accounts for observed comprehension effects.

A second theoretical position she gleaned from self-questioning literature, Wong calls *schema theory*. Schema theory is a more focal approach to active processing of prior knowledge. Whereas active processing theories treat self-questioning broadly, superficially, and quite generally, schema theories propose a specific knowledge-retrieving, knowledge-organizing function to self-questioning. In other words, reading comprehension involves some degree of spontaneous association between what is read and prior knowledge that is, or could be, related. The logical and narrative structure of the text constrains and shapes which associations are selected and used to construct meaning. Although Wong is vague about how self-questioning functions in this theoretical framework, we infer that there may be at least two functions, both serving to regulate cognitive processing of prose in a manner consistent with students' understanding of the task or problem set before them.

The first function might be called an associative search/retrieval function. That is, students, realizing that associating text with prior knowledge is desirable and facilitating, might be taught to prompt themselves to conduct such a search with questions like: "What is a hurricane? What do I know about hurricanes? What do I think about when I think about hurricanes?"

The second function could be considered as being a monitoring/managerial function. To manage prose processing, students may need to learn that their associated memories are two-edged. They certainly can assist comprehension, but they also can distract, diffuse, and distort unless those associations relevant to reading a particular text are selected for attention as others are discarded. Thus, in monitoring, students are being called on to make a judgment of relevance with recall of each potentially relevant association. Self-questions might be posed in the form: "Is remembering (that I was in a storm with my father last summer) going to help me (understand, answer questions about, finish on time) this (story, chapter, article, passage)?"

Additionally, students must be taught that certain kinds of text features (e.g., main characters, main ideas, plot, problem-resolution, agent-action, story grammar) can serve as prompts or guidelines for editing and organizing associations. Self-questions can be posed first to guide identification of these comprehension signposts (e.g., "Where does it tell who this is about? Which sentence is the topic sentence?"), whereupon location of the desired information can prompt additional questions helpful for sorting through or generating associations (e.g., "Does the main character do what I did or would do in the same situation? Is there anything in the text that talks about things I know about this topic?").

The third theoretical position discussed by Wong is oriented around metacognitive theory. Wong attributed the elaboration of this position mostly to Flavell and Brown. Metacognition, in this context, is a broad set of adaptive capabilities, including self-questioning, that permit individuals to organize and allocate cognitive resources most effectively to reading or studying tasks. In Wong's estimation, the notions of informed and self-controlled strategy training introduced by Brown and Palincsar (1982) are among the most important products of metacognition theory. Informing students about how strategies can and should work for them will enhance maintenance and generalization. However, Wong agrees that it is important to craft strategy training so that strategy selection and use become self-controlled.

She therefore views self-questioning as performing two different functions. The first relates to activating and structuring manipulation of content-relevant information. The second metacognitive function of self-questions creates and maintains a kind of executive oversight of progress in solving problems or completing tasks. Specifically, Wong argues that such self-induced monitoring of comprehension during reading, for example, can alert learning disabled students to erroneous or inadequate understanding of text and thereby trigger selection of appropriate and corrective strategies.

Instructional Implications

Wong feels, and her own research demonstrates, that there is adequate evidence that teaching students to question themselves during reading can enhance or improve performance. However, she also indicates that there are serious constraints on applying this conclusion indiscriminately. First, she argues persuasively that, regardless of theoretical orientation, knowledge possessed by students seriously constrains the degree to which self-questioning can activate facilitating prose comprehension processes. In other words, there is a reciprocity between knowledge and its use during prose processing that is a bit like a chicken–egg problem for teachers. Students must possess relevant background and foundation knowledge at each stage of acquisition of new knowledge. Regardless how generally effective a particular search/retrieval strategy might be, its utility will be diminished for a particular learning disabled student who lacks prerequisite knowledge. On the other hand, teaching such prerequisite knowledge necessarily entails teaching learning disabled students to be strategic in using whatever knowledge they already possess. The point of entry into this cyclical process of acquisition is unclear. Wong both acknowledges and expands on this problem in discussing the apparent constraints on use of self-questions by metacognitively deficient students. Usefulness of self-questions, she concludes, can be thwarted by lack of general awareness about how such questions can or should function or about why one is reading a specific text in the first place. Thus, although we may now have insight that strategies employing self-questioning can facilitate performance on learning tasks, and we have some idea how to teach those strategies, it is still unclear how to build in learning disabled students, at least by means of a short-term instructional intervention, those metacognitive abilities that seem absolutely critical in more success-ful learners.

Summary

There are important similarities between Sternberg's *metacomponents* and related constructs used by others we have discussed, such as *meta-cognitive knowledge* (Flavell & Wellman, 1977; Flavell, 1979) and *execu-tive functioning* (Brown, 1975; Butterfield & Belmont, 1977). All are con-cerned with mechanisms permitting individuals to coordinate, orchestrate, and press for efficient operation of different mental functions. All of the metacognition constructs proposed thus far try, unsuccessfully we think, to depict how *knowledge*, in some complex, self-referenced way, impacts not only the efficiency of mental processes, but also the elaboration of older and the acquisition of new processes. Simply stated, all meta-mental constructs attempt to describe awareness of one's own cognition as this awareness interacts with or otherwise affects processes of cognitive change over time and experience. Although these theoretical formulations are not, strictly speaking, individual difference learning models, their emerg-ence has altered how we view learning phenomena regarding learning disabled students. More to the point, they have strongly influenced how we interpret learning failure—more in terms of developing or modifiable competencies and less in terms of permanent, structural defects.

It is not surprising, therefore, that all the researchers we have discussed remain optimistic about designing instructional interventions to teach or promote metacognitive knowledge about and control of strategies. But, they are individually and collectively unable to propose a comprehensive intervention designed explicitly for learning disabled students. In par-ticular, the precise specification and sequencing of instructional elements, whether to teach task-specific cognitive strategies or global metacognitive (self-regulating) abilities, remains an empirical question at best if not a profound theoretical problem (e.g., see Meichenbaum, 1985)

As we assess the empirical literature, there are three serious obstacles facing further development of metacognition theory. First, the phenom-ena of acquiring metacognitive abilities, as understood in the extant body of research, is developmentally complex. It is clear to us that develop-ment of cognitive strategies and development of metacognitive knowledge about and control over these strategies must occur in parallel or in some irreducibly reciprocal manner. One implication is that instructional elements that relate to circumscribed, highly task-specific cognitive tactics (we prefer the limits connoted by this term to the more encompassing connotation of *strategy*) must be related differently at different phases of skill/knowledge acquisition to accommodate differences in knowledge previously acquired, differences in communicative ability (i.e., *teach-*

ability, broadly speaking), and differences in global (including meta-cognitive) self-awareness (including self-esteem, attributions for learning success and failure, natural or intrinsic motivation). Further, the issue of when and how to focus and sequence teaching on metacognitive, rather than tactical responses to tasks and problems, pivots on the troubling duality of the construct of metacognition itself; at once a component cognitive process and also an executive manager of component cognitive processes.

Second, we discern a complex and often invisible, but always present, transpersonal character in metacognition research. That is, the teacher, trainer, or research investigator is neither a disinterested neutral party nor an automatic program that mechanically and uniformly guides learner behavior. Rather, even under nominally standardized training conditions, it would be an unusual researcher indeed who did not make some attempt to accommodate individual differences by contingently modifying or supplementing explanatory or other instructional communications (e.g., see Shepherd & Gelzheiser, 1987; Turnure, 1987). Simply stated, "what we see" in metacognitive training research is probably not "what we get."

Third, there is an obvious and troubling problem surrounding the questionable ecological validity of metacognition research to date. More-over, the problem is deeper than the general failure to define and dif-ferentiate clearly learning disabled students in their natural classroom environments. Whatever strategy or metacognitive strategy instruction is employed, necessarily must be related consistently to a larger array of considerations that occupy the thinking of real people, teachers as well as children, performing in natural circumstances. These considerations include, but are not limited to, the meaning(s) of the social setting in which activity occurs; the stated or inferred purpose(s) for activity, per-sonal, collaborative, or others' intention(s), motivation(s) for participat-ing, performing, and excelling; and presence of distracting or competing demands for time and energy.

Thus, in the most general terms, obstacles to development of meta-cognitive theory may be capsulated as follows. Picking apart the teach-able cognitive components that contribute to successful learning, difficult as that may be, is only the first half of the problem. The second half involves fitting the various instructional elements related to each of these components into a logically integrated, developmentally appropriate, practical instructional plan. We feel strongly that this is primarily a theoretical, not an engineering, problem that must be addressed in a new generation of theoretically elaborated metacognition research.

These considerations of obstacles sketch a much more complex and transactional reality to cognitive and metacognitive functioning than has been acknowledged by these six researchers. We now address this more complex conceptualization and offer some tentative recommendations.

Limitations of Metacognitive Theory to Date

In the history of research on learning disabilities there have been few concepts that have captured the attention and gripped the theoretical imagination of researchers quite so powerfully and pervasively as the related concepts of production, strategy, or metacognitive deficiency. Only the rival conceptualization that learning disabilities are a collection of specific, innate, neurogenic disorders has a longer and equally prominent history.

However, despite fine scholarship by the investigators discussed in this chapter, and many others, a fair analysis of the net impact of this vast body of work on practice would conclude that it has been miniscule. In their analysis of difficulties faced in applying strategy instruction in real classrooms, and despite their more sanguine conclusions, Pressley and his colleagues (Goodchild, et al., 1989 and Symons, et al., 1989) presented strong arguments that essentially support this view.

In our view, one of the chief reasons for this unhappy circumstance is research tradition in learning disabilities that freely borrows, but fails to adapt to *school circumstances*, theoretical positions from psychology (e.g., neuropsychology, developmental psychology, cognitive psychology). Education tends to be a field of scholarship that imports more than it exports, that receives ideas more than it conceives its own. Although some might disagree, we believe this view even more persuasively characterizes special education. Simply stated, mental and behavioral handicaps historically have been seen as manifestations of innate pathologies, defects, and abnormalities. Under this key assumption, medically oriented researchers hunt for causes in the neuroanatomy or neurochemistry of individual children. Similarly, psychologists search for differences in cognition, temperament, or personality—always presuming that etiology is within children or, if it is not, that "environment" simply provokes expression of individual mental or emotional differences. Thus, metacognition is primarily conceived as something that exists as part of "mind." Moreover, because it is perceived as executive manager of all cognitive and behavioral functioning, it naturally has become the prime suspect for the failure by some children who otherwise are thought to be intelligent, to learn academic skills "normally."

It is not surprising that so little research on metacognition has been situated in *naturally constituted*, ongoing school classrooms during learning of real academic content. Psychologists typically avoid the research "noise" attendant to natural environments. In any case, application of their research is regarded by some psychologists as mere engineering. That is, describe what needs to be done in sufficient detail and "train" teachers to do it. This is not to suggest that research grounded in psychology is not valuable. Quite the contrary. Psychological constructs and theories have always been a rich source of testable hypotheses about the nature of learning disabilities. However, classroom environments, multiple and diverse individuals involved in complex cognitive and social transactions, make them qualitatively, not just quantitatively, distinct from psychological laboratories.

Unfortunately, this psychologically based approach has not resulted in much measurable benefit to educational practice and specifically to education of learning disabled students. The problem is not only that teachers are not programmable like so many computers, nor that their information processing capabilities and productivity during teaching is infinitely more complex than our best computer models; rather, the problem is that psychology provides no theory of teaching, no theory of the school context of teaching and learning, and no theory of dynamic development and change in teaching and learning as a response to changing student-generated or institution-generated demands. Despite some noteworthy attempts (e.g., Corno, 1986; Corno & Mandinach, 1983), integrating theories of personal cognition and metacognition with theories of transpersonal instructional interaction is simply beyond the reach, if not beyond the grasp, of most extant psychological paradigms.

This analysis of the current status of metacognition theories and research with respect to learning disabilities is not meant as a criticism of psychologists who, after all, are limited by professional design to address some and not other issues. Nor is it a lamentation of despair that the problems faced are too complex and therefore insoluble. Rather, it is intended as a caution and reminder that *laboratory-based* theory generation research on metacognition (i.e., comtemporary theory), however elegant, has produced qualitatively different theory than would have *classroom-based* theory generation research. It is our contention that metacognitive theory and instructional research created in natural contexts will result in more meaningful changes in the teachability of learning disabled students than have been realized to date. It is encouraging to note that the most recent metacognitive research appears to be shifting in this direction. Our own research (Larson, 1985, 1989a, 1989b; Larson & Gerber, 1987) supports the power and efficacy of a natural, context-based metacognitive training curriculum for learning disabled students. Moreover, before major changes in teacher preparation, curriculum, materials, and school structure are contemplated, it is obvious that all instructional approaches must be validated in natural school contexts (Pressley, Goodchild, et al., 1989).

As the concept has been employed, metacognition refers to both knowledge and awareness, and simultaneously to some mechanism of self-control and self-regulation. Metacognitive awareness as a conscious experience of our own cognition is intuitively understandable. We have feelings and sensations that we recognize, for example, that we understand, that we know, that we are trying to remember, that we are paying attention, and so on. We can see, after some reflection (as in this para-

graph), what we think and how we believe we think in different circumstances. Metacognitive knowledge of person, task, and strategy variables,
also conceptually tractable, is best understood as the cumulative result of
experiences that yield such awareness. Despite more than 10 years of
research, though, it remains obscure how development of metacognitive
knowledge and awareness relate to development of self-regulation.

Understanding this relationship is absolutely critical for designing
appropriate instructional interventions for learning disabled students. In
fact, the excellent programs of research conducted by investigators we
have discussed in this chapter tend to converge on the same issue: What
strategy instruction model holds the best promise for inducing generalized
improvement in strategic, self-regulated behavior for children perceived
as learning handicapped?

Although the authors we reviewed in this chapter and many others
have published literally hundreds of studies on cognitive or metacognitive
training, it is surprising how few have been conducted with a carefully
described population of handicapped students. Fewer still have been
conducted in natural classroom environments using academic learning
tasks typical of such environments (Gerber, 1988). Therefore, our fund
of knowledge about how to improve long-term learning outcomes for
handicapped students is much more impoverished than might be expected
(see Pressley, Goodchild, et al., 1989; Pressley, Symons, et al., 1989, for
a more optimistic view). In general, research concerned with metacognition, in the abstract, has been tested for "fit" by using it etiologically to
explain observed characteristics of learning disabled individuals.

Part of the difficulty with this approach, we believe, stems from conceptual and theoretical rigidity and unquestioned assumptions about the
underlying constructs of strategy and production deficiency (Shepherd &
Gelzheiser, 1987; Shepherd, Gelzheiser, & Solar, 1985) as the valid
bedrock for conceptualizing metacognition and strategy instruction
(Gerber, 1983; Gerber & Hall, 1989; Hall, Gerber, & Stricker, 1989).
Production or *strategy deficiency* are psychological constructs that were
developed to describe *within-individual* phenomena thought to account
for successful performance on memory or problem-solving tasks. The
difficulty obtaining generalized transfer or maintenance or flexible control
of strategies led to the realization that some mechanism (i.e., metacognition), again presumably psychological, directed and orchestrated
strategy use.

Need for an Elaborated Model of Metacognition

We believe that all strategy training employs a trainer whose own understanding, knowledge, and communicative competence is as much at issue
as these same characteristics in the trainee. The "meta" aspects of resulting cognitive activity by learners stands in nontrivial relationship to

the cognitive activity of trainers/teachers and the social context that binds them to one another.

The traditional psychological approach searching for a within-person mechanism is inherently blind to the possibility that "meta" cognition is really a form or trace of a *social co-cognition*. This is the socially mediated psychological interface between teacher and student, and it is unique to all human, teacher–learner relationships (including parent–child and expert tutor–novice adult relationships). We suggest that it is a *transpersonal* and not an intrapersonal phenomenon. In this view, the indicators of self awareness, knowledge, and control during relevant tasks are psychological residua of co-cognitive episodes in an ongoing social relationship. An elaborated model of metacognition as a social exchange phenomenon is needed that accounts explicitly for the influence of teacher, classroom, and school variables on learning processes of students perceived as learning disabled. Such a model is especially critical for explaining teaching–learning in learning disabled students in light of the increasing recognition that learning disability is an interaction, as opposed to a within-child, phenomenon between student, teacher, and classroom context.

Indeed, historical and persistent problems with achieving transfer and generalization of strategy use have led to design of metacognitive interventions based on considerably more attention to the nature of strategy instruction than to the mere scheduling or concatenation of training elements. This in turn has prompted us to conclude that variations in teaching are part of the problem, not merely the technical means of its solution. It is therefore not surprising that the interventions with the best empirical support, and that are acknowledged thus far as coming closest to the ideal, namely the *reciprocal teaching* of Palincsar and Brown (1984) and the *direct explanation* approach of Roehler and Duffy (1984), are extraordinarily complex from the perspective of teachers. They require an active, cognitive effort from teachers. For example, applying these approaches requires that teachers attempt in real time to model students' relevant learning characteristics and level of acquisition, examine their own relevant content and teaching knowledge, identify strategies, formulate instructional plans, probe or test assumptions of these plans, monitor students' affective as well as cognitive responses, and modify some or all of their approach as needed.

The point to be made, however, is not only that this kind of cognitively active teaching is exceedingly complex. It is, and in real classrooms can be approximated only by many instructional interactions over the course of time (e.g., see Gerber, 1988). The major point, though, is that such teaching involves a unique cognitive engagement and exchange, largely by means of communicative (in its broadest sense) efforts by both students and teachers, all enclosed and defined for participants by the specific social context of the classroom. Current metacognitive research, particularly as it aspires to influence special education, fails to show sufficient appreciation of this fact. We propose not only that specific contexts of social, communicative exchange foster acquisition of meta-cognitive knowledge, but also that metacognition itself is fundamentally a socially complex phenomenon. In this sense, all academic learning is inherently social learning with socially negotiated meaning for instructional participants.

Need for a Social Model of Teaching

Cognitive–behavioral training techniques were originally designed intui-tively. Use of presentation-modeling, reinforced imitation, reinforcement for better approximations or correct or effective use were expedients. Their theoretical basis was in the work done by Michenbaum who in turn had used the experimental work of Vygotsky. The thrust of Vygotsky's work was that adults use language in the course of their caregiving that mediates the environment for young children. The concept of mediation was central to Vygotsky's theory. According to Vygotsky, language used by adult caregivers accomplishes two functions. It not only labels objects and actions, but also depicts in its grammar a structure of relationships among those objects and actions. Second, it controls the behavior of children while in the midst of experiencing these relationships. This control is established by representing desirable behavior and its contin-gencies in language. The result, according to Vygotsky, is that normally developing young children are not only guided by their caregiver's ver-balizations but also they *internalize*, as thought, these same behavior-regulating statements. It is in this way that young children's thinking as well as their behavior becomes self-controlled. It is in this way that they accumulate a number of schema for solving problems in the material world. The precise mechanism of internalization is theoretically and practically problematic (Meichenbaum, 1985).

We think that two important but seldom analyzed assumptions underlie adoption of Vygotsky's formulation to teaching learning disabled students. In the technical drift of modern research on metacognition, these as-sumptions appear not to have had much impact. First, *instructional language* used by teachers is a unique language form, and serves the same functions accomplished by a caregiver's verbalized cognitive–behavioral guidance. In fact, it could be said that teaching, in its purest expression, is cognitive–behavioral guidance that intends to establish both a special lexicon and action–grammar that will be internalized by students so that their future academic problem-solving will be similarly facilitated.

Second, there is a *social relationship* that binds teacher and student together, that motivates teachers and students to invest effort. This re-lationship must be durable because knowledge transmission and learning require a substantial chain of instructional episodes that are, in part, paced by the individually variable rate of development of students. Moreover, the quality of relationship, how it is interpreted by participants, with what affect they approach interaction and exchange, conditions the necessary motivation of both. Teachers must be willing to exert effort necessary to obtain evidence of knowledge acquisition by their students. Students must be willing to be guided through performance on tasks that not only may have little initial meaning or importance, but also that entail substantial risks for failure, loss of self-esteem and social status, and psychological "pain".

This kind of social requisite for learning is often problematic for the learning disabled child. Learning disabled students are characterized by how little they give in social and instructional exchange with teachers. They are often described as passive, dependent, non–help-seeking learners. Consequently, the social relationship of difficult-to-teach students is frequently without much easily recognized, positive incentive for long-term, mutual commitment. It is also without the basis for effective communication, explanation, and instruction that forms the mechanism of metacognitive growth.

Social Metacognition as a Social Construct

We propose an alternative model of metacognition to address some of the weaknesses of current models. It is constructed from the perspective of learning handicapped students responding to their interpretation of performance demands imposed on them by specific social relationships (e.g., parent, teacher, authority figure) and social contexts (e.g., home, classroom, on the street). There are two novel features in this model. The first is that mechanisms for motivation and attribution formation are embedded in the nature of social exchange, not in the instructional plan per se. That is, the meaningfulness of performance demands to learning handicapped students, and the degree to which incentives for effort are recognized or influence their performance, depends on how social relationships in a particular context are defined and mediated by the communications and behaviors of teachers. There are many practical manifestations, again from the students' perspective, of the worthwhileness of participation and effort. For example, do teachers explain and reexplain without negative affect for the effort reexplanation entails? Do they structure and support (through a scaffold of critical information, models, examples, hints, feedback) problem solving so that some definable level of success is guaranteed? Do teachers permit and validate students' communications, views, formulations, hesitancies, need for time, or primitive (i.e., immature or ineffective) learning tactics?

The second novel feature is the implicit replacement of a single, stable, or linearly developing metacognitive or executive component with a contingent, competitive, and episodic cognitive activation that results in a coordinated response to learning demands. That is, how can metacognition be both a component and simultaneously the main organizing principle of cognition? The underlying notion here that information processing does not follow a strict assembly-type production process, but rather a massive, distributed, and parallel set of processes, has gained increased support among some cognitive psychologists (e.g., see Mahoney & Lyddon, 1988; Mahoney & Nezworski, 1985). The central idea of this alternative perspective is that it is difficult to conceive of a finite, delineated, and yet omnipresent "executive" component that alone accounts for coordinated cognitive effort in complex information (i.e., social) environments. It is as if one executive was assigned direct and total control of all of the complex, interrelated activities, from communication to manufacturing, in a given industry. To stretch the analogy, the alternative view, much like that of classical economics, holds that each of the elemental production units or activities within an industry develop contingent, modifiable, structured relationships with others in response to the aggregated effects of each unit's activity. It is as if Adam Smith wrote *The Competence of Individuals* about cognitive development and organization within individuals instead of *The Wealth of Nations* about economic development and organization in society.

The analogy helps to explain some of the difficulties arising from a more limited information processing approach. First, it helps to account for the episodic competence of learning disabled and mentally retarded children. Conversely, it also helps to explain the lack of ecological validity in most training studies. Natural (i.e., social) learning probably does not occur in the discrete bundles of performance that are the focus of psychological experimentation, and it certainly occurs over much longer periods of time than researchers typically can or want to commit.

Second, it helps to explain why, as Shepherd and Gelzheiser (1987) point out, that the internal validity of cognitive strategy instruction experiments varies with the social degree and type of explanation and assistance provided by experimenters over and above their intended intervention design. That is, the total activating information in an experimental task is underestimated by researchers who view metacognition as an oversight function directed only toward understanding and regulating tasks as the researcher defines them. We hypothesize that the total activating information exists in a systematic social and cognitive relationship between teacher (researcher) and student (subject). By only keeping their eye on student variables, researchers effectively lose sight of half the information. Moreover, much of this information is not supplied in terms or forms that relate strictly to the academic content of the task. Such a system helps to frame the relative success of reciprocal teaching and direct explanation as new-generation strategy instruction approaches.

Finally, a less-reified perspective on executive, or metacognitive, processes appreciates that generalized competence is relative, that it is socially established from successive problem-solving experiences mediated and evaluated by a succession of social agents (parent, teacher, friend, mentor). The implication of this view, therefore, is that students perceived as being learning handicapped cannot be trained in a single episode to be more metacognitively effective, nor even in a series of highly focused episodes. Rather, our view is that such students need much more extensive experience in supported learning episodes than schooling typically provides (Gerber, 1988): episodes that not only have greater temporal contiguity, but also episodes that map for the student a more coherent set of social guidelines and constraints on processes of generating, monitoring, and evaluating one's own performance in problem-solving situations.

Where do We Go from Here?

We have posed the hypothesis that metacognitive development grows out of socially based, intensive, transpersonal exchanges between teachers and students. Moreover, with learning disabled students (and perhaps with many other students) metacognitive learning is not episodic but rather requires sustained and long-term development opportunities across school contexts and certainly over years of schooling.

Following from these assumptions, as we see it, future special education research efforts in the area of metacognition should continue to evaluate instructional training approaches of ecologically valid tasks, but we must also begin to identify and explain the variables in real classrooms that impede and/or enhance the ability of teachers and schools to make socially based and sustained contributions to the metacognitive development of learning disabled children. How can the school context be manipulated so that teachers are provided with skills and ongoing opportunity to engage each learning disabled child in the intensive, social, and long-term effort required for this difficult-to-teach student's metacognitive development? As we have argued in the prior section, such research effort and, more importantly, metacognitive-learning disabled *theory generation* necessitates that research be conducted in natural classroom settings. In her provocative analysis of cognitive research, Farnham–Diggory (1986) concluded:

It is failure, aberrations, or "bothersomeness" on school tasks that precipitates the designation of a child as learning disabled. As researcher, it is our job to enter the scene right there. Knowing what we do about automatic and controlled processing, it is our job to figure out how that accounts for behavior on particular school tasks. (p. 134)

Where do we go from here? As Farnham–Diggory said, "Time, Now, For a Little Serious Complexity."

References

Andrews, G. R., & Debus, R. L. (1978). Persistence and the causal perception of failure: Modifying cognitive attributions. *Journal of Educational Psychology*, *70*, 154–166.

Bobrow, D. G. (1975). Dimensions of representation. In D. G. Bobrow & A. Collings (Eds.), *Representation and understanding: Studies in cognitive sciences.* New York: Academic Press.

Borkowski, J. G., Carr, M., Rellinger, E., & Pressley, M. (1990). Self-regulated cognition: interdependence of metacognition, attributions, and self-esteem. In B. Jones & L. Idol (Eds.), *The dimensions of thinking and cognitive instruction.* Hillsdale, NJ: Erlbaum.

Borkowski, J. G., & Cavanaugh, J. C. (1979). Maintenance and generalization of skills and strategies by the retarded. In N. R. Ellis (Ed.), *Handbook of mental deficiency, psychological theory and research* (2nd Ed., pp. 569–617). Hillsdale, NJ: Erlbaum.

Borkowski, J. G., Johnston, M. B., & Reid, M. K. (1986). Metacognition, motivation, and the transfer of control processes. In S. J. Ceci (Ed.), *Handbook of cognition, social and neuropsychological aspects of learning disabilities.* Hillsdale, NJ: Erlbaum.

Borkowski, J. G., Johnston, M. B., & Reid, M. K. (1987). Metacognition, motivation, and controlled performance. In S. J. Ceci (Ed.), *Handbook of cognitive, social and neurological aspects of learning disabilities.* Hillsdale, NJ: Erlbaum.

Borkowski, J. G., & Kurtz, B. E. (1984). Metacognition and special children. In J. B. Gholson & T. L. Rosenthal (Eds.), *Applications of cognitive developmental theory* (pp. 193–213). New York: Academic Press.

Borkowski, J. G., Reid, M. K., & Kurtz, B. E. (1984). Metacognition and retardation: Paradigmatic, theoretical, and applied perspectives. In R. Sperber, C. McCauley, & P. Brooks (Eds.), *Learning and Cognition in the Mentally Retarded* (pp. 55–76). Baltimore: University Park Press.

Brown, A. L. (1972). A rehearsal deficit in retardates' continuous short term memory: Keeping track of variables that have few or many states. *Psychonomic Science*, *29*, 373–376.

Brown, A. L. (1973). Temporal and contextual cures as discriminative attributes in retardates' recognition memory. *Journal of Experimental Psychology*, *98*, 1–13.

Brown, A. L. (1974). The role of strategic behavior in retardate memory. In N. R. Ellis (Ed.), *International review of research in mental retardation* (Vol. 7, pp. 55–104). New York: Academic Press.

Brown, A. L. (1975). The development of memory: Knowing, knowing about knowing, and knowing how to know. In H. W. Reese (Ed.), *Advances in child development and behavior* (Vol. 10, pp. 103–152). New York: Academic Press.

Brown, A. L. (1978). Knowing when, where, and how to remember: A problem of metacognition. In R. Glaser (Ed.), *Advances in instructional psychology* (Vol. 10). Hillsdale, NJ: Erlbaum.

Brown, A. L., & Barclay, C. R. (1976). The effects of training specific mnemonics on the metamnemonic efficiency of retarded children. *Child Development, 47,* 71–80.

Brown, A. L., & Campione, J. C. (1984). Three faces of transfer: Implications for early competence, individual differences, and instruction. In M. Lamb, A. Brown, & B. Rogoff (Eds.), *Advances in developmental psychology* (Vol. 3). Hillsdale, NJ: Erlbaum.

Brown, A. L., Campione, J. C., Bray, N. W., & Wilcox, B. L. (1973). Keeping track of changing variables: Effects of rehearsal training and rehearsal prevention in normal and retarded adolescents. *Journal of Experimental Psychology, 101,* 123–131.

Brown, A. L., Campione, J. C., & Day, J. D. (1951). Learning to learn: On training students to learn from texts. *Educational Researcher, 10,* 14–21.

Brown, A. L. Campione, J. C., & Murphy, M. D. (1974). Keeping track of changing variables: Long-term retention of a trained rehearsal strategy by retarded adolescents. *American Journal of Mental Deficiency, 78,* 446–453.

Brown, A. L., & DeLoache, J. S. (1977). *Skills, plans, and self-regulation.* Report No. 48.

Brown, A. L., & Palincsar, A. S., (1982). Inducing strategic learning from texts by means of informed, self-control training. *Topics in Learning and Learning Disabilities, 2*(1), 1–17.

Brown, A. L., Palincsar, A. S., & Armbruster, B. B. (1984). Instructing comprehension-fostering activities in interactive learning situations. In H. Mandl, N. Stein, & T. Trabasso (Eds.), *Learning from texts.* Hillsdale, NJ: Erlbaum.

Butterfield, E. C., & Belmont J. M. (1977). Assessing and improving the cognitive functions of mentally retarded people. In I. Bigler & M. Sternlict (Eds.), *The psychology of mental retardation: Issues and approaches.* New York: Psychological Dimensions.

Campione, J. C., & Brown, A. L. (1977). Memory developed in educable retarded children. In R. V. Kail & J. W. Hagen (Eds.), *Perspectives on the development of memory and cognition* (pp. 367–406). Hillsdale, NJ: Erlbaum.

Cawley, J. F. (Ed.) (1985). *Developmental teaching of mathematics for learning disabled.* Rockville, MD: Aspen Systems.

Corno, L. (1986). *The metacognitive control components of self-regulated learning.* Paper presented at the annual meeting of the American Educational Research Association, San Francisco, CA.

Corno, L., & Mandinach, E. B. (1983). The role of cognitive engagement in classroom learning and motivation. *Educational Psychologist, 18*(2), 88–108.

Danner F. W. (1976). Children's understanding of intersentence organization in the recall of short descriptive passages. *Journal of Educational Psychology, 68,* 174–183.

Day, J. D. (1980). *Training summarization skills: A comparison of teaching methods.* Doctoral Dissertation, University of Illinois, Urbana, IL.

DeCorte, E., & Verschaffel, L. (1981). Children's solution processes in elementary arithmetic problems: Analysis and improvement. *Journal of Educational Psychology, 73*(6), 765–779.

Duffy, G. G., Roehler, L. R., Meloth, M. S., Putnam, J., & Wesselman, R. (1986). The relationship between explicit verbal explanations during reading skill instruction and student awareness and achievement: A study of reading teacher effects. *Reading Research Quarterly*, *21*(3), 237–252.

Dweck, C. S. (1975). The role of expectations and attributions in the alleviation of learned helplessness. *Journal of Personality and Social Psychology*, *31*, 674–685.

Dweck, C. S., & Goetz, T. E. (1978). Attributions and learned helplessness. In J. H. Harvey, W. Ickes, & R. F. Kidd (Eds.), *New directions in attribution research* (Vol. 2) Hillsdale, NJ: Erlbaum.

Dweck, C. S., & Licht, B. G. (1980). Learned helplessness and intellectual achievement. In J. Garber & E. P. Seligman (Eds.), *Human helplessness: Theory and application*. New York: Academic Press.

Farnham–Diggory, S. (1986). Time, now, for a little serious complexity. In S. J. Ceci (Ed.), *Handbook of cognitive, social, and neuropsychological aspects of learning disabilities* (Vol. 1, pp. 123–158). Hillsdale, NJ: Erlbaum.

Fisher, M. A., & Zeaman, D. (1973). An attention-retention theory of retardate discrimination learning. In N. R. Ellis (Ed.), *International review of research in mental retardation* (Vol. 6, pp. 169–256). New York: Academic Press.

Flavell, J. H. (1978). Metacognitive development. In J. M. Scandura & C. J. Brainerd (Eds.), *Structural/process theories of complex human behavior* (pp. 213–146). Alphen a.d. Rijn, The Netherlands: Sijtoff and Noordhoff.

Flavell, J. H. (1979). Metacognition and cognitive monitoring: A new area of cognitive—development inquiry. *American Psychologist*, *34*(10), 906–911.

Flavell, J. H., Friedrichs, A. G., & Hoyt, J. D. (1970). Developmental changes in memorization processes. *Cognitive Psychology*, *1*, 324–340.

Flavell, J. H., & Wellman, H. M. (1977). Metamemory. In R. Kail & J. Hagen (Eds.), *Perspectives on the development of memory and cognition* (pp. 3–33) Hillsdale, NJ: Erlbaum.

Forrest, D. L., & Waller, T. G. (1980). *What do children know about their reading and study skills?* Paper presented at the annual meeting of the American Educational Research Association, Boston.

Fowler, J. W., & Peterson, P. L. (1981). Increasing reading persistence and altering attributional style of learned helpless children. *Journal of Educational Psychology*, *73*(2), 251–260.

Garner, R. (1981). Monitoring of passage inconsistency among poor comprehenders: A preliminary test of the "Piecemeal Processing" explanation. *Journal of Educational Research*, *74*, 159–162.

Garner, R. & Kraus, C. (1982). Good and poor comprehender differences in knowing and regulating reading behaviors. *Educational Research Quarterly*, *6*, 5–12.

Gerber, M. M. (1983). Learning Disabilities and cognitive strategies: A case for training or constraining problem-solving. *Journal of Learning Disabilities*, *16*, 255–260.

Gerber, M. M. (1988). Cognitive-behavioral training in the curriculum: Time, slow learners, and basic skills. In E. L. Meyen, G. A. Vergason, & R. J. Whelan (Eds.), *Effective instructional strategies for exceptional children* (pp. 45–64). Denver, CO: Love Publishing.

Gerber, M. M. & Hall, R. J. (1987). Information processing approaches to studying spelling deficiencies. *Journal of Learning Disabilities*, *20*(1), 34–42.

Gerber, M. M., & Hall, R. J. (1989). Cognitive-behavioral training in spelling for learning handicapped students. *Learning Disability Quarterly*, *12*(3), 159–171.

Ghatala, E. S., Levin, J. R. Pressley, M., & Goodwin, D. (1986). A componential analysis of the effects of derived and supplied strategy monitoring in children. *Journal of Experimental Child Psychology*, *41*, 76–92.

Ghatala, E. S., Levin, J. R., Pressley, M., & Lodico, M. G. (1985). Training cognitive strategy monitoring in children. American *Educational Research Journal*, *22*, 1998–16.

Graham, S., & Freeman, S. (1986). Strategy training and teacher vs. student-controlled study conditions: Effects on LD students spelling performance. *Learning Disability Quarterly*, *9*(1), 15–22.

Hall, R. J., Gerber, M. M., & Stricker, A. (1989). Cognitive training: Implications for spelling instruction. In J. N. Hughes & R. J. Hall (Eds.), *Cognitive-behavioral psychology in the schools*: A comprehensive handbook (pp. 347–388). New York: Guilford Publications, Inc.

Hansen, J. (1981). The effects of inference training and practice on young children's comprehension. *Reading Research Quarterly*, *16*, 391–417.

Harris, K. R., Graham, S., & Freeman, S. (1988). Effects of strategy training on metamemory among learning disabled students. *Exceptional Children*, *54*(4), 332–338.

Kreutzer, M. A., Leonard, C., & Flavell, J. H. (1975). An interview study of children's knowledge about memory. *Monographs of the Society for Research in Child Development*, *40*(1, Serial No. 159).

Kurtz, B. E., & Borkowski, J. G. (1984). *Children[15] metacognition: Exploring relations between knowledge, process, and motivational variables. Journal of Experimental Child Psychology*, *37*(2), 335–354.

Larson, K. (1985). The effects of cognitive training for social competence in learning disabled and non-learning disabled delinquents. *Dissertation Abstracts International*, *46/04*, 948-A.

Larson, K. (1989a). Youthful offender's success on parole: The efficacy of teaching social problem solving skills. In S. Duguid (Ed.), *Yearbook of Correctional Education* (pp. 279–298). Published by Simon Fraser University, B. C., Canada and the Correctional Education Association.

Larson, K. (1989b). Problem solving training for enhancing school achievement in high-risk young adolescents. *Remedial and Special Education*, *10*(5), 32–42.

Larson, K., & Gerber, M. (1987). Effects of social metacognitive training for enhancing overt social behavior in LD and low-achieving delinquents. *Exceptional Children*, *54*(3), 201–211.

Licht, B. G. (1983). Cognitive motivational factors that contribute to the achievement of learning-disabled children. *Journal of Learning Disabilities*, *16*(8), 483–490.

Lloyd, J. W., Saltzman, N. J., & Kauffman, J. M. (1981). Predictable generalization in academic learning as a result of preskills and stategy training. *Learning Disability Quarterly*, *4*, 203–216.

Lodico, M. G., Ghatala, E. S., Levin, J. R., Pressley, M., & Bell, J. A. (1983). The effect of strategy-monitoring training on children's selection of effective memory strategies. *Journal of Experimental Child Psychology*, *35*, 263–277.

Luria, A. R. (1976). *Cognitive development: Its cultural and social foundations*. Cambridge, MA: Harvard University Press.

Mahoney, M. J., & Lyddon, W. J. (1988). Recent developments in cognitive approaches to counseling and psychotherapy. *The Counseling Psychologist*, *16*(2), 190–234.

Mahoney, M. J., & Nezworski, M. T. (1985). Cognitive-behavioral approaches to children's problems. *Journal of Abnormal Child Psychology*, *13*(3), 467–476.

Markman, E. (1973). *Factors affecting the young child's ability to monitor his memory*. Unpublished doctoral dissertation, University of Pennsylvania.

Meichenbaum, D. (1985). Teaching thinking: A cognitive-behavioral perspective. In S. F. Chipman, J. W. Segal, & R. Glaser (Eds.), *Thinking and learning skills* (Vol. 2, pp. 407–426). Hillsdale, NJ: Erlbaum.

Moynahan, E. D. (1973). The development of knowledge concerning the effect of categorization upon free recall. *Child Development*, *44*, 238–246.

Murphy, M. D., & Brown, A. L. (1975). Incidental learning in preschool children as a function of level of cognitive analysis. *Journal of Experimental Child Psychology*, *19*, 509–523.

Palincsar, A. S. (1986a). Metacognitive strategy instruction. *Exceptional Children*, *53*(2), 118–124.

Palincsar, A. S. (1986b). The role of dialogue in scaffolded instruction. *Educational Psychologist*, *21*, 73–98.

Palincsar, A. S., & Brown, A. L. (1984). Reciprocal teaching of comprehension fostering and monitoring activities. *Cognition and Instruction*, *1*(2), 117–175.

Paris, S. G. (1978). *Metacognitive development: children's regulation of problem solving skills*. Paper presented at the annual meeting of MPA, Chicago.

Paris, S. G., Cross, D. R., & Lipson, M. Y. (1984). Informed strategies for learning: A program to improve children's reading awareness and comprehension. *Journal of Educational Psychology*, *76*(6), 1239–1252.

Paris, S. G., Wasik, B. A., & Van der Westhuizen, G. (1988). Metametacognition: A review of research on metacognition and reading. In J. E. Readence & R. S. Baldwin (Eds.), *Diaglogues in literacy research: Thirty-seventh yearbook of the National Reading Conference* (pp. 143–166). The National Reading Conference, Inc.

Pressley, M., Borkowski, J. G., & O'Sullivan, J. T. (1985). Children's metamemory and the teaching of memory strategies. In D. L. Forrest-Pressley, G.E. MacKinnon, & T. G. Waller (Eds.), *Metacognition, cognition, and human performance* (pp. 111–153). New York: Academic Press.

Pressley, M., Goodchild, F., Fleet, J., Zajchowski, R., & Evans, E. D. (1989). The challenges of classroom strategy instruction. *The Elementary School Journal*, *89*(3), 301–342.

Pressley, M., Levin, J. R., & Delaney, H. D. (1982). The mnemonic keyword method. *Review of Educational Research*, *52*, 61–92.

Pressley, M., Ross, K. A., Levin, J. R., & Ghatala, E. S. (1984). The role of strategy utility knowledge in children's strategy decision making. *Journal of Experimental Child Psychology*, *38*, 491–504.

Pressley, M., Symons, S., Snyder, B. L., Cariglia-Bull, T. (1989). Strategy instruction research comes of age. *Learning Disability Quarterly*, *12*(1), 16–30.

Reeve, R. A., & Brown, A. L. (1985). Metacognition reconsidered: Implications for intervention research. *Journal of Abnormal Child Psychology*, *13*(30), 343–356.

Reid, M. K., & Borkowski, J. G. (1984). *A cognitive-motivational training program for hyperactive children.* Unpublished manuscript, University of Notre Dame, Notre Dame, IN.

Roehler, L. R., & Duffy, G. G. (1984). Direct explanation of comprehension processes. In G. G. Duffy, L. R. Roehler, & J. Mason (Eds.), *Comprehension instruction: Perspectives and suggestions* (pp. 265–280). New York: Longman.

Russell, R. L., & Ginsburg, H. P. (1984). Cognitive analysis of children's mathematics difficulties. *Cognition and Instruction, 1,* 217–244.

Salatas, H., & Flavell, J. H. (1976). Behavioral and metamnemonic indicators of strategic behaviors under remember instructions in first grade. *Child Development, 47,* 81–89.

Shepherd, M. J., & Gelzheiser, L. M. (1987). Strategies and mnemonics go to school. In *Memory and learning disabilities. Advances in learning and behavioral disabilities* (Suppl. 2, pp. 245–261). Greenwich, CT: JAI Press, Inc.

Shepherd, M. J., Gelzheiser, L. M., & Solar, R. A. (1985). How good is the evidence for a production deficiency among learning disabled students? *Journal of Educational Psychology, 77*(5), 553–561.

Short, E. J., & Ryan, E. B. (1984). Metacognitive differences between skilled and less skilled readers: Remediating deficits through story grammar and attribution training. *Journal of Educational Psychology, 76,* 225–235.

Slife, B. D., Weiss, J., & Bell, T. (1985). Separability of metacognition and cognition: problem solving in learning disabled and regular students. *Journal of Educational Psychology, 77*(4), 437–445.

Sternberg, R. J. (1980). Sketch of a componential subtheory of human intelligence. *The Behavioral and Brain Sciences, 3,* 573–614.

Sternberg, R. J. (1984). Toward a triarchic theory of human intelligence. *The Behavioral and Brain Sciences, 7,* 269–315.

Tenney, Y. J. (1975). The child's conception of organization and recall. *Journal of Experimental Child Psychology, 19,* 100–114.

Turnure, J. E. (1987). Social influences on cognitive strategies and cognitive development: The role of communication and instruction. *Intelligence, 11,* 77–89.

Vygotsky, L. S. (1978). *Mind and society: The development of higher psychological processes.* M. Cole, V. John-Steiner, S. Scribner, & E. Souberman (Eds. & trans.), pp. 19–133. Cambridge, MA: Harvard University Press.

Weiner, B. (1972). *Theories of motivation: From mechanism to cognition.* Chicago: Rand-McNally.

Weiner, B. (1979). A theory of motivation for some classroom experiences. *Journal of Educational Psychology, 71,* 3–25.

Wellman, H. M. (1978). Tip of the tongue and feeling of knowing experiences: A developmental study of memory monitoring. *Child Development, 48*(1), 13–21.

Winograd, P. (1984). Strategic difficulties in summarizing texts. *Reading Research Quarterly, XIX*(4), 404–425.

Wong, B. Y. L. (1979). Increasing retention of main ideas through questioning strategies. *Learning Disability Quarterly, 2,* 42–47.

Wong, B. Y. L. (1985). Self-questioning instructional research: A review. *Review of Educational Research, 55*(2), 227–268.

Wong, B. Y. L. (1986). Metacognition and special education: A review of a view. *Journal of Special Education*, *20*, 9–29.

Wong, B. Y. L., & Jones, W. (1982). Increasing metacomprehension in learning-disabled and normally-achieving students through self-questioning training. *Learning Disability Quarterly*, *5*, 228–240.

Wong, B. Y. L., & Wong, R. (1986). Study behavior as a function of metacognitive knowledge about critical task variables: An investigation of above average, average and learning-disabled readers. *Learning Disability Research*, *1*, 101–111.

Wood, D., Bruner, J. S., & Ross, G. (1976). The role of tutoring in problem solving. *Journal of Child Psychology and Psychiatry*, *17*, 89–100.

Yussen, S. R., & Levy, V. M., Jr. (1975). Developmental changes in predicting one's own span of short-term memory. *Journal of Experimental Child Psychology*, *19*, 502–508.

6
Adults with Learning Disabilities

Henry B. Reiff and Paul J. Gerber

Most introductions to issues in learning disabilities begin with a history of research. In discussing adults with learning disabilities, it might be equally appropriate to examine the research of history. Few topics related to educational problems have received the historical retrospectives granted to adults with purported learning disabilities, and few historical treatments have engendered such controversy regarding basic validity. Individuals throughout history undoubtedly have had learning problems, if not specific learning disabilities. The confusion arises because specific learning disability is a relatively new term that can only be applied through conjecture or speculation. Moreover, it is a term that is relatively synonymous with medical, psychological, and educational terminology of the past. Attempts to identify famous historical figures represent a growing concern to those in the field, while at the same time providing learning disabled individuals with positive role models.

Famous Adults with Learning Disabilities

It is not uncommon to hear remarks such as "Einstein, Churchill, Degas, and others were learning disabled." At national and state learning disability conferences, posters with pictures of famous historical personalities who had learning problems are readily available, and more pictures and names are added each year. Certainly parents and learning disabled individuals themselves can take comfort in knowing that such influential figures are suspected of having learning disabilities. Professionals, too, have jumped on the bandwagon through a liberal sprinkling of casual references to famous scientists, artists, politicians, and philosophers presumed to be learning disabled.

Adelman and Adelman (1987) caution against posthumous diagnoses based on sketchy information, and warn that inadequate historical scholarship creates myths, which no matter how appealing, may be eventually counterproductive. Aaron, Phillips, and Larsen (1988) have countered the Adelmans' argument and provide a rationale for pursuing this kind of study. Their research indicates that four famous men, Thomas Edison, Woodrow Wilson, Hans Christian Andersen, and Leonardo da Vinci, indeed had cognitive, neuropsychological, and biological characteristics associated with developmental reading disability. Perhaps the important question becomes how they managed to compensate and succeed handsomely, while not letting these characteristics prove dysfunctional. This question is even more elusive than a posthumous diagnosis because only a firsthand account will suffice for an explanation.

Adelman and Adelman (1987) suggest that researchers need to find living examples of inspirational models who can offer their particular strategies for coping and succeeding. The Adelmans' challenge is receiving a growing response. Adults with learning disabilities who have attained remarkable achievement are being recognized and honored through such organizations as the National Institute for Dyslexia and the Orton Dyslexia Society. Increasingly, at national and state learning disability conferences, panels of successful professionals with learning disabilities have served as "role models." Testimonials range from pure inspiration to a "how-to" guide of success in adulthood. Sharing personal experiences is a source of support and strength for many adults with learning disabilities. Recent studies of highly successful adults with learning disabilities (cf. Gerber & Ginsberg, 1987–1990) support the thesis that sharing firsthand experience may prove beneficial in helping others understand and cope with their own learning disabilities.

Longitudinal and Follow-Up Studies

A number of studies have addressed issues concerning adults with learning disabilities through longitudinal and follow-up research. Reviews of these studies by Gerber, Reiff, and Ginsberg (1988); Horn, O'Donnell, and Vitulano (1983); and Spreen (1988) found differing explanations and descriptions of learning disabilities in adulthood, largely because of methodological shortcomings, differing emphases, and inconsistencies from one study to the next. Nevertheless, certain consistencies can be gleaned from this body of research. The most striking commonality involves the persistence of learning disabilities into adulthood. The consistency of this finding suggests that learning disabilities represent more of a developmental deficit than a lag or delay. Despite this persistence, clear prognoses for adult outcomes are tenuous. Occupational outcomes and employment rates differed within and between studies. Spreen (1988) concluded that intervention efforts could not predict outcomes whereas Gerber et al. (1988) suggested that effective intervention efforts, coupled with favorable social ecologies, were more likely to result in successful adult adaptation.

The available literature of longitudinal and follow-up studies suggests that a learning disability is a lifelong condition that has various manifestations in adulthood. Academic issues become less important to most adults, mainly because the relevance to daily functioning diminishes in the adult years. Vocational and social issues assume greater import in later life (Gerber & Reiff, in press). Additionally, new obstacles are imposed in meeting the demands of daily life independently. It is not enough to conclude that learning disabilities persist; what must be explored are the unique ways in which this persistence interferes with adult life.

Prognoses

A tacit assumption formerly existed that learning disabilities simply disappeared at the onset of adolesence. This outlook was promulgated by a wide variety of professionals associated with the field of learning disabilities. A school-age emphasis and academic skills orientation resulted in a lack of awareness about the adult population. Beginning with the federal initiative of transition from school to work (Will, 1984), the field began to divert attention to the development of programs and services beyond the school-age years, albeit with a focus on late adolesence and early adulthood. This movement has gained further momentum by the change in name in 1983 of the Association for Children with Learning Disabilities (ACLD) to the Association for Children and Adults with Learning Disabilities. In 1989, the name was changed again to the Learning Disabilities Association (LDA) to make the statement of its mission less cumbersome. In the third decade since Dr. Sam Kirk in 1963 introduced the term learning disabilities, a recognition has evolved that adults also can be affected by learning disabilities.

Prognoses for adult life cover a continuum ranging from functional limitations to functional capabilities. Functionally limited adults with learning disabilities are typically unemployed or underemployed, live at home with parents, and have limited social opportunities and less than satisfying interpersonal relationships. At the other end of the spectrum, some adults with learning disabilities have achieved eminence in their chosen professions and have been able to maintain stable and happy marital and family relationships. They typically are satisfied with the quality of their lives.

Outcomes are as diverse for this population as for nondisabled individuals, although studies do indicate a greater degree of functional limitations in learning disabled adults. The persistence of disorders in the learning process undoubtedly makes overall adult adjustment more challenging. Polloway, Smith, and Patton (1984) note that the presence of cognitive deficits characteristic of learning disabilities are predictive of lower analytic ability and limited responses to job demands, such as acquiring new skills above current ability level.

Coming of Age

Issues concerning adults with learning disabitities received a significant amount of attention during the 1980s. In 1982, the ACLD national conference had as its theme "Coming of Age," which acknowledged the learning disabled adult issue. Later in the same year, the National Institute for Handicapped Research (NIHR) held a state-of-the-art conference about adults with learning disabilities. It was the first time that a governmental entity acknowledged this issue in the field of learning disabilities. The purpose of the meeting was to formulate a research agenda about adults with learning disabilities. The conference generated seven items that set forth a broad framework for research during the decade (Gerber, 1983; Gerber & Mellard, 1985). The seven items listed in priority were to: (a) identify the condition of learning disabilities at adulthood; identify the subgroups and where they are located; determine severity factors and how professionals should work with multihandicapped individuals who have a learning disability, (b) determine what social skills are at issue with learning disabled adults, (c) identify the vocational skills that are at issue for learning disabled adults, (d) conduct a state-of-the-art conference to determine what programs exist for learning disabled adults, (e) establish definitions of community adjustment, and determine which ones apply to learning disabled adults, (f) develop strategies for involving the family in order to help remedy the problems facing learning disabled adults, and (g) identify and investigate the setting demands in postsecondary training.

Other noteworthy activities followed. As a result of adults with learning disabilities becoming eligible for vocational rehabilitation services on the basis of the disability itself, another state-of-the-art conference was held in 1985 to address the rehabilitation needs of clients with learning disabilities. This meeting helped gear up a system for a disabled population that previously had not been served.

The growing momentum around this issue also received significant support from a position paper entitled "Adults with Learning Disbilities: A Call to Action," developed by the National Joint Committee on Learning Disabilities (NJCLD) in 1985. The NJCLD is a committee of cooperating organizations active in the field of learning disabilities and related disorders. The nine specific recommendations to the entire field are presented in Table 6.1.

TABLE 6.1. Recommendations of the National Joint Committee on Learning Disabilities (1985).

1. Programs must be initiated to increase public and professional awareness and understanding of the manifestations and needs of adults with learning disabilities.
2. Selection of appropriate education and vocational training programs and employment for adults with learning disabilities is predicated on a clear understanding of how their condition influences their learning and performance.
3. Throughout the school years, individuals with learning disabilities must have access to a range of program and service options that will prepare them to make the transition from secondary to postsecondary or vocational training settings.
4. Alternative programs and services must be provided for adults with learning disabilities who have failed to obtain a high school diploma.
5. Adults with learning disabilities must have an active role in determining the course of their postsecondary or vocational efforts.
6. Consistent with the Rehabilitation Act of 1973 and regulations implementing Section 504 of that Act, appropriate federal, state, and local agencies, as well as postsecondary and vocational training programs, should continue the development and implementation of effective programs that will allow adults with learning disabilities the opportunity to attain career goals. Also, consistent with Section 504, postsecondary programs, colleges, vocational schools, employers, and governmental agencies should be aware of the nondiscriminatory testing requirements for the handicapped.
7. The development of systematic programs of research that will address the status and needs of adults with learning disabilities is essential for the provision of appropriate services.
8. Curricula must be developed and incorporated in preparation programs for professionals in such disciplines as education, vocational and rehabilitative counseling, social work, psychology, medicine, and law to inform these professionals about the problems and needs of adults with learning disabilities.
9. Mental health professionals must be aware of the unique personal, social, and emotional difficulties that individuals with learning disabilities may experience throughout their lives.

Theoretical Constructs

Educational Construct or Legitimate Syndrome?

Issues surrounding students with learning disabilities tend to focus primarily on educational difficulties. This focus is not surprising since the term learning disabilities is technically an educational construct and was consciously popularized that way. In an operational sense, learning disabilities is not so much a syndrome of common behavioral characteristics as a description of behavioral products or manifestations within the context of the educational system. Students are identified as learning disabled if their educational achievement is not commensurate with their presumed abilities. Simply stated, it is a term used to describe students who, without a primary handicapping condition, fail to negotiate the demands of the educational system. Traditionally, only the interaction of the student with the educational system could result in the diagnosis of learning disabilities. Once the student exited the system, a legitimate question arose: Did learning disabilities continue to exist? The operational manifestations had vanished. When the context for failure had vanished, the construct of a disability became somewhat nebulous, if not moot.

Clearly, many adults with learning disabilities do encounter significant difficulties with adjustment to adult life. From a developmental perspective, then, learning disabilties can be construed as a syndrome of characteristics having different manifestations at different developmental periods and within differing social milieus. During the school years, the manifestations are relatively clear-cut. In adulthood, developmental expectations and outcomes become more multifaceted. The same processing deficits or underlying characteristics that impeded educational success may impair vocational, social, and emotional functioning as well as interfere with the exigencies of daily living. In some cases, the effects of a learning disability become even more debilitating in adulthood. These types of problems form the basis for a definition for some researchers: "Learning disabilities in adults can be viewed as a psychoeducational phenomenon that can seriously impair vocational and social effectiveness" (J. Smith, 1988, p. 52). If such problems can be traced to the same learning differences that made school so difficult, a case may be made for discussing the impact of learning disabilities in adulthood.

The question becomes more intriguing for those adults, perhaps identified as learning disabled in school, who show no signs of being disabled in adult life. Even though characteristics persist, can they truly be considered indicative of a disability if they do not impair adult functioning? Does a learning disability describe a theoretical mode or style of cognitive processing, or is the the issue of "disability" inexorably connected to a product, an evaluation of less than adequate functioning? Aaron et al. (1988) remind us that the resolution is a matter of perspective or definition. A definition emanating from a dysfunctional model perhaps excludes adults who do not have functional limitations. On the other hand, a definition based on the difference model where learning disabilties are "viewed as representing an extreme position within the normal range of variation in human information processing strategies" (p. 537) incorporates adults who have managed to compensate and become functionally capable.

This chapter does not resolve the controversy of what constitutes a disability. Rather, we offer the controversy as a framework to help the reader understand the subjective reality of the term *disability*. As part of the data collection on highly successful adults with learning disabilities (Gerber & Ginsberg, 1987–1990), one of the writers spent a fascinating morning interviewing a woman who terms herself as being learning disabled. She knows of what she speaks for she is an internationally recognized scholar in the field of language learning disabilties, whose research and writing have established her preeminence in the field. Her diagnosis is not self-imposed; she was placed in special education classes throughout her education before college. The writer, however, felt more than a little uncomfortable labeling her as handicapped or disabled. In the very area where learning disabilities are usually manifested, academia, she evidenced no indications of failure. She reads almost painfully slowly, but she has managed not to let this aspect of her learning style interfere with her scholarly productivity. In fact, she has been able to use her own experiences of having lived with an unusual learning style to gain insights that are perhaps unavailable to most other professionals. In the presence of this colleague, whose accomplishments dwarf most professionals' contributions to the field, we had trouble resolving this fundamental issue of what is a disability.

Problems with Definitions

The problems with definitions in the field of learning disabilities are well documented and far from resolved (see chapter 1). There are those who argue that definitions are too liberal in their inclusion of persons who do not belong. Others proffer requisite components dealing with intelligence ranges, neurological development, discrepancies between ability and achievement, and other criteria. This debate has been waged largely outside the learning disabled adult arena. In a pragmatic sense, this is due to the paucity of research in this area, the dearth of programs designed specifically for adults with learning disabilities, and the relatively recent acknowledgment of the importance of the issue itself. Only the Rehabilitation Services Administration (RSA) has adopted a formal definition in order to establish eligibility for services. Their definition is fitting to its mission and vocational focus:

A specific learning disability is a disorder in one or more of the central nervous system processes involved in perceiving, understanding, and/or using concepts through verbal (spoken or written) language or nonverbal means. This disorder manifests itself with a deficit in one or more of the following areas: attending, reasoning, processing, memory, communication, reading, writing, spelling, calculation, coordination, social competence and social maturity. (RSA, 1989)

As has been mentioned in this chapter, the NIHR conference in 1982 had as its first research agenda item the establishment of a definition for adults with learning disabilities. The formulation of an agreed-upon definition has not occurred, despite the need for a workable and logical means of conceptualizing and identifying adults with learning disabilities. Unfortunately, operational definitions for adults are still based on the cumbersome and controversial definition of PL 94–142 and, to a lesser extent, the definition of the NJCLD. Both are targeted at the school-age years while having components relevant to the adult years. They may be of limited value to adults with learning disabilities as the current definitions continue to be less than satisfactory to many in the field (Silver, 1988).

Beyond the need to validate eligibility for vocational rehabilitation services, a framework exists to diagnose learning disabilities in adults. More and more adults are seeking accommodations for their learning disabilities in university courses, in entry level tests in education and business, and for licensure examinations in careers and professions. These requests can be granted only after verification that a learning disability is present. Moreover, some parents of children with learning disabilities are requesting testing to validate long-suspected learning disabilities in themselves. In the absence of a definition for adults, clinicians are left to their best judgments. At present and for the foreseeable future, the issue of definition at the adult level is in a chaotic state.

Issues in Identification and Labeling

It is possible to identify adults with learning disabilities through traditional psychometric measures. Postsecondary educational programs routinely use assessment batteries to identify young adults with learning disabilities, and a number of clinics throughout the country use similar means to identify adults of any age. In one of the most comprehensive programs for college students with learning disabilities at California State University, Northridge, eligibility criteria for identifying college students with learning disabilities include significant intracognitive discrepancy or significant aptitude–achievement discrepancy(ies), at least one standard score in the average range of aptitude, and an average or greater score in at least one academic area (all as measured on technically adequate, standardized tests). Cohen Factor scores are used in helping to determine intracognitive discrepancy. In addition, clinical judgment may be exercised in up to 10% all students tested. Table 6.2 presents some of the standardized and diagnostic tests frequently employed in ascertaining the existence of learning disabilities in adults.

Hoskins and Wren (1989) are advocates of the therapeutic value of diagnosis at the postsecondary level. They contend that the diagnostic process can open new options, providing opportunities to understand the self as learner, and opens the door to planning for successful learning. This outlook is fundamental to providing appropriate educational services in postsecondary programs. Many in the field now contend that labels do not need to follow diagnosis automatically; rather, appropriate services should be geared to individual needs and not to categories of disabilities.

The issue of the real meaning of *disabled* or *handicapped* is far more than a semantic argument. Disabilities often exist more in the mind of the

TABLE 6.2. Measures frequently used to identify adults with learning disabilities.

Ability tests
  Slosson Intelligence
  Watson–Glaser Critical Thinking Appraisal
  Wechsler Adult Intelligence Scale (WAIS–R)
  Woodcock–Johnson Psychoeductional Battery—Cognitive Tests
Achievement tests
  Stanford Achievement Test
  Wide Range Achievement Test (WRAT)
  Woodcock–Johnson Psychoeductional Battery—Achievment Tests
Diagnostic tests
  Border Test of Reading–Spelling Patterns
  Gray Oral Reading Test
  Diagnostic Anaylsis of Reading Errors (DARE)
  Key Math
  Keystone Visual Survey Tests
  Writing sample
  Stanford Diagnostic Reading Test
  Wepman Auditory Discrimination Test

observer than in actual adaptive functioning. Perhaps a more acceptable perspective is to conceive of people labeled learning disabled as people with learning differences. The constellation of these differences even may represent a syndrome, albeit a highly diffuse one. For some, these learning differences may predispose or cause significant difficulties with adult functioning in the more traditional sense of a handicapping condition. For others, these differences become largely inconsequential to daily activities, and adult functioning is not impaired. All have characteristics associated with definitions and conceptualizations of learning disabilities. Whether or not an individual with these characteristics is, in fact, disabled is ultimately a matter of personal choice or perspective, a subjective response.

Some adults who have been identified as learning disabled reject the term. They acknowledge that they learn differently, but they do not see themselves as disabled. The term *disability* puts the blame on the victim instead of investigating the myriad possibilities of why some individuals have trouble with reading, writing, math, and so on. As one adult who describes himself as illiterate but not disabled says, "It's time to get off the backs of innocent chidren (and adults). No matter what you call a special education kid, 'learning disability,' 'learning handicap,' it comes out nigger to me, period" (Gerber & Ginsberg, 1987–1990). Other adults find leaving school as a relief because they can blend into anonymity in a larger social milieu.

Conversely, the term occasionally is embraced by some adults, especially those unidentified during school. In many cases, they grew up feeling they were stupid and all alone. Nobody understood what was going on with them. The discovery of the term learning disabilities can be a tremendous relief. Finally, they are able to stop blaming themselves and to realize that their difficulties are part of a recognized syndrome shared by many others, including some who accomplished remarkable feats during their lifetime. It grants them normal or above normal intelligence, while offering an explanation for the difficulties they have encountered. One adult who did not know that he had a learning disability happened to read an article called, "The Hidden Handicap" in *Psychology Today*. He immediately saw himself and, for the first time, realized that he was not a freak and that he was not to blame for his difficulties. The realization of himself as an adult with learning disabilities allowed him "to learn about my disability and come to grips with it" (Gerber & Ginsberg, 1987–1990).

Developmental Perspectives

The field only now has reached a point where enough research exists to delineate characteristics take the form of difficulties encountered in adult life. Few would disagree that the learning difficulties imposed by learning disabilities persist throughout the lifespan.

Some studies have investigated the persistence of specific characteristics. Bowen and Hynd (1988) evaluated dichotic listening ability in 24 learning disabled adults and ascertained that these adults showed similar deficits in lateralized selective auditory linguistic processing as children with learning disabilities. In another study, normative data from intellectual testing, academic achievement, and neuropsychological measures based on a sample of 100 adults with learning disabilities revealed a cognitive profile similar to that of children with learning disabilities (McCue, Shelly, & Goldstein, 1986). A number of studies have offered evidence that testing scores and learning patterns are consistent throughout the lifespan (Kroll, 1984); specific academic characteristics, such as uneven performance profile, language difficulties, poor writing, math problems, and organizational shortcomings persist as well (Blalock, 1981; Haig & Patterson, 1981).

In school, most students with learning disabilities are reminded on a daily basis of how their particular deficits interfere with success at school. In adulthood, the relationship between deficits and problems in daily life may not be so explicit. Blalock (1981) found that persistent problems associated with learning disabilities included oral language (auditory perception, comprehension, pronunciation, memory, and metalinguistics), reading (decoding and comprehension), written language (handwriting, spelling, syntax, morphology, mechanics, and connected writing formulation), mathematics (calculation and language-related problems), nonverbal abilities (orientation, visual–motor skills, and social perception), and thinking and reasoning skills. These problems were related to vocational, social, emotional, and daily living difficulties in adulthood. Despite such a plethora of self-reported difficulties, many adults with learning disabilities fail to comprehend the relation between these difficulties and problems encountered in diverse aspects of adult life. Blalock (1981) contends that perhaps the most persistent characteristic is an inability to profit from experience.

For many, specific difficulties seem to worsen in adulthood. Gerber et al. (1990) asked 133 adults with learning disabilities to indicate if characteristics found on the three most commonly used definitions of learning disabilities remained stable, got better, or got worse over time. "An overwhelming trend in the data shows that subjects rated their specific problems as getting worse rather than better when comparing school-age to adult years" (p. 6). Several clinical studies lend insight into the manifestations of these difficulties in adulthood. Persistent problems with reading and writing may preclude reading manuals, writing memos, letters, and reports, and writing and cashing checks (Johnson & Blaock, 1987). In adulthood, math deficits interfere with financial management such as paying bills, maintaining records, reconciling bank statements, filing income taxes, and handling money (Siegel, 1974), reading graphs and charts, estimating, approximating, predicting, and making change, determining the price of sale items, calculating tips, following recipes, using measuring devices (e.g., thermometers and gauges), and setting alarm clocks (Johnson & Blalock, 1987).

Another consideration from the developmental perspective concerns the changing manifestations of learning disabilities throughout the life-span. At the core of an adult developmental perspective is adaptation to life events. Not only does the focus shift from academic difficulties in childhood to vocational, social, and independent living concerns in adulthood but whole new areas of potential adaptive dysfunction may arise in the adult years for individuals with learning disabilities. Rourke, Young, and Leenaars (1989) have identified a syndrome of deficits in neurological functioning referred to as nonverbal learning disorder, which may predispose those afflicted to adolescent and adult depression and suicide risk. These individuals experience difficulties with mechanical arithmetic, but are capable in reading and spelling. Although they do have problems with nonverbal communication, school is usually not over-whelming and many make it through college. Crises often begin in entering the job market. Social ineptitude ruins interviews and interferes with job performance. Rourke and colleagues go on to describe other manifestations of the syndrome in adulthood, such as general coping and problem-solving difficulties, as well as interpersonal failures. Such charac-teristics have been related to suicide in adolescents and adults. The authors do not suggest that the nonverbal learning disability syndrome automatically predisposes suicide, but they do point out that manifesta-tions of suicide risk are markedly higher for adults with this syndrome. In any case, the change in manifestations from one developmental period to others is significant, if not alarming.

As much as these descriptions offer a down-to-earth understanding of how learning disabilities may affect adults, they nevertheless do a disservice by offering largely a perspective of pathology. Characteristics become associated with what individuals cannot do. Although some adults with learning disabilities are disabled, in fact, by the inability to handle such demands of adult living, many others find extremely successful ways of coping. Descriptions of adults with learning disabilities need to include not only those areas that present potential problems, but also the way that many adults have managed to work around these problems and overcome their deficits.

The Hidden Handicap

It has become almost a cliche to call learning disabilities "the hidden handicap." This moniker developed because individuals with learning disabilities have few overt indications of a handicapping condition. Within the educational system, however, less opportunities exist to hide the disability. For a student who has been identified as learning disabled, the disability becomes, in fact, somewhat visible; frequently, parents, teachers, peers, and often the student himself are acutely aware of the presence of a disabling condition.

For adults, the hidden quality allows a choice as to whether the condition is acknowledged or not. Once free of the educational system, many adults reject the label and may not consider themselves as disabled (Gerber, 1986). Services for learning disabled adults are underdeveloped and thus limited when compared to more severe disabling conditions, and many adults with learning disabilities decide not to seek services (Zetlin & Hosseini, 1989). Other adults have never been identified because they do not seem to exhibit any overt characteristics; yet, a certain amount of quality in their lives may be lacking due to these more subtle limitations. They may not be aware that, theoretically, they might be classified as learning disabled. Hence, studies on learning disabled adults are limited, in a sense, to those individuals who choose to identify themselves to researchers. Others may truly be hidden. In some cases they suffer from a sense of isolation and desolation. In other cases, they cope extremely well, their particular learning deficits seeming not to interfere with day-to-day life.

Severity

Another common thread running through many studies is the emphasis on the importance of the severity of the disability in determining deficits in adulthood. Severely learning disabled children tend to become severely disabled adults who often are unable to overcome the obstacles of their disabilities, and these problems are exacerbated in persons of lower intelligence. A recent study comparing differing outcomes of learning disabled adults (Minskoff, Hawks, Steidle, & Hoffmann, 1989) corroborates the use of severity as a significant factor relating not only to academic deficits but to vocational adjustment as well. The authors contend that adults with learning disabilities receiving vocational rehabilitation services may constitute a homogeneous group of persons with severe deficits. Of six factors relating to severity, level of intelligence proved to be one of the most critical.

Interviews with learning disabled adults (Gerber & Reiff, in press) add qualitative evidence to the significance of severity for adult prognosis. Of the adults in this study, those with the most severe disabilities were having the most difficult time in adulthood. Problems with attention, comprehension, self-esteem, self-concept, and social skills contributed to inadequate academic skills and a lack of a high school degree, leaving them as prisoners of their diabilities with few pathways to escape. Vocational planning remains a problem, perhaps explaining why Minskoff, Hawks, Steidle, and Hoffmann (1989) found this group needing the services of vocational rehabilitation.

Despite the preponderance of severely disabled adults who have difficulty with life adjustment, Gerber and Reiff (in press) caution against equating degree of accomplishment with a lesser degree of severity. Many successful learning disabled adults have been determined to succeed against the odds, often great odds. Severity has been countered with unusually hard work, an active awareness of strengths and weaknesses, and often intricate and elaborate systems of accommodation and compensation. Even though they have made remarkable achievements in chosen professions or interests, the daily struggle to perform despite a severe disability may exact a heavy toll at some point on the spectrum of adult adjustment.

Social Ecologies

The majority of studies clearly indicate that learning disabilities persist in adulthood. Despite the acknowledged persistence of learning disabilites, some investigators contend that problems related to learning disabilities do not have to be a life-long condition. In reviewing four studies of adults with childhood diagnoses of learning disabilities, Bruck (1987) concluded that in regard to the subjects' literacy skills, academic outcomes, occupational outcomes, and social/emotional adjustments, learning disabilities did not impair adult functioning if adequate treatment had been provided during childhood. Certainly, the traits associated with learning disabilities do not simply disappear, but evidence does suggest that these traits do not have to be dysfunctional provided that adequate treatment exists.

Adequate treatment seems to be more than a specific remedial/ instructional technique or program. Rather, it seems that the most optimistic prognoses evolve from a background of positive and supportive social ecologies. Gerber et al. (1988) cited several studies detailing positive adult outcomes. From these studies, the profile that emerges of the successful learning disabled adult reflects a relatively middle-class to affluent background, a supportive family, and a positive educational experience, usually beyond grade school. Yet entrepreneurs often have little or no positive experiences in school from which to draw at all.

In their ethnographic study of nine learning disabled adults (Gerber & Reiff, in press), successful adults noted a positive school experience as a criticial event that led to a "turnaround" in terms of self-esteem and coping skills. "All had siginficant difficulty in elementary school. A dramatic shift for all these young adults took place when they entered private secondary schools with programs for students with learning disabilities. These programs provided for important educational successes and social skill development. All felt that the reading and language skills acquired in the specialized programs opened up the adult world by allowing them to participate in activities requiring reading. The eventual placement in effective (and expensive) programs evidences family support" (Gerber & Reiff, in press). Additionally, these adults reported a sympathetic family life, where interest existed to find appropriate educational opportunities. As one adult in the Greber and Reiff (in press) ethnographic study exhorted, "You've got to have a mother that pushes you and pushes you and says, 'You're going to do it,' and 'I'm going to stand behind you as long as it takes to do it.'" Conversely, the least successful adults had generally negative memories of school, and, in one case, the informant specifically mentioned that her family life was not always a source of support. Even though educational services may be a crucial factor for successful adult outcomes, an alarming number of learning disabled adolescents do not avail themselves of these opportunities (Zigmond & Thornton, 1985).

The Making of Adults with Learning Disabilities

Educational Histories

The educational histories of adults with learning disabilities are as varied as their individual life stories. Despite differences in placements, types of instruction, labels, and even success or failure, the most consistent experience revolves around an intense dislike of school, at least at some point during their education (Gerber & Ginsberg, 1987–1990). One adult with learning disabilities remembers, "Mostly school was a horrible, humiliating experience of trying to hide somewhere and avoid being picked on and asked questions and being embarrassed by teachers."

For those who are able to take advantage of postsecondary educational opportunities, higher education often fosters a positive change in attitude. The flexibility inherent in many college programs, the chance to pursue an area of interset in depth, and the increased independence and concomitant strengthening of autonomy are all factors that can make college and graduate school satisfying and rewarding. Higher education allows students with learning disabilities to use a greater spectrum of compensatory mechanisms than were available from kindergarten to high school. For example, many learning disabled college students have been able to pass a seemingly overwhelming course by auditing the course, sometimes more than once, before taking the course for credit.

In recent years, colleges have become more responsive to the needs of students with learning disabilities. Directories of two and four-year colleges (cf. Fielding, 1981), guides to postsecondary education (cf. Straughn & Colby, 1985), and other resources identify many postsecondary educational programs for learning disabled students. These programs tend to share the philosophy that college students with learning disabilities can be successful if they receive appropriate educational support services. As the brochure for Learning Disability Program at California State University, Northridge, states, "Support services are intended to provide learning disabled students with the same opportunity for success and achievement as their non-learning disabled peers—an opportunity that allows students with learning disabilities to be judged on the basis of their ability, rather than disability."

Offering special services at the postsecondary level has garnered considerable success. Most programs offer an assessment and diagnosis of the student's specific learning difficulties. Services offered include career planning and placement, professional counseling, test accommodations, educational support specialists, auxiliary aids, compensatory assistance, workshops, peer tutoring, support groups and, in some cases, special housing arrangements. A number of these programs claim that the learning disabled students who take advantage of support services maintain higher grade point averages than their nondisabled peers.

Life Outside the Classroom

The virtually unlimited possibilities of growing up are experienced by individuals with learning disabilities. All have good and bad experiences outside the classroom. Some recall these events of childhood with nostalgia; others harbor little fondness for earlier years. Yet a commonality of most adults with learning disabilities is that they can recall specific, painful incidents outside the classroom that were related to their learning disabilities. In many cases, a great deal of energy is spent in adulthood trying to resolve the effects of this hurt. As one 48-year-old adult with learning disabilities reflected, "I'm in the process of healing" (Gerber & Ginsberg, 1987–1990). Until we can compare their experiences with matched samples of adults who are not learning disabled, we cannot state with certainty if childhood is more difficult or more painful for those with learning disabilities. Nevertheless, the following accounts of life outside the classroom give some idea of what it's like to grow up with a learning disability (Gerber & Ginsberg, 1987–1990).

"I was ridiculed a great deal, especially by guys I was competing with in sports. I think they were just as uncomfortable with my inability to learn. So were the girls."

"I was somewhat immature growing up and had awkward social skills."

"I had some very close friends. The rest of it sucked. I was never invited to anything, never a part of anything."

"I have always felt like I didn't belong to this planet and I was always from somewhere else and I really didn't fit here. Even though I learned to walk and talk like the people that lived here, I really didn't belong here."

Learning Disabilities in the Adult World

Career/Vocation

Career and vocational accomplishments are perhaps society's primary indices for establishing one's degree of success in the adult world. As a result, career and vocational issues assume a large role in determining the effect of learning disabilities in adulthood. In many ways, adults with learning disabilities potentially may be less disabled in the work force than in an educational environment. In school, the very areas of weakness of most learning disabled individuals are stressed; the workplace provides many possibilities of reasonable accommodation where a specific learning disability does not need to have such visible and negative consequences.

Studies indicate that adults with learning disabilities are represented on the full continuum of vocational outcomes (Gerber & Reiff, in press; Rogan & Hartman, 1976). Little research has compared vocational outcomes of adults with learning disabilities to control groups of non-learning disabled adults. However, at least one study of learning disabled adults reported only a 36% employment rate (Hoffmann et al., 1987), certainly a significantly different outcome than nondisabled populations. Some studies offer evidence that unemployment figures are not significantly different, but unemployment figures alone do not accurately depict vocational outcomes. Many adults with learning disabilities are underemployed, often stuck in dead-end jobs that do not tap into their true vocational potential. The available data suggest that as a group, adults with learning disabilities have a lower mean job status than non-learning disabled individuals (Gerber et al., 1988).

Components of Success

A striking paradox in the concept of learning disabilities is the enormous success that some adults with learning disabilities have achieved. Learning disabled individuals become doctors, lawyers, educators, CEOs, entrepreneurs, policymakers, and , in short, anything that is deemed to represent success. When successful adults with learning disabilities are asked what was the key to their success, their initial response is almost always "determination." One entrepreneur prioritized the factors for success: "Tenacity is more valuable than knowledge and skills." A prominent psychologist with learning disabilities firmly stated, "I never stop trying. I have an incredible amount of persistence." Nevertheless, blind determination alone may not be sufficient. Successful adults with learning disabilities chart the course of their ambitiousness through actively integrating other factors (Gerber & Ginsberg, 1987–1990).

In a national study of highly successful learning disabled adults (Gerber & Ginsberg, 1987–1990), the investigators identified a number of key themes which were common to success. These themes included the over-riding theme, control, and two sets of themes labeled internal decisions and external manifestations. Internal decisions included the desire to succeed, being goal oriented, and reframing of the learning disabilities experience in a positive and productive way.

External manifestations were all ways of being adaptable. Adaptability included persistence, a set of coping mechanisms called learned creativity, goodness of fit: matching one's abilities with their environment, and a social ecology of personal support designed to facilitate success.

Beyond the glamour of highly visible success, many learning disabled adults are testaments to the quiet, everyday success representative of the American dream, gainfully employed in jobs that grant both personal and financial satisfaction. In a study by Kokaska and Skolnik (1986), 10 learning disabled adults in occupations such as sanitation technician, special education teacher, professional musician, and heating and air-conditioning contractor gave employment suggestions similar to those used by highly successful individuals. This group recommended selecting a career emphasizing strengths, selecting jobs that allow for one's personal style, building interpersonal skills, accepting the fact of having to work harder and longer, and being honest with oneself.

Another factor for success involves locating jobs where employers will make allowances for workers with learning disabilities. According to one survey of employer attitudes toward hiring adults with learning disabilities, 71% of the employers were willing to make special allowances (Minskoff, Sautter, Hoffmann, & Hawks, 1987). Nevertheless, the researchers concluded that the employers had more positive attitudes toward those with physical disabilities rather than learning disabilities.

Factors of Failure

The very entry into the vocational world—finding and getting a job—proves elusive to many adults with learning disabilities. In a survey by Hoffmann et al. (1987), 381 adults with learning disabilities rated "filling out job applications," "knowing where to go to find a job," and "knowing how to get job training" as their top vocational problems. In addition, the service providers to these adults viewed them as having more significant job problems than were perceived by the adults themselves. It is not uncommon for individuals with learning disabilities to fail at a task without understanding why. Nevertheless, observers have noted specific vocational deficits.

Brown (1980) has identified problems that contribute to vocational failure in learning disabled adults. Inefficiency, errors, accident proneness, difficulty with academic skills, problems in learning a sequence of tasks, time problems, and social skill problems are all characteristics of learning disabled adults that can impair job effectiveness. These problems become more acute in job situations where weaknesses rather than strengths are exploited, and there is limited recourse to compensations and adaptations. Inasmuch as successful adults with learning disabilites have been able to find a "goodness of fit" between job demands, their own abilities, and available resources, unseuccessful adults often are not able to forge such a propitious match.

For one adult with learning disabilities, not recognizing the need for such a match led him to working as a delivery truck driver, even though he had specific difficulties with reading maps and directionality. It was not unusual for him to become lost and arrive late. He also had difficulty in reading the delivery tickets and making sure orders were correct (Gerber & Reiff, in press). In a study of career preferences of secondary students with learning disabilities (Reiff, Evans, & Anderson, 1990), the investigators ascertained that these students did not take "goodness of fit" factors into account in choosing careers. The study recommended that greater emphasis on career awareness and training might enable many young adults with learning disabilities to select more appropriate and satisfying vocations. A number of needs assessments of adults with learning disabilities (cf., ACLD, 1982; Hoffmann et al., 1987) have shown that the need for career counseling and education is consistently rated a priority.

Social

The effect of learning disabilities on social satisfaction is an overriding concern in adulthood. A number of studies have documented that the most visible manifestation of adult learning disabilities lies in problems with social skills (Gerber & Zinkgraf, 1982; Rogan & Hartman, 1976). Social skills not only have a bearing on interpersonal relationships, but are a major determinant of job satisfaction. Many adults with learning disabilities encounter failure in the workplace due to problems in getting along with employers and fellow employees more than to vocational incompetence per se. Conversely, some of the most successful adults have used their sophisticated social skills adeptly to lay a foundation for vocational achievement. Although most adults with learning disabilities struggle with a variety of social situations, many have adapted and compensated to find satisfaction in their social lives.

Components of Success

It is possible that some adults with learning disabilities have a predilection toward effective social functioning. Rourke (1982) has postulated that individuals with a mixture of perceptual processing deficits and cognitive and social strengths are among various possible subtypes of learning disabilities. Certainly, a number of adults with learning disabilities seem to be "naturally" charming individuals, who show no apparent difficulty with negotiating many types of social situations. Many social situations do not demand the reading, writing, and math skills that are problematic. Individuals with effective social skills, in essence, may choose not to have a disabling condition in a variety of social circumstances.

The effects of learning disabilities on social functioning are nonetheless recognizable in most cases. Individuals who are happy with their social lives rely on a variety of adaptive and coping mechanisms. Disclosure of having learning disabilities can be a critical factor. Usually confidants are chosen carefully, but it is the freedom of not having to hide a learning disability that allows for positive social interaction. Playing scrabble would be difficult, if not humiliating, for many individuals with very poor reading and spelling skills; one young woman is able to participate because her friend knows of her learning disability: "I play scrabble with my friend all the time. I say, 'Now tell me if this is right.' And I say out the word and she goes, 'No, it's backward but it's right.' Or I'd come up with a word and spell it. She goes, 'That's not a word!' I'd say, 'It looks right in my brain.' But they know" (Gerber & Reiff, in press).

At some level, social satisfaction is achieved through at least a degree of self-acceptance. A sense of humor, especially the ability to laugh at oneself, can be an essential social coping skill. One adult's description of his outlook on coping with learning disabilities in social situations was:

"My way of dealing with it is to laugh about it, and not only laughing about it, but to make everybody else laugh about it. I can definitely laugh at myself. I think I'm the funniest person I know" (Gerber & Reiff, in press).

Favorable social ecologies, including sources of emotional support, a sense of being successful in some area, and a positive educational experience, seem to be critical factors, at some point, for social success in many adults with learning disabilities (Gerber & Reiff, in press). Many of the components of favorable social ecologies represent alterable variables that do not have to be negatively influenced by learning disabilities. The prognosis for social success in the adult years undoubtedly will improve when positive social ecologies are fostered throughout personal development.

Factors of Failure

For many adults with learning disabilities, social difficulties represent the greatest hurdle to a satisfying life. Lack of close personal friendships, feelings of isolation and aloneness, discomfort in social gatherings, and a sense of boredom and frustration with recreational and leisure time are frequently reported (Gerber et al., 1988). Such social shortcomings are really not so surprising in light of the wealth of literature suggesting that social skills deficits may be intrinsically related to learning disabilities in some cases. Among the many social behaviors linked directly to learning and processing problems are deficits in nonverbal social communication (Bryan, 1977), the use of pragmatic language (Wiig & Harris, 1974), sensitivity to subtlety (Gerber & Zinkgraf, 1982), and a realization of other people's moods (Lerner, 1985). These kinds of difficulties generally are classified as social misperception.

Moreover, since systematic social skills remediation is a relatively new concern in the field, many adults received no assistance in overcoming what may be inherent and life-long social problems. These difficulties do not necessarily stabilize over time, for repeated social failings tend to exacerbate maladaptive social behavior, increasing feelings of alienation and decreasing the willingness to engage actively in social situations. "If the future is anticipated with a sense of defeat, it is likely that less effort will be put into strategies and ways of dealing with potential problems" (Polloway et al., 1984, p. 270). Added to the equation is the tendency of many learning disabled individuals to be less than insightful, if not oblivious, to cause and effect. The result is often a confused, bewildered, and angry adult who feels abused by the world around him.

Blalock (1981) observed 38 adults in a program providing services for learning disabilities over a period of 5 years. More than half the group reported social problems. Many had difficulty making and sustaining friendships. Of particular concern to many young adults with learning disabilities are problems with dating and shyness (Gerber and Reiff, in press; Hoffmann et al., 1987). One young man in Gerber & Reiff's (in press) study said he has problems talking to girls and is afraid that he will stutter. He assumes that he will make a bad impression. "I have a small vocabulary, and so whenever I use big words sometimes I forget how to use them. And I'll say the wrong word. And sometimes I'll forget what I'm getting at, and then I'll forget which way I'm going. So the chicks will just sit there and look at me." Another young man summed up his problems with establishing relationships by stating, "Right now, my social life is kind of bleak."

In Blalock's (1981) study, specific characteristics associated with learning disabilities seemed to have a direct impact on participation in social activities. For some, reading weaknesses prohibited involvement in word and card games played by peers. Others experienced setbacks due to oral language deficits. They had trouble following conversations, understanding jokes, or making conversation. Nonverbal difficulties created problems in such areas as learning to dance and finding their way around new places. Social imperception may have played the most insidious role; Blalock states that many of these adults tended to alienate others, but were not even aware of it.

Even in cases where social skills deficits may not be an inherent condition, learning disabled adults may be more at risk to miss essential experiences in the development of appropriate and "typical" social behavior. For some, specialized and segregated education resulted in a deprivation of normal social interaction with nonhandicapped peers. Others were rejected to a point that they stopped trying or were simply not allowed to participate in the usual social experiences. For some highly successful adults with learning disabilities, the very drive and determination that led them to academic and career success impeded their social development. In school, they had to work much harder than their classmates just to keep up. They worked so hard they simply did not have time to participate in social activities with their peers. A lawyer with learning disabilities describes this aspect of growing up: "I think that because I spent so much time on my studies, I had less time to spend in development of social graces, less time to develop just hanging out. I missed out on a part of living. Has it impacted my life even to this day? Yeah, no question about the fact that it's helped mold my profile of social activity" (Gerber & Reiff, in press).

The extreme end on the continuum of social failing may be represented by incarcerated adults with learning disabilities. School failure, differential treatment, and susceptibility hypotheses have been proffered as explanations for high prevelency rates (ranging from 26% to 73%) of learning disability among delinquents (Larson, 1988). Yet Larson contends that social cognitive problem-solving deficits may be the salient characteristic in learning disabled individuals that can lead to such serious trouble. Problems with controlling impulses, defining and solving problems, evaluating consequences, and monitoring performance are characteristics of learning disabilities that also typically are reported in criminal offenders. Hoffman et al. (1987) give some indication of the pervasiveness of such behaviors in responses from a group of 381 learning disabled adults. The most frequently reported social skills problem was talking or acting before thinking.

Larson and Gerber (1987) offer some hope that certain types of social cognitive deficits, particularly problems with impulse control, are amenable to change. In a study that employed metacognitive training to increase adaptive behavior in learning disabled and non-learning disabled delinquent youth (ages 16–19), the researchers found evidence to support the hypothesis that deficiencies in social metacognition increase the risk for maladaptive behavior in individuals with learning disabilities. Hence, approaches that captialize on developing metacognitive awareness and control may represent opportunities for some adults with learning disabilities to engage in more satisfying social interaction. Approaches that demonstrate effectiveness are likely to be embraced inasmuch as adults with learning disabilities themselves and observers of their behavior have expressed a desire for assistance through social skills training (ACLD, 1982; Hoffmann et al., 1987).

Emotional

In a series of interviews with highly successful adults with learning disabilities (Gerber & Ginsberg, 1987–1990), the researchers noted an almost universal characteristic of this population was a degree of anger, usually stemming from some hurt connected with having learning disabilities. One successful entrepreneur summed up feelings repeated by almost all those interviewed: "I have been as angry as anybody locked up in a cage." In vocational terms, all had been able to turn this anger into a productive source of motivation. Many credit at least some of their success to an intense desire to prove themselves, and to show the world that they weren't "dumb." The same entrepreneur stated that feelings of inferiority and weakness caused him to overcompensate in his drive to succeed. He added, "I took a psychological posture of who the good guys were and who the bad guys were. I wasn't going to let the literate world beat me. They were wrong."

In some cases, adults are able to parlay this drive and determination into a recognition that learning disabilities may have played a positive role in their lives. A successful dentist shared this perspective: "You know, there's a plus side to it. Maybe if I didn't have difficulty with reading, maybe I wouldn't be so determined, and maybe I wouldn't have accomplished as much, or maybe I wouldn't have wanted to accomplish

as much. There's a lot of good. There's a lot of plus that comes out"
(Gerber & Reiff, in press).

Not all adults with learning disabilities are able to use anger, hurt,
pain, or frustration as part of the basis for succeeding. Many are
discouraged from attempting almost any challenge, and seem to live in a
world where emotions ranging from confusion and bewilderment to
despair are common and sometimes dominant. Even those who have
experienced material and vocational success usually report that they have
paid an emotional price in dealing with learning disabilities.

Components of Success

Emotional success is quite difficult to define and listing its components is
problematic. To a large degree, success must be viewed in relation to
severity and prognosis for satisfactory adult functioning. Thus, an adult
severely involved with learning disabilities who functions independently
in a personal and vocational sense can be viewed as successful. More and
more adults are emerging from school-age programming and finding
greater self-acceptance through success after accessing postsecondary or
higher education training. The emotional underpinning to this success is
varied and not easily generalized, although some traits do seem to have
commonalities.

In the adults with learning disabilities studied by Gerber and Ginsberg
(1987–1990), it was clear that self-acceptance was an ingredient of
success. Those individuals, who through introspective processes
understood their strengths and weaknesses and how they related to their
social and vocational milieus, were able to adapt and compete in adult
life. Out of self-acceptance emerges a belief in self that has been shaped
through a combination of encouragement of significant others. either in
childhood or adulthood (or both). Motivation is galvanized by
perseverance, fueled by a string of successes from a long list of risk-taking
actions. The key to success then becomes the notion that success will be
there, despite small failures along the way. Successful outcomes
ultimately will occur if things are done in the unique way fitting to the
adult with learning disabilities. When success begets success, the impact
on self-concept and self-esteem is positive and cumulative. Obstacles of
the past become an opportunity for creative problem solving, and mastery
of these situations reinforce a broader and stronger foundation for self-
actualization.

Self-acceptance is the key to emotional contentment and stability for
anyone: adults with learning disabilities are no exception, but perhaps
they face additional obstacles that tend to exacerbate the process of
self-acceptance. For some, self-acceptance is related to success as defined
by external standards. This perspective might prove debilitating to adults
whose disabilities significantly interfere with various aspects of func-

tioning. For those whose self-acceptance is based more on personal notions of worth, the ability to admit to having weaknesses as well as strengths may be a key to emotional health.

Factors of Failure

Personal problems with frustation, lack of self-confidence, control of emotion and temper, and depression are not uncommon among adults with learning disabilities (Hoffmann et al., 1987). These problems can and do interfere with vocational success, social well-being, and fulfilling interpersonal relationships. Some emotional difficulties appear to be residual from painful experiences while growing up; others clearly are related to present-day frustrations and, in some cases, to the confusion of not understanding why things do not work out. although adult support groups are springing up throughout the country, many adults with learning disabilities feel isolated and are perhaps unaware or unwilling to take advantage of these services. In the Hoffmann et al. (1987) survey of 381 adults with learning disabilities, the researchers found it noteworthy that practically none of the respondents had taken part in a social skills or self-help support group.

Many learning disabled adults are overwhelmed by feelings of stupidity and a lack of self-esteem. S. L. Smith (1988) points out that these adults often cope by developing masks of supercompetence, helplessness, invisibility, clowning, and so forth to hide their hurt. Although the masks afford a sense of protection, they also can cause added stress. Blalock's (1981) study gives other examples of the effort involved in hiding or avoiding the problem: "Husbands took reports home for wives to write, dictionaries were stashed in every possible location, friends were called to spell a word, secretaries asked to 'make a note of this, I'm in a hurry,' etc" (p. 38).

The psychological energy spent in trying to hide the disability, the concomitant sense of deceit, and the fear of being discovered all can take an emotional toll. Even highly successful adults with learning disabilities retain a sense that they are frauds in the real world who will be punished or humiliated if their disability is discovered. One adult with a severe reading disability, who has recently gone public concerning his problem, remembers the terrible cost of covering up this deficiency. "I know that it was very important that I not tell people that I couldn't read or write. If they found out . . . Even when I won the blue ribbon, it really wasn't quite mine. I stole it in a sense. I stole first base. And I'm on third base. And I'm coming home. But if I told somebody before I'd learned to read, even with all my worldly successes they would still discount me because something was wrong with me. So psychologically and emotionally, we're left in our childhood. And we're left in the emotions and fears of our childhood" (Gerber & Ginsberg, 1987–1990).

Another source of frustration facing some adults with learning disabilities arises from an inability to comprehend causality or to understand why a situation does not turn out the way it was anticipated. Adults with learning disabilities have shown a tendency to overestimate their abilities on specific tasks (Wilhardt & Sandman, 1988). This trait can lead to experiences of failure. The frustration is exacerbated because of not knowing why they failed. Adults with learning disabilities have reported feeling confused about why things always seem so difficult (Blalock, 1981).

The global manifestation of such difficulties takes the form of increased anxiety. Whereas some individuals are able to make use of anxiety to increase motivation and performance, most do not function more effectively with psychological stress. In some cases, higher than normal levels of anxiety are not merely the result of emotional lability; rather, specific processing problems connected to learning disabilities may play a role. A number of adults have described feelings of near panic in large social gatherings, not because of emotional reactions, but because of being overwhelmed by sensory stimuli.

Daily Living

For adults with learning disabilities, problems do not disappear simply because deficits with reading, writing, and math may not be as noticeable in day-to-day activities. Whether these difficulties interfere with or diminish satisfaction is largely a combination of compensatory strategies and attitude. The importance of attitude cannot be overstated. For some problem areas, compensatory strategies may not readily available, but a positive and determined attitude can overcome potential setbacks. In the case of the language scholar with learning disabilities to whom we referred in the early part of the chapter, she loves to read for pleasure, despite a reading rate of about five pages per hour. She refuses to let her rate be disability; she will not allow herself to be denied the same opportunities for enjoyment given to nondisabled readers.

Some adults feel that learning disabilities do not affect their daily living to any great degree, but they may be diminishing the impact by simply avoiding or not taking part in many activities where the learning disability would have an impact. Deficits in writing cease to be a problem in daily life if one chooses not to write.

As with all other areas of adult functioning, problems in daily living may be related in part to the severity of the disability. Consistent with the notion that adults with leaning disabilities receiving vocational rehabilitation services may be homogeneous group with severe deficits (Minskoff et al., 1989) is the finding of Hoffmann et al. (1987) that problems with money and banking tended to be more significant for the adults with learning disabilities in vocational rehabilitation. In the Gerber and Reiff (in press) study, the adults with the most severe learning disabilities coped less successfully with money and banking than the other learning disabled adults. To some extent, the problems themselves were not dissimilar between the groups, but the ability to compensate and employ effective strategies differed. Writing checks had become so overwhelming because of spelling the amount that one young lady tried not to use checks, whereas a more successful adult with equally poor spelling kept a "crib" sheet in his checkbook and was not limited in his checkwriting.

Frequently reported problems with daily living, in addition to those previously described, include giving and following directions, reading signs and maps, driving, keeping track of time, domestic and professional organization skills, cooking, wardrobe coordination, and being overwhelmed by shopping (Blalock, 1981; Gerber & Ginsberg, 1987– 1990; Gerber & Reiff, in press). As with all other areas of functioning, many adults with learning disabilities are able to cope remarkably and ingeniously, whereas others are victims to the limitations imposed by the disability. The foundation for overcoming problems in daily living lies in a realization and understanding of the varied effects of learning disabilities in a very broad array of settings and circumstances.

Summary

Controversy and confusion surround the study of adults with learning disabilities. Disagreement ranges from historical diagnoses to formulating definitions. The very concept of who is an adult with learning disabilities is nebulous and largely is determined by one's particular theoretical orientation. Manifestations of learning disabilities change with stages in development. The operational construct of learning disabilities in the school-age years may not effectively identify learning disabilities in adulthood. Despite the different manifestations of learning disabilities in adulthood, the severity of the disability and the impact of social ecologies may offer longitudinal prognoses.

As much as individuals are born with learning differences, the educational system may be largely responsible for creating disabilities out of differences. For most adults with learning disabilities, school was an often painful experience, although some found greater success in postsecondary educational opportunities. Life outside the classroom also could be difficult and alienating.

In the adult world, learning disabilities may have an impact on vocational, social, emotional, and day-to-day functioning. In all of these areas, adults with learning disabilities have demonstrated considerable success as well as debilitating failure. Much of the available data suggests that increased success in areas of adult functioning is possible once critical factors to successful adjustment are analyzed and understood. At present, this realization is far from complete. A need for further extensive research of adults with learning disabilities clearly exists.

The purpose of this chapter has been to introduce the reader to the major issues related to adults with learning disabilities. The authors have intended to infuse a perspective that is based in a belief of what people can accomplish despite their disabilities rather than what limits people because of their disabilities. Models of pathology simply may not be appropriate for conceptualizing adults with learning disabilities. A recognition of course exists that limitations imposed by learning disabilities can be very real, yet the achievements of this population suggest that traditional expectations of failure represent a limited understanding of human resilience.

References

ACLD. (1982, September, October). ACLD vocational committee survey of learning disabled adults: Preliminary report. *ACLD Newsbriefs*, pp. 10–13.

Aaron, P. G., Phillips, S., & Larsen, S. (1988). Specific reading disability in historically famous persons. *Journal of Learning Disabilities, 21*, 523–538.

Adelman, K. A., & Adelman, H. S. (1987). Rodin, Patton, Edison, Wilson, Einstein: Were they really learning disabled? *Journal of Learning Disabilities, 20*, 270–279.

Blalock, J. W. (1981). Persistent problems and concerns of young adults with learning Disabilities. In W. M. Cruickshank & A. A. Silver (Eds.), *Bridges to tomorrow: The best of the ACLD*, Vol. 2 (pp. 35–56). Syracuse, NY: Syracuse University Press.

Bowen, S. M., & Hynd, G. W. (1988). Do children with learning disabilities outgrow deficits in selective auditory attention? Evidence from dichotic listening in adults with learning disabilities. *Journal of Learning Disabilities, 21*, 623–631.

Brown, D. (1980). *Steps to independence for people with learning disabilities.* Washington, DC: Closer Look Parents' Campaign for Handicapped Children and Youth/National Institute of Education. (ERIC Document Reproduction Service No. ED 203605).

Bruck, M. (1987). The adult outcomes of children with learning disabilities. *Annals of Dyslexia, 37*, 252–263.

Bryan, T. (1977). Learning disabled children's comprehension of nonverbal communication. *Journal of Learning Disabilities, 10*, 501–506.

Fielding, P. M. (Ed.) (1981). *A national directory of four year colleges, two year colleges and post high school training programs for young people with learning disabilities* (4th ed.). Tulsa, OK: Partners in Publishing.

Gerber, P. J. (1983). Conference summary and generation of final research priorities. In *The special rehabilitation needs of learning disabled adults* (pp. 50–61). Washington, DC: The National Institute for Handicapped Research.

Gerber, P. J. (1986). The learning disabled adult nexus: European perspectives and emerging American trends. *Journal of Learning Disabilities, 19*(1), 2–4.

Gerber, P. J., & Ginsberg, R. (1987–1990). *Identifying alterable patterns in workplace success for highly successful learning disabled adults.* United States Department of Education. Grant funded by National Institute for Disability Rehabilitation Research, 84.133G.

Gerber, P. J., & Mellard, D. (1985). Rehabilitation of learning disabled adults: Recommended research priorities. *Journal of Rehabilitation, 51*(1), 62–64.

Gerber, P. J., & Reiff, H. B. (in press). *Speaking for themselves: Ethnographic interviews with adults with learning disabilities.* Ann Arbor, MI: University of Michigan Press.

Gerber, P. J., Reiff, H. B., & Ginsberg, R. (1988). Longitudinal and follow-up studies of learning disabled adults: Methodological considerations. *Thalamus— Publication of the International Academy for Research in Learning Disabilities, 6*(1), 1–32.

Gerber, P. J., Schnieders, C. A., Paradise, L. V., Reiff, H. B., Ginsberg, R., & Popp, P. A. (1990). Persisting problems of adults with learning disabilities: Self-reported comparisons from school-age and adult years. *Journal of Learning Disabilities, 23*(9), 570–573.

Gerber, P. J., & Zinkgraf, S. (1982). Social perception ability in learning disabled and nonhandicapped students. *Learning Disability Quarterly, 5*, 135–139.

Haig, J. M., & Patterson, B. H. (1981). *An overview of adult learning disabilities.* Washington, DC: National Institute of Education (ERIC No. 197563).

Hoffman, F. J., Sheldon, K. L., Minskoff, E. H., Sautter, S. W., Steidle, E. F., Baker, D. P., Bailey, M. B., & Echols, L. D. (1987). Needs of learning disabled adults. *Journal of Learning Disabilities, 20*, 43–52.

Horn, W., O'Donnell, J., & Vitulano, L. (1983). Long-term follow-up studies of learning disabled persons. *Journal of Learning Disabilities, 16*, 542–555.

Hoskins, B., & Wren, C. (1989, February). *The therapeutic value of diagnosis: The other side of the labeling issue.* Paper presented at The Fifth Annual Conference on the Learning Disabled Adult, Northridge, CA.

Johnson, D. J., & Blalock, J. W. (1987). *Adults with learning disabilities: Clinical studies.* Orlando, FL: Grune & Stratton.

Kokaska, C. J., & Skolnik, J. (1986). Employment suggestions from LD adults. *Academic Therapy, 21*, 573–577.

Kroll, L. G. (1984). LDs—What happens when they are no longer children? *Academic Therapy, 20*, 133–148.

Larson, K. A. (1988). A research review and alternative hypothesis explaining the link between learning didability and delinquency. *Journal of Learning Disabilities, 21*, 357–363.

Larson, K. A., & Gerber, M. M. (1987). Effects of social metacognitive training for enhancing overt behavior in learning disabled and low achieving delinquents. *Exceptional Children, 54*, 201–211.

Lerner, J. (1985). *Learning Disabilities: Theories, diagnosis, and teaching stategies* (4th ed.). Boston, MA: Houghton-Mifflin.

McCue, M. P., Shelly, C., & Goldstein, G. (1986). Intellectual, academic, and neuropsychological performance levels in learning disabled adults. *Journal of Learning Disabilities, 19*, 233–236.

Minskoff, E. H., Hawks, R., Steidle, E. F., & Hoffmann, F. J. (1989). A homogeneous group of persons with learning disabilities: Adults with severe learning disabilities in vocational rehabilitation. *Journal of Learning Disabilities, 22*, 521–528.

Minskoff, E. H., Sautter, S. W., Hoffmann, F. J., & Hawks, R. (1987). Employer attitudes toward hiring the learning disabled. *Journal of Learning Disabilities, 20*(1), 53–57.

National Joint Committee on Learning Disabilities. (1986). Adults with learning disabilities: A call to action. *Learning Disabilities Quarterly, 9,* 164–168.

Polloway, E. A., Smith, J. D., & Patton, J. R. (1984). Learning disabilities: An adult developmental perspective. *Learning Disability Quarterly, 11*(3), 265–273 (reprinted from *8*(2), 1984).

RSA. (1989, August). *Evaluation of services provided for individuals with specific learning Disabilities* (Vol. 1: Final report). Washington, DC: Department of Education, Contract No. 300-87-0112.

Reiff, H. B., Evans, E., & Anderson, P. L. (1989, October). *Vocational preferences of secondary students with learning disabilities.* Paper presented at the International Conference of the Council for Learning Disabilities (CLD), Denver, CO.

Rogan, L., & Hartman, L. (1976, December). *A follow-up study of learning disabled children as adults.* Final report (Project #443CH60010, Grant #OEG-0-74-7453). Washington, DC: Bureau of Education for the Handicapped, U.S. Department HEW.

Rourke, B. P. (1982). Central proccessing deficiencies in children: Toward a neuropsychological model. *Journal of Clinical Neuropsychology, 4,* 1–18.

Rourke, B. P., Young, G. C., & Leenaars, A. A. (1989). A childhood learning disability that predisposes those afflicted to adolescent and adult depression and suicide risk. *Journal of Learning Disabilities, 22,* 169–175.

Siegel, E. (1974). *The exceptional child grows up.* New York: E. P. Dutton.

Silver, L. B. (1988). A review of the Federal Government's Interagency Committee on Learning Disabilities report to the U.S. Congress. *Learning Disabilities Focus, 3*(2), 73–80.

Smith, J. O. (1988). Social and vocational problems of adults with learning disabilities: A review of the literature. *Learning Disabilities Focus, 4*(1), 46–58.

Smith, S. L. (1988). Masking the feeling of being stupid. *Pointer, 32*(3), 18–22.

Spreen, O. (1988). Prognosis of learning disability. *Journal of Consulting and Clinical Psychology, 56,* 836–842.

Straughn, C., & Colby, M. (1985). *Lovejoy's college guide for the learning disabled.* New York: Simon & Schuster.

Wiig, E., & Harris, S. (1974). Perception and interpretation of nonverbally expressed emotions by adolescents with learning disabilities. *Perceptual and Motor Skills, 38,* 239–245.

Wilhardt, L., & Sandman, C. A. (1988). Performance of nondisabled adults and adults with learning disabilities on a computerized multiphasic cognitive battery. *Journal of Learning Disabilities, 21,* 179–185.

Will, M. (1984). *OSERS programming for the transition of youth with disabilities: Bridges from school to working life.* Washington, DC: United States Department of Education.

Zetlin, A. G., & Hosseini, A. (1989). Six post-school case studies of mildly learning handicapped young adults. *Exceptional Children, 55,* 405–411.

Zigmond, N., & Thornton, H. (1985). Follow-up of postsecondary age learning disabled graduates and drop-outs. *Learning Disabilities Research, 1,* 50–55.

Part 2
Theory

7
Neuropsychological Theories of Learning Disabilities

W. GRANT WILLIS, STEPHEN R. HOOPER, and BRENDA H. STONE

The concept of a learning disability has a long history, but it has been over only the past three decades that this concept has seen a steady proliferation of research investigating its associated neuropsychological factors (Hooper & Willis, 1989; Rourke, 1985). One major research trend emerging from these efforts is that a learning disability is now considered a generic classification that represents a heterogeneous group of disorders. This trend already has been incorporated into the most recent attempts to define this phenomenon, with a major emphasis being placed on known or suspected neurological aspects. Empirical support for this conceptualization has begun to emerge from multiple levels of analysis, including findings obtained from behavioral, physiological, and anatomical studies (Hiscock & Kinsbourne, 1987).

The conceptual and empirical neuropsychological basis of learning disabilities has facilitated productive contemporary thought about this group of disorders. Currently, several neuropsychological models of learning disabilities have been proposed. These models are valuable because they provide frameworks for guiding future research efforts and current clinical practices. This chapter reviews the neuropsychological basis of learning disabilities, discusses selected neuropsychological models that have been advanced from this perspective, and outlines associated conclusions in terms of their implications for research and practice.

Neuropsychological Basis of Learning Disabilities

It is clear that neuropsychology plays a prominent role in contemporary thinking about learning disabilities (Gaddes, 1985; Hooper & Willis, 1989; Hynd, Connor, & Nieves, 1988; Knights & Bakker, 1976), but the neuropsychological basis of learning disabilities conceptually is rooted in its historical foundation. In addition, those definitional issues discussed in chapter 1 that currently plague the diagnosis of learning disabilities have contributed to contemporary conceptualizations.

Empirical research that addresses the neuropsychological basis of learning disabilities strengthens the conceptual understanding of this group of disorders. This research now has been conducted at a variety of levels of analysis, each of which addresses different constructs and uses different methods. This section reviews the neuropsychological basis for learning disabilities from conceptual and empirical perspectives.

Conceptual Basis

The chronicle of learning disabilities includes early attempts to accumulate case-study data for individuals afflicted with various kinds of learning problems. Several such attempts are found in medical literature (e.g., ophthalmology journals) that is well over a century old. These early attempts provided information from which several theories were advanced. Although most of these theories no longer are tenable, they served an important purpose by helping to establish a conceptual basis for learning disabilities.

Early Case Studies

Kirk (1963) generally is recognized as coining the term *learning disability*, but the study of individuals with specific learning difficulties has a clinical and research legacy dating back more than 100 years. At that time, several investigators presented case-study data depicting learning problems of a specific nature. Kussmaul (1877) was among the first scientists to report a patient who, although having no visual impairment, was unable to read words. Later, Hinshelwood (1895) described two adult cases and, subsequently, two child cases (Hinshelwood, 1900, 1902). Despite similar referral concerns, all of these patients manifested a relatively different set of symptoms. In comparing these cases, Hinshelwood was perhaps the first investigator to recognize the heterogeneity of specific learning difficulties and to assert the importance of a thorough assessment in delineating differences among such cases.

Morgan (1896) was among the first to describe an adolescent case with specific learning problems. He reported that after 7 years of instruction, a 14-year-old boy could read only letters and single syllables. The adolescent's writing to dictation also was poor. In 1898 Bastian described another adolescent with similar symptoms. Despite adequate speech and language skills, athletic prowess, and good arithmetic skills, this 18-year-old boy consistently manifested word reversals in reading and severe deficiencies in spelling.

Other cases reported at the turn of the century further emphasized the heterogeneous nature of specific learning deficits, with several of these case reports postulating the presence of a familial component that was contributing to the learning difficulties (Fisher, 1905; Hinshelwood, 1909;

Stephenson, 1905). Jackson (1906) was among the first from the United States to contribute to this evolving literature. He described two additional cases and noted a greater frequency of specific reading problems among males than females.

Given these early case reports, a knowledge base about specific learning problems (i.e., reading) was beginning to be established by the early 1900s. By this time, accumulated data suggested that learning disabilities: (a) were present in children, adolescents, and adults with relatively intact cognitive functions, (b) occurred more frequently among males than females, (c) were heterogeneous in terms of symptom manifestation, differentially affecting reading, spelling, and higher order cognitive functioning, (d) were generally unresponsive to traditional learning opportunities and instructional settings, (e) appeared to have a familial component, and (f) required a comprehensive clinical assessment for accurate diagnosis (Hooper & Willis, 1989).

Although most of these early case studies suggested that learning problems were heterogeneous in nature, nearly all of the research that followed primarily focused on single-factor theories. These theories, most of which stemmed from the work of Orton (1928, 1937), sought to identify a single deficient process that contributed to the learning problem. These studies often contributed to a multitude of disparate explanations for these disorders.

Single-Factor Theories

Although many works have been devoted to single-factor theories (e.g., Satz, Rardin, & Ross, 1971), as well as other chapters in this volume, three of the most prominent theories are noted here: (a) delayed development in cerebral dominance (Orton, 1928, 1937; Satz et al., 1971), (b) visual–perceptual deficits (Frostig, 1964; Kephart, 1971; Lyle & Goyen, 1968, 1975), and (c) auditory–perceptual deficits and associated language inefficiencies (de Hirsch, Jansky, & Langford, 1966; Stanovich, 1988a). Of course, other single-factor theories also have evolved. Some link learning disabilities to poor intersensory integration (Birch & Belmont, 1964, 1965), others to poor or inefficient attention (Dykman, Ackerman, Clements, & Peters, 1971; Hynd, Obrzut, Hynd, & Connor, 1978), and still others to deficient memory skills (Brainerd, Kingma, & Howe, 1986; Cohen & Netley 1981; Nelson & Warrington, 1980; Torgesen, 1988).

Delayed Cerebral Dominance

Although the case-study approach provided support for the notion of learning disabilities, it was not until 1928 that a theoretical basis for learning problems was advanced. Orton (1928, 1937), using an objective approach to assessment, described children who exhibited difficulties with letter sequences, letter differentiation, and letter juxtapositions. Orton attributed these difficulties to a neurodevelopmental failure in establishing cerebral dominance. Based on his clinical observation that there was a higher incidence of reading problems in children with mixed handedness, Orton proposed that the left cerebral hemisphere failed to achieve functional superiority in these children. In turn, Orton stated that this was directly related to deficiencies in information processing, ultimately leading to problems in reading.

Although not without merit, Orton's theory was oversimplified and illogically founded (see Corballis & Beale, 1983), and his concept of incomplete (or delayed) cerebral dominance now has been refuted empirically (Benton, 1975; Kinsbourne & Hiscock, 1981). Instead, more complex theories of learning problems have emerged from hemispheric studies using dichotic-listening and visual-half-field paradigms (McKeever & Van Deventer, 1975; Witelson & Rabinovitch, 1972; YeniKomshian, Isenberg, & Goldstein, 1975). In fact, Thomson (1984) outlined five different research models that have emerged since Orton's original work. These are: (a) a lack of left hemisphere specialization for language abilities, (b) the concept of maturational delays in cerebral specialization, (c) impairment in the left hemisphere, (d) interference of the right hemisphere with the development of the left, and (e) inefficient interhemispheric integration. Several of these lines of research have been challenged, but Orton's theory was seminal in stimulating more than 50 years of scientific investigations.

Visual–Perceptual Deficits

Closely related to Orton's delayed cerebral dominance model were several theories implicating deficits in visual–perceptual abilities (Bender, 1956, 1957; Frostig, 1964; Hermann, 1959; Kephart, 1971). Bender (1956, 1957) implicated poor figure–ground visual perception in reading deficits whereas Kephart (1971) and Frostig (1964) proposed that faulty visual–motor integration was the underlying cause. Hermann (1959) believed higher order visual–spatial processing deficits primarily were responsible for the learning difficulties, but added an interesting speculation that these specific deficits were genetically based.

Initially, considerable support was generated for these visual–perceptual theories (Lyle, 1969; Lyle & Goyen, 1968, 1975). Additional support came from longitudinal investigations searching for precursors of learning disabilities (Satz, Taylor, Friel, & Fletcher, 1978). For example, data from the Florida Longitudinal Project (Satz et al., 1978) suggested that deficits in visual–perceptual and visual–motor functioning, particularly during kindergarten and the early primary grades, were the best predictors of later learning problems. Other studies advanced the notion that disabled learners showed faulty eye movements, particularly during reading. These studies claimed that reading disabled children had eye movements that were erratic and brief (Bouma & Legein, 1977) with excessive fixations (Pavlidis, 1978; Pirozzolo & Rayner, 1978), regressions (Elterman, Abel, Daroff, Dell'Osso, & Bornstein, 1980), and return-sweep inaccuracies (Pirozzolo, 1979). Still other studies, however, failed to replicate these findings (e.g., Brown et al., 1983).

A number of investigators suggested that visual–perceptual deficits were not the sole cause of learning problems (Benton, 1975; Nielson & Ringe, 1969; Vellutino, 1978). In addition to significant methodological concerns for much of this research in general, Vellutino noted that many visual–perceptual problems in both younger and older poor readers were secondary to deficiencies in verbal–mediation strategies. Exclusive of Pirozzolo's (1979) work with eye movement patterns, the visual–perceptual deficit model was unable to account for the multiple deficits found in many learning disabled individuals.

Auditory–Perceptual/Language Deficits

Auditory–perceptual deficiencies and language deficits also have been linked to poor reading (Goldberg & Schiffman, 1972; Henry, 1975; Mann & Brady, 1988; Stanovich, 1988a) and deficient spelling (Clark, 1970; Silver, 1968; Valtin, 1973). For example, Curtiss and Tallal (1988) have suggested that reading disabled children had poorer auditory perception, and that this adversely affected the development of phonic skills, efficient auditory processing, and, ultimately, reading performance.

Extending the basic auditory–perceptual deficit theories to understanding learning disabilities, other investigators have discovered deficits in the related domains of language abilities and linguistic competence. Vellutino (1979) and associates (Vellutino, Steger, DeSetto, & Phillips, 1975; Vellutino, Steger, Kaman, & DeSetto, 1975), for example, presented evidence using verbal and nonverbal learning tasks consistent with the idea that reading disabled children have primary difficulties in verbal learning, verbal abstraction, and generalization of verbal information. Blank and Bridger (1964, 1966) obtained similar findings in their work with disabled readers and verbal classification more than 25 years ago. Phonological deficits also have been proposed as being responsible for learning and reading impediments (Denckla & Rudel, 1976a, 1976b; Fox & Routh, 1980; Montgomery, 1981; Shankweiler & Liberman, 1972; Stanovich, 1988a) as have other linguistic factors such as syntactic competence (Wiig, Semel, & Crouse, 1973), semantic knowledge (Waller, 1976), and the use of one's internal lexicon (Ellis & Miles, 1981).

This theory continues to be prominent in the field of learning disabilities; however, other investigators have challenged these results (Hammill & Larsen, 1974; Richardson, DiBenedetton, & Bradley, 1977). Similar to the criticisms raised against all single-factor theories, it is clear that the auditory–perceptual/language deficit theories do not account for all of the psychoeducational problems manifested by deficient learners.

Criticisms

As can be surmised, none of these single-factor theories has been able to explain the broad spectrum of learning deficiencies that can be manifested. In fact, as the number of single-factor theories and, more recently, multiple-factor theories (e.g., subtyping) has increased, several investigators have proposed that the search for specific underlying causes is too simplistic, given the complexities of the central nervous system (Hynd et al., 1988; Hynd & Hynd, 1984; Olson, Kliegl, & Davidson, 1983; Olson, Kliegl, Davidson, & Foltz, 1985). Olson et al. (1983, 1985), for instance, proposed that differences among learning disabled individuals are distributed continuously rather than distinctly, as would be characteristic of subtypes.

Olson et al. (1985) found individual differences to be present both within and between groups of normal and disabled readers. These investigators also noted that phonological skill level was related significantly to reading style in disabled readers, a finding not characteristic of normal controls. Further, these investigators stated that specific reading problems were attributed to particular situations at designated points of performance on multiple dimensions. This suggests that learning disabilities not only reflect continuous variability but also are dynamic, a finding supported by Spreen and Haaf (1986). Similarly, Hynd et al. (1988) reasoned that, conceptually, each individual case could display a qualitatively different profile of specific neurolinguistic abilities depending on where a specific functional system was disrupted.

This case-study methodology has been advocated for developing individualized treatment programs (Raim & Adams, 1982; Wilson & Baddeley, 1986). Raim and Adams stated that "a case study can help to clarify for the student the puzzling contradictions and the range of irregularities that characterize the learning disabled child" (p. 116). Case studies also support Salvia and Ysseldyke's (1981) "ecology of the child" in the development of appropriate treatment alternatives. Although the case-study approach requires further refinement, the concept of a continuum of cognitive processes is an interesting one because it suggests that subcategorization of variables may be artificial, equivocal, and, ultimately, less useful in diagnosis and treatment.

Summary

Early case studies and single-factor theories (as well as progress in refining definitions) have provided a foundation for conceptualizing learning disabilities multidimensionally from a neuropsychological perspective. Each of the single-factor theories gained some limited support, but none was able to explain satisfactorily the full range of problems presented by individuals with learning impediments. It is likely that each of these single-factor theories addressed a specific dysfunctional component or, perhaps, neurological substrate in the learning process and, from that perspective, contributed to an improved understanding of that functional system and its interactive complexities. The clinical presentation of many of the early case studies, and the sheer number of single-factor theories, provided a good foundation for multidimensional investigations of learning disabilities. This foundation began to be forged with the emergence, through case studies, of syndromes directly related to specific learning problems and, as discussed in chapter 1, continues to be emphasized in the most recent definition of learning disabilities (Interagency Committee on Learning Disabilities, 1987), a definition that also clearly acknowledges the presumed neurological basis of these disorders.

There are many challenges (e.g., definitional issues, operational diagnostic criteria) that must be addressed if the study of this group of disorders is to persevere and improve. In particular, the Regular Education Initiative, which advocates a new service-delivery system based on individual needs of students, has been seriously questioned about general guidelines for evaluating, identifying, and treating learning disabled students (Lerner, 1987). Even so, it has forced the learning disability field to examine its own history and current status, and to recognize the many problems confronted by this field (see Association for Children and Adults with Learning Disabilities, 1986; McCarthy, 1987; Reynolds, Wang, & Walberg, 1987; Will, 1986). The status of the field currently appears to be in flux, if not in jeopardy, given the Regular Education Initiative, and it is unclear what directions will emerge from this proposed legislative challenge.

Empirical Basis

Currently, empirical support for the neuropsychological basis of learning disabilities is accumulating to strengthen the conceptual understanding of this group of disorders. At the behavioral level, perceptual and cognitive abilities have been measured using dichotic listening, visual–half-field, and dichaptic procedures (Hannay, 1986; Jeeves & Baumgartner, 1986). Although not reviewed here, these abilities also have been measured using time-sharing paradigms (Kinsbourne & Hiscock, 1983). Analysis at the physiological level, which is designed to measure brain functioning, has included electrophysiological measures, regional cerebral blood flow, and positron emission tomography (Hynd & Willis, 1988). The measurement of neuroanatomical structure has been accomplished by procedures such as computed tomography, magnetic resonance imaging, and autopsy. Although neuropsychological models of learning disabilities require synthesis (but not necessarily congruence) across all of these levels of analysis, inappropriate generalizations of research from one level of analysis to another should be avoided. For example, neuroanatomical structure should not be inferred from behavioral data because errors of this kind can lead to inaccurate conclusions. To date, most of the empirical research on learning disabilities has been conducted in the area of developmental dyslexia, and a review follows that is organized according to level of analysis.

Behavioral Level of Analysis

Hemispheric lateralization has been an important concept in the study of learning disabilities ever since Orton (1928, 1937) suggested that severe reading disability was due to incomplete cerebral dominance. Although Orton's original ideas about progressive lateralization received minimal empirical support, they did stimulate a great deal of research on the relationship between cerebral lateralization and learning disabilities. Most of the work with children has used noninvasive behavioral procedures (i.e., dichotic listening, visual-half-field, dichaptic procedures). The premise of these procedures is that measured perceptual asymmetries reflect underlying hemispheric asymmetries.

Dichotic Listening

The dichotic-listening procedure involves presenting different auditory stimuli simultaneously to each ear. Because most of the fibers in the auditory system are contralateral, information presented to the left ear projects first to the right hemisphere, and information presented to the right ear projects first to the left hemisphere. The right-ear advantage (REA), which is found in most children, is considered indicative of a left hemisphere dominance for language (Obrzut, Hynd, Obrzut, & Leitgeb, 1980). In the 1970s, dichotic-listening tasks were used to examine groups of learning disabled children who were thought to be incompletely lateralized. Results of several early studies were equivocal. A few found a REA for learning disabled children (Bryden, 1970; Leong, 1976; Yeni-Komshian, Isenberg, & Goldstein, 1975) whereas others found no significant perceptual asymmetry for the learning-disabled group (Witelson & Rabinovich, 1972; Zurif & Carson, 1970). Not only were results of these studies inconclusive, but many had methodological problems, some drew inappropriate conclusions, and very few tested for differences in the REA between normal and disabled groups (Satz, 1976).

The dichotic-listening procedure also has been used to examine ear asymmetry as a function of age. Satz et al. (1971) found that both younger and older reading disabled and normal children had a significant REA, but the REA was significantly greater in the older, normal reading group. These investigators concluded that the brain becomes more functionally lateralized with age, but at a slower rate in disabled readers. In general, these findings have not been confirmed. Other studies that compared the performance of learning disabled and normal children at different ages found no changes in ear asymmetry that could be attributed to development (Hynd, Obrzut, Weed, & Hynd, 1979; Obrzut et al., 1980). These studies also found no difference in degree of cerebral lateralization between learning disabled and normal children.

Morris, Bakker, Satz, and Van der Vlugt (1984) stated that results of studies that originally were used to infer lateralization also could be interpreted as supporting the view that learning disabled children use different cognitive strategies and may have differences in selective attention. Their rationale for this inference was that there are both theoretical and methodological problems in much of the dichotic-listening research. For example, reanalysis of the same data sample can provide support for many different hypotheses. Moreover, components of the dichotic-listening paradigm, such as stimulus materials (e.g., multiple digits, CV combinations, word pairs), number of stimulus pairs presented at each trial, number of trials, rate of presentation, and kind of response required (e.g., free recall, directed), differed from study to study, making comparisons between studies difficult and adversely affecting reliability (see also Segalowitz, 1986). Other problems are related to statistical design and analysis. For example, definitions of what constitutes a REA are unclear (i.e., significant differences usually are not addressed), inappropriate task difficulty may result in floor or ceiling effects, and subject selection (e.g., age, gender, handedness, definition of learning disabilities) often is inconsistent across studies. Finally, according to Morris et al., a significant problems with most dichotic-listening studies is the use of cross-sectional rather than longitudinal data to support development models. Morris et al. concluded that the free-recall dichotic-listening paradigm is not recommended for use with children.

Obrzut, Hynd, Obrzut, and Pirozzolo (1981) used a directed-attention condition to help control for attentional biases and the use of strategies. Based on their findings, these investigators suggested that learning disabled children may, in fact, have attentional deficits. More importantly, these children may have problems with the simultaneous processing of verbal information. It was speculated that this simultaneous-processing deficiency may be related to defects associated with the corpus callosum. Of course, this kind of speculation (i.e., inferring anatomical structure from behavioral data) must be viewed cautiously.

Visual–Half-Field and Dichaptic Procedures

Visual–half-field and dichaptic procedures also have been used to investigate hemispheric asymmetry in learning-disabled children. The visual–half-field technique involves using a tachistoscope to present stimuli to either the right visual field (RVF) or to the left visual field (LVF). Because information is transmitted contralaterally, stimuli perceived in the RVF are projected to the left cerebral hemisphere, and vice versa. As with the dichotic-listening research, however, results of investigations using lateralized tachistoscopic presentations have been equivocal. For example, Marcel, Katz, and Smith (1974) used a tachistoscope to present words to either the LVF or the RVF (i.e., unilateral presentation) and found a significant RVF asymmetry (i.e., left hemisphere) in both good and poor readers. The asymmetry, however, was more pronounced in the good readers. The authors concluded that the learning disabled children processed linguistic stimuli more symmetrically than the normal children. In other words, functional cerebral lateralization appeared less well established for the learning disabled children.

Kershner (1977) found similar results in a study with gifted, average, and dyslexic readers. He used a bilateral presentation procedure (i.e., stimuli presented simultaneously to both the RVF and the LVF). All three groups had a significant RVF advantage; however, the gifted and average readers demonstrated significantly more asymmetry than the dyslexic group. In both the Marcel et al. (1974) and Kershner studies, words within a visual field were presented horizontally. For this reason, an alternative to the deficient cerebral lateralization explanation could be associated with the use of inefficient scanning and encoding strategies by the deficient readers.

Yeni-Komshian et al. (1975) presented numerals and vertically oriented words to both average and deficient readers. The deficient readers actually showed a larger RVF advantage than the average readers for both numerals and words. The reason for this unusual result, however, was that the deficient readers showed larger left–right discrepancies than the average readers. The two groups did not differ significantly on the RVF scores; the major difference between the groups was found on the LVF scores. Deficient readers had more difficulty with stimuli projected to the right visual cortex. These investigators suggested the possibilities that either deficient readers suffer from a processing deficit in the right hemisphere or transmission of information from the right to the left hemisphere is inefficient or degraded. The results of this study suggest the potential importance of the right hemisphere in the reading process.

Witelson (1976, 1977) combined visual–half-field and dichaptic procedures to investigate differences in hemispheric specialization for spatial functions between good and poor readers. The dichaptic procedure involves tactual stimulation. In this study the subjects were required to feel two different nonsense shapes simultaneously for 10 seconds, one with each hand, and then to identify the shapes from a visual display. The visual–half-field task required the subjects to view two pictures of people, presented unilaterally, and to determine whether the pictures were the same or different. Witelson also used a dichotic-listening paradigm to investigate linguistic functioning. She concluded that poor readers had the typical pattern of left hemisphere representation of linguistic functions, normal readers had the expected right hemisphere specialization for spatial processing, but poor readers might have had a lack of right hemisphere specialization for spatial processing or might have had bilateral spatial processing. Witelson speculated that this bilateral involvement might have interfered with the left hemisphere's processing of its own specialized functions (e.g., linguistics).

Pirozzolo and Rayner (1979) presented words and faces tachistoscopically to the left and right hemispheres of normal and disabled readers. Both average and disabled readers showed a right hemisphere advantage for face recognition. Although the average readers recognized words presented to the RVF (i.e., left hemisphere) with greater accuracy than those presented to the LVF (i.e., right hemisphere), the disabled readers did not show this asymmetry. The results of this study did not support Witelson's (1976, 1977) hypothesis that disabled readers have bilaterally represented spatial functions.

Visual–half-field studies have had many of the same methodological problems as dichotic-listening studies (Segalowitz, 1986; Young & Ellis, 1981). According to Segalowitz, measurement error is likely to be high in most lateralization tasks, and the tasks themselves may not discriminate to an appropriate degree. Comparisons among studies are difficult because of varying task components (e.g., control of fixation, stimulus materials, kind of response). Subject selection is probably the major problem of any research dealing with a learning disabled population. As discussed in chapter 1, the term *learning disability* has many definitions. Even when the population is narrowed to dyslexia, various definitions are used. Research supporting the existence of specific subtypes of dyslexia further complicates the matter (Hooper & Willis, 1989). These varying definitions also make comparisons among studies difficult because the similarity of learning disabled groups is questionable.

Conclusions

Despite the methodological problems with the perceptual asymmetry research, conclusions have been reached and new directions have been established. Based on research at the behavioral level of analysis, the conclusions that can be drawn are that there is little evidence supporting a deficient pattern of cerebral lateralization for learning disabled children. There also is little support for the idea that these children are developmentally delayed in lateralization. More likely, discrepancies in perceptual asymmetries might be due to differences in attention, memory, and the use of strategies (Corballis & Beale, 1983; Hiscock & Kinsbourne, 1982; Morris et al., 1984; Obrzut et al., 1981; Watson &

Engle, 1982; Young & Ellis, 1981). Obrzut et al. also speculated that asymmetries may have a neuroanatomical basis. More carefully controlled behavioral studies might help to clarify the neuropsychological mechanisms inherent in learning disability, but analyses at the physiological and anatomical levels are needed for a more accurate indication of how these mechanisms work.

Physiological Level of Analysis

The physiological level of analysis allows a more direct assessment of brain activity and bypasses the need for many of the assumptions that are made at the behavioral level (Springer & Deutsch, 1985). Electrophysiological measures have been used in an attempt to differentiate learning disabled from normal individuals. These measures include the electroencephalogram, which is a continuous recording of brain activity; the measurement of event-related potentials, which uses a signal-averaging paradigm; and the probe event-related potential method, which combines the major advantages of the electroencephalogram and event-related potential (Languis & Wittrock, 1986). Other physiological measures that have been used include regional cerebral blood flow and, to a limited extent, positron emission tomography.

Electrophysiological Measures

Electroencephalogram (EEG). According to Galin (1989), EEG work with the reading disabled population has been hampered by three problems, the first two of which are similar to the problems encountered at the behavioral level of analysis. First, comparison of results across studies is difficult because of differing definitions of the subject population. Second, the assessment of dysfunctional reading is difficult because many strategies are involved in reading and investigators are not sure how normal children and adults actually read. Finally, investigators are unsure of the functional significance of EEG variables.

In 1978, Hughes reviewed 10 EEG studies of dyslexics and reported a high frequency of abnormalities (ranging from 27 to 88%). In a critique of this review, however, Conners (1978) questioned whether, with such a wide range of abnormality, the terms *abnormality* and *dyslexia* could have the same meaning across studies. He also noted that kinds of abnormalities differed from study to study; epileptic spikes were found in some studies, slow waves in others. One of Conners's most interesting findings was the fact that the correlation between the percentage of abnormalities found in the dyslexics and the date when the study was published was $-.91$. Conners interpreted this finding to mean that earlier studies included subjects with problems other than reading disability.

More recent studies have examined potentially subtler electrophysiological differences between normal and learning disabled children (e.g., differences in coherence, patterns of activation, evoked potential features) (Galin, 1989). John et al. (1977) developed a procedure called neurometrics, in which principles of numerical taxonomy are applied to the analysis of EEG and event-related potentials (see also John, 1989). Using a large sample, John et al. reported that neurometric EEG measures discriminated between normal and learning disabled children. When Yingling, Galin, Fein, Peltznam, and Davenport (1986) applied the neurometrics procedure to a group of carefully screened dyslexics and a matched comparison group, however, the procedure did not discriminate between groups. These investigators concluded that dyslexia was not associated with the specific neurometric abnormalities found in a more heterogeneous learning disabled population.

Galin (1989) reported that many EEG studies have suffered from methodological flaws. These studies included children with frank neurological symptoms not related to dyslexia, used small samples, failed to correct for multiple significance tests, did not include independent cross-validation samples, and introduced an interdependence between bands by using relative-power rather than absolute-power spectra. Bradshaw and Nettleton (1983) stated that most EEG measures have not been adequately standardized. The techniques used, placement of electrodes, and kind of tasks vary from study to study. For this reason, Bradshaw and Nettleton argued that much EEG work necessarily is descriptive.

Using a carefully chosen sample of dyslexic children and normal comparison children, and resolving other methodological issues, Galin (1989) and his associates conducted a series of investigations to examine the relationship between EEG activity and dyslexia. Subjects were examined under three conditions: (a) at rest, (b) during an active task (i.e., block design and narrative speech), and (c) during oral and silent reading. In the at-rest condition, no difference was found between dyslexics and normal readers in either absolute delta or theta activity, suggesting that dyslexia was not associated with abnormal slowing. According to Galin (1989), previous studies had reported slow-wave activity in dyslexics. He argued that these earlier results were a statistical artifact of the relative-power measure.

In the active-task condition, the dyslexic children showed the same task-dependent asymmetry of EEG alpha as normal readers, indicating that anomalous patterns of hemispheric activation are not necessarily associated with dyslexia (Galin, 1989; Galin, Herron, Johnstone, Fein, & Yingling, 1988). Galin, Ornstein, Herron, and Johnstone (1982), however, cautioned that alpha is an indication of whether or not a particular brain region is actively engaged; it is not a measure of how well that region is performing. Moreover, Galin et al. (1988) emphasized that the amount of cytoarchitectonic disorganization necessary to disrupt normal amplitude and spectrum of the EEG is not known. Galin concluded that although EEG results indicated that dyslexics do not have abnormal patterns of lateralization, these results did not rule out the possibility of deficits that might affect competence.

In the reading condition, unexpected EEG differences between dyslexics and normal readers were found. These differences involved interactions between the two groups and kind of reading (oral or silent). EEG theta and low-beta power were higher during oral reading than during silent reading in both groups, but the change in power between oral and silent reading was significantly smaller for the dyslexic children. Additional analyses revealed that low beta was related to speaking and that theta was related to reading. The functional significance of theta and beta is not known, and the clinical significance of the EEG differences between normal and dyslexic readers is not understood. The results of this study, however, shed new light on the relationship between brain activity and reading disability.

Event-Related Potentials (ERPs). One advantage of the EEG is that it is a continuous measure and can be used to study ongoing activity in the brain; however, because the EEG is a continuous measure, changes that relate to the occurrence of specific events are difficult to detect (Springer & Deutsch, 1985). In order to make these changes visible, a computer is used to average the waveform records after repeated presentations of the same stimulus and an ERP is produced (Springer & Deutsch, 1985). The ERP includes a cluster of components (i.e., those that occur from about 100 to 500 msec after the stimulus) that are associated with the cognitive processing of the stimulus event (Languis & Wittrock, 1986). Waveforms are labeled by their latency in milliseconds after the onset of the stimulus and by their positive or negative electrical property.

Significant differences in the left temporal P300 waveform have been found between dyslexics and age-matched normal comparison subjects (Duffy, Denckla, Bartels, & Sandini, 1980; Duffy, Denckla, Bartels, Sandini, & Keissling, 1980). Although patterns of EEG activity did not differ during baseline conditions, the EEG activity of dyslexics and normals appeared to differ during reading and listening tasks, particularly in Broca's area, the left temporal region, Wernicke's area, and the angular gyrus. Johnstone et al. (1984) criticized the Duffy, Denckla, Bartels, Sandini, and Keissling study on several issues. The study examined silent, but not oral, reading and neither difficulty level nor handedness was controlled. In addition, a large number of statistical tests were performed on a small sample, obfuscating firm conclusions based on statistical significance.

Probe Event-Related Potentials (Probe-ERPs). Galin and Ellis (1975) developed the probe-ERP paradigm, combining the major advantages of the EGG and ERP methods. The probe-ERP involves the presentation of task-irrelevant probe stimuli (e.g., tone pips or light flashes) while the subject performs a primary cognitive task (Languis & Wittrock, 1986). The conclusions of the probe-ERP studies rely on the assumption that a brain region is less responsive to the probe stimulus when that region is engaged by a concurrent task (Johnstone et al., 1984). Languis and Wittrock (1986) cautioned that habituation to the probe stimuli is a potential problem with this technique and must be considered when interpreting results.

Johnstone et al. (1984) used the probe-ERP method to study dyslexic and normal readers and found differences in regional brain activity during reading. Dyslexics showed a significant amplitude decrease in the 250 to 350 msec range while reading difficult material, but the normal readers did not show this effect. The investigators also were able to identify ERP components that were sensitive to the different demands of oral and silent reading. Dyslexics showed greater asymmetry during oral than silent reading, but the controls showed the opposite effect. Johnstone et al. concluded that the probe-ERP method was effective in studying regional brain processes during reading and that their study had taken a step toward determining whether there are ERP features specific to dyslexics and specific to the reading process.

Regional Cerebral Blood Flow

Regional cerebral blood flow (rCBF) gives valid information about localized cortical activity during cognition (Maximilian, Prohovnik, Risberg, & Hakansson, 1978). This activity can be measured by monitoring the buildup and washout of inhaled ^{133}Xe gas in cerebral tissue (Pirozzolo & Papanicolaou, 1986). According to Pirozzolo and Papanicolaou, rCBF studies have shown differential hemispheric involvement in verbal and spatial tasks. This method has been used with a learning disabled population (Hynd, Hynd, Sullivan, & Kingsbury, 1987). Unfortunately, the invasive nature of the rCBF technique does not lend itself for use with children because it involves the inhalation of a radioactive isotope.

Investigations with reading disabled adults, however, have found interesting results. Here, rCBF was used to show that reading silently or orally activated different regions of the brain (Lassen, Ingvar, & Skinhoj, 1978); therefore, using the technique to localize dysfunction in dyslexia was a logical next step (Rumsey et al., 1987). Wood, Flowers, Naylor, and Felton (1988) studied rCBF during task activation in 50 adult dyslexics and 60 comparison subjects. Subjects listened to words and responded with a finger press if the words were exactly four letters long. Wood et al. found that activation in the region of the left temporal lobe was significantly greater for normals than for dyslexics. In contrast, activation in the region of the right angular gyrus was significantly greater for dyslexics than for normals.

Rumsey et al. (1987) measured rCBF under three task conditions in 14 male adults with severe developmental dyslexia and their comparison subjects. No group differences were found on a number-matching task. On a semantic classification task, however, the dyslexics showed an increased hemispheric asymmetry (i.e., left greater than right), and on a line orientation task, the dyslexics showed a reduced anteroposterior difference when compared to comparison subjects. The investigators concluded that the hemispheric asymmetry could be the result of less efficient processing of information or inadequate integration between the two hemispheres. The reduced anteroposterior difference may have been the result of frontal underactivation.

Huettner, Rosenthal, and Hynd (1989) examined rCBF patterns in normal adults during the reading of narrative text. Narrative text was used because the investigators contended that this task better reflected the cortical activity important in reading (e.g., semantic, pragmatic, emotional, and imagery components). Huettner et al. stated that rCBF studies that found left frontal or left perisylvian activation during reading used either single-word or semantic-recall tasks, which may not have activated all the neurocognitive processes used in reading (Maximilian et al., 1978; Rumsey et al., 1987; Wood, Taylor, Penney, & Stump, 1980). The results of this study indicated that there was bihemispheric involvement during the reading of narrative text. The investigators suggested that by systematically controlling various linguistic and semantic components of reading, it may be possible to derive a more accurate picture of the processes involved in fluent reading.

Hynd et al. (1987) used the narrative-text task to examine rCBF patterns in two adult men representing different subtypes of developmental dyslexia (i.e., surface and deep). For matched controls, a significant involvement of the right hemisphere was evident during the reading of the text. Both dyslexics had less significant degrees of metabolic change in rCBF during the activation task than normal comparison subjects. The investigators interpreted these results cautiously, however, because few subjects were involved and significant intrasubject variability tends to occur in blood flow studies.

Cerebral blood flow techniques are not without their problems. Springer and Deutsch (1985) noted that measuring blood flow is an indirect way of measuring cerebral metabolism. Blood flow may not be responsive enough to rapid variations in brain activity; techniques that measure the distribution of metabolic tracers may be needed to capture these variations. Additionally, rCBF techniques do not provide adequate information about subcortical structures; they give a two-dimensional measurement of three-dimensional activity (Bradshaw & Nettleton, 1983; Rumsey et al., 1987). Resolution also remains a problem that is inherent to these techniques.

Positron Emission Tomography

In contrast to rCBF, positron emission tomography (PET) is a technique that provides both improved spatial resolution and three-dimensional data by imaging localized metabolic activity (Bradshaw & Nettleton, 1983; Rumsey et al., 1987). Because PET is a relatively new technique, however, few studies have been conducted to investigate patterns of activity in the learning disabled population.

One of the few studies that has used PET to examine regional cerebral metabolic rates in dyslexics and normal adults was conducted by Gross-Glenn et al. (1988). Subjects participated in an oral word-reading task. Relative metabolic activity was significantly higher in the left periinsular cortex for the normal group than for the dyslexic group. Moreover, the normal group evidenced greater bilaterally symmetric metabolic activity than the dyslexic group, particularly in the region of the anterosuperior temporal cortex.

Although PET seems to hold promise for future research, there may be instances when it would not be the preferred procedure. PET does provide better spatial resolution than rCBF, but as Bradshaw and Nettleton (1983) noted, PET is less sensitive in temporal terms, requiring sustained measurements of more than 20 minutes. This length of time may lead to practice effects in cognitive laterality tasks. According to Bradshaw and Nettleton, the EEG is more discriminative than either rCBF or PET in temporal terms, whereas it is less discriminative than either in spatial terms (i.e., for temporal: EEG > rCBF > PET; but for spatial: EEG < rCBF < PET). Thus, depending on the task demands, rCBF may be a useful compromise.

Conclusions

As with the perceptual asymmetry research, conclusions and new directions also have been found at the physiological level of analysis. Once again, no support has been found for deficient patterns of lateralization in the learning disabled population; however, the possibility of structural damage not detected by electrophysiological measures has not been excluded. Patterns of cortical activity have been significantly different between normal and disabled readers during reading, although some of these results have been task-dependent (e.g., reading words vs. narrative text, silent vs. oral reading). Further research is needed in this area. Right hemisphere involvement in the reading process, which has emerged as a new direction at the behavioral level of analysis, also has received support at the physiological level. The possibility that dyslexics process information inefficiently or have inadequate integration between the two hemispheres also has received support.

Anatomical Level of Analysis

Inferences about neuroanatomy can be made from the results of behavioral and physiological studies, but the question of whether anatomical asymmetries are the basis for functional asymmetries still remains unanswered. Are learning disabilities related to some underlying neuroanatomical anomaly? Investigations at the anatomical level of analysis are needed to determine whether functional brain asymmetries have a structural basis.

Brain morphology can be investigated either post mortem or in the living brain. Neuroimaging techniques such as computed tomography (CT) and magnetic resonance imaging (MRI) are used to examine the living brain. A CT scan uses an x-ray beam and an array of detectors to calculate the densities of tissue in particular cross-sections of the brain. MRI does not use radiation, but instead uses radio waves and a strong magnetic field to generate cross-sectional images of the brain. Both neuroimaging methods have been used to examine brain structure in the learning disabled population.

Neuroimaging Studies

In an extensive review of neuroimaging studies, Hynd and Semrud-Clikeman (1989) stated that the results of CT and MRI investigations suggest that dyslexics have alterations in normal patterns of brain asymmetry. These alterations take the form of an increased incidence of symmetry in the region of the planum temporale (i.e., a region on the floor of the lateral sulcus) and parieto-occipital cortex. Hynd and Semrud-Clikeman concluded that these results provided limited evidence for a correlation with developmental dyslexia.

Hynd and Semrud-Clikeman (1989) considered the evidence to be limited partly because of the many methodological problems associated with the eight studies (seven CT and one MRI) that have been published since 1976. First, across studies, subjects were grouped according to different criteria (e.g., patterns of cerebral asymmetry or clincially defined subgroups). In some studies the grouping variable did not identify discretely different populations and in other studies it did not accurately characterize the dyslexic syndrome. Second, half of the studies had no comparison group. In studies that did have a comparison group, the ratio of comparison subjects to dyslexics varied greatly from study to study. It was questionable in some studies whether the comparison subjects actually represented the normal population. No clinic populations representative of other neurodevelopmental disorders were included, making it impossible to demonstrate that observed abnormalities in brain morphology were unique to dyslexia. Third, Full-Scale IQ was not reported for some studies. In other studies, some dyslexic subjects had IQs that fell below the normal range. Fourth, although handedness was reported in most studies, specific measures of handedness were not cited. Fifth, most of the studies required the dyslexic subjects to have normal intelligence and a 2-year delay in measured reading achievement. Tests used to measure reading, however, varied from study to study. In some cases the tests did not assess all components of reading, and in other cases reading tests with poor psychometric properties were used. Delays in reading achievement were not documented in some studies, and reading achievement was reported in grade-equivalent scores rather than standard scores in other studies. Sixth, in four of the seven CT studies the kind of scanner used was not mentioned. This is important because older scanners had slow scan times, poor resolution, and thick sections. Some studies were not specific about the scan sections that were examined. Finally, well controlled quantifiable procedures were not always used when evaluating the scans for brain morphology. When used, interrater reliability was not always high.

Despite these methodological problems, one consistent finding emerged. In six of the eight studies, the typical hemispheric asymmetry that favors the left planum temporale region was significantly diminished and there was an increased degree of symmetry in the parieto-occipital region (Hynd & Semrud-Clikeman, 1989). Of course, because these neuroimaging studies did not include comparison groups with a different clinical disorder, it is not possible to assert that this increased symmetry is unique to developmental dyslexia.

Post Mortem Studies

The relationship between brain morphology and developmental dyslexia also can be studied post mortem. Unfortunately, the evidence of neuropathology in developmental dyslexia is based on a small number of cases (Hynd & Willis, 1988). In 1968, Drake reported the first case of neuropathology associated with dyslexia. This report has been criticized, however, because of poorly described findings and because it was not clear whether a learning disability was the subject's primary problem (Hynd & Semrud-Clikeman, 1989; Hynd & Willis, 1988). For this reason, neuropathological evidence for dyslexia primarily is based on case studies reported by Galaburda and his associates (Galaburda & Eidelberg, 1982; Galaburda & Kemper, 1979; Galaburda, Sherman, Rosen, Aboitiz, & Geschwind, 1985). Even these studies, however, are not without problems. Hynd and Semrud-Clikeman reviewed the post mortem studies and noted the following methodological limitations: (a) the discrepancy between ability and reading achievement was not always well documented, making the diagnosis of dyslexia questionable, (b) reading achievement often was reported in grade-equivalent scores rather than standard scores, making comparisons with IQ difficult, (c) evidence of a language delay was not independently determined, (d) cases with diagnoses other than learning disability were not excluded, (e) randomly selected brains of normal learners were not included, and (f) gestational and developmental histories were not documented. One additional limitation concerns researcher expectancy. For example, these researchers not only knew the kinds of neurodevelopmental anomalies that might occur in a reading disabled population, but they also knew a priori that the brains under examination were from dyslexic subjects.

These methodological problems necessitate a cautious approach when evaluating the results of this post mortem research; however, several interesting findings have emerged. Consistent with the neuroimaging research, the post mortem studies suggested that symmetry in the region of the planum temporale and parieto-occipital cortex is found with significantly greater frequency than in the normal population (Hynd & Semrud-Clikeman, 1989). What is not known is whether this pattern of symmetry is unique to the dyslexic population. In fact, 25% of the standard autopsy population has symmetrical plana (Rosen, Sherman, & Galaburda, 1986). Because only about 6% of the population is dyslexic, this leaves a large percentage of nondyslexics with symmetrical plana. According to Rosen et al., symmetric plana may be one component necessary for dyslexia but additional factors also may be required. Including other clinical comparison groups in these studies would help to isolate patterns that are unique to developmental dyslexia (Hynd & Semrud-Clikeman, 1989).

Another interesting finding was bilateral disruption in the medial geniculate nucleus and posterior nucleus of the thalamus (Eidelberg & Galaburda, 1982; Galabruda et al., 1985). Because these nuclei may be related to language, Hynd and Semrud-Clikeman (1989) hypothesized that these nuclei might be involved in allocating and focusing resources on dichotic-listening tasks. Significant involvement of frontal regions bilaterally also was found (Galaburda et al., 1985). According to Hynd and Semrud-Clikeman, there is increasing evidence that the right anterior cortex is involved to a significant degree in a functional linguistic system; thus, the right hemisphere as well as the left may be involved in developmental dyslexia.

Conclusions

Analysis at the anatomical level has not provided definitive answers to the role neuroanatomy plays in learning disabilities. For example, it still is not known whether anatomical asymmetries found post mortem are the basis for functional asymmetries, largely because little was known about the functional asymmetries of subjects before death. What the anatomical research has provided is evidence that areas generally associated with language appear to be more symmetrical across hemispheres in the dyslexic than in the normal population. Support also has been found for involvement of the thalamus, supplementary motor area, and frontal lobes in the reading process.

Summary

Information from all three levels of analysis indicates that learning disabled individuals are neurologically different from non-learning disabled individuals. Although definitive answers have not yet been discovered, progress has been made in determining patterns of central nervous system dysfunction. Untenable theories (e.g., incomplete cerebral lateralization) have been discarded, and new hypotheses (e.g., differential patterns of cortical activation) have replaced them. Advances in technology should provide less invasive and more precise methods to investigate brain–behavior relationships at the anatomical and physiological levels. With improved selection of samples, inclusion of tasks that control for attentional biases and strategies, and use of more sophisticated designs, research at the behavioral level also has the potential to add significantly to our understanding of the neuropsychological basis of learning disabilities.

Neuropsychological Models of Learning Disabilities

The conceptual and empirical neuropsychological bases of learning disabilities provide a solid foundation from which to advance theoretical explanatory models for this group of disorders. Two of these models are discussed here. As noted previously, such models are important because they guide both research and clinical practice. For example, neuropsychological models of learning disabilities suggest differential hypotheses to be tested and clinical interventions to be attempted. In this section, two concepts that are fundamental to understanding neuropsychological models of learning disabilities (i.e., functional brain organization and functional systems) are introduced and two neuropsychological models are illustrated.

Fundamental Concepts

Functional Brain Organization

Perhaps one of the most influential neuropsychological models of cognitive processing was introduced by Luria (1970). He proposed a framework that comprises three basic functional units of the brain: (a) the subcortical, (b) the posterior cortical, and (c) the anterior cortical. Figure 7.1 shows the regions of the brain included in each of these units as well as the hierarchical organization of zones within the cortical units. Each unit is distinctive in terms of its differentiated function. There are extensive interconnections within and among units, however, and these interconnections provide the anatomical basis for the mutual

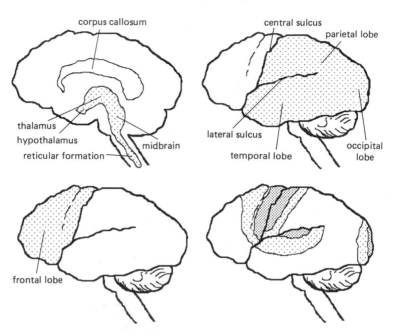

FIGURE 7.1. Luria's three functional units of the brain. *Top Left*: subcortical unit. *Top right*: posterior cortical unit. *Bottom left*: anterior cortical unit. *Bottom right*: hierarchical organization within cortical units (primary zones darkly shaded, secondary zones lightly shaded, tertiary zones unshaded cerebral cortex). Adapted with permission from Hynd, G. W., & Willis, W. G. (1988). *Pediatric neuropsychology* (p. 107). Orlando, FL: Grune & Stratton.

interdependence of the units. Each unit both influences and is influenced by the other units. Luria emphasized that all three units always are involved in the performance of any behavior, an assertion that markedly contrasts with a strictly localizationist perspective on neuropsychology.

Subcortical Unit

The subcortical unit of the brain (illustrated in the top left diagram of Fig. 7.1) functionally is specialized for the "maintenance of . . . [an] *optimal level of cortical tone* . . . essential for the organized course of mental activity" (Luria, 1973, p. 45). This functional concept, or *activating system* (Brodal, 1981), anatomically is associated with the brain stem reticular formation, which is a group of cells within regions of the medulla, pons, and midbrain. The morphological features of this functional unit implicate its role in all conscious and autonomic activity (Brodal, 1981; Luria, 1973) and support the notion that it is involved in the activation, inhibition, and regulation of the central nervous system. Its system of projection fibers serves to interconnect this unit of the brain with more superior (as well as inferior) neuroanatomical structures, again attesting to its mutual interdependence with the cortical units of the brain.

Posterior Cortical Unit

The posterior cortical unit of the brain (illustrated in the top right diagram of Fig. 7.1) functionally is specialized for the reception, analysis, and storage of information. The neuroanatomical substrate for this functional unit is the cortex of the parietal, occipital, and temporal lobes. Within this functional unit is a hierarchy of zones: primary, secondary, and tertiary (see the bottom right diagram of Fig. 7.1).

There is one primary zone within each of the three lobes of this unit, and each primary zone essentially is surrounded by a secondary zone. The major tertiary zone within this unit is demarcated by the area where all three lobes overlap, a region that corresponds to the angular gyrus. The functions of the primary and secondary zones within each lobe are limited to a particular modality. For example, zones within the parietal lobe functionally are specialized for the reception, analysis, and storage of kinesthetic and somatosensory information; zones within the occipital lobe for visual information; and zones within the temporal lobe for auditory information. In contrast, the tertiary zones function to synthesize this information across modalities.

More specifically, the primary (or projection) zones discriminate among stimuli and influence sensory reception to insure optimal perception. The secondary (or association, gnostic) zones, in contrast, are relatively more integrative and are adapted to relaying afferent impulses to tertiary zones for further synthesis. Thus, lesions of the primary zones frequently result in specific sensory deficits, whereas lesions of the secondary zones are likely to result in disorganized perceptions within and among complex groups of unimodal stimuli (Luria, 1970). Finally, the tertiary zones functionally are specialized to integrate stimuli across modalities. According to Luria (1973), this integrative function is associated with thinking abstractly and with memorizing information, both of which are cognitive processes that include converting successive stimuli into simultaneously processed groups. Thus, lesions of the tertiary zones of this unit are likely to disrupt simultaneous (i.e., holistic) cognitive processes (Luria, 1980).

Anterior Cortical Unit

The anterior cortical unit (illustrated in the bottom left diagram of Fig. 7.1) also comprises three hierarchical zones. In this case, however, it is the tertiary zones that guide the functions of the secondary and primary zones, rather than vice versa as with the posterior cortical unit. The tertiary zones of the anterior cortical unit of the brain functionally are specialized to "play a decisive role in the formation of intentions and programmes, and in the regulation and verification of the most complex forms of human behaviour" (Luria, 1973, p. 84). Such behavior includes speech and higher order cognitive processes, which are characterized partially by the successive synthesis of information. Secondary zones functionally are specialized to prepare motor programs and to organize movement, whereas the primary zones functionally are specialized to execute the most basic elements of motoric activity. The neuroanatomical substrate for this functional unit is the cortex of the frontal lobes.

Functional Systems

Clearly, the human central nervous system is highly specialized for function. This fact, however, often is misconstrued to suggest that particular regions of the brain operate independently. Currently, for example, there is an abundance of popular press literature that dichotomously characterizes the two cerebral hemispheres and suggests that individuals primarily may be *left-brained* or *right-brained*. Such literature renders a disservice to the discipline of neuropsychology by its oversimplification, and it is especially problematic when applied to treatments for individuals afflicted with learning disabilities. In addition to impeding progress in understanding brain–behavior relationships, this kind of misconstruction is inconsistent with the concept of a neuropsychological functional system that provides the substrates for behavior, a fundamental concept elaborated in detail by Luria (1980).

Thus, although even the neonatal brain is highly differentiated for function, the neural substrates for these functions correspond to systems of components rather than to discrete regions. These components operate interdependently toward a unified result. One approach to neuro-psychological evaluation is to investigate the integrity of functional systems by examining their component parts. In order to use this approach effectively, clinicians must be able qualitatively to analyze complex systems of behavior according to these individual components. Additionally, it often is useful to know the neuroanatomical bases for those components. This is a difficult task because there is less than an optimal research base.

Ontogenetic Issues

The problem of an inadequate research base is particularly true for child and adolescent populations. Moreover, especially for higher order cognitive processes such as spelling, arithmetic, and reading, relationships among components of functional systems may change developmentally. For example, during early stages of postnatal development, relatively direct and associative processes dominate. During later stages, however, more complex integration related to speech and higher order cognitive processes dominate.

On the basis of this cognitive developmental progression, Vygotsky (1960) was among the first to speculate that cerebral lesions that are associated with relatively basic sensory processes and that occur during early childhood adversely affect higher order cognitive functioning. This is because the foundation for the higher order cognitive functioning is disrupted. Similar lesions that occur during adulthood, however, are expected to have a much more circumscribed effect because the functional systems that subserve the higher order cognitive functions already are formed. Consequently, Vygotsky proposed that during early stages of development, cerebral lesions primarily disrupt hierarchically higher components of functional systems subserved by the affected region whereas during later stages of development, cerebral lesions primarily disrupt hierarchically lower components that may be regulated by the affected region. Vygotsky's hypothesis is a reasonable one, but there currently is limited empirical evidence to support it (Rutter, 1981).

On the basis of electrophysiological data, Valsiner (1983) also argued that relationships among components of functional systems may change developmentally. Supporting evidence was provided by Merola and Liederman (1985), who found that the degree to which conflicting portions of simultaneous tasks were processed separately by the cerebral hemispheres increased with age. Thus, although additional validating research is required, evidence is accumulating that suggests a dependent relationship between development and interactions among components of functional systems.

Even though its experiential basis was primarily established with adult patients, Luria's (1970) theory of functional brain organization provides a useful framework for conceptualizing potential brain–behavior relationships throughout the lifespan. Given the marked discontinuities in human development, however, a complete understanding of child and adolescent brain–behavior relationships, especially those that concern higher order cognitive functions, is not a simple matter of generalization from research with adult samples. Instead, additional research is required that evaluates established theories in consideration of these developmental discontinuities.

For example, the development of primary, secondary, and tertiary cortical zones follows an ontogenetic course. Based on morphological evidence, Luria (1980) suggested that primary cortical zones appear mature by birth, secondary zones by the first few months postnatally, and tertiary zones by the first few years postnatally. Within child and adolescent populations, however, specific functions subserved by the major units of the brain, especially the tertiary zones, are currently ill-defined.

Some preliminary findings have begun to surface, however, linking specific cognitive functions to selected aspects of neurodevelopment. Passler, Isaac, and Hynd (1985) and Becker, Isaac, and Hynd (1987) found evidence suggesting a developmental progression of behaviors associated with frontal lobe development in children from about ages 5 to 12 years. Using a similar methodology, Heverly, Isaac, and Hynd (1986) found a developmental progression in tactile–visual discrimination functions and associated parietal lobe development. Although these efforts are noteworthy, more research delineating specific structure–function linkages clearly is needed, particularly with respect to its application to learning disabilities.

Proposed Models

To date there have been few attempts to develop models that encompass the neuropsychological aspects of learning disabilities. Even so, there are two models that have been proposed to explain the phenomenon of learning problems. One of these models, the Wernicke–Geschwind model, has its origins in the neurological and neurolinguistic literature and largely is associated with specific reading disabilities. The other, Rourke's nonverbal learning disability model, has its origins in neuropsychology.

Wernicke–Geschwind Model

Luria (1980) considered reading (as well as writing) to be a special form of speech activity. According to this conception, the reading process begins with the visual perception and analysis of a grapheme. The grapheme is recoded to its phonemic structure, which subsequently is comprehended. The automaticity of this process varies as a function of development. Thus, during initial stages of reading, all of the operations noted are incorporated in a clear, serial fashion. During later stages, however, graphemes may come to elicit direct comprehension of written words or even entire phrases, essentially eliminating intermediate phonemic analysis and synthesis.

When the process of reading is considered in this fashion, a number of components of a substrate functional system are implicated. For example, Hynd and Hynd (1984) suggested that graphemes are registered in the occipital lobes where they are associated with known letters or words. This information then is shared with input from other sensory modalities in the region of the left angular gyrus. Linguistic–semantic comprehension of this multimodal integration of information may be subserved in the region of the planum temporale and Wernicke's area of the temporal lobe. Finally, the comprehended information potentially is communicated to Broca's area through the arcuate fasciculus, an

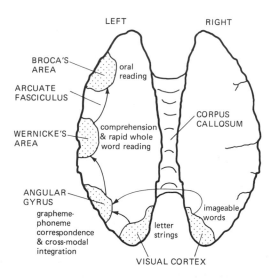

FIGURE 7.2. The brain as viewed in horizontal section illustrating the Wernicke–Geschwind neurolinguistic model of a functional system for reading. Adapted with permission from Hynd, G. W., & Hynd, C. R. (1984). Dyslexia: Neuroanatomical/neurolinguistic perspectives. *Reading Research Quarterly*, *19*, 482–498.

intrahemispheric band of connecting fibers. This putative functional system for reading, illustrated in Figure 7.2, is referred to as the Wernicke–Geschwind model (Mayeux & Kandel, 1985).

Based on this model, Hynd and Hynd (1984) hypothesized that particular subtypes of dyslexia (see Marshall, 1984) could follow from dysfunctions involving particular associated components and interconnections. For example, developmental surface dyslexia, which is characterized by an overreliance on phonological rules, may result from an impaired process in semantic access to what is read. This may be related to a disruption of pathways associated with Wernicke's area. Developmental phonological dyslexia, which is characterized by an inability to apply phonological rules, may be due to an impaired process in grapheme-to-phoneme conversions. This may be related to a disruption of pathways associated with the angular gyrus. Other subtypes of dyslexia also have been proposed based on this functional system, and specific treatment options have been suggested (Hynd, 1986).

Although there is limited empirical validation for the Wernicke–Geschwind model (Hynd et al., 1988), some supporting evidence has emerged from the electrophysiological, neuroimaging, and post mortem studies previously reviewed. Of these three kinds of studies, the post mortem studies perhaps provide the strongest support for this neural substrate. As already noted, however, these results are compromised by a number of methodological problems.

Additionally, Hynd and Semrud-Clikeman (1989) emphasized the obvious inconsistencies between this neurolinguistically based functional system and the neuropathological data. Although the Wernicke–Geschwind model stresses the involvement of the bilateral–posterior and left perisylvian cortices, evidence from the post mortem and neurometabolic studies implicates bilateral–frontal and left perisylvian cortical regions. Moreover, this model does not involve supplementary motor cortex or subcortical areas whereas data from electrophysiological and post mortem studies suggest that these regions may be part of the functional system for reading. Further, as noted earlier, the post mortem studies by Galaburda and colleagues (Galaburda & Eidelberg, 1982; Galaburda et al., 1985) suggested involvement of the medial geniculate nucleus and posterior nuclei bilaterally in the thalamus (see also Landau, Goldstein, & Kleffner, 1960). Given the purported relationship between these subcortical structures and the primary auditory and inferior parietal cortices (Kelly, 1985a, 1985b), these findings suggest linkages to the auditory linguistic deficits typically seen in developmental dyslexia (Hynd & Cohen, 1983; Sidtis et al., 1986).

The bilateral involvement of the anterior cortex also deserves mention, especially given the extensive afferent input that these regions receive from thalamic nuclei (e.g., medial–dorsal thalamic nucleus). These is accumulating evidence that these bilateral frontal regions also are involved in a functional linguistic system (Hynd & Semrud-Clikeman, 1989). Specifically, it has been proposed that the affective and paralinguistic features of language functionally are linked to the right frontal and central perisylvian cortices (Bhatnagar & Andy, 1983; Ross, 1985). The previously noted studies conducted by Hynd and colleagues (Hynd et al., 1987; Huettner et al., 1989) also have demonstrated considerably more involvement of the right central and posterior cortices during the reading of narrative text than would be predicted by the Wernicke–Geschwind model. The efficacy of a right hemisphere theory for reading deficits has been debated by Shallice (1988) as well.

Finally, given accumulating evidence that postulates a functional system for arithmetic (see Deloche & Seron, 1987; Hooper & Willis, 1989) that is quite similar to this putative functional system for reading and perhaps language as well, comparisons with other clinical subgroups are particularly important. For example, it is possible that these functional systems subserve a general cognitive–academic function (e.g., crystallized intelligence) and are not specific to particular academic processes. Such a hypothesis is supported by the relatively robust finding that general cognitive abilities (e.g., Full-Scale IQ) are among the strongest predictors of specific neuropsychological test performance (Hynd, Snow, & Becker, 1986; Hynd & Willis, 1988). Obviously, further research is needed to address these inconsistencies in the literature. It is clear, however, that the Wernicke–Geschwind model has contributed much toward advancing the understanding of learning disabilities.

Nonverbal Learning Disabilities Model

Rourke (1987, 1988b, 1989) has proposed what appears to be one of the first truly neuropsychologically based models for conceptualizing learning disabilities. This model is derived behaviorally as opposed to neurologically. It is based on selected aspects of a theory of differential hemispheric functioning advanced by Goldberg and Costa (1981). Relying primarily on data and speculative evidence derived from adult samples, Goldberg and Costa asserted that the right hemisphere is relatively more specialized for intermodal integration whereas the left hemisphere is more specialized for intramodal integration. Neuroanatomically, these investigators postulated that intramodal integration may be related to a higher ratio of gray matter (i.e., neuronal mass and short nonmyelinated fibers) to white matter (i.e., long myelinated fibers) characteristic of the left hemisphere, whereas intermodal integration may be related to the lower ratio characteristic of the right hemisphere.

Rourke (1987) modified this model by applying a developmental perspective and, given his previous findings with respect to learning disability subtypes (see Rourke, 1985), extended it to account for nonverbal learning disabilities. Rourke hypothesized that involvement of the white matter of the right hemisphere (i.e., lesioned, excised, or dysfunctional white matter) interacts with developmental parameters to result in nonverbal learning disabilities. He reasoned that although a significant lesion in the right hemisphere may be *sufficient* to produce a nonverbal learning disability, it is the destruction of white matter (i.e., matter associated with intermodal functions) that is *necessary* to produce these learning disabilities. Further, it is important to note that the white matter fibers are an integral part of the three principal neuraxes: commissural fibers (i.e., right-to-left interhemispheric connections), association fibers (i.e., anterior-to-posterior intrahemispheric connections), and projection fibers (i.e., superior-to-inferior connections).

Rourke (1988b) stated that the "integrity of white matter (i.e., long myelinated fibers) function would appear to be (a) necessary for the *development* of systems within both hemispheres, and (b) crucial for both the *development* ant the *maintenance* of those functions subserved primarily by systems within the right hemispheral systems, but (c) not necessary for the *maintenance* of some functions subserved primarily by systems within the left hemisphere" (p. 314, emphasis original). Generally, the nonverbal learning disability syndrome would be expected to develop under any circumstance that interferes significantly with the

TABLE   7.1. Neuropsychological,   academic,   and   social–emotional/adaptive characteristics of individuals with nonverbal learning disabilities.

Domain	Strengths	Weaknesses
Neuropsychological	Simple, repetitive motor functions Auditory perception Selective auditory attention Rote memory and learning Speech and language phonology, blending, and segmentation	Complex psychomotor functions (bilateral, but more prominent on left side) Tactile and visual perception Selective tactile and visual attention Exploratory and novel learning Tactile and visual memory Language pragmatics and paralinguistic skills
Academic	Reading decoding Spelling, with errors showing good phonemic equivalents Graphomotor functions (later in development	Reading comprehension Mechanical arithmetic Math reasoning Graphomotor functions (earlier in development) Academic subjects requiring novel problem solving and integration of information (e.g., science)
Social–Emotional/ Adaptive		Extreme difficulty adapting to new situations Social judgment Social perceptions Social interactions Prone to internalizing forms of psychopathology (e.g., depression)

Adapted with permission from Rourke, B.P. (1988). The syndrome of nonverbal learning disabilities: Developmental manifestations in neurological disease, disorder, and dysfunction. *Clinical Neuropsychologist*, *2*, 293–330.

functioning of right hemispheric functional systems or with access to those systems (e.g., agenesis of the corpus callosum). Functionally, the characteristics of such an individual, which Rourke noted should be observable by approximately ages 7 to 9 years (Rourke, 1988a; Rourke, Young, & Leenaars, 1989), implicate neuropsychological, academic, and social–emotional/adaptive domains. These characteristics are listed in Table 7.1.

Neuropsychologically, individuals with nonverbal learning disabilities tend to present a distinct profile of strengths and weaknesses. Relative strengths include auditory perception, simple motor functions, and intact rote verbal learning. Selective auditory attention, phonological skills, and auditory–verbal memory also appear intact. Neuropsychological deficits include bilateral tactile–perception problems and motor difficulties that usually are more marked on the left than on the right side of the body, visual–spatial organization problems, and nonverbal problem-solving difficulties. Paralinguistic aspects of language also are impaired (e.g., prosody, pragmatics). Academically, these individuals evidence adequate word decoding and spelling, with most misspellings being good phonetic equivalents. Graphomotor skills eventually appear age-appropriate, but are delayed early in development. Marked academic deficits tend to be manifested in mechanical arithmetic, mathematical reasoning, and reading comprehension. Academic subject areas such as science also tend to be impaired largely due to reading comprehension deficiencies and deficits in nonverbal problem solving.

Perhaps one of the most interesting aspects associated with this syndrome is that there appears to be a strong relationship with social–emotional and adaptive behavior deficits. These individuals present great difficulty adapting to novel situations and manifest poor social perception and judgment, which results in poor social interaction skills. There appears to be a marked tendency for these individuals to engage in social withdrawal and social isolation as age increases and, consequently, they are at risk for internalized (i.e., overcontrolled) forms of psychopathology. In fact, Rourke et al. (1989), Bigler (1989), and Kowalchuck and King (1989) all noted the increased risk that these individuals have for depression and suicide. Fletcher (1989) also noted that these disorders and behaviors could be attenuated, minimized, or perhaps even prevented by recognizing this syndrome and treating these individuals accordingly. Although these behaviors previously have been documented among children with learning disabilities (Gerber & Zinkgraf, 1982), their relationship with neuropsychological findings only recently has been asserted (Rourke, 1989; Spreen, 1989; Voeller, 1986; Weintraub & Mesulam, 1983). The emphasis placed on social–emotional functioning by this model also is consistent with the most recent definition of learning disabilities (Interagency Committee on Learning Disabilities, 1987) that implicates social skill deficits as major components in this group of learning disorders.

Rourke (1987) proposed this model as a first approximation of a developmental neuropsychological model for nonverbal learning disabilities. Given its neuroanatomical and neuropsychological bases, this model is noteworthy, particularly as it may contribute to conceptualizations of differential diagnosis and, perhaps, to issues of severity related to nonverbal learning disabilities. Further, the model has incorporated significant developmental components that address the timing of the disruption of the white matter and hypothesized outcomes. The model also provides a vehicle for studying how the syndrome might be manifested during adulthood. This latter developmental component is particularly insightful given the recent surge in activity devoted to the learning disabled adult (Spreen, 1987).

Summary

At present, the number of neuropsychological models proposed to understand learning disabilities is few, but the ones that have been proposed have been robust with respect to generating research. The Wernicke–Geschwind model has been useful in demonstrating the importance of language functions and linguistic processes to learning and learning problems, especially in the reading domain. The empirical findings associated with this model have been equivocal, however, and its localization perspective perhaps has presented an overly simplified view of the reading process. Even so, neurolinguistic models continue to provide productive findings and should continue to help guide clinical practice and research.

More recently, Rourke (1987, 1988b, 1989) proposed a model to understand another group of individuals with qualitatively different problems. His nonverbal learning disabilities model has its basis in the neuropsychological subtype literature and in a theory of hemispheric functioning that is neuroanatomically based. Given its emphasis on nonverbal learning disabilities, this model appears to contrast markedly against the Wernicke–Geschwind model. The hemispheric differences proposed by Goldberg and Costa (1981), however, actually suggest that this model may complement linguistic-based models, providing explanations for language-based deficiencies as well.

Although relatively new in comparison to the Wernicke–Geschwind model, this model appears to have good potential for understanding specific subgroups of learning disorders, with the present emphasis being on nonverbal learning disabilities. In addition, given its developmental orientation, it has the added advantage of attempting to understand this kind of learning disability throughout the lifespan. These developmental and neuroanatomical components, in tandem, place learning disabilities as well as other kinds of developmental disorders (e.g., autism) in a broader context. Its inclusion of an affective component is unique and also makes this model noteworthy. Although the ultimate utility of this model remains to be determined, it has provided the field of developmental neuropsychology with firm direction, particularly in regard to a comprehensive understanding of a specific kind of learning disability.

Despite meta-analytic findings of Kavale and Nye (1985/1986), which cite a lack of support for neuropsychological approaches to learning disabilities, these models illustrate the importance of a neuropsychological perspective in attempting to understand this heterogeneous group of disorders. The origins of these models seem to extend from apparently opposite, although by no means mutually exclusive, vantage points. For example, the Wernicke–Geschwind model originated in neurological bases of learning and subsequently incorporated functional aspects of learning. In contrast, the nonverbal learning disability model originated in functional neuropsychological syndrome analysis and subsequently incorporated the neurological bases of this syndrome. Considered collectively, these models provide strong rationale for investigating learning disabilities from a neuropsychological perspective. Further, both of these models have stimulated much activity and discussion in the literature regarding the heterogeneity of this group of disorders. Finally, as with all conceptual models in the clinical literature, their ultimate utility will rest in their contributions to etiology, prognosis, and treatment. Although both models have made strides in these directions, further research continues to be required.

Conclusions

The neuropsychological basis of learning disabilities has been firmly established both conceptually and empirically, and neuropsychological models have been proposed to help explain this heterogeneous group of disorders. The historical foundation for learning disabilities includes early case studies of these disorders as well as single-factor theories that attempted to account for associated symptoms. This foundation provides a solid conceptual basis for understanding learning disabilities multidimensionally from a neuropsychological perspective. As discussed in chapter 1, this conceptual basis has been recognized for many years in evolving definitions of learning disabilities, and now clearly is acknowledged in the most recent definition of these disorders.

Empirical research conducted at behavioral, physiological, and anatomical levels of analysis has strengthened this conceptual basis. Although this research is plagued by multiple methodological problems and has been overly focused on dyslexia, some interesting conclusions have been derived. For example, at a behavioral level of analysis, once-popular hypotheses suggesting that learning disabled individuals were deficient or developmentally delayed in terms of cerebral lateralization generally have not been supported. At a physiological level of analysis, patterns of cortical activity have differentiated dyslexics from normal readers, at least in some specific conditions, and the right cerebral hemisphere has been implicated in the reading process. At an anatomical level of analysis, brain regions associated with language have been shown to be more symmetrical across hemispheres in dyslexic than normal populations, and the thalamus and frontal lobes have been implicated in the reading process.

Currently, explanatory models of learning disabilities have been advanced from these conceptual and empirical neuropsychological bases. Luria's (1970, 1973, 1980) theories of functional brain organization and functional systems are fundamental to these neuropsychological models of learning disabilities because they provide useful frameworks for conceptualizing brain–behavior relationships more generally and throughout the lifespan. The two complementary models discussed (i.e., the Wernicke–Geschwind model and the nonverbal learning disability model) appear to be useful explanatory tools, and they should help to guide learning disabilities research and practice.

Implications

Given the marked discontinuities in human development, understanding brain–behavior relationships, particularly in children, truly is a complex matter. It is clear that there is no direct relationship between extent of brain impairment and behavioral deficit. Instead, this relationship is moderated by a variety of factors, some that are known or suspected, such as the age of the individual and the site of the lesion, and others that currently are unknown. Of course, in the case of learning disabilities, there usually are not definitive or classical neurological hard signs of brain impairment. Even so, the empirical research from behavioral, physiological, and anatomical levels of analysis reviewed here suggests a variety of sometimes subtle and sometimes frank indications of a presumed neurobiological substrate for this group of disorders. Clearly, a neuropsychological perspective on learning disabilities represents a viable conceptualization that carries implications for assessment, diagnosis, and treatment.

The consideration of a comprehensive and detailed neuropsychological profile for a learning disabled individual necessarily involves a thorough evaluation. The research conducted to date indicates that one must consider neurocognitive, linguistic, social–emotional, and academic factors in such an evaluation. Although research evidence is useful in delineating these factors, individual differences undermine broad generalizations. Each case must be investigated individually and thoroughly in order to establish the important links between diagnosis and prognosis and between prognosis and treatment.

Hynd et al. (1988) advocated that such a neuropsychological evaluation should reflect tasks constructed around a wide array of functions. Moreover, such an evaluation should include tasks on which the learning disabled individual performs poorly (e.g., linguistic). Hynd et al. also suggested that this evaluation should be flexible in order to address referral questions efficiently and to relate directly to the research that supports the heterogeneity of learning disabilities. It is important to recognize that the neuropsychological evaluation of individuals with learning disabilities should not occur in isolation. Clinicians who conduct these evaluations should be open to the possibility of interactive effects of other variables (e.g., social–emotional factors). Here, it is important for evaluations to include thorough histories and descriptions of learning problems, the circumstances under which they occur, and the concerns and expectations of all involved (e.g., parent, teachers, child). It is perhaps best that these kinds of evaluations occur within multidisciplinary frameworks.

Finally, Lyon, Moats, and Flynn (1988) noted that it is important to the ecological validity of evaluations that assessment strategies relate to specific suggestions for intervention. Longitudinal studies will be especially important to help establish these links. In contrast, however, Stanovich (1988b) cogently argued that methods used for learning disability diagnosis do not need to be directly related to educationally relevant interventions. Additionally, in emphasizing the importance of basic (as opposed to applied) research in the field of learning disabilities, Swanson (1988) asserted that it is not necessarily the case that investigations that lack ecological validity cannot contribute to ecologically valid theories of learning disabilities, including those that address treatment intervention (see also Kavale, 1988).

In conclusion, the most recent definition of learning disabilities places a heavy emphasis on underlying or presumed neurological dysfunction as a major contributor to this group of disorders. This perspective is supported by much of the evolving empirical research as well as by early case studies. Neuropsychological models provide a strong foundation from which to understand learning disabilities, and are consistent with a multidimensional perspective on these disorders. A neuropsychological orientation also facilitates conceptualizing learning disabilities within developmental parameters. Here, both qualitative and quantitative differences in learning patterns of younger and older children are acknowledged. Thus, it provides a foundation for the early prediction of learning disabilities. Moreover, it suggests reasons why some children seem to develop learning disabilities as they grow older and helps to explain a potential later emergence of a learning disability (e.g., perhaps during adolescence).

Rourke's (1987, 1988b, 1989) model of nonverbal learning disabilities is especially instructive because it addresses many of these issues. All models are important because they provide the basis for guiding future research as well as current practice. Continued refinement of neuropsychological theories of learning disabilities is required, of course, but it is clear that considering the relationship between neurological deficits or dysfunctions and potential learning disabilities has provided a productive avenue to advance our understanding of this heterogeneous group of disorders.

References

Association for Children and Adults with Learning Disabilities (1986). Position statement on a regular education/special education initiative. *Academic Therapy*, 22, 99–103.

Bastian, H. C. (1898). *A treatise on aphasia and other speech defects.* London: H. K. Lewis.

Becker, M. G., Isaac, W., & Hynd, G. W. (1987). Neuropsychological development of nonverbal behaviors attributed to "frontal lobe" functioning. *Developmental Neuropsychology, 3,* 275–298.

Bender, L. A. (1956). *Psychology of children with organic brain disorders.* Springfield, IL: Charles C. Thomas.

Bender, L. A. (1957). Specific reading disabilities as a maturational lag. *Bulletin of the Orton Society, 7,* 9–18.

Benton, A. L. (1975). Developmental dyslexia: Neurological aspects. In W. J. Friedlander (Ed.), *Advances in neurology* (Vol. 7, pp. 1–47). New York: Raven Press.

Bhatnagar, S., & Andy, O. J. (1983). Language in the nondominant right hemisphere. *Archives of Neurology, 40,* 728–731.

Bigler, E. D. (1989). On the neuropsychology of suicide. *Journal of Learning Disabilities, 22,* 180–185.

Birch, H. G., & Belmont, S. (1964). Auditory-visual integration in normal and retarded readers. *American Journal of Orthopsychiatry, 34,* 852–861.

Birch, H. G., & Belmont, S. (1965). Auditory-visual integration, intelligence, and reading ability in school children. *Perceptual and Motor Skills, 20,* 295–305.

Blank, M., & Bridger, W. H. (1964). Cross-modal transfer in nursery school children. *Journal of Comparative and Physiological Psychology, 58,* 227–282.

Blank, M. & Bridger, W. H. (1966). Deficiencies in verbal labeling in retarded readers. *American Journal of Orthopsychiatry, 36,* 840–847.

Bouma, H., & Legein, C. P. (1977). Foveal and parafoveal recognition of letters and words by dyslexics and average readers. *Neuropsychologia, 15,* 69–80.

Bradshaw, J. L., & Nettleton, N. C. (1983). *Human cerebral asymmetry.* Englewood Cliffs, NJ: Prentice-Hall.

Brainerd, C. J., Kingma, J., & Howe, M. L. (1986). Long-term memory development and learning disability: Storage and retrieval loci of disabled/nondisabled differences. In S. J. Ceci (Ed.), *Handbook of cognitive, social, and neuropsychological aspects of learning disabilities* (pp. 161–184). Hillsdale, NJ: Lawrence Erlbaum.

Brodal, A. (1981). *Neurological anatomy in relation to clinical medicine* (3rd ed.). New York: Oxford University Press.

Brown, B., et al. (1983). Predictive eye movements do not discriminate between dyslexic and control children. *Neuropsychologia, 21,* 121–128.

Bryden, M. P. (1970). Laterality effects in dichotic listening: Relations with handedness and reading ability in children. *Neuropsychologia, 8,* 443–450.

Clark, M. M. (1970). *Reading difficulties in school.* Harmondsworth: Penguin Press.

Cohen, R. L., & Netley, C. (1981). Short term memory deficits in reading disabled children in the absence of opportunity for rehearsal strategies. *Intelligence, 5,* 69–76.

Conners, C. K. (1978). Critical review of "Electroencephalographic and neurophysiological studies in dyslexia." In A. L. Benton & D. Pearl (Eds.), *Dyslexia: An appraisal of current knowledge* (pp. 251–261). New York: Oxford University Press.

Corballis, M. C., & Beale, I. L. (1983). *The ambivalent mind: The meuropsychology of left and right*. Chicago: Nelson-Hall.

Curtiss, S., & Tallal, P. (1988). Neurolinguistic correlates of specific developmental language impairment [Abstract]. *Journal of Clinical and Experimental Neuropsychology*, *10*, 18–19.

de Hirsch, K., Jansky, J., & Langford, W. (1966). *Predicting reading failure*. New York: Harper & Row.

Deloche, G., & Seron, K. (Eds.). (1978). *Mathematical disabilities: A cognitive neuropsychological perspective*. Hillsdale, NJ: Lawrence Erlbaum.

Denckla, M. B., & Rudel, R. (1976a). Naming of pictured objects by dyslexic and other learning disabled children. *Brain and Language*, *3*, 1–15.

Denckla, M. B., & Rudel, R. (1976b). Rapid "automatized" naming (RAN): Dyslexia differentiated from other learning disabilities. *Neuropsychologia*, *14*, 471–479.

Duffy, F. H., Denckla, M. B., Bartels, P. H., & Sandini, G. (1980). Dyslexia: Regional differences in brain electrical activity by topographic mapping. *Annals of Neurology*, *7*, 412–420.

Duffy, F. H., Denckla, M. B., Bartels, P. H., Sandini, G., & Kiessling, L. (1980). Dyslexia: Automated diagnosis by computerized classification of brain electrical activity. *Annals of Neurology*, *7*, 421–428.

Dykman, R. A., Ackerman, P. T., Clements, S. D., & Peters, J. E. (1971). Specific learning disabilities: An attentional deficit syndrome. In H. R. Myklebust (Ed.), *Progress in learning disabilities* (Vol. 2, pp. 56–93). New York: Grune & Stratton.

Eidelberg, D., & Galaburda, A. M. (1982). Symmetry and asymmetry in the human posterior thalamus. I: Cytoarchitectonic analysis in normal persons. *Archives of Neurology*, *39*, 325–332.

Ellis, N. C., & Miles, T. R. (1981). A lexical encoding deficiency 1: Experimental evidence. In G. Th. Pavlidis & T. R. Miles (Eds.), *Dyslexia research and its applications to education* (pp. 177–215). New York: Wiley.

Elterman, R. D., Abel, L. A., Daroff, R. B., Dell'Osso, S. F., & Bornstein, J. L. (1980). Eye movement patterns in dyslexic children. *Journal of Learning Disabilities*, *13*, 16–21.

Fisher, J. H. (1905). Case of congenital word-blindness (inability to learn to read). *Ophthalmic Review*, *24*, 315–318.

Fletcher, J. M. (1989). Nonverbal learning disabilities and suicide: Classification leads to prevention. *Journal of Learning Disabilities*, *22*, 176, 179.

Fox, B., & Routh, D. K. (1980). Phonemic analysis and severe reading disability in children. *Journal of Psycholinguistic Research*, *9*, 115–119.

Frostig, M. (1964). *Frostig Developmental Test of Visual Perception*. Palo Alto, CA: Consulting Psychologists Press.

Gaddes, W. H. (1985). *Learning disabilities and brain function: A neuropsychological approach* (2nd ed.). New York: Springer–Verlag.

Galaburda, A. M., & Eidelberg, P. (1982). Symmetry and asymmetry in the human posterior thalamus. II: Thalamic lesions in a case of developmental dyslexia. *Archives of Neurology*, *39*, 333–336.

Galaburda, A. M., & Kemper, T. L. (1979). Cytoarchitectonic abnormalities in developmental dyslexia: A case study. *Annals of Neurology*, *6*, 94–100.

Galaburda, A. M., Sherman, G. F., Rosen, G. D., Aboitiz, F., & Geschwind, N. (1985). Developmental dyslexia: Four consecutive patients with cortical anomalies. *Archives of Neurology, 35,* 812–817.

Galin, D. (1989). EEG studies in dyslexia. In D. J. Bakker & H. van der Vlugt (Eds.), *Learning disabilities, Vol. 1: Neuropsychological correlates and treatment.* Amsterdam: Swets Publishing.

Galin, D., & Ellis, R. (1975). Asymmetry in evoked potentials as an index of lateralized cognitive processes: Relation to EEG alpha asymmetry. *Neuropsychologia, 13,* 45–50.

Galin, D., Herron, J., Johnstone, J., Fein, G., & Yingling, C. (1988). EEG alpha asymmetry in dyslexics during speaking and block design tasks. *Brain and Language, 35,* 241–253.

Galin, D., Ornstein, R., Herron, J., & Johnstone, J. (1982). Sex and handedness differences in EEG measures of hemispheric specialization. *Brain and Language, 16,* 19–55.

Gerber, P. J., & Zinkgraf, S. A. (1982). A comparative study of social-perceptual ability in learning disabled and nonhandicapped students. *Learning Disability Quarterly, 5,* 374–378.

Goldberg, E., & Costa, L. D. (1981). Hemisphere differences in the acquisition and use of descriptive systems. *Brain and Language, 14,* 144–173.

Goldberg, H., & Schiffman, G. (1972). *Dyslexia: Problems of reading disabilities.* New York: Grune & Stratton.

Gross-Glenn, K., Duara, R., Yoshii, F., Barker, W. W., Chen, J. Y., Apicella, A., Boothe, T., & Lubs, H. A. (1988). PET-scan reading studies of familial dyslexics [Abstract]. *Journal of Clinical and Experimental Neuropsychology, 10,* 34–35.

Hammill, D. D., & Larsen, S. C. (1974). The effectiveness of psycholinguistic training. *Exceptional Children, 41,* 5–15.

Hannay, H. J. (Ed.). (1986). *Experimental techniques in human neuropsychology.* New York: Oxford University Press.

Henry, A. (1975). Specific difficulties in reading. *Remedial Education, 10,* 81–85.

Hermann, K. (1959). *Reading disability: A medical study of word-blindness and related handicaps.* Copenhagen: Munksgaard.

Heverly, L. L., Isaac, W., & Hynd, G. W. (1986). Neurodevelopmental and racial differences in tactual-visual (cross-modal) discrimination in normal black and white children. *Archives of Clinical Neuropsychology, 1,* 139–145.

Hinshelwood, J. (1895). Word-blindness and visual memory. *Lancet, 1,* 1506–1508.

Hinshelwood, J. (1900). Congenital word-blindness. *Lancet, 2,* 1564–1570.

Hinshelwood, J. (1902). Congenital word-blindness with reports of two cases. *Ophthalmic Review, 21,* 91–99.

Hinshelwood, J. (1909). Four cases of congenital word-blindness occurring in the same family. *British Medical Journal, 2,* 1229–1232.

Hiscock, M., & Kinsbourne, M. (1982). Laterality and dyslexia: A critical view. *Annals of Dyslexia, 32,* 177–228.

Hiscock, M., & Kinsbourne, M. (1987). Specialization of the cerebral hemispheres: Implications for learning. *Journal of Learning Disabilities, 20,* 130–143.

Hooper, S. R. & Willis, W. G. (1989). *Learning disability subtyping: Neuropsychological foundations, conceptual models, and issues in clinical differentiation*. New York: Springer–Verlag.

Huettner, M. I. S., Rosenthal, B. L., & Hynd, G. W. (1989). Regional cerebral blood flow (rCBF) in normal readers: Bilateral activation with narrative text. *Archives of Clinical Neuropsychology*, *4*, 71–78.

Hughes, J. R. (1978). EEG and neurophysiological studies in dyslexia. In A. L. Benton & D. Pearl (Eds.), *Dyslexia: An appraisal of current knowledge* (pp. 205–240). New York: Oxford University Press.

Hynd, C. R. (1986). Educational intervention in children with developmental learning disorders. In J. E. Obrzut & G. W. Hynd (Eds.), *Child neuropsychology: Vol. 2. Clinical practice* (pp. 265–297). Orlando, FL: Academic Press.

Hynd, G. W., & Cohen, M. (1983). *Dyslexia: Neuropsychological theory, research, and clinical differentiation*. New York: Grune & Stratton.

Hynd, G. W., Connor, R. T., & Nieves, N. (1988). Learning disability subtypes: Perspectives and methodological issues in clinical assessment. In M. G. Tramontana & S. R. Hooper (Eds.), *Assessment issues in child neuropsychology* (pp. 281–312). New York: Plenum.

Hynd, G. W., & Hynd, C. R. (1984). Dyslexia: Neuroanatomical/neurolinguistic perspectives. *Reading Research Quarterly*, *19*, 482–498.

Hynd, G. W., Hynd, C. R., Sullivan, H. G., & Kingsbury, T. B. (1987). Regional cerebral blood flow (rCBF) in developmental dyslexia: Activation during reading in a surface and deep dyslexic. *Journal of Learning Disabilities*, *20*, 294–300.

Hynd, G. W., Obrzut, J. E., Hynd, C. R., & Connor, R. (1978). Attentional deficits and work attributes preferred by learning disabled children in grades 2, 4, and 6. *Perceptual and Motor Skills*, *47*, 643–652.

Hynd, G. W., Obrzut, J. E., Weed, W., & Hynd, C. R. (1979). Development of cerebral dominance: Dichotic listening asymmetry in normal and learning disabled children. *Journal of Experimental Child Psychology*, *28*, 445–454.

Hynd, G. W., & Semrud-Clikeman, M. (1989). Dyslexia and brain morphology. *Psychological Bulletin*, *106*, 447–482.

Hynd, G. W., Snow, J., & Becker, M. G. (1986). Neuropsychological assessment in clinical child psychology. In B. Lahey & A. Kazdin (Eds.), *Advances in clinical child psychology*. New York: Plenum.

Hynd, G. W., & Willis, W. G. (1988). *Pediatric Neuropsychology*. Orlando, FL: Grune & Stratton, Inc.

Interagency Committee on Learning Disabilities. (1987). *Learning disabilities: A report to the U. S. Congress*. Washington, DC: Author.

Jackson, E. (1906). Developmental alexia (congenital word-blindness). *American Journal of Medical Science*, *131*, 843–849.

Jeeves, M., & Baumgartner, G. (Eds.). (1986). Methods in neuropsychology [Special issue]. *Neuropsychologia*, *21*(1).

John, E. R. (1989). *Neurometric evaluation of brain function in normal and learning disabled children*. Ann Arbor: University of Michigan Press.

John E. R., Karmel, B. Z., Corning, W. C., Easton, P. Brown, D., Ahn, H., John, T., Harmony, T., Prichep, L., Toro, A., Gerson, I., Bartlett, F.,

Thatcher, R., Kaye, H., Valdes, P., & Schwartz, E. (1977). Neurometrics. *Science*, *196*, 1393–1410.

Johnstone, J., Galin, D., Fein, G., Yingling, C., Herron, J., & Marcus, M. (1984). Regional brain activity in dyslexic and control children during reading tasks: Visual probe and event-related potentials. *Brain and Language*, *21*, 233–254.

Kavale, K. A. (1988). Epistemological relativity in learning disabilities. *Journal of Learning Disabilities*, *21*, 215–218.

Kavale, K. A., & Nye, C. (1985/1986). Parameters of learning disabilities in achievement, linguistic, neuropsychological, and social/emotional domains. *Journal of Special Education*, *19*, 443–458.

Kelly, J. P. (1985a). Anatomical basis of sensory perception and motor coordination. In E. R. Kandel & J. H. Schwartz (Eds.), *Principles of neural science* (2nd ed.)(pp. 222–243). New York: Elsevier.

Kelly, J. P. (1985b). Auditory system. In E. R. Kandel & J. H. Schwartz (Eds.), *Principles of neural science* (2nd ed., pp. 396–408). New York: Elsevier.

Kershner, J. R. (1977). Cerebral dominance in disabled readers, good readers and gifted children: Search for a valid model. *Child Development*, *48*, 61–67.

Kephart, N. C. (1971). *The slow learner in the classroom* (2nd ed.). Columbus, OH: Charles E. Merrill.

Kinsbourne, M., & Hiscock, M. (1981). Cerebral lateralization and cognitive development: Conceptual and methodological issues. In G. W. Hynd & J. E. Obrzut (Eds.), *Neuropsychological assessment and the school-age child: Issues and procedures* (pp. 125–166). New York: Grune & Stratton.

Kinsbourne, M., & Hiscock, M. (1983). Asymmetries of dual-task performance. In J. B. Hellige (Ed.), *Cerebral hemisphere asymmetry* (pp. 255–334). New York: Praeger.

Kirk, S. A. (1963). Behavioral diagnosis and remediation of learning disabilities. In *Proceedings of the Conference on Exploration into the Problems of the Perceptually Handicapped Child*. Chicago: Perceptually Handicapped Children.

Knights, R. M., & Bakker, D. J. (Eds.). (1976). *The neuropsychology of learning disorders: Theoretical approaches*. Baltimore, MD: University Park Press.

Kowalchuk, B. & King, J. D. (1989). Adult suicide versus coping with nonverbal learning disorder. *Journal of Learning Disabilities*, *22*, 177–179.

Kussmaul, A. (1877). Disturbance of speech. *Cyclopedia of Practical Medicine*, *14*, 581.

Landau, W. M., Goldstein, R., & Kleffner, F. R. (1960). Congenital aphasia: A clinicopathologic study. *Neurology*, *10*, 915–921.

Languis, M., & Wittrock, M. C. (1986). Integrating brain-behavior relationships. In J. E. Obrzut & G. W. Hynd (Eds.), *Child neuropsychology: Vol. 1. Theory and research* (pp. 209–239). Orlando, FL: Academic Press.

Lassen, N. A., Ingvar, D. H., & Skinhoj, E. (1978). Brain function and blood flow. *Scientific American*, *239*, 62–71.

Leong, C. K. (1976). Lateralization in severely disabled readers in relation to functional cerebral development and synthesis of information, In R. M. Knights & D. J. Bakker (Eds.), *Neuropsychology of learning disorders: Theoretical approaches* (pp. 221–231). Baltimore, MD: University Park Press.

Lerner, J. W. (1987). The regular education initiative: Some unanswered questions. *Learning Disabilities Focus*, *3*, 3–7.

Luria, A. R. (1970). Functional organization of the brain. *Scientific American*, *222*, 66–78.

Luria, A. R. (1973). *The working brain: An introduction to neuropsychology*. New York: Basic Books.

Luria, A. R. (1980). *Higher cortical functions in man*. New York: Basic Books.

Lyle, J. G. (1969). Reading retardation and reversal tendency: A factorial study. *Child Development*, *40*, 833–843.

Lyle, J. G., & Goyen, J. (1968). Visual recognition development lag and strephosymbolia in reading retardation. *Journal of Abnormal Psychology*, *73*, 25–29.

Lyle, J. G., & Goyen, J. (1975). Effects of speed of exposure and difficulty of discrimination on visual recognition of retarded readers. *Journal of Abnormal Psychology*, *84*, 673–676.

Lyon, G. R., Moats, L., & Flynn, J. M. (1988). From assessment to treatment: Linkage to interventions with children. In M. G. Tramontana & S. R. Hooper (Eds.), *Assessment issues in child neuropsychology* (pp. 113–142). New York: Plenum.

Mann, V. A. & Brady, S. (1988). Reading disability: The role of language deficiencies. *Journal of Consulting and Clinical Psychology*, *56*, 811–816.

Marcel, T., Katz, L., & Smith, M. (1974). Laterality and reading proficiency. *Neuropsychologia*, *12*, 131–139.

Marshall, J. C. (1984). Toward a rational taxonomy of the developmental dyslexias. In R. N. Malatesha & H. A. Whitaker (Eds.), *Dyslexia: A global issue* (pp. 45–58). The Hague: Nijhoff.

Maximilian, V. A., Prohovnik, I., Risberg, J., & Hakansson, K. (1978). Regional blood flow changes in the left cerebral hemisphere during word pair learning and recall. *Brain and Language*, *6*, 22–31.

Mayeux, R., & Kandel, E. R. (1985). Natural language, disorders of language, and other localizable disorders of cognitive functioning. In E. R. Kandel & J. H. Schwartz, (Eds.), *Principles of neural science* (2nd ed., pp. 688–703). New York: Elsevier.

McCarthy, J. M. (1987). A response to the regular education/special education initiative. *Learning Disabilities Focus*, *1*, 75–77.

McKeever, W. F., & Van Deventer, A. D. (1975). Dyslexic adolescents: Evidence of impaired visual and auditory language processing. *Cortex*, *11*, 361–378.

Merola, J. M., & Liederman, J. (1985). Developmental changes in hemispheric independence. *Child Development*, *56*, 1184–1194.

Montgomery, D. (1980). Do dyslexics have difficulty accessing articulatory information? *Psychological Research*, *43*, 235–245.

Morgan, W. P. (1896). A case of congenital word-blindness. *British Medical Journal*, *2*, 1978.

Morris, R., Bakker, D., Satz, P., & Van der Vlugt, H. (1984). Dichotic listening ear asymmetry: Patterns of longitudinal development. *Brain and Language*, *22*, 49–66.

Nelson, H. E., & Warrington, E. K. (1980). An investigation of memory functions in dyslexic children. *British Journal of Psychology*, *71*, 487–503.

Obrzut, J. E., Hynd, G. W., Obrzut, A., & Leitgeb, J. L. (1980). Time-sharing and dichotic listening asymmetry in normal and learning-disabled children. *Developmental Psychology*, *17*, 118–125.

242   W. Grant Willis, Stephen R. Hooper, and Brenda H. Stone

Obrzut, J. E., Hynd, G. W., Obrzut, A., & Pirozzolo, F. J. (1981). Effect of directed attention on cerebral asymmetries in normal and learning disabled children. *Developmental Psychology*, *17*, 118–125.

Olson, R. K., Kliegl, R., & Davidson, B. J. (1983). Dyslexic and normal readers' eye movements. *Journal of Experimental Psychology: Human Perception and Performance*, *9*, 816–825.

Olson, R. K., Kliegl, R., Davidson, B. J., & Foltz (1985). Individual and developmental differences in reading disability. In T. E. Mackinnon & G. E. Waller (Eds.), *Reading research: Advances in theory and practice* (Vol. 4, pp. 2–64). New York: Academic Press.

Orton, S. T. (1928). Specific reading disability-strephosymbolia. *Journal of the American Medical Association*, *90*, 1095–1009.

Orton, S. T. (1937). *Reading, writing and speech problems in children*. New York: Norton.

Passler, M. A., Isaac, W., & Hynd. G. W. (1985). Neuropsychological development of behaviors attributed to frontal lobe functioning in children. *Developmental Neuropsychology*, *1*, 349–370.

Pavlidis, G. Th. (1978). The dyslexic's erratic eye movements: Case studies. *Dyslexia Review*, *1*, 22–28.

Pirozzolo, F. J. (1979). *The neuropsychology of developmental reading disorders*. New York: Praeger.

Pirozzolo, F. J., & Rayner, K. (1978). The neural control of EM in acquired and developmental reading disorder. In G. Avakian-Whitaker & H. A. Whitaker (Eds.), *Advances in neurolinguistics and psycholinguistics*. New York: Academic Press.

Pirozzolo, F. J., & Rayner, K. (1979). Cerebral organization and reading disability. *Neuropsychologia*, *17*, 485–491.

Pirozzolo, F. J., & Papanicolaou, A. C. (1986). Plasticity and recovery of function in the central nervous system. In J. E. Obrzut & G. W. Hynd (Eds.), *Child neuropsychology: Theory and research* (Vol. 1, pp. 141–154). San Diego, CA: Academic Press.

Raim, J., & Adams, R. (1982). The case study approach to understanding learning disabilities. *Journal of Learning Disabilities*, *15*, 116–118.

Reynolds, M., Wang, M., & Walberg, H. (1987). The necessary restructuring of special and regular education. *Exceptional Children*, *53*, 391–396.

Richardson, E., DiBenedetton, B., & Bradley, C. M. (1977). The relationship of sound blending to reading achievement. *Review of Educational Research*, *47*, 319–334.

Rosen, G. D., Sherman, G. F., & Galaburda, A. M. (1986). Biological interactions in dyslexia. In J. E. Obrzut & G. W. Hynd (Eds.), *Child Neuropsychology: Vol. 1. Theory and research* (pp. 155–173). Orlando, FL: Academic Press.

Ross, E. D. (1985). Modulation of affect and nonverbal communication by the right hemisphere. In M-M. Mesulam (Ed.), *Principles of behavioral neurology* (pp. 239–257). Philadelphia: F. A. Davis Company.

Rourke, B. P. (Ed.). (1985). *Neuropsychology of learning disabilities: Essentials of subtype analysis*. New York: Guilford Press.

Rourke, B. P. (1987). Syndrome of nonverbal learning disabilities: The final common pathway of white-matter disease/dysfunction. *Clinical Neuropsychologist*, *1*, 209–234.

Rourke, B. P. (1988a). Socio-emotional disturbances of learning-disabled children. *Journal of Consulting and Clinical Psychology*, *56*, 801–810.

Rourke, B. P. (1988b). The syndrome of nonverbal learning disabilities: Developmental manifestations in neurological disease, disorder, and dysfunction. *Clinical Neuropsychologist*, *2*, 293–330.

Rourke, B. P. (1989). *Nonverbal learning disabilities: The syndrome and the model*. New York: Guilford Press.

Rourke, B. P., Young, G. C., & Leenaars, A. A. (1989). A childhood learning disability that predisposes those afflicted to adolescent and adult depression and suicide risk. *Journal of Learning Disabilities*, *22*, 169–175.

Rumsey, J. M., Berman, K. F., Denckla, M. B., Hamburger, S. D., Kruesi, M. J., & Weinberger, D. R. (1987). Regional cerebral blood flow in severe developmental dyslexia. *Archives of Neurology*, *44*, 1144–1150.

Rutter, M. (1981). Psychological sequelae of brain damage in children. *American Journal of Psychiatry*, *139*, 21–33.

Salvia, J., & Ysseldyke, J. E. (1981). Assessment in special and remedial education (2nd ed.). Boston: Houghton Mifflin.

Satz, P. (1976). Cerebral dominance and reading disability: An old problem revisited. In R. M. Knights & D. J. Bakker (Eds.), *The neuropsychology of learning disorders: Theoretical approaches* (pp. 273–294). Baltimore, MD: University Park Press.

Satz, P., Rardin, D., & Ross, J. (1971). An evaluation of a theory of specific developmental dyslexia. *Child Development*, *42*, 2009–2021.

Satz, P., Taylor, H. G., Friel, J., & Fletcher, J. M. (1978). Some developmental and predictive precursors of reading disabilities: A six year follow-up. In A. L. Benton & D. Pearl (Eds.), *Dyslexia: An appraisal of current knowledge* (pp. 315–347). New York: Oxford University Press.

Segalowitz, S. J. (1986). Validity and reliadility of noninvasive lateralization measures. In J. E. Obrzut & G. W. Hynd (Eds.), *Child neuropsychology: Vol 1. Theory and research* (pp. 191–208). Orlando, FL: Academic Press.

Shallice, T. (1988). *From neuropsychology to mental structure*. New York: Cambridge University Press.

Shankweiler, D., & Liberman, I. Y. (1972). Misreading: A search for causes. In J. F. Kavanagh & I. G. Mattingly (Eds.), *Language by ear and by eye. The relationship between speech and reading* (pp. 293–317). Cambridge, MA: MIT Press.

Sidtis, J. J., Portenoy, R. K., Jarden, J. O., Lipton, R. B., Kurtzbert, D., Rottenberg, D. A., & Foley, M. (1986. February). *Behavioral, metabolic, and electrophysiologic correlates of compulsive thalamic self-stimulation*. Paper presented at the annual meeting of the International Neuropsychological Society, Denver, CO.

Silver, A. A. (1968). Diagnostic considerations in children with reading disability. In G. Natchez (Ed.), *Children with reading problems: Classic and contemporary issues in reading disability* (pp. 240–250). New York: Basic Books.

Spreen, O. (1987). *Learning disabled children growing up: A follow-up into adulthood*. Lisse Netherlands: Swets & Zeitlinger/Oxford University Press.

Spreen, O. (1989). The relationship between learning disability, emotional disorders, and neuropsychology: some results and observations. *Journal of Clinical and Experimental Neuropsychology*, *11*, 117–140.

Spreen, O., & Haaf, R. G. (1986). Empirically derived learning disability subtypes: A replication attempt and longitudinal patterns over 15 years. *Journal of Learning Disabilities*, *19*, 170–180.

Springer, S. P., & Deutsch, G. (1985). *Left brain, right brain*. New York: W. H. Freeman and Company.

Stanovich, K. E. (1988a). Explaining the differences between the dyslexic and the garden-variety poor reader: The phonological-code variable-difference model. *Journal of Learning Disabilities*, *21*, 590–604.

Stanovich, K. E. (1988b). Science and learning disabilities. *Journal of Learning Disabilities*, *21*, 210–214.

Stephenson, S. (1905). Six cases of congenital work-blindness affecting three generations of one family. *Ophthalmoscope*, *5*, 482–484.

Swanson, H. L. (1988). Toward a metatheory of learning disabilities. *Journal of Learning Disabilities*, *21*, 196–209.

Thomson, M. E. (1984). *Developmental dyslexia: Its nature, assessment, and remediation*. London: Edward Arnold.

Torgesen, J. K. (1988). Studies of children with learning disabilities who perform poorly on memory span tasks. *Journal of Learning Disabilities*, *21*, 605–612.

Valsiner, J. (1983). Hemispheric specialization and integration in child development. In S. J. Segalowitz (Ed.), *Language functions and brain organization* (pp. 321–343). New York: Academic Press.

Valtin, R. (1973). *Report of research on dyslexia in children*. Paper presented at the annual meeting of the International Reading Association, Denver, CO.

Vellutino, F. R. (1979). *Dyslexia: Theory and research*. Cambridge, MA: MIT Press.

Vellutino, F. R., Steger, J. A., DeSetto, L., & Phillips, F. (1975). Immediate and delayed recognition of visual stimuli in poor and normal readers. *Journal of Experimental Child Psychology*, *19*, 223–232.

Vellutino, F. R., Steger, J. A., Kaman, M., & DeSetto, L. (1975). Visual form perception in deficient and normal readers. *Cortex*, *11*, 22–30.

Voeller, K. K. S. (1986). Right hemisphere deficit syndrome in children. *American Journal of Psychiatry*, *143*, 1004–1009.

Vygotsky, L. S. (1960). *Development of the higher mental functions*. Moscow: Izd. Akad. Ped. Nauk ASFSR.

Waller, T. G. (1976). Children's recognition memory for written sentences: A comparison of good and poor readers. *Child Development*, *47*, 90–95.

Watson, E. S., & Engle, R. W. (1982). Is it lateralization, processing strategies, or both that distinguishes good and poor readers? *Journal of Experimental Child Psychology*, *34*, 1–19.

Weintraub, S., & Mesulam, M. M. (1983). Developmental learning disabilities of the right hemisphere: Emotional, interpersonal, and cognitive components. *Archives of Neurology*, *40*, 463–468.

Wiig, E. H., Semel, M. S., & Crouse, M. B. (1973). The use of English morphology by high-risk and learning disabled children. *Journal of Learning Disabilities*, *6*, 457–465.

Will, M. C. (1986). Educating children with learning problems: A shared responsibility. *Exceptional Children*, *52*, 411–416.

Wilson, B., & Baddeley, A. (1986). Single case methodology and the remediation of dyslexia. In G. Th. Pavlidis & D. F. Fisher (Eds.), *Dyslexia: Its neuropsychology and treatment* (pp. 263–277). New York: Wiley.

Witelson, S. F. (1976). Abnormal right hemisphere specialization in developmental dyslexia. In R. M. Knights & D. J. Bakker (Eds.), *Neuropsychology of learning disorders: Theoretical approaches* (pp. 233–255). Baltimore, MD: University Park Press.

Witelson, S. F. (1977). Developmental dyslexia: Two right hemispheres and none left. *Science, 195*, 309–311.

Witelson, S. F., & Rabinovich, M. S. (1972). Hemispheric speech lateralization in children with auditory-linguistic deficits. *Cortex, 8*, 412–426.

Wood, F., Flowers, L., Naylor, C., & Felton, R. (1988). Regional cerebral blood flow during orthographic task activation in adult dyslexics [Abstract]. *Journal of Clinical and Experimental Neuropsychology, 10*, 34.

Wood, R., Taylor, B., Penny, R., & Stump, D. (1980). Regional cerebral blood flow response to recognition memory versus semantic classification tasks. *Brain and Language, 9*, 113–122.

Yeni-Komshian, G. H., Isenberg, D., & Goldstein, H. (1975). Cerebral dominance and reading disability: Left visual field deficits. *Neuropsychologia, 13*, 83–94.

Yingling, C. D., Galin, D., Fein, G., Peltznam, D., & Davenport, L. (1986). Neurometrics does not detect neurologically normal dyslexics. *Electroencephalography and Clinical Neurophysiology, 63*, 426–430.

Young, A. W., & Ellis, A. W. (1981). Asymmetry of cerebral hemispheric function in normal and poor readers. *Psychological Bulletin, 89*, 183–190.

Zurif, E. F., & Carson, G. (1970). Dyslexia in relation to cerebral dominance and temporal analysis. *Neuropsychologia, 8*, 351–361.

8
The Visual Deficit Hypothesis

WILLIAM LOVEGROVE

Historical Antecedents of the Theory

For some years it has been widely accepted that reading disability is not attributable to visual deficits; nor do normal and specifically disabled readers (SRDs) differ systematically in terms of visual processing (Benton, 1962; Vellutino, 1979a, 1979b). Possibly the most important reason for rejecting the involvement of visual deficits in specific reading disability is the consistent failure by many researchers to find differences between SRDs and controls on a wide range of visual tasks (see Benton, 1962; Vellutino, 1979a, 1979b for reviews). In the last 10 years, however, there have been a number of developments that challenge this position.

The research of Vellutino and colleagues has been subject to a number of methodological criticisms (Fletcher & Satz, 1979a, 1979b; Willows, Kershner, & Corcos, 1986). Consequently, a "no visual deficit" position based on that research becomes tenuous. This is made more so by the recent work of Willows (1988). She replicated some of Vellutino's experiments taking care to overcome the methodological problems limiting his work. Her data from tasks similar to those used by Vellutino show that disabled readers do have deficits in early visual processes as well as in visual memory.

At the same time there have been major developments in theories of vision and their application to reading that provide a more meaningful theoretical context in which to consider this issue. The following section outlines one recent approach to vision that has been applied to the issue of reading.

Current Theoretical Position

In this section a theory of vision based on extensive physiological and psychophysical research is outlined. This approach, referred to as *spatial frequency analysis*, has already proved useful in integrating apparently

246

disparate data within the area of infant perception (Banks & Salapatek, 1981). An extension of this theory, which proposes the existence of two subsystems within the human visual system, is then outlined. These subsystems are commonly referred to as the *transient and sustained systems*. Finally, an attempt to relate this approach to the reading process is described.

Spatial Frequency Analysis

One recent approach in vision research (Campbell, 1974; Graham, 1980) indicates the existence of parallel pathways or channels in the human visual system. Each channel is specialized to process information about particular features of visual stimuli.

The characteristics of channels frequently have been investigated using patterns like those shown in Figure 8.1. Such patterns are usually called sine-wave gratings. Three properties of these patterns are of interest in this chapter:

1. Spatial frequency, which refers to the number of cycles (one dark plus one light bar) per degree of visual angle (c/deg). Spatial frequency is higher on the right than the left in Figure 8.1. Spatial frequency can be thought of in terms of stimulus size.
2. Orientation of the grating to the right or left of vertical.
3. Contrast, which refers to the difference between the maximum and minimum luminances of the grating. It is a measure of the ratio of the brightest to the darkest section of the pattern.

Research within a spatial frequency framework has proved useful for a number of reasons. The first relates to the properties of the channels referred to earlier. Each channel is sensitive to a narrow range of spatial frequencies or stimulus widths.

low (general)   medium   high (details)

FIGURE 8.1. Sine-wave gratings commonly used in vision research concerned with spatial frequency channels. Low spatial frequencies are shown on the left and high spatial frequencies on the right.

A second reason for researching within a spatial frequency framework relates to its usefulness with various clinical groups whose visual deficits have not been diagnosed with more traditional techniques. As an example, the commonly used acuity tests, which measure the smallest resolvable detail, only measure functioning of those channels sensitive to high spatial frequencies (or small stimulus sizes). It is possible that a person may function normally in these channels but show a deficit in other channels, which may be important in a world comprising small and large objects. This has been demonstrated with some multiple sclerosis patients for spatial frequency (Regan, Silver, & Murray, 1977) and orientation (Regan, Whitlock, Murray, & Beverley, 1980) and for some patients with cerebral lesions (Bodis-Wollner, 1972).

Spatial frequency or size-sensitive channels are relevant to reading because when we read we process both general (low spatial frequency) and detailed (high spatial requency) information in each fixation. We extract detailed information from an area approximately five to six letter spaces to the right of fixation. Beyond this we also extract visual information but only of a general nature such as word shape (Rayner, 1975). These two types of size information must in some way be combined.

An extension of the spatial frequency approach that incorporates the temporal properties of spatial frequency channels is now outlined. This division is believed to be important in combining the two types of size information involved in reading as outlined above.

Sustained and Transient Channels

It has been shown that spatial frequency channels differ in their temporal properties. In a typical experiment subjects are shown patterns like those in Figure 8.1 flickering at various rates. Subjects are required to set contrast levels so that they can see just the flicker or pattern. When low spatial frequency gratings are moving quickly, we see flicker at lower contrasts than pattern but experience the reverse at high spatial frequencies. Separate measures can be taken for flicker and pattern detection thresholds at a range of spatial and temporal frequencies. Thus, we can plot sensitivity functions for pattern and flicker thresholds at a range of spatial frequencies. Several investigators have shown that the two sensitivity functions (for pattern and flicker) are independent functions of temporal and spatial frequency (King-Smith & Kulikowski, 1975). We are more sensitive to rapid temporal changes at low spatial frequencies and to stationary or slowly moving stimuli at high spatial frequencies. The two functions obtained from such experiments are believed to measure two subsystems in the visual system, the transient and sustained subsystems. An extensive discussion of the properties of

TABLE 8.1. General properties of the sustained and transient subsystems.

Sustained system	Transient system
Most sensitive to high spatial frequencies	Most sensitive to low spatial frequencies
Most sensitive to low temporal frequencies	Most sensitive to high temporal frequencies
Slow transmission times	Fast transmission times
Responds throughout stimulus presentation	Responds at stimulus onset and offest
Predominates in central vision	Predominates in peripheral vision
The sustained system may inhibit the transient system	The transient system may inhibit the sustained system

these systems and how they are identified can be found in Breitmeyer (1988).

The properties of these two subsystems have been identified and are shown in Table 8.1.

It is believed that both the transient and the sustained systems respond to stimuli with intermediate spatial frequencies depending on contrast level. At very low spatial frequencies only the transient system appears to be involved, whereas at very high spatial frequencies only the sustained system functions.

It has been demonstrated physiologically (Singer & Bedworth, 1973) and psychophysically that the two systems mutually may inhibit each other (Breitmeyer & Ganz, 1976). In particular, if the sustained system is responding when the transient system is stimulated, the transient will terminate the sustained activity. These two subsystems and the interactions between them may serve a number of functions essential to the reading process. Recent discussions of possible physiological substrates of these subsystems in cat and monkey are available (Breitmeyer, 1988).

In summary, it has been proposed that the transient system is predominantly a flicker or motion system transmitting information about stimulus change and general shape. The spatial information it transmits is coarse and thus well suited for transmitting peripheral information in reading. The sustained system is predominantly a pattern system transmitting information about stationary stimuli. In reading the sustained system should be most important in extracting detailed information during fixations and the transient system in extracting general information from the periphery. Below we shall see that the two systems also interact in important ways.

Sustained and Transient Channels and Reading

When reading, the eyes move through a series of rapid eye movements called *saccades*. These are separated by fixation intervals when the eyes are stationary. Saccadic eye movements are generally in the direction of

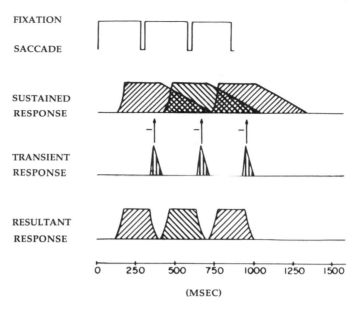

FIGURE 8.2. A hypothetical response sequence of sustained and transient channels during three 250-msec fixation intervals separated by 25 msec saccades (panel 1). Panel 2 illustrates persistence of sustained channels acting as a forward mask from preceding to succeeding fixation intervals. Panel 3 shows the activation of transient channels shortly after each saccade, which exerts inhibition (arrows with minus signs) on the trailing, persisting sustained activity generated in prior fixation intervals. Panel 4 shows the resultant sustained channel response after the effects of the transient-on-sustained inhibition have been taken into account. From "Unmasking Visual Masking: A look at the 'Why' behind the veil of the 'How'" by B. G. Breitmeyer, *Psychological Review*, 1980, *82*, 52–69. Copyright 1980 by the American Psychological Association. Permission to reprint granted.

reading, that is, from left to right when reading English. Sometimes the eyes also move from right to left in what are called *regressive eye movements* or *regressions*. The average fixation duration is approximately 200 to 250 msec for normal readers and it is during these stationary periods that information from the printed page is seen. The average saccade length is six to eight characters, or about 2° of visual angle (Rayner & McConkie, 1976). Saccadic eye movements function to bring unidentified regions of text into foveal vision for detailed analysis during fixations. Foveal vision is the area of high acuity in the center of vision extending approximately 2° (6–8 letters) around the fixation point on a line of text. Beyond the fovea acuity drops off rather dramatically.

The role of transient and sustained subsystems in reading has been considered by Breitmeyer (Breitmeyer 1980, 1983, 1988; Breitmeyer &

Ganz, 1976). Figure 8.2 represents the hypothesized activity in the transient and sustained channels over a sequence of three fixations of 250 msec duration separated by two saccades of 25 msec duration each.

The sustained channel response occurs during fixations and may last for several hundred milliseconds. This response provides details of what the eye is seeing. The transient channel response is initiated by eye movements and lasts for much shorter durations. Consequently, both systems are involved in reading. The duration of the sustained response may outlast the physical duration of the stimulus. This is one form of visible persistence produced by activating sustained channels. It can attain values of several hundred milliseconds and increases with increasing spatial frequency (Bowling, Lovegrove, & Mapperson, 1979; Meyer & Maguire, 1977).

If sustained activity (as shown in Fig. 8.2, panel 2) generated in a preceding fixation persists into the succeeding one, it would interfere with processing there. In this case, what may happen when reading a line of print requiring one, two, or three fixations is illustrated in Figure 8.3 (adapted from Hochberg, 1978).

Consequently, it is evident that for tasks such as reading, persistence across saccades presents a problem as it may lead to superimposition of successive inputs. Breitmeyer proposes that the problem posed by visible persistence is solved by rapid saccades as shown in the bottom two panels of Figure 8.2. Saccades not only change visual fixations, they also activate short latency transient channels (panel 3) that are very sensitive to stimulus movement. This, in turn, inhibits the sustained activity that would persist from a preceding fixation and interfere with the succeeding one (Breitmeyer & Ganz, 1976; Matin, 1974). The result is a series of clear, unmasked, and temporally segregated frames of sustained activity, each one of which represents the pattern information contained in a single fixation as shown in panel 4 of Figure 8.2.

In these terms, clear vision on each fixation results from interactions between the sustained and transient channels. Consequently, the nature of transient-sustained channel interaction seems to be important in facilitating normal reading. Any problem in either the transient or the sustained system or in the way they interact may have harmful consequences for reading.

Evidence Supporting the Theory

The possibility of a visual deficit in SRDs recently has been systematically investigated within a spatial frequency analysis framework. The following is not a complete review of all recent research but a selection of some of the more systematic programs conducted within a spatial frequency framework. Much of this has been directed at the functioning of the

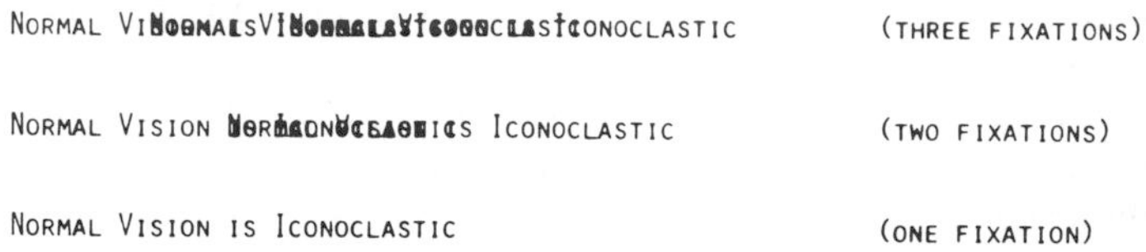

NORMAL VI**NORMAL**S**VI****NORMAL****VIS**+**GO****NOCL****AS**†**C**ONOCLASTIC   (THREE FIXATIONS)

NORMAL VISION **N**OR**MAON**V**CEAON**I**CS** ICONOCLASTIC   (TWO FIXATIONS)

NORMAL VISION IS ICONOCLASTIC   (ONE FIXATION)

FIGURE 8.3. The perceptual masking effects of temporal integration of persisting sustained activity from preceding fixation intervals with sustained activity generated in succeeding ones when the reading of a printed sentence requires one, two, or three fixations. Here, as in panel 2 of Fig. 8.2, the effects of transient-on-sustained inhibition have not been taken into account. From "Unmasking Visual Masking: A Look at the 'Why' behind the Veil of the 'How,'" by B. G. Breitmeyer, *Psychological Review*, 1980, *82*, 52–69. Copyright 1980 by the American Psychological Association. Permission to reprint granted.

transient and sustained systems in normal and specifically disabled readers.

Low-Level Visual Processing in Controls and SRDs

Visible persistence is one measure of temporal processing in spatial frequency channels and refers to the continued perception of a stimulus after it has been physically removed. This is assumed to reflect ongoing neural activity initiated by the stimulus presentation. In adults, duration of visible persistence increases with increasing spatial frequency (Bowling et al., 1979; Meyer & Maguire, 1977). This pattern of temporal activity has been linked to global-to-local processing in human vision (Lovegrove, Lehmkuhle, Baro, & Garzia, 1991) where the general form (global information) is seen before the detail (local information).

Several studies have compared SRDs and controls on measures of visible persistence. It has been shown that SRDs aged from 8 to 15 years have a significantly smaller increase in persistence duration with increasing spatial frequency than do controls (Badcock & Lovegrove, 1981; Lovegrove, Heddle, & Slaghuis, 1980; Slaghuis & Lovegrove, 1985). This effect is normally only found with stimulus durations of 100 msec or greater and is strongest with stimulus duratons of 200 to 350 msec (Badcock & Lovegrove, 1981; Slaghuis & Lovegrove, 1985). This difference between the groups is quite large and may well produce difficulties at higher processing levels.

There is little evidence that the magnitude of differences is less in older than in younger SRDs, indicating that this difference is not simply a result of a developmental lag. The results are consistent with the proposal of a transient system deficit in SRDs (see Slaghuis & Lovegrove, 1986a). This is argued to be the case because a manipulation known to reduce transient system activity—uniform field flicker masking (Breitmeyer, Levi, & Harwerth, 1981)—has a much greater effect on visible persistence in controls than in SRDs. Furthermore, uniform field flicker masking reduces the persistence differences between the two groups (Slaghuis & Lovegrove, 1984).

A second measure on which the two groups have been compared measures the minimum contrast (refer to Fig. 8.1) required to see a pattern. Contrast sensitivity (the reciprocal of the minimum contrast required for detection), plotted as a function of spatial frequency, is referred to as the contrast sensitivity function (CSF). Generally, sensitivity is greatest for intermediate spatial frequencies (2–6 c/deg) and less for low and high spatial frequencies. It has been proposed that the CSF represents the combined activity of several spatial frequency channels at threshold (Blakemore & Campbell, 1969).

Pattern CSFs have been measured in at least five separate samples of SRDs and control readers with ages ranging from 8 to 14 years. It has generally been shown that SRDs are less sensitive than controls at low (1.0–4 c/deg) spatial frequencies (Lovegrove, Bowling, Badcock, & Blackwood, 1980; Lovegrove, Martin, Bowling, Badcock, & Paxton, 1982; Martin & Lovegrove, 1984). In some studies the two groups do not differ in contrast senstivity at higher (12–16 c/deg) spatial frequencies (Lovegrove et al., 1980) and in others SRDs are slightly more sensitive than controls in that range (Lovegrove et al., 1982; Martin & Lovegrove, 1984). It has been shown that the difference between the groups in the patterns of sensitivity is greatest with stimulus durations ranging from 150 to 500 msec (Lovegrove et al., 1980). This parallels the differences between the groups on the measures of visible persistence.

It should be noted that the magnitude of differences between the groups on measures of pattern CSF is not as great as that found on measures of visible persistence (see Lovegrove, Martin, & Slaghuis, 1986). The finding of a small but consistent sensitivity loss at low spatial frequencies in SRDs is consistent with the proposal of a transient system deficit as argued by Lovegrove et al. (1982).

The pattern CSF data are consistent with the visible persistence data reported above. SRDs are less sensitive than controls at low spatial frequencies but not at high spatial frequencies, where they are sometimes more sensitive. As the pattern CSF experiments use a two-alternative temporal forced choice procedure, the differences between the groups are unlikely to result from criterion differences. The finding that SRDs are at least as sensitive as controls at high spatial frequencies is also consistent with the general finding that SRDs have normal or correctable-to-normal acuity. It helps to explain why some studies have, and some have not, found differences in visual processing between the two groups. The presence or absence of differences should reflect the channels whose activity have been measured.

A third approach has measured transient system functioning more directly than shown in the previous two sections. It has been argued that flicker thresholds are mediated by the transient system. Consequently, flicker thresholds under a range of conditions have been measured in SRDs and controls. In these experiments subjects are shown a sine-wave grating counterphasing, that is, moving from right to left and back the distance of one cycle at whatever speed the experimenter chooses. Subjects are required to detect the presence of the flicker. In a number of experiments SRDs have been shown to be less sensitive than controls to counterphase flicker (Brannan & Williams, 1988; Martin & Lovegrove, 1987, 1988). The differences between the groups sometimes become larger as the temporal frequency increases. This is a direct measure of transient system processing and distinguishes very well between individuals in the two groups (Martin & Lovegrove, 1987).

A further series of experiments has been conducted comparing sustained system processing in controls and SRDs (see Lovegrove et al., 1986). Using similar procedures, equipment, and subjects as the experiments outlined above, this series has failed to show any significant differences between the two groups. This implies that either there are no differences between the groups in the functioning of their sustained systems or that such differences are smaller than the transient differences demonstrated.

In summary, three converging lines of evidence suggest a transient deficit in SRDs. The results are internally consistent and consistent with the proposal of a transient deficit. The differences between the groups are quite large and discriminate well between individuals in the different groups, with approximately 75% of SRDs showing reduced transient system sensitivity (Slaghuis & Lovegrove, 1985). At the same time, evidence to date suggests that the two groups do not differ in sustained system functioning. The two findings taken together may help to explain some of the confusion reported in the literature over many years. In these terms, whether or not differences are found will depend on which system is investigated.

Higher Level Perceptual Processes and SRDs

A number of researchers have outlined how the transient and sustained systems may be involved in higher level perceptual processes than those discussed above (Breitmeyer & Ganz, 1976; Weisstein, Ozog, & Szoc, 1975). Williams and colleagues have recently investigated the question of how a transient deficit may manifest itself in higher level perceptual processes. Some of their research will now be reviewed. Their general conclusion is that SRDs manifest difficulties on a large number of perceptual tasks, most of which are believed to involve the transient system.

Williams and Bologna (1985) compared the two groups on a perceptual grouping task previously used by Pomerantz and Garner (1973). They found that SRDs showed a greater perceptual grouping effect than controls. This suggests a lack of flexibility in shifting attention from the transient to the sustained system. In a further experiment, Brannan and Williams (1987) measured the ability to use information provided by a cue to target location. They found the groups differed in their ability to use the cue when the cue preceded the target by less than 50 msec, with SRDs being less efficient than controls. In a temporal order judgment experiment Williams and colleagues showed poor readers required longer intervals between two successive stimuli to make accurate judgments about which of two simple stimuli was presented first (Brannan & Williams, 1988; May, Williams, & Dunlap, 1988). These researchers have also investigated visual search. Whereas Katz and Wicklund (1972) failed to find differences between the two reading groups in their study, Williams, Brannan, and Lartigue (1987) did. SRDs were slower in their search behavior at all locations. Each of these results indicates a poor temporal resolution in disabled readers—a difficulty expected if SRDs do have a transient deficit.

In an important study Williams, Molinet, and LeCluyse (1989) plotted the time course of transient-sustained interactions. A standard way of measuring the temporal properties of transient-sustained interactions is to use a metacontrast masking paradigm (Breitmeyer & Ganz, 1976). In metacontrast masking, a target is presented briefly followed at various delays by a spatially adjacent masking stimulus. The experiment measures the effect of the mask on the visibility of the target. The target is affected by both the temporal and spatial proximity of the mask. It is normally found that the visibility of the target first decreases and then increases as the pattern mask follows it by longer and longer delays. Breitmeyer and Ganz (1976) and Weisstein et al. (1975) have argued that metacontrast masking is due to the inhibition of the sustained response to the target by the transient response to the mask. This happens in much the same way sustained persistence is terminated by transient activity during reading, as is shown in Figure 8.2.

Maximal masking occurs when the transient response to the mask and the sustained response to the target overlap most in time in the visual system. This occurs in metacontrast when the mask follows the target by a certain interval. The point of maximal masking, then, provides an index of the relative processing rates of the target sustained response and the mask transient response. If the difference in rate of transmission is small, the dip in the masking function occurs after a short delay and vice versa. The magnitude of masking provides an index of the strength of transient-on-sustained inhibition. Additionally, metacontrast is normally stronger in peripheral than in central viewing presumably because of the preponderance of transient pathways in peripheral vision. It should be noted that this is the same mechanism proposed to be involved in saccadic suppression (the suppression of sustained activity during eyemovements) as discussed earlier in relation to Figures 8.2 and 8.3.

In an experiment using line targets Williams, Molinet, and LeCluyse (1989) showed that maximal masking occurred at a shorter delay in SRDs than in controls. This result is direct evidence that SRDs have a slower transient system or at least a smaller difference between the rates of processing for their transient and sustained systems than controls. They also found that in peripheral vision SRDs experienced almost no metacontrast masking, which further supports this position. The magnitude of masking was also less in central vision, showing that the transient inhibition was also weaker. Further evidence supporting timing differences between the transient and sustained systems in controls and SRDs has been provided in a subsequent metacontrast experiment where subjects had to identify a target letter. The mask was also letters but could combine with the target to form a word or a nonword (Williams, Brannan, & Bologna, 1988). Both of these studies provide clear evidence of temporal differences between the two groups contributing to high-level perceptual problems.

Temporal resolution may also be investigated using masking by light where the mask is a uniform light field. Here the masking is normally attributed to a reduction in the contrast of the target when the light of the mask is added to it. When comparing good and poor readers using this paradigm, Williams, LeCluyse, and Bologna (1990) found that in central vision SRDs experienced masking over a significanlty longer duration than controls. This again suggests poor temporal resolution in SRDs compared to controls. In peripheral vision, however, SRDs showed very little masking. With intermediate delays between mask and target it was found that SRDs experience no masking at all but facilitation where the mask made the target easier rather than harder to see. A similar result had been reported previously (Geiger & Lettvin, 1987). The latter interpreted their data in terms of attentional differences between the groups. Williams et al. argue that it is unlikely that their results reflect attentional differences and interpret them in terms of visual differences. Clearly, SRDs and controls differ in terms of the relative sensitivity of the central and peripheral visual systems. Although this total data set is consistent with a transient deficit, it also indicates that the visual problem in SRDs may extend beyond the transient system.

In summary, there are now many studies that have investigated higher level perceptual processing in good and poor readers. The results from this wide range of measures confirm the finding of a transient deficit in SRDs. They also suggest that there may be other deficits (visual and higher level), but the precise nature of these is not yet clear.

Stability of Ocular Dominance and Reading

Stability of ocular dominance has frequently been measured by presenting separate images to each eye and slowly separating them by a range of techniques (Bigelow & McKenzie, 1985; Stein & Fowler, 1982). Eventually fusion of the two images breaks down and the eye in which the image is seen to move is regarded as the nondominant eye. Normally this procedure is followed 10 times and stability of ocular dominance is defined as having the same eye dominant on 80% of the trials.

A number of studies have shown that disabled readers are more likely than controls to have instability of ocular dominance (Bigelow & McKenzie, 1985; Stein & Fowler, 1982). Not all studies, however, have found this relationship (Newman, Wadsworth, Archer, & Hockly, 1985). The possible implications of instability of ocular dominance for reading have been explained by Stein and his colleagues. Furthermore, they have proposed a remedial procedure based on their findings. The relationship of instability of ocular dominance to the other measures discussed here is not yet known.

Summary of Experimental Results

Three lines of evidence suggesting a transient deficit in SRDs have been outlined. Williams has considered whether as a consequence SRDs would show visual processing differences on a number of higher level perceptual tasks involving the transient system. On a large number of measures she has shown this to be the case. In addition, she has shown that some of the deficits are more complicated than simply a transient deficit. Exactly how this is so requires further research. Many SRDs also manifest instability of ocular dominance. Furthermore, these same subjects do not show differences on a number of measures of sustained system functioning.

How Well does the Theory Account for the Current Data?

This question can be considered in two related ways. The first concerns whether the sustained-transient framework can account for the conflicting data on vision and reading ability. The second is whether this approach fits with the more extensive literature on reading and other processing areas such as memory and especially language. This chapter primarily addresses the first issue but some attention is given to the second issue under the heading of Limitations of the Theory.

Over the years a substantial number of studies have reported differences in visual processing between good and poor readers. Several researchers (Blackwell, McIntyre, & Murray, 1983; Di Lollo, Hanson, & McIntyre, 1983; Hoien, 1980; Lovegrove & Brown, 1978; Stanley & Hall, 1973) have shown that masking occurs over longer durations in SRDs than in controls. Mason, Pilkington, and Brandau (1981) have shown SRDs to have difficulties with order rather than item information. Hyvarinen and Laurinen (1980) have measured spatial and temporal processing across spatial frequencies. They generally found that disabled readers were less sensitive than controls without specifying whether this difference was greater at certain spatial frequencies. Mecacci, Sechi, and Levi (1983) and May, Lovegrove, Martin, and Nelson (1991) have shown differences between the groups in terms of visual evoked potentials to either checkerboards or sine-wave gratings.

The difficulty, however, is that for almost every study showing differences between the two groups another study may be cited failing to show differences. For example Arnett and Di Lollo (1979), Fisher and Frankfurter (1977), Morrison, Giordani, and Nagy (1977), and Manis and Morrison (1982) have all conducted studies with short-duration stimuli without finding any significant differences between groups. Howell, Smith, and Stanley (1981) and Smith, Early, and Grogan (1986) failed to show spatial–frequency-specific differences in visible persistence between the two groups.

An obvious question is whether it is possible to reconcile these different sets of results in any way. There are a number of ways of attempting to do this. There is the general methodological problem with accepting null findings where a decision has to be made about the relative weight to be placed on significant versus nonsignificant findings. The view taken here is that more weight should be attached to significant findings. There are methodological criticisms of particular experiments that have failed to find significant differences (see, e.g., Slaghuis & Lovegrove, 1986a). There is also the possibility that different results have been obtained because of the different selection procedures that have been used to select the subjects in various studies. These and related methodological issues have been discussed by Gross and Rothenberg (1979). Despite all of these possible explanatory factors, it is unlikely that an acceptable post hoc resolution of the conflicting data is to be found. It makes more sense in the context of this chapter to make predictions about what should be found on a range of different tasks depending on whether or not transient or sustained processing is being measured. The recent systematic research programs discussed here suggest that this framework goes some way toward producing a coherent picture.

It may be stated, therefore, that although there is a large amount of data consistent with the argument presented here, there are also substantial data inconsistent with it. The consistent data are generally more recent and have formed part of one of a systematic programs of research. If the argument presented here is valid, it is possible to make clear predictions about the types of visual tasks on which SRDs should do worse and/or better than controls.

It is important to note in this context that recent research has not simply demonstrated SRDs performing more poorly than controls on all measures of visual processing. SRDs have been shown to perform at least as well as or even better than controls on some tasks, such as high spatial frequency sensitivity, visual acuity, and the oblique effect (Lovegrove et al., 1986). Generally this is thought to be the case on tasks measuring sustained system functioning. Further experimentation will determine whether or not this is so.

Limitations of the Theory

The major limitation of the present position is not in terms of it as a theoretical position that explains the visual performance of disabled readers and controls. Rather, it is in terms of how the current position relates to the following issues:

1. unitary deficit theories of reading disability
2. whether visual processing problems may be causually related to reading disability
3. the relationship of visual deficits to other processing difficulties.

Unitary Theories of Reading Disabilities

It has frequently been argued that it is extremely unlikely that there is only a single cause of reading disability (Fletcher & Satz, 1979a). Rather, there are probably many contributing factors both within a child and between children. This general argument is as applicable to theories based on visual deficits as it is to any other deficit theory. Thus, it is unlikely that most SRDs fail to read solely because of visual deficits. It is necessary to consider how various problems may interact.

In principle, it is possible that within a multiple causal model of reading difficulties one or a few contributing factors are more primary than the others. For example, if there is a basic information processing problem of any kind that makes reading difficult, this in turn may lead to emotional or behavioral problems related to reading. After continual failure at reading the secondary emotional or behavioral problems may become more important than the primary information processing difficulty. Nevertheless, if this deficit is at the first processing stage, the theoretical possibility exists that problems at the first stage contribute to problems at various later stages of processing. It is therefore tempting to speculate that for many children a visual difficulty is a primary contributing factor that interacts with higher levels of processing. As yet, this has not been established and awaits further research. The presence of visual deficits in so many SRDs makes this issue worth pursuing in order to learn how the visual deficits relate to other problems.

Are Visual Deficits Causally Related to Reading Disability?

Obviously, the presence of a difference in visual processing between normal readers and SRDs does not establish a cause–effect relation. This argument has recently been explained in detail by Hulme (1988). Some of his points are:

1. the types of errors commonly made by disabled readers reflect phonological recoding errors rather than visual errors
2. differences between the two groups on a range of visual measures have not been found
3. the tasks used in the experiments reported here lack face validity in relation to reading
4. generally SRDs perform more poorly on a large range of measures (other than visual) that are accepted as not being causally related to reading
5. the most effective demonstration of causality is to evaluate a remediation program derived from the hypothesized deficit.

Although most of these comments are individually at least partially acceptable, the sum of them is not, for the following reasons.

1. Hulme (1988) correctly notes that SRDs typically make phonological errors and this appears to reflect a common problem in these readers. Blaxall and Willows (1984) have shown that type of error made in reading changes markedly with difficulty level. Under conditions of increasing difficulty, SRDs also make more visual errors than controls. For this reason the issue of interpreting errors is more open than suggested by Hulme (1988). Furthermore, the relationship between visual and phonological errors is still to be fully explored (Barron, 1986).

2. A major component of Hulme's claim is derived from the argument proposed most strongly in the literature by Vellutino (1979b) that SRDs do not manifest any difficulties in visual processing. Although Vellutino's argument is not based solely on his own research, much of it is. As has been noted above, Vellutino's research in this area has been subjected to a number of cogent methodological criticisms. Furthermore, a recent replication of some of his experiments (Willows, 1988) has shown differences between SRDs and controls on tasks similar to those used by Vellutino. This questions Vellutino's research even further. Consequently, this is not a solid base on which to mount an argument.

3. Hulme has expressed concern that the sorts of measures used in the research programs discussed here lack face validity in terms of the reading process. This is almost certainly true. Whether this is important or not depends on the view taken about the appropriate way to choose tasks to study visual processing in good and poor readers. Our approach has been to use tasks that have a strong theoretical link with reading but that do not simply mimic the reading process. Our hope has been to identify the basic mechanisms involved in vision generally and reading in particular. The eventual outcome of this approach will be determined by the validity of the theoretical framework leading to the choice of tasks.

An alternative approach is to use tasks that are similar to what a child has to do in reading. Although this is appealing in terms of face validity, studies of this sort have frequently suffered from two criticisms. The first is that often tasks have been chosen in a theoretical vacuum, making interpretation of results difficult. Second, studies that do this are open to the criticism that they only find significant differences because of the strong correlation between reading and the experimental tasks chosen. It is not always clear that the results tell much more than that the groups have been validly chosen. Both approaches have advantages and disadvantages. To date, the theoretical approach adopted in this chapter has provided sufficiently new data to encourage us to pursue our mechanism-based approach.

4. The fourth argument presented by Hulme (1988) is to place our findings in the general category of results that show that SRDs are poorer performers than controls. He correctly notes that this in itself is an uninteresting result as it is well known that many of the tasks on which SRDs perform less well are not causally related to reading. He argues that it is likely visual deficits are not either. His claim that all we have done is to show that SRDs perform less well than controls is incorrect. Our argument for a transient deficit is based on two general findings. The first is the poorer performance of SRDs on a range of tasks that tap transient functioning or transient-sustained interactions. The other is on the finding that they perform as well as or better than controls on a number of tasks presumed to measure sustained functioning. It is the selective nature of the deficit that is the main finding of interest here.

5. Hulme argues finally that the most effective demonstration of causality is to mount interventions based on the hypothesized deficit. If the intervention is successful, it is valid to assume that the deficit is causally related. This conclusion is reasonable. He also argues that if the intervention is unsuccessful, the deficit is not causally related. This conclusion is not logically sound as it assumes that the deficit is amenable to remediation. If the deficit is hard-wired, it may not be amenable to any environmental manipulations even though the deficit is quite real. A classic case here is the exercise treatment proposed by Doman, Spitz, Zvcman, Delacato, and Doman (1960) for various forms of brain

damage. Here there is a clear understanding of the nature of the problem but the neurological damage is not responsive to stimulation. Despite this reservation about the logic of the argument, the spatial filtering work by Williams discussed below offers a possible approach to remediation.

In these terms, regardless of Hulme's arguments, the question of causality is still an open one especially in terms of the amount that is still to be learned about how the early stages of reading interact. At this time it is not possible to say that the visual deficits discussed here do cause reading difficulties. There are a few ways of showing this to be the case. One would be to show that remediation procedures based on this knowledge actually improve reading. This issue will be taken up in a later section. Another way would be to show that there is a direct link between a transient deficit and problems in phonological recoding.

The Relation of Visual Deficits to Other Deficits

There is extensive evidence that SRDs perform worse than controls in a number of other areas, especially in aspects of phonological recoding and memory. It becomes important to ask what, if any, is the relation between the transient system deficits and these other processing areas.

In a recent study on 58 SRDs and 62 controls measures of transient system processing, phonological recoding, and working memory were collected. These measures were subjected to a factor analysis. The results (Lovegrove, McNicol, Martin, Mackenzie, & Pepper, 1988) showed that some of the phonological recoding measures loaded on the same factor as the measures of transient processing used. This shows some relation between the two processing areas but, of course, does not reveal the precise nature of that relation. Until this relation is further clarified it is premature to reject the possibility of a link between visual and phonological errors in reading. The measures of working memory used did not load on the same factor as did the transient system measures and the phonological recoding measures. This study thus provides some preliminary evidence of a link between phonological recoding and visual processing in SRDs but the exact nature of this relation is still to be determined.

Treatment Implications

Little work has yet been done on the remedial implications of a transient deficit. There is preliminary evidence, however, on two fronts. One interpretation of a transient deficit is based on the fact that processing time increases with increasing spatial frequency. It has been argued that such an arrangement may be important in facilitating global-to-local perceptual processing (Lovegrove et al., 1991). In these terms the timing difference between messages from the transient and sustained systems is functionally important. The asynchrony between the two messages and not the absolute timing is the relevant measure. As has been discussed above, this asynchrony is significantly less in SRDs than controls, as measured by duration of visible persistence and metacontrast. Williams and colleagues have conducted a number of experiments testing whether modifying the relative timing would influence higher order perceptual processes in SRDs.

Their basic rationale is as follows. If SRDs do not have an optimal temporal asynchrony between inputs from the transient and sustained systems, they will experience perceptual difficulties. If there is a way of establishing an appropriate asynchrony, many of these perceptual difficulties should disappear. There are theoretically at least two ways of doing this. One is to speed up the transient system and the other is to slow down the sustained system. Williams and colleagues attempted to slow down the sustained system messages relative to the transient messages by spatial filtering, which is known to reduce contrast of high but not low spatial frequencies. Slowing down the high spatial frequency input without affecting the low spatial frequency input in this way should increase the temporal separation between the two systems.

They attempted this first on a visual search task on which SRDs had been shown to be significantly slower than controls (Williams et al., 1987). Whereas the blur had no significant effect on normal adults or children, it significantly decreased search time for SRDs. This effect was not due to any learning or order effects because it was reversible when the spatial filter was repeatedly removed and replaced. The effect was immediate and large.

A similar procedure was applied in the metacontrast study with letters described above. That study showed the masking peak to occur at a shorter interval in SRDs than controls in the unblurred condition. This is what would be expected if the former have a transient deficit. Under conditions of spatial filtering the metacontrast functions of SRDs essentially normalized as their peak masking occurred at the same delay interval as it did for controls. This is a clear demonstration of a change in the time course of transient-sustained interactions under conditions of spatial filtering.

On two measures of visual processing, therefore, a visual manipulation guided by the notion of a transient deficit has been successful in normalizing visual processing in SRDs. This naturally leads to the question of whether such a manipulation would actually improve reading ability. This possibility is currently under investigation. The answer, of course, will go a long way to answering the question raised by Hulme (1988).

There is some evidence to suggest a second remedial implication. It is known that the transient system dominates in peripheral vision whereas the sustained system is more important in central vision. Much of the data discussed above indicate that SRDs may have difficulties integrating central and peripheral information. Lovegrove and MacFarlane (1990) have recently investigated this possibility. They presented reading material to controls and SRDs in a number of formats. In one condition only one word at a time was presented on the screen and it was always in the same position (the no–eye movements condition). In the second there was only one word at a time on the screen; its position successively moved across the screen in a way that approximated reading but there was never any peripheral information present as the fixated word was being viewed (the forced–eye movement condition). In the third there was a line of print present at all times (the eye-movement condition). Controls showed greatest accuracy in the eye-movement condition. By contrast, SRDs performed best in the single word condition and became significantly worse in the eye-movement condition. Similar results with reading comprehension have been reported by Williams and Le Cluyse (1990). This suggests directly that SRDs do have a problem integrating central and peripheral information and that they read better when they only have to process central information. Therefore, any procedure that facilitates this should help SRDs in learning to read.

Conclusions

The data reported in the last 10 years show convincingly that many SRDs have a particular visual deficit. It has also been shown that it is unlikely that the transient deficit results from being unable to read (Lovegrove et al., 1986) although it is not yet known how it may contribute to reading difficulties. This deficit appears to be present in a large percentage of disabled readers and not just for a subgroup frequently referred to as visuospatial dylslexics. There is still a lot of work to be done before knowing how this processing difficulty relates to other difficulties. To date there are some interesting preliminary findings on remedial implications that suggest that this approach warrants further research.

Future Directions

There are a number of obvious directions to pursue. One of the most important, of course, is to pursue the spatial filtering work commenced by Williams. It is essential to know the extent to which the findings with perceptual measures generalize to reading. It is also important to know how prevalent this problem is and how many children may benefit from some form of spatial filtering. Similarly, it is of interest to ask if there are other procedures available for varying the relative timing of the transient and sustained messages.

Another useful direction would be to determine the extent to which the timing problem identified here is part of a general timing problem in SRDs. It has been shown (Tallal & Stark, 1981) that many of these readers have timing problems in audition. This raises the possibility of a general timing problem that may allow integration of research findings from a number of areas.

Finally, if the spatial filtering procedures fulfill their early promise, it would be essential to develop measures that identify transient deficits in prereaders so that advantage of this procedure may be taken before a number of possible secondary problems develop.

References

Arnett, J. L., & Di Lollo, V. (1979). Visual information processing in relation to age and reading ability. *Journal of Experimental Child Psychology*, *27*, 143–152.

Badcock, D. R., & Lovegrove, W. (1981). The effect of contrast, stimulus duration and spatial frequency on visible persistence in normal and specifically disabled readers. *Journal of Experimental Psychology: Human Perception and Performance*, *7*, (3), 495–505.

Banks, M. S., & Salapatek, P. (1981). Infant pattern vision: A new approach based on the contrast sensitivity function. *Journal of Experimental Child Psychology*, *31*, 1–45.

Barron, R. (1986). Word recognition in early reading: A review of the direct and indirect access hypotheses. *Cognition*, *24*, 93–119.

Benton, A. L. (1962). Dyslexia in relation to form perception and directional sense. In J. Money (Ed.), *Reading disability: Progress and research needs in dyslexia* (pp. 81–102). Baltimore: Johns Hopkins Press.

Bigelow, E., & McKenzie, B. (1985). Unstable ocular dominance and reading ability. *Perception*, *14*, 329–335.

Blackwell, S., McIntyre, D., & Murray, M. (1983). Information processing from brief visual displays by learning disabled boys. *Child Development*, *54*, 927–940.

Blakemore, C., & Campbell, F. W. (1969). On the existence of neurones in the human visual system selectively sensitive to the orientation and size of retinal images. *Journal of Physiology*, *203*, 237–260.

Blaxall, J., & Willows, D. (1984). Reading ability and text difficulty as influences on second graded oral reading errors. *Journal of Educational Psychology*, *76*, 330–341.

Boder, E. (1973). Developmental dyslexia: A diagnostic approach based on three atypical reading patterns. *Developmental Medicine and Child Neurology*, *15*, 663–687.

Bodis-Wollner, I. (1972). Visual acuity and contrast sensitivity in patients with cerebral lesions. *Science*, *178*, 769–771.

Bowling, A., Lovegrove W., & Mapperson, B. (1979). The effect of spatial frequency and contrast on visible persistence. *Perception*, *8*, 529–539.

Brannan, J., & Williams, M. (1987). Allocation of visual attention in good and poor readers. *Perception and Psychophysics*, *41*, 23–28.

Brannan, J., & Williams, M. (1988). The effects of age and reading ability on flicker threshold. *Clinical Visual Sciences*, *3*, 137–142.

Breitmeyer, B. G. (1980). Unmasking visual masking: A look at the "why" behind the veil of "how." *Psychological Review*, *87*, (1), 52–69.

Breitmeyer, B. G. (1983). Sensory masking, persistence and enhancement in visual exploration and reading. In K. Rayner (Ed.), *Eye movements in reading: Perceptual and language processes*. New York: Academic Press.

Breitmeyer, B. G. (1988). *Reality and relevance of sustained and transient channels in reading and reading disability*. Paper presented to the 24th International congress of Psychology, Sydney, Australia.

Breitmeyer, B. G., & Ganz, L. (1976). Implications of sustained and transient channels for theories of visual pattern making, saccadic suppression and information processing. *Psychological Review*, *83*, 1–36.

Breitmeyer, B. G., Levi. D. M., & Harwerth, R. S. (1981). Flicker masking in spatial vision. *Vision Research*, *21*, 1377–1385.

Campbell, F. W. (1974). The transmission of spatial information through the visual system. In F. O. Schmidt & F. S. Worden (Eds.), *The Neurosciences Third Study Program* (pp. 95–103), Cambridge, MA: The MIT Press.

Di Lollo, V., Hanson D., & McIntyre, J. (1983). Initial stages of visual information processing in dyslexia. *Journal of Experimental Psychology: Human Perception and Performance*, *9*, 923–935.

Doman, J., Spitz, E., Zucman, E., Delecato, C., & Doman, G. (1960). Children with severe brain injuries: Neurological organization in terms of mobility. *Journal of the American Medical Association*, 174, 257–262.

Fisher, D. F., & Frankfurter, A. (1977). Normal and disabled readers can locate and identify letters: Where's the perceptual deficit? *Journal of Reading Behaviour*, *10*, 31–43.

Fletcher, J. M., & Satz, P. (1979a). Unitary deficits hypotheses of reading disabilities: Has Vellutino led us astray? *Journal of Learning Disabilities*, *12*(3), 155–159.

Fletcher, J. M., & Satz, P. (1979b). Has Vellutino led us astray? A rejoinder to a reply. *Journal of Learning Disabilities*, *12*, 168–171.

Graham, N. (1980). Spatial frequency channels in human vision. Detecting edges without edges detectors. In C. S. Harris (Ed.), *Visual coding and adaptability* (pp. 215–262). Hillsdale, NJ: Lawrence Erlbaum Associates Inc.

Geiger, G., & Lettvin, J. (1987). Peripheral vision in persons with dyslexia. *New England Journal of Medicine*, *316*, 1238–1243.

Gross, K., & Rothenberg, S. (1979). An examination of methods used to test the visual perceptual deficits of dyslexia. *Journal of Learning Disabilities*, *12*, 36–43.

Hochberg, J. E. (1978). *Perception*. Englewood Cliffs, NJ: Prentice-Hall.

Hoien, T. (1980). The relationship between iconic persistence and reading disabilities. In Y. Zotterman (Ed.), *Dyslexia: Neuronal, cognitive and linguistic aspects* (pp. 93–107). Oxford: Pergamon Press.

Howell, E. R., Smith, G. A., & Stanley, G. (1981). Reading disability and visual spatial frequency specific effects. *Australian Journal of Psychology*, *33*(1), 97–102.

Hulme, C. (1988). The implausibilty of low-level visual deficits as a cause of children's reading difficulties. *Cognitive Neuropsychology*, *5*, 369–374.

Hyvarinen, L., & Laurinen, P. (1980). Opthamological findings and contrast sensitivity in children with reading difficulties. In Y. Zotternman (Ed.), *Dyslexia: Neural, cognitive and linguistic aspects* (pp. 117–119). Oxford: Pergamon Press.

Katz, L., & Wicklund, D. (1971). Word scanning rate for good and poor readers. *Journal of Educational Psychology*, *63*, 363–367.

King-Smith, P. E., & Kulikowski, J. J. (1975). Pattern and flicker detection analysed by threshold summation. *Journal of Physiology, London. 249*, 519–549.

Lovegrove, W. J., Bowling, A., Badcock, D., & Blackwood, M. (1980). Specific reading disability: Differences in contrast sensitivity as a function of spatial frequency. *Science, 210*, 439–440.

Lovegrove, W., Bowling, A., Slaghuis, W., Geeves, E., & Nelson, P. (1986). Contrast sensitivity scores of pre-readers as predictors of reading ability. *Perception and Psychophysics, 40*, 440–444.

Lovegrove, W. J., & Brown, C. (1978). Development of information processing in normal and disabled readers. *Perceptual and Motor Skills, 46*, 1047–1054.

Lovegrove, W., Heddle, M., & Slaghuis, W. (1980). Reading disability: Spatial frequency specific deficits in visual information store. *Neuropsychologia, 18*, 111–115.

Lovegrove, W., Lehmkuhle, S., Baro, J., & Garzia, R. (1991). The effect of uniform-field flicker and blur on the global precedence effect *Bulletin of the Psychonomic Society, 29*, 289–291.

Lovegrove, W., & MacFarlane, T. (1990). The effect of text presentation on reading in dyslexic and normal readers. *Perception, 19*, 368.

Lovegrove, W., Martin, F., Bowling, A., Badcock, D., & Paxton, S. (1982). Contrast sensitivity functions and specific reading disability. *Neuropsychologia, 20*, 309–315.

Lovegrove, W., Martin, F., & Slaghuis, W. (1986). A theoretical and experimental case for a residual deficit in specific reading disability. *Cognitive Neuropsychology, 3*, 225–267.

Lovegrove, W., McNicol, D., Martin, F., Mackenzie, B., & Pepper, K. (1988). *Phonological recoding, memory processing and memory deficits in specific reading disability*. In Vickers, D. & Smith, A. (Eds.) Human information processing measures, mechanisms and models. New York: Elserier Science Publishers 65–79.

Manis, F. R., & Morrison, F. J. (1982). Processing of identity and position information in normal and disabled readers. *Journal of Experimental Child Psychology, 33*(1), 74–86.

Martin, F., & Lovegrove, W. (1984). The effects of field size and luminance on contrast sensitivity differences between specifically reading disabled and normal children. *Neuropsychologia, 22*, 73–77.

Martin, F., & Lovegrove, W. (1987). Flicker contrast sensitivity in normal and specifically-disabled readers. *Perception, 16*, 215–221.

Martin, F., & Lovegrove, W. (1988). Uniform and field flicker in control and specifically disabled readers. *Perception, 17*, 203–214.

Mason, M., Pilkington, C., & Brandau, R. (1981). From print to sound: Reading ability and order information. *Journal of Experimental Psychology: Human Perception and Performance, 7*, 580–591.

Matin, E. (1974). Saccadic suppression: A review and an analysis. *Psychological Bulletin, 81*, 899–915.

May, J., Lovegrove, W., Martin, F., & Nelson, W. (1991). Pattern-elicited visual evoked potentials in good and poor readers Clinical Vision Sciences, 6, 131–136.

May, J., Williams, M., & Dunlop, W. (1988). Temporal order judgements in good and poor readers. *Neuropsychologia, 26*, 917–924.

Mecacci, L., Sechi, E., & Levi, S. (1983). Abnormalities of visual evoked potentials by checkerboards in children with specific reading disability. *Brain and Cognition, 2*, 135–143.

Meyer, G. E., & Maguire, W. M. (1977). Spatial frequency and the mediation of short-term visual storage. *Science, 198*, 524–525.

Morrison, F., Giordani, B., & Nagy, J. (1977). Reading disability: An information processing analysis. *Science, 196*, 77–79.

Newman, S., Wadsworth, J., Archer, R., & Hockly, R. (1985). Ocular dominance, reading and spelling ability in school children. *British Journal of Ophthalmology, 69*, 228–232.

Rayner, K. (1975). The perceptual span and peripheral cues in reading. *Cognitive Psychology, 7*, 65–81.

Rayner, K., & McConkie, G. W. (1976). What guides a reader's eye movements? *Vision Research, 16*, 829–837.

Regan, D., Silver, R., & Murray, T. J. (1977). Visual acuity and contrast sensitivity in multiple sclerosis-hidden visual loss. *Brain, 100*, 563–579.

Regan, D., Whitlock, J. A., Murray, T. J., & Beverley, K. J. (1980). Orientation-specific losses of contrast sensitivity in multiple sclerosis. *Investigative Ophthalmology and Visual Science, 19*, 324–328.

Singer, W., & Bedworth, N. (1973). Inhibitory interaction between X and Y units in the cat lateral geniculate nucleus. *Brain Research, 49*, 291–307.

Slaghuis, W., & Lovegrove, W. J. (1984). Flicker masking of spatial frequency dependent visible persistence and specific reading disability. *Perception, 13*, 527–534.

Slaghuis, W., & Lovegrove, W. J. (1985). Spatial-frequency mediated visible persistence and specific reading disability. *Brain and Cognition, 4*, 219–240.

Slaghuis, W., & Lovegrove, W. J. (1986a). The critical duration in spatial-frequency-dependent visible persistence and specific reading disability. *Bulletin of the Psychonomic Society, 24*, 416–418.

Slaghuis, W., & Lovegrove, W. J. (1986b). The effect of physical flicker on visual persistance in normal and specifically disabled readers. *Australian Journal of Psychology, 38*, 1–11.

Smith, A., Early, F., & Grogan, S. (1986). Flicker masking and developmental dyslexia. *Perception, 15*, 473–482.

Stanley, G., & Hall, R. (1973). Short-term visual information processing in dyslexics. *Child Development, 44,* 841–844.

Stein, J., & Fowler, S. (1982). Diagnosis of dyslexia by a new indicator of eye dominance. *British Journal of Ophthalmology, 66,* 332–336.

Tallal, P., & Stark, R. (1981). Speech acoustic-cue discrimination abilities of normally developing and language-impaired children. *Journal of the Acoustical Society of America, 69,* 568–574.

Vellutino, F. R. (1979a). The validity of perceptual deficit explanations of reading disability: a reply to Fletcher and Satz. *Journal of Learning Disabilities, 12,* 160–167.

Vellutino, F. R. (1979b). *Dyslexia: Theory and research.* London: MIT Press.

Weisstein, N., Ozog, G., & Szoc, R. (1975). A comparison and elaboration of two models of metacontrast. *Psychological Review, 2,* 325–342.

Williams, M., & Bologna, N. (1985). Peripheral grouping in good and poor reasers. *Perception and Psychophysics, 36,* 367–374.

Williams, M., Brannan, J., & Bologna, N. (1988). *Perceptual consequences of a transient subsystem visual deficit in the reading disabled.* Paper presented to the 24th International congress of Psychology, Sydney, Australia.

Williams, M., Brannan, J., & Lartigue, E. (1987). Visual search in good and poor readers. *Clinical Vision Sciences, 1,* 367–371.

Williams, M., & Le Cluyse, K. (1990). Perceptual consequences of a transient processing deficit in reading disabled children. *Journal of the American Optometry Association, 61,* 111–121.

Williams, M., Le Cluyse, K., & Bologna, N. (1990). Masking by light as a measure of visual integration time and persistence in normal and disabled readers. *Clinical Vision Sciences, 5,* 335–343.

Williams, M., Molinet, K., & LeCluyse, K. (1989). Visual masking as a measure of temporal processing in normal and disabled readers Clinical Vision Sciences, *4,* 137–134.

Willows, D. (1988). *Disabled and normal readers' visual processing and visual memory of item and spatial-order information in unfamiliar symbol strings.* Paper presented to the 24th International congress of Psychology, Sydney, Australia.

Willows, D., Kershner, J., & Corcos, E. (1986). *Visual processing and visual memory in reading and writing disabilities: A rationale for reopening a closed case.* Paper presented as part of a symposium "The role of Visual Processing and Visual Memory Reading and Writing" at the Annual Meeting of the American Educational Research Association in San Francisco, April 1986.

Willows, D. (1988). *Disabled and normal readers' visual processing and visual memory of item and spatial-order information in unfamiliar symbol strings.* Paper presented to the 24th International congress of Psychology, Sydney, Australia.

Willows, D., Kershner, J., & Corcos, E. (1986). *Visual processing and visual memory in reading and writing disabilities: A rationale for reopening a closed case.* Paper presented as part of a symposium "The role of Visual Processing and Visual Memory Reading and Writing" at the Annual Meeting of the American Educational Research Association in San Francisco, April 1986.

9
Phonological Deficits in Dyslexia: A "Sound" Reappraisal of the Verbal Deficit Hypothesis?

CHARLES HULME and MARGARET SNOWLING

Early theories concerned with children's reading problems stressed the importance of visual problems as explanations of reading failure. Cases of reading difficulty consistently were attributed to problems of visual memory and perception by pioneers such as Hinshelwood (1895, 1917) and Orton (1937). These theories about visual problems causing dyslexia went unchallenged for many years, despite an absence of any good supporting evidence. In the last 20 years or so, problems with the view that a visual deficit can explain most reading problems have grown, and there also has been growing evidence pointing to the importance of language problems. The evidence for visual problems has been reviewed elsewhere (Hulme, 1987, 1988; see Lovegrove, this volume). We restrict ourselves here to the evidence for the importance of verbal problems.

Impairments in language skills are common in dyslexic children. Parental reports show that they often learn to talk later than normal and, in interviews, they may show evidence of less complex language than normal children of the same age; it is also common for dyslexic children to show higher performance, than verbal, IQ scores (Rutter, Tizard, & Whitmore, 1970).

The position that deficits in underlying verbal skills cause reading problems was first explicitly stated by Vellutino (1979) and was termed the *verbal deficit hypothesis*. In his book, he reviewed many studies up to that time, such as those dealing with crossmodal integration, temporal sequencing, and visual perception and memory, which he argued could be parsimoniously interpreted as consistent with a general verbal deficit in dyslexic children.

Current Theoretical Position

Our current theoretical position could be seen as a descendent of the view that language problems are important as causes of dyslexia. In essence, our view is a refinement of this position, which now seems far too broad.

Language is a complex system that can break down in different ways. Linguists stress the different levels of analysis necessary for adequately describing language processing. In particular, we need to distinguish between semantic processes concerned with meaning, syntactic processes concerned with grammar, phonological processes concerned with the sound structure of language, and pragmatics concerned with language use. These different levels of language clearly interact during processing. In dyslexic children, there is considerable evidence for the primary deficit being in phonological processing. In what follows, we will review evidence concerning deficits in language skills in dyslexic children and consistently draw out the idea that the primary problem is at the level of phonology.

Evidence Supporting the Theory

During the last 10 years, there have been two distinct approaches to the study of dyslexia. The first approach has been concerned with explaining dyslexia in terms of deficits in underlying cognitive processes. Work in this field has focused on processes that are assumed to be necessary for learning to read, for example, memory and perceptual processes. The second approach has instead focused directly on the written language skills of dyslexic children. The assumption here has been that qualitative differences between the reading and spelling strategies of dyslexic and normal children will give insight into the nature of the dyslexics' difficulties. In the following sections we review studies reflecting these different approaches and go on to argue that the most fruitful way of interpreting them is within a developmental framework that unites them (Hulme & Snowling, 1988; Snowling, 1987).

Cognitive Deficits

Phonological Awareness

Phonological awareness refers to the ability to reflect explicitly on the sound structure of spoken words. This can be assessed in a variety of tasks, such as asking children to pronounce words when phonemes are deleted from them, identifying the odd word out of a list that share common sound components, transposing sounds within games such as Pig Latin or in Spoonerism tasks, and sound segmentation and blending tasks (see Goswami & Bryant, 1990, and Wagner & Torgeson 1987, for recent reviews).

Most research on phonological awareness has been concerned with its predictive relationship to reading in unselected samples of children. There is considerable evidence showing that phonological awareness tasks are among the best predictors of reading skill and, typically, these relationships can be shown to account for significant amounts of variance in reading skill, even after the effects of intelligence have been partialled out.

The strongest evidence for a link between phonological awareness and learning to read has been produced by Bradley and Bryant. In their first study, they compared a large group of dyslexic children with normal children of the same reading age and IQ (Bradley & Bryant, 1978). Their task involved asking the children to categorize words according to their sounds. On each trial, the children heard four words and had to decide which was the odd one out. In one series, the similar words had the same final phoneme (weed, peel, need, deed), in another they shared the same middle phoneme (nod, red, fed, bed), and in the last series, they shared the opening phoneme (sun, see, sock, rag). The results were clear; the dyslexic children were much worse on this auditory task than the normal children who were some $3\frac{1}{2}$ years younger, but read at the same level. This established that dyslexic children have difficulty in categorizing words on the basis of their sound and that this difficulty is not simply a consequence of their poor reading skills.

Bradley and Bryant (1983) set out to test whether difficulties with sound categorization were a cause of reading difficulties. This was a longitudinal study. At the beginning, the sound categorization ability of more than 400 4- and 5-year-old children was assessed before they started to learn to read. More than 3 years later, their reading and spelling ability and verbal intelligence were assessed. Performance on the sound categorization task was predictive of later reading scores, even when measures of intelligence and memory were taken into account.

To try to check that this correlation between early sound categorization skills and reading reflected a causal influence, Bradley and Bryant included a training study. Sixty-five children who initially were poor at sound categorization were split into four groups. One group was trained in sound categorization, and a second in addition to this was taught letter–sound correspondences. There were also two control groups: one group was taught to group words according to semantic categories and the other received no training.

After training that was spread over 2 years, the group that had been taught sound categorization and letter–sound correspondences was some 8 to 10 month ahead of the taught control group in reading scores. The group that had been taught only to categorize sounds was about 4 months ahead of the control group in reading, but this difference was not statistically significant.

These results fail to clinch the argument for the causal role of sound categorization in learning to read. To prove this would require evidence that the group taught only to categorize words on the basis of their sound was significantly ahead of the group taught to categorize on the basis of meaning. There was a tendency for this to happen, but not to a statistically reliable degree. The group taught to categorize sounds and to link letters to sounds showed impressive improvements but it is difficult to be sure of the source of these gains. A skeptic might argue that this was entirely due to training in letter–sound correspondences. This, after all, is directly a part of teaching people to read and spell. It might be that this group's success depends on having both sound categorization and letter–sound training. But, we cannot tell. To establish this would require another group being given the letter–sound training alone.

Nonetheless, the association between phonological awareness and reading ability is robust, having been obtained in a number of studies. Lundberg, Olofsson, and Wall (1981) gave a large group of Swedish children a battery of measures of phonological awareness. They found that these tests were predictive of reading scores $1\frac{1}{2}$ years later. A similar result to this has also been obtained by Stanovich, Cunningham, and Cramer (1984), who found that a battery of measures of phonological awareness administered before starting to learn to read predicted success in reading a year later. The different tests of phonological awareness were highly intercorrelated, suggesting that they were measuring some common underlying skill.

More recently, attention has been drawn to the fact that different types of phonological awareness may develop at different rates and bear different relationships to the process of learning to read. This argument has been developed most fully by Goswami and Bryant (1990). Their argument depends on recognizing that there are different levels of analysis for spoken words and awareness of these develops at different rates. One of the larger speech units, the syllable, is familiar. However, words can also be divided into subsyllabic units; namely, onset and rime. Within each syllable of English, the rime comprises the vowel and succeeding consonants, if any; the onset refers to the consonant or cluster that precedes the vowel. So, for example, the monosyllabic word "string" consists of an onset, /str/, and a rime, /ing/. Treiman (1983, 1985) has shown that adults and children find it easier to segment words into onset and rime units (e.g., cri-sp) than into units that cut across these segments (e.g., cri-sp). One task that taps young children's sensitivity to rimes is rhyme detection; for example, asking children to pick the odd (nonrhyming) word out from a group of four spoken words (Bradley & Bryant, 1978). As we have seen, this task can be performed quite adequately by 4- and 5-year-olds, before they have learned to read, and is highly predictive of their later success in reading and spelling. The ability to segment words by phonemes appears later, possibly as a consequence of learning to read. It is difficult task for young children and shows serious impairment in dyslexic children. Goswami and Bryant (1990) argue, after a review of many studies, that it is awareness of onset and rime that is crucial to learning to read, whereas awareness of smaller speech segments (phonemes) arises at least partly as a consequence of learning to read. Hence, illiterate adults who have never had the opportunity to learn to read are poor on tasks requiring segmentation of words into phonemes (Morais, Bertelson, Cary, & Alegria, 1986).

Verbal Memory Problems

Verbal memory is one area of language function that has been investigated a great deal in dyslexic children. This is not surprising because learning to read is a massive feat of verbal memory and it is clear that problems in this area are likely causes of reading problems.

Short-Term Memory

A common measure of short-term memory is digit span: the number of digits a child can repeat in correct serial order immediately after hearing them. As is usual in short-term memory tasks, here the person has to remember a small amount of information for a relatively short time, and the order of recall is important. There is ample evidence that dyslexic children typically do poorly on digit-span tests and other measures of short-term memory (Hulme, 1981; Jorm, 1983; Siegal & Linder, 1984). Moreover, the claim has often been made that their memory problems are attributable to difficulties with the use of phonological codes (Shankweiler, Liberman, Mark, Fowler, & Fischer, 1979). This claim was based on findings that they did not exhibit the classic phonemic confusability effect in short-term memory (memory for lists of rhyming items being shorter than memory for lists of nonrhyming items).

The validity of this claim was first questioned by Hall, Wilson, Humphreys, Tinzman, and Bowyer (1983), who showed that, provided the level of task difficulty was equated for good and poor readers, they were equally susceptible to phonemic confusability effects in memory. A seriers of studies by Johnston and colleagues provide corroborative evidence (Johnston, 1982; Johnston, Rugg, & Scott, 1987; Holligan & Johnston, 1988). For example, Johnston et al. (1987) compared groups of poor readers (of average or below average intelligence) with age-matched and reading-age matched controls on memory span tests, having first adjusted task difficulty for each child by pretesting performance on memory for lists of dissimilar items. Performance of the four groups at two age levels (8 and 11 years) was then assessed when recalling strings of phonemically similar letters (e.g., b, c, d, g, p). All groups here showed a phonemic similarity effect. It can be concluded that dyslexic children are, on average, subject to impairments of verbal short-term memory, although it does not seem that they use different coding processes. Thus, dyslexic and normal readers show evidence of speech-based coding of information as assessed by the occurrence of the phonemic similarity effect (see Hulme & Tordoff, 1989, for discussion of the mechanisms responsible for this effect and its development).

In the light of these deficits, an important question is how short-term memory problems might hinder learning to read. Short-term memory is often held to serve as a working memory system when reading (Baddeley & Hitch, 1974), the idea being that this system is used to keep track of the order of words in phrases and sentences (Kleiman, 1975). Impairments of short-term memory might therefore be expected to lead to problems in the comprehension of prose, particularly when word order is crucial to the meaning. However, there is no evidence that dyslexic children have any particular difficulty with reading prose, over and above those attributable to their difficulties in identifying words.

It is less obvious how short-term memory problems could create difficulties in learning to identify individual words, which is where, we would argue, the retarded reader's problems lie (cf. Aaron, 1989). One possibility, however, is that these problems lead to difficulties with phonic blending. When decoding a word that is not known, the child must produce a set of possible pronunciations for the letters in the word. These separate sounds then must be blended to produce a possible pronunciation for the word as a whole. Beginning readers can often be heard to go through this process overtly. Torgeson and Wagner (1989) showed that beginning readers find blending tasks easier if the individual sound segments are presented at a fast rate, thereby reducing memory load. Thus, it is indeed possible that short-term memory problems could make the blending procedure difficult for dyslexic children.

Torgeson, Rashotte, Greenstein, Houck, and Portes (1988) tested this possibility. They compared a group of dyslexic children selected for their low digit-span scores with normal readers and a group of dyslexic children with normal digit spans, on a sound blending test from the Illinois Test of Psycholiguistic Abilities. In this test, series of words and nonwords are spoken to the child, one at a time, in segmented form (e.g., "b-a-g") and the child is asked to say the word (bag). The dyslexic children with low spans did much worse on this task than the normal readers or the dyslexic children with normal spans, who did not differ. Therefore it seems likely that, at least for some dyslexic children, their short-term memory problems contribute to the difficulties they have with phonics.

An alternative explanation for the short-term memory problems of dyslexic children is that they are a consequence, rather than a cause, of their reading problems. Perhaps learning to read brings improvements in short-term memory. One approach to this is to compare dyslexic children with normal children of the same reading age. When this is done, the groups do not differ on short-term memory tasks, but it is always possible that this is because of the age advantage then accruing to the dyslexics.

A better approach is to conduct longitudinal studies where memory is assessed before children start to learn to read. The evidence from this sort of study on the whole suggests that memory difficulties precede reading difficulties. Jorm, Share, MacLean, and Matthews (1984) gave a large group of 5-year-olds a sentence memory task on entry to school. They tested all the children again on the memory test when they were almost 7 years old, and also gave them an IQ and a reading test. Memory scores at first testing correlated with later reading scores when the effects of age and IQ were partialed out. This indicates that good memory scores before learning to read are predictive of later success in reading and is consistent with the possibility of a causal influence of memory ability on reading ability. It is worth noting that the memory test used here involving sentences differs from conventional short-term memory tasks that involve meaningless strings of items. This difference may be important. It could be argued that memory for sentences is a sensible thing to assess and might reasonably be expected to correlate with reading ability. The task is not directly comparable with conventional tests of short-term memory, however, and probably places a greater emphasis on long-term memory and language comprehension skills. However, Mann and Liberman (1984) assessed memory in kindergarten children for unrelated strings of words before the children started reading and found that this did correlate with reading scores 1 year later.

In conclusion, it seems quite possible that the short-term memory problems commonly found in dyslexic children do contribute to their difficulties in learning to read. The most obvious way in which this might come about is because of difficulties with phonic blending. In addition, short-term memory problems may lead to difficulties in holding partially decoded words in mind while they are compared with the pronunciations of words retrieved from long-term memory. The idea that short-term memory problems are causally related to reading problems is far from firmly established, however. It is clear that there is an association between short-term memory problems and reading problems. The slight inconsistencies in the evidence on this probably reflect the fact, demonstrated by Torgeson et al. (1988), that these problems are not characteristic of all dyslexic children. The time would now seem ripe for studies designed to show that this association reflects a causal link between memory problems and reading problems. The natural way to do this would be to conduct training studies that attempt to improve the short-term memory abilities of dyslexic children. If such training were effective and led to improvements in reading, this would be good evidence for a causal connection.

Long-Term Memory

Even if short-term memory problems were of no consequence as causes of reading difficulties, it might still be the case that problems with more durable forms of memory were important. Rather surprisingly, studies of long-term memory in dyslexic children are less common than those of short-term memory.

One long-term memory task that has been studied a good deal is paired-associate learning. Here the child has to make an arbitrary association between a stimulus and a response. The most relevant task to learning to read is visual–verbal paired-associate learning. Here the child has to learn a name to go with some visual stimulus (often an abstract shape). The evidence from paired-associate tasks is clear: when these tasks involve a verbal component, dyslexic children almost invariably perform more poorly than normal children of the same age (for a review of these studies see Hulme, 1981).

It is plausible that difficulties of this sort could lead to problems in learning to read. In the early stages of learning to read, children may develop a considerable sight vocabulary by simply learning arbitrary associations between certain patterns of letters and their spoken counterparts. A child who has difficulty with paired-associated learning will have difficulty at this most elementary stage in learning to read. The other major way of learning to read is by phonics. Here the child learns rules that relate the letters used to spell words to their constituent sounds. A necessary step for this to happen is that the child learns the sounds of the letters. This, again, is an example of paired-associate learning, and many dyslexic children have profound difficulty in mastering the names and sounds of letters.

Another way of exploring the long-term memory system of normal and dyslexic readers is by the use of recognition memory or cued recall tasks. Here the evidence is relatively consistent in pointing to the tendency for normal readers to make use of phonological memory codes and for this tendency to be reduced in dyslexics (Byrne & Shea, 1979; Mark, Shankweiler, Liberman, & Fowler, 1977). However, Olson, Kliegl, Davidson, and Davies (1984) found that this phonetic confusability effect decreased with age for normal readers but increased for dyslexics. This showed that the dyslexics were delayed in the acquistition of these codes, but that they were by no means completely deficient. These findings, together with analyses of error data in this experiment, are compatible with the hypothesis that the absence of phonological coding strategies at a specific developmental stage might induce the use of compensatory (visual) memory strategies.

In line with this "compensation" hypothesis, Rack (1985) found differences between dyslexic 12- to 13-year-old dyslexics and younger reading-age matched controls, suggesting that dyslexics used orthographic codes in cued recall whereas normal readers used phonological codes. In the first part of this experiment, subjects carried out a rhyme judgment task on pairs of words and, in the second part, they were shown one item from each pair and were asked to recall the item that had appeared with it previously. Pairs of items were of four types: rhyming and orthographically similar (farm–harm), rhyming and orthographically dissimilar (rose–goes), nonrhyming and orthographically similar (how–low), and nonrhyming and orthographically dissimilar (farm–boat). The experiment was completed with both auditory and visual presentation, the results being essentially similar; that is, dyslexic and normal readers performed as well as each other in the rhyme judgments and their overall levels of recall were the same (note that the normal children were younger). However, although normal readers recalled a greater number of the rhyming stimuli, regardless of orthographic similarity, the dyslexics recalled more of the orthographically similar items, irrespective of rhyming similarity. These results suggested that the dyslexics were relying less on the use of phonological memory codes than their younger reading-age matched controls. A similar result was reported by Holligan and Johnston (1988) comparing 8-year-old poor readers with age-matched and reading-age matched controls. In a recognition memory task, following written rhyme judgments, the poor readers tended to choose orthographically similar pairs whereas the normal control group chose phonologically similar pairs.

Thus, it is quite plausible that dyslexic readers have difficulty with the use of phonological codes in long-term memory. These difficulties could create significant problems during reading that require the ongoing retrieval of phonological information in response to the visual input of printed words. Interestingly, a consequence of learning to read will be to provided dyslexics with alternative coding strategies, based on the visual appearance of words, which may facilitate their performance on certain cognitive tasks.

Naming Deficits

Another task that requires the retrieval of phonological information from long-term memory is naming. Word-finding difficulties are often reported in dyslexic children and experimental studies using rapid automatized naming tasks (RAN) usually report deficiencies in dyslexics. The classic study of this was by Denckla and Rudel (1976), who gave normal children and dyslexic children random lists of objects, colors, letters, and numbers to name as fast as possible. The dyslexic children were much slower here and, although the appropriate analysis is not reported, it looks as though the older dyslexic children were actually slower than younger normal children of the same reading age. The dyslexic children's difficulty here is probably not simply a consequence of their poor reading skill.

Extending these findings, Katz (1986) used a clinical test, the Boston Naming Test, to compare the performance of dyslexic 8-year-old readers with average and good readers of the same age. This test requires the naming of pictuted objects that are presented without contextual cues. The dyslexic children were less able to label the objects, and they had particular difficulty with low-frequency names and polysyllabic words. In fact, naming performance correlated with reading skill even when the children's receptive understanding of the names was controlled. In an extension of this study, Rubin, Zimerman, and Katz (1989) found that poor readers did not differ from good readers in their ability to select the initial phonemes or rhymes of object names that they had not produced spontaneously, and they were equally able to use initial phoneme prompts to retrieve the names. There was, however, a slight tendency for the poor readers to do less well when provided with a rhyming cue, but it is difficult to make any strong interpretation of this group difference because the number of items that were cued this way was extremely small. Overall, these findings from studies of naming deficits are consistent with the view that dyslexic children experience relatively specific problems in retrieving phonological information from long-term memory.

One difficulty with these studies by Denckla and Katz and his colleagues is that they did not include a reading-age comparison group. Without this control group, the possibility that the naming problems are a consequence of the reading difficulty cannot be ruled out. To address this question, Snowling, van Wagtendonk, and Stafford (1988) asked dyslexic children to name objects either after picture presentation or after a spoken definition. These authors compared the performance of the dyslexics with that of children of the same age as well as with children of a similar level of reading ability. All subjects found it more difficult to name the items after a spoken definition, but the group differences in performance were similar on both tasks. Essentially, dyslexics made more naming errors than children of the same age and a similar number to children of the same reading level.

To confirm this finding, a second experiment carefully matched dyslexic children with normal readers of the same age who also scored at the same level on the British Abilities Scales Test of Word Definitions (a vocabulary test). The two groups were then presented with a receptive vocabulary test in which one of four pictures had to be selected to match a spoken word and, subsequently, with a naming task. The results were clear-cut; the dyslexics did as well as the control group on the receptive vocabulary test, but made more errors on the naming task.

In summary, dyslexic children have naming difficulties that are unexpected, given their age and IQ, and are out of line with their receptive vocabulary. This suggests that they have difficulty in retrieving the phonological representations of words that they know. However, since they do not seem to be any worse at this than younger children of the same reading age, this might be a consequence of their reading difficulty. Logically, however, such a possibility does not seem particularly appealing. There seems to be no compelling theoretical reason to expect reading to produce such changes in retrieval from long-term memory. An alternative view is that these naming deficits are one manifestation of an underlying weakness in information-processing systems dealing with phonological information that is causally related to these children's reading difficulties. We now turn to consider another type of evidence relevant to such a view.

Repetition Deficits

Clinical reports often comment on the tendency for dyslexic children to mispronounce words or, spontaneously, to "spoonerize; for example, saying "par cark" for "car park." Miles (1983) felt that these minor articulation difficulties were of diagnostic significance, and included a repetition task in a test battery designed to identify dyslexic individuals.

Snowling (1981) asked dyslexic children to repeat a series of words of two, three, and four syllables and also a series of analogous nonwords derived from the words by changing one or two phonemes to others that were made either in the same place in the mouth or in the same manner. She compared their performance with that of a group of younger normal readers who were matched with the dyslexics in terms of reading ability. Interestingly, although the dyslexics were as good as the control group when repeating the words, they made significantly more errors when repeating the nonwords. This difficulty was interpreted in terms of problems with the segmentation operations required for compiling a new motor articulation program. When such programs existed, as for real words, dyslexics were able to access them—it was the nonlexical, phonological procedures that caused difficulty. Arguably, these difficulties could be attributed to perceptual problems such that dyslexics failed to "hear" the novel materials properly. This explanation seemed unlikely as, in a separate experiment, the dyslexics were found to discriminate complex nonwords from distractors differing by a single phoneme as well as controls.

Snowling, Goulandris, Bowlby, and Howell (1986) extended these findings to confirm that dyslexic children have specific difficulty with nonword repetition. In this experiment, subjects were required to repeat high-frequency words such as *dog* and *trick*, low-frequency words such as *glades* and *chef*, and nonwords made up by changing the first phoneme of the high-frequency words, such as *tog* and *drick*. All of the stimuli were of one syllable, and they were presented either in a clear background or with noise masking that was designed to reduce the signal-to-noise ratio. The dyslexic children were 10-year-olds, reading on average at the 8-year level. They were compared with a group of normal 10-year-old readers (chronological age-matched controls) and a group of normal 8-year-old readers who were reading at the same level (reading-age matched controls).

The first clear finding of the study was that although noise masking increased the error rate in the repetition task, it did so to the same extent for dyslexics as for normal readers. Therefore, it could be concluded that the dyslexics did not have any differential difficulty with the auditory perception of the word and nonword stimuli they had to repeat. However, there were interesting group differences with respect to the repetition of different stimulus types. None of the three groups had any difficulty in repeating high-frequency words but, interestingly, the dyslexics could repeat low-frequency words only as well as the younger reading-age matched controls. This was an unexpected finding to which we will return. However, of central importance was the groups' performance in nonword repetition. Here dyslexic children made more errors, not only more than children of the same age, but also more than younger children reading at the same level. This was a striking finding that confirmed earlier reports of nonword repetition deficits in dyslexic children. The problems could not be attributed to perceptual difficulties because the dyslexics were affected no more by noise masking than the control group, and it could not be attributed to peripheral articulation difficulties because in that case their pronunciation of all words should have been affected. The conclusion that they had specific difficulties with the segmentation processes required in order to assemble a new motor program therefore seemed the most likely explanation.

It could be argued that a direct consequence of this difficulty in processing nonwords for pronunciation would be a delay in the acquisition of new lexical entries in the spoken language system. Initially, all unfamiliar words are "nonwords' to a young child, until, through learning, lexical entries are created for them. Dyslexics' difficulty in repeating low-frequency items, relative to age-matched controls fits in with this hypothesis, suggesting that they might be slower to expand their spoken vocabulary of words than expected given their IQ. Also consonant with this view is the finding of naming difficulties in dyslexics.

Perceptual Problems

The cognitive deficits with which we have been concerned arguably could be related to difficulties first in establishing, and later in accessing, adequate phonological representations. A number of studies have suggested that these problems may themselves be perceptual in origin. That is, developmental difficulties with speech perception could interfere with phonological processing. The difficulty of demonstrating such perceptual deficits, however, is marked because, if they exist at all, they are undoubtedly subtle. Moreover, it is possible that these difficulties predate the stage at which dyslexic readers are identified and, because of maturational changes, may largely have been resolved by the time these children are identified as having reading difficulties. Nonetheless, a few studies provide suggestive evidence on this issue.

Brandt and Rosen (1980) investigated the perception of stop consonants (e.g., d) by dyslexic and normal readers. They found that the dyslexics performed like children at an earlier developmental stage, a finding similar to that of Godfrey, Syrdal-Lasky, Millay, and Knox (1981), who found that dyslexics were inconsistent in their phonetic classification of auditory cues in both discrimination and identification tasks. More recently, Reed (1989) carried out several experiments that pointed to the existence of a perceptual deficit in some dyslexic children.

In Reed's study, dyslexics had more difficulty in determining the order in which two stop consonants or two brief tones was presented than normal readers of the same age (7–10 years). In contrast, temporal order judgments that involved steady-state vowels caused no difficulty. Similarly, the dyslexic children had more difficulty with a word identification task in which an auditorily presented word had to be matched with one of two pictures, differing by a single phoneme; for example, *goal* paired with the picture representation of *goal* and *bowl*. They were also less consistent in their phonemic categorization of stimuli, as evidenced by poorer identification of syllables in synthetic speech that were near a phoneme category boundary, as well as by poorer discrimination of syllable pairs that crossed the category boundary. Taken together, these findings seemed to suggest that the dyslexic children had difficulty with the perception of brief auditory cues, a difficulty that could plausibly account for their impaired performance on a range of phonological processing tasks.

So far, the evidence we have reviewed paints a fairly clear pitcure as to the cognitive deficits that are characteristic of dyslexic children. Foremost among these are difficulties with the processing of speech sounds, which undoubtedly would interfere with the child's developing awareness of the phonological structure of words and also with the establishment of adequate phonological representations of spoken words. Without such representations, phonological memory problems are to be anticipated, as are naming difficulties. However, most significantly in the case of dyslexic children, we would argue that these deficits are directly implicated in reading failure. We now turn to this evidence.

Written Language Deficits

Developmental models focusing on the acquisition of literacy provide an important framework within which to examine the reading and spelling skills of dyslexic children. Marsh, Friedman, Welch, and Desberg (1981) and Frith (1985) view the child as passing through a series of stages or phases before becoming fully literate, each stage building on the previous one. In the initial stage, it is widely held that reading is visually based and proceeds by the use of partial cues. According to Frith and also Seymour and Elder (1988), children in this early "logographic" phase make visual reading errors because they remember words according to features like first leters, *wish* for *water*, or word length, *gentlemen* for *grandmother*. It is also important to note that at this stage the child has no strategies for deciphering unfamiliar printed words (other than by visual approximation to known words), and spelling is rudimentary, perhaps restricted to a few rote words.

The next stage, the alphabetic, is one in which the child begins to be able to decode, according to Marsh et al. (1981) first, by the application of sequential left to right decoding rules (k + a + m), and then by using hierarchical decoding strategies (k + a + m + e = "kaim"). Frith (1985) is less specific about the strategies that the child will use, but recognizes the importance of the child's emerging knowledge of letter–sound correspondences. Indeed, the child's awareness of the alphabetic principle —the relationships between sounds and letters as embodied in print—also brings with it the ability to spell, or at least to transcode phonetically spoken words into written ones.

The final stage the orthographic, is characterized by both automaticity and flexibility. Reading and spelling proceed independently of sound at this stage and, according to Marsh et al., lexical analogies can be used both in reading and spelling.

At the present time, there is considerable debate not only as to whether it is appropriate to view reading development as a series of stages (Stuart and Coltheart, 1988; Ehri, 1989), but also as to the processing characteristics of children's reading and spelling at different points in development (Campbell, 1985; Goswami, 1988). It is not our aim here to enter into this debate. However, we would note that the development of reading must be viewed as the acquisition of two distinct systems: (a) a lexical system for the processing of familiar printed words and (b) a secondary phonological reading system that the child can use to decipher unfamiliar words. We shall remain agnostic about the extent to which these systems develop or function independently. Suffice it to say that there is ample evidence that children make use of a sight vocabulary when reading, and they also can resort to the use of phonological strategies when presented with unfamiliar words. Furthermore, it seems clear that awareness of the phonological structures of words will be central to the development of decoding competence since this relies on knowledge of letter–sound correspondences. It can be predicted, therefore, that dyslexics will have more difficulty with the acquisition of phonological reading strategies than normally developing children.

Phonological Deficits in Reading

A number of different methodologies have been used to evaluate the use of phonological reading strategies in reading. These include lexical decision tasks, tests of written rhyme judgment, the pronunciation of regular and irregular words, and nonword reading. The experiments we shall review here largely focus on direct tests of word and nonword reading in which dyslexic children have been compared with controls groups, matched either for chronological age or for reading age.

Evidence from Single-Word Reading Tasks

Words in English orthography vary in the directness of mapping sound onto spelling. Some words (e.g., *cat*) have a simple pattern where each phoneme is represented by a single letter; in other cases, more complex, but nevertheless rule-governed, relationships apply (e.g., *pine*, where the terminal vowel lengthens the middle vowel); and in yet other cases, the relationship between spelling and sound is quite obscure (e.g., *yacht*). Experimental studies often contrast regular words with irregular (or exception) words. The logic here is that irregular words should be read less well by children and adults according to the extent to which they use rules about spelling patterns in order to decode words. If dyslexics are poor at doing this, they might be expected to show little difference in their ability to read regular and irregular words, as compared to normal children reading at the same level.

One of the first studies to compare directly the performance of dyslexic readers with reading-age matched control groups when reading regular and irregular words was reported by Frith and Snowling (1983). This experiment also included a comparison with able autistic children who were good readers. The results indicated that dyslexic children were not susceptible to a regularity effect in their reading. While normal readers read a greater number of regular than matched irregular words, dyslexic children did not. It is also relevant that normal readers took less time to read the regular words, but this time advantage was not apparent in the data from the dyslexic children.

Seidenberg, Bruck, Fornarolo, and Backman (1985) addressed the issue of decoding processes in dyslexic readers along similar lines. In their experiment, groups of good, poor, and dyslexic readers (defined by exclusionary criteria) were asked to read 80 monosyllabic words, 40 of which were exceptions (e.g., *paid*, *have*), 20 of which had ambiguous spelling patterns (e.g., *clown*, *thrown*) and 20 of which were regular (e.g., *hope*). They also read 60 nonwords, matched to a subsample of the words. In the experiment as a whole, dyslexic readers did not differ from the unselected group of poor readers, but both groups made more errors than the good readers.

The authors use these results to argue against the diagnostic significance of the term *dyslexic reader* (see Wolf, 1986, for a critique). For present purposes, we do not wish to enter this debate. Seidenberg et al. (1985) go on to discuss differences in the pattern of errors between the dyslexic and good readers. Dyslexics made more errors on vowels than on consonants, and they made more totally inappropriate pronunciations for vowels in regular words and nonwords. There was less tendency for dyslexics to make regularizations (reading by the strict application of letter–sound rules; e.g., glove as *gloave*), and they made more substitutions in the reading of consonants. These data are broadly consistent with the view that dyslexics have difficulty with phonological reading strategies; however, they are difficult to interpret because the levels of performance for the two groups differed. It is conceivable, indeed, even to be expected on the basis of developmental models of reading acquisition, that children reading at different levels will make qualitatively different patterns of error. Thus, there is little specific that can be learned about the reading characteristics of dyslexic children from this study, although it is worth noting that the performance of the dyslexics was fairly homogeneous and did not suggest marked individual differences in reading strategy.

Extending work along these lines, Szeszulski and Manis (1987) asked dyslexic readers to read regular and irregular words and nonwords but this time they compared their performance with that of normal readers who were reading at the same grade level. This was a reading-age match design and included comparisons at 2nd- and 4th-grade levels. Among children reading at the 2nd-grade level there were some interesting group differences; there was a larger regularity effect for normal readers, although the effect was apparent in both groups, and the dyslexics made fewer rule-based pronunciations of nonwords than the control group. At the higher reading-age level, the interpretation of the word and nonword data is complicated by the presence of ceiling effects and, unfortunately, latency data are not available. Essentially then, these data can be regarded as supportive of the hypothesis that dyslexics are deficient in their use of phonological reading strategies. Like Seidenberg et al. (1985), Szeszulski and Manis (1986) did not find significant heterogeneity in their dyslexic data.

Hence, the results from group comparisons of dyslexic and normal readers suggest that dyslexics are less skilled in the use of decoding strategies, particularly those that relate vowel patterns to their phonological correspondences. Unfortunately, a number of methodological problems permeate this area, including the lack of appropriate comparison groups and the presence of ceiling effects relating to the use of inappropriately easy stimuli. Rather than dwelling on these now, we turn to examine the evidence on nonword reading in dyslexia.

Evidence from Nonword Reading

One advantage of focusing on nonword reading in comparisons of dyslexic and normal readers is that nonwords are unfamiliar items. Reading them therefore requires tapping into the processes that are used in learning to read which, by implication, are deficient in dyslexic readers.

Nonword reading, we would argue, gives a relatively direct indication of phonological reading skill. However, it is important to interpret performance in nonword reading in relation to word-reading skill. Developmentally, it is usual to see an increase in decoding skill, as measured by nonword reading. An interesting aspect of dyslexia is to determine whether this same relationship holds.

Many studies have addressed the question of nonword reading in dyslexia in the last 10 years. We are therefore forced here to give a brief review that we hope, nonetheless, presents a balanced picture. An early study by Snowling (1980) used a cross-modal matching task to assess nonword reading skill. In the critical condition, subjects first saw a written nonword and then they heard a spoken nonword, and their task was to say whether the two stimuli were the same or not. The stimuli were all single-syllable nonwords containing four letters, and the letters corresponded to either three (torp) or four (sint) phonemes (when pronounced with a Southern English accent). Dyslexics differed from reading-age matched normal readers in this critical visual–auditory matching condition; the dyslexics had great difficulty in recoding the nonwords into phonological form. In a second study, Snowling (1981) asked subjects to read monosyllabic and disyllabic nonwords containing either no, one or two consonant clusters, and she recorded the time that they took to pronounce the stimuli in groups of six. Stimuli without clusters included *wut* and *tegwop*; stimuli containing one cluster included *blem* and *twamket*. Overall, the dyslexics were slower and more error-prone than reading-age matched controls when reading the nonwords aloud; however, the phonological structure of the nonwords was an important factor influencing performance. Dyslexics found the longer and more complex words particularly difficult.

A number of studies along similar lines corroborated the above findings. In a straightforward experiment, Baddeley, Ellis, Miles, and Lewis (1982) presented subjects with single-syllable words and non words, (e.g., stane, frute, dake, selt). The groups performed similarly no real words but the dyslexics made more errors in nonword reading than reading-age matched controls. Likewise, Kochnower, Richardson, and DiBenedetto (1983), DiBenedetto, Richardson, and Kochnower (1983), Siegel and Ryan (1988), and Holligan and Johnston (1988) reported nonword reading deficits in dyslexics compared with younger reading-age matched controls.

A slightly different approach was adopted by Olson, Kliegel, Davidson, and Foltz (1985), who assessed phonological reading skill using a task in which subjects had to choose which two nonwords would sound like a real word if were read out loud (*caik–dake*). This task involved recoding nonwords and recognizing when there was a match between the phonological form and that of a familiar word. The dyslexic readers were significantly worse than the normal readers on this phonological choice task. However, they also were given a test of lexical (or orthographic) knowledge. Here they had to examine two letter strings that sounded the same and identify the correctly spelled version, as opposed to a homophonic misspelling (*street–streat*). This lexical/orthographic task required specific knowledge of the conventionally correct spelling of words. Dyslexic children did not differ from the reading-age matched comparison group on the orthographic task, suggesting that their phonological difficulties were, to some extent, independent of their orthographic knowledge. Thus, like the studies requiring nonword pronunciation, these findings support the notion that dyslexics have specific difficulty with the phonological aspects of decoding and suggest that they may reach their level of reading competence by relying more on a visual approach to reading than normal children. The finding that they are more likely to make errors in the pronunciation of vowel segments of words and less likely to make regularization errors in single-word reading is consistent with this view.

Although the evidence presented so far is undoubtedly persuasive, there have been a fair number of failures in replicating the finding of nonword reading deficits in dyslexia. The first of these to appear was that of Beech and Harding (1984), who asked dyslexics and a reading-age matched control group to read matched regular words, exception words, and nonwords based on Baron's (1979) materials. Examples of matched trios were: *suffer* (R), *sugar* (E) and *suther* (N); *nome* (R), *come* (E) and *bome* (N); and *signal* (R), *sign* (E) and *signeb* (N). The groups performed similarly on the two word measures; however, they also read the nonwords equally poorly. This led the authors to conclude that the dyslexic readers should be characterized as developmentally delayed rather than deficient in phonological reading skills. In a similar vein, Treiman and Hirsh-Pasek (1985) gave subjects matched sets of single-syllable regular, exception, and nonwords (*bone, done, yone*), again based on Baron's (1979) materials. Contrary to the nonword deficit hypothesis but in line with the results of Beech and Harding (1984), dyslexic readers performed similarly to younger normal readers on measures of regular, exception word, and nonword reading.

The next failure to find a nonword reading deficit in dyslexia was reported by Johnston, Rugg, and Scott (1987), using a sentence verification task. In one condition subjects saw sentences containing a nonword; for example, "She loast her bike." The nonwords were controls for pseudohomophones that were used in a second condition (Can you poast this letter?). In another condition, the subjects read sentences containing inappropriate words, such as "He went to boy a book." These were the controls for sentences containing an inappropriate homophone, for example, "She ran down the rode.". It is important to note that the fact that the nonwords were presented in context changes the nature of the task somewhat, as there is evidence that poor readers might particularly benefit from this manipulation (Pring and Snowling, 1986). However, more relevant is that the subjects were asked to read the distractor nonwords on a subsequent occasion. At both age levels, performance on the nonword task was equivalent for dyslexic and normal readers.

Finally, Vellutino and Scanlon (1987), provide the strongest evidence against the nonword reading deficit hypotheis, at least in terms of sample size. In this study, 75 dyslexic readers and 75 normal readers, matched for reading grade, were asked to read nonwords. The groups performed similarly on this task. A smaller study by Baddeley, Logie, and Ellis (1988) asked subjects to read words and nonwords that were created by changing one letter in each of 20 different real words. Dyslexics and reading-age matched normal readers were similar in terms of their nonword reading performance. However, it should be noted that the dyslexics read the words relatively better than the control group, calling into question the adequacy of the reading-age match. Nonetheless, the apparently larger word–nonword difference was not statistically significant, and a group of 32 dyslexics, from which an IQ matched sample was drawn, showed a word and nonword reading level that was similar to that of the normal comparison group. Thus, this study found no evidence of a specific nonword reading deficit in dyslexics.

Reviewing these seemingly disparate findings on the status of phonological reading deficits in dyslexia, Snowling and Rack (in press) have discussed a variety of methodological issues. An important factor that seemed to distinguish studies that found a nonword reading deficit from those that did not was age, particularly the age of the readers in the normal comparison group. When normal readers of approximately 7 years of age were tested, their nonword reading skill was poor and, therefore, the probability of finding dyslexic/normal reader differences was reduced. More importantly, the nature and complexity of the nonwords used to assess phonological reading strategies were crucial elements as well as the way in which they were presented. There was a greater probability of finding dyslexic deficits on nonwords that were phonologically complex, containing more than one syllable and/or consonant clusters, and on nonwords that were visually dissimilar to words. The chances of finding dyslexic deficits were reduced when nonwords were presented in the context of visually similar words and where priming effects, therefore, may have come into play.

In short, although a number of studies have challenged the view, there is considerable empirical support for the position that dyslexic children have specific difficulties with the acquisition of phonological reading strategies. This is particularly true when a stringent criterion of normal IQ is applied in the selection of dyslexic readers and when they are compared with normal readers matched for reading comprehension (Aaron, 1989). This does not rule out the possibility, however, that some dyslexics may develop their use of grapheme–phoneme correspondence rules after an initial setback and use them in a number of reading tasks; for example, in lexical decision (Holligan & Johnston, 1988).

Spelling Deficits

In comparison with the wealth of studies addressing the reading capabilities of dyslexic children, there have been relatively few empirical studies of their spelling performance. Early studies, such as those of Naidoo (1972), Boder (1973), and Nelson and Warrington (1974), pointed to two patterns of spelling performance associated with dyslexia. First, there appear to be children who spell phonetically and who therefore have significant difficulties with an irregular orthography such as English. Second, there are dyslexics who have more serious problems in that their spelling errors are dysphonetic; that is, fail to portray the sound sequence of the word correctly. Later studies corroborate this picture, but few have investigated the processing skills associated with the different patterns of deficit.

An exception to this is the work of Frith (1980), who compared dyslexic children with normal spellers as well as with children who read well but who had specific spelling problems (referred to as group B spellers). The dyslexic spellers were characterized as having problems on a number of phonological tasks, which is consistent with much of the evidence reviewed above. Interestingly, the problems of the group B spellers appeared to be due primarily to the way in which they processed words during reading, even though they were relatively good readers. They were not as good as normal readers who were good spellers in profreading and in detecting "e"'s in letter-cancellation tasks. These results, together with the finding that they were also not as good at nonword reading, suggest that the group B spellers tended to process words holistically and without detailed visual attention to their letter-by-letter structures. A problem with this interpretation is that Perin (1983), working with a similar group of adolescent poor spellers, found that this group also had problems on tasks requiring explicit phoneme segmentation. It is therefore plausible that their spelling problems originated from reading difficulties in common with other dyslexics, but that they had largely resolved their earlier reading problems by the time that their spelling was studied.

Clearly there is room for a good deal more systematic work that examines the ability of dyslexic children to spell and relates findings to the underlying processing skills of dyslexics.

Adequacy of the Theory

The two themes that have dominated the field of research on dyslexia during the 11 years since the publication of Vellutino's verbal deficit hypothesis have provided us with a relatively consistent picture of the cognitive characteristics of dyslexic readers and of their predominant reading strategies. Dyslexic children have difficulties with tasks that require explicit phonological awareness, verbal memory, and naming skills; additionally, they experience subtle difficulties with speech perception and production. Studies of their reading have suggested that their problems are mainly with the development and use of phonological strategies. Taken together, it is tempting to draw parallels between their underlying cognitive skills and their reading performance. However, a major problem encountered in doing so is that the findings are based entirely on group studies. By their very nature, group studies average across subjects and therefore overlook individual differences. These individual differences are of potential importance in theorizing about the specific impact of cognitive deficits on the acquisition of reading and spelling processes and, more generally, in evaluating the adequacy of the phonological deficit hypothesis.

Although good evidence in favor of distinct subtypes is certainly lacking (Olson et al., 1985; Treiman & Hirsh-Pasek, 1985; Seymour, 1986), possibly the most systematic approach to the study of individual differences among dyslexics has revealed important variations in their reading and spelling skills. Researchers using a cognitive–neuropsychological approach have provided unequivocal evidence that individual dyslexic children, studied at one point in time, can vary qualitatively with respect to their patterns of reading (and spelling) performance. First, developmental dyslexics who have a specific problem with phonological reading strategies, as revealed by their superior word reading ability compared to their nonword reading skill, have been likened to neurological patients with acquired phonological dyslexia after brain damage (Campbell & Butterworth, 1985; Seymour & MacGregor, 1984; Temple & Marshall, 1983). In contrast, dyslexics who have relatively less difficulty with phonological reading strategies but have problems with direct lexical strategies, as evidenced by problems with the reading of irregular words, have been labeled developmental surface dyslexics (Coltheart, Masterson, Byng, Prior, & Riddoch 1983) or developmental morphemic dyslexics (Seymour, 1986).

The findings of cognitive–neuropsychological studies have enchanced our understanding of the different ways in which reading can break down after brain damage and, to some extent, as the consequence of developmental difficulties, but attempts to link these impairments with underlying processing deficits have been limited. Campbell and Butterworth (1985) speculated that the problems encountered by their subject, R.E., a developmental phonological dyslexic, stemmed from this individual's inability to carry out phonemic parsing because of her extremely limited short-term memory capacity. However, since R.E. was already an adult by the time she was studied, much of their argument remains conjecture, as does that of Funnell and Davidson (1989), who have recently described a similar case.

Moreover, even within one so-called subtype, there is variation: Snowling, Stackhouse, and Rack (1986) described seven developmental phonological dyslexics, all of whom read nonwords significantly less well than expected, given their word recognition levels. Closer examination of the phonological skills of the individuals case by case suggested that the precise locus of their deficit affected the nature of the "dyslexia" that they exhibited. Among dyslexics of lower reading age, this could be seen clearly by an examination of their spelling errors. Perhaps most importantly, it might be deduced that phonological skills are a good predictor of future prognosis. In order to explore this possibility, longitudinal studies are needed for the purpose of mapping the cognitive profiles of individual dyslexic children and conducting ongoing follow-up of these children for an extended period of time to discern their eventual outcome in terms of reading and spelling processes.

To this end, one of the children originally studied by Snowling et al. (1986), J.M., has been followed now for 6 years. When first assessed, J.M. had problems primarily with output phonology (segmentation, memory, and repetition difficulties), and these difficulties persist to date, although he is now 14 years old (Hulme & Snowling, 1991). Interestingly, J.M. still cannot read nonwords effectively, and his spelling is markedly dysphonetic, despite several years of remediation that included phonics training (Snowling & Hulme, 1989). One aspect of J.M.'s performance that may be of importance is that his visual skills are excellent. We have therefore speculated that he has learned to read by relying on his visual strengths. This compensatory route apparently was unavailable to another developmental dyslexic, J.A.S., who was studied as an adult by Goulandris and Snowling (1991). Unlike J.M., J.A.S. had mastered letter–sound rules but in her reading she confused homophones (e.g., pair–pare, pair–pear), and her spelling was extremely phonetic. Another interesting difference between J.A.S. and J.M. was that J.A.S. had severe visual memory deficits. We are forced to assume that these deficits played some role in her reading failure.

Potentially, then, individual case studies provide powerful tools for exploring the relationships between cognitive deficits and reading failure. The case of J.M. provides excellent confirmation for the picture emerging from group studies—there is a highly specific association between phonological deficits in the processing of both spoken and printed words. This approach is equally useful in identifying the development and use of compensatory strategies and in determining how these are linked with individual strengths and weaknesses within dyslexic individuals, a point well illustrated by the contrasting patterns found in J.M. and J.A.S.

A possible objection to the argument we have put forward, both with respect to single case and group studies, is that we have focused solely on the processing of single words in spoken language and in reading tasks. We would argue that our reasons for doing so are precisely because there is relatively little evidence that dyslexics have more global language difficulties than linguistically normal individuals, and, where dyslexics' difficulties seem more extensive, this is attributable precisely to processing limitations of the types we have discussed. For instance, reports of narrative speech deficits in dyslexia are most likely traceable to word-finding (naming) deficits at the single word level (Davenport, Yingling, Fein Galin, & Johnstone, 1986). It falls to us to expand briefly on this argument before discussing the implications of our hypothesis for treatment.

First, the argument that dyslexics principally show deficits with the phonological aspects of language has been advanced. However, a number of recent studies have suggested difficulties with syntactic processing. Bowey (1986), for example, showed that there was a strong correlation between a measure of syntactic awareness and decoding skill, and that good readers performed at a higher level on tasks designed to tap the ability to judge grammatical well-formedness than poor readers. A problem with these studies, and others of similar ilk, is that it is possible that certain syntactic structures—for example, relative clauses—are only encountered with any degree of frequency in written language. It follows that poor readers will have had less exposure to these situations than good readers and, hence, will have difficulty in dealing with them. Without data from reading-age matched controls, it is not possible to judge the validity of these findings.

Similarly, there have been a number of reports concerning the language comprehension abilities of dyslexic readers (Byrne, 1981; Stein, Cairns, & Zurif, 1984). Together, these studies have contributed to the formulation of the "structural lag hypothesis"; that is, that dyslexics are delayed in their acquisition of certain syntactic structures (Shankweiler & Crain, 1986). However, recent work has suggested that, rather than lacking knowledge of certain syntactic structures that emerge late in language acquisition, poor readers are subject to processing limitations that cause comprehension failure in particular contexts. In this regard, Macaruso, Bar-Shalom, Crain, and Shankweiler (1989) presented groups of good and poor 7-year-old readers with spoken sentences containing temporal terms; for example, "Before you push the car, push the horse" and "After you pick up the truck, pick up the horse." The subjects were asked to move toys in line with the instructions in the test sentences.

In the first experiment, the comprehension of sentences in which there was conflict between conceptual order and order of mention was tested and compared with that of sentences in which there was correspondence between conceptual order and order of mention. Overall, the poor readers made more errors than the good readers, especially ordering errors, and their main difficulty was in processing sentences containing the term *after*. Nonetheless, their overall success rate was high (some 75% of sentences were comprehended correctly). This goes against the hypothesis that poor readers have a general lag in syntactic development. Thus, a second experiment explored their performance when processing load was varied in one of two ways.

The first manipulation of processing load was brought about by adding pronominal modifiers to half of the test sentences; for example, "Push the second smallest horse before you push the car." The second manipulation was of context, so that subjects were first asked to choose one of the toys and then this item was included in the subordinate clause, thereby making the context helpful. Poor readers were found to make more errors with the interpretation of the complex noun phrases than with the simple versions, and also to have fewer problems in the context conditions. Overall, the results went against the structural lag hypothesis and suggested instead that poor readers are subject to processing limitations. It can be argued that these processing limitations arise because of their phonological deficits and, more specifically, their memory coding problems.

Turning to written language processing, there is virtually no evidence that dyslexic children have difficulties with syntactic or comprehension processes that cannot be explained by the basic difficulty that they have with decoding skills (Perfetti, Goldman, & Hogaboam, 1979; Stanovich, 1986). In fact, Stanovich (1980) argued that poor readers are likely to use context more during reading than good readers, to compensate for their slow decoding speed. In line with this position, Frith and Snowling (1983) found that dyslexic readers were as good as reading-age matched controls at selecting the missing words in a written text, using a modified cloze procedure. Furthermore, they were able to answer questions that were posed about the text after the exercise better than the children in the control group. This ability to comprehend text well holds in single-case studies also. J.M., the developmental phonological dyslexic whom we described above, had extreme difficulty in using phonological reading strategies. Nonetheless, we found him to be perfect when required to complete cloze tasks or to detect anomalies in written text, and also in answering questions requiring either recall of factual material from the text or inferences based on it (Snowling & Hulme, 1989).

In short, experiments exploring language processing beyond the single-word level have failed to find deficits in dyslexia that cannot be explained in terms of relatively low-level phonological difficulties such as word-finding and short-term memory problems. These data underscore the specificity of the problem facing dyslexic readers, a problem that resides in the processing of speech-based material and one that has an impact on the development of phonological coding capacities for both written and spoken language.

Treatment Implications

Despite the enormous number of published studies on developmental dyslexia, there has been scarcely any research directed at the question of how best to treat these difficulties. A number of studies carried out in dyslexia clinics in the United Kingdom, using variants of multisensory teaching techniques, have reported gains in reading performance but these studies have lacked appropriate experimental controls, limiting their validity (Andrews & Shaw, 1986; Hornsby & Miles, 1980). In Canada, Lovett, Ransby, and Barron (1988) compared the effectiveness of three teaching regimes: one provided training in word recognition and decoding skills, one in both oral and written skills, and one in "classroom survival skills," an alternative treatment control. There was a posttraining advantage for those readers receiving the training in word recognition and decoding who had been defined as accuracy disabled and rate disabled. Once again, however, it is difficult to evaluate the specific aspects of treatment that led to gains, given the realistic but thus uncontrolled teaching regimes.

The predominant approach to teaching dyslexic children recognizes their difficulty with sounds. The most popular teaching schemes embody highly structured phonic teaching, with explicit emphasis on learning to relate spelling patterns to sound (Hornsby, 1985). There is, however, a dearth of empirical evidence to substantiate claims for the effectiveness of these approaches. Moreover, there is reason to suppose that these methods, which involve teaching children to decode words phoneme by phoneme, will place a burden on skills of phonemic awareness, short-term memory, and sound blending, all of which tend to be deficient in dyslexic children (Wagner & Torgeson, 1987). It may be the case that some dyslexic children fail to respond to these programs for reasons related to the extent and severity of their (phonological) impairment, and learn to read using an alternative whole-word approach. Certainly J.M., whom we discussed earlier, has been taught by these methods; yet, he has evidently learned to read slowly and without developing phonological reading strategies (Snowling & Hulme, 1989).

A possible reason for the failure of phonic methods to help J.M. and some other dyslexics is that the traditional phonic approach to teaching these children is based on a crude theoretical position: Dyslexic children are deficient in phonic skills, and these skills need to be taught to them explicitly. In fact, these techniques simply may place excessive demands on many dyslexic children's ability to deal with speech sounds. The work described earlier concerned with phonological awareness and the distinction between the subsyllabic units, onset, and rime is relevant here.

The predictive relationship between the ability to detect rhymes and learning to read most likely arises because children use their knowledge of the shared sound similarities between words to categorize the written versions of these words. Hence, knowing that *train, brain,* and *main* rhyme may allow a child to read *brain* and *main* by analogy with *train* (Goswami, 1988) and to spell them alike. This work leads naturally, therefore, to a tentative suggestion for a method for teaching dyslexic children to read and spell. Since we know that sensitivity to rhyme normally develops before sensitivity to phonemic units, teaching methods should capitalize on the relative ease of segmenting words into onset and rime units. Analysis of words into onset and rime units should increase sensitivity to mappings between groups of letters and sound segments (e.g., /ight/ is pronounced /ite/), and thereby facilitate the learning of spelling patterns to sound relationships. In essence, teaching through onset-rime divisions may represent a fruitful new approach because it will encourage the development of analytic reading strategies without overburdening the dyslexic's weak phonological skills.

There is some preliminary evidence from experimental studies to support this approach to teaching. Bradley and Bryant (1983) found that training children to categorize words according to their sounds (onsets and rimes), in combination with training in representing the sounds of words with letters, led to significant improvements in these children's reading and spelling skills. More recently, Wise, Olson, and Treiman (1990) have looked directly at teaching normal children to read words divided into onset and rime units. Using a computer, the word to be learned was presented on a monitor screen and groups of letters within the word could be separately highlighted. At the same time, a text-to-speech system would produce the sound of the part of the word that was highlighted. Sometimes, the division of the word coincided with the onset-rime division; sometimes, it did not. They found that words taught by separating them into onset and rime were learned better than those that were not. However, this was far from a realistic teaching study. The children were seen only once, and we do not know whether such learning would be durable or show generalization. Nevertheless, this study provides an excellent starting point for more realistic teaching studies. Since it seems possible that methods based on the onset-rime distinction may prove particularly useful for dyslexic children, research into this possibility is urgently needed.

Conclusions and Future Directions

There can be little doubt in our minds that research in this field has made massive strides forward in recent years. The research reviewed here indicates with some precision the range of phonological deficits that affect many dyslexic children. Furthermore, there are good grounds for believing that these phonological deficits play a role in causing these children's reading difficulties. What, then, should research in the near future try to achieve?

There are three issues that stand out as being important and worthy of more scrutiny. The first is to continue to forge explicit links between underlying phonological deficits and problems in learning to read and spell. By now there is no doubt that many dyslexic children experience difficulties with a wide variety of phonological skills, such as phonological awareness, short- and long-term verbal memory processes, and nonword repetition. A major issue is to relate these deficits more explicitly to the patterns of reading and spelling difficulties in these children.

The second issue follows directly from the first and concerns the problem of individual differences. The charge that experimental psychologisits too often ignore individual differences among their subjects is far from novel. In the field of dyslexia, it is potentially very important, however. It is a truism that dyslexic children, just as normal children, differ. We critically need more precise information about these differences and the origin (in terms of underlying cognitive porcesses) of different patterns of reading and spelling problems. Such knowledge is of great theoretical interest in terms of understanding the cognitive processes involved in learning to read. In practical terms, such knowledge certainly will have an important bearing on the development of teaching techniques.

This brings us to our final issue, which concerns remediation. We have spent relatively little time in this chapter talking about remediation. This, we would argue, is an unfortunate reflection on our current state of knowledge. The body of research in this area largely has been focused on the difficulties that characterize dyslexic children rather than how these difficulties can be treated. To some extent, this is defensible; before trying to tackle a problem, it is undoubtedly useful to have an accurate description of its nature. Having read our views on this subject, we hope people will agree with our view that we now know a considerable amount about the nature of dyslexia and that the time is now ripe to turn to studies that will directly confront treatment. We have made some fairly specific suggestions concerning the implications of current knowledge about the cognitive deficits in dyslexic children for teaching. It is to be hoped that in the near future these important practical issues are given more attention in research studies. Studies of treatment and its effectiveness, in the long term, are powerful ways of assessing the adequacy of our current theories about the underlying causes of dyslexia.

References

Aaron, P. G. (1989). Qualitative and quantitative differences among dyslexic, normal and non dyslexic poor readers. *Reading and Writing*, *1*, 291–309.

Andrews, N. & Shaw, J. (1986). The efficacy of teaching dyslexics. *Child: Care, Health and Development*, *12*, 53–62.

Baddeley, A. D., Ellis, N. Miles, T., & Lewis, V. (1982). Developmental and acquired dyslexia: A comparison. *Cognition*, *11*, 185–195.

Baddeley, A. B., & Hitch, G. (1974). Working memory. In G. H. Bower (Ed.), *The psychology of learning and motivation* (Vol. 8, pp. 47–90). New York: Academic Press.

Baddeley, A. D., Logie, R., & Ellis, N. (1988). Characteristics of developmental dyslexia. *Cognition*, *29*, 197–228.

Baron, J. (1979). Orthographic and word specific mechanisms in children's reading of words. *Child Development*, *50*, 60–72.

Beech, J. R., & Harding, L. M. (1984). Phonemic processing from a developmental lag viewpoint. *Reading Research Quarterly*, *19*, 357–366.

Boder, E. M. (1973). Developmental dyslexia: A diagnostic approach based on three atypical reading-spelling patterns. *Developmental Medicine and Child Neurology*, *15*, 663–687.

Bowey, J. A. (1986) Syntactic awareness in relation to reading skill and ongoing reading comprehension. *Journal of Experimental Child Psychology*, *41*, 282–299.

Bradley, L., & Bryant, P. E. (1978). Difficulties in auditory organisation as a possible cause of reading backwardness. *Nature*, *271*, 746–747.

Bradley, L., & Bryant, P. E. (1983). Categorising sounds and learning to read: A causal connexion. *Nature*, *301*, 419–421.

Brandt, J. & Rosen, J. (1980). Auditory-phonemic perception in dyslexia: Categorised identification and discrimination of stop consonants. *Brain and Language*, *9*, 324–327.

Bryant, P. E., & Bradley, L. (1985). *Children's reading problems*. Oxford: Blackwell.

Byrne, B. (1981). Deficient syntactic control in poor readers: Is a weak phonetic memory code responsible? *Applied Psycholinguistics*, *2*, 201–212.

Byrne, B., & Shea, P. (1979). Semantic and phonetic memory codes in beginning readers. *Memory and Cognition*, *7*, 333–338.

Campbell, R. (1985), When children writen non-words to dictation. *Journal of Experimental Child Psychology*, *40*, 133–151.

Campbell, R., & Butterworth, B. (1985). Phonological dyslexia and dysgraphia in a highly literate subject; A developmental case with associated deficits of phonemic awareness and processing. *Quarterly Journal of Experimental Psychology*, *37A*, 435–475.

Coltheart M., Masterson, J., Byng, S., Prior, M., & Riddoch, J. (1983). Surface dyslexia. *Quarterly Journal of Experimental Psychology*, *35A*, 469–496.

Davenport, L., Yingling, C., Fein, G., Galin D., & Johnstone, J. (1986). Narrative speech deficits in dyslexics. *Journal of Clinical and Experimental Neuropsychology*, *8*, 347–361.

Denckla, M. B., & Rudel, R. G. (1976). Rapid automatized naming: Dyslexia differentiated from other learning disabilities. *Neuropsychologia*, *14*, 471–479.

Dibenedetto, B., Richardson, E., & Kochnower, J. (1983). Vowel generation in normal and learning disabled readers. *Journal of Educational Psychology*, *75*, 576–582.

Ehri, L. (1989). Reconceptualising the development of sight-word reading and its relationship to decoding. In P. Gough (Ed.), *Reading acquistition*. London: Erlbaum.

Frith U. (1980). Unexpected spelling problems. In U. Frith (Ed.), *Cognitive processes in spelling*. London: Academic Press.

Frith, U. (1985). Beneath the surface of developmental dyslexia. In K. E. Patterson, J. C. Marshall, & M. Colthear (Eds.), *Surface dyslexia*. London: Routledge & Kegan-Paul.

Frith, U., & Snowling, M. (1983). Reading for meaning and reading for sound in autistic and dyslexic children. *British Journal of Developmental Psychology*, *1*, 329–42.

Funnell, E., & Davidson, M. (1989). Lexical capture: A developmental disorder of reading and spelling. *Quarterly Journal of Experimental Psychology*, *41A*, 471–487.

Godfrey, J., Syrdal-Lasky, A., Millay, K., & Knox, C. (1981). Performance of dyslexic children on speech perception test. *Journal of Experimental Child Psychology*, *32*, 401–424.

Goswami, U. (1988). Orthographic analogies and reading development. *Quarterly Journal of Experimental Psychology*, *40A*, 239–268.

Goswami, U., & Bryant, P. (1990). *Phonological skills and learning to read*. London: Erlbaum.

Goulandris, N., & Snowling, M. (1991). Visual memory deficits: A possible cause of developmental dyslexia? *Cognitive Neuropsychology*, *8*, 127–154.

Hall, J., Wilson, K., Humphreys, M., Tinzman, M. & Bowyer, P. (1983). Phonemic similarity effects in good vs. poor readers. *Memory and Cognition*, *11*, 520–527.

Hinshelwood, J. (1895). Word-blindness and visual memory. *Lancet*, *2*, 1564–1570.

Hinshelwood, J. (1917). *Congenital word-blindness*. London: Lewis.

Holligan, C., & Johnston, R. S. (1988). The use of phonological information by good and poor readers in memory and reading tasks. *Memory and Cognition*, *16*, 522–542.

Hornsby, B. (1985). A structured phonetic-linguistic method for teaching dyslexics. In Snowling, M, (Ed.), *Children's Written Language Difficulties* (pp. 119–133). Windsor: NFER-Nelson.

Hornsby, B., & Miles, T. (1980). The effects of a dyslexia centered teaching programme. *British Journal of Educational Psychology*, *50*, 236–242.

Hulme, C. (1981). *Reading retardation and multi-sensory teaching*. London: Routledge & Kegan Paul.

Hulme, C. (1987). Reading retardation. In J. R. Beech & A. M. Colley (Eds.), *Cognitive apporaches to reading*, (pp. 94–128). Chichester: Wiley.

Hulme, C. (1988). The implausibility of low-level visual deficits as a cause of children's reading difficulties. *Cognitive Neuropsychology*, *5*, 369–374.

Hulme, C., & Snowling, M. (1988). The classification of children's reading difficulties. *Developmental Medicine and Child Neurology*, *37*, 167–169

Hulme, C., & Snowling, M. (1991). Deficits in output phonology cause developmental phonological dyslexia. *Mind and Language*, *6*, 130–134.

Hulme, C., & Tordoff, V. (1989). Working memory development: The effects of speech rate, word length and acoustic similarity on serial recall. *Journal of Experimental Child Psychology*, *48*, 1–19.

Johnston, R. S. (1982). Phonological coding in dyslexic readers. *British Journal of Psychology*, *73*, 455–460.

Johnston, R. S., Rugg, M., & Scott, S. (1987). Phonological similarity effects memory span and developmental reading disorders: The nature of the relationship. *British Journal of Psychology*, 78, 205–211.

Jorm, A. F. (1983). Specific reading retardation and working memory: A review. *British Journal of Psychology*, 74, 311–342.

Jorm, A. F., Share D. L., MacLean R., & Matthews, R. (1984). Phonological confusability in short-term memory for sentences as a predictor of reading ability. *British Journal of Psychology*, 75, 393–400.

Katz, R. (1986) Phonological deficiencies in children with reading disability: Evidence from an object naming task. *Cognition*, 22, 225–57.

Kleiman, G. N. (1975). Speech recoding in reading. *Journal of Verbal Learning and Verbal Behaviour*, 14, 323–339.

Kochnower, J., Richardson, E., & DiBenedetto, B. (1983). A comparison of the phonic decoding ability of normal and learning disabled children. *Journal of Learning Disabilities*, 16, 348–351.

Lovett, M., Ransby, M., & Barron, R. (1988). Treatment, subtype and word type in dyslexic children's response to remediation. *Brain and Language*, 34, 328–349.

Lundberg, I., Olofsson, A., & Wall, S. (1981). Reading and spelling skills in the first school years predicted from phonemic awareness skills in kindergarten. *Scandinavian Journal of Psychology*, 21, 159–173.

Macaruso, P., Bar-Shalom, E., Crain, S., & Shankweiler, D. (1989). Comprehension of temporal terms by good and poor readers. *Language and Speech*, 32, 45–67.

Mann, V., & Liberman, I. Y. (1984). Phonological awareness and verbal short-term memory: Can they presage early reading success? *Journal of Learning Disabilities*, 17, 592–599.

Mark, L. S., Shankweiler, B., Liberman, I., & Fowler, C. (1977). Phonetic recoding in the beginning reader. *Memory and Cognition*, 5, 623–9.

Marsh, G., Friedman, M., Welch, V., & Desberg, P. (1981). *A cognitive-developmental theory of reading acquisition. Reading research: Advances in theory and practice, 3.* New York: Academic Press.

Miles, T. (1983). *Dyslexia: The pattern of difficulties*. London: Granada.

Morais, J., Bertelson, P., Cary, L., & Alegria, J. (1986). Literacy training and speech segmentation. *Cognition*, 24, 45–64.

Naidoo, S. (1972). *Specific dyslexia*. London: Pitman Publishing.

Nelson, H., & Warrington, E. K. (1974). Developmental spelling disability and its relation to other cognitive abilities. *British Journal of Psychology*, 65, 265–74.

Olson, R. K., Kliegl, R., Davidson, B. J., & Davies, S. (1984). Development of phonetic memory codes in disabled and normal readers. *Journal of Experimental Child Psychology*, 37, 187–206

Olson, R. K., Kliegl, R., Davidson, B. J., & Foltz, G. (1985). Individual and developmental differences in reading disability. In T. G. Waller (Ed.), *Reading research: Advances in theory and practice* (Vol. 4). New York: Academic Press.

Orton, S. T. (1937). *Reading*, writing and speech problems in children. London: Chapman and Hall Ltd.

Perfetti, C., Goldman, S., & Hogaboam, T. (1979). Reading skill and the identification of words in dscourse context. *Memory and Cognition*, 7, 273–82.

Perin, D. (1983). Phonemic segmentation and spelling. *British Journal of Psychology*, *74*, 129–44.

Pring, L., & Snowling, M. (1986). Developmental changes in word recognition: an information processing account. *Quarterly Journal of Experimental Psychology*, *38A*, 395–418.

Rack, J. (1985). Orthographic and phonetic coding in normal and dyslexic readers. *British Journal of Psychology*, *76*, 325–340.

Reed, M. (1989). speech perception and the discrimination of brief auditory cues in reading disabled children. *Journal of Experimental Child Psychology*, *48*, 270–292.

Rubin, H. Zimerman, S., & Katz, R. (1989). Phonological knowledge and naming ability in children with reading disability. *Reading & Writing*, *1*, 393–404.

Rutter, M., Tizard, J., & Whitmore, K. (Eds.) (1970). *Education, health and behaviour*. London: Longmans

Seidenberg, M., Bruck, M., Fonarolo, B., & Backman M. (1985). Word recognition processes of poor and disabled readers: Do they necessarily differ? *Applied Psycholinguistics*, *6*, 161–180.

Seymour, P. H. K. (1986). *Cognitive analysis of dyslexia*. London: Routledge and Kegan Paul.

Seymour, P. H. K., & Elder, M. (1988). Beginning reading without phonology. *Cognitive Neuropsychology*, *3*, 1–36.

Seymour P. H. K., & MacGregor, C. (1984). Developmental dyslexia: A cognitive experimental analysis of phonological, morphemic and visual impairments. *Cognitive Neuropsychology*, *1*, 43–82.

Shankweiler, D., & Crain, S. (1986). Language mechanisms and reading disorder: A modular approach. *Cognition*, *24*, 139–164.

Shankweiler, D., Liberman, I., Mark, L., Fowler, C., & Fischer, F. (1979). The speech code and learning to read. *Journal of Experimental Psychology*: *Human Learning and Memory*, *5*, 531–45.

Siegel, L., & Linder, B. (1984). Short-term memory processes in children with reading and arithmetic disabilities. *Developmental Psychology*, *20*, 200–207.

Siegel, L. S., & Ryan, E. B. (1988). The development of grammatical sensitivity and phonological skills in normally achieving and learning disabled children. *Developmental Psychology*, *24*, 28–37.

Snowling, M. (1980). The development of grapheme-phoneme correspondences in normal and dyslexic readers. *Journal of Experimental Child Psychology*, *29*, 294–305.

Snowling, M. (1981). Phonemic deficits in developmental dyslexia. *Psychological Research*, *43*, 219–234.

Snowling, M. J. (1983). The comparison of acquired and developmental disorders of reading. *Cognition*, *14*, 105–118.

Snowling, M. (1987), *Dyslexia: A cognitive developmental perspective*. Oxford: Basil Blaskwell.

Snowling, M., Goulandris, N., Bowlby, M., & Howell, P. (1986). Segmentation and speech perception in relation to reading skill. *Journal of Experimental Child Psychology*, *41*, 489–507.

Snowling, M., & Hulme, C. (1989). A longitudinal case study of developmental phonological dyslexia. *Cognitive Neuropsychology*, *6*, 379–401.

Snowling, M. J., & Rack, J. P. (in press). Dyslexia: Deficits in grapheme-phoneme correspondence? In J. Stein (Ed.), *Vision and Visual Dyslexia*.

Snowling, M. J., Stackhouse, J., & Rack, J. P. (1986). Phonological dyslexia and dysgraphia: A developmental analysis. *Cognitive Neuropsychology, 3*, 309–339.

Stanovich, K. E. (1986). Cognitive processes and the reading problems of learning-disabled children: Evaluating the assumption of specificity. In J. Torgeson & B. Wong (Eds.), *Psychological and educational perspectives on learning disabilities*. New York: Academic Press.

Stanovich, K. E., Cunningham, A. E., & Cramer, B. B. (1984). Assessing phonological skills in kindergarten children: Issues of task comparability. *Journal of Experimental Child Psychology, 38*, 175–190.

Stein, C., Cairs, H., & Zurif, E. (1984). Sentence comprehension limitations related to syntactic deficits in reading-disabled children. *Applied Psycholinguistics, 5*, 305322.

Stuart, M., & Coltheart, M. (1988). Does reading develop in a sequence of stages? *Cognition, 30*, 139–181.

Szeszulski, P., & Manis, F. (1987). A comparison of word recognition processes in dyslexic an normal readers at two different reading age levels. *Journal of Experimental Child Psychology, 44*, 364–376.

Temple, C., & Marshall, J. (1983). A case study of developmental phonological dyslexia. *British Journal of Psychology, 74*, 517–533.

Torgeson, J., Rashottte, C., Greenstein J., Houck, G., & Portes, P. (1988). Academic difficulties of learning disabled children who perform poorly on memory span tasks. In H. L. Swanson (Ed.), *Memory and learning disabilities: Advances in learning and behavioral disabilities*. Greenwich, CT: JAI Press.

Torgeson, J., & Wagner, R. (1989). Blending and segmentation processes in beginning readers. *Journal of Experimental Child Psychology, 49*, 364–376.

Treinman, R. (1983). The structure of spoken syllables: Evidence from novel word games. *Cognition, 15*, 49–74.

Treiman, R. (1985). Onsets and rimes as units of spoken syllables: evidence from children. *Journal of Experimental Child Psychology, 39*, 161–181.

Treiman, R., & Hirsh-Pasek, K. (1985). Are there qualitative differences in reading behavior between dyslexics and normal readers? *Memory and Cognition, 13*, 357–364.

Vellutino, F. R. (1979). *Dyslexia: Theory and research*. Cambridge: MIT Press.

Vellutino, F. R., & Scanlon, D. M. (1987). Phological coding, phonological awareness and reading ability: evidence from a longitudinal and experimental study. *Merrill-Plamer Quarterly, 33*, 321–364.

Wagner, R., & Torgeson, J. (1987). The nature of phonological processing and its causal role in the acquisition of reading skill. *Psychological Bulletin, 101*, 192–212.

Wise, B., Olson, R., & Treiman, R. (1990). Subsyllabic units as aids in beginning readers word learning: Onset-rime versus post-vowel segmentation. *Journal of Experimental Child Psychology, 49*, 1–19.

Wolf, M. (1986). The question of essential differences in developmental dyslexia: A response to Seidenberg, Bruck, Fonoralo & Backman. *Applied Psycholinguistics, 7*, 69–75.

10
The Inactive Learner Hypothesis: Myth or Reality?

Elizabeth J. Short, Christopher W. Schatschneider, and Sarah E. Friebert

Learning disabled children have often been characterized as inactive or passive problem solvers as compared to their non-learning disabled peers (Meltzer, Solomon, & Fenton, 1987; Short, Cuddy, Friebert, & Schatschneider, 1989). Many researchers interested in the inactive learner hypothesis (Torgesen, 1977) have focused on the domain of problem solving because it enables an examination of students' ability to formulate or define problems, their selection and implementation of strategies designed to solve these problems, and their ability to evaluate their progress toward achieving task goals (Pressley, 1986; Pressley, Borkowski, & Schneider, 1987; Ryan, Short, & Weed, 1986; Sternberg, 1977; Stone & Michals, 1986, Swanson, 1988). The finding that learning disabled students are less proficient than their non-learning disabled counterparts in academic performance can be expanded to include observations that learning disabled students are ineffective in planning, problem representation, self-monitoring, and approaching the task in an organized fashion (Hallahan & Bryan, 1981; Torgesen, 1982). Learning disabled students are not only less efficient in problem solving per se, but they are also less flexible in their selection of task-appropriate strategies than their non-learning disabled peers. They tend to adhere rigidly to one aspect of the problem, experiencing great difficulty shifting their attention from one dimension of a problem to another (Short, Friebert, & Andrist, 1990). Finally, learning disabled students seem to have developed a limited strategic repertoire. They appear to be unaware of the utility of a variety of strategies and fail to monitor the effectiveness of the particular strategy adopted (Brown & Palincsar, 1982; Flavell, 1979).

Given the vast array of problem-solving differences between learning disabled and non-learning disabled students in both academic and social situations, it is not surprising that learning disabled learners have been described as "inactive learners" and "other regulated" (Torgesen, 1982). Self-regulated learning involves active participation on the part of the learner in planning and monitoring the learning process (Corno, 1986). As such, a self-regulated learning style is a prerequisite for successful learning. This chapter examines the utility of the inactive learner hypothesis for explaining the academic and social failures of learning disabled students. Whereas the authors acknowledge the fact that no one theory or hypothesis to date can completely account for every learning disabled student's academic and social failure, the inactive learner hypothesis can be offered as a partial explanation for many learning disabled children's failure. Support for the inactive learner hypothesis will be drawn from research on cognition, metacognition, and motivation. The plethora of treatment approaches for learning disabled children identified as inactive learners speaks to the appeal of this hypothesis and to the optimism of the field. Yet, disenchantment with the hypothesis has surfaced for a variety of reasons, including sample heterogeneity and variable treatment effects.

Historical Antecedents of the Theory

Learning disabled children have been consistently distinguished by one feature: an incongruity between their expected academic achievement based on their mental ability and their actual performance in the learning situation (Short et al., 1989; Short, Feagans, McKinney, & Applebaum, 1984). The main issue has been to determine what specific factor(s) or deficit(s) interferes between normal mental ability and impaired independent achievement (Short et al., 1989). Numerous suggestions have been made regarding the causal factors responsible for this discrepancy, including specific cognitive deficits, specific strategic deficits, and specific motivational deficits (Ryan et al., 1986). However, no consensus has been reached regarding the ultimate cause of learning disabilities.

An examination of the historical roots of the inactive learner hypothesis reveals recurring themes with new twists. Before 1968, when Kirk coined the term *learning disabilities*, learning disabled students were studied under the rubric of underachievement. The sentiment at the time was that students failed in school due to some faulty transactional pattern at home. The assumption was that emotional factors blocked the learning process (Kessler, 1988). Thus, the home environment and the mother, in particular, was blamed for the learning failure of the child. Dissatisfied with this approach, Cruickshank (1977) argued that not all learning failures stemmed from faulty transactional patterns in the home, but might instead be the result of brain injury. With this reevaluation, the locus of the deficit was shifted from the other to the self. Then in 1963, Kirk introduced the construct of learning disabilities in an attempt to shift the emphasis from speculation about the causes of learning failure to identification and treatment of the learning problems themselves (Taylor, 1988).

Under the direction of Samuel Kirk, the National Advisory Committee on Handicapped Children put forth an operational definition of learning disabilities in 1968. The definition cites that children with learning disabilities show deficits in one or more of the psychological processes involved in learning, and further specifies that these deficits are not caused by physical handicaps, mental retardation, or from environmental disadvantages (Taylor, 1988).

According to Keogh (1987), all subsequent definitions included the same premise: learning disabled students' learning problems are due to deficits in one or more psychological processes. Yet, disagreement arose as to which process was most important to the identification of learning disabilities. Definitions ranged from specific syndromes at one end of the spectrum to more global learning problems at the other end. Neurological deficits in brain functioning were held forth as a causal explanation for the ability–performance discrepancy by those researchers and educators arguing for specific deficits (Rourke, 1985). A flurry of activity was generated during the first decade of learning disabilities research, as efforts were repeatedly directed toward the isolation of the "true" cognitive process responsible for learning disabilities. Nonetheless, at the end of the first decade, we were no closer to the "true" cognitive process responsible for learning disabilities than we are today. It was at the end of this decade that Joseph Torgesen proposed his inactive learner hypothesis (Torgesen, 1977). This hypothesis falls at the opposite end of the definitional continuum from the specific deficit camp, in that it argues that a passive learning style may account for all learning disabled students' failures, regardless of any specific cognitive deficit.

Current Theoretical Perspective

In 1977, Torgesen proposed a different explanation for the reported differences in psychological functions found between learning disabled and non-learning disabled groups. He argued that the performance deficits observed in learning disabled students on tasks assumed to measure specific psychological abilities directly may be due to inefficient use of an existing function and not to a specific ability deficit. He stressed that a distinction between deficits in ability and deficits in performance must be made. Performance deficits could be due to either lack of ability or failure to use existing ability. Deficits resulting from lack of ability mean that the individual is biologically impaired in performing a function. In contrast, performance deficits resulting from production deficits (Flavell, 1977) occur when an individual is capable of performing the function but is not efficiently using available resources. It is important to note that the theory does not deny the existence of ability deficits in some learning disabled students; rather, it calls into question the assumption that observed deficits in functioning are solely due to deficits in ability.

In addition to the argument that learning disabled students' failure on academic tasks is often a byproduct of their inactive approach to learning, Torgesen offered a possible explanation for the characteristic IQ–achievement discrepancy found in learning disabled students. He proposed that the discrepancy observed between intelligence and achievement may be, in fact, the result of differences in the type of learning required by the task. Since it is essentially a measure of skills obtained outside the classroom, intelligence may be viewed, however, as incidentally learned (Flavell, 1971). Once in the classroom, a child must engage in self-conscious or intentional learning and must develop active learning strategies. Discrepancies may occur when comparing IQ scores based on incidental learning with achievement scores based on intentional learning. The discrepant score may not be due to any specific cognitive deficit, but may result instead from factors that influence the ability to use efficient learning strategies. Individuals who have difficulties actively learning new material and developing new strategies to accommodate learning may be considered *inactive learners*. Torgesen's reconceptualization of learning disabilities thus shifted the emphasis from pinpointing specific deficits in perception and cognitive abilities to explaining how nonspecific factors influence learning.

Evidence for the Theory

The concept of the inactive learner has received increased research attention since Torgesen introduced it in 1977 (Bender, 1987). Interest has focused not only on the possibility of cognitive deficits, but also on the metacognitive and motivational factors that influence cognitive performance. Recently, Short and Weissberg-Benchell (1989) explained the significance of cognitive, metacognitive, and motivational factors for successful learning in their Triple Alliance Model. According to the Triple Alliance Model, skilled learners must achieve a delicate balance between cognitive, metacognitive, and motivational processes. Active learners form effective alliances so that metacognitive and motivational forces augment their cognitive skills. In contrast, inactive learners form faulty alliances between cognitive, metacognitive, and motivational skills. This model offers direct support for the inactive learner hypothesis from a number of different perspectives. First, the model proposes that inactivity in learning may occur because of cognitive deficiencies. In addition, performance deficits may result from metacognitive deficiencies. These deficiencies in self-regulated skills would dramatically affect the learner's ability to demonstrate cognitive competence. Performance deficits may be also caused by a faulty motivational style. In the latter two cases, the performance deficit appears to be the same on the surface. However, an examination of the deep structure reveals different etiology (Bray, 1985).

The subsequent sections will describe the evidence for the inactive learning style based on cognitive, metacognitive, and motivational findings.

Cognitive Deficits

Deficits in memory and attentional skills in learning disabled populations have been attributed to both structural and strategic deficits (Short & Weissberg-Benchell, 1989). Although structural deficits seem not to support the inactive learner hypothesis directly, neither do they negate the possibility that poor performance is the net result of the absence of strategies.

Torgesen has conducted several investigations in the area of memory that indicate that many learning disabled students do not use effective memorization strategies to aid task performance. In one study, 2nd grade students classified as good and poor readers were compared on sequential recall tasks (Torgesen & Goldman, 1977). The two groups were shown drawings of common objects, with the experimenters pointing to a variety of pictures. After a 15-second delay, during which time the child's eyes were closed, the child was asked to point to the objects previously selected. Poor readers were less efficient in their recall of the objects than their skilled reader counterparts. Since this difference was attributed to failure to employ verbal rehearsal as a strategy, poor readers' passivity on the task was assumed to be responsible for their poor performance. This assumption was validated further by Torgesen and Goldman (1977), who observed that task performance could be improved substantially by brief training in verbal rehearsal. These results concerning passivity in learning have been replicated repeatedly by Torgesen and his colleagues (Torgesen, Murphy, & Ivy, 1979). In these studies, passivity in learning seemed to be due to a failure to use strategic knowledge.

Support for the inactive learner hypothesis can be drawn from the memory literature, but it also exists in the attentional literature. Deficits in attention observed in learning disabled populations are quite variable and appear to affect learning in different ways (Keogh & Margolois, 1976). In an observational study conducted by McKinney and Feagans (1983), learning disabled children were shown to be deficient in task-oriented behaviors such as concentration, attention, and task persistence. The variability of their attentional skills was highlighted further in another observational study (Freidman, Cancelli, & Yoshida, 1988). Learning disabled children exhibited less on-task behavior than their non-learning disabled peers in the classroom setting, but when placed in a resource room, the learning disabled students were observed to be on-task just as often as their non-learning disabled peers. The authors argue that attention to task is not stable, but is specific and variable depending on classroom setting, type of instruction, and involvement of peers. Taken together, these studies suggest that learning disabled students possess the ability to sustain their attention in academic contexts, but fail to do so consistently as a function of situational factors.

Training studies have met with considerable success in improving the attending behavior of learning disabled students across a variety of situations (Hallahan, Kneedler, & Lloyd, 1983). The strategy employed involved the self-monitoring of attention skills. Students were asked to record on-task and off-task behaviors at certain prescribed time intervals. In addition to self-monitoring, this behavior modification technique made use of charting and reinforcers to change maladaptive classroom behavior. The fact that such straightforward training improved the attending behaviors of the learning disabled students suggests that they possess the ability to attend, but fail to do so without assistance.

Taken together, support for strategy deficits or inactive learning in learning disabled populations has been demonstrated across a variety of tasks. Memory tasks include those involving words (Bauer, 1977), digits (Torgesen & Houck, 1980), sentences (Kee, Worden, & Throckmorton, 1984), and narratives (Wong & Jones, 1982). Attentional tasks include sustained attention (Hallahan et al., 1983) and selective attention (Short et al., 1990). These strategic deficits bear direct relevance to the inactive learner hypothesis in that the observable performance of learning disabled students often greatly underestimates the actual competence of these students. In addition, brief strategy training often dramatically improved the academic performance of learning disabled students. The presence of a strategic deficit does not preclude the possibility that structural differences exist between some learning disabled and non-learning disabled learners (Pascul-Leone, 1970). However, the data suggest that a substantial number of learning disabled learners fail to process information strategically and do not take advantage of existing capacities (Chi, 1977; Short & Weissberg-Benchell, 1989).

Metacognition

Metacognitive factors have been implicated consistently as critical elements in the development of an active learning style. Metacognition can be defined as the student's awareness of his/her own cognition and the techniques employed to regulate cognitive skills (Brown, 1978). The sensitivity or awareness aspect of metacognition refers to the learner's awareness of person, task, and strategy variables that affect cognitive performance (Flavell & Wellman, 1977). The assumption is that with each new educational experience, students acquire more information about strengths and weaknesses in the self as a learner, the ease or difficulty of an array of tasks, and the range of application for a variety of strategies. The second aspect of the definition refers to the self-regulation of learning: how students use their knowledge of the self, strategy, and task variables to plan, implement, monitor, and regulate task performance (Brown, Bransford, Ferrara, & Campione, 1983; Flavell, 1981). Without adequate knowledge about person, task, and strategy variables, it would be difficult to imagine how a student would become self-regulated in the learning process.

A number of studies have shown that learning disabled students lack sufficient metacognitive knowledge in a variety of domains, including attention (Loper, Hallahan, & Ianna, 1982), memory (Borkowski, Peck, Reid, & Kurtz, 1983), reading (Short & Ryan, 1984; Wong & Jones, 1982), problem solving (Short et al., 1990), and language (Feagans & Short, 1986). Perhaps more relevant to the inactive learner hypothesis, however, are the deficits observed in the self-regulation aspect of metacognition. In a recent study of self-regulation abilities among non-learning disabled, learning disabled, and mentally retarded students, Short, Schatschneider, Cuddy, Evans, Dellick, and Basili (1991) provide considerable evidence for the inactive learner hypothesis. Students were asked to perform a series of analogies twice, first on their own (independent), and second while thinking aloud. Performance measures included the number of correctly solved analogies in the independent and the think-aloud condition. In addition, protocols recorded from the think-aloud performance were scored qualitatively for self-regulated learning (i.e., problem definition, strategic awareness, and amount of adult assistance via prompts), as well as for verbal ability (i.e., fluency and complexity). The assumption was that the self-regulated learner strategically would be aware, would represent the problem space adequately, and would require only minimal adult assistance in problem solving.

Two pieces of data from this study support the inactive learner hypothesis. First, learning disabled students were superior in their problem-solving performance under the think-aloud condition as compared to the independent condition. Although the verbalizations were left to the discretion of the learner, encouraging students to talk through the problem appeared to foster a more active style of processing. A second piece of evidence supporting the theory was obtained from the think-aloud protocols. Despite no differences in verbal fluency among the three groups, non-learning disabled students demonstrated superior skills in all aspects of self-regulation. While learning disabled and mentally retarded students did not differ in terms of their ability to define the problem, learning disabled students demonstrated greater awareness of task-appropriate strategies than did their mentally retarded counterparts. In addition, learning disabled subjects required more prompting than either the non-learning disabled or the mentally retarded students. This finding on the amount of adult assistance required by learning disabled learners is consistent with the inactive learner hypothesis. Despite the fact that learning disabled students possessed the requisite strategic awareness to solve the problems correctly, they required substantial assistance from the experimenter in order to demonstrate this competence. In addition, they failed to use their strategic awareness to help in the representational phase of problem solving. These findings suggest that the learning disabled students are quite aware of task-appropriate strategies, but experience great difficulty gathering appropriate information to solve a problem. When provided with adult assistance, learning disabled students are capable of demonstrating considerable improvement in problem solving as compared to their independent performance.

Metacognitive theory has been quite informative about when, where, and why learning disabled students lapse into a passive learning style (Pressley, 1991). Active learning clearly requires effort on the part of the learner; however, effort is often not sufficient for successful academic performance (Clifford, 1984). According to Pressley's Good Strategy User model, learning disabled students may lapse into an inactive style of learning when they lack (a) concrete processing goals, (b) the self-monitoring skills necessary to evaluate these goals, (c) motivation and/or are anxious, or (d) the background knowledge and strategic repertoire necessary for success.

Why learning disabled students lapse into an inactive style of processing is the subject of some debate. According to the Triple Alliance Model, the passivity results from a faulty alliance between cognitive skills and metacognitive skills. On the one hand, if strategic attempts by the learner meet with repeated failure, the learners' strategic repertoire is limited to methods that do not meet with success. Failure thus conveys the implicit message that strategic effort cannot enhance limited cognitive ability. On the other hand, limited cognitive ability may preclude the spontaneous development and application of strategies designed to enhance learning. This again leaves the learning disabled students with a restricted strategic repertoire with which he/she must operate. Metacognitive theorists would argue that the development of an active learning style necessitates consideration of how cognitive skills, metacognitive skills, and motivational style interact to affect learning (Brown et al., 1983).

Motivational

Motivational deficits in learning disabled students have also been consistently implicated as a factor in their academic failure. The motivational deficits explored by researchers and educators alike are too numerous to list. However, two aspects of motivation, self-concept and attributional style, are particularly noteworthy in terms of supporting the inactive learner hypothesis.

Self-Concept

All problem solvers form self-schemata about their strengths and weaknesses in both academic and social domains (Hagen, Barclay, & Newman, 1982). These self-schemata shape an individual's performance in a variety of ways, including task selection, task persistence, and task orientation. Research on individual differences in self-schemata has concluded that learning disabled students have poor self-perceptions as compared to their non-learning disabled peers. In addition, some data exist for generalized perceptions of low competence across a variety of academic and nonacademic domains (Butkowsky & Willows, 1980). According to the Triple Alliance Model, poor self-concept would lend itself to the adoption of a passive learning style because of a faulty alliance between cognitive and motivational domains. If the learning disabled student perceives him/herself either to be lacking in competence or to be of questionable competence in an academic or social situation, then it should not be surprising that he/she will appear passive in problem solving in order to circumvent the risk of failure. That is, the learner forms a connection between cognitive and motivational skills that prevents him/her from demonstrating existent cognitive competence.

Experimental support for this contention that lack of self-confidence may be responsible, in part, for the passive learning style adopted by learning disabled students has been quite extensive. For example, Donahue, Pearl, and Bryan (1980) demonstrated that learning disabled students' poor referential communication skills were not a function of their cognitive ability (i.e., ability to judge adequacy of cues), but instead appeared to be a function of their negative self-appraisal. Given the task of selecting a target picture from a set of four pictures based on either adequate or inadequate clues, learning disabled students were less apt to question the speaker in the inadequate clue conditions compared to their non-learning disabled counterparts. Donahue et al. (1980) ruled out the possibility that cognitive failure prevented subjects from judging the adequacy of the messages. That is, no differences between learning disabled and non-learning disabled students emerged on their ability to differentiate adequate from inadequate cues. Donahue and her colleagues argued that learning disabled students failed to request further clarification from the speaker because they assumed that the faulty communication was the result of their own inability to comprehend the message. Thus, low self-esteem perpetuated a vicious cycle of failure for the learning disabled students (Torgesen, 1980). Because of repeated failure in social situations, learning disabled students become discouraged about asking questions and adopt a passive communication style instead. This passivity leads to further failure through inactivity which, in turn, reinforces belief in low ability (Licht & Kistner, 1986). Future research should examine the pervasiveness of the debilitative effects of the self-schemata on cognitive performance.

Attributional Style

The impact of attributional style on academic performance has been a subject of much interest for the past two decades (Weiner, 1979). More specifically, researchers and educators have been interested in how perceptions about causality in success and failure situations influence future academic behavior. Causality has been explored in three ways: locus, stability, and control (Weiner, 1979). Factors that are commonly implicated as important causal explanations in learning disabled and non-learning disabled populations include ability, effort, task demands, and luck (Licht, 1983).

Since learning disabled students are apt to experience chronic failure in both academic and social arenas, they come to perceive the causes for their successes and failures in maladaptive ways. Failure is seen as being inevitable, as resulting from lack of ability (stable, internal, and uncontrollable), and as unchangeable (Jacobsen, Lowery, & DuCette, 1986). Success is seen as being unlikely, as resulting from luck or ease of the task (temporary, external, and uncontrollable), and again as unchangeable. This maladaptive attributional profile does not allow learning disabled students to interpret success in a positive light, and thereby to feel a sense of pride in their accomplishments. Similarly, their interpretation of failure as an inevitable consequence of their low ability lends itself to self-doubt, helplessness, and shame. Given this profile of the learning disabled student, it should not be surprising that learning disabled students lack task persistence, self-confidence, and independence in learning (Kistner, Osborne, & LeVerrier, 1988). Unless learning disabled students recognize the importance of their own effort in overcoming failure situations, they are not apt to engage actively in the process of learning.

The important role that attributional processes play in promoting an active style of learning has been highlighted recently by the Triple Alliance Model (Short & Weissberg-Benchell, 1989). According to the model, maladaptive attributional patterns affect both cognitive performance and metacognitive knowledge in several ways, including discouraging task analysis, task persistence, and optimal task selection.

Learning disabled children's faulty attributional pattern leads to the belief that failure is beyond their control and that task outcomes cannot be changed. As a result, no attempt to engage in active task analysis is made. In contrast, active learners develop corrective hypotheses regarding poor performance because they believe task outcome is within their control (Pearl, Bryan, & Herzog, 1983). Moreover, as task difficulty increases, learning disabled children attribute their successes to luck and their failures to poor ability, whereas skilled children attribute successes to high effort and failure to task difficulty (Aponick & Dembo, 1983). Thus, failure to engage in effective task analysis would affect negatively both the exercise of current cognitive skills and the development of effective task-appropriate metacognitive strategies.

Maladaptive attributions also impact on performance by affecting students' task selection. In a study by Fyans and Maehr (1979), elementary school children were asked to choose one of three angle-matching tasks. Although in reality the tasks did not differ, children were told that success for one task could be achieved by ability, for another task by effort, and for a third task by luck. Children chose tasks in accordance with their beliefs regarding the causes of their own successes and failures. In other words, those children who believed that success was due to ability tended to choose ability tasks, and so forth. The implication drawn from this study is that learning disabled children would not select tasks that challenge either their ability or their effort since they do not perceive these variables to be causally important. Here again, cognitive skills are not exercised.

Maladaptive attributions have also been shown to affect task persistence (Butkowsky & Willows, 1980). Challenging tasks may prove to be too difficult for learning disabled students, discouraging effort and strategic behavior. Lack of effort and passivity in the learning environment will not enable the improvement of skills and success to be achieved. Easy tasks will not encourage effort either, since tasks need to be sufficiently challenging so that students can achieve success with some effort. Once students recognize the importance of task persistence for academic success, an effective alliance between motivation, cognition, and metacognition will be formed. The net result of this effective alliance is active, strategic learning.

How Well Does the Theory Account for the Current Data in the Field?

Although learning disabled students often have been characterized as passive in learning situations, more recent investigations have called into question the adequacy of the hypothesis for classifying learning disabled students. In particular, two bodies of literature can be examined to determine the adequacy of the inactive learner hypothesis: (a) the subtyping literature, and (b) the cognitive strategy literature. The question of interest is, "Are all learning disabled learners inactive?" Thus, we are looking for data that suggest learning disabled students are active processors of information.

Empirical classification research has shown great promise in capturing the variability that exists within learning disabled samples (Speece &

Cooper, 1991). Subtyping efforts directed at understanding the variability in learning disabled students' performance have been quite numerous and informative (McKinney, 1988). Recent subtyping work conducted by Speece and her colleagues (Speece, McKinney, & Applebaum, 1985; McKinney & Speece, 1986) directly addresses this question of whether all learning disabled students are inactive learners. Sixty-three school-identified learning disabled students were rated by their teacher on several dimensions of classroom behavior, including independence/dependence, task orientation/distractibility, extraversion/introversion, and considerateness/hostility. The noteworthy dimensions for our hypothesis are the first two. Using the method of hierarchical cluster analysis, Speece et al. (1985) identified seven distinct patterns of strengths and weaknesses based on classroom behavior. Thirty-five percent of the sample was rated by teachers as having normal behavior. That is, about one third of the sample displayed no passivity in learning. In contrast, approximately 40% of the sample displayed maladaptive behavior that would support the inactive learner hypothesis. This inactive subset of the sample was composed of an attention deficit subtype (29%) and a with-drawn subtype (11%). Although both groups would fit the criterion for an inactive learner, the educational implications of subgroup membership are quite different. McKinney and Speece (1986) demonstrated that the longitudinal consequences of inactivity due to attentional problems are much more severe than those due to socially withdrawn behavior. In sum, the important results from this study are twofold: one, not all learning disabled students can be characterized by passivity in learning; and two, the implications of this symptom can be understood only in terms of the cause. Inactivity in learning that stems from both behavior problems and attentional deficits has serious educational consequences for the learning disabled student.

Although considerable evidence from the cognitive strategy literature can be offered in support of the inactive learner hypothesis, data also can be offered as evidence against the theory. In one such study, Havertape and Kass (1978) explored the strategic differences in problem-solving performance between adolescent learning disabled and non-learning disabled students using the think aloud methodology. Analysis of the think aloud protocols revealed that 33% of the learning disabled students gathered appropriate information to solve the problem, whereas 80% of the non-learning disabled students gathered relevant task information. In addition, 40% of the learning disabled students indicated comprehension of the problem, whereas 80% of the non-learning disabled students indicated comprehension. Also, 16% of the learning disabled students used logical and efficient steps to solve the problems, whereas 57% of the non-learning disabled students approached the problem in a logical and efficient fashion. It should be noted that instead of approaching the problem in a logical fashion, 40% of the learning disabled students could be considered inactive in their problem-solving approach in that they were impulsive and random in their responses. Finally, and perhaps most noteworthy, even when learning disabled students were using task-appropriate strategies, they were not likely to complete the problem successfully. By employing the think aloud technique, Havertape and Kass (1978) discovered that the problem-solving inadequacies experienced by some learning disabled students were due to an inactive or passive approach to the task; however, for other learning disabled students, failure was not due to inactivity at all. Instead, their failure in problem solving appeared to be attributable to the inefficient implementation of strategies. Without the think aloud technique, the factors responsible for differences in performance (i.e., passivity, inefficient strategies) could not have been isolated.

Taken together, the evidence from the subtyping literature and the strategy training literature suggests that, whereas passivity may be characteristic of learning disabled students in general, it is inaccurate to assume that all learning disabled students approach learning in a passive fashion. In addition, the passivity observed in learning disabled students is symptomatic of some underlying cause. The causes for passivity may be manifested in any number of ways, including faulty attributions, lack of strategic knowledge, rigid strategic repertoire, narcissistic fantasy, and so forth. As noted by Torgesen (1987), without a clear guiding theory, our research questions will be essentially random guesses. The inactive learner hypothesis, which acknowledges a broad array of nonspecific factors that could contribute to learning failure, is perhaps too loose a hypothesis to allow for an adequate test.

Limitations of the Theory

The assumption underlying both the inactive learner hypothesis (Torgesen, 1977) and the production deficiency hypothesis (Flavell, 1971) is that observed performance underestimates actual competence. More specifically, this discrepancy between observed and expected performance has been attributed to failure to employ strategies actively. Thus, the learning disabled student's academic failure is assumed to result from a generalized absence of strategic behavior. As a result of this assumption, a flurry of activity centered around the development of strategy interventions has been noted.

Recently, Bray (1985) has challenged this approach of emphasizing strategy deficiencies and treatments designed to foster "good strategy users" (Pressley et al., 1987). While the inactive learner hypothesis focused attention on the development of strategic approaches for all learners, Bray's notion of "production anomalies and strategic competence" has turned researchers'/educators' attention to the study of strategic competence on a more broad-based level. In other words, Bray argues that the emphasis should be on when learners can use a strategy and when they cannot, rather than on the strategy itself. The concept of *production anomalies* argues for an examination of strategic flexibility or the point at which learners' strategies break down.

Bray's point about production anomalies is well taken, particularly with learning disabled populations. Although learning disabled learners have been assumed to be deficient in their use of strategies across a wide array of tasks, this is not synonymous with a sheer absence of strategic behavior (i.e., inactive learning). This distinction was made clear by the two previously mentioned studies employing the think aloud technique (Havertape & Kass, 1978; Short et al., 1991). One criticism of the theory therefore results from its focus on generalized passivity within the child.

The inactive learner hypothesis has lost favor in the field of learning disabilities for several other reasons as well. The trend over the past decade has been toward definitional specificity, measurement specificity, and causal specificity. Due to the heterogeneous nature of learning disabled populations, progress has been difficult to achieve. Dissatisfied researchers and practitioners have moved away from global definitions and hypotheses. Instead, they have focused their attention on the identification of specific subgroups of learning disabled students who share similar processing deficits. By focusing on carefully crafted subgroups of learning disabled students who possess similar profiles of strengths and weaknesses across a variety of cognitive tasks, experimenters can assess more adequately the effectiveness of interventions (Speece & Cooper, 1991).

A third limitation of the inactive learner hypothesis is that no clear means of measurement was put forth by the theory. One possible way to measure inactivity might be to observe the spontaneous use of strategies among learning disabled students. At any rate, specificity in measurement has been an important issue for all practitioners interested in classification. However, no uniform measure has been agreed on to date.

A fourth drawback to the theory is its failure to specify whether the characteristic passivity is a primary cause of learning disabilities or simply the consequence of learning failure. The inactive learner hypothesis "lumped" learning disabled students together based on their global characteristic of passivity. In the field, the focus of our interventions turned toward increasing active learning without a clear view of what factors were causing the inactivity. Learning disabled students' passivity ostensibly could be attributed to a variety of factors, including lack of knowledge about strategies, laziness, and defensiveness (Kessler, 1988). Treatment approaches designed to change the passivity of learning disabled students should target the cause and not simply the symptom of the behavior.

When all aspects are considered together, the inactive learner hypothesis clearly has been useful in that it directed our attention to aspects of the learner that are quite malleable (e.g., passive style, strategic repertoire, and motivational style). However, although the hypothesis offered some hope of remediating the learning disabled student's learning failure, several shortcomings were noted. These include (a) treatment imprecision, (b) definitional imprecision, (c) measurement imprecision, and (d) causal imprecision.

Treatment Implications

Promoting active self-regulated learning in learning disabled children is a formidable challenge to educators and parents. Although promising techniques are currently available, their efficacy for all learning disabled students is questionable. All intervention techniques presented here have been designed to place the locus of control in the hands of the student and are therefore incompatible with an inactive learning style. Although interventions ideally are designed to give the student ultimate responsibility for learning, developmental considerations often preclude yielding total responsibility for learning. That is, young learners may not have the necessary self-regulatory skills needed to learn effectively on their own. Nonetheless, these interventions have shown great promise in promoting active learning. Interventions can be directed at both the institutional and individual level.

Institutional Interventions

Too often our educational system fosters dependence, rather than independence, in learning. At almost every level of the educational ladder, students look to their teachers for goal-setting, strategy selection/implementation, and monitoring/evaluation. This style of passive learning is often unknowingly reinforced by teachers focused on classroom gains instead of individual learner gains. While this criticism legitimately can be levied at regular education, it is perhaps even more noteworthy when one examines special education programs. All handicapped learners have individual educational plans (IEPs) developed for them by teachers and parents. These IEPs establish daily, monthly, and yearly goals for the students, with the skills and strategies to be accomplished clearly delineated. Typically, these IEPs are developed without input from the student and therefore represent a clear-cut example of "other regulation." With this in mind, it is apparent that programmatic changes must be undertaken for self-regulated learning to develop.

One such change has been suggested by Van Reusen (1984), who advocated for learning disabled adolescents' active participation in the formulation of their IEPs. Support for the characteristic passivity of learning disabled students was obtained by Van Reusen (1984) when he observed that adolescent learning disabled students participated at a minimal level during IEP meetings when allowed the opportunity to advocate for themselves. He further noted that with training in self-advocacy techniques, learning disabled adolescents were able to provide valuable insights into their learning problems and were quite capable of goal-setting behaviors not otherwise demonstrated. Thus, the IEP came to function as a cooperative contract between the student and his/her parents and teachers, rather than as a perfunctory, externally applied learning directive.

A second institutional change designed to foster an active, self-regulated learning style in learning disabled students involves loosening the structure of the learning environment. Although clear structure in classrooms has been shown to be correlated positively with achievement gains (Cullinan, Lloyd, & Epstein, 1981), the presence of clear structure also seems to increase the learner's dependence on the teacher for organizing tasks, overall decision making, and error detection and correction. Thus, highly structured learning environments appear to foster both the adoption of an external locus of control and feelings of learned helplessness (Schumaker, Deshler, & Ellis, 1986).

Research support for the powerful effect of classroom structure on learning and motivation is quite consistent (Schunk, 1985). Three types of classrooms have been shown to affect students' performance in diverse ways: (a) competitive learning (i.e., ego-involved learning), (b) mastery learning (i.e., task-involved learning), and (c) cooperative learning (i.e., group approach). Covington and Omelich (1981) demonstrated that the goal of learning in a mastery setting is to increase knowledge and comprehension whereas the goal of learning in a competitive setting is to avoid failure rather than to pursue knowledge. In addition, because mastery-learning settings allow for the retesting of skills, students are more apt to set realistic goals. Allowing students to set realistic goals reaps great motivational benefits, particularly for learning disabled students (Schunk, 1984, 1985; Tollefson, Tracy, Johnson, Farmer, & Buenning, 1984). In addition, the retesting and monitoring process increases students' grade aspirations and confidence as well as their beliefs in the value of effort for success (Covington & Omelich, 1981; Nicholls, 1984). Further, learning disabled students placed in resource rooms or self-contained classrooms (where learning goals are individualized) perceive themselves to be more academically competent than those learning disabled children placed in regular classrooms (Renick, 1985).

Cooperative learning appears to have powerful effects as well, although the data are less conclusive. Cooperative learning settings seem to be most beneficial for children with low self-concepts because when a group succeeds, all group members feel a sense of pride and satisfaction (Ames & Felker, 1979). Provided groups succeed in the identification of problem goals and selection of task-appropriate strategies, the cooperative learning structure would be optimal for learning disabled students in that effective problem-solving skills can be both modeled and practiced in a nonthreatening environment. If the group fails, however, learning disabled students may assume responsibility for this failure, thereby diminishing the probability of their active group involvement in the future.

Taken together, the data on mastery and cooperative learning environments suggest that the structure of both the resource room and the regular classroom should be loosened somewhat to allow students to practice their skills in problem identification, strategy selection, self-monitoring, and strategy revision. Immediate learning goals may have to be sacrificed temporarily while students refine their self-regulatory skills. Unless students feel free to exercise these newfound self-regulatory skills, they will remain "other regulated" or "outer directed" (Zigler, 1966).

Individual Interventions

Interventions aimed at modifying the learner's passive behavior are too numerous to list in their entirety. A subset of these interventions include self-instructional training (Meichenbaum, 1977), daily learning logs (D'Arcy, 1981), and the think-aloud technique (Short et al., 1991). All of these interventions are designed to enable teachers to promote a general awareness of the cognitive, metacognitive, and motivational processes involved in learning.

Self-instructional training typically is aimed at two levels of behavior: a global or task-independent level and a specific or task-dependent level (Brown et al., 1983). Global self-instructions are designed to promote active, self-regulated learning across a variety of problem-solving situations. The assumption is that by employing self-verbalizations, the learner will become more active and self-regulated in the problem-solving process. Although self-instructional training techniques are quite diverse in terms of content, a common focus and set of key ingredients are usually retained. Self-instructional approaches commonly focus on problem identification, solution strategies, and support strategies. That is, the self-instructional package usually enables the learner to target a problem for solution, identify a strategy for solving the problem, and muster sufficient attention and motivation to perform the task. Key ingredients to self-instructional packages include verbal directions, modeling, feedback, prompting, systematic fading, and often physical demonstrations. Initially, the self-instructional approach is learned through interaction with the skilled other. This socioinstructional approach allows the self to gain control over learning (Belmont, 1989).

Despite the widely accepted notion that self-instructions greatly improve the problem-solving skills of the learner, few studies have systematically explored the way in which individual difference variables influence the efficacy of self-instructional training. In a recent article by Whitman (1987), the relationship of individual difference variables to the self-instructional process was delineated. Two variables thought to influence greatly the efficacy of self-instructional training were the learners' knowledge base and linguistic ability. To illustrate this point, a self-instructional story grammar technique was shown to be quite effective in promoting reading competence among poor readers (Short & Ryan, 1984). By capitalizing on the learners' prior knowledge of story structure, this story grammar strategy minimized the burden placed on working memory by the trained strategy. The important role played by verbal competence in self-instructional training was illustrated by White, Pascarella, and Pflaum (1981), who showed that self-instructional techniques proved ineffective in promoting reading comprehension unless 2nd grade proficiency had been demonstrated. Thus, active learning can be promoted through the use of self-instructional techniques, provided the learners possess adequate background knowledge and linguistic skills to use the strategies.

A second type of intervention aimed at promoting an active learning style is referred to as self-monitoring. An example of a training technique designed to promote self-monitoring is the use of learning logs (Bondy, 1984). Research by D'Arcy (1981) clearly supports the utility of learning logs for promoting active learning. Students were asked to think about their academic activities daily and write about points of confusion, generate questions for further clarification and self-study, and summarize insights gained from the activity. The shift from product to process learning seemed to encourage an active learning style in students. These learning logs appear to be an effective means for teaching cognitive skills as well as for instilling a self-regulated and motivated approach to learning for skilled learners. Research is still needed on the utility of this method with learning disabled and young learners. Nonetheless, learning logs may be a promising intervention and diagnostic technique with learning disabled students.

Another promising intervention with the inactive learner is the think-aloud technique. Think-aloud techniques require teachers to verbalize the thought processes and strategies that they are using to tackle a specific problem-solving situation (Whimbey & Lochhead, 1986). By thinking aloud, teachers demonstrate their own effective strategies for tackling novel and/or difficult problems. Not only can teachers demonstrate task-appropriate strategies, but they also can model critical coping and repair strategies. This technique has been shown to be an effective way to enhance the problem-solving performance of some learning disabled students (Short et al., 1991) as well as proving to be an important diagnostic tool for assessing the problems encountered during the problem-solving process (Short et al., 1989b).

In summary, numerous treatment approaches have been developed in response to the inactive learner hypothesis. These treatment approaches have been quite successful at improving the problem-solving performance of a variety of learners (e.g., skilled, learning disabled, mentally retarded attention deficit disorder) in a variety of domains (e.g., math, reading, problem solving, writing). Despite the proliferation of seemingly effective treatment programs, however, little attention has been paid to the individual difference variables that appear to interact with treatment outcome.

Conclusions and Future Directions

The inactive learner hypothesis once held theoretical and educational appeal in that it was an all-inclusive theory, but it now appears in hindsight to be plagued with the common problems of the field. These problems include imprecision in sample definition, measurement, and causality. As a result of these problems, interventions aimed at remediating learning disabled students' inactive approach to learning have focused primarily on the development of cognitive and motivational strategies. Considerable progress has been made toward delineating the strategic repertoire of the skilled learner, but the library of strategies available to the learning disabled student remains somewhat of a mystery (Short & Weissberg-Benchell, 1989; Wong, 1985). According to the inactive learner hypothesis, learning disabled students can be characterized by passivity and therefore should appear nonstrategic. Yet evidence clearly exists that this is only applicable to a subgroup of the learning disabled population (Havertape & Kass, 1978; Speece et al., 1985).

So what is the future of our inactive learner hypothesis? Although his comments were not specifically targeted to the inactive learner hypothesis, Torgesen's (1987) recent discussion on the future of learning disabled research seems quite applicable. First, our efforts to describe the inactivity of learning disabled students should be couched in theory. Precise theoretical predictions must be generated about the cause(s) of this inactivity. Once these predictions are made, subgroups of learning disabled students should be carefully selected to test our hypotheses, and samples should be described in great detail to assure future replicability of these findings. On one hand, it is reasonable to imagine a subgroup of learning disabled students whose inactivity primarily is due to the absence of metacognitive knowledge and strategies. An equally reasonable possibility would be a subgroup of learning disabled students whose inactivity is the result of emotional and/or motivational deficits. An adequate test of these predictions depends on precision in both sample selection and measurement. The future of the inactive learner hypothesis as a viable descriptive and experimental tool, therefore, lies in our ability to classify reliable subgroups of inactive learners and to pinpoint the underlying cause(s) for this inactivity.

References

Ames, C., & Felker, D. (1979). An examination of children's attributions and achievement related evaluations in competitive, cooperative, and individualistic reward structures. *Journal of Educational Psychology, 71*, 413–420.

Aponick, D., & Dembo, M. (1983). LD and normal adolescents' causal attributions of success and failure at different levels of task difficulty. *Learning Disability Quarterly, 6*, 31–39.

Bauer, R. A. (1977). Memory processes in children with learning disabilities: Evidence for deficient rehearsal. *Journal of Experimental Child Psychology, 24*, 415–430.

Belmont, J. M. (1989). Cognitive strategies and strategic learning: The socio-instructional approach. *American Psychologist, 44*, 142–148.

Bender, W. N. (1987). Behavioral indicators of temperament and personality in the inactive learner. *Journal of Learning Disabilities, 30*(2), 301–305.

Bondy, E. (1984). Thinking about thinking: Encouraging children's use of metacognitive processes. *Childhood Education, 60*(4), 234–238.

Borkowski, J. G., Peck, V. A., Reid, M. K., & Kurtz, B. (1983). Impulsivity and strategic transfer: Metamemory as a mediator. *Child Development, 54*, 459–473.

Bray, N. W. (1985). *Why are the mentally retarded strategically deficient?* Symposium presented at the 18th annual Gatlinburg Conference on Research and Theory in Mental Retardation and Developmental Disabilities, Gatlinburg, TN.

Brown, A. L. (1978). Knowing when, where, and how to remember. In R. Glaser (Ed.), *Advances in instructional psychology* (Vol. 1, pp. 77–167). Hillsdale, NJ: Lawrence Erlbaum & Associates.

Brown, A. L., Bransford, J. D., Ferrara, R. A., & Campione, J. C. (1983). Learning, remembering, and understanding. In P. H. Mussen (Ed.), *Handbook of child psychology: Cognitive development* (Vol. III, pp. 77–166). New York: John Wiley & Sons.

Brown, A. L., & Palincsar, A. S. (1982). Inducing strategic learning from texts by means of informed, self-control training. *Topics in Learning and Learning Disabilities, 2*, 1–18.

Butkowsky, I. S., & Willows, D. M. (1980). Cognitive-motivational characteristics of children varying in reading ability: Evidence for learned helplessness in poor readers. *Journal of Educational Psychology, 72*, 402–422.

Chi, M. T. (1977). Age differences in memory span. *Journal of Experimental Child Psychology, 23*, 266–271.

Clifford, M. M. (1984). Thoughts on a theory of constructive failure. *Educational Psychologist, 19*, 108–120.

Corno, L. (1986). The metacognitive control components of self-regulated learning. *Contemporary Educational Psychology*, *11*, 333–346.

Covington, M. V., & Omelich, C. L. (1981). As failures mount: Affective and cognitive consequences of ability demotion in the classroom. *Journal of Educational Psychology*, *71*, 169–182.

Cruickshank, W. M. (1977). Some issues facing the field of learning disabilities. *Journal of Learning Disabilities*, *10*, 57–64.

Cullinan D., Lloyd, J., & Epstein, M. H. (1981). Strategy training: A structured approach to arithmetic instruction. *Exceptional Education Quarterly*, *2*, 41–50.

D'Arcy, P. (1981). Putting your own mind to it. *Forum for the Discussion of New Trends in Education*, *23*, 38–40.

Donahue, M., Pearl, R., & Bryan, T. (1980). Learning disabled children's conversational competence: Responses to inadequate messages. *Applied Psycholinguistics*, *1*, 387–403.

Feagans, L., & Short, E. J. (1986). Longitudinal assessment of referential communication skills in normally achieving and learning disabled children. *Developmental Psychology*, *22*, 177–183.

Flavell, J. H. (1971). What is memory development the development of? *Human Development*, *14*, 272–278.

Flavell, J. H. (1977). Cognitive Development. Englewood Cliffs, NJ: Prentice Hall.

Flavell, J. H. (1979). Metacognition and cognitive monitoring: A new era of cognitive-developmental inquiry. *American Psychologist*, *34*, 906–911.

Flavell, J. H. (1981). Cognitive monitoring. In W. P. Dickson (Ed.), *Children's oral communication skills*. New York: Academic Press.

Flavell, J. H., & Wellman, H. M. (1977). Metamemory. In R. V. Kail & J. W. Hagen (Eds.), *Perspectives on the development of memory and cognition* (pp. 3–33). Hillsdale, NJ: Erlbaum & Associates.

Friedman, D. L., Cancelli, A. A., & Yoshida, R. K. (1988). Academic engagement of elementary school children with learning disabilities. *Journal of School Psychology*, *26*, 327–340.

Fyans, L., & Maehr, M. (1979). Attributional style, task selection, and achievement. *Journal of Educational Psychology*, *71*, 499–507.

Hagen, J. W., Barclay, C. R., & Newman, R. S. (1982). Metacognition, self knowledge, and learning disabilities: Some thoughts on knowing and doing. *Topics in Learning and Learning Disabilities*, *2*, 19–26.

Hallahan, D. P., & Bryan, T. H. (1981). Learning disabilities. In J. M. Kaufman & D. P. Hallahan (Eds.), *Handbook of Special Education* (pp. 141–164). Englewood Cliffs, NJ: Prentice-Hall.

Hallahan, D. P., Kneedler, R. D., & Lloyd, J. W. (1983). Cognitive behavior modification techniques for learning-disabled children: Self instruction and self monitoring. In J. D. McKinney & L. Feagans (Eds.), *Current topics in learning disabilities*. Norwood, NJ: Ablex Publishing.

Havertape, J. F., & Kass, C. E. (1978). Examination of problem solving in learning disabled adolescents through verbalized self-instructions. *Learning Disability Quarterly*, *1*, 94–100.

Jacobsen, B., Lowrey, B., & DuCette, J. (1986). Attributions of learning-disabled children. *Journal of Educational Psychology*, *78*, 59–64.

Kee, D., Worden, P. E., & Throckmorton, B. (1984). Sentence demonstration ability in reading disabled vs. normal college students. *Bulletin of the Psychonomic Society, 22*, 183–185.

Keogh, B. K. (1987). A shared attribute model of learning disabilities. In S. Vaughn & C. Bos (Eds.), *Research in learning disabilities: Issues and future directions*. Boston: Little, Brown & Co.

Keogh, B. K., & Margolois, J. (1976). Learn to labor and wait: Attentional problems with children with learning disorders. *Journal of Learning Disabilities, 9*, 276–286.

Kessler, J. W. (1988). *The Psychopathology of Childhood*. Englewood Cliffs, NJ: Prentice Hall.

Kistner, J., Osborne, M., & LeVerrier, L. (1988). Causal attributions of LD children: Developmental patterns and relation to academic progress. *Journal of Educational Psychology, 80*, 82–89.

Licht, B. (1983). Cognitive-motivational factors that contribute to the achievement of learning-disabled children. *Journal of Learning Disabilities, 16*, 483–490.

Licht, B. G., & Kistner, J. A. (1986). Motivational problems of learning-disabled children: Individual differences and their treatment implications. In J. K. Torgesen & B. Y. L. Wong (Eds.), *Psychological and educational perspectives on learning disabilities* (pp. 225–255). New York: Academic Press.

Loper, A. B., Hallahan, D. B., & Ianna, S. O. (1982). Meta-attention in learning disabled and normal students. *Learning Disabilities Quarterly, 5*, 29–36.

McKinney, J. D. (1988). Research on conceptually and empirically derived subtypes of specific learning disabilities. In M. C. Wang, M. C. Reynolds, & H. J. Walberg (Eds.), *The handbook of special education: Research and practice* (Vol. 2, pp. 253–281). Oxford, England: Pergamon Press.

McKinney, J. D., & Feagans, L. (1983). Adaptive classroom behavior of learning disabled children. *Journal of Learning Disabilities, 16*, 360–367.

McKinney, J. D., & Speece, D. L. (1986). Academic consequences and longitudinal stability of behavioral subtypes of learning disabled children. *Journal of Educational Psychology, 78*, 365–372.

Meichenbaum, D. (1977). *Cognitive behavior modification: An integrative approach*. New York: Plenum Press.

Meltzer, L. J., Solomon, M. A., & Fenton, T. (1987, August). *Problem solving strategies in children with and without learning disabilities*. Paper presented at the 95th Annual Convention of the American Psychological Association, New York.

Nicholls, J. (1984). Conceptions of ability and achievement motivation: A theory and its implications for education. In S. Paris, D. Olson, & H. Stevenson (Eds.), *Learning and motivation in the classroom* (pp. 211–237). Hillsdale, NJ: Erlbaum & Associates.

Pascul-Leone, J. (1970). A mathematical model for the transition rule in Piaget's developmental stages. *Acta Psychologia, 32*, 301–345.

Pearl, R., Bryan, T., & Herzog, A. (1983). Learning disabled and nondisabled children's strategy analysis under high and low success conditions. *Learning Disability Quarterly, 6*, 67–74.

Pressley, M. (1986). The relevance of the good strategy user model to the teaching of mathematics. *Educational Psychologist, 21*, 139–161.

Pressley, M. (1991). Can learning disabled children become good strategy users?: How can we find out? In L. Feagans, E. J. Short, & L. Meltzer (Eds.), *Subtypes of learning disabilities: Theoretical perspectives and research* (pp. 137–161). Hillsdale, NJ: Lawrence Erlbaum & Associates.

Pressley, M., Borkowski, J. G., & Schneider, W. (1987). Cognitive strategies: Good strategy users coordinate metacognition and knowledge. In R. Vasta & G. Whitehurst (Eds.), *Annals of Child Development* (Vol. 4, pp. 89–129). Greenwich, CT: JAI Press.

Renick, M. J. (April, 1985). *The development of learning disabled children's self-perceptions*. Paper presented at the biannual meeting of the Society for Research in Child Development, Toronto.

Rourke, B. P. (1985). *Learning disabilities in children: Advances in subtype analysis*. New York: Guilford Press.

Ryan, E. B., Short, E. J., & Weed, K. A. (1986). The role of cognitive strategy training in improving the academic performance of learning disabled children. *Journal of Learning Disabilities*, *19*, 521–529.

Schumaker, J. B., Deshler, D. D., & Ellis, E. S. (1986). Intervention issues related to the education of LD adolescents. In J. K. Torgesen & B. Y. L. Wong (Eds.), *Psychological and educational perspectives on learning disabilities* (pp. 329–365). New York: Academic Press.

Schunk, D. (1984). Sequential attribution feedback and children's achievement behaviors. *Journal of Educational Psychology*, *76*, 1159–1169.

Schunk, D. (1985). Self-efficacy and classroom learning. *Psychology in the Schools*, *22*, 208–223.

Short, E. J., Cuddy, C. L., Friebert, S. E., & Schatschneider, C. W. (1989). The diagnostic and educational utility of thinking aloud during problem solving. In H. L. Swanson, & B. Keogh (Eds.), *Learning disabilities: Theoretical and research issues* (pp. 93–109). Hillsdale, NJ: Lawrence Erlbaum & Associates.

Short, E. J., Feagans, L., McKinney, J. D., & Applebaum, M. I. (1984). Longitudinal stability of LD subtypes based on age- and IQ-achievement discrepancies. *Learning Disability Quarterly*, *9*, 214–225.

Short, E. J., Friebert, S. E., & Andrist, C. G. (1990). Individual differences in attentional processes as a function of age and skill level. *Learning and Individual Differences*, *2*, 389–402.

Short, E. J., & Ryan, E. B. (1984). Metacognitive differences between skilled and less skilled readers: Remediating deficits through story grammar and attributional training. *Journal of Educational Psychology*, *76*, 225–235.

Short, E. J., Schatschneider, C., Cuddy, C. L., Evans, S. W. Dellick, D. M., & Basili, L. A. (1991). The effects of thinking aloud on the problem-solving performance of bright, average learning disabled, and developmentally handicapped students. *Contemporary Educational Psychology*, *16*, 139–153.

Short, E. J., & Weissberg-Benchell, J. (1989). The triple alliance for learning: Cognition, metacognition, and motivation. In C. McCormick, G. Miller, & M. Pressley (Eds.), *Cognitive strategy research: Implications for the curriculum* (pp. 33–63). New York: Springer-Verlag.

Speece, D. L., & Cooper, D. H. (1991). Retreat, regroup, advance? An agenda for empirical classification research in learning disabilities. In L. Feagans, E. J. Short, & L. Meltzer (Eds.), *Subtypes of learning disabilities: Theoretical perspectives and research* (pp. 33–52). Hillsdale, NJ: Lawrence Erlbaum & Associates.

Speece, D. L., McKinney, J. D., & Applebaum, M. I. (1985). Classification and validation of behavioral subtypes of learning disabled children. *Journal of Educational Psychology*, *77*, 67–77.

Sternberg, R. J. (1977). *Intelligence, information processing, and analytical reasoning: The componential analysis of human abilities.* Hillsdale, NJ: Lawrence Erlbaum & Associates.

Stone, A., & Michals, D. (1986). Problem-solving skills in learning disabled children. In S. J. Ceci (Ed.), *Handbook of cognitive, social, and neuropsychological aspects of LD* (Vol. 1, pp. 291–316). Hillsdale, NJ: Lawrence Erlbaum & Associates.

Swanson, H. L. (1988). Learning disabled children's problem solving: Identifying mental processes underlying intelligent performance. *Intelligence*, *12*, 261–278.

Taylor, H. G. (1988). Learning disabilities. In E. J. Mash & L. G. Terdal (Eds.), *Behavioral assessment of childhood disorders* (pp. 402–450). New York: The Guilford Press.

Tollefson, N., Tracy, D., Johnson, E., Farmer, A., & Buenning, M. (1984). Goal setting and personal responsibility training for learning disabled adolescents. *Psychology in the Schools*, *21*, 224–233.

Torgesen, J. K. (1977). The role of nonspecific factors in the task performance of learning-disabled children: A theoretical assessment. *Journal of Learning Disabilities*, *10*, 27–34.

Torgesen, J. K. (1982). The learning-disabled child as an inactive learner: Educational implications. *Topics in Learning and Learning Disabilities*, *2*(1), 45–51.

Torgesen, J. K. (1987). Thinking about the future by distinguishing between issues that have resolutions and those that do not. In S. Vaughn & C. Bos (Eds.), *Research in learning disabilities: Issues and future directions*. Boston: Little, Brown & Co.

Torgesen, J. K., & Goldman, T. (1977). Verbal rehearsal and short-term memory in reading-disabled children. *Child Development*, *48*, 56–60.

Torgesen, J. K., & Houck, G (1980). Processing deficiencies in learning-disabled children who perform poorly on the digit span task. *Journal of Educational Psychology*, *72*, 141–160.

Torgesen, J. K., Murphy, H., & Ivey, C. (1979). The effects of an orienting task on the memory performance of reading disabled children. *Journal of Learning Disabilities*, *12*, 396–401.

Van Reusen, A. K. (1984). *A study on the effect of training learning disabled adolescents in self-advocacy procedures for use in the IEP conference.* Unpublished doctoral dissertation. Lawrence: University of Kansas.

Weiner, B. (1979). A theory of motivation and attribution for some classroom experiences. *Journal of Educational Psychology*, *75*, 530–543.

Whimbey, A., & Lochhead, J. (1986). *Problem solving and comprehension: A short course in analytic reasoning.* San Francisco, CA: Freeman.

White, C. V., Pascarella, E. T., & Pflaum, S. W. (1981). Effects of training in sentence construction on the comprehension of learning disabled children. *Journal of Educational Psychology*, *73*, 697–704.

Wong, B. Y. L. (1985). Metacognition and learning disabilities. In D. L. Forrest-Pressley, G. E. MacKinnon, & T. G. Waller (Eds.), *Metacognition, cognition, and human performance* (Vol. 2, pp. 137–180). New York: Academic Press.

Wong, B. Y. L., & Jones, W. (1982). Increasing metacomprehension in learning disabled and normally achieving students through self questioning training. *Learning Disability Quarterly*, 5, 228–240.

Zigler, E. (1966). Research on personality structure in the retardate. In N. R. Ellis (Ed.), *International review of research in mental retardation* (Vol. 1, pp. 77–108). New York: Academic Press.

11
Genetics

JIM STEVENSON

The role of genetic factors has become a central research question in psychology both in relation to nomothetic and ideographic aspects of development. This represents a marked change from the situation in the early 1970s when skepticism about research on what was termed the *nature–nurture controversy* was at its highest. Since then a growing volume of research activity has centered on the significance of genetic differences in determining individual differences in development. This has included work on IQ and temperament/personality. Reading disability has also been the subject of considerable activity.

One of the factors encouraging this reemergence has been the development of sophisticated methods for formulating and testing theories about the combined action of genetic and environmental effects on development (Hay, 1985; Plomin, 1986). There has been a parallel burgeoning in the understanding of the molecular basis of gene action. This has led to what has been called the *new genetics* (McGuffin, 1987). Reading disability has been the subject of a range of research activity from the population level biometric genetic analysis to the subcellular level chromosomal or even molecular genetic investigations.

These findings on the genetic influences on reading have been reviewed periodically (e.g., Childs & Finucci, 1983; Finucci & Childs, 1983; Finucci, Guthrie, Childs, Abbey, & Childs, 1976; Pennington & Smith, 1983, 1988; Smith, 1986). There have been a number of more general reviews of the program of genetic research into human behavioral and psychological variations (Loehlin, Willerman, & Horn, 1988; Ludlow & Cooper, 1983; Vandenberg, Singer, & Pauls, 1986).

Historical Antecedents of the Theory

A particular landmark in human behavioral genetics was the publication by Jinks and Fulker (1970) of an article that clearly demonstrated the value of applying the biometric techniques of population genetics to human psychological characteristics. Genetic research before that time tended to rely on simple Mendelian (single major gene effects) explanations of the impact of genetic factors. The literature on reading disability had been sparse (e.g., Bakwin, 1973; Hallgren, 1950; Zerbin-Rudin, 1967), although from an early stage the familial nature of reading disability had been noted (Hinshelwood, 1907; Thomas, 1905).

The pre-1970s research had concentrated almost exclusively on twins. Unfortunately, these early twin studies suffered from a number of methodological inadequacies (see Stevenson, Graham, Fredman, & McGloughlin, 1987 for a critique). These early studies indicated that the concordance for monozygotic twin pairs (MZ) was approaching 100% and dizygotic pairs (DZ) was about 30%. Such findings are consistent with all reading difficulties stemming from genetic causes. However, since the methodological failings were in the direction favoring the detection of genetic effects, these early studies need to be looked at as of historical interest only.

The new behavior genetics based on population genetics has a long pedigree. The analytic approach of partitioning the variance observed in the phenotype into components of heritable (additive) genetic effects, nonheritable (nonadditive effects, such as dominance), and various types of environmental influence has its origins in work on animal breeding developed by Sewell Wright in the 1920s. These biometric model building approaches have reached a considerable level of complexity. Fain, Spuhler, and Kimberling (1986) have provided an introduction to the application of these approaches to learning disability data. There has been controversy over the application of such path models (Karlin, Cameron, & Chakraborty, 1983). However, the validity of such an approach has been robustly defended (Cloninger, Rao, Rice, Reich, & Morton, 1983). It is clear that such model fitting approaches are of considerable importance and relevance to developmental psychology in general (Plomin, DeFries, & Fulker, 1988).

There have been methodological and analytic advances using alternatives to genetic model building. For example, DeFries and Fulker (1985, 1988b) have demonstrated the value of a multiple regression procedure to estimate the size of genetic effects. This form of analysis has provided the most convincing evidence to date of genetic influences on reading disability (DeFries, Fulker, & LaBuda, 1987). The regression procedure is particularly valuable when dealing with twin data obtained from samples identified by the presence of at least one learning disabled twin. More generally, it allows estimates to be made of genetic effects in the general population when the only sample of twins available is restricted to those from clinic cases or extreme groups. It is also a flexible technique that has been applied to questions of age related changes in the heritability of reading disability (Wadsworth, Gillis, DeFries, & Fulker, 1989), to sex differences in heritability (DeFries, Gillis, & Wadsworth, in press), and to the comparison of heritability of spelling disability in two different twin samples (DeFries, Stevenson, Gillis, & Wadsworth, in press).

The developments in molecular biology have provided geneticists with powerful procedures for investigating genetic effects. Some of these, such as genetic markers, are considered in more detail below and the field has been reviewed in relation to language-related disorders by Kimberling (1983).

Current Theoretical Position

Single Major Gene Effects

It is important to emphasize again that genetic influences on development can be distinguished in terms of their impact on normal developmental progression and on individual differences. This distinction is important as a basis for quantitative biometric genetic analysis, since it is solely concerned with partitioning variance in a characteristic (phenotype) into its constituent parts, that is, those due to genetic variation (genotype) and those due to environmental variation and experiences. In single gene analysis this distinction between individual differences and normal developmental progression is seen at its most stark. The theory assumes that a different allele (i.e., different forms of a gene at a particular locus) are having a major adverse impact on normal development.

Smith and Goldgar (1986) have argued that if such a single gene can be isolated and characterized it would enhance our understanding of genetic mechanisms at the level of the individual rather than the population. This could have a decisive impact on the counseling for individuals once the genetic properties of dominance and penetrance were established. The technique for identifying the presence of such single major genes is called *segregation analysis*.

This technique is an extension of the principles of Mendelian inheritance. If single major genes are present, then the pattern of characteristics observed in the offspring should conform to expected ratios. The genetic theory allows for interaction between genes at different loci (epistasis), which produces variable penetrance; that is, the likelihood that the gene is expressed is modified by the presence of other genes. Dominance effects also need to be considered, that is, interactions between alleles at the same locus. Smith and Goldgar (1986) provide a succinct introduction to the method of segregation analysis.

A major difficulty in using segregation analysis with reading disability is the problem of clearly defining the phenotype. Just what is the reading disability being investigated? This creates a number of problems. First, many of the early studies did not use a clear operational definition of reading problems. Rather than using standardized test procedures, teachers and parents were often asked to judge whether an individual had a literacy problem. Second, in some studies difficulties in other aspects of development were used to identify a proband (i.e., an individual in a family pedigree that is considered to show the characteristic of interest). Hallgren (1950), for example, used a history of language difficulties as identifying a possible proband. Third, it is becoming clear that reading disability is heterogeneous. If different genetic mechanisms are operating to produce different types of problems, then these need to be distinguished within a pedigree before applying segregation analysis. These issues of specifying the phenotype are pervasive in genetic research on learning disabilities and have hampered progress. It can be argued that the identification of types of reading disability will result from the research program on genetic factors. There is a need for a process of cross-referencing so that the results of laboratory research into cognitive deficits feeds into genetic research and the results of genetic research on the phenotype are added into experimental studies.

Polygenic Models

Although single major gene effects are likely to be most familiar to the nonspecialist, not least because of their association with the classical genetic analyses of Mendel, they may be of far less importance than systems of genetic effects produced by the combined action of a number of genetic loci (polygenic inheritance). The analysis of such influences requires the application of complex mathematical model fitting procedures (Fain et al., 1986).

The usual case is when the psychological characteristics are considered to be caused by a continuously varying underlying attribute called *liability*. Variations in liability are due to the joint effects of genetic and environmental influences. When the magnitude of the underlying liability exceeds a certain value, then the psychological attribute is shown. The simplest case is when the characteristic itself is subject to continuous variation. In this case a threshold does not have to be incorporated into the model. In reading disability there is a strong divergence of opinion about the appropriate way to conceptualize the distribution of reading ability. Rutter and Yule (1975) have argued that there is clear evidence for discontinuity in the distribution. This has been challenged by van der Wissel and Zegers (1985). Bryant and Bradley (1985) have also argued that reading should be viewed as a continuously distributed ability. They go on to suggest that the underlying cognitive capability that produces this variation is phonological awareness, which is itself continuously distributed. Wagner has also suggested the significance of phonological processing ability as a determiner of variation in reading skill (Wagner, 1986; Wagner & Torgesen, 1987).

Yule (1985) argues that the original finding that the excess of specific reading retardation is not simply due to measurement artifacts. This has been confirmed by Stevenson (1988), who showed that in a number of different samples a hump was found at the lower end of the distribution of reading and spelling achievement in relation to intelligence. This was also true of measures of phonological processing, such as non–word reading.

There is no necessary link between a discontinuous distribution of reading scores and genetic causation. The underlying liability might be due to the effect of a single major environmental influence. A hypothetical example could be the presentation of a model of recreational reading by the parents. The extent or frequency of their reading for pleasure may be irrelevant. The lack of exposure of the child to such a model may be all that is necessary for reading disability to occur. Similarly, the absence of a hump in the distribution may not indicate the absence of genetic effects. The crucial issue is the degree of the alleles' impact on liability.

Whether a threshold has to be postulated or not also depends on other effects, such as sex. It has often been postulated that sex differences in the prevalence of a particular characteristic are the product of a sex difference in the threshold for the expression of a condition. The underlying liability is the same but the position of the threshold on the distribution of liability is different for the two sexes. It is such a situation that results in the greater incidence of affected relatives in the family histories of the less affected sex. Individuals from the less affected sex require a greater liability through genetic or environmental loadings in order for the condition to be manifest.

The quantitative genetic approach attempts to partition the variance in the phenotype (V_P) into a simple linear function of genetic variance (V_G) and two types of environmental variance: common environment (V_{CE}) and specific environment (V_{SE}). It is also necessary to complete this breakdown by including error variance (V_e). This can be expressed in the following equation:

$$V_P = V_G + V_E + V_e \qquad (1)$$

The subdivision of the environmental contribution yields:

$$V_P = V_G + V_{CE} + V_{SE} + V_e. \qquad (2)$$

The classic twin study can provide data to provide estimates of the genetic, common, and specific environmental components. The logic of this procedure is as follows. The correlation between sets of scores will be a function of the causal factors that are common to the two sets of scores. When the scores being correlated come from identical (MZ) twins reared together in the same family, the common causal factors are V_G and V_{CE} (Equation [3]). For fraternal (DZ) twins reared in the same family, again

V_{CE} is a common factor but from genetic theory we know they only share $0.5 \, V_G$ (Equation [4]).

$$r_{MZ} = V_G + V_{CE} \tag{3}$$

$$r_{DZ} = 0.5V_G + V_{CE}. \tag{4}$$

By subtraction,

$$r_{MZ} - r_{DZ} = 0.5V_G$$

$$V_G = 2(r_{MZ} - r_{DZ}). \tag{5}$$

Substituting in [3]

$$r_{MZ} = 2(r_{MZ} - r_{DZ}) + V_{CE}$$

$$V_{CE} = r_{MZ} - 2(r_{MZ} - r_{DZ}). \tag{6}$$

With twin data alone the effects of the specific environment and error variance cannot be separated. From Equation (2) and setting V_P equal to 1 we obtain:

$$1 = V_G + V_{CE} + (V_{SE} + V_e).$$

Substituting from Equation (3),

$$1 = r_{MZ} + (V_{SE} + V_e)$$

$$V_{SE} + V_e = 1 - r_{MZ}. \tag{7}$$

Therefore in Equations (5), (6), and (7) we have a means of estimating the contribution of genetic, common, and specific environmental influences, respectively, to the variation in a characteristic.

This is a necessarily simplified account of genetic analysis. There are a number of texts that provide a good introduction to behavior genetics (e.g., Hay, 1985; Plomin, 1986; Plomin, DeFries, & McClearn, 1990). Further elaborations of quantitative genetic analyses applied to learning disabilities can be found in Fain et al. (1986). They discuss liability and threshold models and the fitting of linear models such as that in Equation (2) to genetic data using path analysis.

Evidence Supporting the Theory

Reading in Subjects with Chromosomal Anomalies

The most general evidence that genetic factors contribute to learning disabilities comes from studies on chromosomal abnormality. If individuals with an abnormal chromosomal pattern are also found to have relatively specific deficiencies in their reading ability, then genetic factors have been crudely implicated in those deficiencies. The abnormalities associated with autosomal anomalies are usually severe (e.g., Down syndrome), whereas the sex chromosome anomalies may have only subtle cognitive effects and may be unsuspected. The sex chromosome anomalies may also be quite common. For examples, 47, XXY may occur in as many as 1 in 800 live male births. It is to be expected that the best evidence on genetic involvement in reading comes from studies of sex-chromosome anomalies (Bender, Puck, Salbenblatt, & Robinson, 1986a; Netley, 1983). Boys who are 47, XXY score significantly below matched controls on auditory short-term memory and reading skills (Bender, Puck, Salbenblatt, & Robinson, 1986b). Importantly, this sample of 14 47, XXY cases did not show similar significant deficits in intelligence, perception, and language.

The relative specificity of this link between 47, XXY and reading difficulties is highlighted by the failure to establish any specific reading deficits in 45, XO girls (Turner's syndrome) who show a specific spatial deficit, although there is some evidence indicating that 47, XYY boys may show a somewhat similar pattern of reading deficit to 47, XXY boys (Bender et al., 1986a). Additional evidence of the involvement of sex chromosomes with reading comes from the work demonstrating a link between fragile X and language disorders (Bregman, Dykens, Watson, Ort, & Leckman, 1987; Newell, Sanborn, & Hagerman, 1984).

Multiple Anomaly Syndromes

The identification of specific reading disabilities in individuals with chromosomal anomalies is direct evidence for genetic involvement in reading disability. Similar but less direct evidence comes from children with multiple anomaly syndromes (Shprintzen & Goldberg, 1986) and from what has come to be known as the study of behavioral phenotypes of children with known genetic disorders. Here, specific types of learning disability can be used to aid diagnosis. Further, the link between syndromes with a known genetic origin and reading disability is consistent with the notion that genetic factors can influence such cognitive processes. For example Shprintzen and Goldberg (1986) give the example of some lysosomal storage disease (such as Hurler–Scheie compound syndrome), where mental retardation is often absent but learning disabilities are present.

Genetic Effects Shown in Brain Structure and Function

If genetic factors are to influence reading ability there should be a chain of effects that link gene action, nerve cell structure, and function that should show themselves in differences in the biochemical characteristics, neurophysiology, neuroanatomy, and neuropsychology of reading disabled children. There is accumulating evidence of neurological distinctiveness of reading disabled children. For example, Geschwind and Galaburda (1987) have claimed some evidence that shows developmental dyslexics have discernible neuroanatomical anomalies in the region of the planum temporale of the left hemisphere. Abnormal cortical evoked potentials both to visual (Connors, 1971) and auditory stimulation (Weber & Ommen, 1977) of reading disabled children have been reported. Interestingly, Byring and Jarvilehto (1985) have demonstrated a particularly strong evoked potential effect in poor spellers in their early adolescence. Other supposed neurophysiological deficits in reading disabled children have not been substantiated. Vestibular dysfunction has been proposed as important for learning disabilities. However, a carefully conducted study by Polatajko (1985) failed to demonstrate any vestibular dysfunction in 40 learning disabled children compared to normal controls.

It appears that the evidence from such investigations of possible neurophysiological/neuropsychological mechanisms mediating genetic effects on reading implicate language-related structures and functions rather more than those concerned with processing visual information. This search for the mechanisms underlying reading disorders is starting to use instruments and techniques that allow a far more sensitive monitoring of brain structure and functioning than has been possible hitherto. Petersen, Fox, Posner, Mintum, and Raichle (1988) have demonstrated the power of positron emission tomography to identify regions of the cortex that are active during different aspects of normal reading. According to this study, the temporoparietal region is *not* activated by nonword auditory stimuli but is implicated in phonological coding. This study concerned reading by normal subjects but, as Marshall (1988) has commented, this represents an exciting convergence of interest between neurophysiology and cognitive neuropsychology.

Genetic Marker Studies

One of the potentially most important findings in the genetics of learning disabilities has been the identification of a specific genetic site for a form of familial dyslexia. This autosomal dominant disability has been traced to this locus by the use of genetic linkage analysis (Smith, Kimberling, Pennington, & Lubs, 1983; Smith, Pennington, Kimberling, & Ing, 1990). This technique traces whether a particular characteristic tends to be inherited within a family alongside other characteristics of known genetic origin and with a known location in the genome. Genes that are physically close to one another tend to be inherited together. A characteristic that is of uncertain origin can be confirmed as genetic if such linkage occurs. The absence of linkage could mean either that the trait being considered has no genetic basis or that the gene responsible is distant from known marker genes. Smith et al. (1983) used a wide range of 23 biochemical and chromosome banding heteromorphisms to establish that within nine families exhibiting three-generational transmission of reading disability, all but one family showed linkage between reading disability and a locus on the short arm of chromosome 15. As more families have been added to this series the linkage to a site on chromosome 15 has weakened. Some families show a stronger link to chromosome 6 (Smith, Pennington, Kimberling, & Ing, 1990). Subsequent studies on these families (Pennington et al., 1986) have suggested that the form of reading disability affected is similar to phonological dyslexia (Beauvois & Derouesne, 1979). This adds further support for the value of the two-route model of reading that has been applied so successfully to acquired dyslexia (Coltheart, Patterson, & Marshall, 1988; Patterson, Marshall, & Coltheart, 1985).

Although this work on genetic markers is of considerable interest, the relevance of these findings to the majority of reading disabled children has yet to be established. Few families show the clear three-generational pattern used to identify the sample for these particular linkage studies. There is also some doubt about how clearly the linkage has been established (Plomin, 1989). Nevertheless, this work has stimulated a great deal of interest in the notion that high level cognitive tasks such as reading could be affected by a single gene locus.

How Well does the Theory Account for the Current Data on Learning Disabilities?

The main data on genetic effects in learning disabilities come from two sources: segregation analysis applied to family pedigrees and from the study of twins. To date there have been no adoption studies concentrating on reading, although the children from the Colorado Adoption Project (Plomin, DeFries, & Fulker, 1988) are coming to the age where reading can be assessed.

Family Data

A number of early attempts were made to apply segregation analysis to pedigrees of families containing reading disabled individuals. A variety of single major gene mechanisms were suggested, for example, autosomal dominant (Hallgren, 1950), sex-limited autosomal dominant (Zahalkova, Vrzal, & Kloboukova, 1972) and sex-linked inheritance on the X chromosome (Symmes & Rapoport, 1972). The findings of these studies are of limited value due to a number of methodological difficulties, including the adequacy of definitions of reading disability, ascertainment biases in the selection of families, and weaknesses in the analyses performed.

Finuccci et al. (1976) studied 20 pedigrees and identified a further complication, that of genetic heterogeneity. The pattern of inheritance within the families was not consistent with a single genetic mechanism but rather with a number of modes of genetic influence. It was not until data became available from the Colorado Family Reading Study that segregation analyses could be undertaken to distinguish different types of genetic mechanisms operating on single gene effects in families (DeFries, Singer, Foch, & Lewitter, 1978; Foch, DeFries, McClearn, & Singer, 1977; Lewitter, DeFries, & Elston, 1980). They concluded from a study of 133 families that different genetic systems were influencing the transmission of reading disability. This is the most sophisticated segregation analysis undertaken to date. The data from these families have been subjected to different data analysis methods. For example, LaBuda, Vogler, DeFries, and Fulker (1985) used multivariate path analysis of reading ability to show that symbol-processing speed and spatial/reasoning measures in these and control families was consistent with heterogeneity of reading disorders. However, their results also showed some common familial influences on the different components of reading ability.

Other large data sets have been established, for example by Borges-Osorio and Salzano (1987) in Brazil. They found no evidence for a simple single major gene influence on disabilities in reading and writing, although they have yet to submit their data to formal segregation analysis. Finally, Lundberg and Nilsson (1986) have shown the potential of unusual sources of family data such as church records, which can provide data on literacy in many generations of a family.

The combined effect of genetic and common environmental family effects are sufficiently strong to increase greatly the risk of reading disability in the offspring of affected parents. Vogler, DeFries, and Decker (1985) have provided evidence from the Colorado Family Reading Study that, depending on the rate of reading in the population, the ralative risk for boys with an affected parent ranges from 3.91 to 9.73. This relative risk is the ratio of the probability of the child becoming disabled if the parent is reading disabled or is a normal reader. The relative risk for girls varies from 8.89 to 13.33. Vogler et al. (1985) note that the sex with the lower absolute risk (girls are 4 times less likely to have a reading problem) have the higher relative risk when there is evidence of an affected parent. However a study by Shaywitz, Shaywitz, Fletcher and Escobar (1990) suggests that the gender ratio in reading disabled children is less marked amongst research identified samples than in referred cases. The odd sex ratios in families of reading disabled children (Tallal, Ross, & Curtiss, 1989) has not been replicated in an analysis of data from 5 independent samples (Wadsworth, DeFries, Stevenson, Gilger, & Pennington, 1991). It is clear that the identification of sex related genetic effects is affected both by the definition of reading ability that is used and by the method of ascertainment of the samples. Until the impact of these methodological aspects are better understood, the estimation of relative risk by sex in the families of affected children needs to be treated with caution.

Twin Data

There are three types of twin design that have been used to identify genetic influences on reading. First, there is the orthodox comparison of concordance rates for reading problems in MZ twin pairs and in DZ twin pairs. Such data are obtained in twin samples where at least one member of a twin pair shows a reading disability. Second, there is the estimation of genetic effects from the comparison of within-pair similarity in reading ability using data from samples of twins not selected for the presence of reading difficulty. Third, there is a recently developed multiple regression-based procedure (DeFries & Fulker, 1985). The power of this last technique is that it can provide estimates of genetic effects on disability and on individual differences across the full range of ability from the same data set (DeFries & Fulker, 1988a). It circumvents some of the arbitrary definitions of reading disorder inherent in the concordance procedure.

As mentioned above, the twin studies published before the late 1970s had indicated an almost 100% concordance for reading problems in MZ twin pairs and approximately 30% in DZ pairs. A study of 285 twin pairs from the general population ascertained from hospital birth records and school registers found a somewhat different pattern (Stevenson et al., 1987). The twins were studied within a few months of their 13th birthdays. The concordance rates showed only modest evidence for genetic influences on reading, whereas for spelling quite strong genetic effects were apparent. It was argued that because reading disability is defined by an arbitrary cut-off score on a continuous scale of reading underachievement, just one concordance rate cannot be calculated to provide unequivocal evidence of genetic influences.

Accordingly, Stevenson et al. also analyzed their data to produce estimates of within-pair similarity across the entire range of ability. The following estimates were obtained for the parameters in Equation (2): V_G = 0.29, V_{CE} = 0.22, V_{SE} = 0.33, V_e = 0.15. The distinction between V_{SE} and V_e can be made on the basis of a previous reliability exercise that established the likely measurement error with these tests on 13-year-olds. As with the concordances, the results for spelling were more marked: V_G = 0.73, V_{CE} = 0.02, V_{SE} = 0.16, V_e = 0.09. It is important to note that in both these analyses the effects of IQ have been controlled using multiple regression before the genetic analyses. This might account for the estimate of V_G for reading being lower than that derived from data provided by Harris (1982) on twins. In her study the intraclass correlations were $r_{MZ} = 0.93$ and $r_{DZ} = 0.59$, which yields the following estimates: $V_G = 0.68$, $V_{CE} = 0.25$, and $(V_{SE} + V_e) = 0.07$. However, it may also be that V_G is higher in reading for younger children. The twins in Harris (1982) were in first and second grade, whereas those in Stevenson et al. (1987) were 13 years old. The differential impact of remedial teaching on improving reading rather than spelling could alter within-pair similarity. This could produce an increase in the V_{SE} estimate and a decline in V_G with age for reading but a maintained high V_G for spelling.

The other large-scale twin study on reading using systematic ascertainment is the Colorado Reading Project (DeFries, Fulker, & LaBuda, 1987; LaBuda & DeFries, 1988a; LaBuda, DeFries, & Fulker, 1986). Using the multiple regression method developed by DeFries and Fulker (1985), the score of a cotwin is predicted from those of proband twins plus other terms such as the degree of genetic relatedness. This produced estimates of $V_G = 0.52$ and $V_{CE} = 0.39$ for individual differences in reading ability (LaBuda & DeFries, 1988b). This figure for V_G is somewhat higher than the 0.30 figure obtained for the genetic contribution to reading disability originally obtained from the same sample. However, a subsequent report (DeFries et al., 1987) has given a somewhat higher figure of 0.40 for heritability of the reading disability, what they term h_g^2. The values for V_{CE} and V_{SE} for disability were 0.35 and 0.25, respectively.

The data from these two twin studies have been merged and subjected to joint analyses. The heritability of disability ($h^2{}_g$) for spelling was almost identical in the Colorado (0.62) and London (0.61) studies giving an overall value for the heritability of spelling disability of 0.62 ± 0.13 (p $<.001$) (DeFries, Stevenson, Gillis, & Wadsworth, in press). This result was even more striking given the differences in the way subjects were identified and the use of different spelling measures in the two samples.

Using the Colorado twin sample, Ho and Decker (1988) have confirmed the findings from family studies (LaBuda et al., 1988) that similar familial processes are acting on aspects of information processing such as symbol processing speed, sequential memory, and reading per se. This strongly suggests a common set of genetic influences on a wide range of reading-related abilities. These same genetic effects then may also play a role in producing the information processing deficits seen in reading disabled children.

At the same time, Ho, Gilger, and Decker (1988) have also proposed that one particular subtype of dyslexia can be identified for which genetic influences are particularly strong. Bannatyne (1971) observed that children with a specific profile of abilities, where spatial ability was better than conceptual ability and the processing of sequential information was weakest of all, constitute a subtype of dyslexia that was familial. Subsequently in a systematic family study, Decker and Corley (1984) could not adequately differentiate this profile as more familial than other types of reading disability. Ho et al. (1988) used the Colorado Twin Study of Reading Disability sample to test more directly for genetic effects on this proposed "genetic dyslexia" subtype. The sample was too small to identify reliably the degree of heritability for the Bannatyne subtype to allow comparisons of heritability with other forms of dyslexia. However, the concordance rates in 9 MZ pairs was 67% and in 10 DZ pairs was 30%, at least indicative of a genetic influence for this form of disability.

Both the Colorado and London twin studies highlight the significance of environmental factors in producing individual differences in reading. They also indicate that a single dominant fully penetrant major gene cannot be responsible for most cases of reading disability. This means that the locus on chromosome 15 identified by Smith et al. (1983) must be affecting a relatively small proportion of the population of reading disabled children.

There is an important question that has been raised over the value of twins as a source of data on effects on reading that apply to the general singleton population. Johnson, Prior, and Hay (1984) have studied reading and language development in 18 same-sex male twin pairs. Using the Neale Analysis of Reading Ability, it was found that the twins showed a high rate of reading difficulties, for example, accuracy reading age was below chronological age in 72% of twins. Furthermore, the early language competence of these children was a good predictor of the degree of reading underachievement in relation to IQ. Hay (1985) concludes that these results preclude the generalization of results on reading from twins to singletons because a particular experience of early language delay has a distinctive detrimental effect on twins, reading ability. The main concern about the value of twin data is when effects are found more commonly in twin pairs of one zygosity type. The findings Johnston, Prior, and Hay (1984) do not suggest such effects. As far as genetic estimates are concerned, the impact of language delays in both MZ and DZ pairs tend to inflate the estimates of common environmental effects and thereby underestimate genetic effects. So, although caution is necessary when generalizing from findings on twins to the general population (Hay, O'Brien, Johnston, & Prior, 1894), twin pairs remain an invaluable tool for the analysis of genetic influences on reading ability and disability (Harris, 1986).

Limitations on the Theory

A recurring difficulty in genetic research into reading disabilities has been the clear specification of the disability being studied. Some of these stem from the problems of identifying equivalent reading problems in families in whom individuals have a wide age range. However, many problems stem from the failure to establish diagnostic and nosological groups within the field of learning disabilities. The distinction between specific reading retardation and reading backwardness has yet to gain universal acceptance. Even where clear evidence is present in the distribution of reading score to support the notion of a distinct group of reading underachievers (Stevenson, 1988), this is not necessarily reflected in differences in the reading process itself (Fredman & Stevenson, 1988).

Amid this confusion, genetic studies may play a role in clarifying the important distinctions that need to be made in development of a classificatory framework for reading difficulties. Pennington (1986) has listed a number of features of a marker phenotype, that is, a definition of reading disability that may differ from standard diagnostic criteria but that is ideally suited to genetic research. These are complete penetrance, early onset, developmental persistence, bimodality, and differentiation within pedigrees, that is, some relatives should *not* show the phenotype and be clearly distinguishable and dissociated from other disabilities (e.g., hyperactivity). Pennington applies these criteria to developmental dyslexia and concludes that phoneme awareness and segmentation skills, verbal short-term memory, and lexical retrieval are all candidates for a marker phenotype for reading disability. He suggests that there may even be a common underlying deficit producing disability in all three aspects of processing verbal information.

This is an important review of the relevant research and the targeting of these three characteristics seems sensible. However, the approach advocated by Pennington (1986) is not based on an overall model of the reading process. Indeed, much of the research into genetic factors in reading disability is largely atheoretical. The procedure in, for example, the Colorado Reading Project, is to use a battery of psychometrically developed reading related tests. A single dimension or discriminant is used to derive a score for genetic analysis. The use of such data reduction methods does not take into account the ways in which different components of the reading process may be related to one another.

Another alternative is to use an explicit model to test for where an individual may be failing in the reading process. This therefore does not rely on assumptions of a common basis for most reading difficulties. It recognizes that individuals may differ in the origin and nature of their reading difficulty. The literature on acquired dyslexias provides a significant precedent for this approach. In the field of cognitive neuropsychology it has been demonstrated that by careful examination of the language difficulties of brain damaged adults, types of reading failure can be shown to disassociate. The dissociation provides evidence in support of a two-route model of the reading process. By carefully constructing list of words and nonwords for the subjects to read, specific aspects of weakness can be identified.

It is clear from the work of Coltheart, Masterson, Byng, Prior and Riddoch (1983) and Temple and Marshall (1983) that some developmental dyslexics can also be placed into the surface and phonological categories, respectively. However, it is equally clear that until such a model includes a developmental component, the typology will not fit the range of reading problems found among developmental dyslexics. The theoretical formulation of Frith (1985) goes some way toward this goal.

The genetic analysis of reading disability has started to recognize the need to test forms of disability that are derived from an overall model of the normal reading process. The work of Pennington et al. (1986) is a move in this direction and one that is likely to be more fruitful than continuing to follow a main effects model that underlies the psychometric approach that has dominated genetic research to date.

A significant component of genetic research is the clarification it can provide concerning th potency and type of environmental influence on cognitive development in general, and reading in particular (Rutter, 1985). At the simple level of distinguishing between common and specific environmental effects, genetic research can guide the search for important environmental influences. These estimates for the effects of experiential factors are deduced from the similarities between relatives (especially twins) alone. They do not require the direct measurement of aspects of the environment itself. It is here that genetically oriented researchers fail to take advantage of the opportunity to go on to investigate which aspects of experience actually contribute to reading difficulties. In particular, twins provide a unique opportunity to investigate the role of specific or nonshared environmental characteristics (Bronfenbrenner, 1986).

One such analysis (Stevenson & Fredman, 1990) showed that the estimates for common environmental effects obtained from twin similarity agreed with the proportion of the variance that could be explained by direct measurement of aspects of the family and social experiences of the twins. It was particularly revealing that once intelligence was controlled using a regression procedure then aspects of common environment had little to contribute. That is, family characteristics and features of parental interest in education and engagement in reading were related to the twins' general level of intellectual ability. The important influences specifically on reading were more attributable to the nonshared environment.

It should be noted that these twins were 13 years of age. There may be important family or parental effects specifically on reading that show themselves in the initial stages of learning to read (Hewison, Tizard, & Schofield, 1982). However, these results agree with those of Stevenson, Lee, Stigler, and Lucker (1984), who found that at age 11 years there was little in the family backgrounds or in parent–child interaction of children in Japan, Taiwan, and the United States that differentiated between good and poor readers.

As we come to establish the role of genetic effects on a range of abnormal characteristics in children (Rutter et al., 1990a, 1990b) the potential for common genetic causation becomes salient. In particular, in reading it is clear that two commonly associated characteristics, language and conduct disorders, are also subject to genetic influences. Howlin and Rutter (1987) have reviewed the links between language disorders and reading, but as yet none of the genetically informative studies have attempted to investigate this association using more sophisticated classifications of types of language disorder (Bishop, 1987). One particular aspect that is worth pursuing is the possibility of a genetically produced developmental lag that might commonly underlie both language and reading disorders (Bishop & Edmundson, 1987; Stanovich, Nathan, & Zolman, 1988).

Treatment Implications

At present it is premature to suggest that the program of genetic research into reading disorders has made any major contribution to treatment. There are, however, a number of general implications that it suggests for the way reading disabilities are conceptualized and managed.

First, genetic research has thrown light onto the role of environmental or nongenetic influences. The differentiation of common (shared) or specific (nonshared) environmental influences provides an important step in the development of models of nongenetic influences. This may in turn help to identify and interpret the significance of experiential effects on reading and possibly contribute to remediation or prevention.

Second, the clarification of genetic factors has led to the possibility of firmer guidelines on the identification of children at risk for reading disability. This means that greater importance needs to be given to obtaining family data when assessing children. Vogler, DeFries, and Decker (1985) showed the relative risks for subjects with an affected parent. They conclude that a family history should be taken in conjunction with other indicators of risk of reading disorders such as diagnostic test battery results, teacher ratings, and congenital and perinatal abnormalities. The implication here is both that problems in reading may be more clearly diagnosed at an earlier age and that the possibility exists for identifying children during the preschool years who also may be highly at risk for reading disability. Preventive programs for such children could then be introduced (Stevenson, 1989).

Third, although as yet clear results have not been achieved, it is likely that the extension of genetically informative research designs into studies of the identification and classification of reading disability will be fruitful.

There are a number of studies that are now looking at the relationship between subtypes of reading and genetic etiology. Decker and Bender (1988) suggest that already it is clear, first, that in reading phenotypic homogeneity does not reflect genetic homogeneity. That is, the same reading disorder can have caused by different genetic mechanisms: the example of phonological dyslexia will be discussed below. Second, genetic homogeneity does not produce phenotypic homogeneity. That is, environmental factors can have a strong effect to offset the genetic predisposition to develop reading disability.

This leads to the fourth and final general implication of recent genetic research. There is a need to abandon the view that genetic factors are immutable and fix from conception the developmental history of the child. None of the recent genetic studies confirm the very high (almost 100%) heritability found in the early twin literature. This means that there is much scope for environmental effects. The more we come to understand genetic control over development, the clearer it is that this results in a continuing interplay between genetic systems that change during the lifespan and complex environmental effects, some of which are themselves mediating genetic processes. An example is the correlation between the genetic transmission of a reading disabled parent to his children and the environment such a parent provides in terms of reading instruction and models for the value and importance of literacy.

As yet, genetic research cannot identify which types of reading process are more or less remediable, nor can it provide strong guidelines for planning remediation. The implications are greater for prevention and for developing the general view of the operation of etiological factors in reading disability.

Conclusions and Future Directions

The results of genetically oriented research over the past decade have led to a number of clear conclusions. There is genetic heterogeneity in reading disabilities. There are a number of independent genetic mechanisms that are affecting reading competence; some are linked to the X chromosome and others are clearly autosomal.

There is also the phenomenon of the same phenotype being produced by different genetic mechanisms. This is illustrated by the dominant autosomal single major gene identified by Smith et al. (1983) on chromosome 15. The pattern of reading deficit in families in whom this gene is present is consistent with phonological dyslexia (Pennington et al., 1986). In addition to this single gene there are indications of a possibly polygenic system that influences phonological processing. Using data from the Colorado Twin Study, Olson, Wise, Conners, Rack, and Fulker (1989) found a heritability for phonological coding of 0.46. This contrasts with a heritability for whole word or orthographic reading ability that is essentially zero.

Data from the Stevenson et al. (1987) twin study support these findings. The child's ability to read nonwords aloud (e.g., OWT, OAN) was measured. The intraclass correlations for MZ twins was 0.61 and for same-sex DZ pairs was 0.36, yielding a heritability estimate of 0.50. It could be argued that this putative genetic effect was a result of general intelligence being under a degree of genetic influence. Therefore, the scores were regressed onto WISC–R IQ and the residuals taken. These IQ-independent measures of phonological route functioning were used to calculate heritability. The r_{MZ} was 0.58 and r_{DZ} was 0.28; thus, after IQ was controlled, the heritability rose to 0.60. To test these same twins' abilities to read via a whole word route, they were asked to read irregular words aloud (e.g., ANSWER, LAUGH) (see Fredman & Stevenson, 1988 for further details of the test construction and administration). These words cannot be read using the phonological route since by definition they do not conform to normal phoneme–grapheme correspondences. The heritability for the reading of such irregular words was 0.04 (r_{MZ} = 0.49, r_{DZ} = 0.47). When IQ was controlled this fell to zero (r_{MZ} = 0.38, r_{DZ} = 0.38).

The significance of genetic influences on phonological route processing was further illustrated in an analysis using the multiple regression procedure of DeFries and Fulker (1985, 1988b) to identify the heritability of phonological disability (Stevenson, in press). This analysis produced non-significant values of h^2_g for orthographic disability and values of h^2_g of 0.74 ± 0.38 (P < .05) and 0.74 ± 0.38 (P < .05) for two different components of phonological processing; non-word reading and homophone recognition respectively. An intriguing feature of these results was these represent *two independent* aspects of phonological ability each influenced by genetic factors.

There is nongenetic evidence that suggests that phonological processing (Wagner & Torgesen, 1987) and phonological awareness (Bryant & Bradley, 1985) are strong determinants of reading ability in a large part of the population. The neuroanatomical evidence on developmental dyslexics (Geschwind & Galaburda, 1987) suggests that the planum temporale of the left hemisphere is the site of a range of histological abnormalities. The PET studies of normal reading implicate the temporoparietal region of the left hemisphere as responsible for phonological coding.

It is plausible that these two genetic mechanisms, single major gene on chromosome 15 and a polygenic system, affect reading via their impact on the structure and functioning of this region of the left hemisphere. This suggestion can only be made tentatively at this stage but does at least make a case for the need to consider different genetic mechanisms that produce similar reading deficits.

It is clear that as techniques in molecular genetics proceed and the process of mapping the human genome progresses, the scope for genetic marker studies will increase. It is likely that such research will continue to be applied to other aspects of child disorders. Autism is one such condition that is of considerable genetic interest (Folstein & Rutter, 1988). Here the evidence implicates a genetic effect on language ability. Although reading disability is not of central interest in the case of autism, the possibility of identifying epistasis (i.e., the interaction between genes at different sites) and pleiotropy (i.e., genes having multiple effects on the phenotype) means that within such a genetic research program clarification may emerge of the role of genetic factors in other language-related fields, such as reading.

The importance of longitudinal research in dyslexia has been highlighted by Finucci (1986). DeFries (1988) has demonstrated the value of longitudinal research in establishing links between reading deficits during middle childhood and those in early adulthood. A central part of this issue of stability in reading disability is the role of genetic factors in maintaining the deficit. A major omission from the current data on genetic factors in reading is the absence of a longitudinal twin study. Such a study using measures derived from developmental models of dyslexia, such as that of Frith (1985), is likely to be of the utmost interest and would complement the data on age-related changes in the genetic contribution to IQ produced by Wilson (1983) and by Fulker, DeFries, and Plomin (1988).

References

Bakwin, H. (1973). Reading disability in twins. *Developmental Medicine and Child Neurology*, *15*, 184–187.

Bannatyne, A. (1971). *Language reading and learning disabilities*. Springfield, IL: Charles C. Thomas.

Beauvois, M.-F., & Derouesne, J. (1979) Phonological alexia: three dissociations. *Journal of Neurology, Neurosurgery and Psychiatry*, *42*, 1115–1124.

Bender, B. G., Puck, M. H., Salbenblatt, J. A., & Robinson, A. (1986a). Cognitive development of children with sex chromosome abnormalities. In S. D. Smith (Ed.), *Genetics and learning disabilities* (pp. 175–204). London: Taylor and Francis.

Bender, B. G., Puck, M. H., Salbenblatt, J. A., & Robinson, A. (1986b). Dyslexia in 47, XXY boys identified at birth. *Behavior Genetics*, *16*, 343–354.

Bishop, D. V. M. (1987). The causes of specific developmental language disorder ("developmental dysphasia"). *Journal of Child Psychology and Psychiatry*, *28*, 1–8.

Bishop, D. V. M., & Edmundson, A. (1987). Specific language impairment as a maturational lag: Evidence from longitudinal data on language and motor development. *Developmental Medicine and Child Neurology*, *29*, 442–459.

Borges-Osorio, M. R. L., & Salzano, F. M. (1987). Frequencies of language disabilities and their family patterns in Porto Alegre, Brazil. *Behavior Genetics*, *17*, 53–69.

Bregman, J. D., Dykens, E., Watson, M., Ort, S. I., & Leckman, J. F. (1987). Fragile X syndrome: Variability of phenotypic expression. *Journal of the American Academy of Child and Adolescent Psychiatry*, *26*, 463–471.

Bronfenbrenner, U. (1986). Ecology of the family as a context for human development: Research perspectives. *Developmental Psychology*, *22*, 723–742.

Bryant, P., & Bradley, L. (1985). *Childrens reading problems: Psychology and education*. Oxford: Blackwell.

Byring, R., & Jarvilehto, T. (1985). Auditory and visual evoked potentials of school boys with spelling disabilities. *Developmental Medicine and Child Neurology*, *27*, 141–148.

Childs, B., & Finucci, J. M. (1983). Genetics, epidemiology and specific reading disability. In M. Rutter (Ed.), *Developmental neuropsychiatry* (pp. 507–519). New York: Guilford Press.

Cloninger, C. R., Rao, D. C., Rice, J., Reich, T., & Morton, N. E. (1983). A defense of path analysis in genetic epidemiology. *American Journal of Human Genetics*, *35*, 733–756.

Coltheart, M., Masterson, J., Byng, Prior, M., & Riddoch, J. (1983). Surface dyslexia. *Quarterly Journal of Experimental Psychology*, *35*, 469–595.

Coltheart, M., Patterson, K., & Marshall, J. C. (1988). *Deep dyslexia* (2nd ed.). London: Routledge & Kegan Paul.

Connors, C. K. (1970). Cortical visual evoked response in children with learning disorders. *Psychophysiology*, *7*, 418–428.

Decker, S. N., & Bender, B. G. (1988). Converging evidence for multiple genetic forms of reading disability. *Brain and Language*, *33*, 197–215.

Decker, S. N., & Corley, R. P. (1984). Bannatyne's "genetic dyslexic" subtype: A validation study. *Psychology in the Schools*, *21*, 300–304.

DeFries, J. C. (1988). Colorado Reading Project: Longitudinal analyses. *Annals of Dyslexia*, *38*, 120–130.

DeFries, J. C., & Fulker, D. W. (1985). Multiple regression analysis of twin data. *Behaviour Genetics*, *15*, 467–473.

DeFries, J. C., & Fulker, D. W. (1988a). Multiple regression analysis of twin data: Etiology of deviant scores versus individual differences. *Acta Geneticae Medicae et Gemellologiae*, *37*, 1–13.

DeFries, J. C., & Fulker, D. W. (1988b). Multiple regression analysis of twin data: Etiology of deviant scores versus individual differences. *Acta Genetica et Gemellologiae*, *37*, 205–216.

DeFries, J. C., Fulker, D. W., & LaBuda, M. C. (1987). Evidence for a genetic aetiology in reading disability of twins. *Nature*, *329*, 537–539.

DeFries, J. C., Gillis, J. J., & Wadsworth, S. J. (in press). Genes and genders: a twin study of reading disability. In A. M. Galaburda (Ed.), *The extraordinary brain: neurobiologic issues in developmental dyslexia*. Cambridge, Mass.: MIT Press.

DeFries, J. C., Singer, S. M., Foch, T. Y., & Lewitter, F. I. (1978). Familial nature of reading disability. *British Journal of Psychiatry*, *132*, 361–367.

DeFries, J. C., Stevenson, J., Gillis, J. J., & Wadsworth, S. J. (in press). Genetic etiology of spelling deficits in the Colorado and London twin studies of reading disability. *Reading and Writing*.

Fain, P. R., Spuhler, K. P., & Kimberling, W. J. (1986). Quantitative genetics and learning disabilities. In S. D. Smith (Ed.), *Genetics and learning disabilities* (pp. 21–46). London: Taylor and Francis.

Finucci, J. M. (1986). Follow-up studies of developmental dyslexia and other learning disabilities. In S. D. Smith (Ed.), *Genetics and learning disabilities* (pp. 97–124). London: Taylor and Francis.

Finucci, J. M., & Childs, B. (1983). Dyslexia: family studies. In C. L. Ludlow & J. A. Cooper (Eds.), *Genetic aspects of speech and language disorders* (pp. 157–168). New York: Academic Press.

Finucci, J. M., Guthrie, J. T., Childs, A. L., Abbey, H., & Childs, B. (1976). The genetics of specific reading disability. *Annals of Human Genetics*, *40*, 1–23.

Foch, T. Y., DeFries, J. C., McClearn, G. E., & Singer, S. M. (1977). Familial patterns of impairment in reading disability. *Journal of Educational Psychology*, *69*, 316–329.

Folstein, S. E., & Rutter, M. L. (1988). Autism: Familial aggregation and genetic implications. *Journal of Autism and Developmental Disorders*, *18*, 3–30.

Fredman, G., & Stevenson, J. (1988). Reading processes in specific reading retarded and reading backward 13 year olds. *British Journal of Developmental Psychology*, *6*, 97–108.

Frith, U. (1985) Beneath the surface of surface of surface dyslexia. In K. E. Patterson, J. C. Marshall, & M. Coltheart (Eds.), *Surface dyslexia: Neuropsychological studies of phonological reading* (pp. 301–330). London: Lawrence Erlbaum.

Fulker, D. W., DeFries, J. C., & Plomin, R. (1988). Genetic influence on general mental ability increase between infancy and middle childhood. *Nature*, *336*, 767–769.

Geschwind, N., & Galaburda, A. M. (1987). *Cerebral lateralisation: Biological mechanisms, associations and pathology*. Cambridge, MA: MIT Press.

Hallgren, B. (1950). Specific dyslexia: A chlinical and genetic study.*Acta Psychiatrica and Neurologia Scandinavica*, *65*(Suppl. 1), 1–287.

Harris, E. L. (1982). Genetic and environmental influences on reading achievement: A study of first and second grade twin children. *Acta Geneticae Medicae et Gemellologiae*, *31*, 64–116.

Harris, E. L. (1986). The contribution of twin research to the study of the etiology of reading disability. In S. D. Smith (Ed.), *Genetics and learning disabilities* (pp. 3–20). London: Taylor and Francis.

Hay, D. A. (1985). *Essentials of behaviour genetics*. Oxford: Blackwells. Hay, D. A., O'Brien, P. J., Hohnston, C. J., & Prior, M. (1984). The high incidence of reading disability in twin boys and its implications for genetic analyses. *Acta Geneticae Medicae et Gemellologiae: Twin Research*, *33*, 223–236.

Hewison, J., Tizard, J., & Schofield, W. (1982). Collaboration between teachers and parents in assisting children's reading. *British Journal of Educational Psychology*, *52*, 1–15.

Hinshelwood, J. (1907). Four cases of congenital word-blindness occurring in the same family. *British Medical Journal*, *1*, 608–609.

Ho, H. Z., & Decker, S. N. (1988). Cognitive resemblance in reading disabled twins. *Developmental Medicine and Child Neurology*, *30*, 99–107.

Ho, H. Z., Gilger, J. W., & Decker, S. M. (1988). A twin study of Bannatyne's "genetic dyslexic" sub-type. *Journal of Child Psychology and Psychiatry*, *29*, 63–72.

Howlin, P., & Rutter, M. (1987). The consequences of language delay for other aspects of development. In W. Yule & M. Rutter (Eds.), *Language development and disorders* (pp. 271–294). Clinics in Developmental Medicine No 101–102. Oxford: Mac Keith Press.

Jinks, J. L., & Fulker, D .W. (1970). Comparison of the biometrical genetical, MAVA and classical approaches to the analysis of human behaviour. *Psychological Bulletin*, *73*, 311–349.

Johnston, C., Prior, M., & Hay, D. (1984). Prediction of reading disability in twin boys. *Developmental Medicine and Child Neurology*, *26*, 588–595.

Karlin, S., Cameron, E. C., & Chakraborty, R. (1983). Path analysis in genetic epidemiology: A critique. *American Journal of Human Genetics*, *35*, 695–732.

Kimberling, W. J. (1983). Linkage analysis of communication disorders. In C. L. Ludlow & J. A. Cooper (Eds.), *Genetic aspects of speech and language disorders* (pp. 151–156). New York: Academic Press.

LaBuda, M. C., & DeFries, J. C. (1988a). Genetic and environmental etiologies of reading disability: A twin study. *Annals of Dyslexia*, *38*, 131–138.

LaBuda, M. C., & DeFries, J. C. (1988b). Genetic etiology of reading disability: Evidence from a twin study. In G. T. Pavlidis (Ed.), *Dyslexia: A neuropsychological and learning perspective*. New York: John Wiley.

LaBuda, M. C., DeFries, J. C., & Fulker, D. W. (1986). Multiple regression analysis of twin data obtained from selected samples. *Genetic Epidemiology*, *3*, 425–433

LaBuda, M. C., Vogler, G. P., DeFries, J. C., & Fulker, D. W. (1985). Multivariate familial analysis of cognitive measures in the Colorado Family Reading Study. *Multivariate Behavioral Research*, *20*, 357–368.

Lewitter, F. I., DeFries, J. C., and Elston, R. C. (1980). Genetic models of reading disability. *Behaviour Genetics*, *10*, 9–30.

Loehlin, J. C., Willerman, L., & Horn, J. M. (1988). Human behaviour genetics. *Annual Review of Psychology*, *39*, 101–133.

Ludlow, C. L., & Cooper, J. A. (Eds.) (1983). *Genetic aspects of speech and language disorders*. New York: Academic Press.

Lundberg, I., & Nilsson, L. G. (1986). What church examination records can tell us about the inheritance of reading disability. *Annals of Dyslexia*, *36*, 217–236.

Marshall, J. C. (1988). The life blood of language. *Nature*, *331*, 560–561.

McGuffin, P. (1987). The new genetics and childhood psychiatric disorder. *Journal of Child Psychology and Psychiatry*, *28*, 215–222.

Netley, C. (1983). Sex chromosome abnormalities and the development of verbal and non-verbal abilities. In C. L. Ludlow & J. A. Cooper (Eds.), *Genetic aspects of speech and language disorders* (pp. 179–196). New York: Academic Press.

Newell, K., Sanborn, B., & Hagerman, R. (1984) Speech and language dysfunction in the fragile-X syndrome. In R. Hagerman & P. McBogg (Eds.), *The fragile X syndrome: Diagnosis, biochemistry and treatment* (pp. 175–200). Denver: Spectra.

Olson, R. K., Wise, B., Conners, F., Rack, J., & Fulker, D. (1989). Specific deficits in component reading and language skills: Genetic and environmental influences. *Journal of Learning Disabilities*, *22*, 339–348.

Patterson, K. E., Marshall, J. C., & Coltheart, M. (Eds.) (1985). *Surface dyslexia: Neuropsychological and cognitive studies of phonological reading* London: Lawrence Erlbaum.

Pennington, B. F. (1986). Issues in the diagnosis and phenotype analysis of dyslexia: Implications for family studies. In S. D. Smith (Ed.), *Genetics and learning disabilities* (pp. 69–96). London: Taylor and Francis.

Pennington, B. F., McCabe, L., Smith, S. D., Lefly, D. L., Bookman, M. O., Kimberling, W. J., & Lubs, H. A. (1986). Spelling errors in adults with a form of familial dyslexia. *Child Development, 57*, 1001–1013.

Pennington, B. F., & Smith, S. D. (1983). Genetic influences on learning disabilities and speech and language disorders. *Child Development, 54*, 369–387.

Pennington, B. F., & Smith, S. D. (1988). Genetic influences on learning disabilities: An update. *Journal of Consulting and Clinical Psychology, 56*, 817–823.

Petersen, S. E., Fox, P. T., Posner, M. I., Mintum, M., & Raichle, M. E. (1988) Positron emission tomographic studies of the cortical anatomy of single-word processing. *Nature, 331*, 585–589.

Plomin, R. (1986). *Development, genetics and psychology.* Hillsdale, NJ: Lawrence Erlbaum.

Plomin, R. (1989). Environment and genes: Determinants of behavior. *American Psychologist, 44*, 105–111.

Plomin, R., DeFries, J., & Fulker, D. W. (1988). *Nature and nurture during infancy and early childhood.* Cambridge: Cambridge University Press.

Plomin, R., DeFries, J. C., & McClearn, G. E. (1990). *Behavioral genetics: a primer.* Second Edition. New York: W.H. Freeman.

Polatajko, H. J. (1985). A critical look at vestibular dysfunction in learning disabled children. *Developmental Medicine and Child Neurology, 27*, 283–292.

Rutter, M. L. (1985). Family and school influences on cognitive development. *Journal of Child Psychology and Psychiatry, 26*, 683–704.

Rutter, M., Bolton, P., Harrington, R., Le Couteur, A., Macdonald, H., & Simonoff, E. (1990a). Genetic factors in child psychiatric disorders: I. A review of research strategies. *Journal of Child Psychology and Psychiatry, 31*, 3–38.

Rutter, M., Macdonald, H., Le Couteur, A., Harrington, R., Bolton, P., & Bailey, A. (1990b). Genetic factors in child psychiatric disorders: II. Empirical findings. *Journal of Child Psychology and Psychiatry, 31*, 39–84.

Rutter, M. and Yule, W. (1975) The concept of specific reading retardation. *Journal of Child Psychology and Psychiatry, 16*, 181–197.

Shaywitz, S. E, Shaywitz, B. A., Fletcher, J. M., & Escobar, M. D. (1990). Prevalence of reading disability in boys and girls. *Journal of the American Medical Association, 264*, 998–1002.

Shprintzen, R. J., & Goldberg, R. B. (1986). Multiple anomaly syndromes and learning disabilities. In S. D. Smith (Ed.), *Genetics and learning disabilities* (pp. 153–174). London: Taylor and Francis.

Smith, S. D. (Ed.) (1986). *Genetics and learning disabilities.* London: Taylor and Francis.

Smith, S. D., & Goldgar, D. E. (1986). Single gene analyses and their application to learning disabilities. In S. D. Smith (Ed.), *Genetics and learning disabilities* (pp. 47–68). London: Taylor and Francis.

Smith, S. D., Kimberling, W. J., Pennington, B. F., & Lubs, H. A. (1983). Specific reading disability: Identification of an inherited form through linkage analysis. *Science, 219*, 1345–1347.

Smith, S. D., Pennington, B. F., Kimberling, W. J., & Ing, P. S. (1990). Familial dyslexia: Use of genetic linkage to identify subtypes. *Journal of the American Academy of Child and Adolescent Psychiatry*, *29*, 204–213.

Stanovich, K. E., Nathan, R. G., & Zolman, J. E. (1988). The developmental lag hypothesis in reading: Longitudinal and matched reading-level comparisons. *Child Development*, *59*, 71–86.

Stevenson, H. W., Lee, S., Stigler, J., & Lucker, G. W. (1984). Family variables and reading: A study of mothers of poor and average readers in Japan, Taiwan and the United States. *Journal of Learning Disabilities*, *17*, 150–156.

Stevenson, J. (1988) Which aspects of reading ability show a "hump" in their distribution? *Applied Cognitive Psychology*, *2*, 77–85.

Stevenson, J. (1989) Language development and delays and the predictors of later reading failure. In M. Brambring, F. Losel, & H. Skowronek (Eds.), *Children at risk: Assessment and longitudinal research* (pp. 295–309). Berlin: de Gruyter.

Stevenson, J. (in press) Which aspects of processing text mediate genetic effects? *Reading and Writing*

Stevenson, J., & Fredman, G. (1990). The social environment correlates of reading ability. *Journal of Child Psychology and Psychiatry*, *31*, 681–698.

Stevenson, J., Graham, P., Fredman, G., & McLoughlin, V. (1987). A twin study of genetic influences on reading and spelling and ability and disability. *Journal of Child Psychology and Psychiatry*, *21*, 283–292.

Symmes, J. S., & Rapoport, J. L. (1972). Unexpected reading failure. *American Journal of Orthopsychiatry*, *42*, 82–91.

Tallal, P., Ross, R., & Curtiss, S. (1989). Unexpected sex-ratios in families of langauge/learning-impaired children. *Neuropsychologia*, *27*, 987–998.

Temple, C., & Marshall, J. C. (1983). A case study of developmental phonological dyslexia. *British Journal of Psychology*, *74*, 517–533.

Thomas, C. (1905). Congenital word-blindness and its treatment. *Ophthalmoscope*, *3*, 380–385.

Vandenberg, S. G., Singer, S. M., & Pauls, D. L. (1986). *The heredity of behaviour disorders in adults and children*. New York: Plenum Press.

van der Wissel, A., & Zegers, F. E. (1985) Reading retardation revisited. *British Journal of Developmental Psychology*, *3*, 3–9.

Vogler, G. P., DeFries, J. C., & Decker, S. N. (1985). Family history as an indicator of risk for reading disability. *Journal of Learning Disabilities*, *18*, 419–421.

Wadsworth, S., DeFries, J. C., Stevenson, J., Gilger, J. W., & Pennington, B. F. (1991) Gender ratios among reading-disabled children and their siblings. Submitted for publication.

Wadsworth, S. J., Gillis, J. J., DeFries, J. C., & Fulker, D. W. (1989). Differential genetic aetiology of reading disability as a function of age. *The Irish Journal of Psychology*, *10*, 509–520.

Wagner, R. K. (1986). Phonological processing abilities and reading: Implications for disabled readers. *Journal of Learning Disabilities*, *19*, 623–630.

Wagner, R. K., & Torgesen, J. K. (1987). The nature of phonological processing and its causal role in the acquisition of reading skills. *Psychological Bulletin*, *101*, 192–212.

Weber, B. A., & Ommen, G. S. (1977). Auditory and visual evoked responses in children with familial reading disabilities. *Journal of Learning Disabilities*, *10* 153–158.

Wilson, R. S. (1983). The Louisville Twin Study: Developmental synchronies in behaviour. *Child Development*, *54*, 298–316.

Yule, W. (1985). Comments on van der Wissel & Zegers: Reading retardation revisited. *British Journal of Developmental Psychology*, *3*, 11–14.

Zahalkova, M., Vrzal, V., & Kloboukova, E. (1972). Genetical investigations in dyslexia. *Journal of Medical Genetics*, *9*, 48–52.

Zerbin-Rudin, E. (1967). Congenital word blindness. *Bulletin of the Orton Society*, *17*, 47–54.

12
Information Processing Models

ROBERT T. SOLMAN and KEITH E. STANOVICH

Historical Antecedents of the Theory

Growth in the research studying the cognitive processes operating in fluent reading has been substantial in the last 10 years. A number of powerful models of fluent reading have been developed (e.g., Just & Carpenter, 1980; Lesgold & Perfetti, 1981; Rayner & Pollatsek, 1989; Thibadeau, Just & Carpenter, 1982), and our knowledge of how the fluent reader operates has been extended. In this chapter, we will sketch some of the progress that has been made in using these models to understand reading disability.

Reading disability is the most prevalent and, arguably, the most harmful type of learning disability. In a highly verbal society being unable to read not only has negative educational consequences but, all too frequently, it also has harmful social outcomes (see Tregurtha, 1988). It is of paramount importance that its cause be isolated, and much recent work conducted within an information processing analysis of the reading process has begun to converge on a general set of conclusions. Research from a wide variety of paradigms is pointing to phonological processes as the main locus of the disability.

Cognitive tasks are divided into a number of processes and information stores through information processing analyses. For example, they usually include a sensory store for the temporary storage of the input, perceptual and recognition processes and short-term memory, various central processing manipulations and long-term memory, and a process of response selection. The flow of information is in the one direction from the input, through the various stages of manipulation and transformation to the output, but allowance usually is made for feedback or interactions from the later or higher stages to influence processing at the earlier stages. Decomposing a complex cognitive task in this manner facilitates theoretical advance by detailing how variables selectively influence specific stores, stages, and processes (Fodor, 1983; Posner, 1978). In the case of the complex information processing task of reading, information processing researchers usually have looked for the causes of failure in four classes of cognitive processes: visual processes, the use of context to facilitate word recognition, phonological processes, and memory and comprehension strategies. The last of these cognitive processes is concerned primarily with text integration and comprehension in long-term or semantic memory, and the first three are concerned with information processing operations at the word level.

There is now considerable evidence to suggest that the cognitive processes involved in word decoding, or the information processing operations carried out at the word level, contribute strongly to variance in reading ability. There is a strong relationship between reading comprehension and a child's ability to recognize and decode words, particularly in the early school grades. Stanovich, Cunningham, and Feeman (1984b) found substantial correlations between reading comprehension and word recognition speed and accuracy across a wide variety of studies, and recent research suggests that these relationships arise because word decoding ability is necessary for comprehension (see Stanovich, 1982a for a review). Although poor word decoding skills may be a consequence of limited exposure to text, they also appear to be a major cause of reading failure (Aaron, 1989; Bertelson, 1986; Morrison, 1987; Perfetti, 1985; Siegel & Faux, 1989). A decoding deficit is found in poor readers even when differential exposure to text is eliminated (Guthrie & Tyler, 1976), and the relationship is apparent at the earliest stages of skill acquisition (Biemiller, 1970; Groff, 1978).

Researchers have examined visual processes, the use of context to facilitate word recognition, and phonological processes in their attempts to specify the locus of the dyslexic's word decoding problem and consequent reading disability.

Early Visual Processes

Deficits in early visual information processing operations frequently have been proposed in the reading disability literature as an important cause of reading failure. In particular, erratic eye movements frequently have been put forward as a source of reading failure, despite the fact that the data have failed to support this hypothesis. As early as 1958, Tinker concluded that erratic eye movements result from, and are not a cause of, reading difficulties. This conclusion was supported by Taylor (1965), and more recent studies have put it beyond reasonable doubt (Rayner, 1978, 1985). The consensus of researchers in the field is that erratic eye movements are caused by reading difficulties. They are unlikely to be a contributing factor to reading failure, although it is possible that they play a role in a small number of cases of reading disability. In these cases erratic eye movements may be part of the cause, but such cases are likely to be exceptions.

Sequencing and reversal errors (e.g., b/d, was/saw) also have been considered indicative of visual processing problems. However, several investigations have demonstrated that they are not a unique diagnostic feature of reading disability (see Stanovich, 1982a for a discussion of how reliance on case studies as evidence can be misleading). The systematic study of the distribution of error types across reading ability has indicated that poor readers make more errors of all types, but that their number of reversal errors, as a proportion of the total number of errors, is no higher than that displayed by good readers. Also, the data obtained in these investigations suggest that it is verbal/linguistic factors, rather than visual ones, that give rise to the sequencing and reversal errors (Calfee, 1977; Fischer, Liberman, & Shankweiler, 1978; Shankweiler & Liberman, 1972; Vellutino, 1979).

Visual perception is obviously more complicated than just those processes involved in the control of eye movements and the production of reversal errors. Many different tasks have been used to study visual perception (e.g., visual masking, visual search, flicker fusion, perceptual grouping, etc.), and some studies have demonstrated a relationship between reading ability and visual processing (Gross & Rothenberg, 1979; Mazer, McIntyre, Murray, Till, & Blackwell, 1983). In contrast, however, many studies have failed to find a relationship (Arnett & DiLollo, 1979; Ellis, 1981; Gupta, Ceci, & Slater, 1978; Hulme, 1981; Mitchell, 1982; Morrison & Manis, 1982; Swanson, 1983). Several reviews of this literature have converged on the conclusion that visual processing abilities are, at best, weakly related to reading acquisition (Carr, 1981; Rutter, 1978; Vellutino, 1979). Also, it is generally accepted that visual perception training programs have been ineffective in promoting reading acquisition (Coles, 1978; Kavale & Mattson, 1983; Vellutino, 1979).

In view of the weight of past evidence, current opinion in the reading disability field is that early visual processes do not play a significant causal role in reading disability (Aman & Singh, 1983; Stanovich, 1986a; Vellutino, 1979). However, some of the studies reported by Lovegrove (this volume), as well as an investigation by Solman and May (1990) indicating reading skill differences in a spatial location task, will keep the debate about the possible role of visual processing deficits open, at least for the immediate future. Lovegrove (this volume) argues that more recent attempts at demarcating visual processing deficits in some children theoretically are more well formulated than earlier attempts (see Hulme, 1988 for a contrary opinion). The goal for future research in this area will be to demarcate reliably a subgroup of children with visual problems that can be separated from any possible language problems and that are demonstrated to be a cause of poor reading performance rather than a spurious correlate.

Contextual Processes that Facilitate Word Recognition

The ability to use contextual information to facilitate word recognition during reading is often proposed as a critical determinant of reading ability. This use of context (i.e., its use to speed ongoing word recognition during reading) should be distinguished from its use to facilitate the memory and comprehension of text (Bransford & Johnson, 1973). In the past, this distinction frequently has been blurred, and a sensible and accurate interpretation of research findings has been difficult.

Arguably, the most influential theory that relates reading development and the use of context to facilitate word recognition is the one developed by Goodman (1965, 1976) and Smith (1971). They proposed that sensitivity to redundancy in the form of the semantic and syntactic cues in previously processed text allows the reader to develop hypotheses about the words that are to come. These hypotheses can be confirmed by sampling only a few features from the upcoming words' visual representation. Goodman and Smith hypothesized that fluent readers are better at this psycholinguistic guessing game than poor readers because they are better able to use the contextual redundancy in the previously processed text to facilitate recognition of the upcoming words. Although this theory has enjoyed unprecedented popularity and has had a significant, but misleading impact on educational practice, it is not supported by the empirical evidence.

Good readers may be better at using contextual information to aid comprehension, but this is not the case when the information is to be used to aid word recognition. Many studies employing a wide variety of paradigms have failed to show that good readers rely more on context for word recognition than poor readers. This includes studies of oral reading errors (Allington & Fleming, 1978; Biemiller, 1979; Juel, 1980; Perfetti & Roth, 1981; Whaley & Kibby, 1981), timed text reading (Biemiller, 1977–1978; Stanovich, Cunningham, & Feeman, 1984a), text disruption manipulations (Allington & Strange, 1977; Schwartz & Stanovich, 1981), single-word priming (Schvaneveldt, Ackerman, & Semlear, 1977; Simpson, Lorsbach, & Whitehouse, 1983), sentence priming (Perfetti & Roth, 1981; Stanovich, Nathan, West, & Vala-Rossi, 1985; Stanovich, West, & Feeman, 1981; West & Stanovich, 1978), and paragraph priming (Perfetti, Goldman, & Hogaboam, 1979).

The studies reported by Perfetti et al. (1979) provide a good example of the importance of distinguishing hypotheses about contextual effects that are operating at the level of word recognition from those that are influencing text integration and comprehension. They found that good readers who demonstrated smaller context effects than poor readers when recognizing words were superior on a clozelike prediction task. This suggests that although the more skilled readers possess better text-level prediction abilities than less skilled readers, these abilities are not used to assist them in the recognition of words. In fact, the word recognition carried out by skilled readers is largely an automatic process that does not need contextual facilitation. Automatic word recognition is necessary if sufficient attention is to remain available for allocation to text integration and comprehension processes (Perfetti, 1985; Stanovich, 1982b, 1984, 1986b).

Experiments show that poor readers are not experiencing difficulty because they cannot use context to assist in recognizing words. The argument used to support the hypothesis that poor readers are bad at using context as an aid for word recognition has been based on the observation that these children appear to plod through text. They are slow, do not appear to use context, and understand little. It has been assumed incorrectly that this results from their having learned inefficient strategies, such as an overreliance on "phonics" (as argued by Goodman), and having failed to learn contextual strategies. The evidence clearly contradicts this view (Liberman, 1982; Mitchell, 1982; Perfetti & Roth, 1981; Rayner & Pollatsek, 1989; Richardson, DiBenedetto, & Adler, 1982; Stanovich, 1984, 1986b; Stanovich, Cunningham, & Feeman, 1984a). When poor readers understand the context, they reliably show context effects on word recognition. However, in most cases their slow and inaccurate word decoding processes degrade the contextual information to the point where it cannot be understood and used. In other words, their failure to use context under these circumstances is a consequence of their poor decoding skills. When they understand the context, they use it in the same way as the good readers.

In a longitudinal study, Stanovich, Cunningham, and Feeman (1984a) showed that when less skilled 1st graders reach the reading stage where they can decode a particular passage with the same speed and accuracy as a group of skilled readers, they demonstrate just as much context facilitation. Failure at Goodman's "psycholinguistic guessing game" does not explain reading failure. The ability to access rapidly and automatically individual word meanings on a graphophonemic basis is much more important.

The Current Theoretical Consensus

The current consensus in the reading literature is that the ability to access rapidly and automatically individual word meanings on a graphophonemic basis is critically implicated in reading failure (Aaron, 1989; Barron, 1981; Chall, 1979; Gough, 1981; Gough & Hillinger, 1980; Juel, 1983; Kamhi & Catts, 1989; Liberman, 1982; Mitchell, 1982; Morrison, 1987;

Perfetti & Roth, 1981; Stanovich, 1982a, 1986b; Vellutino, 1979). Additionally, the locus of this word decoding deficiency, and consequent reading disability, is to be found in the domain of phonological skills. The evidence supporting phonological processing deficits as the primary cause of specific reading disability or dyslexia has been summarized by Stanovich (1988a, 1988b), who notes that both theoretical interest in this learning disability and justification of differential educational treatments for its remediation have been based on the assumption that it is caused by a specific, rather than a general, processing problem. The differences between dyslexia and a reading problem that is associated with low assessed IQ and poor performance in other areas (sometimes referred to as "garden-variety" poor reading; see Gough & Tunmer, 1986) can be conceptualized within what has been termed the phonological-core variable-difference model (Stanovich, 1988b).

The phonological-core variable-difference model rests on the assumption of specificity in learning disabilities (Hall & Humphreys, 1982; Stanovich, 1986a, 1986b). In the case of the dyslexic child, the assumption is that there is an information processing deficit that is specific to the reading task. In short, the deficit must not extend too far into other domains of cognitive functioning. It must be domain-specific (Cossu & Marshall, 1986) rather than a process that operates across a wide variety of domains. This requirement has directed the search for a flaw in the dyslexic's word recognition processes, and the data indicate that it is the phonological processing that forms the basis of the dyslexic pattern of reading disabled performance.

The reason that the existence of localized, faulty phonological processing by the specifically reading disabled child is found frequently in conjunction with more general cognitive deficits can be illustrated by considering the gradation of reading deficiency from the dyslexic to the "garden-variety" poor reader. As we move from the extreme dyslexic toward the "garden-variety" poor reader, the poor reader without aptitude/achievement discrepancy (see Gough & Tunmer, 1986), we move from a processing deficit localized in the phonological core to the global deficits demonstrated by the latter. Therefore, the cognitive differences displayed by any group of poor readers will depend on the composition of the group. If they are a carefully selected group of extreme dyslexics, the differences between them and good readers will consist of deficits located only in the phonological core. As the group becomes more mixed with an increasing number of "garden-variety" poor readers, the cognitive deficits detected will increase in number until they reach the large number of deficits demonstrated by a group consisting of only the latter. The model explains why almost all information processing investigations of reading disability have uncovered phonological deficits but, because of the mixed composition of many of the groups of disabled readers, they have also found deficits in other areas as well.

Evidence Supporting the Theory

Phonological processing tasks tap into mechanisms responsible for the efficient or inefficient functioning of the critical word processing module in reading. There is a considerable body of evidence that links deficits in performance on these tasks with reading disability. For example, less skilled readers have difficulty making explicit reports about sound segments at the phonemic level, they display naming difficulties, their utilization of phonological codes in short-term memory is inefficient, and their categorical perception of certain phonemes may be other than normal (Kamhi & Catts, 1989; Liberman & Shankweiler, 1985; Mann, 1986; Pennington, 1986; Wagner & Torgesen, 1987; Werker & Tees, 1987; Williams, 1984). However, of more importance is the evidence indicating that this linkage is a causal one, with deficiencies in phonological processing causing specific reading disability (Bradley & Bryant, 1985; Maclean, Bryant, & Bradley, 1987; Perfetti, 1985; Stanovich, 1986b, 1988a, 1988b). Both longitudinal correlational studies (Bradley & Bryant, 1985; Bryant, Bradley, Maclean, & Crossland, 1989; Maclean et al., 1987; Perfetti, Beck, Bell, & Hughes, 1987; Torneus, 1984), and experimental investigations (Bradley & Bryant, 1985; Fox & Routh, 1984; Lundberg, Frost, & Peterson, 1988; Olofsson & Lundberg, 1985; Treiman & Baron, 1983) have strongly indicated this causal connection. In the experimental investigations, phonological processing skills have been manipulated by training groups of young children in them and then comparing their performances in word recognition and spelling to the performances of untrained groups. The results of these comparisons have shown reliable advantages for trained groups.

An important aspect of phonological processing tasks is that they predict reading ability better than comprehensive, standardized intelligence tests (Mann, 1984; Stanovich, Cunningham, & Feeman, 1984b; Zifcak, 1981). Stanovich (1988a) calculated that the median correlation between reading ability and intelligence measures was .34 for beginning readers, whereas the correlation between reading and phonological processing measures was .52. Also, phonological processing is a relatively unique or independent predictor of reading ability. Several researchers (Bradley & Bryant, 1985; Lundberg, Olofsson, & Wall, 1980; Mann, 1984; Tunmer & Nesdale, 1985) have shown that phonological processing measures account for a statistically significant proportion of the variance in reading ability after the variance associated with intelligence and other cognitive tasks has been partialed out. Even after removing the variance accounted for by chronological age, a picture vocabulary test, the WISC–R, and a memory test, Bradley and Bryant (1985) found that their sound categorization task contributed a significant increase in explained variance.

The longitudinal correlation investigations linking phonological awareness measures and reading ability, independent of other cognitive measures, and the positive consequences of experimental training in phonological processing skills indicate that phonological measures tap into something very different from the cognitive processes measured by standard intelligence, cognitive, and reading readiness tasks. In other words, phonological awareness skill relatively is dissociated from other higher level cognitive skills. It is the most likely locus for the mechanism leading to specific reading disability, as it depresses reading but not other global intellectual skills.

How Well does the Theory Account for the Current Data?

From the earliest stages of skill acquisition, phonological processes are strongly linked to reading ability. Children at some point must acquire skill at breaking the spelling-to-sound code of the language if they ever are to gain the reading independence that eventually leads to the significant levels of practice that are prerequisite to fluent reading (LaBerge & Samuels, 1974). There are several prerequisite and facilitating subskills that are critical to success at spelling-to-sound code breaking. One such subskill is the ability to discriminate letters, the visual segments of words. Acquisition of this subskill usually is not a difficulty for problem readers, but letters must be mapped onto phonemic segments, and it is at this point that they encounter difficulty. They first must become aware of the phoneme as the basic unit of the spoken word. Phonological segmentation skills that are based on linguistic awareness at the phonemic level are strongly linked to the speed of initial reading acquisition and to reading disability (Bradley & Bryant, 1978, 1983; Fox & Routh, 1976, 1980, 1983; Liberman, 1973, 1982; Liberman & Shankweiler, 1979; Kamhi & Catts, 1989; Mann, 1984; Rozin & Gleitman, 1977; Share, Jorm, Maclean, & Matthews, 1984; Stanovich, Cunningham, & Cramer, 1984; Treiman & Baron, 1981; Williams, 1980), and the evidence indicates that this skill is causally related to later reading skill (Bradley & Bryant, 1983; Bryant et al., 1989; Fox & Routh, 1976; Goldstein, 1976; Mann, 1984; Perfetti et al., 1987; Treiman & Baron, 1981; Williams, 1980, 1984).

Studies carried out by Fox and Routh (1980, 1983) provide good examples of the importance of phonological awareness skills, both as a determining factor in the ease of initial reading acquisition and as an indicator of reading disability. A group of 1st graders were tested on a phonemic segmentation task that required them to "say a little piece of" a one-syllable word. Average readers had no difficulty with this task, but the poor readers could not segment the words. When followed up after 3 years, all the children then were able to segment phonemes, but those who had failed the task when they were in 1st grade suffered from fairly severe reading problems. They were more than 2 years behind the IQ-matched control group in reading achievement and displayed a tendency to produce "bizarre" dysphonetic spelling errors.

The development of the spelling-to-sound connections that are necessary for word decoding on a phonological basis naturally is delayed by early difficulty in becoming aware of phonemes as the segments of spoken words. It is therefore not surprising that the ability to access the lexicon accurately and rapidly via phonological coding is strongly related to reading skill, and the absence of facility at this level is strongly associated with reading disability (Barron, 1980, 1981; Hogaboam & Perfetti, 1978; Jorm & Share, 1983; Perfetti & Hogaboam, 1975). This connection has been demonstrated in a wide variety of tasks that tap facility at grapheme-to-phoneme conversion. For example, numerous studies have shown that the speed and accuracy with which poor and disabled readers name pseudowords (i.e., pronounceable nonwords) is inferior to the speed and accuracy demonstrated by good readers (e.g., Jorm & Share, 1983; Perfetti & Hogaboam, 1975).

Snowling (1980) administered a number of tasks to a group of dyslexic children, rigorously categorized as such after extensive psychometric testing, and to a group of younger normal children who were matched on reading level. There were, of course, some similarities in the performances of the groups, but the dyslexics were markedly inferior on a visual–auditory matching task with nonsense words that mimicked the grapheme–phoneme conversion process in reading. Also, while performance on this visual–auditory matching task was correlated significantly with reading level in the reading-level matched normals, there was no relationship with reading level in the dyslexic group. Snowling (1981) followed up these children after a year and found that the dyslexics were inferior to the younger reading-level matched normals at naming nonsense words (i.e., pronounceable nonwords). In commenting on these findings, Snowling suggested that normal development in reading is characterized by both an increase in grapheme–phoneme decoding ability and in the size of sight vocabulary, whereas in dyslexics the sight vocabulary increases but the development of grapheme–phoneme decoding ability is severely delayed.

As well as providing a more efficient mode of word recognition, facility at grapheme–phoneme conversion may assist short-term memory. Reading requires that sequences of words be held in short-term memory while comprehension processes operate to integrate these words into a meaningful conceptual structure that can be stored in long-term memory. A phonetic code is the most stable short-term memory code for this purpose (Baddeley, 1966; Conrad, 1964). Therefore, the ability to form rapidly a stable phonological code in short-term memory might be expected to be related to reading comprehension (Perfetti & Lesgold, 1977; Perfetti & McCutchen, 1982). Research on phonological confusability effects in memory has shown that the inferior performance of disabled readers is probably due to inefficient phonological coding of stimuli or an inability to maintain a phonological code in working memory (Brady, Shankweiler, & Mann, 1983; Byrne, 1981; Olson, Davidson, Kliegl, & Davies, 1984). They display memory deficits on tasks where the stimuli are easily verbally labeled or named, but not on tasks where the stimuli are not verbally codable and must be maintained in some form of visual representation (Hulme, 1981; Katz, Shankweiler, & Liberman, 1981; Swanson, 1983). This indicates that the memory deficit suffered by disabled readers is not a general memory deficiency, but rather a specific deficiency caused by their poor phonological coding abilities.

Limitations of the Theory

The dyslexic suffers from a specific deficiency in the operation of phonological coding processes is a simple theory, but there are a number of potentially complicating pieces of evidence that threaten to limit its explanatory scope. It appears to be the case that a small group of dyslexic readers exists whose core deficit is in the orthographic processing and lexical knowledge domain. Work on acquired reading disability has revealed the existence of this surface dyslexia (Patterson, Marhall, & Coltheart, 1985), and multivariate investigations have indicated that efficient phonological processing is necessary, but is not sufficient for achieving advanced levels of word recognition (Juel, Griffith, & Gough, 1986; Tunmer & Nesdale, 1985). It is not clear what the actual problems are in orthographic processing by these dyslexics. This relatively small group of specifically reading disabled children with orthographic processing problems need to be considered separately from those more numerous phonologically disabled dyslexics. Recent genetic analyses have indicated that the phonological deficit is more highly heritable than the orthographic deficit (Olson, Wise, Conners, Rack, & Fulker, 1989).

A more subtle complicating factor than the existence of a separate group of orthographic dyslexics is the absence of a fully articulated developmental model of specific reading disability. This development is complicated by the presence of "Matthew effects" in reading (Stanovich, 1986b). The early acquisition of reading skill results in reading/academic experiences that facilitate the development of other cognitive structures that, in turn, lay the foundation for successful reading achievement at more advanced levels. There are many "rich-get-richer and poor-get-poorer" phenomena that result from the interaction of the cognitive characteristics of children and their home and academic environments

(Stanovich & West, 1989). The result of these interactions is that the early modular or localized deficit displayed by the dyslexic can grow into generalized cognitive, behavioral, and motivational problems. In the course of development, the dyslexic demonstrates an increasingly more global cognitive deficit and becomes harder to distinguish from the "garden-variety poor" reader. This complication can weaken the argument for a localized phonological deficit and needs to be addressed in future research.

Treatment Implications

Although there appears to be a genetic component underlying the phonological deficit suffered by dyslexics (Olson et al., 1989), this does not mean that environmental factors are irrelevant, which is a mistaken inference commonly made in the educational literature (Angoff, 1988; Stanovich, 1989). It is clear that reading ability improves with exposure to print (Stanovich & West, 1989), even in the case of severe phonological deficiency. Some remediated adult dyslexics have achieved, albeit with great effort, normal (or even above normal) levels of word recognition (Campbell & Butterworth, 1985; Rudel, 1981). This suggests that improved reading instruction and greater reading experience may compensate for a phonological deficit. However, this appears to be a bypassing of the problem rather than a correction. Although these adults have achieved a high level of word recognition through extended practice, they remain deficient in phonological coding tasks, such as reading pronounceable nonwords. This does not mean necessarily that phonological processing cannot be improved, but it does indicate that reading experience alone does not appear to be sufficient to improve it in dyslexics.

Research on the remediation of phonological problems has taken two directions. The first approach, which has been referred to earlier, is to train prereaders in segmental language skills. Bradley and Bryant (1983) found a trend for trained prereaders to perform better at reading in the early grades than their classmates who had not received practice as prereaders in segmental language tasks. This trend later was confirmed in a major study by Lundberg, Frost, and Peterson (1988). These latter researchers also found that segmental language training improved later reading development and, in addition, reduced the likelihood of reading difficulties for children at risk.

The second approach to remediation uses an emphasis on the mapping between orthographic segments and subword speech segments during reading practice. If phonological coding can be improved significantly in children who are failing at reading by using this approach, then a major cause of difficulty with word recognition could be ameliorated. However, some studies have suggested that the usual types of phonics training during reading practice are not effective with readers with severe phonological processing deficits (Campbell & Butterworth, 1985; Lyon, 1983). A more concentrated and effective approach to the improvement of phonological training and segmental language skills may be needed with these children.

Olson and his colleagues (Olson, Foltz, & Wise, 1986; Olson & Wise, 1987) have developed a computer-based program to teach phonological coding and language segmentation. This program provides segmented orthographic and speech feedback for reading disabled children when they encounter difficult words. Each orthographic segment is highlighted in reverse-video and synchronized with the presentation of the corresponding speech segment. The initial short-term studies showed that the children did learn to read the words on which they requested feedback, and some early results from a long-term training study also have indicated that the training program can teach phonological coding and language segmentation to dyslexics (Olson, Wise, Connors, & Rack, 1990; Wise Olson, Anstett, Andrews, Terjak, Schneider, Kostuch, & Kriho, 1989).

Conclusions

The evidence suggests that the dyslexic or specifically disabled reader suffers from a lack of phonological awareness that impairs his ability to segment, analyze, and synthesize phonologically the speech stream. This skill is related crucially to the ability to decode words by phonological recoding, and accounts for the word-level processing deficits of the dyslexic. Also, deficient phonological recoding skills probably contribute to the poor performance of specifically disabled readers on short-term memory tasks and, in turn, this difficulty contributes to poor comprehension. Reading comprehension relies on access to rapidly formed and maintained phonological codes in short-term memory, and dyslexic readers have difficulty with these processes.

While efforts will continue to uncover evidence of reliably distinguishable dyslexic subtypes with orthographic or visual processing deficits, efforts are being increased to develop remediation techniques for the vast majority of dyslexic children who are characterized by phonological deficits. Programs of early prevention that have focused on phonological skills have shown some success (Bradley & Bryant, 1985). Computer-based methods aimed at increasing the print exposure and phonological skills of the older dyslexic likewise have met with some success (Wise et al., 1989). Progress in this area has not been of the "breakthrough" type, but more like a slow but steady accretion of information and techniques. Although dyslexia has proven to be a vexing research problem, recent progress gives us a reason for considerable optimism.

References

Aaron, P. G. (1989). *Dyslexia and hyperlexia.* Dordrecht, The Netherlands: Kluwer Academic.

Allington, R., & Fleming, J. (1978). The misreading of high frequency words. *Journal of Special Education, 12,* 417–421.

Allington, R., & Strange, M. (1977). Effects of grapheme substitutions in connected text upon reading behavior. *Visible Language, 11,* 285–297.

Aman, M., & Singh, N. (1983). Specific reading disorders: Concepts of etiology reconsidered. In K. Gadow & I. Bialer (Eds.), *Advances in learning and behavioral disabilities* (Vol. 2, pp. 1–47). Greenwich, CT: JAI Press.

Angoff, W. H. (1988). The nature–nurture debate, aptitudes, and group differences. *American Psychologist, 43,* 713–720.

Arnett, M., & DiLollo, V. (1979). Visual information processing in relation to age and to reading ability. *Journal of Experimental Child Psychology, 27,* 143–152.

Baddeley, A. (1966). Short-term memory for word sequences as a function of acoustic, semantic, and formal similarity. *Quarterly Journal of Experimental Psychology, 18,* 362–365.

Barron, R. (1981). Reading skills and reading strategies. In A. Lesgold & C. Perfetti (Eds.), *Interactive processes in reading* (pp. 299–327). Hillsdale, HJ: Erlbaum.

Barron, R. (1980). Visual-orthographic and phonological strategies in reading and spelling. In U. Frith (Ed.), *Cognitive processes in spelling* (pp. 195–213). London: Academic Press.

Bertelson, P. (1986). The onset of literacy: Limited remarks. *Cognition, 24,* 1–30.

Biemiller, A. (1970). The development of the use of graphic and contextual information as children learn to read. *Reading Research Quarterly, 6,* 75–96.

Biemiller, A. (1977–1978). Relationships between oral reading rates for letters, words, and simple text in the development of reading achievement. *Reading Research Quarterly, 13,* 223–252.

Biemiller, A. (1979). Changes in the use of graphic and contextual information as functions of passage difficulty and reading achievement level. *Journal of Reading Behavior, 11,* 307–319.

Bradley, L., & Bryant, P. (1978). Difficulties in auditory organization as a possible cause of reading backwardness. *Nature, 271,* 746–747.

Bradley, L., & Bryant, P. (1983). Categorizing sounds and learning to read: A causal connection. *Nature, 301,* 419–421.

Bradley, L., & Bryant, P. E. (1985). *Rhyme and reason in reading and spelling.* Ann Arbor: University of Michigan Press.

Brady, S., Shankweiler, D., & Mann, V. (1983). Speech perception and memory coding in relation to reading ability. *Journal of Experimental Child Psychology, 35,* 345–367.

Bransford, J., & Johnson, M. (1973). Consideration of some problems in comprehension. In W. G. Chase (Ed.), *Visual information processing* (pp. 383–438). New York: Academic Press.

Bryant, P. E., Bradley, L., Maclean, M., & Crossland, D. (1989). Nursery rhymes, phonological skills and reading. *Journal of Child Language*, *16*, 407–428.

Byrne, B. (1981). Deficient syntactic control in poor readers: Is a weak phonetic memory code responsible? *Applied Psycholinguistics*, *2*, 201–212.

Calfee, R. (1977). Assessment of independent reading skills: Basic research and practical applications. In A. S. Reber & D. L. Scarborough (Eds.), *Toward a psychology of reading* (pp. 289–323). Hillsdale, HJ: Erlbaum Associates.

Campbell, R., & Butterworth, B. (1985). Phonological dyslexia and dysgraphia in a highly literate subject: A developmental case with associated deficits of phoneme processing and awareness. *The Quarterly Journal of Experimental Psychology*, *37*, 435–475.

Carr, T. (1981). Building theories of reading ability: On the relation between individual differences in cognitive skills and reading comprehension. *Cognition*, *9*, 73–113.

Chall, J. (1979). The great debate: Ten years later, with a modest proposal for reading stages. In L. Resnick & P. Weaver (Eds.), *Theory and practice of early reading* (Vol. 1, pp. 29–55). Hillsdale, NJ: Erlbaum Associates.

Coles, G. (1978). The learning disabilities test battery: Empirical and social issues. *Havard Educational Review*, *48*, 313–340.

Conrad, R. (1964). Acoustic confusions in immediate memory. *British Journal of Psychology*, *55*, 75–84.

Cossu, G., & Marshall, J. C. (1986). Theoretical implications of the hyperlexia syndrome: Two new Italian Cases. *Cortex*, *22*, 579–589.

Ellis, N. (1981). Visual and name coding in dyslexic children. *Psychological Research*, *43*, 201–218.

Fischer, F., Liberman, I., & Shankweiler, D. (1978). Reading reversals and developmental dyslexia: A further study. *Cortex*, *14*, 496–510.

Fodor, J. (1983). *Modularity of mind*. Cambridge, MA: MIT Press.

Fox, B., & Routh, D. (1976). Phonemic analysis and synthesis as word attack skills. *Journal of Educational Psychology*, *68*, 70–74.

Fox, B., & Routh, D. (1980). Phonemic analysis and severe reading disability. *Journal of Psycholinguistic Research*, *9*, 115–119.

Fox, B., & Routh, D. (1983). Reading disability, phonemic analysis, and dysphonic spelling: A follow-up study. *Journal of Clinical Child Psychology*, *12*, 28–32.

Fox, B., & Routh, D. K. (1984). Phonemic analysis and synthesis as word attack skills: Revisited. *Journal of Educational Psychology*, *76*, 1059–1064.

Goldstein, D. (1976). Cognitive-linguistic functioning and learning to read in pre-schoolers. *Journal of Educational Psychology*, *68*, 680–688.

Goodman, K. (1965). A linguistic study of cues and miscues in reading. *Elementary English*, *42*, 639–643.

Goodman, K. (1976). Reading: A psycholinguistic guessing game. In H. Singer & R. Ruddell (Eds.), *Theoretical models of processes of reading* (pp. 479–508). Newark, DE: International Reading Association.

Gough, P. (1981). A comment on Kenneth Goodman. In M. Kamil (Ed.), *Directions in reading: Research and instruction* (pp. 20–25). Clemson, SC: National Reading Conference.

Gough, P., & Hillinger, M. (1980). Learning to read: An unnatural act. *Bulletin of the Orton Society*, *30*, 171–196.

Gough, P. B., & Tunmer, W. E. (1986). Decoding, reading, and reading disability. *Remedial and Special Education*, *7*, 6–10.

Groff, P. (1978). Should children learn to read words? *Reading World*, *17*, 256–264.

Gross, K., & Rothenberg, S. (1979). An examination of methods used to test the visual perceptual deficit hypothesis of dyslexia. *Journal of Learning Disabilities*, *12*, 409–416.

Gupta, R., Ceci, S., & Slater, A. (1978). Visual discrimination in good and poor readers. *Journal of Special Education*, *12*, 409–416.

Guthrie, J., & Tyler, S. (1976). Psycholinguistic processing in reading and listening among good and poor readers. *Journal of Reading Behavior*, *8*, 415–426.

Hall, J., & Humphreys, M. (1982). Research on specific learning disabilities: Deficits and remediation. *Topics in Learning and Learning Disabilities*, *2*, 68–78.

Hogaboam, T., & Perfetti, C. (1978). Reading skills and the role of verbal experience in decoding. *Journal of Educational Psychology*, *70*, 717–729.

Hulme, C. (1981). The effects of manual training on memory in normal and retarded readers: Some Implications for multi-sensory teaching. *Psychological Research*, *43*, 201–218.

Hulme, C. (1988). The implausability of low-level visual deficits as a cause of children's reading difficulties. *Cognitive Neuropsychology*, *5*, 369–374.

Jorm, A., & Share, D. (1983). Phonological recoding and reading acquisition. *Applied Psycholinguistics*, *4*, 103–147.

Juel, C. (1980). Comparison of word identification strategies with varying context, word type, and reader skill. *Reading Research Quarterly*, *15*, 358–376.

Juel, C. (1983). The development and use of mediated word identification. *Reading Research Quarterly*, *18*, 306–327.

Juel, C., Griffith, P. L., & Gough, P. B. (1986). Acquisition of literacy: A longitudinal study of children in first and second grade. *Journal of Educational Psychology*, *78*, 243–255.

Just, M., & Carpenter, P. (1980). A theory of reading: From eye fixations to comprehension. *Psychological Review*, *87*, 329–354.

Kamhi, A., & Catts, H. (1989). *Reading disabilities: A developmental language perspective*. Boston: College-Hill Press.

Katz, R., Shankweiler, D., & Liberman, I. (1981). Memory for item order and phonetic recoding in the beginning reader. *Journal of Experimental Child Psychology*, *32*, 474–484.

Kavale, K., & Mattson, P. (1983). "One jumped off the balance beam": Meta-analysis of perceptual-motor training. *Journal of Learning Disabilities*, *16*, 165–173.

LaBerge, D., & Samuels, S. (1974). Toward a theory of automatic information processing in reading. *Cognitive Psychology*, *6*, 293–323.

Lesgold, A., & Perfetti, C. (1981). *Interactive processes in reading*. Hillsdale, NJ: Erlbaum Associates.

Liberman, I. (1973). Segmentation of the spoken word and reading acquisition. *Bulletin of the Orton Society*, *23*, 65–77.

Liberman, I. (1982). A language-oriented view of reading and its disabilities. In H. Myklebust (Ed.), *Progress in learning disabilities* (Vol. 5, pp. 81–101). New York: Grune & Stratton.

Liberman, I., & Shankweiler, D. (1979). Speech, the alphabet and teaching to read. In L. Resnick & P. Weaver (Eds.), *Theory and practice of early reading* (Vol. 2, pp. 109–132). Hillsdale, NJ: Erlbaum Associates.

Liberman, I. Y., & Shankweiler, D. (1985). Phonology and the problems of learning to read and write. *Remedial and Special Education, 6,* 8–17.

Lundberg, I., Frost, J., & Peterson, O. (1988). Effects of an extensive program for stimulating phonological awareness in preschool children. *Reading Research Quarterly, 23,* 263–284.

Lundberg, I., Olofsson, A., & Wall, S. (1980). Reading and spelling skills in the first school years predicted from phonemic awareness skills in kindergarten. *Scandinavian Journal of Psychology, 21,* 159–173.

Lyon, G. R. (1983). Subgroups of learning disabled readers: Clinical and empirical identification. In H. R. Myklebust (Ed.), *Progress in learning disabilities* (Vol. V, pp. 103–134). New York: Grune & Stratton.

Maclean, M., Bryant, P., & Bradley, L. (1987). Rhymes, nursery rhymes, and reading in early childhood. *Merril-Palmer Quarterly, 33,* 255–281.

Mann, V. (1984). Reading skill and language skill. *Developmental Review, 4,* 1–15.

Mann, V. (1986). Why some children encounter reading problems. In J. Torgesen & B. Wong (Eds.), *Psychological and educational perspectives on learning disabilities* (pp. 87–113). New York: Academic Press.

Mazer, S., McIntyre, C., Murray, M., Till, R., & Blackwell, S. (1983). Visual persistence and information pick-up in learning disabled children. *Journal of Learning Disabilities, 16,* 221–225.

Mitchell, D. (1982). *The process of reading: A cognitive analysis of fluent reading and learning to read.* New York: John Wiley.

Morrison, F. J. (1987). The nature of reading disability: Toward an integrative framework. In S. Ceci (Ed.), *Handbook of cognitive, social, and neuro-psychological aspects of learning disabilities* (pp. 33–62). Hillsdale, NJ: Erlbaum.

Morrison, F., & Manis, F. (1982). Cognitive processes and reading disability: A critique and proposal. In C. Brainerd & M. Pressley (Eds.), *Program in cognitive development research* (Vol. 2, pp. 59–94). New York: Springer-Verlag.

Olofsson, A., & Lundberg, I. (1985). Evaluation of long term effects of phonemic awareness training in Kindergarten. *Scandinavian Journal of Psychology, 26,* 21–34.

Olson, R., Davidson, B., Kliegl, R., & Davies, S. (1984). Development of phonetic memory in disabled and normal readers. *Journal of Experimental Child Psychology, 37,* 187–206.

Olson, R. K., Foltz, G., & Wise, B. (1986). Reading instruction and remediation with the aid of computer speech. *Behavior Research Methods, Instruments, and Computers, 18,* 93–99.

Olson, R. K., & Wise, B. (1987). Computer speech in reading instruction. In D. Reinking (Ed.), *Computers and reading: Issues for theory and practice* (pp. 156–177). New York: Teachers College Press.

Olson, R. K., Wise, B., Connors, F., & Rack, J. (1990). Organization, heritability, and remediation of component word recognition and language skills in disabled readers. In T. H. Carr & B. A. Levy (Eds.), *Reading and its development: Component skills approaches* (pp. 261–316). New York: Academic Press.

Olson, R., Wise, B., Conners, F., Rack, J., & Fulker, D. (1989). Specific deficits in component reading and language skills: Genetic and environmental influences. *Journal of Learning Disabilities*, *22*, 339–348.

Patterson, K., Marshall, J., & Coltheart, M. (1985). *Surface dyslexia*. London: Erlbaum.

Pennington, B. F. (1986). Issues in the diagnosis and phenotype analysis of dyslexia. In S. D. Smith (Ed.), *Genetics and learning disabilities* (pp. 69–96). San Diego: College-Hill Press.

Perfetti, C. (1985). *Reading ability*. New York: Oxford University Press.

Perfetti, C., Goldman, S., & Hogaboam, T. (1979). Reading skill and the identification of words in discourse context. *Memory and Cognition*, *7*, 273–282.

Perfetti, C., & Hogaboam, T. (1975). Relationship between single word decoding and reading comprehension skill. *Journal of Educational Psychology*, *56*, 461–469.

Perfetti, C., & Lesgold, A. (1977). Discourse comprehension and sources of individual differences. In M. Just & P. Carpenter (Eds.), *Cognitive processes in comprehension* (pp. 141–183). Hillsdale, NJ: Erlbaum.

Perfetti, C., & McCutchen, D. (1982). Speech processes in reading. In N. Lass (Ed.), *Speech and language: Advances in basic research and practice* (Vol. 7, pp. 237–269). New York: Academic Press.

Perfetti, C., & Roth, S. (1981). Some of the interactive processes in reading and their role in reading skill. In A. Lesgold & C. Perfetti (Eds.), *Interactive processes in reading* (pp. 269–297). Hillsdale, NJ: Erlbaum Associates.

Perfetti, C. A., Beck, I., Bell, L., & Hughes, C. (1987). Phonemic knowledge and learning to read are reciprocal: A longitudinal study of first grade children. *Merril-Palmer Quarterly*, *33*, 283–319.

Posner, M. (1978). *Chronometric explorations of mind*. Hillsdale, NJ: Erlbaum.

Rayner, K. (1978). Eye movements in reading and information processing. *Psychological Bulletin*, *85*, 618–660.

Rayner, K. (1985). Do faulty eye movements cause dyslexia? *Developmental Neuropsychology*, *1*, 3–15.

Rayner, K., & Pollatsek, A. (1989). *The psychology of reading*. Englewood Cliffs, NJ: Prentice Hall.

Richardson, E., DiBenedetto, B., & Adler, A. (1982). Use of the decoding skills test to study differences between good and poor readers. In K. Gadow & I. Bialer (Eds.), *Advances in learning and behavioral disabilities* (Vol. 1, pp. 25–74). Greenwich, CT: JAI Press.

Rozin, P., & Gleitman, L. (1977). The structure and acquisition of reading II: The reading process and the acquisition of the alphabetic principle. In A. Reber & D. Scarborough (Eds.). *Toward a psychology of reading* (pp. 55–141). Hillsdale, NJ: Erlbaum Associates.

Rudel, R. G. (1981). Residual effects of childhood reading disabilities. *Bulletin of the Orton Society, 31*, 89–102.

Rutter, M. (1978). Prevalence and types of dyslexia. In A. Benton & D. Pearl (Eds.), *Dyslexia: An appraisal of current knowledge* (pp. 5–28). New York: Oxford University Press.

Schvaneveldt, R., Ackerman, B., & Semlear, T. (1977). The effect of semantic context on children's word recognition. *Child Development*, *48*, 612–616.

Schwartz, R., & Stanovich, K. (1981). Flexibility in the use of graphic and contextual information by good and poor readers. *Journal of Reading Behavior*, *13*, 263–269.

Shankweiler, D., & Liberman, I. (1972). Misreading: A search for causes. In J. Kavanagh & I. Mattingly (Eds.). *Language by ear and eye* (pp. 106–133). Cambridge: MIT Press.

Share, D., Jorm, A., Maclean, R., & Matthews, R. (1984). Sources of individual differences in reading acquisition. *Journal of Educational Psychology*, *76*, 1309–1324.

Siegel, L. S., & Faux, D. (1989). Acquisition of certain grapheme-phoneme correspondences in normally achieving and disabled readers. *Reading and Writing: An Interdisciplinary Journal*, *1*, 37–52.

Simpson, G., Lorsbach, T., & Whitehouse, D. (1983). Encoding and contextual components of word recognition in good and poor readers. *Journal of Experimental Child Psychology*, 161–171.

Smith, F. (1971). *Understanding reading*, New York: Holt, Rinehart and Winston.

Snowling, M. (1980). The development of grapheme-phoneme correspondence in normal and dyslexic readers. *Journal of Experimental Child Psychology*, *29*, 294–305.

Snowling, M. (1981). Phoneme deficits in developmental dyslexia. *Psychological Research*, *43*, 219–234.

Solman, R. T., & May, J. G. (1990). Spatial localization discrepancies: A visual deficiency in poor readers. *The American Journal of Psychology*, *103*, 243–263.

Stanovich, K. E. (1982a). Individual differences in the cognitive processes of reading 1: Word decoding. *Journal of Learning Disabilities*, *15*, 485–493.

Stanovich, K. E. (1982b). Individual differences in the cognitive processes of reading II: Text-level processes. *Journal of Learning Disabilities*, *14*, 549–554.

Stanovich, K. (1984). The interactive-compensatory model of reading: A confluence of developmental, experimental, and educational psychology. *Remedial and Special Education*, *5*, 11–19.

Stanovich, K. E. (1986a). Cognitive processes and the reading problems of Learning disabled children: Evaluating the assumption of specificity. In J. Torgesen & B. Wong (Eds.), *Psychological and educational perspectives on learning disabilities* (pp. 87–113). New York: Academic Press.

Stanovich, K. E. (1986b). Matthew effects in reading: Some consequences of individual differences in the acquisition of literacy. *Reading Research Quarterly*, *21*, 360–407.

Stanovich, K. E. (1988a). The right and wrong places to look for the cognitive locus of reading disability. *Annals of Dyslexia*, *38*, 154–177.

Stanovich, K. E. (1988b). Explaining the difference between the dyslexic and the garden-variety poor reader: The phonological-core variable-difference model. *Journal of Learning Disabilities*, *21*, 590–612.

Stanovich, K. E. (1989). Various varying views on variation. *Journal of Learning Disabilities*, *22*, 366–369.

Stanovich, K., Cunningham, A., & Cramer, B. (1984). Assessing phonological awareness in kindergarten children: Issues of task comparability. *Journal of Experimental Child Psychology*, *38*, 175–190.

Stanovich, K., Cunningham, A., & Feeman, D. (1984a). The relationship between early reading acquisition and word decoding with and without context: A longitudinal study of first-grade children. *Journal of Educational Psychology*, *76*, 668–677.

Stanovich, K., Cunningham, A., & Feeman, D. (1984b). Intelligence, cognitive skills, and early reading progress. *Reading Research Quarterly*, *19*, 278–303.

Stanovich, K. E., Nathan, R. G., West, R. F., & Vala-Rossi, M. (1985). Children's word recognition in context: Spreading activation, expectancy, and modularity. *Child Development*, *56*, 1418–1429.

Stanovich, K. E., & West, R. F. (1989). Exposure to print and orthographic processing. *Reading Research Quarterly*, *24*, 402–433.

Stanovich, K., West, R., & Feeman, D. (1981). A longitudinal study of sentence context effects in second-grade children: Tests of an interactive-compensatory model. *Journal of Experimental Child Psychology*, *32*, 185–199.

Swanson, L. (1983). A study of nonstrategic linguistic coding on visual recall of learning disabled readers. *Journal of Learning Disabilities*, *16*, 209–216.

Taylor, S. (1965). Eye movements while reading: Facts and fallacies. *American Educational Research Journal*, *2*, 187–202.

Thibadeau, R., Just, M., & Carpenter, P. (1982). A model for the time course and content of reading. *Cognitive Science*, *6*, 157–203.

Tinker, M. (1958). Recent studies of eye movements in reading. *Psychological Bulletin*, *55*, 215–231.

Torneus, M. (1984). Phonological awareness and reading: A chicken and egg problem. *Journal of Educational Psychology*, *70*, 1346–1358.

Treiman, R., & Baron, J. (1981). Segmental analysis ability: Development and relation to reading ability. In T. Waller & G. Mackinnon (Eds.), *Reading research: Advances in theory and practice* (Vol. 3, pp. 100–120). New York: Academic Press.

Treiman, R., & Baron, J. (1983). Phonemic-analysis training helps children benefit from spelling-sound rules. *Memory and Cognition*, *11*, 382–389.

Tregurtha, A. (1988). *Between dark and daylight. An autobiography by Andrew Tregurtha*. Sydney: Collins.

Tunmer, W. E., & Nesdale, A. R. (1985). Phonemic segmentation skill and beginning reading. *Journal of Educational Psychology*, *77*, 417–427.

Vellutino, F. (1979). *Dyslexia: Theory and research*. Cambridge: MIT Press.

Wagner, R. K., & Torgesen, J. K. (1987). The nature of phonological processing and its causal role in the acquisition of reading skills. *Psychological Bulletin*, *101*, 192–212.

Werker, J. F., & Tees, R. C. (1987). Speech perception in severely disabled and average reading children. *Canadian Journal of Psychology*, *41*, 48–61.

West, R., & Stanovich, K. (1978). Automatic contextual facilitation in readers of three ages. *Child Development*, *49*, 717–727.

Whaley, J., & Kibby, M. (1981). The relative importance of reliance on intraword characteristics and interword constraints for beginning reading achievement. *Journal of Educational Research*, *74*, 315–320.

Williams, J. (1980). Teaching decoding with an emphasis on phoneme analysis and phoneme blending. *Journal of Educational Psychology*, *72*, 1–15.

Williams, J. (1984). Phonemic analysis and how it relates to reading. *Journal of Learning Disabilities*, *17*, 240–245.

Wise, B., Olson, R., Anstett, M., Andrews, L., Terjak, M., Schneider, V., Kostuch, J., & Kriho, L. (1989). Implementing a long-term computerized remedial reading program with synthetic speech feedback. *Behavior Research Methods, 21*, 173–180.

Zifcak, M. (1981). Phonological awareness and reading acquisition. *Contemporary Educational Psychology, 6*, 117–126.

Part 3
Treatment

13
Behavioral Approaches

Nirbhay N. Singh, Diane E. D. Deitz, and Judy Singh

Behavioral approaches to the remediation of academic deficits in students with learning disabilities involve the use of stimulus-control and reinforcement-based procedures to produce the desired gains in academic behavior. The specific techniques used are derived from a model that emphasizes environmental variables as controllers of behavior, and that eschews the use of intervening variables such as psychological processes as explanatory or heuristic tools (Skinner, 1950). Traditionally, subject variables have been accorded little importance, and the assessment of academic deficits is usually restricted to a functional analysis of those deficits in relation to their antecedents and consequences for the student's behavior in the learning situation. Of course, the lack of emphasis in this model on the diagnosis of the disorder as to cause or classification means that little is known about the generalizability of the effects of behavioral approaches across diagnostic groups or subgroups. Indeed, students with learning disabilities appear to be a heterogeneous group with regard to their etiology, related behavior problems, and academic deficits. However, it remains to be demonstrated that diagnostic subgroups do require differential academic remediation.

According to Lahey and his colleagues (Lahey & Johnson, 1977; Treiber & Lahey, 1983), there are three primary tenets of behavioral approaches to the remediation of academic deficits in students with learning disabilities. These include (a) individualization and mastery, (b) direct teaching of the deficit rather than of some inferred deficit, and (c) an emphasis on continuous assessment during remediation that provides the basis for the modification of the intervention program, as needed.

This chapter presents a comprehensive review of behavioral approaches, with the intention of providing a useful, structured guide to most of the strategies that have been used to remediate reading and spelling deficits in students with learning disabilities. We did not strive to include only students who can be identified exclusively as learning disabled because the actual definition of learning disabilities used by the researchers in published studies has been rather variable (Singh & Beale,

375

1988). However, most of the students in these studies would meet the federal criteria for learning disability.

Reading

Behavioral approaches have been used in the acquisition and remediation of reading by students with learning disabilities. Most of the studies have focused on the enhancement of reading proficiency through the reinforcement of accuracy, and the correction of errors during oral reading. The students in these studies had progressed beyond the elementary stage of reading, although proficient decoding of words was still problematic for some of them. The efficacy of behavioral strategies for increasing comprehension in students with learning disabilities has been evaluated in fewer studies. However, the acquisition of initial reading skills by students with learning disabilities has not been researched much at all.

We will review the literature on initial reading (word recognition), oral reading, and comprehension. The aim is not to provide an exhaustive review of the literature but to alert the reader to the variety of behavioral strategies that are available for remediating reading deficits in students with learning disabilities. Occasionally, the efficacy of a procedure will be discussed with reference to students with other mildly handicapping conditions because the same procedures often are used successfully with them as well as with those who are learning disabled. Furthermore, the general conclusions derived from the academic remediation literature are applicable to students across a variety of mildly handicapping conditions.

Word Recognition

Most students do not have any problems in learning to read basic sight words through traditional teaching methods, such as trial-and-error learning (Etzel & LeBlanc, 1979; McGee & McCoy, 1981). In the typical trial-and-error learning situation, the teacher models the pronunciation of a new word and then reinforces the student's correct responses to the word. All incorrect responses are corrected but not reinforced. For those students who have difficulty learning through this method, the teacher has to use alternative teaching procedures. One such class of procedures, usually termed stimulus control, is derived from basic studies in discrimination learning. Stimulus control refers "to the extent to which the value of an antecedent stimulus determines the probability of occurrence of a conditioned response" (Terrace, 1966, p. 271). Although studies using stimulus control methods typically have not employed students with learning disabilities, the procedures used are applicable across children with a variety of disabilities.

Errorless Discrimination Learning Procedures

A number of errorless discrimination learning procedures are available that can be used to teach basic sight words. In all of these procedures, the students are initially provided training on an easy discrimination that is gradually made more difficult or complex by systematically changing the discriminative stimuli. Procedures pertinent to the present discussion include stimulus fading, stimulus shaping, superimposition and fading, and prompting.

Stimulus Fading

Terrace (1963) demonstrated that difficult discriminations can be taught virtually without errors by the gradual shifting of control from one dimension to another through a procedure called stimulus fading. This procedure can be used to teach both letters and words to students with learning disabilities. For example, in letter discrimination training, the criterion letter (e.g., the letter A) can be presented at full intensity, and then, a second letter (e.g., B) can be systematically faded in until an A-B discrimination is established. An alternative format would be to enhance the size (i.e., the salience) of letter A, but not B, during initial training and then to fade A systematically to criterion size.

For example, Rincover (1978) taught children with autism to discriminate between the letters J and S by increasing the salience of J but not S. The salience of J was increased by exaggerating the crossbar on the J, and when the discrimination between the two letters was established, the exaggeration was faded. Furthermore, Rincover (1978) taught the children to discriminate between three-letter words (e.g., *jar-son*) by initially exaggerating the first letter of the target word (i.e., the crossbar on J) and then fading the exaggeration on subsequent trials. Egeland and Winer (1974) and Egeland (1975) reported that, when compared to a trial-and-error method, children made fewer errors on letter discrimination when using a fading procedure. In another study, Lancioni, Ceccarani, and Oliva (1981) taught words by initially increasing the salience of the first letter of each word, which was faded once the discrimination between the words was established.

Schimek (1983) used stimulus fading procedures to teach a student with learning disabilities to discriminate between three digraphs *ch*, *th*, and *sh*. Initially, the visual digraph *th* was presented with a visual cue and the student was asked to repeat its sound. Then the visual cue was gradually faded, with the student being reinforced for making errorless discriminations. A similar procedure was used with the other two digraphs.

Stimulus Shaping

The major difference between stimulus fading and stimulus shaping procedures is that whereas stimulus fading involves no change in the topography of the training or the criterion stimulus, stimulus shaping involves critical changes in the topography of the criterion stimulus. In stimulus shaping, the initial training stimulus, which may not resemble the criterion stimulus but is easily discriminated by the student, is gradually shaped over successive training trials to form the criterion stimulus.

Stimulus shaping can be used to teach simple sight words to children (LeBlanc, Etzel, & Domash, 1978). Initially, a pictorial stimulus is presented, which is gradually shaped to form a word. For example, to teach the word *log*, a line drawing of a log is initially presented, and then, in successive phases, the letters *l*, *o*, and *g* are shaped from the line drawing of *log*. In a variation of this procedure, Miller and Miller (1968, 1971) used a stimulus-shaping procedure, called symbol accentuation, to teach sight words to students with mental retardation. In addition, Miller and Miller (1971) found stimulus shaping to be more effective than a trial-and-error procedure in teaching sight words to children. Jeffree (1981) provided further confirmation of the efficacy of this approach. Finally, Smeets, Lancioni, and Hoogeveen (1984) demonstrated the superiority of stimulus shaping over fading and nonfading procedures in sight word recognition by children.

Superimposition and Fading

Another procedure that can be used to teach words to children involves the superimposition of two stimuli (a training stimulus and a prompt), followed by the fading of the prompt. For example, a word (e.g., *apple*) and a picture prompt (i.e., a picture of an apple) are presented together as a complex stimulus, and the student is told what the word is. Typically, the picture controls the student's response because it is the easier stimulus to discriminate. In successive trials or sessions, the picture is gradually faded out of the complex stimuli, and only the word is left. Once the picture is faded, the control is shifted from the picture to the word, and the child responds to the word.

A number of studies have used this technique to teach sight word vocabulary to children. Corey and Shamow (1972) compared the effects of superimposition alone or paired with fading of the prompt on the acquisition and retention of sight words. They found that young children learned and retained more words when both procedures were used. Similar results were reported by Dorry and Zeaman (1973, 1975). In another study, Dorry (1976) found that fading the prompt alone was just as effective as simultaneously fading out the picture prompt and fading in the word. In an extension of this line of research, Walsh and Lamberts

(1979) compared the efficacy of the fading procedure with a stimulus-shaping reading program (Edmark Reading Program). Although the students learned sight words in both procedures, they performed better with stimulus shaping.

Delayed Prompting

In delayed prompting, a complex stimulus is presented, but in successive trials or sessions, the presentation of the second stimulus (i.e., the prompt) is systematically delayed or faded on a temporal dimension (Touchette, 1971). In one variation of this procedure, the training stimulus (e.g., the word *apple*) is presented, and after a delay, a prompt (e.g., a picture of an apple) is presented. The student's response is under the control of the word if the response is before the prompt, and under the control of the picture if the response follows the prompt.

Delayed prompting procedures have been used to teach letter and word recognition skills to children. McGee and McCoy (1981) evaluated the effects of trial-and-error, fading, and delayed-prompting procedures in teaching oral reading responses to students with mental retardation. Greater acquisition and retention were evident with both fading and delayed prompting than with the trial-and-error procedure. In another study, Bradley-Johnson, Sunderman, and Johnson (1983) found delayed prompting to be more effective than fading in teaching easily confused letters to young children.

Extrastimulus and Intrastimulus Prompting

An added or extrastimulus prompt can be used to facilitate a child's reading. For example, a picture, an object, or pointing by the teacher can be used to facilitate a child's learning of a new word. Stimulus prompts that are additional to the training stimulus are termed extrastimulus prompts, and it is assumed that the child will continue to respond correctly when the extrastimulus prompt is withdrawn (Schreibman, 1975; Schreibman, Charlop, & Koegel, 1982). Intrastimulus prompts are those that involve increasing the salience of the training stimulus itself.

Extrastimulus prompts in the form of pictures are typically used in basal readers for young children (Samuels, 1967, 1970). However, the current research literature suggests that using extrastimulus prompts may have detrimental effects on the reading performance of some children (Koegel & Rincover, 1976; Saunders & Solman, 1984). These children fail to transfer from the extrastimulus prompt to the training stimulus because of a blocking effect of the extrastimulus prompts (Singh & Solman, 1990). Comparative studies show that children perform better when intrastimulus rather than extrastimulus prompts are used (Schreibman, 1975; Wolfe & Cuvo, 1978).

Modeling

Modeling has been used to teach sight words to students with learning disabilities. For example, in one study, 5th grade students tutored younger students in reading words through modeling and imitation (Chiang, Thorpe, & Darch, 1980). Words written on flashcards were used as the stimulus. The tutor modeled the correct pronunciation of each word, and then the tutee repeated it. The tutee then said each word by himself, with the tutor providing corrective feedback. The results showed that educationally significant gains in word recognition were made by the tutees. In another study, word recognition was increased in two students with learning disabilities through antecedent and contingent modeling (Hendrickson, Roberts, & Shores, 1978). Freeman and McLaughlin (1984) provide another example of the use of modeling procedures in enhancing sight word reading. They reported increased sight word recognition by six students with learning disabilities through the modeling of vocabulary words using a tape recorder.

Summary

Only a few studies are available on the remediation of word recognition skills in students with learning disabilities. However, there are many procedures that have been validated with students who have mildly handicapping conditions, and these procedures can be used to increase the word recognition skills of students with learning disabilities.

Oral Reading

Oral reading is an integral part of instruction in most reading curricula. It is useful for a number of reasons, including (a) as a medium for instruction and remediation, (b) as an indicator of reading achievement, and (c) as a diagnostic tool for reading problems. In addition, oral reading ability appears to be highly correlated with comprehension, with studies showing a clear relationship between oral reading fluency and comprehension (Doehring, 1977; Perfetti & Hogoboam, 1975; Singh & Singh, 1986a). As noted by Jenkins (1979, p. 69), "oral reading can be considered one legitimate measure of reading ability."

In this section, we provide an overview of behavioral approaches to the remediation of oral reading errors, focusing on antecedent and consequent procedures.

Antecedent Strategies

Although most studies on academic remediation have used response-contingent error-correction procedures, antecedent strategies also have proved to be effective in producing educationally significant behavior change (Glynn, 1982). A number of antecedent strategies have been used to increase learning disabled students' proficiency in oral reading, as well as in comprehension.

Antecedent Modeling

In the antecedent modeling of basic sight words, the teacher presents a word to the child and says, "This word is . . . ," and then asks, "What word is this?" Hendrickson et al. (1978) used this procedure to teach basic sight words to two students with learning disabilities. In addition, they found that antecedent modeling was more effective than a contingent modeling procedure. A similar strategy can be used as an error correction procedure during oral reading of textual material (e.g., a story). Indeed, this procedure was used to improve student's oral reading of basal readers in a study by Smith (1979).

Phonics Instruction

Phonics instruction can be used either as an antecedent strategy for word recognition or as a consequent, error correction strategy (Singh & Singh, 1988). For example, Lovitt and Hurlburt (1974) evaluated the effects of prior phonics instruction on the oral reading proficiency of four students with learning disabilities. They reported that phonics instruction enhanced the children's performance on five phonics tasks and increased their overall oral reading proficiency.

Previewing

A number of studies have shown that reading accuracy can be improved if students are allowed to preview the text before reading it orally. The commonly used previewing procedures either require the teacher or a peer to introduce and highlight significant aspects of the story or have the student silently read the passage before reading it aloud.

The efficacy of a number of previewing procedures in improving oral reading accuracy has been demonstrated in several studies with students who had mildly handicapping conditions (e.g., Rose, 1984; Singh & Singh, 1984). For example, Rose and Sherry (1984) evaluated the effects of two previewing procedures on the oral reading performance of five adolescents with learning disabilities. During silent previewing, the student read the assigned reading passage before reading it aloud, and during listening previewing, the teacher read the assigned selection aloud, with the student following along silently before the student reading the passage aloud. Both previewing procedures were more effective than a baseline control, with the listening previewing producing higher rates of correct reading than silent previewing.

In a related study, Rose and Beattie (1986) used an alternating treatments design to evaluated the effects of two previewing procedures on the oral reading performance of four elementary-aged boys with learning disabilities. During listening previewing, the teacher read the assigned passage aloud while the student followed along silently before reading the passage aloud, and during taped previewing, the student listened to prerecorded reading passages while following along silently before reading the passage aloud. The students' rate of words read correctly was higher under the two previewing conditions when compared to a no-previewing control condition. In addition, the rate was higher under the listening procedure when compared to the taped procedure.

Sachs (1984) also evaluated the effects of two previewing activities, a concept analysis activity and a motivation statement, on the oral reading performance of 36 students, 12 of whom were formally identified as learning disabled. Results showed that the concept analysis activity was superior to the motivation statement in reducing graphophonemic, syntactic, and semantic errors of these students.

Salend and Nowak (1988) used peer-previewing to enhance the oral reading performance of three students with learning disabilities. During the previewing intervention, the peer previewer read aloud a randomly assigned passage from a book while the student listened and followed along using a photocopy of the passage. The peer was instructed to read clearly and slowly. The student was required to read to the teacher once the peer previewer completed reading the assigned passage. Results showed a substantial increase in the oral reading skills of the students.

Summary

There is a small literature attesting to the efficacy of antecedent error correction procedures in the remediation of oral reading errors of students with learning disabilities.

Consequent Strategies

A number of consequent error correction strategies have been used to increase the oral reading skills of students with learning disabilities. In addition, other procedures used with children who have mildly handicapping conditions may be equally applicable to students with learning disabilities. Given that there are a number of descriptive and evaluative reviews of this literature (e.g., Hansen & Eaton, 1978; Hansen & Lovitt, 1977; Lahey, 1977; Rose, Koorland, & Epstein, 1982; Ross, 1981; Singh & Singh, 1986b), we present here only a brief discussion of the procedures that can be used effectively with this population.

General Feedback

Simply providing feedback often results in increased academic performance (Perkins, 1988). For example, Thorpe, Chiang, and Darch

(1981) provided group and individual feedback for oral reading accuracy to 16 students, 7 of whom had learning disabilities. Under the group condition, the mean reading error rate of the group was plotted daily on a graph, and during the individual condition each individual's error scores were plotted. It was found that providing a graphic display of reading errors increased the accuracy of the students' oral reading during both individual and group conditions.

Reinforcement

A number of studies have shown that token or tangible reinforcement procedures can be used to increase oral reading accuracy (e.g., Billingsley, 1977; Jenkins, Barksdale, & Clinton, 1978; Lahey & Drabman, 1974; Lahey, McNees, & Brown, 1973). For example, Billingsley (1977) evaluated the effects of self-imposed and externally imposed schedules of reinforcement on the oral reading performance of eight students with learning disabilities. Results showed that the students increased their oral reading proficiency under both reinforcement conditions when compared to baseline. Further, some students performed better under the self-imposed reinforcement condition whereas others performed better under the externally imposed conditions, with a few showing no preference.

The specific effects of reinforcement have been demonstrated in a study by Swanson (1981), who found that comprehension increased when it was targeted for reinforcement but not when oral reading accuracy was reinforced. This study confirmed and extended earlier research (e.g., Jenkins et al., 1978; Roberts & Smith, 1980) that suggested that reinforcement has specific effects on the behavior that is reinforced without producing concomitant changes in other academic behaviors. That is, when oral reading accuracy is reinforced, little or no improvement occurs in comprehension and vice versa.

Attention to Errors

It is well established that teacher attention to oral reading errors increases the accuracy of oral reading of students. For example, in a study with 11-year-old students who were learning disabled, McNaughton and Delquadri (1978) examined the effects of immediate teacher attention to error words on the number of errors and self-corrections made by these students. The results showed that, when compared to baseline, there was a reduction in oral reading errors and an increase in self-corrections during intervention.

Other studies have shown that delayed teacher attention may be more effective than immediate attention to errors (McNaughton & Glynn, 1981; Singh, Winton, & Singh, 1985). It was reported in these studies that delaying teacher attention by 5 or 10 seconds after an error is made by the student, or waiting until the end of the sentence, dramatically decreases oral reading errors and increases self-corrections. One explanation is that the time delay involved in this procedure stops the teacher from preempting the student in making appropriate corrections as a result of using contextual cues.

Drill

Drill requires the teacher to supply the correct word when an error is made, and then to print all error words on index cards and present individually to the student at the end of the oral reading session. Words are removed from the deck as they are correctly pronounced. The teaching continues until the student successfully completes the entire error-word deck without a mistake on two consecutive presentations.

The efficacy of drill has been compared to a number of other error correction procedures. For example, in a comparative study, Jenkins and Larson (1979) found isolated word drill to be more effective than other error-correction procedures (e.g., word meaning, sentence repeat, word supply, and end-of-page review) in increasing the oral reading accuracy of students with learning disabilities. In another study, drill (flash cards) was used in addition to other procedures in a cross-age tutoring program (Chiang et al., 1980). The procedures were effective in increasing the word recognition skills of students with learning disabilities.

O'Shea, Munson, and O'Shea (1984) found word drill and phrase drill to be superior to word supply in increasing students' recognition of words in isolation, but phrase drill was found to be more effective than word drill in increasing their recognition of words in context. In another study, drill and modeling procedures were used to increase oral reading accuracy and comprehension (Roberts & Smith, 1980).

Rosenberg (1986) compared a drill procedure against phonic drill and word supply in a study with four students with learning disabilities. In the word supply condition, the teacher supplied the correct word when the student made an error and then the student was asked to repeat that word and continue reading. The phonic drill procedure was similar to the standard drill procedure except that the teacher paid particular attention to the phonic elements of the error word by sounding out each element of the word. It was found that drill was more effective than word supply and phonic drill.

Word Analysis and Word Supply

Word analysis and word supply are used extensively with beginning readers (Singh, 1990). Word analysis requires the teacher to direct the child's attention to the phonetic elements of the error word and to "sound out" the word. Word supply requires the teacher to "supply" or tell the child the correct word following an error.

Comparative studies of the use of these two procedures with students labeled as learning disabled have produced mixed results: one study reported word supply to be more effective in increasing oral reading accuracy (Rose, McEntire, & Dowdy, 1982), and another (Meyer, 1982) showed no difference. To complicate matters further, Singh and Singh (1985) found word analysis to be more effective than word supply with students who were moderately mentally retarded. As noted by Singh and Singh (1988), the word analysis procedure provides enhanced reading proficiency over time because initially, it takes the student much longer to master the phonic elements of the language. However, once this is achieved, the student is able to use this knowledge to decode new words independently.

Directed Rehearsal

Overcorrection, a package of procedures originally devised for decreasing maladaptive behavior, has been found to be effective in enhancing a number of academic behaviors (Singh, 1985). In a recent reappraisal of this procedure, it was noted that the term *directed rehearsal* may be more appropriate when the procedure is used as an educational intervention (Lenz, Singh, & Hewett, 1991). Thus, in this chapter the term *directed rehearsal* will be used instead of overcorrection.

Singh, Singh, and Winton (1984) used directed rehearsal to increase the oral reading accuracy of students who were moderately mentally retarded. In this procedure, each incorrectly read word is repeated five times, and the sentence in which the word occurs is correctly repeated once. Directed rehearsal has been found to be effective in both individual (Singh et al., 1984) and group training formats (Singh, 1987), and to be more effective than isolated word drill (Singh & Singh, 1986c) in increasing oral reading accuracy of students with mental retardation. Given that directed rehearsal is effective with students who are mentally retarded, it is more than likely that the procedure will be as effective with those who are learning disabled.

Summary

The efficacy of some consequent strategies for enhancing oral reading accuracy and comprehension appears to be well established with students who are learning disabled. Although the earlier studies were methodologically flawed in several respects (see Gadow, Torgesen, & Dahlem, 1983), more recent and better controlled studies provide the basis for this conclusion. In addition to the studies reviewed above, there are others that have used a combination of antecedent and consequent strategies to facilitate oral reading in children with reading problems, including those with learning disabilities (e.g., Darch & Gersten, 1985; Fleisher & Jenkins, 1978; Limbrick, McNaughton, & Glynn, 1985;

Thorpe & Borden, 1985). These studies suggest that behavioral procedures can be used to produce educationally significant gains in the oral reading accuracy of students with learning disabilities.

Reading Comprehension

Reading comprehension is often defined as the understanding, evaluating, and utilizing of information and ideas expressed in print. As such, it can be thought of as an interactive process between the author and the reader. We can differentiate at least four different types of comprehension activities that the reader can engage in: literal, interpretation, critical reading, and application of what is read.

In literal comprehension, the reader is interested in getting the primary, direct, or the most literal meaning of the text. Literal comprehension does not require much thinking on the part of the reader because only the facts presented in the text are of concern. Interpretation requires the reader to "read between the lines," and derive interrelationships between the ideas and experiences expressed by the author, although these may not be directly stated in the text. Critical reading requires the reader not only to interpret the text but also to evaluate what is read. The evaluation can be across several dimensions, including quality, value, and accuracy. Finally, application is when the reader is able to use in his own life some aspect of the author's ideas and experiences.

Behavioral Strategies

A number of behavioral strategies have been used to increase comprehension skills in students with learning disabilities. Although the type of comprehension targeted has been rarely specified in most studies, most of them have concentrated on either literal comprehension or interpretation, or their combination.

Previewing and Prereading Activities

The effects of previewing difficult short stories on both learning disabled and high-ability students' comprehension has been investigated by Graves and his colleagues (Graves & Cooke, 1980; Graves, Cooke, & LaBerge, 1983; Graves & Palmer, 1981). These studies showed that previewing of the text greatly facilitates students' comprehension. Similar facilitative effects on the comprehension of learning disabled students have been reported in a number of studies of prereading activities. For example, Sachs (1983) compared the effects of three prereading activities: a modified directed reading activity, a modified concept activity analysis, and a worksheet activity. The modified directed reading activity was used to arouse the students' interest, assist them to relate their experiential backgrounds to the concepts of the story through vocabulary development, and set a purpose for the story. The concept analysis activity was used to enhance the students' ability to comprehend the story's central concept by drawing on their background of experience and prior knowledge. The worksheet activity was used as a control condition, and consisted of the students and teacher working together on three word-attack wordsheet pages selected from the wordbooks of the basal series used for the study. Results showed that both active prereading interventions produced higher scores on critical comprehension when compared to the worksheet activity.

Pflaum, Pascarella, Auer, Augustyn, and Boswick (1982) evaluated the effects of four comprehension-facilitating aids on the comprehension scores of 99 normally achieving and learning disabled students. The four conditions were: word identification and meaning aids, sentence aids, purpose-setting aids, and prior knowledge aids. Results showed that the learning disabled students showed a greater improvement under the sentence aid condition than under the prior knowledge condition. Indeed, the overall results showed that microlevel aids (word and sentence conditions) produced higher comprehension scores than the macrolevel aids (purpose setting and prior knowledge conditions). These results suggest that students with learning disabilities benefit from specific, microlevel comprehension instruction.

Chang, Williams, and McLaughlin (1983) reported that comprehension can be improved if learning disabled students are required to read the target text orally to the teacher, who simply corrects mispronunciations or word substitutions. Jenkins, Heliotis, Haynes, and Beck (1986) reported that the comprehension of both normally achieving and learning disabled children can be increased if they are required to summarize, or restate, the contents of each paragraph before the comprehension test. These findings were replicated under controlled conditions in another study with 32 elementary learning disabled students (Jenkins, Heliotis, Stein, & Haynes, 1987).

Content Area Instruction

Darch and Gersten (1986) compared the effects of two prereading conditions designed to increase high school learning disabled students' comprehension. One group of students was provided prereading activities based on a basal approach to teaching comprehension and the other group received instruction using an advance organizer in the form of a text outline designed to assist students processing information from the text. The results showed that students receiving instruction using an advance organizer increased their comprehension skills much more than the students taught with the basal approach.

In a related study, Darch and Carnine (1986) examined the relative effectiveness of two approaches to teaching literal comprehension to learning disabled students during content area instruction. One group of students was presented information via visual spatial displays while the other group was presented content via text. In both treatments, the students studied content in groups and were given explicit study strategies. Results showed that students using the visual display approach showed far greater gains in comprehension than the text group of students. However, there was no difference between the two groups when their comprehension was tested on an untaught passage.

Question Prompts

A number of studies have shown that story mapping can be used to enhance the comprehension of normal, low achieving, and learning disabled students (e.g., Idol, 1987). Basically, the story mapping strategy involves the provision of a series of questions that direct the student's attention to important and interrelated aspects of the reading passage.

In two related studies, Wong (1979, 1980) evaluated the effectiveness of question prompts in increasing learning disabled students' comprehension. Question prompts require the teacher to provide the students with the questions before they read the target text. In the first study (Wong, 1979), 30 normally achieving and 30 learning disabled students were tested in groups of three. The students were given a printed sheet containing a Japanese folktale. The experimenter read the story orally, with the students following the printed story visually. For the experimental subjects, the experimenter read each question that preceded its target paragraph before reading the paragraph itself. The same questions were printed on the copies of the story given to the children in this treatment condition. The copies of the story given to the control subjects contained no questions. Immediately after the experimenter finished reading the story, the students were asked to recall as much of the story as possible by writing it down. Results showed that the learning disabled students improved their comprehension and retention of the main ideas of the story with question prompts. Essentially similar results were obtained by Wong (1980) in a more elaborate follow-up study that dealt with inferential comprehension rather than identification of main ideas as in the previous study. These results were interpreted in terms of Torgesen's (1977) theory of the learning disabled student as an inactive learner.

Clark, Deshler, Schumaker, Alley, and Warner (1984) reported that learning disabled students could improve their comprehension if they engaged in self-questioning during the reading of the target text. In addition, comprehension was facilitated if the students were able to visualize the contents of the target text. The effectiveness of self-questioning, particularly if combined with story structure training, has been reported in another study with learning disabled students (Griffey, Zigmond, & Leinhardt, 1988). These results also can be explained within Torgesen's (1977) framework of the inactive learner.

The results of a study by Dyck and Sundbye (1988), however, appear to be at variance with this theory. Learning disabled students performed equally well on comprehension questions under two conditions. In the first, the story was made more explicit by adding supportive information to it, and in the second, by asking inference questions at the end of episodes to guide the students in orally making similar elaborations of the entire text. The inactive learner theory would have been supported if the question condition proved superior to the text explicit condition.

Vocabulary Instruction

Pany and Jenkins (1978) investigated the effects of vocabulary instruction on the reading comprehension of students with learning disabilities. Three instructional conditions that varied in the amount of direct instruction provided were evaluated. The three conditions were: meanings from context (no direct instruction), meanings given (the students were told the meaning of preselected words from the reading passage), and meanings practiced (direct instruction on word meaning via a flash card technique). The results showed that while the meanings practiced condition did improve the students' scores on vocabulary, there was no differential effect of the three intervention conditions on story comprehension. Similar results were reported in a follow-up study in which vocabulary instruction failed to influence comprehension scores as assessed by cloze tests and story recall (Pany, Jenkins, & Schreck, 1982).

Bos, Anders, Filip, and Jaffe (1989) have suggested that the lack of comprehension effects in the above studies "may be related to the limited breadth of instruction and depth of processing during the vocabulary instruction" (p. 384). Bos et al. (1989) tested their explanation in a study that evaluated two methods of vocabulary instruction with 50 learning disabled students. They contrasted semantic feature analysis and interactive instructional strategy with the dictionary method, a commonly used vocabulary acquisition technique. The semantic feature analysis emphasizes broad instruction and deep processing that is tied to the structure of the passage content, and the dictionary method focuses on associating words with their definitions. Results showed that the students in the semantic feature analysis instructional condition had significantly greater measured comprehension than those in the dictionary instruction condition.

Study Skill Training

Teaching students study skills techniques, such as the Survey, Question, Read, Recite, and Review (SQ3R) procedure (Robinson, 1941), can improve their reading comprehension. In an evaluation of the SQ3R procedure, Alexander (1985) found that learning disabled students were able to increase their story-retelling scores through the use of this procedure.

Summary

The effectiveness of several strategies have been evaluated for their ability to enhance the comprehension of students with learning disabilities. Some strategies were chosen specifically to test empirically Torgesen's (1977) theory of the learning disabled student as an inactive learner; others were chosen because they have been found to be useful with normal and low achieving students.

Spelling

Given that methods of compensation are fewer and less effective, spelling may be even more sensitive to the existence of language disabilities than reading (Wallace & McLaughlin, 1988). Whereas spelling offers no opportunity for clues, reading may offer contextual, structural, or configuration clues to the student (Lerner, 1985). Also, because words are spelled either correctly or incorrectly, teachers cannot give the student the "benefit of the doubt" as often occurs in reading when a student's pronunciation of a word closely approximates the correct pronunciation (Hallahan, Kauffman, & Lloyd, 1985). Therefore, poor readers generally are poor spellers (Carpenter & Miller, 1982; Lerner, 1985; Mercer, 1987), yet poor spellers may be good, average, or poor readers.

Importance of Spelling

Although the importance of spelling ability may be debated, both the educational and public communities reward spelling achievement and punish lack of achievement (Graham & Miller, 1979). Spelling is used in correspondence as part of many jobs and is part of every academic content area (Hammil, 1990). Lack of spelling achievement often impedes the educational, occupational, and social status of individuals. In some professions, such as teaching, poor spelling simply is unacceptable.

A crucial component of writing, spelling ability allows the writer to follow a line of thought without interruptions to address spelling uncertainties. (One of the great ironies of life is the dictionary system, which requires a close approximation of the spelling of a word in order to ascertain how it is spelled.) When writing notes to ourselves, such as a list of tasks to complete by the end of the day, the importance of spelling is minimal as long as we can retrieve the information we need. At any given time, "zucchini" probably is represented a myriad of ways on various grocery lists. However, once writing is directed to others, spelling becomes important. Rightly or wrongly, many of us adjust our opinions of peoples' intelligence and general competence if they misspell words in their personal or professional written communications.

Definitions of Spelling

Because spelling is so objective, the term *spelling* has a consistent meaning for the great majority of people. However, definitions of spelling reflect some variation. Brueckner and Bond (1955) defined spelling as the ability to produce in written or oral form the correct letter arrangement of words. A similar definition was offered by Mercer (1987), who defined spelling as the forming of words through the traditional arrangement of letters. Hanna, Hodges, and Hanna (1971) addressed spelling as the process of encoding or rendering spoken words into written symbols.

Graham and Freeman (1985) presented a more complex definition of spelling. They view spelling as a euphemism for a variety of skills including the ability to recognize, recall, reproduce, or obtain orally or in written form the correct sequence of letters in words. Perhaps the best definition of spelling is that of Hallahan, Kauffman, and Lloyd (1985), who included components of different definitions to form a concise yet comprehensive description. They described spelling as a process that requires a person to produce in oral or written form the correct sequence of letters that form a particular word. The correct sequence of letters is produced by converting phonemes (sounds) into graphemes (written letters). Phonemes may be covertly produced, or thought, as well as heard.

Of particular importance in the Hallahan et al. definition is attention to covertly produced stimuli for spelling. Once we no longer participate in formal spelling instruction as part of our academic training, most spelling behavior in which most of us engage is covertly cued.

Spelling and English

In contrast to the different opinions on how spelling should be defined is the consistent opinion that the English language is challenging for spellers (Collins, 1983; Hallahan et al., 1985; Wallace & McLaughlin, 1988). The difficulties involved in spelling English constitute a primary reason why so many persons experience spelling problems. The 26 letters of the alphabet form 44 phonemes for which there are 251 different spellings (Hull, 1976; Mercer, 1987). The existence of 1,800 English homonyms and numerous words with irregular spelling patterns extends the problem (Collins, 1983).

English spelling simply cannot be learned by rote memory or solely through phonemic decoding. Numerous linguists and reading and spelling researchers have delineated a structure composed of several levels that constitute the English spelling system. On the surface level, rules of phoneme–grapheme correspondence are applied. The deeper, more critical level is based on the application of morphological relationships (Bailet, 1990; N. Chomsky, 1970; Stubbs, 1980).

Morphographs are the smallest units of words that are meaningful (e.g., root words, suffixes, prefixes) (Maggs, McMillan, Patching, & Hawke, 1981). A morphograph is not the same as a syllable or phoneme since typically a phoneme can be spelled more than one way. Maggs et al. (1981) cited two advantages of using morphographs to teach spelling: (a) morphographs either maintain the same spelling in different words or change in predictable ways, and (b) there are far fewer morphographs than words and this results in a faster rate of learning. According to Dixon (1976), more than 75 words can be spelled using just 12 morphographs: able, re, arm, claim, er, ing, dis, cover, ed, order, un, and ness. In summary, the regularities in English spelling are related to morpholoigical relationships rather than surface phonology (Johnson, 1988; Schwartz & Doehring, 1977).

Spelling and Learning Disabled Students

Partly because of the difficulties inherent in the English language, spelling often becomes a tedious chore that leads to the confusion and bewilderment of many students (Gerber & Hall, 1987). Spelling causes extraordinary difficulties for students who are learning disabled. Failure to acquire the skills necessary to spell accurately and rapidly is one of the most common characteristics of students labeled as learning disabled (Gerber, 1984; Gerber & Hall, 1987; Poplin, Gray, Larsen, Banikowski, & Mehring, 1980). In fact, despite considerable variability in selection criteria, surveys of students identified as learning disabled consistently resulted in academic profiles in which spelling was one of the weakest, if not the weakest, skill (Gerber & Hall, 1987).

The spelling problems of students with learning disabilities are evident throughout their academic programs. Using sophisticated regression analyses to look at ability versus achievement, Cone, Wilson, Bradley, and Reese (1985) found that spelling problems became evident in the early elementary years and persisted as a serious problem throughout the school years. A large body of literature attests to the differences between the spelling proficiency of normally achieving students and students labeled as learning disabled (Carlisle, 1987; Cook, 1981; Fischer, Shankweiler, & Liberman, 1985; Schwartz & Doehring, 1977). Poplin et al. (1980) looked at skills relating to written expression across three age groups of normally achieving and learning disabled students and found significantly lower scores for the learning disabled students, especially for the more objective skills such as spelling.

Another body of spelling literature addresses the way in which we learn to spell. Good spellers begin to form spelling rules before the beginning of formal spelling instruction (Schwartz & Doehring, 1977). Normally achieving students proceed by testing and revising these rules and by forming additional rules (Bailet, 1990; Beers, 1980; C. Chomsky, 1979; Templeton, 1980). Spelling impairment may reflect the inability of learning disabled students to formulate and revise rules at the normal rate (Moats, 1983; Read, 1975). A number of persons agree that the spelling problems of students identified as learning disabled are based on a delay in the rate of acquisition of morphological rules rather than unique, idiosyncratic response patterns (Gerber, 1984; Nelson, 1980; Vogel, 1983). The errors of a group of dyslexic subjects were no more inaccurate or orthographically illogical than the errors of normally achieving students (Nelson, 1980).

However, other researchers found that learning disabled students manifested different error patterns than normally achieving students. In a sequence of case studies reported by Cook (1981), the error patterns of both normally achieving and learning disabled students showed significant strategy shifts, but some of the learning disabled students deviated markedly from the normal developmental course (Bailet, 1990). Carpenter (1983) sought to determine if spelling error patterns of 30 disabled readers differed from that of 40 younger able readers and 37 same-age able readers. Discriminant analyses indicated distinguishing patterns between disabled readers and same-age able readers. The use of phonetic strategies was the major difference between the two groups with the learning disabled students generating more unrecognizable spellings for both regular and irregular words.

The Carpenter (1983) study was one of a considerable number of studies designed to assess the degree of phonetic accuracy of good and poor spellers (Carpenter & Miller, 1982; Finucci, Isaacs, Whitehouse, & Childs, 1983; Firth, 1980; Moats, 1983). A number of researchers have documented methodological problems that occurred in these studies (Bailet, 1990; Bookman, 1984; Carlisle, 1987; Gerber & Hall, 1987; Moats, 1983). Perhaps most important was a point made by Bailet (1990): the premise of phonetic accuracy oversimplifies and misrepresents the spelling process, because English spelling is governed by higher order, morphological rules. Students with spelling difficulties lack the spontaneous ability to identify and apply these morphological rules.

Regardless of whether the spelling errors of learning disabled students result from a delay in skill acquisition or differences in the way spelling strategies are formulated and revised, the errors must be addressed through systematic and direct instruction.

Spelling Instruction

Traditional classroom spelling programs that use a basal spelling series often are unsuccessful with students identified as learning disabled (Collins, 1983; Wallace & McLaughlin, 1988). A typical week of spelling in the public schools consists of independent study and completion of workbook exercises Monday through Thursday with a test on Friday. This format of study-test is ineffective for many students (Bryant, Draben, & Gettinger, 1981; Reith, Axelrod, Anderson, Hathaway, Wood, & Fitzgerald, 1974).

Some students do not require much instructional effort from their teachers. Surveys of classroom practice revealed that American students receive little specific spelling instruction (Gerber & Hall, 1989). Those who learn despite lack of instruction are considered normal achievers and those who do not are considered learning disabled. Instead of providing spelling instruction, teachers often rely on incidental learning (Hammil, Larsen, & McNutt, 1977). To say that this approach is difficult to understand is an understatement. Students are not expected to teach themselves in any other major academic area.

Because of this lack of spelling instruction, the design of spelling texts becomes even more important. Yet evaluations of basal spelling texts by researchers generally lead to concern. Graham (1983) cited inadequate spelling texts as one reason for unsatisfactory spelling progress. Cronnel and Humes (1980) found a minimal amount of instructional practice in spelling texts and Cohen (1969) found numerous activities that were irrelevant or inappropriate. According to Collins (1983), many spelling programs promote phonics-based instruction, failing to discriminate between reading (a decoding process in which students respond to a tangible stimulus) and spelling (an encoding process in which students respond to words that are spoken or thought). Finally, few textbook writers and publishers have incorporated research results in their spelling programs. Given this picture of instructional and textbook inadequacies, we do not find it surprising that learning disabled students evidence particular weakness in spelling.

We have discussed briefly some of the discrepancy and error-pattern research conducted with students identified as learning disabled. In the following section, intervention research will be discussed.

Spelling Interventions

Unlike the vast amount of literature that addresses the spelling discrepancies and error patterns of persons with learning disabilities, the intervention research is limited. A summary of this research is presented in Table 13.1, and includes studies from 1978 to the present time. Most of

TABLE 13.1. Spelling intervention studies (1978–1991).

Study	N	Description	CA	Grade Level	GES	IQ	Description	Example	Measure
Bailet (1990)	14	NA	x̄ 11.6	6th	7.9	104	Real words with suffixes	|Press|ure	Number of spelling errors in the largest portion of words
	14	NA	x̄ 9.6	4th	4.4	102			
	14	LD/PR	x̄ 11.8	6th	4.0	105	Nonsense words with suffixes	|Frisk|ed	
	7	LD/GR	x̄ 11.8	6th	4.7	105			
Bailet & Lyon (1985)	1	LD	42	—	5.0	102	Words with letters that change sound if suffix added. Base and suffix-adding words	Discuss Discussion	Percentage of words spelled correctly
Bryant, Drabin, & Gettinger (1981)	64 (randomly assigned to four groups)	LD	x̄ 10	NR	2.2 (reading)	93	Irregular words	Cough	Number of words spelled correctly
Foxx & Jones (1978)	29 (across four grade-level groups)	PS	NR	4th, 5th, 7th, & 8th	NR	NR	Spelling tests from grade-level texts	NR	Percent words spelled correctly
Frank, Wacker, Zeith, & Sagen (1987)	4	LD	x̄ 9.6	NR	1.7	94	Frequently used words. Spelling demons	NR	Percent words spelled correctly. Percent letter sequences correct
Gerber (1986)	11	PS	x̄ 11	1st–9th	NR	NR	Three lists of words varying only in initial consonant, blend, or digraph	Hide Side	Percent words spelled correctly
Gettinger (1985)	9	PS	8–13	3rd–8th	One year or more below grade level	Avg	Regular and irregular words	NR	Number of words spelled correctly

TABLE 13.1. (Cont'd)

Study	Participants						Dependent Variables		
	N	Description	CA	Grade Level	GES	IQ	Description	Example	Measure
Graham & Freeman (1985)	40 (randomly assigned across four conditions)	LD	NR	4th	NR	NR	NR	NR	Number of words spelled correctly
Harris, Graham, & Freeman (1988)	40 (randomly assigned across four conditions)	LD	$\bar{x}$ 10.8	4th	2.5	97	Frequently and infrequently used words	NR	Accuracy of student-predicted performance
Kauffman, Hallahan, Haas, Brame, & Boren (1978)	1	LD	12	NR	NR	NR	Regular and irregular words	NR	Percent words spelled correctly
Nulnan & Gerber (1984)	1	LD	8.5	2nd	1.3 (reading)	120	Words that spelled other words by changing the first consonant	Wish Dish	Number of words spelled correctly. Type of error
Ollendick, Matson, Esveldt-Dawson, & Shapiro (1980) Study 1	2	LD	10 8.5	NR	8.0 1.0	100 96	Words from published reading inventory	NR	Number of words spelled correctly
Study 2	2	ILD	13	NR	10	91	Words from published reading inventory	NR	Number of words spelled correctly
Singh, Farquhar, & Hewett (1991)	4	LD	$\bar{x}$ 15.4	High school	2 yrs below	Normal	Words from published spelling list	NR	Number of words spelled correctly
Wong (1986)	8	PS	NR	6th	NR	NR	Words from spelling curriculum	NR	Number of words spelled correctly

TABLE 13.1. Spelling intervention studies (1978–1991).

| Study | Independent variable(s) | | | Results | Follow-up | Teacher acceptance | Participant acceptance |
	Description	Individual	Trainer				
Bailet (1990)	Student required to write base word before suffix-adding word	I	Author	All groups performed better under treatment conditions	NR	NR	NR
Bailet & Lyon (1985)	Trainer read base word before derived or inflected words	I	NR	Spelling performance improved under treatment conditions	Yes	NR	NR
Bryant, Drabin, & Gettinger (1981)	Number of words taught per day: 3, 4, or 5	I	Author, 4 graduate students	Average total words learned did not differ across groups. Three-word group scored highest on three common words	NR	NR	NR
Foxx & Jones (1978)	Four conditions: (1) Pretest study test (2) Pretest-positive practice (3) Pretest-positive practice (4) Pretest-positive practice-test-positive practice	I	Teachers	For 4th, 7th, and 8th graders, pretest-positive practice-test-positive practice produced the greatest or second greatest gains	Yes	Yes	Yes
Frank, Wacker, Zeith, & Sagen (1987)	Treatment package (interspersal of known words, positive practice, and teacher supervision of study) across group and individual instruction	I and G	Author, teacher	No differences in responding across individual and group instruction	Yes	NR	NR

TABLE 13.1. (Cont'd)

Study	Independent variable(s)			Results	Follow-up	Teacher acceptance	Participant acceptance
	Description	Individual	Trainer				
Gerber (1986)	Contingent imitation of errors and modeling; teacher prompts on word similarities	I	NR	All interventions increased spelling accuracy. Percent correct was higher generally when prompts were added to contingent imitation and modeling	NR	NR	NR
Gettinger (1985)	Cues (highlighting incorrect parts of misspelled words) vs. no cues. Teacher-directed instruction vs. student-directed instruction	I	Author, 3 graduate students	Student-directed instruction incorporating cues produced the highest scores	Yes	NR	NR
Graham & Freeman (1985)	Strategy training across three study conditions: (1) teacher-directed (2) student-controlled (3) teacher-monitored (4) free study (no strategy)	I	Instructor	All groups who received strategy training performed better than the free study group. Performance was not differentially affected by study condition	NR	NR	NR

Study	Conditions		Implementer	Findings			
Harris, Graham, & Freeman (1988)	Four conditions: (1) teacher-directed (2) teacher-monitored (3) student-controlled (4) free study (no strategy)	NR	Teachers	Majority of students across conditions overestimated performance. Accuracy was highest for the teacher-monitored group	NR	NR	NR
Kauffman, Hallahan, Haas, Brane, & Boren (1978)	Modeling vs. modeling plus contingent imitation of errors	I	Teacher	Imitation plus modeling was superior for both regular and irregular words	Yes	NR	NR
Nulnan & Gerber (1984)	Contingent imitation, modeling, and reinforcement	I	Author	Treatment package led to spelling acquisition	NR	Yes	Yes
Ollendick, Matson, Esveldt-Dawson, & Shapiro (1980) Study 1	Positive practice vs. reinforcement plus positive practice vs. control	I	Aide	Positive practice plus reinforcement led to most rapid acquisition	NR	NR	Yes
Study 2	Positive practice vs. traditional instruction vs. reinforcement plus traditional instruction	I	Aide	Positive practice plus reinforcement was most effective	NR	NR	Yes

TABLE 13.1. (Cont'd)

Study	Independent variable(s)			Results	Follow-up	Teacher acceptance	Participant acceptance
	Description	Individual	Trainer				
Singh, Farquhar, & Hewett (1991)	Directed rehearsal vs. known-word interspersal plus directed rehearsal vs. control	I	Graduate Student	Directed rehearsal enhanced spelling performance of all subjects. Interspersal training did not add to efficacy	NR	NR	NR
Wong (1986)	Spelling grid plus self-questioning strategy	G	NR	Accuracy of spelling performance increased	Yes	NR	NR

LD, learning disabled; PR, poor readers; CA, chronological age; I, treatment applied individually; NR, not reported; NA, normally achieving; GR, good readers; GES, grade equivalence score; G, treatment applied to group; Yes, was reported; PS, poor spellers.

the participants in these studies were individuals with learning disabilities. A few participants were described as poor spellers with normal intelligence.

Interventions were based on behavioral or cognitive–behavioral principles. Cognitive behavioral research, which blends two schools of thought previously viewed as incompatible, was included for several reasons. First, interventions that ignore the importance of the unobservable, internal steps we conduct when engaging in complex academic behaviors such as spelling have limited success in promoting the academic success of learning disabled students (Hallahan, Kneedler, & Lloyd, 1983). Second, a body of literature demonstrating the success of cognitive behavior modification (CBM) has been developing. Finally, CBM lends itself to matching learner characteristics (e.g., lack of appropriate strategies) with treatment (e.g., teaching strategy application) (Hallahan et al., 1983). Behavioral characteristics included in CBM include the use of objectives, behavioral definitions of responding, ongoing data collection, task analysis, modeling, reinforcement, teaching to mastery, and corrective feedback. The intervention studies will be discussed briefly, beginning with those that focus on the arrangement of antecedents.

Antecedent Strategies

In a number of studies, the experimenters manipulated antecedent events (e.g., teacher prompts, conditions for studying) in an effort to improve the spelling acquisition of students labeled as learning disabled. An easily controlled antecedent is the number of new words presented per session. Bryant et al. (1981) compared the effects of presenting three, four, or five new words per session to 64 learning disabled students and found the average total words learned was the same across conditions. However, students in the three-word group scored highest on nine common words. Another group of researchers investigated the effectiveness of individual versus group training when using a treatment package consisting of known-word interspersal, positive practive, positive reinforcement, and teacher supervision of study sessions. No differences were found between individual and group training. This lack of difference may reflect that group training consisted of individual instruction conducted with more than one student at a time rather than group-directed instruction. The structure of training sessions also was the focus of Graham and Freeman (1985). These researchers compared three conditions for studying a spelling strategy to free study with no strategy. All students who received strategy training performed better than the free-study group, with no differential effects produced by the study condition.

Additional antecedent interventions were based on strategy application. Wong (1986) looked at the influence of a self-questioning strategy used in conjunction with a spelling grid and found improved spelling performance for eight poor spellers. Bailet (1990) and Bailet and Lyon (1985) directed the attention of learning disabled students to the base word of derived words. In the 1985 study, the spelling accuracy of a learning disabled student was improved when the trainer read the base word before a derived or inflected word the student was asked to spell. These results were replicated in a large follow-up study that included both good and poor readers who were learning disabled. In this study, students were asked to write the base word before writing suffix-adding words.

Consequent Strategies

Another group of studies focused on interventions designed around consequences rather than antecedents. These consequences generally were applied after an incorrect spelling response and included a punishment component. Positive practice, a form of overcorrection in which the person is required to write a misspelled word correctly a multiple number of times, was investigated in several studies. Foxx and Jones (1978) looked at 29 poor spellers in 4th, 5th, 7th, and 8th grades. Four conditions were compared across and within groups: (a) pretest study test, (b) pretest-positive practice, (c) pretest-positive practice test, and (d) pretest-positive practice-test-positive practice. For most participants, the pretest-positive practice-test-positive practice condition produced the greatest or second greatest increase regardless of when presented. Positive practice also was studies by Ollendick, Matson, Esveldt-Dawson, and Shapiro (1980), who conducted two experiments, one with two learning disabled persons and one that included one learning disabled person. In both experiments, positive practice plus reinforcement led to improved spelling performance.

A second consequence of interest to researchers was contingent imitation of errors, a procedure in which the trainer imitates the incorrect response of the subject. Kauffman, Hallahan, Haas, Brame, and Boren (1978) compared modeling the correct spelling to modeling plus contingent imitation. Imitation plus modeling proved more effective both for regular and irregular words. Contingent imitation of errors and modeling also were part of the treatment package investigated by Nulman and Gerber (1984), who added reinforcement of correct responding to their package. The spelling acquisition of a 2nd grade learning disabled student was successfully treated with this package.

Antecedent and Consequent Strategies Combined

A final group of studies included interventions that incorporated both antecedents and consequences. Teacher prompting on word similarities appeared to increase the effectiveness of contingent imitation plus modeling (Gerber, 1986). However, the design of this study did not lead to conclusive results. In another study by Singh, Farquhar, and Hewett (1991), directed rehearsal, which incorporates modeling and positive practice, was evaluated. Directed rehearsal was compared to directed rehearsal plus known-word interspersal. Using an alternating treatments design and incorporating a control condition, the researchers found that directed rehearsal enhanced spelling performance, but interspersal training did not contribute to efficacy. Finally, Gettinger (1985) looked at the effects of highlighting the incorrect parts of misspelled words as well as the effects of teacher-directed versus student-directed instruction. The highest scores were produced for student-directed instruction that incorporated the cueing. Of importance in interpreting this study is the difference between student-determined instruction and student-directed instruction. Through controlling their study, students were applying a sequence of steps provided by the teacher.

Summary and Research Needs

The lack of a comprehensive body of spelling-intervention research with learning disabled students is astonishing for several reasons: (a) spelling problems are a primary characteristic of this population, (b) spelling problems hinder academic, occupational, and social success, (c) spelling has been a focus of academic programming for a very long time, and (d) general research in spelling has been conducted for more than 80 years. A great need exists for systematic and well designed research in this area. A number of aspects should be considered when designing this research:

1. Generalization of effects is of particular importance and should be addressed in all studies; interventions that will generalize beyond the words used in training are essential.
2. Maintenance of skills should be assessed through follow-up data at regular intervals after cessation of training. Skills that are not maintained are of little value.
3. Fidelity to treatment should be evaluated and reported.
4. Research publications should include "technological" descriptions of treatment (Baer, Wolf, & Risley, 1968). A technological description is thorough enough to allow exact replication.
5. Component analyses of treatment packages would lead to precise conclusions about the effectiveness of particular antecedents and consequences included in these packages.
6. Interventions designed to address particular problems identified through research should be pursued; this is a primary goal of cognitive behavioral research.
7. Attention should be given to the general "effective instruction" literature. Surely the characteristics of effective instruction (e.g.,

group instruction, teacher-directed instruction, high levels of student responding) should be considered when designing interventions.

8. Since most spelling researchers agree that spelling is based on morphographic relationships, these relationships offer a natural area for research.
9. Students with spelling problems may work harder to overcome these problems if they are taught the importance of spelling.
10. If possible, evaluations of participant and teacher acceptance should be conducted. Of particular importance is teacher acceptance, as effective interventions are of little benefit unless they are used.

Attention to teacher acceptance could help ameliorate a major problem that concerns researchers. According to several sources (Collins, 1983; Fitzsimmons & Loomer, 1977; Gerber & Hall, 1989), research-supported practices are seldom used by teachers, who continue to operate traditional programs. This problem may require research designed to determine effective methods for getting teachers to implement empirically derived spelling interventions. Of equal importance is the design and implementation of research structured to evaluate carefully the effectiveness of morphographic spelling programs with learning disabled students. Spelling Mastery (Dixon, Englemann, Meier, Steely, & Wells, 1980) is a highly structured program designed to be used with 2nd through 6th graders. This program uses a morphographic approach and incorporates the characteristics of effective instruction. Students who complete this program develop a spelling vocabulary of more than 10,000 words. A similar program, Morphographic Spelling (Dixon, 1976), was designed as a remedial program for use with 4th through 12th graders and adults. Students are trained to use five rules for combining morphographs to spell more than 12,000 words. This program was tested with a large group of students, many of whom were poor spellers, and proved to enhance spelling performance (Maggs et al., 1981). Well designed investigations of the effectiveness of these programs when used with individuals with learning disabilities would yield information that could substantially impact the field.

Individuals with learning disabilities will not learn to spell well unless they receive systematic, teacher-directed instruction. Additional research is required to identify that instruction and to determine methods to ensure teacher implementation.

Epilogue

Given the volume of research on behavioral approaches to the remediation of academic deficits in students with learning disabilities, our review has been selective rather than exhaustive. Because of our own interests, we have concentrated on reading and spelling; however, readers interested in the remediation of mathematics should consult a recent review by Pereira and Winton (1991) on this topic. In addition, because of space considerations, our review of reading research has been directed more at an examination of behavioral remediation strategies rather than a critical appraisal of published studies using these strategies. Readers interested specifically in a critical appraisal of reading research with students who are learning disabled should consult the excellent reviews by Jenkins and Heliotis (1981), Paris, Wixon, and Palincsar (1986), and Weisberg (1988). However, the comparatively smaller literature on behavioral approaches to spelling remediation allowed us to present, in table form, a critical and methodological review of the spelling literature.

References

Alexander, D. F. (1985). The effect of study skill training on learning disabled students' retelling of expository material. *Journal of Applied Behavior Analysis*, *18*, 263–267.

Baer, D. M., Wolf, M. M., & Risley, T. R. (1968). Some current dimensions of applied behavior analysis. *Journal of Applied Behavior Analysis*, *1*, 91–97.

Bailet, L. L. (1990). Spelling rule usage among students with learning disabilities and normally achieving students. *Journal of Learning Disabilities*, *23*, 121–128.

Bailet, L. L., & Lyon, C. R. (1985). Deficient linguistic rule application in a learning disabled speller: A case study. *Journal of Learning Disabilities*, *18*, 162–165.

Beers, J. W. (1980). Developmental strategies of spelling competence in primary school children. In E. Henderson & J. Beers (Eds.), *Developmental and cognitive aspects of learning to spell* (pp. 35–45). Newark, DE: International Reading Association.

Billingsley, F. F. (1977). The effects of self- and externally-imposed schedules of reinforcement on oral reading performance. *Journal of Learning Disabilities*, *10*, 549–555.

Bookman, M. O. (1984). Spelling as a cognitive-developmental linguistic process. *Academic Therapy*, *20*, 21–32.

Bos, C. S., Anders, P. L., Filip, D., & Jaffe, L. E. (1989). The effects of an interactive instructional strategy for enhancing reading comprehension and content area learning for students with learning disabilities. *Journal of Learning Disabilities*, *22*, 384–390.

Bradley-Johnson, S., Sunderman, P., & Johnson, C. M. (1983). Comparison of delayed prompting and fading for teaching preschoolers easily confused letters and numbers. *Journal of School Psychology*, *21*, 327–335.

Brueckner, L., & Bond, G. (1955). *Diagnosis and treatment of learning difficulties*. New York: Appleton-Century-Crofts.

Bryant, N. D., Drabin, I. R., & Gettinger, M. (1981). Effects of varying unit size on spelling achievement in learning disabled children. *Journal of Learning Disabilities*, *14*, 200–203.

Carlisle, J. F. (1987). The use of morphological knowledge in spelling derived forms by learning disabled and normal studies. *Annals of Dyslexia*, *37*, 90–108.

Carpenter, D. C. (1983). Spelling error profile of able and disabled readers. *Journal of Learning Disabilities, 16*, 102–110.

Carpenter, D., & Miller, L. J. (1982). Spelling ability of reading disabled LD students and able readers. *Learning Disability Quarterly, 5*, 65–70.

Chang, S. Q., Williams, R. L., & McLaughlin, T. F. (1983). Differential effects of oral reading to improve comprehension with severe learning disabled and educable mentally handicapped students. *Adolescence, 18*, 619–626.

Chiang, B., Thorpe, H. W., & Darch, C. B. (1980). Effects of cross-age tutoring on word-recognition performance of learning disabled students. *Learning Disability Quarterly, 3*, 11–19.

Chomsky, C. (1979). Approaching reading through invented spelling. In L. B. Resnick & R. A. Weaver (Eds.), *Theory and practice of early reading* (Vol. 2, pp. 43–65). Hillsdale, NJ: Erlbaum.

Chomsky, N. (1970). Phonology and reading. In H. Levin & J. Williams (Eds.), *Basic studies in reading* (pp. 3–18). New York: Harper & Row.

Clark, F. L., Deshler, D. D., Schumaker, J. B., Alley, G. R., & Warner, M. M. (1984). Visual imagery and self-questioning: Strategies to improve comprehension of written material. *Journal of Learning Disabilities, 17*, 145–149.

Cohen, L. (1969). *Evaluating structural analysis method used in spelling books.* Unpublished doctoral dissertation, Boston University.

Collins, M. (1983). Teaching spelling: Current practices and effective instruction. *Direct Instruction News, 7*, 1–15.

Cone, T. E., Wilson, L. R., Bradley, C. M., & Reese, J. H. (1985). Characteristics of LD students in Iowa: An empirical investigation. *Learning Disability Quarterly, 8*, 211–220.

Cook, L. (1981). Misspelling analysis in dyslexia: Observation of developmental strategy shifts. *Bulletin of the Orton Society, 31*, 123–134.

Corey, J. R., & Shamow, J. (1972). The effects of fading on acquisition and retention of oral reading. *Journal of Applied Behavior Analysis, 5*, 311–315.

Cronnell, B., & Humes, A. (1980). Elementary spelling: What's really taught. *Elementary School Journal, 81*, 59–64.

Darch, C., & Carnine, D. (1986). Teaching content area material to learning disabled students. *Exceptional Children, 53*, 240–246.

Darch, C., & Gersten, R. (1985). The effects of teacher presentation rate and praise on LD students' oral reading performance. *British Journal of Educational Psychology, 55*, 295–303.

Darch, C., & Gersten, R. (1986). Direction-setting activities in reading comprehension: A comparison of two approaches. *Learning Disability Quarterly, 9*, 235–243.

Dixon, R. (1976). *Morphological spelling.* Chicago: Science Research Associates.

Dixon, R., Engelmann, S., Meier, M., Steely, D., & Wells, C. (1980). *Spelling mastery* (Levels A–E). Chicago: Science Research Associates.

Doehring, D. G. (1977). Comprehension of printed sentences by children with reading disability. *Bulletin of the Psychonomic Society, 10*, 350–352.

Dorry, G. W. (1976). Attentional model for the effectiveness of fading in training reading vocabulary with retarded persons. *American Journal of Mental Deficiency, 81*, 271–279.

Dorry, G. W., & Zeaman, D. (1973). The use of a fading technique in paired-associate teaching of a reading vocabulary with retardates. *Mental Retardation*, *11*, 3–6.

Dorry, G. W., & Zeaman, D. (1975). Teaching a simple reading vocabulary to retarded children: Effectiveness of fading and nonfading procedures. *American Journal of Mental Deficiency*, *79*, 711–716.

Dyck, N., & Sundbye, N. (1988). The use of text explicitness on story understanding and recall by learning disabled children. *Learning Disabilities Research*, *3*, 68–77.

Egeland, B. (1975). Effects of errorless training on teaching children to discriminate letters of the alphabet. *Journal of Applied Psychology*, *60*, 533–536.

Egeland, B. & Winer, K. (1974). Teaching children to discriminate letters of the alphabet through errorless discrimination training. *Journal of Reading Behavior*, *6*, 143–150.

Etzel, B. C., & LeBlanc, J. M. (1979). The simplest treatment alternative: The law of parsimony applied to choosing appropriate instructional control and errorless-learning procedures for the difficult-to-teach child. *Journal of Autism and Developmental Disorders*, *9*, 361–382.

Fitzsimmons, R., & Loomer, B. (1977). *Spelling research and practice*. Iowa City: Iowa State Department of Public Instruction and University of Iowa.

Finucci, J. M., Isaacs, S. D., Whitehouse, C. C., & Childs, B. (1983). Classification of spelling errors and their relationships to reading ability, sex, grade placement, and intelligence. *Brain and Language*, *20*, 340–355.

Fischer, F. W., Shankweiler, D., & Liberman, Il Y. (1985). Spelling proficiency and sensitivity to word structure. *Journal of Memory and Language*, *24*, 423–441.

Fleisher, L. S., & Jenkins, J. R. (1978). Effects of contextual and decontextualized practice conditions on word recognition. *Learning Disability Quarterly*, *1*, 39–47.

Foxx, R. M., & Jones, J. R. (1978). A remediation program for increasing the spelling achievement of elementary and junior high school students. *Behavior Modification*, *2*, 211–230.

Frank, A. R., Wacker, D. P., Zeith, T. Z., & Sagen, T. K. (1987). Effectiveness of a spelling study package for learning disabled students. *Learning Disabilities Research*, *2*, 110–118.

Freeman, T. J., & McLaughlin, T. F. (1984). Effects of a taped-words treatment procedure on learning disabled students' sight-word oral reading. *Learning Disability Quarterly*, *7*, 49–54.

Firth, U. (1980). Unexpected spelling problems. In U. Firth (Ed.), *Cognitive processes in spelling* (pp. 495–515). New York: Academic Press.

Gadow, K. D., Torgesen, J. K. & Dahlem, W. E. (1983). Learning disabilities. In M. Hersen, V. B. Van Hasselt, & J. L. Matson (Eds.), *Behavior therapy for the developmentally and physically disabled* (pp. 307–331). New York: Academic Press.

Gerber, M. M. (1984). Investigations of orthographic problem-solving ability in learning disabled and normally achieving students. *Learning Disability Quarterly*, *7*, 157–164.

Gerber, M. M. (1986). Generalization of spelling strategies by LD students as a result of contingent imitation/modeling and mastery criteria. *Journal of Learning Disabilities*, *19*, 530–537.

Gerber, M. M., & Hall, R. J. (1987). Information processing approaches to studying spelling deficiencies. *Journal of Learning Disabilities*, *20*, 34–42.

Gerber, M. M., & Hall, R. J. (1989). Cognitive-behavioral training in spelling for learning handicapped students. *Learning Disability Quarterly*, *12*, 159–171.

Gettinger, M. (1985). Effects of teacher-directed versus student-directed instruction and cues for improvind spelling performance. *Journal of Applied Behavioral Analysis*, *18*, 167–171.

Glynn, T. (1982). Antecedent control of behavior in education contexts. *Educational Psychology*, *2*, 215–229.

Graham, S. (1983). Effective spelling instruction. *The Elementary School Journal*, *83*, 560–568.

Graham, S., & Freeman, S. (1985). Strategy training and teacher vs. student controlled study conditions: Effects on LD students' spelling performance. *Learning Disability Quarterly*, *8*, 267–274.

Graham, S., & Miller, L. (1979). Spelling research and practice: A unified approach. *Focus on Exceptional Children*, *12*, 1–16.

Graves, M. F. & Cooke, C. L. (1980). Effects of previewing difficult short stories for high school students. *Research on Reading in Secondary Schools*, *6*, 38–54.

Graves, M. F., Cooke, C. L., & LaBerge, M. J. (1983). Effects of previewing difficult short stories on low ability junior high school students' comprehension, recall, and attitudes. *Reading Research Quarterly*, *18*, 262–276.

Graves, M. F., & Palmer, R. J. (1981). Validating previewing as a method of improving fifth and sixth grade students' comprehension of short stories. *Michigan Reading Journal*, *15*, 1–3.

Griffey, Q. L., Zigmond, N., & Leinhardt, G. (1988). The effects of self-questioning and story structure training on the reading comprehension of poor readers. *Learning Disabilities Research*, *4*, 45–51.

Hallahan, D. P., Kauffman, J. M., & Lloyd, J. W. (1985). *Introduction to learning disabilities*. Englewood Cliffs, NJ: Prentice-Hall, Inc.

Hallahan, D. P., Kneedler, R. D., & Lloyd, J. W. (1983). Cognitive behavior modification techniques for learning disabled children: Self-instruction and self-monitoring. In J. D. McKinney & L. Fregan (Eds.), *Current topics in learning disabilities*. Norwood, NJ: Ablex Publishing Corporation.

Hammil, D. D., (1990). Improving spelling skills. In D. Hammil & N. R. Bartel (Eds.), *Teaching students with learning and behavior problems*. Boston: Allyn and Bacon.

Hammil, D. D., Larsen, S., & McNutt, G. (1977). The effects of spelling instruction: A preliminary study. *Elementary School Journal*, *78*, 67–72.

Hanna, P., Hodges, R., & Hanna, J. (1971). *Spelling: Structure and strategies*. New York: Houghton-Mifflin.

Hansen, C. L., & Eaton, M. D. (1978). Reading. In N. G. Harring, T. C. Lovitt, M. D. Eaton, & C. Hansen, (Eds.), *The fourth R: Research in the classroom*. Columbus, OH: Charles E. Merrill.

Hansen, C. L., & Lovitt, T. (1977). An applied behavior analysis approach to reading comprehension. In J. T. Guthrie (Ed.), *Cognition, curriculum and comprehension*. Newark, DE: International Reading Association.

Harris, K. R., Graham, S., & Freeman, S. (1988). Effects of strategy training. *Exceptional Children*, *54*, 332–338.

Hendrickson, J. M., Roberts, M., & Shores, R. F. (1978). Antecedent and contingent modeling to teach basic sight vocabulary to learning disabled children. *Journal of Learning Disabilities*, 11, 524–528.

Hull, M. (1976). *Phonics for teachers* (2nd ed.). Columbus, OH: Charles E. Merrill.

Idol, L. (1987). Group story mapping: A comprehension strategy for both skilled and unskilled readers. *Journal of Learning Disabilities*, *20*, 196–205.

Jeffree, D. (1981). A bridge between pictures and print. *Special Education: Forward Trends*, *8*, 28–31.

Jenkins, J. R. (1979). Oral reading: Considerations for special and remedial education teachers. In J. E. Button, T. C. Lovitt, & T. D. Rowland (Eds.), *Communications research in learning disabilities and mental retardation* (pp. 67–91). Baltimore: University Park Press.

Jenkins, J. R., Barksdale, A., & Clinton, L. (1978). Improving reading comprehension and oral reading: Generalization across behaviors, settings and time. *Journal of Learning Disabilities*, *11*, 607–617.

Jenkins, J. R., & Heliotis, J. G. (1981). Reading comprehension instruction: Findings from behavioral and cognitive psychology. *Topics in Language Disorders*, *1*, 25–41.

Jenkins, J. R., Heliotis, J., Haynes, M., & Beck, K. (1986). Does passive learning account for disabled readers' comprehension deficits in ordinary reading situations? *Learning Disability Quarterly*, *9*, 69–76.

Jenkins, J. R., Heliotis, J. D., Stein, M. L., & Haynes, M. C. (1987). Improving reading comprehension by using paragraph restatements. *Exceptional Children*, *54*, 54–59.

Jenkins, J. R., & Larson, K. (1979). Evaluating error-correction procedures for oral reading. *Journal of Special Education*, 13, 145–156.

Johnson, D. J. (1988). Review of research on specific reading, writing, and mathematics disorders. In J. F. Kavanagh & T. J. Truss, Jr. (Eds.), *Learning disabilities: Proceedings of the national conference*. Parkton, MD: York Press.

Kauffman, J. M., Hallahan, D. P., Haas, K., Brame, T., & Boren, R. (1978). Imitating children's errors to improve their spelling performance. *Journal of Learning Disabilities*, *11*, 217–222.

Koegel, R. L., & Rincover, A. (1976). Some detrimental effects of using extra stimuli to guide learning in normal and autistic children. *Journal of Abnormal Child Psychology*, *4*, 59–71.

Lahey, B. B. (1977). Research on the role of reinforcement in reading instruction: Some measurement and methodological deficiencies. *Corrective and Social Psychiatry and Journal of Behavior Technology Methods*, *23*, 27–32.

Lahey, B. B., & Drabman, R. S. (1974). Facilitation of the acquisition and retention of sight-word vocabulary through token reinforcement. *Journal of Applied Behavior Analysis*, *7*, 307–312.

Lahey, B. B., & Johnson, M. S. (1977). *Psychology and instruction*. Glenview, IL: Scott, Foresman.

Lahey, B. B., McNees, M. P., & Brown, C. C. (1973). Modification of deficits in reading for comprehension. *Journal of Applied Behavior Analysis*, *6*, 475–480.

Lancioni, G. E., Ceccarani, P., & Oliva, D. (1981). Avviamento alla lettura tramite insegnamento programmato. *Psicologia e Scuola, 7*, 16–27.

Le Blanc, J. M. Etzel, B. C., & Domash, M. A. (1978). A functional curriculum for early intervention. In K. E. Allen, V. A. Holm, & R. L. Schiefelbusch (Eds.), *Early intervention: A team approach* (pp. 331–381). Baltimore: University Park Press.

Lenz, M., Singh, N. N., & Hewett, A. E. (1991). Overcorrection as an academic remediation procedure: A review and reappraisal. *Behavior Modification, 15,* 64–73.

Lerner, J. W. (1985). *Learning disabilities: Theories, diagnosis, and teaching strategies* (4th ed.). Boston: Houghton Mifflin.

Limbrick, E., McNaughton, S., & Glynn, T. (1985). Reading gains for underachieving tutors and tutees in a cross-age tutoring programme. *Journal of Child Psychology and Psychiatry, 26*, 939–953.

Lovitt, T. C., & Hurlburt, M. (1974). Using behavior-analysis techniques to assess the relationship between phonics instruction and oral reading. *Journal of Special Education, 8*, 57–72.

Maggs, A., McMillan, K., Patching, W., & Hawke, H. (1981). Accelerating spelling skills using morphographs. *Educational Psychology, 1*, 49–56.

McGee, G. G., & McCoy, J. F. (1981). Training procedures for acquisition and retention of reading in retarded youth. *Applied Research in Mental Retardation, 2*, 263–276.

McNaughton, S., & Delquadri, J. (1978). Error attention tutoring in oral reading. In T. Glynn & S. McNaughton (Eds.), *Behavior analysis in New Zealand* (pp. 98–122). Auckland, New Zealand: University of Auckland.

McNaughton, S., & Glynn, T. (1981). Delayed versus immediate attention to oral reading errors: Effects on accuracy and self-correction. *Educational Psychology, 1*, 57–65.

Mercer, C. D. (1987). *Students with learning disabilities*. Columbus, OH: Merrill Publishing Company.

Meyer, L. A. (1982). The relative effects of word-analysis and word supply correction procedures with poor readers during word-attack training. *Reading Research Quarterly, 17*, 544–555.

Miller, A., & Miller, E. A. (1968). Symbol accentuation: The perceptual transfer of meaning from spoken to printed words. *American Journal of Mental Deficiency, 73*, 200–208.

Miller, A., & Miller, E. A. (1971). Symbol accentuation, single-track functioning and early reading. *American Journal of Mental Deficiency, 76*, 110–117.

Moats, L. C. (1983). A comparison of the spelling errors of older dyslexic and second grade normal children. *Annals of Dyslexia, 33*, 121–139.

Nelson, H. E. (1980). Spelling errors in normals and dyslexics. In U. Firth (Ed.), *Cognitive processes in spelling* (pp. 475–493). New York: Academic Press.

Nulman, J. H., & Gerber, M. M. (1984). Improving spelling performance by imitating a child's errors. *Journal of Learning Disabilities, 17*, 328–333.

Ollendick, T. H., Matson, J. L., Esveldt-Dawson, K., & Shapiro, E. S. (1980). Increasing spelling achievement: An analysis of treatment procedures utilizing an alternating treatment design. *Journal of Applied Behavior Analysis, 13*, 645–654.

O'Shea, L. J., Munson, S. M., & O'Shea, D. J. (1984). Error correction in oral reading: Evaluating the effectiveness of three procedures. *Education and Treatment of Children*, *7*, 203–214.

Pany, D., & Jenkins, J. R. (1978). Learning word meanings: A comparison of instructional procedures. *Learning Disability Quarterly*, *1*, 21–31.

Pany, D., Jenkins, J. R., & Schreck, J. (1982). Vocabulary instruction: Effects on word knowledge and reading comprehension. *Learning Disability Quarterly*, *5*, 202–215.

Paris, S. G., Wixon, K. K., & Palincsar, A. S. (1986). In E. Rothkopf (Ed.), *Review of research in education* (pp. 91–128). Washington, DC: American Educational Research Association.

Perfetti, C., & Hogoboam, T. (1975). Relationship between single word decoding and reading comprehension skill. *Journal of Educational Psychology*, *67*, 461–469.

Pereira, J. A., & Winton, A. S. W. (1991). Teaching and remediation of mathematics: A review of behavioral research. *Journal of Behavioral Education*, *1*, 3–24.

Perkins, V. L. (1988). Feedback effects on oral reading errors of children with learning disabilities. *Journal of Learning Disabilities*, *21*, 244–248.

Pflaum, S. W., Pascarella, E. T., Auer, C., Augustyn, L., & Boswick, M. (1982). Differential effects of four comprehension-facilitating conditions on LD and normal elementary-school readers. *Learning Disability Quarterly*, *5*, 106–116.

Poplin, M., Gray, R., Larsen, S., Banikowski, A., & Mehring, T. (1980). A comparison of components of written expression abilities in learning and non-learning disabled children at three grade levels. *Learning Disabilities Quarterly*, *3*(4), 46–53.

Read, C. (1975). Lessons to be learned from the preschool orthographer. In E. Lenneberg & E. Lenneberg (Eds.), *Foundations of language development* (Vol. 2, pp. 329–346). New York: Academic Press.

Reith, H., Axelrod, S., Anderson, R., Hathaway, F., Wood, K., & Fitzgerald, C. (1974). Influence of distributed practice and daily spelling on weekly spelling tests. *Journal of Educational Research*, *68*, 73–77.

Rincover, A. (1978) Variables affecting stimulus fading and discriminative responding in psychotic children. *Journal of Abnormal Psychology*, *87*, 541–553.

Roberts, M., & Smith, D. D. (1980). The relationship among correct and error oral reading rates and comprehension. *Learning Disability Quarterly*, *3*, 54–64.

Robinson, F. P. (1941). *Diagnostic and remedial technique for effective study*. New York: Harper.

Rose, T. L. (1984). The effects of previewing on retarded learners' oral reading. *Education and Training of the Mentally Retarded*, *19*, 49–53.

Rose, T. L., & Beattie, J. R. (1986). Relative effects of teacher-directed and taped previewing on oral reading. *Learning Disability Quarterly*, *9*, 193–199.

Rose, T. L., Koorland, M. A., & Epstein, M. H. (1982). A review of applied behavior analysis interventions with learning disabled children. *Education and Treatment of Children*, *5*, 41–58.

Rose, T. L., McEntire, E., & Dowdy, C. (1982). Effects of two error-correction procedures on oral reading. *Learning Disability Quarterly*, *5*, 100–105.

Rose, T. L., & Sherry, L. (1984). Relative effects of two previewing procedures on LD adolescents' oral reading performance. *Learning Disability Quarterly*, *7*, 39–44.

Rosenberg, M. S. (1986). Error-correction during oral reading: A comparison of three techniques. *Learning Disability Quarterly*, *9*, 182–192.

Ross, A. O. (1981). *Child behavior therapy*. New York: Wiley.

Sachs, A. (1983). The effects of three prereading activities on learning disabled students' reading comprehension. *Learning Disability Quarterly*, *6*, 248–251.

Sachs, A. (1984). The effects of previewing activities on oral reading miscues. *RASE*, *5*(3), 45–49.

Salend, S. J., & Nowak, M. R. (1988). Effects of peer-previewing on LD students' oral reading skills. *Learning Disability Quarterly*, *11*, 47–53.

Samuels, S. J. (1967). Attentional processes in reading: The effects of pictures on the acquisition of reading responses. *Journal of Educational Psychology*, *58*, 337–342.

Samuels, S. J. (1970). Effects of pictures on learning to read, comprehension, and attitudes. *Review of Education Research*, *40*, 397–407.

Saunders, R. J., & Solman, R. T. (1984). The effect of pictures on the acquisition of a small vocabulary of similar sight-words. *British Journal of Educational Psychology*, *54*, 265–275.

Schimek, N. (1983). Errorless discrimination training on digraphs with a learning disabled student. *School Psychology Review*, *12*, 101–105.

Schreibman, L. (1975). Effects of within-stimulus and extra-stimulus prompting on discrimination learning in autistic children. *Journal of Applied Behavior Analysis*, *8*, 91–112.

Schreibman, L., Charlop, M. H., & Koegel, R. L. (1982). Teaching autistic children to use extra-stimulus prompts. *Journal of Experimental Child Psychology*, *33*, 475–491.

Schwartz, S., & Doehring, D. G. (1977). A developmental study of children's ability to acquire knowledge of spelling patterns. *Developmental Psychology*, *13*, 419–420.

Singh, N. N. (1985). Overcorrection of academic behavior. In C. Sharpley, A. Hudson, & C. Lee (Eds.), *Proceedings of the Eighth Annual Conference on the Australian Behavior Modification Association* (pp. 382–391). Melbourne, Australia: ABMA.

Singh, N. N. (1987). Overcorrection of oral reading errors: A comparison of individual and group training formats. *Behavior Modification*, *11*, 165–181.

Singh, N. N. (1990). Effects of two error-correction procedures on oral reading errors: Word supply versus sentence repeat. *Behavior Modification*, *14*, 188–199.

Singh, N. N., & Beale, I. L. (1988). Learning disabilities: Psychological therapies. In J. L. Matson (Ed.), *Handbook of treatment approaches in child psychopathology* (pp. 525–553). New York: Plenum Press.

Singh, N. N., Farquhar, S., & Hewett, A. R. (1991). Enhancing the spelling performance of learning disabled students: Task variation does not increase the efficacy of directed rehearsal. *Behavior Modification*, *15*, 271–282.

Singh, N. N., & Singh, J. (1984) Antecedent control of oral reading errors and self-corrections by mentally retarded children. *Journal of Applied Behavior Analysis*, *17*, 111–119.

Singh, N. N., & Singh, J. (1985). A comparison of word supply and word analysis error correction procedures on oral reading by mentally retarded children. *American Journal of Mental Deficiency*, *90*, 64–70.

Singh, N. N., & Singh, J. (1986a). A behavioral remediation program for oral reading: Effects on errors and comprehension. *Educational Psychology*, *6*, 105–114.

Singh, N. N., & Singh, J. (1986b). Reading acquisition and remediation in the mentally retarded. In N. R. Ellis & N. W. Bray (Eds.), *International review of research in mental retardation* (Vol. 14, pp. 165–199). New York: Academic Press.

Singh, N. N., & Singh, J. (1986c). Increasing oral reading proficiency: A comparative analysis of drill and positive practice overcorrection procedures. *Behavior Modification*, *10*, 115–130.

Singh, N. N., & Singh, J. (1988). Increasing oral reading proficiency through overcorrection and phonic analysis. *American Journal of Mental Retardation*, *93*, 312–319.

Singh, N. N., Singh, J., & Winton, A. S. W. (1984). Positive practice overcorrection of oral reading errors. *Behavior Modification*, *8*, 23–27.

Singh, N. N., & Solman, R. T. (1990). A stimulus control analysis of the picture-word problem in children who are mentally retarded: The blocking effect. *Journal of Applied Behavior Analysis*, *23*, 525–532.

Singh, N. N., Winton, A. S. W., & Singh, J. (1985). Effects of delayed versus immediate attention to oral reading errors on the reading proficiency of mentally retarded children. *Applied Research in Mental Retardation*, *6*, 283–292.

Skinner, B. F. (1950). Are theories of learning necessary? *Psychological Review*, *57*, 193–216.

Smeets, P. M., Lancioni, G. E. & Hoogeveen, F. R. (1984). Effects of different stimulus manipulations on the acquisition of word recognition in trainable mentally retarded children. *Journal of Mental Deficiency Research, 28*, 109–122.

Smith, D. D. (1979). The improvement of children's oral reading through the use of teacher modeling. *Journal of Learning Disabilities*, *12*, 172–175.

Stubbs, M. (1980). *Language and literacy: The sociology of reading and writing*. London: Routledge & Kegan Paul.

Swanson, L. (1981). Modification of comprehension deficits in learning disabled children. *Learning Disability Quarterly*, *4*, 189–202.

Templeton, S. (1980). Spelling, phonology, and the older student. In E. H. Henderson & J. W. Beers (Eds.), *Developmental and cognitive aspects of learning to spell: A reflection of word knowledge* (pp. 85–96). Newark, DE: International Reading Association.

Terrace, H. S. (1963). Discrimination learning with and without "errors." *Journal of the Experimental Analysis of Behavior*, *6*, 1–27.

Terrace, H. S. (1966). Stimulus control, In W. K. Honig (Ed.), *Operant behavior: Areas of research and application* (pp. 271–344). New York: Appleton-Century-Crofts.

Thorpe, H. W., & Borden, K. S. (1985). Effect of multisensory instruction upon on-task behaviors and word reading accuracy of learning disabled children. *Journal of Learning Disabilities*, *18*, 279–286.

Thorpe, H. W., Chiang, B., & Darch, C. B. (1981). Individual and group feedback systems for improving oral reading accuracy in learning disabled and regular class children. *Journal of Learning Disabilities*, *14*, 332–334, 367.

Torgesen, J. K. (1977). The role of nonspecific factors in the task performance of learning disabled children: A theoretical assessment. *Journal of Learning Disabilities*, *10*, 27–34.

Touchette, P. E. (1971). Transfer of stimulus control: Measuring the moment of transfer. *Journal of the Experimental Analysis of Behavior*, *15*, 347–354.

Treiber, F. A., & Lahey, B. B. (1983). Toward a behavioral model of academic remediation with learning disabled children. *Journal of Learning Disabilities*, *16*, 111–115.

Vogel, S. A. (1983). A qualitative analysis of morphological ability in learning disabled and achieving children. *Journal of Learning Disabilities*, *16*, 416–420.

Wallace, G., & McLaughlin, J. A. (1988). Written language problems. In G. Wallace & J. McLaughlin (Eds.), *Learning disabilities: Concepts and characteristics* (3rd ed.). Columbus, OH: Merrill Publishing Company.

Walsh, B. F., & Lamberts, F. (1979). Errorless discrimination and picture fading as techniques for teaching sight words to TMR students. *American Journal of Mental Deficiency*, *83*, 473–479.

Weisberg, R. (1988). 1980s: A change in focus of reading comprehension research: A review of reading/learning disabilities research based on an interactive model of reading. *Learning Disability Quarterly*, *11*, 149–159.

Wolfe, V. F., & Cuvo, A. J. (1978). Effects of within-stimulus and extra-stimulus prompting on letter discrimination by mentally retarded persons. *American Journal of Mental Deficiency*, *83*, 297–303.

Wong, B. Y. L. (1979). Increasing retention of main ideas through questioning strategies. *Learning Disability Quarterly*, *2*, 42–48.

Wong, B. Y. L. (1980). Activating the inactive learner: Use of questions/prompts to enhance comprehension and retention of implied information in learning disabled children. *Learning Disability Quarterly*, *3*, 29–37.

Wong, B. Y. L. (1986). A cognitive approach to teaching spelling. *Exceptional Children*, *53*, 169–173.

14
Cognitive–Behavioral Approaches in Reading and Written Language: Developing Self-Regulated Learners

Karen R. Harris, Steve Graham, and Michael Pressley

A Brief Perspective

The movement toward cognitive–behavioral educational interventions for children with significant academic problems has been the result of multiple forces. Although space precludes a thorough history, it is appropriate to acknowledge major impetuses here (see Harris, 1982, Mahoney, 1977, and Meyers, Cohen, & Schleser, 1989 for more detailed histories). Dissatisfaction with traditional behavioral interventions and their underlying assumptions became evident across many fields in the 1960s, including that of learning disabilities. While many important behavioral interventions were identified for special needs children, dissatisfaction arose in part from the limited scope and effectiveness of behavioral interventions that focused on discrete procedures used to change restricted behaviors, and in part from frequent failure to obtain durable and generalizable results (Harris, 1982). From the radical behavioral viewpoint, cognitions had no place in the science of behavior, and the underlying assumption was "the best way to change thoughts and feelings is to change behavior directly; changes in thoughts and feelings will then follow" (Ledwidge, 1978, p. 371). Most cognitivists in turn focused on cognition as the focal point for change and rejected behavioral learning principles in the 1960s.

In the 1970s, however, there was a dramatic new emphasis on integration. Increased ideological and technological flexibility promoted a marriage of what had been viewed as contradictory perspectives, that is, cognitive and behavioral psychologies. Pressure for the integration of knowledge into a prescriptive science forced hard thinking about how to combine powerful affective, behavioral, and cognitive elements, each of which served different but complementary goals. Increased support for a reciprocal influence model, which emphasized the transactional relationship between organismic and environmental influences, further contributed to the emergence of cognitive–behavior modification (CBM) (Harris, 1985).

Bandura's (1969) work on social learning theory, in particular, laid the cornerstone for the view of the individual as responding constructively to a perceived world and the emergence of cognitive–behavioral interventions (Meyers et al., 1989). Meichenbaum's (1977) seminal text on cognitive–behavior modification and the research leading up to it strongly influenced the development of integrated intervention approaches. Meichenbaum emphasized active collaboration on the part of the student, and suggested that modeling, Socratic dialogue, and guided discovery might all be effective means of developing self-regulated learners. In addition, he emphasized both cognitive–functional assessment and the importance of conducting instruction within the "zone of proximal development" (Vygotsky, 1962), consonant with earlier work by Piaget and other cognitive development theorists. Meichenbaum and Asarnow (1979) also noted the importance of affective variables. These variables, including critical aspects of motivation such as adaptive attributions and a mastery orientation, are currently receiving increased attention in cognitive–behavioral models and interventions (Garner & Alexander, 1989; Harris & Pressley, 1991).

Thus, it is no longer appropriate to refer to cognitive–behavioral interventions as simply the integration of cognitive and behavioral change techniques (Harris, 1985). Rather, cognitive–behavioral models operate from a social learning theory based "developmental transactional analysis of behavior" (Meichenbaum & Gilmore, 1984, p. 289). Currently, research on both literacy and expertise is impacting cognitive–behavioral instructional approaches (Harris & Graham, in press).

Assumptions and Components

The overriding goal and common characteristic of CBM interventions is the development of self-regulated learners. A number of cognitive–behavioral interventions have been devised to promote self-regulation; the theoretical basis and operational characteristics of CBM have become clearer as research has progressed. It is important to identify current interrelated assumptions underlying cognitive–behavioral approaches, since these assumptions provide the framework for our discussion of cognitive and cognitive–behavioral approaches to reading and writing for students with learning disorders. They include: (a) affect, behavior, and cognition are transactionally related, (b) children are active participants in the learning process, (c) developmental progressions among affective, behavioral, and cognitive dimensions are critical in the design of interventions, (d) ecological variables, including the situational, cultural, and systems network of which the individual is a part, are also critical concerns, and (e) a purposeful, integrated intervention approach that combines affective, behavioral, and cognitive intervention components within developmental and ecological parameters is necessary when children face significant and debilitating difficulties (Harris, 1985; Wong, Harris, & Graham, 1991). Although attention to these assumptions may not be evident in every investigation, the importance of these assumptions is increasingly evident in the CBM literature and in learning disabled research in general (cf. Hughes & Hall, 1989).

The assumptions underlying CBM bring into focus the need for developmental research that explores the transactional relationships between affect, behavior, and cognition. In Kendall and Braswell's (1982) model, for example, situation-specific expectancies (such as therapeutic expectancies and self-efficacy) are seen as preceding a behavioral event, current concerns occur concomitantly with the event, and causal attributions occur at the culmination of the event. Self-statements, images, and problem-solving can occur at all points throughout the temporal flow. Generalized cognitions, such as an attributional style or belief system, can develop as the result of multiple behavioral events (e.g., recurring failure can promote the belief that one is incompetent). Anticipatory cognitions, including generalized expectancies, may also become part of an individual's cognitive style as the result of repetitions of cognitive-event sequences. Such anticipatory cognitions can then be called into play preceding a behavioral event, either motivating adaptive behavior (e.g., the belief that effort is important to success) or undermining adaptive behavior (e.g., the belief that failure is inevitable). Empirical validation of this model is needed; however, it provides a valuable framework for theory and research.

Cognitive–behavioral models of learning and development, such as that proposed by Kendall and Braswell (1982), have informed strategy instruction interventions. A number of theorists and researchers now suggest that effective strategy instruction in academic domains should include three major components: teaching strategies, development of knowledge about the use and significance of those strategies (metacognitive information about strategies), and provision of executive routines to promote self-regulation of strategic performance (cf. Brown, Campione, & Day, 1981). Variations in the combination and realization of these components have led to several models of learning and instruction (cf. Deshler & Schumaker, 1986, 1988; Graham, Harris, & Sawyer, 1987; Harris & Graham, 1988; Meyers et al., 1989; Palincsar, 1986; Palincsar & Brown, 1984; Pressley, Borkowski, & Schneider, 1989; Siegel, 1982). The recent emphasis on motivation has led to recognition that goal orientations and attitudinal dispositions may profoundly affect the use of learning strategies (Borkowski, Carr, Rellinger, & Pressley, 1990; Brown, 1988; Nolen, 1988). Whereas metacognitive information about strategies can perform both an attributional training and goal setting function (Harris, 1989), explicit attributional retraining and the development of a mastery orientation among students may be critical in obtaining strategic performance (Ames & Archer, 1988; Borkowski et al., 1990; Garner & Alexander, 1989; Pearl, 1985).

CBM and Students with Learning Disabilities: An Appealing Match

Cognitive–behaviorally based models of teaching and learning that focus on motivating students to use learning strategies represent an appealing match to the needs of students with learning disabilities. Although students with learning disabilities represent a heterogeneous population, recent research has indicated that poor performance among these students may frequently be the result of problems in self-regulation of organized, strategic behaviors; behaviors they have the ability to acquire and use (Harris, 1986; Wong, 1982). Children with learning disabilities or other inefficient learners may not make use of effective verbal mediation processes or may not have developed an effective linguistic control system (i.e., they may have difficulties establishing correspondence between saying and doing or in using verbalizations to guide behavior) (Harris, 1986; Zivin, 1979). Students with learning disabilities have also exhibited difficulties in the comprehension of task demands, in the production of effective task strategies, and in the use of strategies to mediate performance (Hallahan, Lloyd, Kauffman, & Loper, 1983; Harris, 1982). In addition to deficits in self-regulation of strategic behavior, some combination of the following characteristics are present among many (although certainly not all) students with learning disabilities: learned helplessness, an external locus of control, unrealistic pretask expectancies, maladaptive attributions, negative task orientations, low levels of motivation, negative task affect, poor problem-solving skills, difficulties with time-on-task and task engagement, impulsivity, and low productivity (Graham & Harris, 1987; Harris, 1982; Wong, Harris, & Graham, 1991). The frequency of multiple, interrelated problems of an affective, behavioral, and cognitive nature among students with learning disabilities provides a compelling argument for the use of multicomponent, integrative CBM interventions.

Although relatively few cognitive–behavioral studies focused on the instruction of academic skills before 1980 (Hobbs, Moguin, Tyroler, & Lahey, 1980), CBM-based strategy instruction has since become a major focus of educational research with the learning disabled and other special needs learners. In this chapter, we review *cognitive* and *cognitive–behavioral* approaches for students with learning disabilities in the areas of reading and writing. Although it is sometimes difficult to distinguish between interventions characterized as cognitive and those termed cognitive–behavioral, more purely cognitive approaches can be described (albeit somewhat simplistically) as attempting to improve academic problem-solving skills through the use of cognitive mediation strategies; the emphasis is on the role of cognition in the mediation of behavior (Hughes & Hall, 1989). Cognitive–behavioral approaches take a broader perspective, emphasizing the reciprocal nature of affect, behavior, and cognition. Recognition of the role of affect and motivation in learning and behavior among cognitive psychologists, however, has made it more difficult to differentiate between purely cognitive and cognitive–behavioral interventions. Further, there is an increasing awareness that distinctions between affect, behavior, and cognition are sometimes artificial and created only to facilitate research and theory. For instance, as Benson and Presbury (1989) noted, it has been traditional to represent "thinking" as cognitive and feeling as affect. Many cognitive psychologists today, however, believe that "feeling, or affect, *is* a cognitive process' (Benson & Presbury, 1989, p. 57). Emotions are viewed as types of thoughts. Thus, it is difficult to classify the interventions reviewed here as cognitive or cognitive–behavioral; labels often have more relationship to the theoretical orientation of the researcher than to the components and procedures used. It is important to note, however, that the long-term goals of most of the researchers whose work is reviewed here include promoting active learning, enthusiastic and responsive teaching, effective teacher–student dialogues, and self-regulated use of powerful strategies.

In the next section we review interventions intended to increase reading comprehension. This will be followed by a review of procedures to promote writing.

Approaches for Improving Reading Comprehension

Cognitive strategy instruction can promote prose comprehension, including the comprehension of students with learning disabilities, at least for students enrolled in the later elementary grades and beyond. Such instruction is successful, in part, because these students often fail to use strategies to understand and remember meaningful materials. In this section, we first review five strategies for improving prose comprehension, ones proven useful with students with learning disabilities. Then we discuss a method for teaching several presumably powerful comprehension strategies to students with learning disabilities, an approach designed to enhance self-regulated learning of strategies that are taught. Finally, cognitive–behavioral packages for reading comprehension are taken up.

Comprehension Strategies that Work with Students with Learning Disabilities

Increasing Students' Knowledge and Use of the Structure of Meaningful Materials: Story Grammar, Summarization, and Question-answering Strategies

Prose is structured. A story typically has a beginning that includes information about the setting and characters. Once the time, place, and players are introduced, some problem arises. Attempts to solve the problem and the reactions of the characters are the heart of the story. Eventually a solution is discovered and the loose ends and subplots are tied up. These components of a story are refered to as story grammar (e.g., Stein & Glenn, 1979). Knowledge of these elements leads to expectations about what will be in a story, expectations that aid understanding.

Although story grammar is known by most good comprehenders, at least implicitly, some children with learning disabilities do not possess such knowledge. One possibility is to teach these students to use story grammar to guide comprehension. This approach has been examined in several recent investigations with good results (Bednarczyk & Harris, 1989; Idol, 1987; Idol & Croll, 1987; Short & Ryan, 1984). In general, story grammar instruction improves both free recall of stories and responses to short-answer questions about stories that are read. Idol's story grammar instruction particularly focuses on the construction of a story summary based on the story grammar elements, with students taught to look explicitly for each element and to record it in a "story map." Thus, story grammar strategies are a special case of summarization, a strategy studied extensively as a mediator of learning from expository texts.

Every exposition contains information varying in importance, from critical to trivial. Mature readers pay more attention to the more critical information. As a result, they tend to remember more important rather than less important information in prose. Nonetheless, evidence is increasing that children in general do not differentially process information in prose to the extent they could; more positively, they can be taught to do so, as can students with learning disabilities. A variety of approaches to summarization have been designed and studied for this purpose.

The simplest is to teach readers to construct single sentences capturing the meaning of entire paragraphs. One sentence is constructed for each paragraph in a text (e.g., Jenkins, Heliotis, Stein, & Haynes, 1987). A much more complex approach is better grounded in theory, however. Brown and Day (1983; see also Bean & Steenwyk, 1984) developed a strategy based on the principles used by mature, sophisticated readers when they summarize text (Kintsch & van Dijk, 1978; van Dijk & Kintsch, 1983). It consisted of executing the following steps:

1. delete trivial information
2. delete redundant information
3. substitute superordinate terms for lists of terms
4. integrate a series of events with a superordinate action term
5. select a topic sentence
6. invent a topic sentence if there is none.

Even more elaborate summarization instruction has been developed by Taylor and her associates for use with long passages (e.g., 1982; Taylor & Beach, 1984). Specifically, Taylor taught children to use text headings, subheadings, and paragraphs to develop an outline. Perhaps the most ambitious approaches to summarization to date have amalgamated the Brown and Day (1983) and Taylor (1982) techniques, with students learning how to summarize paragraphs and learning how to develop outlines relating the ideas covered in the separate paragraphs (e.g., Baumann, 1984; Rinehart, Stahl, & Erickson, 1985).

Some of the summarization instruction is strikingly similar to story grammar training in that students are taught the way a type of text is typically organized and instructed to search for information in the text that fulfills particular functions. For instance, Armbruster, Anderson, and Ostertag (1987) taught 5th grade children the problem/solution structure characterizing many social studies passages. Students were informed they should identify and summarize the problem specified in a passage, the actions taken by people to solve the problem, and the results after these actions, including whether the problem was solved. Moreover, the gains produced by summarization instruction are similar to those produced by story grammar instruction. Free recall of text is improved, as is recall of specific elements in response to short-answer questions.

In short, evidence is growing that children with learning disabilities often do not know the conventional structures underlying stories and expositions; the type of materials they are often responsible for reading, understanding, and remembering. More positively, they can be taught information about these structures and can be taught to use their new knowledge about structure to guide comprehension and learning of material presented in text. To date, the results have been positive, affecting retrieval of information in text given minimal cuing (i.e., free recall) and facilitating recall of specific information in response to factual questions.

Research on another type of structural strategy further illustrates these points. Often, elementary school children are required to answer questions based on information in text. When the child does not know the answer, it would seem obvious to most adults to look back in the text for the answer. It is not obvious, though, to many poor elementary age readers (Garner, Macready, & Wagoner, 1984). Again, however, they can be taught the lookback strategy. Garner, Hare, Alexander, Haynes, and Winograd (1984) taught poor readers that looking back was useful when an answer to a text-adjunct question was not known after reading a text. In addition, the students were also taught how to skim the article to isolate the part of the text that might contain the answer. Appropriate use of looking back increased after such instruction.

Raphael and her associates (Raphael & McKinney, 1983; Raphael & Pearson, 1985; Raphael & Wonnacott, 1985) extended this type of structural training, hypothesizing that poor readers often do not recognize what type of information is required to answer a question accompanying text. Students in grades 4 through 8 were taught to analyze a question to determine if it was tapping factual information, and thus could be answered by information "right there" in the text; if it was asking for an inference, and thus required searching for information in the text and thinking about it; or if it was requesting the reader's opinion, and thus required reflecting on the information in text in light of one's own predilections. Question-answering performance improves after this type of instruction.

Teaching story grammar, summarization, and question-answering strategies improves poor readers' performance, thus indicating that problem readers are not engaging in these processes without instruction, or at least they are not doing so to the extent they could. That it is possible to induce such processing through instruction suggests these deficiencies are not too deep. It is not that poor readers cannot execute these strategies; it is that they have not been taught the procedures (Belmont & Butterfield, 1977) or that they have not learned where and when to apply them. Teaching poor readers about the structural characteristics of text and how to make use of those structural characteristics to enhance understanding and learning from text makes good sense in light of the data to date. But that is not enough, as will become more apparent as we review other strategies that can increase memory and comprehension of what is read.

Increasing Student Elaboration of Prose: Imagery and Questioning Strategies

Researchers interested in elaboration have typically been concerned with getting students to go beyond the information explicitly stated in text in order to code text more completely. A variety of approaches have traditionally been studied, one of the most popular of which is encouraging students to construct mental images representing the content of material read. This procedure is particularly easy to apply to narratives; transforming the story as conveyed text into a vivid "movie of the mind." Although children younger than 8 years of age generally do not benefit from such instructions (see Pressley, 1977), the typical outcome with older students is that learning of text is improved, at least a little. Students who construct images representing the content of stories can usually answer a few more short-answer questions covering the content of stories read than students who read and study stories using their typical methods of coding (e.g., Pressley, 1976). In general, imagery effects on prose learning are obtained regardless of the verbal ability of the child reader (e.g., Cariglia-Bull & Pressley, 1989).

Construction of images not only promotes memory of what is read, but can produce fuller understanding as well. A study by Gambrell and Bales (1986) illustrates this point. In their experiment, students read texts containing internal inconsistencies, with the most important dependent variable being whether students noticed the errors in the text. Students taught to use imagery to code the texts detected more errors than control students permitted to read and study the passages any way they liked, consistent with the hypothesis that imagery increases comprehension.

Other promising methods of elaboration are also being studied. For instance, Davey and McBride (1986) taught 6th grade children to generate questions about the content of text they were reading. In particular, they were encouraged to produce think-type questions that would require integration across different parts of text. Presumably, the production of such questions requires students to make inferences and elaborate text more than when the text is processed as usual. Consistent with this hypothesis, instructions to generate thought questions while reading improved 6th grade children's ability to answer inferential questions that followed reading of passages.

In summary, child readers can often be prompted to respond to text in ways they would not normally employ, with clear comprehension and learning gains the result. Elaboration is a fairly general term capturing a number of operations intended to produce embellished representations of to-be-learned content. In addition to the two forms of elaboration reviewed in this subsection, another group of elaborative strategies is usually considered as a separate category, with this taken up next.

Increasing Use of Prior Knowledge

What a child gets from a book often will be determined by what the child brings to the book; many demonstrations in the literature illustrate that prior knowledge can greatly affect understanding of prose (e.g., Anderson & Pearson, 1984). Prior knowledge creates expectations about what should occur in a text, increasing attention to aspects of text relevant to those expectations. Prior knowledge encourages readers to go beyond the information in the text, making appropriate inferences. It can also facilitate subsequent reconstruction and recall of what was in text. Thus, a student with a lot of knowledge about Judiasm could use that information to direct retrieval after reading the *Diary of Anne Frank*, searching memory for whether there was mention in the *Diary* of various aspects of Jewish customs and history. Anderson (1984) provided a particularly thorough review of how prior knowledge can affect prose processing.

Students with learning disabilities, often fail to use what they know to aid their interpretation and learning of new content. Again, however, it is possible to teach students to access their prior knowledge as they process prose, with this procedure being at the heart of a number of successful interventions (e.g., Au, 1980; Manzo, 1979; Palincsar & Brown, 1984; Tharp, 1982; Wood, Pressley, & Winnc, 1990). Hansen and Pearson's (1983) training is the most frequently cited example of such instruction. They taught 4th grade children to make predictions about content of text to be read, predictions based on what they already knew about the topic of the text. After reading practice texts, students were presented questions requiring inferential processing of the material. These questions required them to combine their own knowledge of the world with information conveyed in the text. Thus, after reading a story about an animal character, they would be asked to predict what kind of actions the character might make if it were human. In summary, over the course of 2 months, students were given meaningful instruction about how to relate what they read to their own knowledge base. After this training, poor 4th grade readers could answer more short-answer questions than control students about text they read.

Development of procedures to encourage students to integrate newly encountered material with prior knowledge is a main contemporary concern of researchers interested in elaboration. Thus, Wood et al. (1989) presented passages about wild animals to students in grades 4 through 8. Each passage contained information about the animal's habitat, food, and habits, as in the following example:

The Western Spotted Skunk lives in a hole in the ground. The skunk's hole is usually found on a sandy piece of farmland near crops. Often the skunk lives alone, but families of skunks sometimes stay together. The skunk mostly eats corn. It sleeps just about any time except between 3 o'clock in the morning and sunrise. The biggest danger to this skunk is the great horned owl.

Students in an elaborative condition were instructed to attempt to determine why each fact stated in each passage would be true for the particular animal in question (e.g., Why would the skunk often live alone? Why would skunks sometimes live in families?) That is, they were to search their prior knowledge about the animal in question and animals similar to it to determine why the fact as stated was sensible. There was a clear main effect in this study: students trained to pose and answer "why" questions while they processed the factual passages remembered more from the passages than students left to their own devices to learn the material. Such a result suggests strongly that elementary students do not spontaneously process expository text in light of their prior knowledge, or at least do not do so as completely as they could. It also suggests that learning of factual text, an ecologically valid task given the demands of schooling, might often be improved by students being encouraged to elaborate what they are reading relative to what they already know. Our understanding of prior knowledge activation strategies is limited at this time; what is known suggests these procedures are powerful, with the effects demonstrated to date likely to stimulate much additional research on these procedures.

Summary

A variety of cognitive strategies have been identified that improve comprehension when elementary grade students, including students with learning disabilities, execute them. The strategies studied to date will continue to be refined; new strategies will be developed and tested. Given that some potent procedures have been identified, how to teach effective strategies so that students use them has become a major concern (see Pressley, Scruggs, & Mastropieri, 1989; Pressley et al., 1989).

How Can Strategies be Taught so that Students Continue to Use Them?

If a student is taught only how to execute a strategy and given some practice doing it, there is little reason to believe the student will continue to use the procedure even in settings and on tasks similar to instructional settings and tasks. A great deal of thought has been given to how instruction might be engineered in order to produce durable use of strategies; a few instructional packages have been produced that yield long-term comprehension benefits. Two are highlighted here, beginning with reciprocal instruction, an instructional package that undoubtedly produced the greatest interest among educators during the 1980s and was designed explicitly for children with serious comprehension difficulties. Explicit cognitive–behavioral strategy instruction is then taken up.

Reciprocal Instruction

Reciprocal instruction was designed for readers who can decode but experience comprehension problems. It involves instruction on four strategies, ones Palincsar and Brown (1984) believed would promote comprehension based on the research evidence available in the early 1980s. Students are taught to *predict* what information might occur in a to-be-read text, to *generate questions* about content as it is read, to *summarize* the material in the text, and to *seek clarification* when comprehension difficulties occur. A hallmark of reciprocal instruction is that teaching is scaffolded (e.g., Manzo, 1969; Vygotsky, 1978; Wood, Bruner, & Ross, 1976)—teachers gradually diminish support as students become more proficient in executing and coordinating the four strategies. At first, the expert completely guides the child's activity, modeling how the strategies can be coordinated during reading of text. At this point, the child is mostly an observer, one member of a reading group. Then, the children in the group attempt the strategies. Students take turns as leader of the group, making predictions, generating questions about the text, seeking clarifications, and summarizing text content. The adult teacher provides supportive cuing, assistance, and additional modeling as required; fellow students also give feedback and help to one another. Instruction from the adult is gradually withdrawn, as student competence in coordinated use of the strategies increases. Throughout instruction the adult provides critical metacognitive information about the strategy, such as commentary about why, when, and where to use the trained strategies. Autonomous execution of the strategies by the child is the goal.

Although this intervention package is well known, there is limited evaluation of it; most of the evaluation has been provided by Palincsar and Brown (e.g., 1984). In general, the available data suggest the treatment does improve the reading comprehension of students who experience comprehension problems. The research to date also makes clear that reciprocal instruction is not a panacea, with modest effects overall and small effects for many students. A recent experimental analysis of reciprocal instruction illustrates these points.

The basic design of Lysynchuk, Pressley, and Vye's (1990) experiment was simple. There was one reciprocal instruction condition and one control condition, replicated at 4th grade and 7th grade levels. Standardized assessments were used to identify students who could read grade-level vocabulary but who performed poorly on comprehension tests. Students in both reciprocal instruction and control conditions met in reading groups of two to five children for 13 sessions. The control participants were treated as much like the reciprocally taught students as possible except they were given no scaffolded instruction of the four comprehension strategies. The control students met the same number of times as the reciprocally instructed students, they were exposed to the same practice materials as the trained students, and they took the same practice tests.

The main concern in the study was whether reciprocal teaching would improve performance on a standardized comprehension test. It did: there was a greater gain in comprehension test performance from pretest to posttest in the trained than in the control condition. Nonetheless, only a minority of reciprocally taught students experienced large gains.

On the one hand, perhaps not much should be expected of an intervention lasting only a few weeks. Alternatively, there are some theoretical reasons to believe that the small treatment effects are due in part to the ways strategies are presented and practiced during reciprocal teaching. First, although there is modeling of the strategies and provision of information about their utility, neither is as extensive or as explicit as could be. Further, instruction is not criterion-based (cf. Graham & Harris, 1989a). In particular, careful checks on whether or not students can execute the strategies autonomously are not made, nor is there any effort to be sure students have encoded the metacognitive content provided to them about the strategies. Similarly, although there is modeling of the coordinated use of the strategies and some practice in coordinating the strategies, there is little understanding at this point of how well students really can use these strategies in an articulated fashion after reciprocal instruction.

In contrast, the cognitive–behavioral approach to reading strategy instruction discussed next is much more explicit, with substantially more detailed teacher checks and feedback. Moreover, there is greater concern for embellishing instruction in ways that theoretically should promote durable use of the trained strategies in a coordinated fashion.

Cognitive–Behavioral Instruction

For more than two decades, a small group of research psychologists and educators has been constructing cognitive–behavioral interventions aimed at improving academic functioning, often with impressive success (for reviews, see Hughes & Hall, 1989; Meichenbaum, 1977; Witt, Elliott, & Gresham, 1988). One of the most visible groups in this effort is at the University of Kansas Learning Disabilities Institute headed by Donald Deshler and Jean Schumaker (cf. Deshler & Schumkaer, 1986, 1988). They have produced an entire strategy instructional curriculum designed to foster skills critical to success in school, including the use of powerful comprehension strategies (e.g., summarization, imagery). The same teaching approach is used with each strategy in the curriculum, one designed to promote masterful and automatic use of strategies, including appropriate generalization of the procedures that are learned.

First, a to-be-acquired strategy is described to students, with the description including important information about how and why the strategy promotes performance and when and where the techniques can be used. The teacher models the strategy by thinking aloud as he or she performs the criterion task. Students then begin to use the strategy with guidance from the teacher. Students verbally rehearse the steps of the strategy until they are known well. Practice and feedback are given with simple materials, progressing gradually to grade-appropriate materials; speed and accuracy are encouraged and corrective feedback continues. Multiple checks are used to determine whether students have mastered strategy execution. Generalization of the strategy is promoted through a variety of mechanisms. Students practice with diverse materials. Students are reminded often about where the strategy can be used. There is practice in using the strategy on class assignments, that is, students are given instruction about how to apply the procedure to the task they are expected to mediate during the school day (and beyond) using the strategy. Students are taught to prompt themselves to use the strategy with self-talk and to be alert to environmental cues indicative that the strategy should be used. Cards summarizing how to execute a strategy may be provided to students for them to carry with them; in part these cue students to continue using the trained procedure and in part they eliminate memory errors that potentially could undermine strategy execution (i.e., the student has an external record of the steps involved in carrying out the procedure). Motivation to use the trained strategies is enhanced by making it obvious the procedure is affecting performance positively. Students chart their learning before and after learning the strategy and are taught to self-reinforce for doing well.

The evidence that the Kansas training regime can be used to promote general use of comprehension strategies is growing (Ellis, Lenz, & Sabornie, 1987a, 1987b). One obvious conclusion from analysis of the work of Deshler and his associates is that generally improved performance does not come easily; effective strategy instruction is multicomponential, involving intensive and extensive teacher–student contact. Consider Deshler and Schumaker's (1986) summary of what is demanded of teachers:

... providing appropriate positive and corrective feedback using organizers throughout the instructional session, ensuring high levels of active academic responding, programming youth involvement in discussions, providing regular review of key instructional points and checks of comprehension, monitoring student performance, requiring mastery learning, communicating high expectations to students, communicating rationales for instructional activities, and facilitating independence (pp. 58–587).

Even though there is little analytical research permitting confident conclusions that each and every component is necessary for strategy instruction to be effective (see Pressley, Forrest-Pressley, & Elliott-Faust, 1988, for details), Deshler and his colleagues have developed their instructional procedures in light of thousands of hours spent teaching students with learning disabilities. They have revised their procedures a number of times, motivated by failures of less complete instructional models to produce general effects (Deshler, 1989). Moreover, the recommendations they are making are consistent with those of others who have succeeded in developing strategy instruction producing general effects.

Virtually all such strategy instructional packages include interactive and direct teaching of strategies and teaching of the strategies in the context where they are to be used. Instructing students to monitor their comprehension is always a key ingredient in such packages, as is provision of metacognitive information about the strategy. Further, there are always efforts to insure that students recognize the benefits that accrue from use of the strategies in question (Symons, Snyder, Cariglia-Bull, & Pressley, 1989).

Although the evidence to date supports the conclusion that extensive and explicit instruction designed to produce self-regulated use of comprehension strategies can promote effective use of these strategies, there is a need for much more research on the components of extensive and explicit instruction that are responsible for maintenance and transfer of strategies. The evidence that does exist, however, suggests that instructional elements long associated with cognitive–behavior modification can play a powerful role in the development of durable comprehension skills (see Bommarito & Meichenbaum, 1978, for an early demonstration, discussed in Meichenbaum & Asarnow, 1979).

One of the most analytical evaluations of the potential contribution of cognitive–behavioral elements to comprehension instruction was provided by Elliott-Faust and Pressley (1986). They were concerned with a particular problem in comprehension, how to increase awareness of inconsistencies in text. Markman (1979) had proposed that awareness of inconsistencies would occur if the internally inconsistent pieces of information were activated simultaneously and compared; the frequent failure of children to detect inconsistencies presumably reflects their failure to coactivate parts of a text concerned with closely related information. Elliott-Faust and Pressley (1986) hypothesized that children could be trained to coactivate different parts of text, with an increase in error detection the result. What is most critical here is that in some conditions of their study, their 3rd grade participants were only provided instruction about how to do comparison processing (referred to as the comparison training condition). In contrast, participants in their most complete treatment condition (referred to here as the self-instruction condition) were taught how to self-instruct comparison of different parts of text with one another. Students learned to use self-instructions designed to remind themselves of the nature of the task, activate comparison strategies, increase adherence to the comparison strategies, and encourage self-evaluation. The experiment also included several control conditions, permitting evaluation of whether the comparison training or self-instruction procedures were effective at all.

Both the comparison training and the self-instruction training produced near ceiling levels of performance, with more than 90% of the passages correctly rated by students (i.e., they found the inconsistencies in inconsistent text, and they reported no inconsistencies in valid passages). Performance in these conditions was well above the level of performance in even the best control condition included in the study.

A main hypothesis in the study was that inclusion of the self-instructional elements would improve durable use of the comparison strategies. This could be assessed since the comparison condition was identical to the self-instruction condition except that the students were not taught to use self-instructional questions. If this hypothesis was correct, performance in a delayed error detection task should be better in the self-instruction condition than in the comparison condition. Thus, 1 week later, students were given another four passages to evaluate. At this delayed testing session, no mention was made of the trained strategies, so that their use would indicate student self-regulated maintenance of the strategies. At this testing, comparison-trained subjects had no advantage relative to the control condition with the highest performance; in contrast, performance in the self-instruction condition continued to be near ceiling (i.e., 95%) and significantly better than performance in the best control condition.

In short, effective long-term use of the comparison strategies required both training of the comparison strategies and instruction about how to self-regulate their use (i.e., self-questioning instruction). The self-questioning routine is an "executive" strategy (Brown, Bransford, Ferrara, & Campione, 1983; Meichenbaum, 1977; Pressley et al., 1988; Pressley, Forrest-Pressley, Elliott-Faust, & Miller, 1985), flagging when and how to apply comparison processes. The careful experimental control in Elliott-Faust and Pressley (1986) permitted the conclusion that it really was the self-instructional questioning that promoted durable use of the comparison strategies.

Summary

Most of the research to date on comprehension has focused on the identification of single strategies promoting understanding of text, with much less concern about teaching self-regulated use of those strategies. The research to date on the development of autonomous use of strategies suggests that it is possible to teach students with learning disabilities comprehension strategies using a multicomponent cognitive–behavioral approach. Although across-study comparisons are always dangerous, the effects produced in studies involving instruction that is more cognitive (e.g., reciprocal teaching) seem modest compared to striking improvements in studies invloving more extensive and explicit modeling, criterion-based instruction, explanatory tutoring, and reinforcement with feedback. Direct comparisons of these two approaches would permit determination of whether more complete cognitive–behavioral instruction is more effective in promoting comprehension than reciprocal instruction. Of course, this specific recommendation simply reflects that in general, much more research is needed on instruction intended to produce self-regulated comprehension.

We close this section by noting that most of the research on comprehension has been cross-sectional, with little concern about documenting how students move from slow, deliberate, and perhaps cumbersome use of comprehension strategies to automatic and facile use of them. Documenting this progression and determining how to maximize the probability that automaticity will occur should also be high priorities. Real world demands often preclude use of a strategy that must be consciously executed, for conscious execution of strategies requires attention that may be required for other processing (e.g., a child in the classroom must not only read what is on the board but attend to teacher and other-student commentary). A significant challenge facing researchers is to determine whether cognitive–behavioral interventions can produce cognitively adept comprehenders who effortlessly respond to the many possible demands of prose processing. The greatest challenges of comprehension strategy instruction have yet to be met.

Approaches for Improving Writing

According to Graham and Harris (1989b), cognitive–behaviorally based approaches are a viable means of improving the writing performance of students with learning disabilities. Recent research on the nature of writing has resulted in the development of reasonably coherent descriptions of the mental processes writers employ when composing. For example, the influential model developed by Flower and Hayes (1980) described writing as a cognitive activity: writing is goal-directed, writing goals are hierarchically organized, and writers accomplish their goals by employing a variety of mental processes—planning, sentence generation, and revision. Students with learning disabilities have considerable difficulty with many of the cognitive processes identified by Flower and Hayes. Evidence collected to date suggests that these students have problems with generating content, framing text, transcription, planning text, and revising. In addition, they appear to have trouble assessing their own capabilities and recognizing what writing strategies and processes are needed and how to regulate their use (Graham & Harris, in press). Thus, cognitive–behavioral approaches to writing instruction offer a good match to current conceptualizations of writing and the characteristics of students with learning disabilities.

In this section we review approaches aimed at providing students with help in carrying out the sophisticated mental processes involved in writing. First, we examine substantive and procedural facilitation, two approaches identified by Scardamalia and Bereiter (1986). Next, research examining the effects of cognitive and cognitive–behaviorally based strategy instruction on students' writing will be reviewed.

Substantive and Procedural Facilitation

With substantive facilitation, an adult or a peer acts as an active collaborator and, in effect, shoulders some of the burden for completing the writing activity (Scardamalia & Bereiter, 1985). By having a collaborator take responsibility for part of the executive load during writing, a student should be able to carry out more sophisticated processes than he normally would when left to his own devices.

Substantive facilitation is common in school-based writing instruction. For example, the traditional procedure of writing comments on students' papers involves the teacher as a collaborator. By identifying a problem in a paper and suggesting a general solution, the student is relieved of this burden and only has to decide on a specific action to remedy the problem. Similarly, suggestions or questions concerning the content of a student's writing during peer conferencing, a common component of the process approach to writing, involves classmates as collaborators. Even though such probes and hints may be subtle, they constitute substantive facilitation in that they involve what the writer has said or intends to say (Scardamalia & Bereiter, 1986).

In procedural facilitation, "help is of a nonspecific sort, related to the student's cognitive processes, but not responsive to the actual substance of what the student is thinking or writing" (Scardamalia & Bereiter, 1986, p. 796). In contrast to substantive facilitation, the student does all of the work, but under conditions that reduce the overall processing burden. By providing cues or routines that lessen the executive demands of the writing task, it is anticipated that procedural facilitation will allow students to make fuller use of the knowledge and skills they already possess.

The Compare–Diagnose–Operate (CDO) routine developed by Scardamalia and Bereiter (1983) provides an example. This procedure includes a system of cues that the student uses to execute important components of the revising process. The student is cued to "Compare" by selecting one card from a series of 11 that best represent his evaluation of a sentence (e.g., People may not believe this). "Diagnosis" is then activated by the instructor, who asks the student to justify his choice. "Operate" is next cued by the use of cards; the student selects one card from a series of six directives (e.g., I'd better leave this part out). Finally, the student implements the selected directive and starts the cycle again with the next sentence. Thus, the CDO procedure provides students with a manageable executive routine designed to affect how they deploy their attention during revising.

Substantive and procedural facilitation can be used in tandem. Conferencing that occurs between the student and teacher during the evolution of a paper often involves both forms of facilitation, for example. To illustrate, MacArthur (1988) is currently examining the effectiveness of a writing curriculum with special needs students that includes student–teacher conferences as an integral part of the program. To help teachers become proficient in conferencing, a series of recommendations and procedures were developed, including the suggestion that teachers ask students questions about what they intend to do next, or about things in the student's paper they do not understand or would like to know more about. Questions about the student's next step direct attention to a procedural decision, while questions concerning content are substantive in nature.

At present, we know little about the impact of substantive and procedural facilitation on how or what students with learning disabilities write. In a recent study by Graham (1989), a simple procedural facilitator was used to prompt students to continue the process of composing. When 4th and 6th grade students with learning disabilities had ostensibly written all that they could, the instructor encouraged them to write more. The introduction of contentless production signals resulted in doubling to tripling of text length and small but significant improvements in quality. It must be noted, however, that the contentless prompts did not always result in the generation of more text, and when they did, a considerable amount of repetitive and irrelevant information was produced.

Graves, Montague, and Wong (1989) have examined the effectiveness of a more sophisticated procedural facilitator with 5th and 6th grade students with learning disabilities. Students were provided with a cue card that listed four story elements: setting, character(s), problem and plan, and ending. They were directed by an instructor to make a check by each element as they included it in their story. Students who were directed to use this procedure produced stories of higher quality than students writing under normal conditions. The addition of a prompt to make the characters think and feel just as people do, however, did not enhance students' performance.

Although enough data are not available to critique adequately the effectiveness of substantive and procedural facilitation with students with learning disabilities, several caveats are in order. First, if students do not possess necessary prerequisite skills or knowledge, substantive and procedural facilitation will have little or no effect on what and how students write. Providing a routine for directing the revising process or using feedback to alert students to problem areas in their text are likely to be unsuccessful if students lack the underlying competence to take advantage of these supports (see, for instance, Pressley, Borkowski, & Schneider's [1989] evaluation of strategy by knowledge-base interactions). Second, the impact of substantive and procedural facilitation also depends on what students internalize. For example, the primary value of procedural facilitation is that it provides external support for a procedure that will eventually be run autonomously (Scardamalia & Bereiter, 1986). It is not clear, however, what students will internalize as a result of practice in using the procedure or how the procedure will be used (i.e., will it be dropped or corrupted?) once the external supports are removed. Third, with substantive facilitation there is the danger that teachers will provide too much help, casting the student in a passive role. Finally, attention needs to be directed at Bereiter and Scardamalia's (1982) claim that procedural facilitators will act as "change-inducing agents" that will promote the development of the cognitive system, particularly cognitive strategies and self-regulatory mechanisms. In our estimation, this assertion is premature; not enough evidence has been put forward to support this claim adequately.

Strategy Instruction

Strategy instruction presumably can be used to help students with learning disabilities gain security in the cognitive processes and subprocesses considered central to effective writing as well as to help them develop more mature and complex composing behaviors (Graham & Harris, 1988). There have been three separate groups of researchers who have systematically investigated the use of writing strategies.

Learning Strategies Curriculum

As we noted previously, Donald Deshler, Jean Schumaker, and their colleagues at the Research Institute at the University of Kansas have developed a strategies curriculum for secondary students with learning disabilities. One strand of their curriculum includes four strategies for improving students' performance on the kinds of writing tasks commonly assigned in school.

One of the strategies, Sentence Writing, deals solely with the production of basic sentence types: simple, compound, complex, and compound–complex (Schumaker & Sheldon, 1985). The strategy includes 14 different formulas, each representing a different sentence structure. When using the strategy, the student first picks a formula, then selects words to fit the formula, and finally checks to make sure the sentence is complete. In addition, students are taught to identify and define a variety of grammatical structures (e.g., independent clause, coordinating conjunction, etc.) that are relevant to the parts of the various sentence formulas.

In our opinion, the Sentence Writing strategy is the least useful of the writing strategies developed by the Kansas group. First, empirical evidence supporting the effectiveness of the strategy is meager (see Graham & Harris, 1989b). Second, the strategy is extremely complicated and requires a great deal of memorization, making it especially susceptible to corruption and misuse over time. Third, current evidence suggests that identifying and defining various parts of speech is not a necessary prerequisite to writing sentences (Graham, 1982). Fourth, there may be much more parsimonious ways of improving the sentence writing skills of students with learning disabilities; for example, sentence combining has proven to be a powerful tool for helping students internalize procedures for writing more complex sentences (Scardamalia & Bereiter, 1986).

Another strategy that the Kansas group has developed for dealing with the production of text is the Paragraph Writing strategy. This strategy includes a series of steps that the student uses to generate a paragraph that lists or describes, shows sequence, compares and/or contrasts, or demonstrates cause and effect. Evidence on the effectiveness of the strategy has been reported by Moran, Schumaker, and Veter (1981) and Schmidt, Deshler, Schumaker, and Alley (reported in Schumaker et al., 1983). In both experiments, the paragraph writing skills of students with learning disabilities improved after strategy training.

A third strategy, Error Monitoring, includes a series of steps that students use to direct the writing process, from generating an initial draft to editing for mechanical errors. The strategy is designed primarily to direct students' attention to the cosmetic and mechanical aspects of writing (capitalization, punctuation, spelling, and appearance), with only limited attention directed at the substance of the composition. Schumaker, Deshler, Alley, Warner, Clark, and Nolan (1982) found that students with learning disabilities who used this strategy improved in their ability to detect and correct not only their own mechanical errors but those of other students as well. It is not clear, however, if the Error Monitoring strategy has an effect on *what* students with learning disabilities write.

The last strategy, Theme Writing, includes a series of steps for writing an integrated composition. We were unable to locate any evidence on the effectiveness of this strategy; however, it closely resembles the prewriting, write, and revising format popular in writing instruction today. The basic advantage of this approach is that it divides the writing task into discrete stages, making the writing task more manageable for poor writers (Graham, 1982). Taken together, the writing strategies developed by the Kansas group represent an ambitious effort to help adolescents who are poor writers develop intentional control over the processes of generating and editing text.

Cognitive Strategy Instruction in Writing Program (CSIW)

Englert, Raphael, and their colleagues at Michigan State University (Englert & Raphael, in press; Englert, Raphael, Anderson, Anthony, Fear, & Gregg, 1988) have developed an expository writing program focusing on the social context in which students write, teaching strategies for performing the writing process, and the role of text structure in planning, organizing, drafting, and revising. Although space does not allow us to give a detailed description here (see Englert et al., 1988), we highlight important components of their approach.

In order to help make writing processes and strategies explicit to students, Englert and her colleagues broke the writing process into separate stages, and "think" sheets were developed to direct what students do during each of the following subprocesses: planning, organizing, writing, editing, and revising. For example, the planning think sheet poses a series of questions that help the writer focus on the audience, purpose for writing, and relevant background knowledge. Different expository text structures are emphasized on the organizing think sheet where a graphic organizer containing questions and keywords associated with the text structure being studied is included. Text structure is again emphasized on the editing think sheet where the student and a peer editor evaluate the students' first draft. Finally, the student uses the revising think sheet to consider how they will change their paper based on their own evaluation and feedback from the peer editor. In addition, recognizing and analyzing specific text structures as well as teacher modeling of the thinking, problem-solving, and self-regulatory processes involved in the use of the think sheets are promoted via written lesson plans designed to illustrate appropriate dialogue and critical lesson elements.

Englert and her colleagues are currently analyzing the effectiveness of the CSIW program; the curriculum is being implemented by teachers in eight schools with learning disabilities and regular education students (Englert et al., 1988). Results from individual case studies, however, have been promising, indicating that the program can have positive effects on both learning disabled students' writing performance and metacognitive knowledge (Englert & Raphael, in press; Englert et al., 1988).

Self-Regulated Strategy Development

Graham, Harris, and their colleagues at the University of Maryland have developed a series of writing strategies that have been field tested with students with learning disabilities in the upper elementary grades. Each of the strategies has been taught via a set of instructional procedures (see Table 14.1) labeled self-regulated strategy development (cf. Graham & Harris, 1987, 1989a; Graham et al., 1987; Harris & Graham, 1988). The instructional stages presented in Table 14.1 can be reordered or combined as needed, are recursive in places, and are not meant to be followed in a "cookbook" fashion. The stages provide a general format and guidelines; flexibility, individualization, and responsive teaching are important aspects of this approach (Harris & Pressley, 1991).

These stages, however, represent merely the bare framework of instruction (Harris, 1989). Affective, behavioral, and cognitive learner and task analyses are carefully conducted to allow subsequent selection of skills and strategies to be taught as well as tailoring of components and procedures to students' capabilities; the goal is to present a "do-able"

TABLE 14.1. Self-regulated strategy development: Basic stages.

Stage 1: *Preskill Development.* Any preskills necessary for understanding, learning, and executing the targeted strategy that are not already in the learner's repetoire are developed.

Step 2: *Review Current Performance Level.* Instructor and student examine and discuss baseline data and any strategies the student currently uses. Negative or ineffective self-statements or strategies can also be discussed. The significance and potential benefits of the proposed instruction are examined. In addition, commitment to participate as a partner and to attempt the strategies is established, and goals are established in a positive, collaborative manner.

Stage 3: *Discuss the Executive Strategy.* The instructor describes the executive strategy. Then the instructor and student discuss advantages of the strategy as well as how and when to use it.

Stage 4: *Model the Strategy and Self-Instructions.* The instructor or a peer models the strategies to be learned, in context. Instructor and student then discuss the model's performance, and the student generates and records his *own* self-instructions to direct the use of the strategy. Instructor and student may also collaborate on any changes that make the strategy more effective.

Stage 5: *Mastery of the Strategy.* The student is required to memorize the steps in the strategy and the self-instructions. Paraphrasing is allowed as long as meaning remains intact.

Stage 6: *Collaborative Practice of Strategy Steps and Self-Instructions.* The student practices the strategy and supporting self-instructions while performing the task. *Self-regulation* procedures such as goal setting, self-monitoring, or self-reinforcement are discussed, decided on, and used throughout this step. Prompts, interaction, and guidance are faded over practice sessions until the student achieves independent performance. Challenging, proximal goals are determined cooperatively, while criterion levels are gradually increased until the final goal is met. Instructor and student plan for transfer and maintenance of the strategy.

Stage 7: *Independent Performance.* Transition to covert self-instructions is encouraged as the student learns to use the strategy independently. Self-regulation procedures are continued, and plans for transfer and maintenance are implemented. Strategy effectiveness and performance are evaluated collaboratively.

Stages are flexible, recursive, and individualized as necessary; instruction is criterion-based rather than time-based.

challenge within the students' capabilities. Instruction emphasizes the student's role as an active collaborator (areas of collaboration include determining goals of instruction, completion of the task, evaluation of the strategy and task performance, and planning for transfer and maintenance) and highly interactive learning between teacher and students, with responsibility for recruiting and applying, monitoring, and evaluating strategies gradually placed on the student. Metastrategy information is emphasized, which is believed to perform both an attributional training and goal setting function. Principles of interactional scaffolding and Socratic dialogue are incorporated. Teachers are enthusiastic and responsive to each child and provide individually tailored feedback. Strategies are explicitly and overtly modeled in context. Self-regulation procedures are taught explicitly. Finally, progression through instruction is criterion-based rather than time-based, and previously taught skills/strategies are routinely reviewed.

Graham, Harris, and their colleagues have examined the effectiveness of several different writing strategies (for a complete review of this line of research, see Graham, Harris, MacArthur, & Schwartz, 1991). For example, in their first investigation (Harris & Graham, 1985), 6th grade students with learning disabilities were taught a strategy for generating specific types of words (action verbs, adjectives, and adverbs) to use in their stories. Students' self-regulation of the strategy was facilitated through the use of criterion goal-setting, self-monitoring procedures, and self-instructional statements (e.g., problem definition statements). Instruction in the use of the strategy resulted in increases in each of the types of words targeted for instruction, the length of text, and the quality of stories. Treatment effects generalized to the students' classroom and were maintained for up to 8 weeks. Although the students remembered the strategy steps, they failed to use the strategy on a probe administered in a new school setting 14 weeks after the completion of training.

Graham and Harris have also developed two prewriting strategies that involve using prefabricated genre frames to generate notes and ideas to be used in the students' subsequent compositions. In an initial story grammar strategy study by Graham and Harris (1989a), 5th and 6th grade students with learning disabilities generated notes in advance of writing by responding to a series of questions related to the basic elements included in most common short stories (e.g., "What does the main character want to do?"). All students participated in instruction in the use of the strategy and supporting self-instructional statements; one half of the students were also taught to use goal-setting and self-monitoring procedures. After instruction, the quality and schematic structure of students' stories improved and they evidenced higher self-efficacy scores. The inclusion of the goal-setting and self-monitoring procedures did not augment either the students' writing or their self-efficacy. The observed effects were generalized to a new setting and were maintained over a 2-week period. Although students with learning disabilities taught to use the strategy were as effective in incorporating story elements into their writing as normally achieving students, the quality of their stories was poorer. In a follow-up study, however, there was no difference in the quality of stories developed by normally achieving students and students with learning disabilities who received the full strategy instruction regime (Sawyer, Graham, & Harris, 1991).

Graham and Harris (1989c) developed a second strategy that used text structure as a guide for generating notes in advance of writing but focused on argumentative essays. The first step in this strategy required the student to consider who will read the text and the purpose for doing the assignment. The student then planned the composition in advance through the use of text structure prompts. Finally, while writing the composition, the student continued the planning process by adding additional ideas and details. After instruction in the use of the strategy, the essays of 6th grade students with learning disabilities were more complete, cohesive, longer, and judged to be of higher quality. Strategy instruction also had a positive effect on students' self-efficacy for writing. Treatment effects were maintained over time and transferred to a new setting. Additionally, although not all of the students with learning disabilities spontaneously transferred the use of the strategy to a second genre, story writing, one session in the use of a slightly modified version of the strategy (story relevant text structure prompts were inserted during the second step) resulted in the desired transfer.

Many writing tasks assigned in school can be characterized as ill-defined problems. In a study conducted with 5th grade students with learning disabilities (Graham, MacArthur, Schwartz, & Voth, 1989), a strategy was designed that included two approaches that can be helpful in dealing with ill-defined problems that require essay responses. The strategy was structured around a means–ends analysis: the student set product goals for what the paper would accomplish and further articulated process goals for achieving the selected product goals. Next, the writing task was broken down into several related subproblems: (a) generate goals, (b) develop notes, (c) organize notes, (d) write and continue planning, and (e) evaluate success in obtaining goals.

Instruction in the strategy had a positive effect on students' writing; essays became more complete, longer, and were judged to be of higher quality. Treatment effects were maintained over time and, as in the Graham and Harris (1989c) investigation, some of the students evidenced transfer to a second genre, story writing. An additional practice session in using the strategy to write stories resulted in transfer for the remaining students. Several of the students became more realistic in their self-efficacy for writing after training, and some changes in the students' metacognitive knowledge were also noted.

As a final illustration of this program of research, Graham and MacArthur (1988) examined the effectiveness of teaching 5th and 6th grade students with learning disabilities a strategy for revising essays that could be used while working on a word processor. The strategy included self-directed prompts for adding relevant textual material, improving the clarity and cohesiveness of the writer's argument, and detecting and correcting mechanical errors. After strategy instruction, students made more revisions and developed papers that were longer and judged to be qualitatively better than compositions produced during baseline. These effects were maintained over time and students were able to adapt the strategy successfully when composing with paper and pencil. Students were also more confident in their ability to write and revise after learning the strategy.

Issues

As indicated by this chapter, strategy instruction has been successfully used to improve the writing of students with learning disabilities. A variety of strategies have been designed that help students establish intentional control over sentence and paragraph production, activate a search of appropriate memory stores for writing content, facilitate the framing and organizing of writing material, support the development of writing goals, and boost the quantity and quality of text revisions. Nonetheless, there remain a number of issues regarding the use of strategy instruction with students with learning diabilities in the area of written language.

Most writing strategy instruction with students with learning disabilities has been conducted by researchers and their staff, not by the students' actual teachers. We are not sure if teachers will view this approach or the writing strategies developed to date as acceptable (cf. Harris, Preller, & Graham, 1990), and thus, it is especially important to examine the effects of strategy instruction within the context of the classroom. What problems and difficulties do teachers encounter in implementing strategy instruction in writing? What social–contextual variables promote or hinder learning disabilities students' acquisition and use of the strategic behaviors central to effective writing? Does adding strategy instruction to other writing programs, such as the currently popular process approach to writing, have an augmental effect?

As with both substantive and procedural facilitation, internalization is also an important issue in strategy instruction. In the revision study by Graham and MacArthur (1988), students choose to ignore certain steps in the strategy or overemphasize others. Further, students used the strategy in slightly different ways, and some of the students made ineffective modifications in the strategy as they used it over time. Finally, the relationship between learning disabilities students' knowledge of writing, knowledge of the writing topic, and utilization of writing strategies needs to be examined (Alexander & Judy, 1988). Incomplete or inaccurate knowledge of writing may interfere with the learning of a writing strategy.

Conclusion

Cognitive–behavioral approaches represent a promising instructional approach for students with learning disabilities and other inefficient learners. A great many challenges and issues remain, however, for both researchers and practitioners in this area. We close with discussion of three areas of critical concern: (a) issues regarding generalization and maintenance of cognitive–behavioral intervention effects, (b) the need for component analyses studies and establishment of intervention integrity, and (c) theoretical issues concerning the nature of CBM-based strategy interventions.

Generalization and Maintenance

Cognitive–behaviorally based academic interventions have frequently proven effective in significantly and meaningfully improving performance among problem learners. Further, these interventions have produced performance gains for mildly handicapped learners, including students with learning disabilities, sometimes to the level of their nonhandicapped peers (cf. Graham & Harris, 1989a; Pressley & Levin, 1986). However, researchers have also hypothesized that CBM interventions would produce evidence of greater generalizablility and durability than obtained with strictly behavioral approaches. Evidence to date (e.g., Elliott-Faust & Pressley, 1986) favors CBM approaches in terms of generalizability and durability but is far from conclusive (Hughes & Hall, 1989). Despite increases in our knowledge about how to promote maintenance and generalization during the last decade, maintenance and generalization sometimes do not occur after CBM instruction (Harris & Pressley, 1991). Such failure may be due to a number of factors, including short-term training, lack of long-term follow-up, narrow content of instruction, questionable relevance of the training tasks, and failure to consider ecological, systems, and agent variables (Harris, 1985; Hughes & Hall, 1989; Meyers et al., 1989).

We suggest, however, researchers consider an additional issue. Little is known about the breadth, depth, and course of the development of maintenance and generalization capabilities in children, and thus there is little but intuition to guide us in setting reasonable criteria and evaluating outcomes in our research (Harris, 1985, 1988; Harris & Pressley, 1991). Our research efforts would profit from further descriptive, developmental studies of skill maintenance and transfer among both exceptional and normally achieving children. Based on what little research has been done, it is becoming increasingly apparent that adults also evidence difficulties with transfer and maintenance; that whereas even young children can learn to transfer, there are multiple variables that can affect propensity to transfer, that metacognition develops with age and is critically implicated in transfer, and that less explicit instruction is needed to promote durable strategy application with older compared to younger normally achieving children (Brown & Kane, 1988; Elliott-Faust & Pressley, 1986; Garner & Alexander, 1989; Harris & Pressley, 1991; O'Sullivan & Pressley, 1984; Pressley & Dennis-Rounds, 1980). In addition to providing insight regarding generalization and maintenance, a rich base of descriptive, developmental research across domains would help to develop assessment methodologies, suggest functional relationships that may increase intervention efficacy, assist in determining developmentally and culturally appropriate definitions of competence, and provide insight about the acquisition of competent behaviors (Harris, 1985). Attention to developmental issues in generalization and maintenance is clearly warranted.

Components Analyses and Intervention Integrity

Little research has been done to determine the relative contributions of CBM components and the variables responsible for change, or to establish cost–benefit relationships among components (Graham & Harris, 1989c; Pressley et al., 1988). The initial research that has been done, however, has provided some interesting results. For instance, Elliott-Faust and Pressley (1986) found support for one of the main theoretical claims of CBM; as noted previously, their study demonstrated clearly that teaching students to self-instruct deployment of strategies and to self-monitor strategy use promoted durable use of those strategies and was superior to simply teaching children the task strategy. Graham and Harris (1989a), on the other hand, did not find support for the theoretically proposed incremental effects of explicit self-regulation procedures over and above self-instructed strategy use and instruction concerning the use and significance of the strategy. They pointed out that the situation is probably more complex than the addition of powerful components to instruction. In particular, how instruction is carried out must also be considered. Instructional characteristics that may help to establish instructional potency include the student's role as an active collaborator, interactive learning, meaningful teacher–student dialogue, gradual transfer of responsibility for effective strategy use, criterion-based instruction, modeling and use of strategies in context and in actual classroom settings, and enthusiastic and responsive teaching. Determining the contributions of both CBM components and the characteristics of instruction in promoting effective strategy use is a major challenge to researchers.

Issues of intervention integrity are related to the need for components analyses and are equally critical to researchers and educators concerned with increasing real-classroom self-regulation among students (Harris, 1988). "Treatment integrity" has been previously defined and discussed in the literature and refers to the degree to which treatment is delivered and carried out (by teachers, trainers, and/or students) as intended. The concept of "intervention integrity" expands on and subsumes treatment integrity in ways that are particularly appropriate to educational strategy instruction and self-regulation research (Harris, 1988). First, intervention integrity requires that each and every component of a strategy intervention is both delivered and carried out as recommended and intended. This is not as simple as it may appear; simplistic, naive conceptualization and construction of CBM interventions can lead (and has led) to ineffective interventions (Harris, 1985). Further, intervention integrity is critical when researchers conduct studies comparing different instructional approaches.

Perhaps more importantly, the proposition that strategy interventions frequently involve multiple processes of change necessitates an expansion of the treatment integrity concept. In any intervention, but particularly in multicomponent interventions, it is necessary to differentiate between therapeutic procedures and therapeutic processes (Harris, 1985). Thus, intervention integrity also refers to the degree to which intervention processes and outcomes are specified and assessed. Establishing intervention integrity therefore requires *assessment of the processes of change as related to both intentions and outcomes*. It should be noted that although CBM strategy interventions frequently include some combination of affective, behavioral, and cognitive targets, outcome assessment is frequently limited to behavioral indices (Harris, 1985). Multiple outcome measures across domains are needed to broaden the focus of analysis, increase confidence in assessment data, and to determine whether or not CBM works for the reasons it is hypothesized to work (Harris, 1985).

To establish intervention integrity, researchers must study the processes of change, which requires both experimental manipulations and reliable dependent measures (Harris, 1986). Establishing intervention integrity can therefore both test and expand the CBM model/theoretical base. Of course, as the processes and targets of change progress on a continuum from observable to inferred, intervention integrity will become more challenging to establish and will create interesting challenges in assessment (Harris, 1988). It is worth meeting these challenges, however, for as the processes and targets of change in strategy interventions progress from assessed to ignored (or assumed), guarantees of intervention integrity are correspondingly reduced.

The Nature of CBM Interventions

Recently, cognitive strategy instruction has been mistakenly described as failing to be constructivistic in nature and thus an approach that should be abandoned by educators of students with learning disabilities (see Harris & Pressley, 1991, for a detailed discussion; Poplin, 1988). Constructivism stresses the importance of children participating fully in the construction of their own knowledge and the need for instruction to take place just slightly beyond the child's current level of performance. Some researchers have argued that a constructivistic approach consisting of guided discovery (of a domain, of strategies, self-instructions, etc.) will be more effective than explicit instruction concerning how and when to use a strategy, especially with respect to generalization and maintenance (cf. Harris & Pressley, 1991; Mayers et al., 1989). Our view is that the beliefs and assumptions underlying CBM are akin to those underlying constructivism, and in fact originate from many of the same theoretical sources (i.e., the work of Piaget, Bandura, and Meichenbaum). Further, discovery approaches may have inherent problems. True discovery is rare, inefficent, and time consuming; it is impossible for students to discover all that they need to know; some students may experience high levels of frustration with discovery approaches, and only a few students may tend to make most of the discoveries within a given group (cf. Harris & Pressley, 1991). In contrast, structured, teacher-directed learning activities have been effective with students with learning disabilities (Hallahan et al., 1983). At this time, however, discovery-oriented and explicit strategy instructional approaches have not been compared directly in experimental tests; such research is needed before valid claims can be made.

Proponents of explicit strategy instruction have provided substantial evidence that it can be used profitably when there is a good match to the learner's needs and characteristics, there is an effective strategy appropriate to the problem, and when teachers can meet the demands that strategy instruction creates (Harris, 1982; Harris & Pressley, 1991). Cognitive–behavioral interventions continue to represent an important and meaningful frontier to learning disabilities researchers and educators.

References

Alexander, P., & Judy, J. (1988). The interaction of domain-specific and strategic knowledge in academic performances. *Review of Educational Research*, *58*, 375–404.

Ames, C., & Archer, J. (1988). Achievement goals in the classroom: Students' learning strategies and motivation processes. *Journal of Educational Psychology*, *80*, 260–267.

Anderson, R. C. (1984). Role of the reader's schema in comprehension, learning, and memory. In R. C. Anderson, D. S. Ogle, and E. G. Carr (Eds.), *Strategic teaching and learning: Cognitive instruction in the content areas* (pp. 73–91). Alexandria, VA: Association for Supervision and Curriculum Development.

Anderson R. C., & Pearson, P. D. (1984). A schema-theoretic view of basic processes in reading. In P. D. Pearson (Ed.), *Handbook of reading research* (pp. 255–291). New York, NY: Longman.

Armbruster, B. B., Anderson, T. H., & Ostertag, J. (1987). Does text strcture/ summarization instruction facilitate learning from expository text. *Reading Research Quarterly*, *22*, 311–346.

Au, K. (1980). Participation structures in a reading lesson with Hawaiian children. *Anthropology and Education Quarterly*, *11*, 91–115.

Bandura, A. (1969). *Principles of behavior modification*. New York: Holt, Rinehart & Winston.

Baumann, J. E. (1984). The effectiveness of a direct instruction paradigm for teaching main idea comprehension. *Reading Research Quarterly, 20*, 93–115.

Bean, T. W., & Steenwyk, F. L. (1984). The effect of three forms of summarization instruction on sixth graders' summary writing and comprehension. *Journal of Reading Behavior, 16*, 297–306.

Bednarczyk, A. M., & Harris, K. R. (1989). *Story grammar instruction for learning disabled students with comprehension problems.* Unpublished raw data. College Park, MD: University of Maryland, Department of Special Education.

Belmont J. M., & Butterfield, E. C. (1977). The instructional approach to developmental cognitive research. In R. V. Kail, Jr., & J. W. Hagen (Eds.), *Perspectives on the development of memory and cognition* (pp. 437–482). Hillsdale, NJ: Lawrence Erlbaum Associates.

Benson, A. J., & Presbury, J. H. (1989). The cognitive tradition in schools. In J. N. Hughes & R. J. Hall (Eds.), *Cognitive behavioral psychology in the schools: A comprehensive handbook* (pp. 37–61). New York: Guilford Press.

Bereiter, C., & Scardamalia, M. (1982). From conversation to composition: The role of instruction in a developmental process. In R. Glaser (Ed.), *Advances in instructional psychology* (Vol. 2, pp. 1–64). Hillsdale, NJ: Lawrence Erlbaum.

Bommarito, J., & Meichenbaum, D. (1978). *Enhancing reading comprehension by means of self-instructional training.* Unpublished manuscript. Waterloo ON Canada: University of Waterloo, Department of Psychology.

Borkowski, J. G., Carr, M., Rellinger, E. A., & Pressley, M. (1990). Self-regulated strategy use: Interdependence of metacognition, attributions, and self-esteem. In B. F. Jones (Ed.), *Dimensions of thinking: Review of research* (pp.53–92). Hillsdale, NJ: Erlbaum Associates.

Brown, A. L. (1988). Motivation to learn and understand: On taking charge of one's own learning. *Cognition and Instruction, 5*, 311–321.

Brown, A. L., Bransford, J. D., Ferrara, R. A., & Campione, J. C. (1983). Learning, remembering, and understanding. In J. H. Flavell & E. M. Markamn (Eds.), *Handbook of child psychology, Vol. III, Cognitive development* (pp. 177–266). New York: Wiley.

Brown, A. L., Campione, J. C., & Day, J. D. (1981). Learning to learn: On training students to learn from texts. *Educational Researcher, 10*, 14–21.

Brown, A. L., & Day, J. D. (1983). Macrorules for summarizing texts: The development of expertise. *Journal of Verbal Learning and Verbal Behavior, 22*, 1–14.

Brown, A. L., & Kane, M. J. (1988). Preschool children can learn to treansfer: Learning to learn and learning from example. *Cognitive Psychology, 20*, 493–523.

Cariglia-Bull, T., & Pressley, M. (1990). Short-term memory differences between children predict imagery effects when sentences are read. *Journal of Experimental Child Psychology, 49*, 384–398.

Davey, B., & McBride, S. (1986). Effects of question-generation training on reading comprehension. *Journal of Educational Psychology, 78*, 256–262.

Deshler, D. D. (1989, April). *The development of the Kansas Learning Strategies Curriculum.* Paper presented at the Annual Meeting of the American Educational Research Association, San Francisco.

Deshler, D. D., & Schumaker, J. B. (1986). Learning strategies: An instructional alternative for low-achieving adolescents. *Exceptional Children*, *52*, 583–590.

Deshler, D. D., & Schumaker, J. B. (1988). An instructional model for teaching students how to learn. In J. L. Graden, J. E. Zins, & M. J. Curtis (Eds.), *Alternative educational delivery systems: Enhancing instructional options for all students* (pp. 391–411). Washington, DC: NASP.

Elliott-Faust, D. J., & Pressley, M. (1986). How to teach comparison processing to increase children's short- and long-term comprehension monitoring. *Journal of Educational Psychology*, *78*, 27–33.

Ellis, E. S., Lenz, B. K., & Sabornie, E. J. (1987a). Generalization and adaptation of learning strategies to natural environments: Part 1, Critical agents. *Remedial and Special Education*, *8*(1), 6–20.

Ellis, E. S., Lenz, B. K., & Sabornie, E. J. (1987b). Generalization and adaptation of learning strategies to natural environments: Part 2, Research into practice. *Remedial and Special Education*, *8*(2), 6–23.

Englert, C. S., & Raphael, T. (in press). Developing successful writers through cognitive strategy instruction. In J. Brophy (Ed.), *Advances in research on teaching*. Greenwich, CT: JAT Press.

Englert, C. S., Raphael, T., Anderson, L., Anthony, H., Fear, K., & Gregg, S. (1988). A case for writing intervention: Strategies for writing informational text. *Learning Disabilities Focus*, *3*, 98–113.

Flower, L., & Hayes, J. (1980). The dynamics of composing: Making plans and juggling contraints. In L. Gregg & E. Steinberg (Eds.), *Cognitive processes in writing* (pp. 31–50). Hillsdale, NJ: Lawrence Erlbaum.

Gambrell, L. B., & Bales, R. J. (1986). Mental imagery and the comprehension-monitoring performance of fourth- and fifth-grade poor readers. *Reading Research Quarterly*, *21*, 454–464.

Garner, R., & Alexander, P. A. (1989). Metacognition: Answered and unanswered questions. *Educational Psychologist*, *24*, 143–158.

Garner, R., Hare, V. C., Alexander, P., Haynes, J., & Winograd, P. (1984). Inducing use of a text lookback strategy among unsuccessful readers. *American Educational Research Journal*, *21*, 789–798.

Garner, R., Macready, G. B., & Wagoner, S. (1984). Readers' acquisition of the components of the text-lookback strategy. *Journal of Educational Psychology*, *76*, 300–309.

Graham, S. (1982). Composition research and practice: A unified approach. *Focus on Exceptional Children*, *14*, 1–16.

Graham, S. (April, 1989). *The role of production factors in learning disabled students' compositions*. Paper presented at Annual Meeting of the American Educational Research Association, San Francisco.

Graham, S., & Harris, K. R. (1987). Improving composition skills of inefficient learners with self-instructional strategy training. *Topics in Language Disorders*, *7*, 66–77.

Graham, S., & Harris, K. R. (1988). Instructional recommendations for teaching writing to exceptional students. *Exceptional Children*, *54*, 506–512.

Graham, S., & Harris, K. R. (1989a). A components analysis of cognitive strategy instruction: Effects on learning disabled students' compositions and self-efficacy. *Journal of Educational Psychology*, *81*, 353–361.

Graham, S., & Harris, K. R. (1989b). Cognitive training: Implications for written language. In J. Hughes & R. Hall (Eds.), *Cognitive behavioral psychology in the schools: A comprehensive handbook.* (pp. 247–279). New York: Guilford Publishing Co.

Graham, S., & Harris, K. R. (1989c). Improving learning disabled students' skills at composing essays: Self-instructional strategy training. *Exceptional Children*, *54*, 201–214.

Graham, S., & Harris, K. R. (in press). Cognitive strategy instruction in written language for learning disabled students. In S. Vogel & B. Levinson (Eds.), *Effective intervention for the learning disabled.* New York: Springer-Verlag.

Graham, S., Harris, K. R., MacArthur, C. A., & Schwartz, S. (1991). Writing and writing instruction for students with learning disabilities: Review of a research program. *Learning Disability Quarterly*, *14*, 89–114.

Graham, S., Harris, K. R., & Sawyer, R. (1987). Composition instruction with learning disabled students: Self-instructional strategy training. *Focus on Exceptional Children*, *20*, 1–11.

Graham, S., & MacArthur, C. (1988). Improving learning disabled students' skills at revising essays produced on a word processor: Self-instructional strategy training. *Journal of Special Education*, *22*, 133–152.

Graham, S., MacArthur, C., Schwartz, S., & Voth, T. (1989, April). *Improving LD students' compositions using a strategy involving product and process goal-setting.* Paper presented at Annual Meeting of the American Educational Research Association, San Francisco.

Graves, A., Montague, M., & Wong, Y. (1989, April). *The effects of procedural facilitation on story composition of learning disabled students.* Paper presented at the Annual Meeting of the American Educational Research Association, San Francisco.

Hallahan, D. P., Lloyd, J. W., Kauffman, J. M., & Loper, A. (1983). Academic problems. In R. J. Morris & T. R. Kratochwill (Eds.), *Practice of child therapy: A textbook of methods* (pp. 113–141). New York: Pergamon Press.

Hansen, J., & Pearson, P. D. (1983). An instructional study: Improving the inferential comprehension of fourth-grade good and poor readers. *Journal of Educational Psychology*, *75*, 821–829.

Harris, K. R. (1982). Cognitive-behavior modification: Application with exceptional students. *Focus on Exceptional Children*, *15*, 1–16.

Harris, K. R. (1985). Conceptual, methodological, and clinical issues in cognitive behavioral assessment. *Journal of Abnormal Child Psychology*, *13*, 373–390.

Harris, K. R. (1986). The effects of cognitive-behavior modification on private speech and task performance during problem solving among learning disabled and normally achieving children. *Journal of Abnormal Child Psychology*, *14*, 63–67.

Harris, K. R. (April, 1988). *What's wrong with strategy intervention research: Intervention integrity.* Paper presented at the Annual Meeting of American Educational Research Association, New Orleans.

Harris, K. R. (March, 1989). *The role of self-efficacy in self-instructional strategy training and the development of self-regulated learning among children with learning disabilities.* Paper presented at the Annual Meeting of the American Educational Research Association, San Francisco.

Harris, K. R., & Graham, S. (1985). Improving learning disabled students' composition skills: Self-control strategy training. *Learning Disability Quarterly*, *8*, 27–36.

Harris, K. R., & Graham, S. (1988). Self-instructional strategy training: Improving writing skills among educationally handicapped students. *Teaching Exceptional Students*, *20*, 35–37.

Harris, K. R., & Graham, S. (in press). Strategy instruction in written language: An integrational model. In M. Pressley, K. R. Harris, & S. Guthrie (Eds.), *Promoting academic competence and literacy: Cognitive research and instruction*. New York: Academic Press.

Harris, K. R., Preller, D., & Graham, S. (1990). Acceptability of cognitive-behavioral and behavioral interventions among teachers. *Cognitive Therapy and Research*, *14*, 573–587.

Harris, K. R., & Pressley, M. (1991). The nature of cognitive strategy instruction: Interactive strategy construction. *Exceptional Children*, *57*, 392–405.

Hobbs, S. A., Moguin, L. E., Tyroler, M., & Lahey, B. B. (1980). Cognitive behavior therapy with children: Has clinical utility been demonstrated? *Psychological Bulletin*, *87*, 147–165.

Hughes, J. N., & Hall, R. J. (Eds.) (1989). *Cognitive-behavioral psychology in the schools: A comprehensive handbook*. New York: Guilford Press.

Idol, L. (1987). Group story mapping: A comprehension strategy for both skilled and unskilled readers. *Journal of Learning Disabilities*, *20*, 196–205.

Idol, L., & Groll, V. J. (1987). Story-mapping training as a means of improving reading comprehension. *Learning Disability Quarterly*, *10*, 214–229.

Jenkins, J. R., Heliotis, J., Stein, M. L., & Haynes, M. (1987). Improving reading comprehension by using paragraph restatements. *Exceptional Children*, *54*, 54–59.

Kendall, P. C., & Braswell, L. (1982). On cognitive-behavioral assessment: Model, measures, and madness. In C. D. Spielberger & J. N. Butcher (Eds.), *Advances in personality assessment* (Vol. 1, pp. 35–82). Hillsdale, NJ: Erlbaum.

Kintsch, W., & van Dijk, T. A. (1978). Toward a model of text comprehension and production. *Psychological Review*, *85*, 363–394.

Ledwidege, B. (1978). Cognitive behavior modification: A step in the wrong direction? *Psychological Bulletin*, *85*, 353–375.

Lysynchuk, L. M., Pressley, M., & Vye, N. J. (1990). Reciprocal teaching improves standardized reading comprehension performance in poor grade-school comprehenders. *Elementary School Journal*, *90*, 469–484.

MacArthur, C. (1988). *A process approach to writing instruction*. College Park, MD: Institute for the Study of Exceptional Children and Youth.

Mahoney, M. J. (1977). Reflections on the cognitive learning trend in psychotherapy. *American Psychologist*, *32*, 5–13.

Markman, E. M. (1979). Realizing that you don't understand: Elementary school children's awareness of inconsistencies. *Child Development*, *50*, 643–655.

Manzo, A. V. (1969). The ReQuest procedure. *Journal of Reading*, *2*, 123–126.

Meichenbaum, D. (1977). *Cognitive-behavior modification: An integrative approach*. New York: Plenum Press.

Meichenbaum, D. H., & Asarnow, J. (1979). Cognitive-behavioral modification and metacognitive development: Implications for the classroom. In P. C. Kendall & S. D. Hollon (Eds.), *Cognitive-behavioral interventions: Theory, research and procedures* (pp, 11–35). New York: Academic Press.

Meichenbaum, D., & Gilmore, J. B. (1984). The nature of unconscious processes: A cognitive-behavioral perspective. In K. Bowers & D. Meichenbaum (Eds.), *The unconscious reconsidered* (pp. 273–298). New York: Wiley.

Meyers, A. W., Cohen, R., & Schleser, R. (1989). A cognitive-behavioral approach to education: Adopting a broad-based perspective. In J. Hughes & R. Hall (Eds.), *Cognitive behavioral psychology in the schools: A comprehensive handbook* (pp. 62–86). New York: Guilford Press.

Moran, M., Schumaker, J., & Vetter, A. (1981). *Teaching a paragraph organization strategy to learning disabled adolescents* (Research Report No. 54). Lawrence: University of Kansas Institute for Research in Learning Disabilities.

Nolen, S. B. (1988). Reasons for studying: Motivational orientations and study strategies. *Cognition and Instruction, 5*, 269–287.

O'Sullivan, J. T., & Pressley, M. (1984). Completeness of instruction and strategy transfer. *Journal of Experimental Child Psychology, 38*, 275–288.

Palincsar, A. S. (1986). The role of dialogue in providing scaffolded instruction. *Educational Psychologist, 21*(1 & 2), 73–98.

Palincsar, A. S., & Brown, A. L. (1984). Reciprocal teaching of comprehension—Fostering and comprehension monitoring activities. *Cognition and Instruction, 1*, 117–175.

Pearl, R. (1985). Cognitive behavioral interventions for increasing motivation. *Journal of Abnormal Child Psychology, 13*, 443–454.

Poplin, M. S. (1988). The reductionist fallacy in learning disabilities: Replicating the past by reducing the present. *Journal of Learning Disabilities, 21*, (7), 389–400.

Pressley, G. M. (1976). Mental imagery helps eight-year-olds remember what they read. *Journal of Educational Psychology, 68*, 355–359.

Pressley, M. (1977). Imagery and children's learning: Putting the picture in developmental perspective. *Review of Educational Research, 47*, 586–622.

Pressley, M., Borkowski, J. G., & Schneider, W. (1989). Good information processing: What it is and how education can promote it. *International Journal of Educational Research, 13*, 857–867.

Pressley, M., & Dennis–Rounds, J. R. (1980). Transfer of a mnemonic keyword strategy at two age levels. *Journal of Educational Psychology, 72*, 575–582.

Pressley, M., Forrest-Pressley, D. L., & Elliott-Faust, D. J. (1988). What is strategy instructional enrichment and how to study it: Illustrations from research on children's prose memory. In F. Weinert & M. Perlmutter (Eds.), *Memory development: Universal changes and individual development* (pp. 101–131). Hillsdale, NJ: Lawrence Erlbaum Associates.

Pressley, M., Forrest-Pressley, D., Elliott-Faust, D. L., & Miller, G. E. (1985). Children's use of cognitive strategies, how to teach strategies, and what to do if they can't be taught. In M. Pressley & C. J. Brainerd (Eds.), *Cognitive learning and memory in children* (pp. 1–47). New York: Springer-Verlag.

Pressley, M., & Levin, J. R. (1986). Elaboration learning strategies for the inefficient learner. In S. J. Ceci (Ed.), *Handbook of cognitive, social, neuropsychological aspects of learning disabilities* (pp. 175–211). Hillsdale, NJ: Erlbaum Associates.

Pressley, M., Scruggs, T. E., & Mastropieri, M. A. (1989). Memory strategy instruction in learning disabilities: Present and future directions for researchers. *Learning Disabilities Research, 4,* 68–77.

Pressley, M., Woloshyn, V., Lysynchuk, L. M., Martin, V., Wood, E., & Willoughby, T. (1990). A primer of research on cognitive strategy instruction: The important issues and how to address them. *Educational Psychology Review, 2,* 1–58.

Raphael, T. E., & McKinney, J. (1983). An examination of fifth- and eighth-grade children's question-answering behavior: An instructional study in metacognition. *Journal of Reading Behavior, 15,* 67–86.

Raphael, T. E., & Pearson, P. D. (1985). Increasing students' awareness of sources of information for answering questions. *American Educational Research Journal, 22,* 217–236.

Raphael, T. E., & Wonnacott, C. A. (1985). Metacognitive training in question-answering strategies: Implementation in a fourth-grade developmental reading program. *Reading Research Quarterly, 20,* 282–296.

Rinehart, S. D., Stahl, S. A., & Erickson, L. G. (1985). Some effects of summarization training on reading and studying. *Reading Research Quarterly, 21,* 422–438.

Sawyer, R., Graham, S., & Harris, K. (1991). *Theoretically based effects of strategy instruction components on learning disabled students' acquisition, maintenance, and generalization of composition skills and self-efficacy.* Manuscript submitted for publication.

Scardamalia, M., & Bereiter, C. (1983). The development of evaluative, diagnostic and remedial capabilities in children's composing. In M. Martlew (Ed.), *The psychology of written language: Developmental and educational perspectives* (pp. 67–95). London: John Wiley.

Scardamalia, M., & Bereiter, C. (1985). Fostering the development of self-regulation in children's knowledge processing. In S. Chiman, J. Segal, ? R. Glaser (Eds.), *Thinking and learning skills: Current research and open questsions* (Vol. 2, pp. 563–577). Hillsdale, NJ: Lawrence Erlbaum.

Scardamalia, M., & Bereiter, C. (1986). Written composition. In M. Wittrock (Ed.), *Handbook of research on teaching* (3rd ed., pp. 778–803). New York: MacMillan.

Schumaker, J., Deshler, D., Alley, G., Warner, M., Clark, F., & Nolan, S. (1982). Error monitoring: A learning strategy for improving adolescent performance. In W. M. Cruickshank & J. Lerner (Eds.), *Best of ACLD* (Vol. 3, pp. 170–183). Syracuse, NY: Syracuse University Press.

Schumaker, J. B., Deshler, D. D., Alley, J. R., & Warner, M. M. (1983). Toward the development of an intervention model for learning disabled adolescents: The University of Kansas Institute. *Exceptional Education Quarterly, 4,* 45–74.

Schumaker, J., & Sheldon, J. (1985). *The sentence writing strategy.* Lawrence: University of Kansas.

Short, E. J., & Ryan, E. B. (1984). Metacognitive differences between skilled and less skilled readers: Remediating deficits through story grammar and attribution training. *Journal of Educational Psychology*, 75, 225–235.

Siegel, I. E. (1982). The relationship between parental distancing strategies and the child's cognitive behavior. In L. M. Laosa & I. E. Siegel (Eds.), *Families as learning environments for children* (pp. 47–86). New York: Free Press.

Stein, N. L., & Glenn, C. G. (1979). an analysis of story comprehension in elementary school children. In R. O. Freedle (Ed.), *New directions in discourse processing* (pp. 53–120). Norwood, NJ: Ablex.

Symons, S., Snyder, B. L., Cariglia-Bull, T., & Pressley, M. (1989). Why be optimistic about cognitive strategy instruction? In C. B. McCormick, G. E. Miller, & M. Pressley (Eds.), *Cognitive strategy research: From basic research to educational applications* (pp. 3–32). New York and Berlin: Springer-Verlag.

Taylor, B. M. (1982). Text structure and children's comprehension and memory for expository material. *Journal of Educational Psychology*, 74, 323–340.

Taylor, B. M., & Beach, R. W. (1984). The effects of text structure instruction on middle-grade students' comprehension and production of expository text. *Reading Research Quarterly*, 19, 134–146.

Tharp, R. G. (1982). The effective instruction of compehension: Results and description of the Kamehameha Early Education Program. *Reading Research Quarterly*, 17, 503–527.

van Dijk, T. A., & Kintsch, W. (1983). *Strategies in discourse comprehension*. New York: Academic Press.

Vygotsky, L. S. (1962). *Thought and language*. Cambridge, MA: MIT Press.

Vygotsky, L. S. (1978). *Mind in society: The development of higher psychological processes*. Cambridge, MA: Harvard University Press.

Witt, J. C., Elliott, S. N., & Gresham, F. M. (1988). *Handbook of behavior therapy in education*. New York: Plenum.

Wong, B. Y. L. (Ed.) (1982). Metacognition and learning disabilities [Special issue]. *Topics in Learning and Learning Disabilities*, 2(1).

Wong, B. Y. L., Harris, K. R., & Graham, S. (1991). Academic applications of cognitive-behavioral programs with learning disabled students. In P. C. Kendall (Ed.), *Child and adolescent therapy: Cognitive-behavioral procedures* (pp. 245–275). New York: Guilford Press.

Wood, D., Bruner, J. S., & Ross, G. (1976). The role of tutoring in problem solving. *Journal of Child Psychology and Psychiatry*, 17, 89–100.

Wood, E. J., Pressley, M., & Winne, P. (1990). Elaborative interrogation effects on children's learning of factual content. *Journal of Educational Psychology*, 82, 741–748.

Zivin, G. (Ed.) (1979). *The development of self-regulation through private speech*. New York: Wiley & Sons.

15
Computer-Assisted Instruction: Potential and Reality

KATHRYN G. KARSH and ALAN C. REPP

Students with learning disabilities are identified primarily on the basis of a discrepancy between their ability and achievement (Hammill, 1990; Mercer, King-Sears, & Mercer, 1990). There are many theories regarding the etiology of this discrepancy; however, the fact remains that these students have difficulty achieving at a level commensurate with their ability in one or more subject areas (Berk, 1983). Research continues to seek to identify the presumed neurological bases for the achievement discrepancies of learning disabled students (cf. Bonnet, 1989). However, researchers and practitioners alike recognize that currently the best approach to remediate these achievement discrepancies is to provide systematic instruction tailored to the assessed needs of learning disabled students (Lessen, Dudzinski, Karsh, & Van Acker, 1989).

To provide systematic instruction, special educators have recognized the need to attend to the principles of effective instruction (Christenson, Ysseldyke, & Thurlow, 1989; Englert, 1984a, 1984b; Rieth & Evertson, 1988; Rieth, Polsgrove, & Semmel, 1981). The characteristics of effective instruction for students with learning disabilities can be summarized as:

1. carefully structured lessons that provide clear objectives, rules, and examples, and include several presentation-demonstration-practice cycles (Rosenshine & Stevens, 1986)
2. high rates of active learning time where students receive numerous opportunities to respond (Greenwood, Delquadri, & Hall, 1984)
3. teaching that maintains a brisk pace throughout the lesson and results in rapid progress through the curriculum (Evertson, 1982)
4. instruction that provides a high success rate with practice activities that result in 80% accuracy or higher (Rosenshine & Stevens, 1986)
5. immediate teacher feedback that provides reinforcement for correct responses and corrective feedback for errors (Gersten, Woodward, & Darch, 1986)
6. instruction that includes careful, frequent monitoring and evaluation of student performance and adjustment of instruction according to those results (Good & Brophy, 1986).

Despite widespread agreement on the importance of these instructional variables for learning disabled students, many of these practices are not implemented by teachers at a level that meets the needs of students (Morsink, Soar, Soar, & Thomas, 1986; Rieth & Frick, 1983; Rieth, Polsgrove, Okolo, Bahr, & Eckert, 1987). For example, an observational study indicated that learning disabled students spent only 12% of their time in school in direct involvement in academic tasks (Thurlow, Graden, Greever, & Ysseldyke, 1982). A number of reasons may exist to explain this situation: (a) insufficient human resources to provide the quantity of direct instruction and practice that these students require, (b) insufficient time to monitor each student's responses and provide individual instruction according to those responses, and (c) the tedium inherent in providing the required amount of practice (Torgeson & Young, 1983).

One alternative that can provide increased opportunities for direct instruction and practice to learning disabled students is computer-assisted instruction (CAI). Remarkable similarities exist between the characteristics of effective teacher instruction and the capabilities of computer-assisted instruction. The following have been identified as important capabilities of CAI that parallel the characteristics of effective teacher instruction:

1. well-sequenced instruction, which teaches to mastery and provides many repetitions (Budoff, Thormann, & Gras, 1984; LeBlanc, Hoko, Aangeenbrug, & Etzel, 1985)
2. high frequency of student responses (Budoff et al., 1984)
3. rapid pace of presentation, which can be individualized for each student (Budoff et al., 1984)
4. repeated practice and demonstration of mastery (Budoff et al., 1984; Torgeson & Young, 1983)
5. immediate feedback, including immediate reinforcement for correct responses and consistent correction procedures for incorrect responses (Budoff et al., 1984; Le Blanc et al., 1985; Torgeson & Young, 1983)
6. individualized instruction, including assessment of prerequisite skills and selection of appropriate teaching sequences (Le Blanc et al., 1985).

In addition, CAI is particularly well suited for some teaching functions, such as individualized drill and practice, which are time consuming for the teacher to implement. The computer has been described as a good motivator for learning disabled students and as a source of high levels of engagement (MacArthur, Haynes, & Malouf, 1986; Thormann, Gersten, Moore, & Morvant, 1986). Computer-assisted instruction can lead to more positive attitudes in conjunction with academic remediation (Kavale & Forness, 1986), particularly when academic work on the computer is compared to similar academic tasks in the classroom (Watkins, 1989).

The appeal of CAI for students with learning disabilities is evidenced by the increase in the number of microcomputers in classrooms for learning disabled students. From 1983 to 1985, for example, the number of microcomputers increased from 65,000 to 200,000 (Blaschke, 1986). It has been estimated that microcomputers are now installed in approximately 96% of all American schools. A recent survey (Malouf, Morariu, Coulson, & Maiden, 1989) found that 38% of the special education teachers used computers directly with their students three or more times a week and 40% used computers once or twice a week.

The types of software used by learning disabled students in their classrooms include, in rank order, (a) drill and practice, (b) academic games, (c) tutorials, (d) extracurricular games, (e) simulations, and (f) programming (Thormann et al., 1986). Of these types, the most common is drill and practice software (Becker, 1983; Maddux, 1984). Although much of the drill and practice software has been heavily criticized (Le Blanc et al., 1985; Carlson & Silverman, 1986), it can provide learning disabled students with the repetition they require in order to attain fluency or automaticity of lower order skills (Torgeson, 1986). Drill and practice programs have been used to teach skills such as word recognition (Jones, Torgeson, & Sexton, 1987), or addition and subtraction facts necessary for higher order skills instruction (Hasselbring, Goin, & Bransford, 1988).

The other two types of software in which the computer assumes an explicit teaching function are tutorials and simulations. Tutorial software enables the computer to become a true tutor of new skills or content. For example, Collins, Carnine, and Gersten (1987) developed a tutorial program to teach basic logical reasoning skills to secondary learning disabled students. The computer provided all the instruction, including the presentation of strategies and examples. Through the software program, the computer also determined whether the student had mastered one set of material and was ready for the next.

Computers also have been recognized as a means to teach problem solving by making simulated laboratory experiences available to learners (Budoff et al., 1984; Lieber & Semmel, 1985). Computer simulation activities have been used successfully to enhance (rather than replace) problem-solving instruction. Woodward, Carnine, and Gersten (1988) demonstrated that a combination of structured teaching and computer simulation was effective in teaching factual-level knowledge, as well as higher level problem-solving skills, to secondary students with mild learning handicaps.

The computer has been used in classrooms to provide academic and extracurricular games to learning disabled students. Teachers have used microcomputer games as a reinforcer to motivate students to complete tasks unrelated to the computer (Rieth, 1986), as well as a source of drill and practice. However, the novelty of the computer games may be an important factor in motivation and reinforcement, and these aspects of the computer game software may be transitory (Chiang, 1986; Romanczyk, 1986). The arcade-like features of the games, including fancy lights, graphics, and sound effects, may actually interfere with learning over time, and thus reduce the drill and practice benefits of the programs (Chiang, 1986; Christensen & Gerber, 1990).

The computer also has been recognized as a source of programming opportunities for students. Programming experiences such as LOGO[2] have been advocated because of their potential to help students move to more abstract levels of thinking, use feedback more effectively, and develop improved attitudes toward learning (Weir & Watt, 1981). However, little empirical research is available at this time to determine the benefits of programming experiences for learning disabled students.

In recent years, educators have watched the use of CAI increase far more rapidly than the research on its use. In many cases, research on CAI has begun after the programs have been developed and marketed. Such a process of development that leads to research rather than research that leads to development is not, however, an unexpected one in an entrepreneurial area that has shown such rapid growth. The fact remains that systematic research that examines the effectiveness of CAI for learning disabled students is only beginning. In the remainder of this chapter we review the existing research on CAI for learning disabled students in order to provide information on using computers in the classroom and to suggest future research directions in examining the effective use of computer technology for these students.

Effectiveness of CAI

One of the often-cited attractions of CAI is that it has the potential to provide instruction that is equivalent to that provided by the teacher. The advantages of a technology that can provide instruction equivalent to that of a teacher are numerous, and among these are increased engagement and learning rates. There are few studies that compare computer interventions against other kinds of educational innovations for learning disabled students (Majsterek & Wilson, 1989; Pogrow, 1988). Reviews of studies conducted with regular education students indicated that traditional teacher instruction supplemented by CAI was more effective than CAI or teacher instruction alone. In addition, although student learning time was reduced in CAI, maintenance was better with traditional teacher instruction (Edwards, Norton, Taylor, Weiss, & Dusseldorp, 1975; Jameson, Suppes, & Wells, 1974; Kulik, Bangert, & Williams, 1983; Visonhaler & Bass, 1972). Most recently, the research on CAI for regular education students has been criticized as being scanty and offering little information on the conditions and circumstances under which we can expect computers to be effective (Bracey, 1988).

In a large-scale study with 250 learning disabled students in grades 1 through 6, McDermott and Watkins (1983) compared CAI spelling or CAI math with conventional classroom instruction for the school year. The findings for the students in the conventional classroom condition, the students in the CAI math condition, and the CAI spelling condition were equivalent, leading the authors to recommend the.approach of finding the most effective combination of teacher and CAI instruction. Lieber and Semmel (1985) also concluded from the results of studies comparing CAI and traditional instruction for mildly handicapped students that CAI should be a supplement rather than a replacement for traditional instruction.

Although general conclusions have been made, the available research on the effectiveness of CAI for learning disabled students is sparse. In addition, the description of the components of the CAI instruction (and teacher instruction in comparative studies) is often incomplete (Majsterek & Wilson, 1989). One approach with the available data is to make some tentative conclusions on the basis of particular academic areas. In the following section we examine the effectiveness of CAI for specific academic areas for the type of skill taught (e.g., reading comprehension, word decoding) and for the type of CAI program used (e.g., drill and practice, tutorial, or simulation).

Reading

The skills that children must learn in reading fall into four broad areas: (a) phonological word analysis, (b) rapid sight word recognition, (c) fluent word processing in text, and (d) comprehension (Torgeson, 1986). The first three skill areas are often grouped together as decoding skills, which most learning disabled students have significant difficulties in acquiring (Stanovich, 1982). In fact, 60% to 80% of all learning disabled students have a primary educational disability in reading (Lyon, 1985).

Efficient decoding skills are necessary for reading comprehension because establishment of fluent decoding skills precedes increases in reading comprehension (Lesgold & Resnick, 1982). Teachers often have difficulty in providing the amount of individualized practice necessary for learning disabled students to develop generalized fluency in decoding skills so that these students may successfully complete higher order comprehension activities.

The computer can provide the opportunities for practice in decoding that the teacher cannot. It has the potential to individualize instruction, monitor the student's responses, and adjust the speed of presentation in order to increase fluency. Computer-assisted instruction in decoding can be either tutorial (where new material is introduced and corrective feedback is given on errors) or drill and practice (where extensive mastery-level practice on previously teacher-taught material is provided). Most of the CAI decoding programs examined to date are drill and practice.

Roth and Beck (1984) reported substantial increases in word reading fluency when a group of poor readers similar to learning disabled readers used the Construct A Word program. This CAI program provided drill and practice in forming real words by matching consonants or consonant blends with word endings (e.g., -un, -ate, -ing). The students worked three or four times a week in 20-minute sessions for 12 weeks, and, at the end of this time, demonstrated increases in sentence comprehension as well as generalized fluency (Roth & Beck, 1984). Similar results were reported by Rashotte and Torgeson (1985) in a study with 4th grade learning disabled students and by Torgeson (1986) in a study with 2nd and 3rd grade learning disabled students.

One important question regarding CAI is whether the improved skills demonstrated during computer use will generalize to traditional paper and pencil tasks. In a study directed toward teaching elementary learning disabled students rapid and accurate decoding (Jones et al., 1987), measures included not only correct decoding of words on the screen, but also individual words on paper as well as words in paragraphs on paper. The Hint and Hunt program was used to provide the computer-based drill and practice. The 10 students in the experimental group received 10 weeks (15 minutes per day) of mastery-level practice on five short vowels and four vowel digraphs and diphthongs contained in single-syllable words. The results showed that the treatment group improved in accuracy and speed on computer-presented words, generalization to untrained words on a computer-presented test, and speed and accuracy on a written paragraph reading test.

These preliminary findings suggest that CAI drill-and-practice programs can be used to build generalized decoding fluency for learning disabled students. Computer-assisted instruction allows the teacher to provide opportunities for practice that can be motivating, individualized, carefully monitored, and speed oriented. However, as a supplement to teacher instruction, the CAI programs must use skills and words that correspond with the student's curriculum, and the programs must evidence adequate instructional design. Additionally, ongoing opportunities to practice the skills must be provided in order to maintain them.

Few studies are available that have examined the effectiveness of CAI in teaching or providing practice in reading comprehension. One reason may be that it has been easier to develop software programs for decoding skills than for comprehension skills. Reading comprehension programs require more branching and memory than drill-and-practice programs (Torgeson, 1986).

In a study that examined the computer as a presentation mode for teaching reading comprehension to learning disabled high school students (Keene & Davey, 1987), no differences were found between text presented on a computer screen and text presented in a book on measures of comprehension and use of five of six comprehension strategies. However, the computer did facilitate use of a comprehension look-back strategy when compared to traditional text. In addition, the students' attitudes toward the reading task were more favorable when they used the computer. Horton, Lovitt, Givens, and Nelson (1989) compared the effectiveness of a study guide presented on computer to traditional note-taking in order to improve textbook comprehension for learning disabled and remedial students in a 9th grade geography class. The computerized study guide produced significantly higher performance than the note-taking condition. In an effort to improve reading comprehension for 10th and 11th grade learning disabled students, Casteel (1988) presented chunked reading passages (grouping words in a sentence into short meaningful phrases of three to five words) on the computer screen and in traditional written text. When both chunked methods were compared to a nonchunked CAI control group, Casteel concluded that such chunking could improve reading comprehension. These studies suggest reading comprehension activities presented in traditional text also can be presented on the computer screen.

The computer has been used to teach content vocabulary to learning disabled students. With a tutorial program that used self-pacing, frequent responding, corrective feedback, sequenced instruction, small teaching sets, and cumulative review, the learning disabled, remedial, and general education high school students in the study showed improvement (Horton, Lovitt, & Givens, 1988). However, although the gain scores for the learning disabled and remedial students were the same, the learning disabled students required more repetitions of the program. Content vocabulary also was taught successfully to high school learning disabled students with a software program by Johnson, Gersten, and Carnine (1987) that used sets of seven practice words and provided individualized systematic review. This program led to significantly faster acquisition than a popular program, Word Attack!, which presented words in sets of 25.

These studies suggest that carefully designed CAI has the potential to be an effective supplement to teacher instruction in reading comprehension, at least in high school classrooms. Presentation of text on computer screen is equivalent to written text. The computer may provide increased individualized learning opportunities for learning disabled students, as in vocabulary development, and may provide teachers with an effective and timesaving means to address the heterogeneity of mainstreamed classes.

Mathematics

Learning disabled students are less proficient than their peers in acquiring basic math skills, and this discrepancy increases with age (Fleischner, Garnett, & Shepherd, 1982). This discrepancy has been noted particularly in the acquisition of basic math facts. The computer has the potential to be a valuable instructional tool for learning disabled students in the area of mathematics. The computer can motivate, increase engagement, provide increased opportunities for individualized instruction, provide immediate reinforcement and feedback, and provide detailed data about the student's performance (Montague, 1987).

In a comparison of traditional instruction and CAI in the resource room, Watkins and Webb (1981) found that a learning disabled group who received CAI (Math Machine) for 10 minutes a day performed significantly better on both standardized and criterion-referenced tests than a learning disabled group who received traditional resource room instruction in math. Although the components of traditional instruction were not reported, the components of the CAI math program included individualized instruction, a comprehensive curriculum organized into a hierarchy of skills, a description of learner outcomes, measurements of progress, strategies for placing the student within the curriculum, and a multisensory learning format. Unfortunately, because the components of traditional instruction were not reported, the conclusions that can be drawn from these results are limited.

In another comparison of CAI and traditional teacher instruction, Trifiletti, Frith, and Armstrong (1984) reported that learning disabled students who received 40 minutes of CAI instruction for 4 months with the Spark-80 Computerized Mathematics System were superior to learning disabled resource room students, both in the number of math skills mastered and the fluency of problem solving. The Spark-80 program used assessment, tutorials, drill and practice, skill games, and word problems. The computer program used specific criteria to make data-based decisions on whether the student should receive tutorial instruction, drill and practice, or word problems. Although the authors reported that the resource room program was workbook oriented (Working with Numbers), no description was given of the teacher instruction or of the criteria for making data-based decisions, thus limiting conclusions about the results.

Mathematics instruction typically falls into two broad categories: computation and problem solving. As previously noted, learning disabled students are often discrepant in their mastery of math facts when compared to their nonhandicapped peers. Many learning disabled students use counting strategies that interfere with higher order processes in problem solving (Hasselbring et al., 1988). Computer-assisted instruction has the potential to provide the drill-and-practice opportunities necessary to develop rapid, effortless, and errorless recall of basic math facts (Hasselbring et al., 1988).

Chiang (1986) investigated the effectiveness of three CAI programs, Multiplication Table, Micro Multiplication, and Treasure Hunt of Facts, to increase six 4th grade learning disabled students' performance on timed probes of multiplication facts. Improvement was found on both the computer (Meteor Multiplication) probes and written probes. However, the improvement was more marked on the paper and pencil probes. Chiang suggested that the students' responding on the computer was made more difficult by finding the correct key, and that this factor may actually interfere with the acquisition of automaticity of math facts. Furthermore, the computer game format, such as found in the Treasure Hunt and Meteor Multiplication programs, which included extraneous graphics and sounds, may not be so effective as simple drill-and-practice programs. This suggestion was verified by Christensen and Gerber (1990) who reported that an arcade-like game format interfered with learning disabled students' performance on computerized drill and practice of basic addition facts.

Although Chiang (1986) demonstrated generalization of multiplication facts presented on the computer to written probes, Howell, Sidorenko, and Jurica (1987) cautioned that drill-and-practice programs alone may be inadequate in effecting lasting changes in the mastery of math facts. In this single-subject study (n = 1), the Galaxy Math and Memory Ease programs were used successively to provide drill and practice in multiplication facts. Although increases in correct responding and decreases in time to respond were found, the results did not maintain over time. The third and most successful intervention involved a teacher instructional strategy, in which the student was taught an algorithm, The Rule of Nines, and the Galaxy Math drill-and-practice program, and these were used for maintenance of gains made.

The limitations of drill and practice were further emphasized by Hasselbring et al. (1988), who found that learning disabled students who came to a CAI drill-and-practice program using counting strategies to answer math facts left the program with the same counting strategies. If, however, the students came to the CAI program from teacher instruction where they were taught not to count, recalling facts at the computer led to automaticity. The authors developed a drill-and-practice program, Fast Facts, that individualized instruction according to an assessment of the student's level of automaticity. Components of the Fast Facts program included small sets of target facts, controlled response times, and interspersed target and maintenance facts. The teacher was able to select the facts to be learned and the speed with which they were presented.

The effectiveness of the Fast Facts program was investigated with three groups of students (n = 160), ages 7 to 14 years. The three groups included learning disabled students who received daily instruction for 10 minutes per day from a computer, a learning disabled contrast group who received daily instruction from the teacher, and nonhandicapped students who received instruction from the teacher. After 49 days of instruction, the learning disabled students in the CAI group showed a 73% increase in the number of facts recalled from memory, the learning disabled contrast students showed no change with teacher instruction, and the nonhandicapped contrast students showed a slight increase. The results for the learning disabled students in the CAI group were maintained for 4 months.

The results of these preliminary investigations of drill-and-practice programs for math suggest that the computer alone is not sufficient to develop automaticity of math facts. Teacher instruction before the CAI drill-and-practice program is needed for CAI to be effective. Additionally, effective CAI programs for math drill and practice must use procedures based on effective instruction and mastery learning. Among these procedures are carefully sequenced instruction, assessment of students' speed and accuracy for determining the next instructional sequence, flexibility in selecting facts to be learned and the speed with which they are presented, small learning sets, and the interspersal of target and maintenance facts.

In contrast to the research on math facts, few software programs are available to teach verbal mathematical problem solving (Montague, 1987). One recent study used a Direct Instruction CAI program on word problem analyses to teach mildly handicapped junior high students a strategy for choosing the correct operation in multiplication and division math story problems. An important question in this study was whether a CAI tutorial program alone could be effective in teaching this higher order skill. The Analyzing Word Problems program used explicit instruction to teach a clearly specified, step-by-step strategy. This program was compared to the Semantic Calculator (Sunburst Communications, 1983), which guided the student through word story problems by asking questions such as "How many?" and "What?". No significant differences were found between the Direct Instruction group and the Semantic Calculator group on the posttest, although in interviews the students favored the Direct Instruction program. The lack of significant differences for the Direct Instruction program could be attributed either to the students' failure to attend to the prompts to use the strategy or to the lack of flexibility (i.e., branching) in the computer program that a teacher could provide. The authors of this study and Montague (1987) concur that until more results are available, CAI programs to teach verbal mathematical problem solving should be used for practice in generalized strategy application and maintenance after the teacher has taught the strategy.

Spelling

The computer has been used both for spelling assessment and instruction for learning disabled students. Hasselbring and Crossland (1981, 1982) reported successful computer-based administration of the Kottmeyer Diagnostic Spelling Test. The computer delivered directions via the computer screen and auditory cassette, and the students typed responses. The computer then provided an error list and diagnostic error analysis for the teacher. When compared to the traditional written response procedure, the computer version was found to be both efficient and cost effective.

In a similar study, however, Varnhagen and Gerber (1984) compared the administration of the Test of Written Spelling on the computer and on paper. The students took less time and spelled more words correctly on the written test. The authors suggested that letter-search time on the computer keyboard may interfere with the actual spelling process.

Three studies have investigated spelling instruction with the computer. Watkins and Webb (1981) reported that the CAI program, the Spelling Machine, and traditional teacher instruction produced comparable results. A CAI program to remediate incorrectly spelled words (Hasselbring, 1984) proved to be slightly better than teacher instruction with feedback. When an error occurred in the CAI program, a model of the error was provided and then a correct model of the word was provided for the student to copy. Morris, Murdock, O'Conner, and St. Peter (1987) reported that in a comparison of teacher instruction and CAI with synthesized speech, teacher instruction was better initially, but CAI led to better retention of spelling skills.

The results comparing teacher instruction and CAI for spelling assessment and instruction are equivocal. Computer-assisted instruction does have the potential, however, of being efficient and cost effective for the teacher. An important variable that should be examined to clarify further these results is the keyboarding skills possessed by the students. Studies that either require subjects to possess prerequisite keyboarding skills or that use alternate response modes (e.g., Touch Window) would be valuable.

Writing

Learning disabled students evidence considerable difficulties with writing tasks (Graham & MacArthur, 1988; Thomas, Englert, & Gregg, 1987) and lack strategies for managing basic planning, composing, and editing (Morocco & Neuman, 1986). With the decade of writing research by Graves (1983, 1985) and others, educators have examined the impact of the computer as a writing tool or word processor on the writing skills of learning disabled students. Potentially, the computer can increase the learning disabled student's motivation for writing, improve text editing skills, and allow the student to concentrate on content first and stylistic and mechanical concerns second (MacArthur, 1988; Morocco & Neuman, 1986).

In a case study described by Morocco and Neuman (1986), learning disabled students learned to revise their writing in resource rooms where they received a process approach to writing instruction (Graves, 1983), combined with the use of a word processor. Word processing facilitated a skills approach to writing (reduction of mechanical errors) as well as a meaning-oriented approach. In a year-long study by Kerchner and Kistinger (1984), a learning disabled experimental group of 4th, 5th, and 6th graders in a resource room used the process approach to writing as proposed by Graves (1983) and Bank Street Writer on the computer. Of the two classes in the control group, one used a language experience approach with no word processing and the other concentrated on spelling skills with sentence dictation. Significant effects for Thematic Maturity, Word Usage, Style, and Written Language Quotient on the Test of Written Language were found for the experimental group.

Although successful use of word processors by learning disabled students has been reported, learning to use these programs can present problems for students (MacArthur & Schneiderman, 1986). Two groups of learning disabled students met for 12 1-hour sessions to learn to use a computer for word processing. One group used the Milliken Word Processor and the other used Cut and Paste. Both programs were chosen for their ease of learning and simplicity of use. Observations of the students during instruction revealed the following types of errors or problems: (a) a hunt-and-peck method of typing that resulted in a typing speed of two to four words per minute, (b) inefficient cursor use and incorrect positioning of the cursor, (c) confusion about the way text is formatted on the screen versus the way it is represented in computer memory and sent to the printer, and (d) problems in loading and saving files, moving and deleting blocks of text, and sending text to the printer. The most persistent problem was confusion about the correct use of spaces and returns. Two general recommendations for using word processors as part of the writing process for learning disabled students were to provide (a) direct instruction in the overall organization of the word processing program, and (b) direct instruction and structured practice on specific points of difficulty.

A comparison of handwriting and word processing methods of text production yielded only minor differences between revisions (MacArthur & Graham, 1987). Regardless of the type of production, revisions were basically surface level (e.g., spelling, punctuation, and capitalization). These results led the authors to conclude that merely providing elementary-aged learning disabled students with practice in using a word processor will not improve revising behavior or written text, and may not free the student from mechanical concerns during the initial composition.

On the basis of this study, Graham and MacArthur (1988) investigated the impact of a six-step revision strategy on the essays produced on a word processor by three learning disabled students in the 5th and 6th grades. Strategy instruction by the teacher increased revising behavior and the length and quality of written products. Maintenance and generalization to paper and pencil were observed, as well as an increase in the students' confidence in writing ability.

The computer is not a writing curriculum or an instructional method for writing, but it may be a tool that affects the writing process and facilitates certain types of writing instruction (MacArthur, 1988). Word processing independent of instruction has little impact on learning disabled students' written products. However, word processing may facilitate revising skills taught by the teacher.

Conclusion

This section has examined the limited research on how learning disabled students benefit from the range of available drill-and-practice, tutorial, and simulation CAI programs. One conclusion from the effectiveness literature thus far is that the computer, at best, provides only a modest advantage when compared to teacher instruction. Some researchers have suggested that currently the computer should be viewed merely as a vehicle of instruction for individualized drill and practice, and that more attention should be directed toward the instructional design within the CAI programs. Through such attention, we may be able ultimately to determine the effectiveness of CAI for learning disabled students across a variety of programs and skill areas.

Instructional Design in CAI

The importance of using principles of learning in CAI applications has been widely recognized (Carnine, 1989; LeBlanc et al., 1985; Thorkildsen & Reid, 1989). Although much research is available on effective teaching practices (cf. Brophy & Good, 1984; Stevens & Rosenshine, 1981; Wittrock, 1986), little is known about the effective application of these practices to CAI software. The capacity of computer software to isolate and control specific instructional variables makes CAI a desirable context in which to examine these variables. The importance of this type of study is underscored by the available research that does suggest that the application of specific instructional design principles to CAI can make a considerable difference in the effectiveness of CAI for learning disabled students (Hasselbring et al., 1988; Torgeson, 1986; Woodward, Carnine, Gersten, Gleason, Johnson, & Collins, 1986). Among the variables that have been examined in CAI for learning disabled students are learning set size, pacing, response mode, prompts, feedback, and reinforcement. Each of these will be discussed below.

Learning Set Size

Le Blanc et al. (1985) have included a high ratio of opportunities to respond to stimulus presentations among a list of optimal teaching procedures in CAI. Repeated practice on any given skill is important in order to achieve mastery learning. Software programs that limit the size of the learning set (e.g., seven vocabulary words or two math facts and their reversals) and provide numerous opportunities to respond to a single skill have been effective for learning disabled students (Hasselbring et al., 1988; Johnson et al., 1987). In addition, software programs that provide cumulative review of learned skills (Johnson et al., 1987) or that intersperse learned skills with target skills (Hasselbring et al., 1988) provide better maintenance of skills.

Pace of Presentation

When new skills are presented to learning disabled students, emphasis is usually on learner-controlled responding. However, once the student demonstrates accuracy, the important focus should be on developing fluency or automaticity (Le Blanc et al., 1985; Torgeson, 1986). Difficulties in slower recognition rates of words or math facts are often impediments to higher order reading or math skills for learning disabled students. The computer is particularly well suited to produce the rate of presentation of stimuli necessary to increase fluency or automaticity. Torgeson (1986) and Hasselbring et al. (1988) demonstrated that drill-and-practice programs that allowed the teacher to adjust the speed level or time allowed for responding led to increased fluency. Hasselbring et al. (1988) suggested that manipulation of controlled response times may be the single most important variable in developing automaticity of math facts.

Response Mode

A basic question in CAI is how students should respond on the computer. One common mode of responding is to use the keyboard to type a response. In a study to increase the sight-word reading vocabulary of learning disabled students, Cohen, Torgeson, and Torgeson (1988) compared a typing condition, which required students to type words into the computer, and a no-typing condition, which required students to press the spacebar. Both versions of the program were effective in improving speed and accuracy of word recognition. The typing condition was more effective in increasing spelling accuracy. However, the students enjoyed the no-typing condition more and were able to attain mastery level of words faster in the no-typing condition. Mouse-controlled responding was investigated by Horton, Lovitt, and Slocum (in press) who reported the successful use of this response mode in the development of a map tutorial software program for high school learning disabled students.

At this time, there is no preferred response mode for CAI. In fact, response mode very well may interact with the type of skill that is being taught. Future research is needed to determine which response mode is appropriate for the specific skill being learned, the value of alternative computer input devices such as touch-sensitive computer screens (Battenberg & Merbler, 1989), and the importance of prerequisite keyboarding skills (MacArthur & Schneiderman, 1986).

Criterion-Related and Extraneous Cues and Prompts

When teaching a new skill, it is important to draw the student's attention to the relevant or critical features of the skill (Le Blanc et al., 1985). As in the analysis of any textual material (Vargas, 1984), consideration must be given to the stimuli that are controlling a student's responding in CAI. With the introduction of extraneous visual and auditory stimuli in many CAI programs, concern exists that these added graphics, pictures, or sound effects may interfere with the student's learning (Chiang, 1986; Christensen & Gerber, 1990; Le Blanc et al., 1985).

Torgeson, Waters, Cohen, and Torgeson (1988) compared the relative effectiveness of three practice variations of a computer program to teach word recognition to 1st, 2nd, and 3rd grade learning disabled students. The three conditions included (a) the word presented with a graphic, (b) the word presented with a graphic and synthesized speech, and (c) the word presented with synthesized speech. All three conditions resulted in significant improvements in accuracy and speed of word identification. No differences were found among the treatments in terms of the types of stimuli that were presented to the student during instruction.

Another study (Kinney, Stevens, & Schuster, 1988) investigated the appropriateness of a prompting procedure (constant time delay) to teach a student to spell the names of 15 states. A time delay procedure transfers stimulus control from a prompt to the stimulus by delaying the presentation of the prompt after the teaching stimulus has been presented. In this study, the computer's voice synthesizer instructed the student to spell the name of a state. If the student did not respond within 6 seconds, the model of the word was presented on the computer screen, and the student had 30 seconds to type the target word and press the return. The constant time delay procedure proved to be an effective strategy that facilitated the transfer of stimulus control from a visual prompt. This procedure also resulted in the generalization and maintenance of the correct spelling to a written task.

Considerably more research is needed to determine how task stimuli should be presented on the computer. More information is needed on the types of criterion-related prompts and fading procedures that increase correct responding in CAI. More research is also needed to examine the effects of extra stimulus prompts, such as sound effects, animated graphics, and so forth, that are present in much of the commercially available software.

Feedback

Research on teaching has revealed that effective teachers provide immediate corrective feedback (Englert, 1984a; Gersten, Carnine, & Woodward, 1987; Rieth et al., 1981). Feedback is particularly important for learning disabled students who make more errors than their non-handicapped peers. Collins et al. (1987) have identified three basic kinds of feedback: (a) minimal, which tells the student whether the answer is right or wrong, (b) basic, which tells the student whether the answer is correct or incorrect, and if incorrect, supplies the correct answer, and (c) elaborated corrective feedback, which provides the student with a set of rules or prompts that will allow the student to come up with the correct answer.

Collins et al. (1987) compared basic and elaborated feedback within the context of a CAI program that taught reasoning skills to learning disabled and remedial high school students. Scores were higher for the elaborated corrections condition for posttests, generalization, and maintenance. Both feedback conditions took the same amount of time, with the authors suggesting that although the elaborated feedback condition may have been time intensive early in the program, it may have prevented errors at a later point. The effectiveness of elaborated feedback was also demonstrated by Hasselbring (1984) in an investigation of a CAI spelling program. When the student erred, the computer presented the incorrect response, modeled the correct response, and then requested the student to spell the word correctly.

Reinforcement

Although reinforcement for correct responding is necessary for learning to occur, too much reinforcer stimulation may interfere with learning (Chiang, 1986; Le Blanc et al., 1985). In a study that used videodisc-enhanced CAI, Thorkildsen and Reid (1989) reported that bonus feedback (i.e., added reinforcers, such as graphic and video routines, which are common in commercial software) had little positive effect on learning disabled students' time-telling. Although posttest scores were remarkably similar for the knowledge of results condition (feedback only as to correct or incorrect) and the bonus feedback condition, the bonus feedback condition required more time to complete the program and interfered with pacing and opportunities to respond.

In an attempt to clarify what kind of reinforcement maximizes learning gains, three reinforcement conditions were compared during a CAI math drill and practice program with four at-risk 2nd grade students (Axelrod, McGregor, Sherman, & Hamlet, 1987). The three reinforcement conditions included a variable ratio (VR-5) games condition, a variable ratio (VR-10) games condition, and a no-games reinforcement condition (i.e., the students were reinforced with compliments on the monitor and number of correct answers). Consistent with previous results, Axelrod et al. (1987) reported that students had more opportunities to respond and more correct responses with the no-games reinforcement condition.

Future Directions for CAI for Learning Disabled Students

Cook (1989) has remarked that many of the investigations of CAI have demonstrated an overemphasis on technology and early implementation without an adequate theoretical focus on instructional design. The limited research on the instructional design of CAI for learning disabled students would suggest that this is the case. Researchers and practitioners alike report that computers do not seem to have a considerable impact on practice and programs (Okolo, Rieth, & Bahr, 1989), and the effectiveness of computers for learning disabled students is still in doubt (Malouf et al., 1989; Pogrow, 1988). Research on CAI for learning disabled students must take a number of directions, which are discussed below.

Software Development

The first and perhaps most obvious need is the development of instructionally sound software. More attention must be given to the variables that promote mastery learning. Software should be developed and tested that attempts to: (a) teach skills in a sequence, (b) provide instruction on skills found deficient in a pretest, (c) train each skill to mastery, (d) provide several levels of instruction (e.g., accuracy, fluency, generalization) for each skill, and (e) provide immediate corrective feedback (Cipani & Kearly, 1986). Evaluation of the software should include not only posttest scores on the computer but also measures of generalization, maintenance, social validation, and efficiency. The software must not only be effective, but must demonstrate evidence of efficient use in classroom settings and compatibility with curriculum.

Collins and Carnine (1988) have emphasized the importance of a field test and revision process in order to develop CAI software for students with learning disabilities.

Recent advances in hardware and authoring languages should allow researchers and developers the opportunity to move from an emphasis on relatively inflexible drill and practice programs to flexible programs that may be tutorially based and modifiable to individual learners. The recent hardware advances allow for more branching and instructional control and a better interface among the lesson format, graphics or animation, sound, and student record keeping. Touch-sensitive computer screens, mouse-controlled responding, and digitized sound also have the potential of improving software development. The technology and authoring languages are available for the development of microcomputer-driven videodisc instruction, which has proven effective in business and industry. A number of studies have already demonstrated the effectiveness of Level I videodisc instruction programs (i.e., operated by the teacher) for learning disabled students (Hasselbring, Sherwood, Bransford, Fleenor, Griffith, & Goin, 1988; Hofmeister, Engelmann, & Carnine, 1986; Kelly, Carnine, Gersten, & Grossen, 1986).

Integration in Classroom

A second area of concern is the integration of CAI into systematic instruction in the classroom (Panyan, Hummel, & Jackson, 1988). Classroom observations have indicated that strategies for integrating CAI with learning disabled students are neither elaborate nor systematically employed by their teachers. This problem, in part, is related to the current status of software development. Teachers are dissatisfied with much of the commercially available software, its limited use (i.e., drill and practice), and the assistance that they must provide students while they are using the software (Neuman, 1989; Okolo et al., 1989; Panyan et al., 1988). Many of the learning disabled students who use the software require teacher assistance because of their inadequate reading skills and inability to understand the errors that they make (Neuman, 1989).

More research attention needs to be given to the classroom environments where CAI is used. Panyan et al. (1989) have suggested that researchers attend to the congruence between classroom curriculum content, instructional objectives, and the modifiability of software programs. Attention must also be given to the types of programs (i.e., drill and practice, tutorial, and simulation) appropriate to different grouping situations, given the limited availability of computers in the classroom (Cosden, Gerber, Semmel, Goldman, & Semmel, 1987; Lieber & Semmel, 1989). For example, Hine, Goldman, and Cosden (1990) provide evidence that supports the use of the computer as a vehicle for learning disabled students to collaborate on writing activities.

The emphasis on teacher training should be less technical and more instructional (Fazio & Polsgrove, 1989). Teachers need simpler documentation and instructions, both in implementing the software and in integrating the software into the existing classroom curriculum. Alternative methods of evaluating software should be explored. Malouf et al. (1989) reported that teachers far prefer examining software to looking at written evaluations of the software.

Alternative Uses of Computer Technology

Another research direction involves examining innovative ways that the computer can enhance traditional teacher instruction. Much of the previous research has examined CAI as a substitute for the teacher. A different focus is to examine ways in which the computer can support traditionally delivered instruction.

An observational study by Rieth and Frick (1983) revealed that teachers of learning disabled students spent 40% of their time teaching and 60% of their time not in contact with students. Much of this time was spent in clerical chores, including correcting students' work. Several authors have reported the successful use of a computer-based networking system to monitor students' responses (Hayden, Wheeler, & Carnine, 1989; Robinson, DePascale, & Roberts, 1989; Woodward, Carnine, Gersten, & Moore, 1987). Students can use small keypads connected to a single computer to answer a teacher's question or worksheet problem. Each student's answer is displayed on the computer screen next to the problem number. Teachers have used this technology successfully to monitor and provide immediate feedback to learning disabled students during both group instruction and independent practice. Implementation of the networking system has led to a higher rate of on-task behavior (Woodward et al., 1987) and increased accuracy for the students (Robinson et al., 1989).

Simulation is another innovative use of computer and videodisc technology that can enhance traditional teacher instruction and thus benefit learning disabled students. Simulation activities that follow explicit teacher instruction can help teach problem-solving skills by quickly demonstrating the effects of different variables and showing causal relationships (Woodward et al., 1988).

Computer technology has the potential to benefit learning disabled students through facilitating improved assessment practices. A computerized curriculum-based measurement system, which provided components of both data collection and skills analysis in spelling instruction, led to teachers' designing more specific instructional programs and effecting better student achievement (Fuchs, Allinder, Hamlett, & Fuchs, 1990). Hofmeister and Lubke (1988) have suggested that the computer can be used to simulate consultation with a human expert (thus, "expert system"). They reported the development of an expert system, CLASS.LD2, to provide assistance in classifying a student as learning disabled. In the future, they suggest that the computer can be used for test interpretation, monitoring student performance, and assisting with behavior management.

The research on CAI for students with lerning disabilities is limited and inconclusive at this time. The extent to which progress will be made will depend on the extent to which the principles of learning and effective instruction will guide future research and implementation. The classroom computer has the potential of both serving explicit teaching functions and enhancing traditional teacher instruction for learning disabled students. The outcome will depend on attention to effective instruction rather than to hardware and technology alone.

Acknowledgments. This research is supported in part by a grant (HI80P80043) from the office of Special Education and Rehabilitation Services of the U.S. Department of Education.

Note. A list of authors and/or publishers of the computer software mentioned in this article is available from the first author. Please send requests to Kathryn G. Karsh, Ed.D., Educational Research & Services Center, 425 Fisk Avenue, DeKalb, Illinois, 60115.

References

Axelrod, S., McGregor, G., Sherman, J., & Hamlet, C. (1987). Effects of video games as reinforcers for computerized addition performance. *Journal of Special Education Technology*, *9*, 1–8.

Battenberg, J. K., & Merbler, J. B. (1989). Touch screen versus keyboard: A comparison of task performance of young children. *Journal of Special Education Technology*, *10*, 24–28.

Becker, H. J. (1983). *School uses of microcomputers.* Baltimore, MD: The Johns Hopkins University Center for Social Organization of Schools.

Berk, R. A. (1983). Toward a definition of learning disabilities: Progress or regress? *Education and Treatment of Children*, *6*, 285–310.

Blaschke, D. (1986). Technology for special education: A national strategy. *Technical Horizons in Education Journal*, *13*, 77–82.

Bonnet, K. A. (1989). Learning disabilities: A neurobiological perspective in humans. *Remedial and Special Education*, *10*, 8–19.

Bracey, G. (1988). Computers and learning: The research jury is still out. *Electronic Learning*, *8*, 28–29.

Brophy, J., & Good, T. (1984). Teacher behavior and student achievement. In M. Wittrock (Ed.), *Third handbook of research on teaching* (3rd ed.). New York: Macmillan.

Budoff, M., Thormann, M. J., & Gras, A. (1984). *Microcomputers in special education: An introduction to instructional applications.* Cambridge, MA: Brookline Books.

Carlson, S. A., & Silverman, R. (1986). Microcomputers and computer-assisted instruction in special classrooms: Do we need the teacher? *Learning Disability Quarterly, 9,* 105–110.

Carnine, D. (1989). Teaching complex content to learning disabled students. *Exceptional Children, 55,* 524–533.

Casteel, C. A. (1988). Effects of chunked reading among learning disabled students: An experimental comparison of computer and traditional chunked passages. *Journal of Educational Technology Systems, 17,* 115–121.

Chiang, B. (1986). Initial learning and transfer effects on microcomputer drills and on LD students' multiplication skills. *Learning Disability Quarterly, 9,* 118–123.

Christensen, C. A., & Gerber, M. M. (1990). Effectiveness of computerized drill and practice games in teaching basic math facts. *Exceptionality, 1,* 149–165.

Christenson, S. L., Ysseldyke, J. E., & Thurlow, M. L. (1989). Critical instructional factors for students with mild handicaps: An integrative review. *Remedial and Special Education, 10,* 21–31.

Cipani, E., & Kearly, P. J., (1986). Designing and evaluating computer-assisted instructional programs using a diagnostic prescriptive model. *Journal of Special Education Technology, 8,* 31–43.

Cohen, A. L., Torgesen, J. K., & Torgesen, J. L. (1988). Improving speed and accuracy of word recognition in reading disabled children: An evaluation of two computer program variations. *Learning Disabilities Quarterly, 11,* 333–340.

Collins, M., & Carnine, D. (1988). Evaluating the field test revision process by comparing two versions of a reasoning skills CAI program. *Journal of Learning Disabilities, 21,* 375–379.

Collins, M., Carnine, D., & Gersten, R. (1987). Elaborated corrective feedback and the acquisition of reasoning skills: A study of computer-assisted instruction. *Exceptional Children, 54,* 254–262.

Cook, E. K. (1989). The use of Macintosh authoring languages in effective computer-assisted instruction. *Journal of Educational Technology Systems, 18,* 109–122.

Cosden, M. A., Gerber, M. M., Semmel, D. S., Goldman, S. R., & Semmel, M. I. (1987). Microcomputer use within micro-educational environments. *Exceptional Children, 53,* 399–409.

Edwards, J., Norton, S., Taylor, S., Weiss, M., & Dusseldorp, R. (1975). How effective is CAI? A review of the research. *Educational Leadership, 33,* 147–153.

Englert, C. S. (1984a). Effective direct instruction practices in special education settings. *Remedial and Special Education, 5,* 38–47.

Englert, C. S. (1984b). Measuring teacher effectiveness from the teacher's point of view. *Focus on Exceptional Children, 17,* 1–14.

Evertson, C. (1982). Differences in instructional activities in higher- and lower-achieving junior English and math classes. *Elementary School Journal, 82,* 329–350.

Fazio, B. B., & Polsgrove, L. (1989). An evaluation of the effects of training special educators to integrate microcomputer technology into math curricula. *Journal of Special Education Technolgy, 10,* 5–13.

Fleischner, J. E., Garnett, K., & Shepherd, M. J. (1982). Proficiency in arithmetic basic facts computation of learning disabled children. *Focus on Learning Problems in Mathematics*, *4*, 47–56.

Fuchs, L. S., Allinder, R. M., Hamlett, C. L., & Fuchs, D. (1990). An analysis of spelling curricula and teachers' skills in identifying error types. *Remedial and Special Education*, *11*, 42–52.

Gersten, R., Carnine, D., & Woodward, J. (1987). Direct instruction research: The third decade. *Remedial and Special Education*, *8*, 48–56.

Gersten, R., Woodward, J., Darch, C. (1986). Direct instruction: A research-based approach to curriculum design and teaching. *Exceptional Children*, *53*, 17–31.

Good, T. L., & Brophy, J. E. (1986). School effects. In M. C. Wittrock (Ed.), *Handbook of research on teaching* (3rd ed., pp. 570–602). New York: Macmillan.

Graham, S. E., & MacArthur, C. (1988). Improving learning disabled students' skills at revising essays produced on a word processor: Self-instructional strategy training. *The Journal of Special Education*, *22*, 133–152.

Graves, D. H. (1983). *Writing: Teachers and children at work*. Exeter, NH: Heinemann Education Books.

Graves, D. (1985). *Breaking ground: Teachers relate reading and writing in the elementary school*. Exeter, NH: Heinemann Educational Books.

Greenwood, C. R., Delquadri, J., & Hall, R. V. (1984). Opportunity to respond and student academic performance. In W. Heward, T. E. Heron, D. S. Hill, & J. Trapp-Porter (Eds.), *Focus on behavior analysis in education*. Columbus, OH: Charles E. Merrill.

Hammill, D. D. (1990). On defining learning disabilities: An emerging consensus. *Journal of Learning Disabilities*, *23*, 74–84.

Hasselbring, T. S. (1984). Using a microcomputer for imitating students' errors to improve spelling performance. *Computer Reading and Language Arts*, *1*, 12–14.

Hasselbring, T. S., & Crossland, C. L. (1981). Using microcomputers for diagnosing spelling problems in learning handicapped children. *Educational Technology*, *21*, 37–39.

Hasselbring, T. S., & Crossland, C. L. (1982). Application of microcomputer technology to spelling assessment of learning disabled students. *Learning Disability Quarterly*, *5*, 80–82.

Hasselbring, T. S., Goin, L. I., & Bransford, J. D. (1988). Developing math automaticity in learning handicapped children: The role of computerized drill and practice. *Focus on Exceptional Children*, *20*, 1–7.

Hasselbring, T., Sherwood, R., Bransford, J., Fleenor, K., Griffith, D., & Goin, L. (1987). An evaluation of a level-one instructional videodisc program. *Journal of Educational Technology Systems*, *16*, 151–169.

Hayden, M., Wheeler, M. A., & Carnine, D. (1989). The effects of an innovative classroom networking system and an electronic gradebook on time spent scoring and summarizing student performance. *Education and Treatment of Children*, *12*, 253–264.

Hine, M. S., Goldman, S. R., & Cosden, M. A. (1990). Error monitoring by learning handicapped students engaged in collaborative microcomputer-based writing. *The Journal of Special Education*, *23*, 407–422.

Hofmeister, A. M., Engelmann, S., & Carnine, D. (1986). Videodisc technology: Providing instructional alternatives. *Journal of Special Education Technology*, *7*, 35–41.

Hofmeister, A. M., & Lubke, M. M. (1988). Expert systems: Implications for the diagnosis and treatment of learning disabilities. *Learning Disability Quarterly*, *11*, 287–291.

Horton, S. V., Lovitt, T. C., & Givens, A. (1988). A computer-based vocabulary program for three categories of student. *British Journal of Educational Technology*, *19*, 131–143.

Horton, S. V., Lovitt, T. C., Givens, A., & Nelson, R. (1989). Teaching social studies to high school students with academic handicaps in a mainstreamed setting: Effects of a computerized study guide. *Journal of Learning Disabilities*, *22*, 102–107.

Horton, S. V., Lovitt, T. C., & Slocum, T. (in press). Teaching geography to high school students with academic deficits: Effects of a computerized map tutorial. *Learning Disability Quarterly*.

Howell, R., Sidorenko, O. E., & Jurica, J. (1987). The effects of computer use on the acquisition of multiplication facts by a student with learning disabilities. *Journal of Learning Disabilities*, *20*, 336–341.

Jameson, D., Suppes, P., & Wells, S. (1974). The effectiveness of alternative instructional media: A survey. *Review of Educational Research*, *44*, 1–67.

Johnson, G., Gersten, R., & Carnine, D. (1987). Effects of instructional design variables on vocabulary acquisition of LD students: A study of computer-assisted instruction. *Journal of Learning Disabilities*, *20*, 206–213.

Jones, K. M., Torgeson, J. K., & Sexton, M. A. (1987). Using computer guided practice to increase decoding fluency in learning disabled children: A study using the Hint and Hunt I program. *Journal of Learning Disabilities*, *20*, 122–128.

Kavale, K. A., & Forness, S. R. (1986). School learning, time, and learning disabilities: The disassociated learner. *Journal of Learning Disabilities*, *19*, 130–138.

Keene, S., & Davey, B. (1987). Effects of computer-presented text on LD adolescents' reading behavior. *Learning Disabilities Quarterly*, *10*, 283–290.

Kelly, B., Carnine, D., Gersten, R., & Grossen, B. (1986). The effectiveness of videodisc instruction in teaching fractions to learning disabled and remedial high school students. *Journal of Special Education Technology*, *8*, 5–17.

Kerchner, L. B., & Kistinger, B. J. (1984). Language processing and word processing: Written expression, computers, and learning disabled students. *Learning Disabilities Quarterly*, *1*, 329–335.

Kinney, P. G., Stevens, K. B., & Schuster, J. W. (1988). The effects of CAI and time delay: A systematic program for teaching spelling. *Journal of Special Education Technology*, *9*, 61–72.

Kulik, J. A., Bangert, R. L., & Williams, G. W. (1983). Effect of computer-based technology on secondary school students. *Journal of Educational Psychology*, *75*, 19–26.

Le Blanc, J. M., Hoko, A., Aangeenbrug, M. H., & Etzel, B. C. (1985). Microcomputers and stimulus control: From the laboratory to the classroom. *Journal of Special Education Technology*, *7*, 23–30.

Lesgold, A. M., & Resnick, L. B. (1982). How reading difficulties develop: Perspectives from a longitudinal study. In J. P. Das, R. F. Mulcahy, & A. E. Wall (Eds.), *Theory and research in learning disabilities* (pp. 155–188). New York: Plenum.

Lessen, E. S., Dudzinski, M., Karsh, K. G., & Van Acker, R. M. (1989). Academic interventions with learning disabled students: A review of published research since Public Law 94–142. *Learning Disabilities Focus, 4*, 106–122.

Lieber, J., & Semmel, M. I. (1985). Effectiveness of computer application to instruction with mildly handicapped learners: A review. *Remedial and Special Education, 6*, 5–12.

Lieber, J., & Semmel, M. I. (1989). The relationship of group configuration to the interactions of students using microcomputers. *Journal of Special Education Technology, 10*, 14–23.

Lyon, G. R. (1985). Educational validation studies. In B. P. Rourke (Ed.), *Neuropsychology of learning disabilities* (pp. 168–193). New York: Guilford Press.

MacArthur, C. A. (1988). The impact of computers on the writing process. *Exceptional Children, 54*, 536–547.

MacArthur, C., & Graham, S. (1987). Learning disabled students' composing under three methods of text production: Handwriting, word processing, and dictation. *Journal of Special Education, 21*, 22–42.

MacArthur, C. A., Haynes, J. A., & Malouf, D. B. (1986). Learning disabled students' engaged time and classroom interaction: The impact of computer-assisted instruction. *Journal of Educational Computing Research, 2*, 189–198.

MacArthur, C. A., & Schneiderman, B. (1986). Learning disabled students' difficulties in learning to use a word processor: Implications for instruction and software evaluation. *Journal of Learning Disabilities, 19*, 248–253.

Maddux, C. D. (1984). Educational microcomputing: The need for research. *Computers in the Schools, 1*, 35–41.

Malouf, D. B., Morariu, J., Coulson, D. B., & Maiden, V. S. (1989). Special education teachers' preferences for sources of software evaluation information. *Journal of Special Education Technology, 9*, 144–155.

Majsterek, D. J., & Wilson, R. (1989). Computer-assisted instruction for students with learning disabilities: Considerations for practitioners. *Learning Disabilities Focus, 5*, 18–27.

McDermott, P. A., & Watkins, M. W. (1983). Computerized vs. conventional remedial instruction for learning disabled pupils. *The Journal of Special Education, 17*, 81–88.

Mercer, C. D., King-Sears, P., & Mercer, A. R. (1990). Learning disabilities definitions and criteria used by state education departments. *Learning Disabilities Quarterly, 13*, 141–147.

Montague, M. (1987). Using microcomputers to teach verbal mathematical problem solving to learning disabled students. *Computers in the Schools, 4*, 121–130.

Morocco, C. C., & Neuman, S. B. (1986). Word processors and the acquisition of writing strategies. *Learning Disabilities Quarterly, 19*, 243–247.

Morris, P. D., Murdock, J. Y., O'Conner, N. M., & St. Peter, S. M. (1987). *Comparing teacher-assisted and computer-assisted instruction for high school students with learning disabilities.* Paper presented at the Ninth International Conference in Learning Disabilities, San Diego, CA.

Morsink, C. V., Soar, R. S., Soar, R. M., & Thomas, R. (1986). Research on teaching: Opening the door to special education classrooms. *Exceptional Children, 53*, 32–40.

Neuman, D. (1989). Computer-based education for learning disabled students: Teachers' perceptions and behaviors. *Journal of Special Education Technology*, *9*, 156–166.

Okolo, C. M., Rieth, H. J., & Bahr, C. M. (1989). Microcomputer implementation in secondary special education programs: A study of special educators', mildly handicapped adolescents', and administrators' perspectives. *The Journal of Special Education*, *23*, 107–117.

Panyan, M. V., Hummel, J., & Jackson, L. B. (1988). The integrating of technology in the curriculum. *Journal of Special Education Technology*, *9*, 109–119.

Pogrow, S. (1988). The computer movement cover-up. *Electronic Learning*, April, 6–7.

Rashotte, C. A., & Torgeson, J. K. (1985). Repeated reading and reading fluency in learning disabled children. *Reading Research Quarterly*, *20*, 180–188.

Rieth, H. (1986). *An analysis of the instructional and contextual variables that influence the efficacy of computer-based instruction for mildly handicapped secondary school students*. Paper presented at the Special Education Technology Conference, Washington, DC.

Rieth, H., & Evertson, C. (1988). Variables related to the effective instruction of difficult-to-teach children. *Focus on Exceptional Children*, *20*, 1–8.

Rieth, N. J., & Frick, T. (1983). *An analysis of the impact of instructional time with different delivery systems on the achievement of mildly handicapped students* (Final Grant Research Report). Bloomington: Indiana University Center for Innovation in Teaching the Handicapped.

Rieth, H. J., Polsgrove, L., Okolo, C., Bahr, C., & Eckert, R. (1987). An analysis of the secondary special education classroom ecology with implications for teacher training. *Teacher Education and Special Education*, *1*, 113–119.

Rieth, H., Polsgrove, L., & Semmel, M. I. (1981). Instructional variables that make a difference: Attention to task and beyond. *Exceptional Education Quarterly*, *2*, 61–82.

Robinson, S. L., DePascale, D., & Roberts, F. C. (1989). Computer-delivered feedback in group-based instruction: Effects for learning disabled students in mathematics. *Learning Disabilities Focus*, *5*, 28–35.

Romanczyk, R. G. (1986). *Direct computer instruction: Issues of assessment, effectiveness, and generalization*. Paper presented at the Special Education Technology Conference, Washington, DC.

Rosenshine, B., & Stevens, R. (1986). Teaching functions. In M. C. Wittrock (Ed.), *Handbook of research on teaching* (3rd ed., pp. 376–391). New York: Macmillan.

Roth, S. F., & Beck, I. L. (1984). *Research and instructional issues of children's decoding skills through a microcomputer program*. Paper presented at the annual meeting of the American Educational Research Association, New Orleans, LA.

Stanovich, K. E. (1982). Individual differences in the cognitive processes of reading I: Word decoding. *Journal of Learning Disabilities*, *15*, 285–492.

Stevens, R., & Rosenshine, B. (1981). Advances in research on teaching. *Exceptional Education Quarterly*, *12*, 1–9.

Thomas, C., Englert, C., & Gregg, S. (1987). An analysis of errors and strategies in the expository writing of learning disabled students. *Remedial and Special Education*, *8*, 21–30.

Thorkildsen, R. J., & Reid, R., (1989). An investigation of the reinforcing effects of feedback on computer-assisted instruction. *Journal of Special Education Technology*, *9*, 125–135.

Thormann, J., Gersten, R., Moore, L., & Morvant, M. (1986). Microcomputers in special education classrooms: Themes from research and implications for practitioners. *Computers in the Schools*, *3*, 97–109.

Thurlow, M. L., Graden, T., Greever, T. W., & Ysseldyke, J. E. (1982). *Academic responding time for learning disabled and non-learning disabled students (Technical Report No. 72)*. Minneapolis: University of Minnesota, Institute for Research on Learning Disabilities.

Torgeson, J. K. (1986). Computers and cognition in reading: A focus on decoding fluency. *Exceptional Children*, *53*, 157–162.

Torgeson, J. K., & Young, K. A. (1983). Priorities for the use of microcomputers with learning disabled children. *Journal of Learning Disabilities*, *16*, 234–237.

Torgeson, J. K., Waters, M. D., Cohen, A. L., & Torgeson, J. L. (1988). Improving sight-word recognition skills in LD children: An evaluation of three computer program variations. *Learning Disability Quarterly*, *11*, 125–132.

Trifiletti, J. J., Frith, G. H., & Armstrong, S. (1984) Microcomputers versus resource rooms for LD students: A preliminary investigation of the effects on math skills. *Learning Disabilities Quarterly*, *7*, 69–76.

Vargas, J. S. (1984). What are your exercises teaching? An analysis of stimulus control in instructional materials. In W. L. Heward, T. E. Heron, D. S. Hill, & J. Trapp-Porter (Eds.), *Focus on behavior analysis in education* (pp. 126–141). Columbus, OH: Charles E. Merrill.

Varnhagen, S., & Gerber, M. M. (1984). Use of microcomputers for spelling assessment: Reasons to be cautious. *Learning Disability Quarterly*, *7*, 266–270.

Visonhaler, J. F., & Bass, R. K. (1972). A summary of ten major studies on CAI drill and practice. *Educational Technology*, *12*, 29–32.

Watkins, M. W. (1989). Computerized drill and practice and academic attitudes of learning disabled students. *Journal of Special Education Technology*, *9*, 167–172.

Watkins, M. W., & Webb, C. (1981). Computer-assisted instruction with the learning disabled students. *Educational Computer Magazine*, *Sept–Oct*, 24–26.

Weir, S., & Watt, D. (1981). LOGO: A computer environment for learning disabled students. *The Computing Teacher*, *8*, 11–17.

Wittrock, M. C. (Ed.) (1986). *Handbook of research on teaching* (3rd ed.). New York: MacMillan.

Woodward, J., Carnine, D., & Gersten, R. (1988). Teaching problem solving through computer simulations. *American Educational Research Journal*, *25*, 72–86.

Woodward, J., Carnine, D., Gersten, R., Gleason, M., Johnson, G., & Collins, M. (1986). Applying instructional design principles to CAI for mildly handicapped students: Four recently conducted studies. *Journal of Special Education Technology*, *8*, 13–26.

Woodward, J., Carnine, D., Gersten, R., & Moore, L. (1987). Using computer networking for feedback. *Journal of Special Education Technology*, *8*, 28–35.

16
Pharmacological Intervention

Michael G. Aman and Johannes Rojahn

The use of pharmacotherapy to treat specific learning disorders is a controversial matter that has stirred heated debate in the literature (e.g., Aman, 1980a; Dykman, 1980; Rimland, 1988; Silver, 1988; Wacker, 1988). Part of the reason for the controversy is that the data bearing on the issue simply are not that clear (especially insofar as the cerebral stimulants are concerned), as we hope to show later in this chapter. Nevertheless, these are important issues because of the sheer numbers of children receiving some form of pharmacotherapy and because of the unknown potential of drugs to influence outcome. Furthermore, this is a timely point at which to reexamine pharmacotherapy, because a substantial number of important empirical drug studies have only recently been published. Although these do not resolve the question of drug efficacy, safety, and so forth, they certainly do bring a much sharper focus to the questions that should be addressed.

In this chapter we discuss both the history and prevalence of pharmacotherapy for treating children with specific learning disorders. This is followed by a brief discussion of nosology and definitional issues as well as design considerations with respect to drug assessment in the learning disabilities. Next, studies of (a) the cerebral stimulants, (b) nootropics (piracetam), and (c) antimotion sickness drugs (the principal drug groups sometimes advocated for treating learning disabled children) are reviewed as well as the other major types of psychotropic drugs. Major unresolved issues impinging on this body of research are then considered, and this is followed by a discussion and overall conclusions. Several prior reviews have appeared on the topic of drug therapy and specific learning disorders (e.g., Aman, 1980b; Aman, 1982a; Barkley & Cunningham, 1978; Gadow, 1983; Rie, Rie, Stewart, & Ambuel, 1976a), and the interested reader may wish to consult these as well for an historical perspective.

History of Pharmacotherapy for Treating Learning Disorders

As noted below, the principal drugs used to treat children with specific learning disabilities are the cerebral stimulants (e.g., methylphenidate [Ritalin], dextroamphetamine [Dexedrine], and magnesium pemoline [Cylert]). The stimulants are now a well established and frequently used treatment for managing acting out behavior in children with Attention Deficit Disorder with Hyperactivity (ADD-H; Campbell & Werry, 1986) (now designated as Attention Deficit Hyperactivity Disorder [ADHD] in the DSM-III-R; American Psychiatric Association, 1987). Historically there has always been a large overlap between hyperactivity and specific learning disorders in the sense that children selected for one type of condition (e.g., ADHD) will also include a large proportion of youngsters with the other problem (i.e., specific learning disorders). Furthermore, the earliest description of ADHD children often focused on Minimal Brain Dysfunction (MBD) as the presumptive cause of their cognitive and behavioral problems (Clements & Peters, 1962; see also chapter 1). MBD in turn could be diagnosed on the basis of a neurological pattern, behavioral disturbances, learning disorders, or some combination of all three (see Aman & Singh, 1983; Rutter, Graham, & Yule, 1970, chapter 1). As MBD was regarded as an indication for pharmacotherapy, it eventuated that many children with either hyperactivity *or* specific learning disabilities were so treated, especially with stimulants such as methylphenidate (Werry, 1974). Going back further still to the earliest report of the use of stimulant drugs to treat children with behavior disorders (Bradley, 1937), it is interesting to note that effects on learning were emphasized as a major category of improvement. For example, Bradley reported:

Fourteen children responded in a spectacular fashion. Different teachers, reporting on these patients . . . agreed that a great increase of interest in school material was noted immediately. There appeared to be a definite "drive" to accomplish as much as possible during the school period, and often to spend extra time completing additional work. Speed of comprehension and accuracy of performance were increased in most cases. (p. 578)

With these historical antecedents in mind, it is perhaps not surprising that physicians gradually began to employ pharmacotherapy, especially with stimulants, with children whose principal presenting complaint was a learning disability. It appears to be a practice that evolved in minute stages, it is essentially unrecorded in the professional journals, and the reasons for this practice have to be inferred from discussions such as those presented above. Nevertheless, in the following section it becomes clear that pharmacotherapy is indeed a common form of treatment in the learning disabilities field.

Prevalence of Psychotropic Drug Prescription in the Learning Disabilities

One of the earliest studies of drug prevalence among learning disabled children was conducted by Hansen and Keogh (1971). They surveyed 229 pupils in programs for educationally handicapped children in southern California and found that 71 (31%) used prescribed medication regularly. Central neurous system (CNS) "tranquilizers" (presumably neuroleptics) such as thioridazine (Mellaril) were the most frequently prescribed medications (71% of cases), followed by CNS stimulants (38%). Gadow (1976) surveyed the teachers of 2,559 early childhood special education (ECSE) children in Illinois about the types of medication taken by these children. Illinois ECSE programs provide educational services for children aged 3 to 5 years who have a variety of problems such as learning disability, emotional disturbance, developmental delay, and physical handicap. Gadow found that 14% of these children received at least one psychotropic and/or anticonvulsant drug during the school year: 6% were taking stimulant drugs, 10% anticonvulsant drugs, 1.4% neuroleptics (major tranquilizers), and 1.3% anxiolytic drugs.

Schain (1972) noted that almost half of the children selected for learning problems in one study actually were regarded as having hyperactive behavior as their principal presenting complaint. This supports the observation, presented earlier, that learning disabilities and hyperactivity tend to overlap, and it also suggests that many learning disabled children tend to receive medication because of the coexisting hyperactivity. Krager, Safer, and Earhart (1979) surveyed children in elementary classes in Baltimore County, Maryland. Of 1,221 students enrolled in public special education schools for mentally retarded, physically handicapped, and emotionally disturbed children, 187 (15.3%) were reported as receiving medication for hyperactivity.

Finally, for the present purposes, the best study of drug prevalence among intellectually average, learning disabled children was probably that conducted by Cullinan, Gadow, and Epstein (1987). Among a group of 962 learning disabled students aged 6 to 18 years, 6.1% were reported as taking psychotropic medication by their teachers. Stimulants accounted for the preponderance of medication, followed distantly by neuroleptics. However, it is likely that these figures underestimate the true prevalence of psychotropic drugs in elementary school learning disabled children, because teachers may well not have been aware of psychotropic drugs in all cases and because of a reluctance by physicians to treat teenage youngsters with stimulants.

To summarize, the numbers of learning disabled children receiving psychotropic medication appear to differ widely with geographic region and administrative designation of educational difficulty. Thus far, the prevalences have ranged from about 6% (Cullinan et al., 1987) to 31%

(Hansen & Keogh, 1971). With the exception of the earliest of these studies (Hansen & Keogh, 1971), the cerebral stimulants, especially methylphenidate, have been the prevalent type of medication reported. Even the most conservative figure of 6% would represent a very large number, in absolute terms, of children affected. However, it would not surprise us if the "real" percentage of elementary school children, administratively classified as learning disabled, who are prescribed psychotropic medication was closer to 10% or more nationwide. Hence, the issue of whether these agents influence academic performance and scholastic achievement is by no means a moot point.

Nosology and Basic Definitions of Learning Disabilities

In chapter 1, Kavale and Forness describe some of the fundamental problems in arriving at a consensus regarding the definition of learning disabilities. Kavale and Forness rightly point out that none of the definitions proposed thus far are without problems, especially when the multiple needs of research, clinical practice, and politics/legislation are all considered concomitantly. Nevertheless, for research to progress in this field we need some shorthand method for describing and comparing the groups of subjects under study. Over the years, a variety of terms have been employed to describe children having reading and other forms of academic difficulty—minimal brain dysfunction and dyslexia are just two examples. Unfortunately, such terms have tended to create more confusion than understanding unless further specified or qualified. For example, minimal brain dysfunction has often been used as a concept that has relied in part on the presence of a learning problem to infer its existence and which at the same time has been used to explain such problems (see chapter 1, Aman & Singh, 1983; Rutter, Graham, & Yule, 1970). The circularity in such an approach is self-evident and not helpful scientifically. In a similar vein, the term *dyslexia* seems to sow confusion, as the existence of the disorder hinges not on a specified degree of disability but instead on a subjective appraisal of "the peculiar and specific nature of the errors in reading and spelling" (Critchley, 1970, p. 11). No single sign or set of signs is definitive but instead a multitude of patterns may be regarded as establishing the syndrome (Reid, 1972); hence, *dyslexia* appears to be in the eye of the beholder.

It seems to us that, without further specification of such terms, their use will necessarily impede the advancement of scientific knowledge in this area. Hence, given the present state of the field, we feel that the use of operational definitions remains the most satisfactory approach for describing subject populations in treatment research. As much of the drug research in this field has involved children with reading disorders, it is useful to review two of the more common operational definitions used to define reading problems, namely reading backwardness and reading retardation. As popularized by Rutter and Yule (1973, 1975; Yule & Rutter, 1970), *reading backwardness* refers to a lag between chronological age and reading age. By convention, a lag of 2 years has often been used to select children for clinically severe reading backwardness, although there is no reason why a different formula could not be used. *Reading retardation* refers to a lag between mental age and reading age, and once again by convention a lag of 2 years has often been used to designate clinically severe groups of such children.[1] It may also be more rational to express this as ratio of reading age to mental age, although the approach still falls under the rubric of reading retardation. Given the definition used for reading backwardness, it is of course possible that children of low ability would be reading at or about the level that would be expected of them in terms of their presumed cognitive ability. In contrast, reading retardation implies that the discrepancy between expected level and attainment level is unexplained (at least in terms of the child's general intellectual ability). As such, the term reading retardation appears to be more consistent with most researchers' concepts of what a learning disability is (Aman & Singh, 1983). With this background in mind then, we may wonder how rigorously children have been screened for studies of pharmacotherapy with children having learning disabilities.

Methodological Issues in Drug Studies

Methodological issues are discussed only briefly here. Sprague and Werry (1971) are often credited with first pointing out the fundamental requirements of a scientifically interpretable study regarding pediatric drug research. Among the criteria specified by Sprague and Werry are the need for placebo-control conditions to minimize expectancy bias and the use of double-blind precautions to prevent raters and subjects from foreknowledge of the drug identities during the study. Sprague and Werry also pointed out the need for random assignment of subjects to drug (or drug order) conditions, standardized (i.e., reliable and valid) assessments of change, and the requirement for correct interential statistics to be applied to determine whether a true drug effect occurred. Finally, Sprague and Werry noted the desirability of standardizing dosage in some

---

[1] Rutter and Yule (1973) have argued that it is appropriate to make some adjustment for the tendency of reading scores to regress toward the group mean when reading performance is predicted by IQ. When conducting population studies, Rutter and Yule have calculated a regression equation for determining expected reading age based on chronological age and IQ. However, this refinement does not alter the basic distinction between reading backwardness and reading retardation as presented here.

way (preferably by blood level determinations or by basing it on the subject's weight) to enable comparisons across studies. In addition to these standards, Aman and Singh (1980) added the strong recommendation that subjects be free of all other medications during drug investigations so that the effects of the drug(s) under study not be obfuscated by drug interactions.

With the possible exception of standardized dosages, these criteria are widely subscribed to today as necessary for a sound drug study. In the reviews that follow, these standards will be applied to evaluate the existing drug studies with learning disabled children.

Review of Drug Research with Learning Disabled Children

The Cerebral Stimulants

As noted earlier, the stimulants are the most commonly prescribed medications used for behavior problems, especially hyperactivity, with children. Eighteen studies could be located that evaluated the stimulants and that included academic performance as a dependent variable (see Table 16.1). Not all of these were designed to evaluate the role of stimulants in learning disabilities, but they are included nevertheless to glean as comprehensive a picture as possible. In the interests of brevity, these studies are referred to by their respective numerals in the table Methylphenidate (Ritalin) was assessed in 13 studies, dextroamphetamine (Dexedrine) in 4 studies, magnesium pemoline (Cylert) in 3, and deanol (Deaner) in 1.

Methodology and Subject Selection

The methodology of these studies, insofar as the Sprague and Werry (1971) drug criteria are concerned, was generally very good. Only one study (entry 2) failed to mention the use of a double-blind control, whereas one other (entry 16) was neither blind nor controlled. In eight studies (1, 7–9, 11–13, 17), subjects were admitted specifically because of the presence of a reading problem. However, in only four of these (7, 11, 12, 17) was the definition of reading disorder rigorous enough to define clinically significant and reasonably homogeneous groups. Subjects were identified for a variety of learning problems of unspecified severity in four others (2, 4, 5, 14). In six studies (3, 6, 10, 15, 16, 18), subjects were admitted because of the presence of Attention Deficit Disorder, whereas in three others participants were screened for both hyperactivity and learning problems (3, 14, 17).

TABLE 16.1. Studies of achievement and academic application using stimulant drugs.

Authors	Subjects	Drugs, group size	Duration	Perceptual-cognitive measures[a]	Achievement measures[a,b]
1. Huddleston, Staiger, Frye, Musgrave, & Stritch (1961)	"Retarded readers" of normal IQ. Primary, secondary, & tertiary level students. Degree of retardation unspecified	Deanol, 75 mg, twice daily (n = 60); placebo (n = 60)	8 weeks	Differential Aptitude Test Clerical speed (1/1) Clerical accuracy (1/1) [2/2]	Gates Survey Reading Test (0/1) [0/1]
2. Conners, Rothschild, Eisenberg, Schwartz, & Robinson (1969)	Children with learning or behavior problems. Extent of learning problem unspecified	Dextroamphetamine (approx. 25 mg/day) (n = 22); placebo (n = 21)	4 weeks	Goodenough–Harris Draw a Person (0/1) Porteus Mazes (1/1) Frostig Test of Perception (2/3) Auditory perception (1/3) Paired associate learning (1/2) Bender Gestalt (0/1) [5/11]	WRAT Reading (0/1) Spelling (0/1) Arithmetic (1/1) Gray Oral Reading (0/1) [1/4]
3. Conrad, Dworkin, Shai, & Tobiessen (1971)	Children screened for hyperactivity. Extent of learning problem unspecified	Dextroamphetamine (10–20 mg/day) (n = 33); placebo (n = 35)	4–6 months	Frostig Test of Perception (3/7) Bender Gestalt (0/1) Spatial Orientation (0/1) Bender Recall (0/1) Temporal Order (0/1) [3/11]	WRAT Reading ↓ (0/1) Arithmetic (0/1) [0/2]

Study	Subjects	Drug/dose	Duration	Tests	WRAT
4. Conners, Taylor, Meo, Kurtz, & Fournier (1972)	Children referred for learning or behavior problem. Extent and type of learning problem unspecified	Dextroamphetamine (20 mg/day) (n = 21); magnesium pemoline (82 mg/day) (n = 21); placebo (n = 21)	8 weeks	Porteus Mazes (1/2) Frostig Test of Perception (3/6) Continuous performance task (0/2) ITPA (0/1) Harris Goodenough Draw-a-Man (0/1) Bender Gestalt (0/1) Paired associate learning (0/1) [4/14]	WRAT Reading (0/1) Spelling (1/1) Arithmetic (0/1) Gray Oral Reading (1/1) Gates Diagnostic Reading (0/1) Comprehension (0/1) Speed ↓ (0/1) Accuracy (0/1) [2/8]
5. Conners (1972)[c]	Children referred for academic problems. Extent and type of learning problem unspecified	Methylphenidate (Dose ?) (n = 29); dextroamphetamine (Dose ?) (n = 24); placebo (n = 22)	8 weeks	Frostig Test of Perception (4/6) Bender Gestalt Draw-a-Man test (1/1) Porteus Mazes (1/2) Speech discrimination (3/3) Continuous performance task (2/2) [11/14]	WRAT Reading (0/1) Spelling (0/1) Arithmetic (0/1) [0/3]
6. Page, Janicki, Bernstein, Curran, & Michelli (1974)	Children selected for hyperkinesis due to MBD. Extent and nature of learning problem unspecified	Magnesium pemoline 2.69 mg/kg/day; placebo (total n = 238)	9 weeks	Lincoln Oseretsky (1/3) Porteus Mazes Test (0/1) Bender Gestalt (0/1) Goodenough-Harris Draw-a-Person (0/1) [1/6]	WRAT Reading (1/1) Spelling (0/1) Arithmetic (1/1) [2/3]

TABLE 16.1. (Cont'd)

Authors	Subjects	Drugs, group size	Duration	Perceptual-cognitive measures[a]	Achievement measures[a,b]
7. Gittleman-Klein & Klein, 1976	Children backward in reading by at least 2 years, free of cross-situational hyperactivity	Methylphenidate (52 mg/day) (n = 29); placebo (n = 32)	4 & 12 weeks	Porteus Mazes (3/4) Visual motor integration (2/2) Visual sequential memory (2/2) Paired associate learning (1/2) Draw-a-Person (0/2) Continuous performance task (1/4) [9/16]	WRAT Reading 4 weeks, 12 weeks (0/2) Arithmetic 4 weeks, 12 weeks (1/2) Spelling 4 weeks, 12 weeks (0/2) Gray Oral Reading 4 weeks, 12 weeks (0/2) [1/8]
8. Rie, Rie, Stewart, & Ambuel, 1976a	Children backward in reading by at least 6 months	Methylphenidate (21.1 mg/day) (n = 28); placebo (n = 28)	12 weeks	ITPA (1/4) Bender Gestalt (0/1) [1/5]	Iowa Test of Basic Skills Word analysis (1/1) Vocabulary (0/1) Reading (0/1) Spelling (0/1) Math 1 (0/2) [1/6]
9. Rie, Rie, Stewart, & Ambuel, 1976b	Children backward in reading by at least 6 months	Methylphenidate (23.1 mg/day) (n = 18); placebo (n = 18)	15 weeks	ITPA (1/4) Bender Gestalt (0/1) [1/5]	Iowa Test of Basic Skills Word analysis (1/1) Vocabulary (1/1) Reading (0/1) Spelling (0/1) Math 1 (0/2) [2/6]

10. Conners & Taylor, 1980	60 children with hyperkinesis due to MBD; 49 regarded as having "learning problems" in school	Magnesium pemoline (n = 19), 2.25 mg/kg/day; Methylphenidate (n = 20), 0.82 mg/kg/day; placebo (n = 21)	8 weeks	Porteus Mazes (0/2) Goodman–Fristoe–Woodcock Test for Auditory Discrimination (0/4) Draw-a-Man Test (1/2) Matching Familiar Figures (0/2) Minnesota Perceptuo-Diagnostic Test (0/2) Continuous performance test (0/6) [1/18]	WRAT Reading (0/1) Spelling (0/1) Arithmetic (0/1) [0/3]
11. Aman & Werry, 1982	Children retarded in reading by at least 2 years, mean deficit of 3.7 years	Methylphenidate (0.35 mg/kg) (n = 15); Diazepam 0.1 mg/kg (n = 15); placebo (n = 15)	6 days	Matching Familiar Figures (0/2) Auditory–Visual Integration (0/2) Continuous performance task (1/3) [1/7]	Neale Analysis of Reading Accuracy (0/1) Comprehension (0/1) Psycholinguistic analysis Self-correction (0/1) Syntax (0/1) Error rate (0/1) Repetition rate (0/1) Prompt rate (0/1) Letter recognition (0/1) Common words (0/1) [0/9]

TABLE 16.1. (Cont'd)

Authors	Subjects	Drugs, group size	Duration	Perceptual-cognitive measures[a]	Achievement measures[a,b]
12. Gittleman, Klein, & Feingold, 1983[d]	Children backward in reading by >1 year	Methylphenidate mean dose 1.19 mg/kg/day (n = 31); placebo (n = 30)	18 weeks; subjects reassessed 2 & 8 months after treatment	Vigilance (1/2) Paired associate learning (0/1) Visual Sequential Memory (1/1) Children's Embedded Figures (0/1) Raven's Matrices (1/1) Matching Familiar Figures (1/2) Porteus Mazes (1/2) Visual Motor Integration (0/1) Draw-a-Person (0/1) [5/12]	Basic Reading Skills (1/23 subtests) Gray Oral Reading Test (0/1) WRAT reading (0/1) Stanford Achievement Tests (1/5) Daniels & Diack Tests (1/10) Non–Reading Achievement Tests: WRAT Arithmetic (0/1) Spelling (0/1) Stanford Achievement Tests: Math Computation (1/1) Math Concepts (0/1) Math Application (1/1) Social Studies (1/1) Science (0/1) Total Math (1/1) [7/48]

13. Ballinger, Varley, & Nolen, 1984	Children with ADDH and backward in reading from 0.5 to 5.5 years (mean 2.4 years)	Methylphenidate, 0.303 and 0.636 mg/kg/day (n = 9); placebo (n = 9)	1 week	Sentence Completion Task (1/1) Letter Matching Task (2/2) [3/3]	Durrell Analysis of Reading Word recognition (0/1) Comprehension (0/1) Words Per minute (0/1) [0/3]
14. Pelham, Bender, Caddell, Booth, & Moorer, 1985	29 children, most of whom had ADDH. 13 subjects below grade level on reading, spelling, and arithmetic; 12 below in spelling only, 4 in reading, and 5 in arithmetic	Methylphenidate, 0.15, 0.30, and 0.60 mg/kg/day (n = 29); placebo (n = 29)	1 week for methylphenidate, 2 weeks for placebo	Nil [0/0]	Arithmetic worksheets Number of problems Attempted (1/1) Number correct (1/1) Reading comprehension Number of problems attempted ↓ (0/1) Number correct (0/1) Number correct/attempted (1/1) Spelling (0/1) Proportion correct (1/1) [4/7]
15. Douglas, Barr, O'Neill, & Britton, 1986	16 children of normal IQ with ADDH	Methylphenidate, 0.3 mg/kg, twice daily (n = 16); placebo (n = 16)	Acute (1 day)	Paired associate learning (1/1) [1/1]	Grade-appropriate arithmetic prolems (4/5) Arithmetic self-corrections (2/3) Grade appropriate spelling ↓ (0/1) Spelling study task (1/2) Word generation task (2/2) Arithmetic problems—classroom (2/3) Word generation task—classroom (1/2) Effort ratings (4/4) [16/22]

TABLE 16.1. (Cont'd)

Authors	Subjects	Drugs, group size	Duration	Perceptual-cognitive measures[a]	Achievement measures[a,b]
16. Famularo & Fenton, 1987[e]	10 children having ADD without hyperactivity. 4 children described as learning disabled, defined as >1 year deficiency in a subject area	Methylphenidate, 0.4 to 1.2 mg/kg/day (n = 10); no drug (n = 10)	1 school term each for predrug, methylphenidate, and postdrug	Nil [0/0]	Grade point average based on composite of reading, spelling, science, and mathematics (1/1) [1/1]
17. Kupietz, Winsberg, Richardson, Maitinsky, & Mendell, 1988; Richardson, Kupietz, Winsberg, Maitinsky, & Mendell, 1988	47 children with ADDH and reading disorder, defined as reading levels ≤75% of expected grade placement (= backwardness)	Methylphenidate, 0.3 mg/kg/day (n = 14), 0.5 mg/kg/day (n = 11), 0.7 mg/kg/day (n = 10); placebo (n = 12)	6 months	Paired associate learning (1/1)[f] Short-term memory[z] (1/2) [2/3]	Reading grade level First 14 weeks (1/1) Second 14 weeks (1/1) ↓ Gates MacGinitie Reading Tests Comprehension (0/1) Vocabulary (0/1) PIAT Comprehension (0/1) Reading Recognition (1/1)[g] Math (0/1)

Study	Sample	Treatment	Duration	Dependent measures		
18. Rapport, Stoner, DuPaul, Kelly, Tucker, & Schoeler, 1988	Children diagnosed as ADDH; 4 had been identified by schools as having learning disabilities	Methylphenidate, 5, 10, 15, 20 mg/day (n = 22); placebo (n = 22)	6 days	Decoding Skills Test Basal vocabulary Raw (1/1)[h] Basal vocabulary, instruction (0/1) Basal vocabulary, frustration (1/1)[h] Phonic patterns, real words (0/1) Phonic patterns, nonsense (0/1) [5/12] Academic Efficiency Score (1/1) [1/1]	Matching familiar figures (1/2) [1/2]	

Note: This table has been adapted by permission from: Aman, M. G. (1982) Psychotropic drugs in the treatment of reading disorders. In R. N. Malatesha & P. G. Aaron (Eds.), *Reading disorders: Varieties and treatments* (pp. 453–471). New York: Academic Press. WRAT, Wide Range Achievement Test; Bender Gestalt, Bender Visual Motor Gestalt Test; ITPA, Illinois Test of Psycholinguistic Abilities; Lincoln Oseretsky, Lincoln Oseretsky Test of Motor Development; PIAT, Peabody Individual Achievement Test.

[a] Excluding WISC. Fractions in parentheses (e.g., 2/4) indicate the proportion of dependent measures showing significant change. Fractions in square brackets [] indicate the total proportion of dependent measures affected by drug in that study.

[b] ↓ Arrow indicates worsening with drug treatment.

[c] The secondary study appearing in this publication (Conners, Rothschild, Eisenberg, Schwartz, & Robinson, 1969) is reported elsewhere in the table.

[d] Results reported for 18-week treatment period.

[e] Not blind, no placebo control.

[f] Significant high dose/placebo difference. Finding present at 1 of 3 time intervals.

[g] Significant at 1 of 3 time intervals.

[h] Significant at 2 of 3 time intervals.

Dosage Levels

Sprague and Sleator (1973, 1975, 1977) have presented data showing that dosage level may be an important consideration in determining clinical response to methylphenidate. Their studies have consistently shown that there appears to be a linear, dose-dependent relationship between dosage and parent and teacher ratings of behavioral improvement. In contrast, however, Sprague and Sleator have consistently observed a curvilinear relationship between performance on a memory recognition task and dose. On a group basis, subjects show steady improvements up to a dose of around 0.30 mg/kg of methylphenidate after which performance is said to decline, especially at high doses such as 1.0 mg/kg. Sprague and Sleator have argued that these findings could have important implications for clinical management (especially in learning impaired children) and that the objective should be to adjust dosage at a moderate level so that both learning and behavior are enhanced.

Only a few other investigators have assessed dose-response relationships, and comparison of results is made difficult by the fact that none of them have precisely replicated Sprague and Sleator's (1973, 1975, 1977) procedures. Gan and Cantwell (1982) tested a group of ADD-H children on a paired associate task, with doses graduating from 0 to 1.0 mg/kg. Like Sprague and Sleator, they observed the greatest enhancement of performance at 0.3 mg/kg. However, Kupietz, Winsberg, Richardson, Maitinsky, and Mendell (1988) observed a trend for performance on recognition memory and paired associate learning to show the greatest improvement with the highest dose used, namely 0.7 mg/kg. Similar linear dose-dependent responses have been reported with a vigilance task (Charles, Schain, & Zelniker, 1981), accuracy on the Matching Familiar Figures Task and academic efficiency (Rapport et al., 1988), and on number of arithmetic problems completed (Pelham, Bender, Caddell, Booth, & Moorer, 1985). Thus, some of the evidence for an inverted U-shaped dose-response curve appears to conflict with the phenomenon observed by Sprague and Sleator. However, it is worth nothing that none of the conflicting studies has replicated their procedures precisely. Furthermore, a number of the tasks used (e.g., vigilance [Charles et al., 1981], arithmetic problems attempted and/or completed [Pelham et al., 1985]) appear to reflect motivational and effort-related changes rather than true cognitive performance on the part of the subjects. Hence, the question of which dosage is optimal is still open to debate, and it may well eventuate that the answer depends in part on the cognitive task chosen. In any case, it seems to the present authors that this remains an important issue and one worthy of investigation insofar as the effects of drugs on achievement is concerned.

With respect to the studies under review, most (2–4, 7–10, 12, 16) used doses higher or markedly higher than those recommended by

Sprague and Sleator as optimal for learning. Two studies (entries 11, 15) employed doses similar to that designated as optimal for cognitive performance, and a further five investigations (13, 14, 16–18) used a range of dose levels that included that suggested by Sprague and Sleator.

Summary of Results

The results for the stimulant studies have been grouped according to the type of dependent measure. Cognitive–perceptual measures other than achievement measures appear in column 5 of Table 16.1; achievement measures and assessments of application to academic tasks appear in column 6. (IQ tests do not appear as dependent variables in Table 16.1 because it has been shown repeatedly that such instruments are highly insensitive to psychotropic drug effects [Sprague & Werry, 1971; Aman, 1984a].) Each type of measure has been summarized to indicate the number of variables assessed (the denominator) and the number found to be significantly improved by the drug under study (the numerator). For example, "(2/4)" would indicate that four variables were analyzed and two of them showed statistically significant drug enhancement. Finally, a pair of square brackets appears at the bottom of each set of variables for an entire study. These signify the total number of variables assessed and the proportion found to be significantly enhanced by pharmacotherapy for that study. This type of summary is useful in that it enables us to evaluate and compare a large volume of data from studies employing different designs and different dependent measures. However, it does tend to give disproportionate weight to single studies that have incorporated a large number of dependent variables (e.g., 12, 15), a potential difficulty to which readers should be alert.

Summarizing over all 18 studies, we find that 51 of 130 (39%) perceptual–cognitive measures showed significant drug enhancement, whereas 43 of 148 (29%) achievement/academic application measures showed significant improvement with pharmacotherapy. Thus, overall, the various perceptual measures and cognitive performance tests were more sensitive to stimulant drugs than achievement and academic application measures. The same approach can be applied to compare the effects of selection procedures (ADHD vs. non-ADHD subjects), severity of learning disability (severe vs. mild/unspecified), dosage levels (high dose vs. low and/or a range of doses), and duration of treatment (acute vs. long-term).

Studies that selected subjects for the presence of ADHD (6, 10, 13–18) tended to have a higher proportion of achievement/scholastic application improved by stimulant drugs than did studies that did not specify ADHD as a selection criterion (1, 2–4, 7–9, 11, 12). The proportions of achievement variables affected were 56% and 15%, respectively. A similar procedure was used to compare studies that employed a stringent definition of learning disorders (7, 11, 12, 17) with those using weak criteria or unspecified types of learning disabilities (1–6, 8–10, 13–16, 18). The percentages of academic variables influenced by treatment were 17% and 42%, respectively. Thus, children with *less* severe learning disorders appear to be more readily affected by stimulant medication. Studies were also divided into high dose experiments (doses well above 0.3 mg/kg methylphenidate or its equivalent) (2–4, 7–10, 12, 16) and low dose experiments or those incorporating a range of doses (11, 13–15, 17, 18). Among the "high dose" studies, 17% of the achievement/application variables were enhanced by stimulant medication, whereas in the remainder 32% of variables showed facilitation. However, interpretation of these findings is not at all straightforward, because improvement within the studies classified as "low dosage" often occurred at higher dose levels within dose studies (13, 14, 17,18). Finally, the studies were categorized according to duration of treatment: 4 weeks or less (2, 11, 13–15, 18) and 8 weeks or longer (1, 3–10, 12, 16, 17). The proportions of improved achievement and/or scholastic application variables as a function of duration of drug treatment were 48% and 21%, respectively, favoring the studies of short duration.

Critique of Studies of Stimulant Drugs

To sum over all studies, a substantial proportion of cognitive–perceptual variables (39%) did change, whereas a smaller proportion of scholastic achievement/application variables (29%) were also affected by pharmacotherapy. Thus, demonstration of drug facilitation of achievement and related performance appears to be more difficult than showing improvements on more specific types of cognitive test. Studies that deliberately screened subjects for ADHD obtained a much greater proportion of scholastic change (56%) than did those employing other entry criteria. This suggests that the presence of Attention Deficit Hyperactivity Disorder as a *primary* presenting complaint may be an important variable potentially capable of moderating response to stimulant therapy. At the same time, it should be noted that a number of follow-up studies of hyperactive children who did receive long-term stimulant therapy have generally been unable to document long-term drug-related scholastic gains (Aman, 1984b; Weiss & Hechtman, 1986).

The findings from studies with severely learning disabled children in comparison with those having milder or unspecified learning problems are somewhat discouraging. Perhaps not surprisingly, they suggest that children having more severe learning disorders are less likely than mildly disabled children to respond to pharmacotherapy with stimulants. In the writers' view, the dosage comparisons do not shed much light on optimal clinical practice regarding dosage adjustment. In our opinion, this is because the dependent variables of interest in these studies tended to reflect greater motivation (or "drive") than acquisition of new learning (e.g., 14, 18). The comparison of studies in terms of duration of treatment actually favored the short-term investigations, an issue we shall return to later.

In our view, the most comprehensive studies of stimulant therapy in learning disabled children were those carried out by Gittelman, Klein, and Feingold (1983, study 12 of Table 16.1) and Richardson, Kupietz, Winsberg, Maitinsky, and Mendell (1988, study 17). Both studies used stringent definitions for subject selection and both assessed changes over relatively long periods of stimulant treatment (18 and 28 weeks, respectively), allowing for the possibility of true gains in achievement. Perhaps most importantly, both studies provided for drug-free assessments of achievement, so that any changes would reflect relatively long-term gains in learning rather than the possible transitory effects of methylphenidate on task performance. At follow-up, Gittelman et al. (12) observed little in the way of sustained reading gains (1 of 34 test variables) whereas Richardson et al. (17) reported improvements on a minority of achievement measures (3 of 10 test variables). It must be noted that Gittelman et al. used considerably higher doses (mean 1.2 mg/kg) than often seen in the literature, but nevertheless it must be concluded that these are rather discouraging findings.

What then can we conclude from the literature about the value of the stimulants for treating children with learning disorders? First, we have some reservations about the actual characterization of results used in some reports. What are reported as "learning" measures in some studies (14, 15, 18) probably reflect more the impact of drug-induced motivation and drive (i.e., performance) rather than new acquisition. This is an important distinction and one that has often been ignored in the past. Thus, many of these studies may have been reiterating the oft-observed short-term effect of stimulants on task performance (especially on vigilance-type tasks) (Aman, 1978) rather than permanent gains in the body of acquired knowledge. This is supported by the fact that gains were, if anything, greater in the short-term than in the long-term studies, a finding that runs counter to what would be expected if skill acquisition were being affected in a material way. Nevertheless, it is reasonable to expect that increases in drive and motivation might translate into academic gains over time. The available evidence from Table 16.1 suggests that such gains, if they do occur, are rather subtle and difficult to measure. The data also suggest that children with true ADHD symptomatology and those with mild learning impairments are more likely to benefit from such therapy than those without coexisting hyperactivity or with severe learning disabilities. This may seem like a small advantage to be gleaned from such therapy, given the substantial interest and research invested in stimulants over the years. On the other hand, perhaps we have been asking too much of a pill to reverse a lifetime of learning impairment. The data, such as they are, at least suggest some potentially profitable avenues for treatment and future research.

The Nootropics

A more recent addition to the pharmacotherapy of learning disabilities are the nootropics, a term derived from the Greek *noos* (mind), and *trepein* (toward) (Dimond & Brouwers, 1976). The nootropics are related chemically to the neurotransmitter gramma-aminobutyric acid (GABA) and it has been suggested that these drugs act on the cerebral cortex and related telencephalic structures and thereby enhance higher cortical functions without apparent stimulant or sedative effects (Giurgea, 1973; Union Chimique Beege 1976, cited from Simeon et al., 1980). Dimond and Brouwers (1976) reported that nootropics improved verbal learning, short-term memory, and performance in normal adults. Other studies have indicated that these drugs might be selectively effective for tasks requiring left hemisphere functioning. In addition, nootropics are said to be well tolerated without causing appreciable side effects. These findings encouraged researchers to investigate the potential of nootropics with populations having diminished mental abilities, such as individuals with geropsychiatric problems, mental retardation, and specific learning disabilities.

Piracetam (2-pyrrolidone acetamide; Nootropil, Nootropyl, Nootrop, Noostan, Barcan) is the most prominent nootropic drug in learning disabilities research. Two recent reviews (Coles, 1987; Gualtieri, Golden, & Fahs, 1983) indicated that contrary to the most promising claims that have been made for piracetam, it has had a modest, if not disappointing record as far as improving cognitive functioning is concerned. One of the reviewers, Coles (1987), generally adopted a skeptical position in his treatment of the pharmacological literature in learning disabilities. But regardless of his polemical style of debate, Coles points out inconsistencies in the studies that are worth considering. His skepticism is specifically targeted toward a series of publications from a large multicenter research project in the United States that was supported by the drug manufacturer, Union Chimique Belge, that is responsible for almost all of the major studies to date.

In preparation for this chapter we conducted a computerized literature search for an exhaustive list of archival publications on the topic. We were able to identify 16 piracetam publications in learning disabilities, which are excerpted in Table 16.2. In the interest of brevity, these studies are referred to hereafter by their identifying numerals in the table. To avoid any possible confusion with Table 16.1, the studies from the two tables are numbered consecutively.

TABLE 16.2. Studies of Piracetam in learning disabled children.

Authors	Subjects	Drugs, group size	Duration	Cognitive/ psychophysiological measures	Achievement measures
19. Wilsher, Atkins, & Manfield, 1979	17-to 24-year-old dyslexic males; controls matched for IQ[a]	LD: piracetam, 1,600 mg daily (n = 9); placebo (n = 7). Controls: piracetam, 1,600 mg daily (n = 6); placebo (n = 8)	3 weeks	Rote/serial learning (3/3) Dichotic listening (1/1) Tachistoscopic visual processing (0/1) [4/5]	Nil [0,0]
20. Simeon et al., 1980	Boys backward in reading, spelling, or arithmetic by >1 year, and PIQ higher than VIQ by 15 or more points	Piracetam, 4,800 mg daily (n = 29), placebo (n = 29)	4 or 8 weeks	Neuropsychological test battery (unspecified): Verbal task (0/1) Nonverbal task (0/1) Sensory task (0/1) [0/4]	Nil [0/0]
21. Volakva, Simeon, Simeon, Cho, & Reker, 1981	Boys backward in reading, spelling, or arithmetic by >1 year, and PIQ higher than VIQ by 15 or more points	Piracetam, 4,800 mg daily (n = 29); placebo (n = 29)	4 or 8 weeks	Power spectral (EEG) analyses: Delta activity increased (1/1) Fast beta activity (0/1) Average EEG frequency increased (1/1) [2/3]	Nil [0/0]
22. Simeon et al., 1983	Boys backward in reading, spelling, or arithmetic by >1 year, and PIQ higher than VIQ by 15 or more points	Piracetam, 4,800 mg daily (n = 29); placebo (n = 29)	4 or 8 weeks	Continuous performance task (0/2) [0/2]	Nil [0/0]

TABLE 16.2. Studies of Piracetam in learning disabled children.

Authors	Subjects	Drugs, group size	Duration	Cognitive/ psychophysiological measures	Achievement measures
23. Wilsher & Milewski, 1983	Reading retarded boys with reading quotients ≤0.85	Piracetam 3,300 mg daily (n = 30); placebo (n = 29)	12 weeks	WISC–R: Similarities (1/1) Vocabulary (0/1) [1/2]	Nil [0/0]
24. Chase, Schmitt, Russel, & Tallal, 1984	Reading retarded boys with reading quotients ≤0.85	Piracetam 3,300 mg daily (n = 28); placebo (n = 27)	12 weeks	WISC–R Digit Span (0/1) Rapid Automatized Naming Test (0/4) Repetition Test (0/3) Token Test (0/2) Paired Associate Learning (0/1) [0/11]	WRAT Spelling (0/1) Free writing (1/2) Gilmore Oral Reading (1/3) Gilmore Composite Reading (2/2) Gates-McKillop Syllabification (0/1) [4/9]
25. Conners et al., 1984	Reading retarded boys with reading quotients ≤ 0.85	Piracetam, 3,300 mg daily (n = 8); placebo (n = 5)	12 weeks	Vigilance task (0/6) Event related potentials (9/24) [9/30]	Nil [0/0]
26. Helfgott, Rudel, & Krieger, 1984	Reading retarded boys with reading quotients ≤ 0.85	Piracetam, 3,300 mg daily (n = 16)	12 weeks	Nil [0/0]	WRAT Reading (0/1) Gilmore Oral Reading (1/1) [1/2]
27. Rudel & Helfgott, 1984	Reading retarded boys with reading quotients ≤0.85	Piracetam, 3,300mg daily (n = 29); placebo (n = 30)	12 weeks	Neimark Memorization Strategy Test: Number recalled (1/1) Clustering (0/1) Organizational strategy (0/1) [1/3]	Nil [0/0]
28. Dilanni et al., 1985	Reading retarded boys with reading quotients ≤0.85	Piracetam, 3,300mg daily (n = 133); placebo (n = 124)	12 weeks	WISC–R Digit Span (0/1) Rapid Automatized Naming Test (0/4) [0/5]	Gilmore Oral Reading (1/3) WRAT Spelling (0/1) Free writing (0/2) Gates-McKillop Syllabification (0/1) [1/7]

Study	Description	Dosage	Duration		
29. Wilsher, Atkins, & Manfield, 1985	Boys retarded in reading or spelling by 2 or more years	Piracetam, 3,300mg daily (n = 21); placebo (n = 19)	8 weeks	Nil [0/0]	British Abilities Scales—Word reading (1/1) Neale Analysis of Reading (2/2) [3/3]
30. Conners et al., 1986	Reading retarded boys with reading quotients ≤0.85	Piracetam, 3,300mg daily (n = 8); placebo (n = 5)	12 weeks	Vigilance task (0/6) Event-related potentials (5/24) [5/30]	Nil [0/0]
31. Helfgott, Rudel, & Kairam, 1986	Reading retarded boys with reading quotients ≤0.85	Piracetam, 3,300mg daily (n = 30); placebo (n = 30)	12 weeks	Paired associate learning (0/5) WISC–R Digit Span (0/1) Rapid Automatized Naming Test (1/4) Neimark Memorization Strategy Test (1/3) [2/13]	WRAT Reading (1/1) [1/1]
32. Tallal, Chase, Russell, & Schmidt, 1986	Reading retarded boys with reading quotients ≤0.85	Piracetam, 3,300mg daily (n = 28); placebo (n = 27)	12 weeks	Rapid Automatized Naming Test (1/4) [1/4]	Gilmore Oral Reading (1/3) Gilmore Composite Reading (2/2) Gates-McKillop Syllabification (0/1) WRAT Spelling (0/1) Free Writing (1/2) [4/9]
33. Conners et al., 1987	Reading retarded children with reading quotients ≤0.85	Piracetam, 3,300mg daily (n = 15); placebo (n = 14)	36 weeks	Vigilance task (1/6) Event-related potentials (4/13) [5/19]	Nil [0/0]
34. Wilsher et al., 1987	Reading retarded children with reading quotients ≤0.85	Piracetam, 3,300mg daily (n = 112); placebo (n = 113)	36 weeks	Nil [0/0]	Gray Oral Reading (2/2) Gilmore Oral Reading (1/3) WRAT–R Reading (1/1) [4/6]

WRAT, Wide Range Achievement Test; WISC–R, Wechsler Intelligence Scale for Children—Revised.
[a] As defined by Thomson, 1977.

Methodology

Overall, the quality of the reviewed piracetam studies for learning disabilities, as far as the Sprague and Werry (1971) criteria are concerned, was very good. All of these studies were conducted in double-blind fashion, using matching placebos. Similarly, all of these studies used acceptable group assignment procedures. Subjects were either randomly assigned to the drug condition (e.g., 19), or a restricted random assignment method was used to assure roughly equal numbers of subjects in each treatment condition (e.g., entry 24).

Several different types of research designs were employed. Typically, these studies included only clinical populations of subjects with learning disabilities, although one study included a healthy control group (19). Drug–placebo crossover designs were adopted in some of the earlier studies (19–22). In one of them, however, carryover effects occurred despite a 3-week washout period between treatment phases (19). The authors interpreted those carryover effects as attributable to piracetam rather than to learning (without elaborating on the rationale of this conclusion), and proceeded to analyze their data in a between-groups fashion, dropping the crossover (i.e., final treatment phase) data. Subsequently, crossover designs disappeared from the learning disability piracetam literature, and the random assignment parallel group design with placebo control became the most popular alternative. The parallel-groups drug trials lasted either 8 (29) or 12 (23–28, 30–32) weeks. In two cases the trials lasted an entire academic year, or 36 weeks (33, 34). In many of the studies, much data was collected and elaborate procedures were employed to reduce, transform, and analyze the data. It was sometimes quite difficult to describe all of the data management procedures undertaken, and in fact too seldom were the published descriptions satisfactory. In those cases where the operations could be adequately identified, statistical analysis varied from being simplistic to highly sophisticated.

As discussed previously, the definition of the subject population is a crucial issue in learning disability research. It can be argued that achievement level should not be defined solely as a lag behind the subject's age, but also with respect to his presumed mental ability. Overall, the definitions of learning disability in the piracetam literature were satisfactory in this respect. None of the 16 studies had defined their subjects merely by a lag between chronological age and reading age. In one subgroup of studies (20–22) learning disability was operationalized as a significant discrepancy between verbal and performance WISC–R IQs, with the verbal IQ being at least 15 points lower; the full WISC–R IQ had to be in the normal range. In addition, the Wide Range Achievement Test (WRAT) reading, spelling, or arithmetic levels had to be at least one grade placement behind age expectation. Other studies selected subjects on the basis of a reading quotient (RQ), which was to be .85 or lower. Two types of reading quotients were used. The first one (RQ_1) was defined as a ratio of reading age to mental age (23, 24, 26–28, 31, 32), whereas the second (RQ_2) included both mental age and chronological age in the denominator but gave double the weight to mental age (25, 30, 33, 34).[2] The majority of studies included only boys, 8 years of age or older, whereas two studies included girls as well (33, 34).

Another feature was the use of well chosen exclusion criteria applied across a large proportion of these studies. Explicitly excluded were subjects who had neurological and emotional problems or who experienced educational deprivation (23, 26–34), and who were receiving other psychoactive medication (23, 28, 32–34). The dosage levels ranged from 1,600 mg to 4,800 mg per day. In the majority of studies a fixed dosage of 3,300 mg was used (23–34). Dosages were fixed throughout irrespective of subjects' weights or responses, and administration was usually twice daily. We were unable to find dose-response studies of piracetam in this population.

Summary of Results

A summary of these 16 publications is complicated by the fact that the results were often inconsistent within and across studies. Furthermore, many measures were used, consisting of standardized instruments and ad hoc tests, many of which were highly interdependent. In addition, it appears that some research groups published their results at different stages of the protocol with inconsistent results. Typically the later versions showed more favorable results in terms of positive drug effects. This suggests that subjects were added to an already existing subject pool to increase inferential power. Although this approach is, of course, not germane to piracetam research, it often left the reviewers wondering what should be taken as the "definitive" study from a certain research series, and how the results from the earlier publications should be treated. As in the previous section of this chapter, we divided the results into two broad groups of outcome variables: nonreading (perceptual– cognitive, behavioral, and electrophysiological) changes and achievement measures.

Perceptual–Cognitive Measures

These measures can be broken down into measures of memory, vigilance, and other performance variables. The only test for long-term memory

---

[2] When the full scale IQ is close to 100, RQ_1 and RQ_2 will produce very comparable quotients. However, when the full scale IQ differs from the normal range, the two quotients are increasingly different. For example, with the IQ below normal, RQ_2—all other variables being equal—tends to be numerically lower than RQ_1.

retrieval was the Rapid Automatized Naming Test (RAN), a nonstandardized measure developed by Denckla and Rudel (1976) that generates four different naming measures. Out of four studies (24, 28, 31, 32), only letter naming scores were found to be significantly different in two instances (31, 32). Color, object, and number naming did not differentiate piracetam from placebo subjects. Short-term memory was investigated with the Neimark Memorization Strategy Test (27, 31) the WISC–R Digit Span subtest (24, 28, 31), a serial learning task (19), a paired associate visual memory task (24), a verbal paired-associate test (31), dichotic listening (19), and the Repetition Test (24). Of these, two of three Neimark test variables, all three nonsense syllables variables, and the dichotic listening measure were enhanced by piracetam. However, none of the other short-term memory tests produced significant results. Thus, 6 of 17 short-term memory test variables were sensitive to piracetam. Vigilance was assessed in four studies (22, 25, 30, 33), but none of these measures improved at traditionally accepted probability levels with piracetam, regardless of the nature of the stimuli. Of all the other cognitive–perceptual measures collected, only the WISC–R Similarities subtest was found to differ significantly between piracetam and placebo groups.

Behavior Ratings

Only two studies (20, 22) included behavior rating scales, namely the Clinical Global Impressions Scale, the Children's Psychiatric Rating Scale, Conners' Parent and Teacher Rating Scales, and the Myklebust Pupil Rating Scale. However, none of these measures indicated bahavioral changes. Thus, it does not appear that piracetam has much if any effect on overt behavior, at least given the medication regime employed in these studies.

Electrophysiological Studies

Electrophysiological studies were conducted primarily by two research teams (21, 22, 25, 30, 33). They were modeled on earlier experiments with normal adults (Misurec & Strnad, 1980) and geriatric patients (Bente, Glatthaar, Ulrich, & Lewinsky, 1978; Vencovsky et al., 1980) that showed that piracetam increased electroencephalogram (EEG) power in certain frequency bands. Since these findings were similar to those observed with stimulant drugs, they were seen as a possible indication that piracetam may increase alertness or decrease fatigue (20–22). Another hypothesis addressed by this EEG research was laterality, specifically the possibility that piracetam may have selective effects on the left hemisphere with its potential relationship to verbal tasks (25, 30, 33). It was found that piracetam caused a decrease in delta activity and an increase in average EEG frequency (20, 21). Also, a proportional relationship between predrug occipital delta activity and a related reduction in delta frequencies was found (22). Conners and his group (25, 30, 33) used event-related potentials (ERPs) in connection with a continuous performance task that required a distinction between letter and nonletter stimuli and several significant changes in ERP parameters were observed. However, EEG methods have been of limited usefulness in explaining the effects of piracetam due to a lack of change on collateral cognitive and perceptual measures.

Achievement Measures

Achievement measures consisted of reading and spelling/writing tests and showed a slightly better success ratio than the perceptural–cognitive measures. The reading tests included the WRAT Reading subtest (26, 31, 34), the British Abilities Scales Word Reading subtest (29), the Neale Analysis of Reading Ability (29), the Gray Oral Reading Test (34), and the Gilmore Oral Reading Test. The scores of the Gilmore Oral Reading Test were compared in two ways: direct scores of reading accuracy and comprehension (24, 26, 28, 32, 34) and composite scores (24, 32), which were transformed and joined to reflect a combination of reading rate, accuracy, and comprehension. Reading comprehension was tested in four studies by the Gilmore Oral Reading and/or the Gray Oral Reading Test. In one study the comprehension score of the Gilmore Oral Reading Test was the only reading measure (28), but this was not affected by the drug. In two other studies both the direct and the composite Gilmore comprehension scores were reported (24, 32), and each time only the composite score was improved by piracetam. Only in one study were the usual Gilmore and the Gray Oral comprehension scores presented together (34), and in that instance both comprehension scores were significantly different between the piracetam and the control group. Thus, strong evidence of piracetam enhancing reading comprehension was found in only one study. These differences were obtained in a large group study with 81 subjects receiving piracetam for 36 weeks and 77 control subjects, and the differences in outcome scores were small. Therefore, it must be questioned whether the improvement observed in this large study can be regarded as clinically significant, and what proportion of individuals actually benefited academically from piracetam. Reading rate and accuracy showed even fewer improvements than comprehension. Writing and spelling achievement was tested by the WRAT Spelling subtest (24, 28, 32), the Gates-McKillop Syllabification test (28, 32), and 5 minutes of free writing (24, 28, 32). Again, the evidence for a therapeutic effect was weak. Writing/spelling tests were only marginally sensitive to piracetam. Only the writing error of the free writing task showed improvement in two (24, 32) of three studies (24, 28, 32).

Conclusion

In summary, after reviewing 16 studies, some of which lasted up to 36 weeks and had large samples of subjects, the conclusion must be that the effect of piracetam in improving performance in learning disabilities is unclear. The differences found in some of the studies were inconsistent and are so far primarily of academic, rather than practical, interest. They are certainly not sufficient to recommend the clinical use of this drug. On the other hand, none of the early claims of piracetam's safety have been repudiated by the studies reviewed here. Even after a 36-week protocol involving 112 subjects taking a 3,300 mg daily dose, no serious adverse effects were observed (28), a finding echoed by others (20), who noted the absence of anorexia and insomnia in their subjects.

Antimotion Sickness Medications

Two psychiatrists, Harold Levinson and Jan Frank, have promoted antimotion sickness medication for treating "dysmetric dyslexic and dyspraxic" individuals. These authors developed a "3-D optical scanner" that shows a moving foreground against a stationary background or, conversely, a stationary foreground against a moving background. According to Frank and Levinson (1976–1977), most dyslexic children perceive the moving stimulus sequence as blurred at much lower speeds than do normal children. Based in part on this observation, Levinson and Frank have speculated that a dysfunction within the cerebellar–vestibular system, rather than the cerebral cortex, is the physiological basis of "dysmetric [meaning inability to arrest a movement at a desired point] dyslexia" (Frank & Levinson, 1977; Levinson, 1980). The authors hypothesize that the cerebellum regulates visual input transmission speed and "coordinates the spatio-temporal order of the sensory input in a manner analogous to its recognized . . . role in regulating and coordinating the motor output" (Frank & Levinson, 1977, p. 422). They further speculate that motion sickness medications (a) act to improve "cerebellar vestibular harmonizing capacity" and (b) that this will make them useful in treating dysmetric dyslexia and dyspraxia (Levinson and Frank's term for developmental dyslexia) (Frank & Levinson, 1977).

Levinson and Frank report that a series of antimotion sickness drugs are useful for treating most dyslexic individuals. These drugs include cyclizine (Marezine), meclizine (Antivert), dimenhydrinate (Dramamine), diphenhydramine (Benadryl), and methylphenidate (Ritalin) (Levinson, 1980). The claimed utility of these is based on a series of clinical anecdotes regarding various patients so treated. Levinson (1980) reports that in one "pilot" study of 280 cases, more than one third of the patients responded favorably to antimotion sickness drug thereapy. In a subsequent study of 200 patients, 77% were said to show some degree of mild to dramatic improvement in dyslexic functioning. The following categories were said to show "positive dysmetric and dysgraphic response patterns" to treatment: reading ability; writing activity; spelling; arithmetic; directionality, spatial organization, and planning; balance and coordination; foreground–background discrimination; speech; memory; time sense; mood; self image; body image; frustration tolerance; anxiety tolerance; socialization; and acceptance of symptoms (Frank & Levinson, 1976–1977).

However, we were able to locate no quantitative data regarding reading or premedication/postmedication reading score comparisons in Levinson and Frank's publications to support their contention that these are useful agents for treating dysmetric dyslexia. In characteristic prose, Levinson (1980) explained his failure to perform properly controlled clinical trials as follows:

Because these pilot pharmacologic studies were entirely exploratory, and thus significantly "blind," an open-ended clinical–qualitative or historical approach was deemed an essential first step. . . . It seemed far wiser for the author to scan, and possibly even sketch, the panoramic clinical response to the antimotion sickness medications before limiting himself in advance to the "blind" but detailed measurements of only a few preselected, singly appearing variables suspended in a completely uncharted scientific cosmos. (p. 236)

Needless to say, Levinson's pilot "studies" fulfill none of the methodological criteria specified by Sprague and Werry (1971). Nevertheless, Levinson and Frank's notions have been publicized in the popular media and Levinson is purported to charge $500 for his diagnostic treatment work-up (cf. Coles, 1987). As of 1976, these authors reported that they had examined more than 1,000 children having specific, primary, or developmental dyslexia (Frank & Levinson, 1975–1976).

Recently at least three scientific comparisons have appeared in the professional literature that challenge Levinson and Frank's theory that large percentages of dyslexic individuals have a visual oculomotor dysfunction. Brown et al. (1983), Polatajko (1987), and Shumway-Cook, Horak, and Black (1987) all tested matched groups of learning disabled and control children in rotational experiments in which either the subjects or their environmental surrounds were experimentally rotated to assess vestibulo-ocular effects. None of these studies observed significant differences in vestibulo-ocular reflexes between learning disabled and control subjects. Polatjko concluded that normal and learning disabled children do not differ in terms of nystagmus elicited by both visual and vestibular input (optokinetic nystagmus), whereas Shumway-Cook et al. concluded that balance and coordination problems could not be attributed to sensory inputs from the vestibular system.

It is also noteworthy that Levinson and Frank included methylphenidate as a member of the antimotion sickness drugs. As noted by Masland and Usprich (1981), Levinson appears to use the term *cerebellar-harmonizing agent* for any drug improving dysmetric functioning, regardless of chemical structure or clinical group to which the drug belongs. Thus, inclusion of methylphenidate appears to be based on circular reasoning. Furthermore, to the extent that methylphenidate was used conjointly with true antimotion sickness drugs, this may have even further confounded Levinson's observations for, as we have already seen, methyphenidate may have some legitimate role to play in treating children with learning disabilities and it also tends to normalize behavior in children with Attention Deficit Disorder.

Recently, Fagan, Kaplan, Raymond, and Edgington (1988) published a controlled study of meclizine, meclizine plus methylphenidate, methylphenidate, and placebo in 12 children with delayed reading and who had at least two indicators of cerebellar dysfunction. Acute administration of meclizine failed to influence overall (group) reading performance, although some individual subjects did show positive fluctuations. This was followed by a 3-month crossover trial with meclizine in six subjects who had shown possible improvements during the acute trial. No drug improvements were found in reading performance, parent and teacher behavior ratings, or saccadic latency or eye tracking errors. However, a significant improvement was found on ocular motor stability during steady fixation. Fagan et al. concluded that optimism for the clinical value of meclizine and its analogues is not justified.

Most of the antimotion sickness drugs have marked antihistaminic proporties. In this regard, it is worth summarizing a study of promethazine (Phenergan, Mepergan), which has been used as both an antimotion sickness and antinausea drug. It is a phenothiazine derivative with a potent antihistaminic action. Zametkin, Reeves, Webster, and Werry (1986) compared the effects of promethazine with baseline conditions and with methylphenidate in eight children with Attention Deficit Disorder. Zametkin et al. found that not only did promethazine fail to improve behavior, but it actually appeared to worsen the behavior of several subjects. Given that there appears to be a marked overlap between the presence of learning disabilities and of hyperactivity in many children, this study suggests even greater caution in the use of drugs that were principally antihistaminic in action.

Antihistamines are also anticholinergic, and it is probably this property that explains their psychotropic action. According to Werry (1980), most drugs with marked anticholinergic effects tend to impair learning performance. Obviously we do not believe that there is an established or even a likely role for the use of antimotion sickness drugs in the treatment of learning disabled children. In fact, we believe that these drugs could be positively harmful to some children, especially those who have marked inattention and overactivity.

Antianxiety Drugs

It has long been noted that there is often an association between learning disabilities (and more specifically, reading disorders) and the presence of high anxiety levels. In an early study, Robinson (1946) surveyed prominent workers concerning emotional and personality factors found in children with specific reading problems. Timidity, extreme self-consciousness, inferiority feelings, and withdrawal were all consistently and frequently cited as correlates of these reading problems. Using different rating instruments, McCarthy and Paraskevopoulos (1969) and Aman (1979) found that teachers rated learning disabled and reading retarded children, respectively, subtstantially higher than controls on subscales related to tension, anxiety, and social withdrawal (see Aman & Singh, 1983, for review of personality correlates in reading disorders). Thus, persistent failure in learning to read or master other academic skills may place learning disabled children at high risk for developing anxiety disorders, and this in turn may interfere with special educational efforts to help such children overcome their learning problems. Conversely, initially high anxiety may interfere with reading acquisition, which may lead to more debilitating anxiety. For this reason some authors (Freed, Abrams, & Peifer, 1959; Millichap, 1968; Westman, Arthur, & Scheidler, 1965) have recommended that benzodiazepines and other anxiolytic drugs may have therapeutic value in learning disabled children.

McNair (1973) and Cole (1986) have reviewed the effects of antianxiety drugs, in particular the benzodiazepines, on learning in adults. In general, both authors concluded that the benzodiazepines tend to impair acquisition in normal subjects. However, the effects of these drugs depend in part on type of task used, and under certain conditions (e.g., stress-inducing) an enhancement may even occur. Research on the cognitive effects of these drugs with children is virtually nonexistent (Rapoport, Mikkelson, & Werry, 1978). Furthermore, the use of such drugs in anxiety disorders in children is relatively unstudied and the results to date are largely equivocal (Werry & Aman, 1980).

Only three studies could be located of the benzodiazepine anxiolytic drugs in children with learning disabilities. Fenelon, Holland, and Johnson (1972) assessed the effects of nitrazepam (Mogadon) in backward readers in a double-blind, placebo-controlled study. they found that nitrazepam reduced the amount of abnormal EEG activity (some of which was of equivocal significance) in these children. Furthermore, the EEG spatial index, which was said to reflect appropriate spatial differentiation in the brain, was significantly increased with nitrazepam. Unfortunately, no measure of reading performance was taken, so that it cannot be determined whether the EEG changes were associated with relevant adaptive changes.

In an extension to this study, Fenelon and Wortley (1973) compared the effects of nitrazepam in reading disabled subjects to those of placebo in normal controls and reading disabled children. The controls were found to have the lowest two-flash fusion thresholds (TFTs), which are said to be inversely related to arousal. Placebo-treated reading disabled subjects had the highest TFTs, and the performance of subjects receiving nitrazepam fell between these groups but tended to approximate that of controls. Unfortunately, no predrug measures were reported so that it cannot be determined whether the three groups would have performed this way regardless of drug condition. As in the previous report (Fenelon et al., 1972), no changes in reading performance were measured.

Finally, in a study summarized previously, Aman and Werry (1982) compared diazepam (Valium), in doses of 0.10 mg/kg, with methylphenidate and placebo in severely reading retarded children (see study 11, Table 16.1). Diazepam reduced omission errors on a continuous performance task and caused improvements on a measure of dynamic tremor, although most cognitive and motor variables were not affected. Both active drugs (methylphenidate and diazepam) caused some trends in the direction of improved reading performance, but none of these comparisons actually reached statistical significance.

Obviously, this is not a satisfactory data base from which to make treatment recommendations. Indeed, the use of the benzodiazepines for any disorder is largely unstudied in children, regardless of the presence or not of a learning disability. At this time, the use of these drugs for treating children with learning disabilities would have to be regarded as experimental unless there were other compelling clinical reasons for employing them.

Neuroleptics (Antipsychotics, Major Tranquilizers)

With the rationale that reading disability may be a manifestation of underlying anxiety and emotional maladjustment, Freed et al. (1959) conducted a trial of neuroleptic drugs in children who were at least 3 years backward in reading. Using a between-groups design, several conditions were compared in the 44 children who took part, as follows: placebo, placebo plus reading instruction, chlorpromazine (Thorazine), chlorpromazine plus reading instruction, and prochlorperazine (Compazine; Stemetil) plus reading instruction. Depending on the measure used, significant reading gains were observed over time for the following comparisons: placebo plus reading instruction, chlorpromazine plus reading instruction, and prochlorperazine plus reading instruction. Although the active drug plus remediation groups performed better than groups receiving other treatment combinations, they did not appear to have surpassed the placebo plus remediation group at statistically significant levels.

Aman (1978) has summarized much of the research on the laboratory cognitive effects of the neuroleptic drugs in children. At higher doses, depression of performance has been noted in attention span, rote verbal learning, response time and accuracy on a recognition memory task, and mental age scores on the Porteus Mazes task. However, lack of effects is a much more common finding overall than depression of function. Furthermore, in one study of haloperidol treatment in hyperactive children and unsocialized aggressive children, it was found that low doses (0.025 mg/kg/day) actually facilitated performance, whereas higher doses (0.05 mg/kg) caused performance decrements (Werry & Aman, 1975). Winsberg and Yepes (1978) noted that studies of neuropleptic drugs in normal adults have frequently observed worsening on cognitive tasks, whereas studies of patients with thought disorders have often shown enhancement of cognitive function. Beyond their use in childhood autism, neuroleptics are occasionally used for the management of hyperactivity (as well as certain other disorders) in children. Depending on the choice of drug and dose, studies have often documented behavioral improvements as assessed by parents, teachers, and doctors (Winsberg & Yepes, 1978). It is not clear whether such behavioral improvements will translate into collateral gains in learning, although most past studies have been negative in this respect (Aman, 1978; Winsberg & Yepes, 1978).

Obviously one study with children having reading disorders is an insufficient basis for making judgments regarding the value of neuroleptics in specific learning disabilities. However, our best guess is that unless there is a compelling reason for employing such agents (e.g., severe hyperactivity) neuroleptics are highly unlikely to improve academic attainment.

Antidepressants

We know of only one study that has evaluated the effects of these drugs on academic performance, this being a study of imipramine in hyperactive boys who were followed up at 1 year (Quinn & Rapoport, 1975). As compared with an unmedicated group, boys receiving imipramine showed no differences on the Wide Range Achievement Test, the Wechsler Intelligence Scale for Children, or the Porteus Mazes test.

Aman (1980b) has reviewed the effects of these drugs on cognitive performance. Several studies have shown antidepressant-induced improvements on vigilance type tasks, such as the Continuous Performance Task. However, most other forms of cognitive tests, such as measures of cognitive style, IQ tests, and perceptual tests, have shown no differences between antidepressant drugs and placebo.

The clinical indications for antidepressants in children may include enuresis, Conduct Disorder, Attention Deficit Hyperactivity Disorder, depression, and separation anxiety (Rapoport & Mikkelsen, 1978). To the extent that these disorders overlap with specific learning disabilities, the antidepressants may impact the academic outcome of these children. However, it would be premature to speculate whether these drugs have any appreciable cognitive effects in and of themselves.

Other Drugs

Megavitamins

The use of vitamin, mineral, and dietary treatments used in the developmental disabilities has been reviewed by Aman and Singh (1988). With the exception of several well known, genetically transmitted metabolic disorders, Aman and Singh were unable to find any mineral or vitamin treatments that unequivocally caused learning or behavioral improvements in children having learning or behavior disorders.

Cott (1971, 1972, 1974) has claimed that a combination of a megavitamin diet high in niacin or niacinamide, ascorbic acid, pyridoxine, and calcium pantothenate (sometimes in combination with an antihypoglycemia diet) may improve behavior and learning disabilities in children. However, we were unable to locate any studies by Cott that demonstrated such an effect. At least three well designed studies, employing a variety of objective measures, have assessed variations of the Cott formula with hyperactive or learning disabled samples (Arnold, Christopher, Huestis, & Smeltzer, 1978; Haslam, Dalby, & Rademaker, 1984; Kershner & Hawk, 1979). None of these studies could document improvements from the vitamin supplements as compared with placebo. Indeed, Haslam et al. observed deterioration due to the active treatment on a measure of disruptive classroom behavior and, furthermore, tests of liver functioning showed a significant elevation of serum transaminase levels.

Codergocrine Mesylate

Codergocrine mesylate (Hydergine) is a naturally occurring combination of three ergot alkaloids frequently used to treat psychomotor disorders associated with old age (Tareen, Bashir, Saeed, & Hussain, 1988). It is thought to increase brain metabolism by affecting certain cerebral enzymes.

Tareen et al. (1988) compared codergocrine mesylate with placebo in a heterogeneous group of children having a variety of behavioral and learning problems. Significant drug effects were reported on a variety of dimensions, including speech, "comprehension," attentiveness, memory, and rate of learning. It is not clear from the paper how these were assessed, although parent and teacher subjective impressions of change appeared to be the basis for comparisons.

Some Relevant Issues

State-Dependent Learning

State-dependent learning is a phenomenon in which material learned under a given drug state is best retrieved (or recalled) under the same drug state. Conversely, material learned under one drug condition may be less accessible if the individual is retested under a different drug condition. State-dependent learning can be demonstrated in humans with a variety of drugs, including alcohol, barbituates, marihuana, anticholinergics, physostigmine, and phenothiazines (Overton, 1968; Weingartner, 1978). This phenomenon could be of practical educational significance because material learned while a child is receiving pharmacotherapy may not transfer well when the child is later tested under no drug or with another medication. Likewise, state-dependent learning might have implications for the later transfer of gains due to behavior therapy or psychotherapy if this is applied while a child is receiving pharmacotherapy.

Probably because of their prevalence, both for treating behavior and learning-related problems, the cerebral stimulants have been the subject of considerable research in this regard. Early studies of possible state-dependent learning due to dextroamphetamine or methylphenidate provided no evidence of the phenomenon either with adults (Hurst, Radlow, Chubb, & Bagley, 1969) or with children (Hallsten, 1970; Aman & Sprague 1974). Subsequently, Swanson and Kinsbourne (1976) did report fairly marked state-dependent learning effects with methylphenidate, but these were said to be confined to subjects showing facilitation due to the drug during acquisition phases of the study (i.e., state dependency occurred only in positive drug responders). Of course, this was a troubling finding, because it suggested that state dependency tended to occur in the very children most likely to receive stimulant therapy. Swanson and Kinsbourne's study was later replicated by Shea (1982), again using methylphenidate as the active drug and again dividing subjects into responders and nonresponders. However, Weingartner, Langer, Gria, and Rapoport (1982) also attemped such a replication by dividing subjects into positive drug responders and nonresponders, and they found no evidence of state dependency with dextroamphetamine. Gan and Cantwell (1982) analyzed their data across all subjects as well as within positive and negative placebo responders and, likewise, noted no interactions between type of drug (methylphenidate or placebo) during acquisition and drug state during recall sessions. Still others, using either methylphenidate or magnesium pemoline, were able to demonstrate no dissociative effects between active drug and placebo, although no effort was made to split the groups as was done by Swanson and Kinsbourne (Becker-Mattes, Mattes, Abikoff, & Brandt, 1985; Steinhausen & Kreutzer, 1981; Stephens, Skinner, & Pelham, 1984).

Thus, of the 10 studies reviewed here, only 2 showed evidence of state-dependent learning, and in the first of these such evidence hinged on a post hoc division of subjects. The only other study that has attempted a similar division (Weingarner et al., 1982) has been unable to replicate the finding. Furthermore, if this were a robust phenomenon, it should emerge as significant irrespective of subgrouping unless the data from nonresponders were in some sense cancelling out the findings observed with responders—that is, the phenomenon should still be observable, but it would be expected to be less powerful. We do not feel that the evidence supports the impression of state-dependent learning with stimulant drugs in children, even within positive drug responders. We are not aware of research into state-dependent effects of drugs other than stimulants in childhood disorders. Dissociation of learning appears to be most readily demonstrated with drugs having marked sedative-hypnotic effects, and these are seldom used in childhood behavioral problems. Thus, state dependency may not be a practical issue, at least with most agents being used at the present time.

Degree of Relationship Between Behavioral and Cognitive Changes

Most children who receive psychotropic medication tend to do so for behavioral control rather than learning enhancement. Regardless of the reason for administering such medication, it is almost always clinically evaluated against the endpoint of the child's apparent behavioral changes. However, this may prove to be a procedure fraught with problems. For example, Rie et al. (1976a) found that parent and teacher ratings of achievement were in fact unrelated to actual achievement as assessed by standardized tests. Gittelman-Klein and Klein (1975) obtained what appears to be an analogous finding in a study of methylphenidate with hyperactive children. They calculated nearly 300 correlations between changes in psychological tests and ratings, by significant others, of clinical change. Only 13 of these correlations were significant, and 7 of the correlations were in the opposite direction to what was predicted! Aman and Turbott (1991) used a battery of cognitive and motor tests in an attempt to predict clinical response to methylphenidate in ADHD children. In general, the psychomotor battery failed to predict clinical outcome and, furthermore, changes on the cognitive–motor tests were mostly unrelated to changes in behavior ratings. A similar lack of relationship between behavioral and cognitive changes has been reported by a number of other investigators, (e.g., Lerer, Lerer, & Artner, 1977; Rapoport, Quinn, Bradbard, Riddle, & Brooks, 1974; Weingartner et al., 1982), although some workers have found a positive relationship between cognitive and behavioral changes (e.g., Rapport et al., 1988; Richardson et al., 1988).

This frequent observation of no relationship between the two spheres is an important issue, as it raises the specter that if behavioral control serves as the sole criterion in determining optimal treatment, then that treatment *may* come at the cost of optimal learning performance. This may help to explain why investigators have had little success showing academic enhancement due to pharmacotherapy thus far. It also suggests that clinicians may need to incorporate some indices (or at least guidelines gleaned from research) to avoid undermining cognitive functioning while achieving behavioral improvement. As suggested previously, adequate medical supervision of the future may demand provision for both cognitive and behavioral assessment when determining the optimal choice of drug and dosage (Aman, 1982a).

Possible Adverse Cognitive Effects of Stimulants

Most research with the cerebral stimulants over the years has focused on their possible beneficial effects and in particular, the enhancement of sustained attention has been a repeated and robust finding (Douglas & Peters, 1979). However, some authors have suggested that stimulant drugs may also be capable of producing adverse cognitive effects. In a thoughtful review, Robbins and Sahakian (1979) attempted to integrate findings with these drugs from both the animal and human research. They suggested that at higher doses the stimulants are capable of narrowing or focusing attention such that stereotypic behavior at moderate to high doses seen in animal studies may be an exaggeration of the effects on attention seen at lower doses with children and adults. Aman (1982b) extended this observation and suggested that the stimulant drugs sometimes cause adverse effects in children having developmental disabilities. Aman argued that many of these individuals initially present with an excessively narrow breadth of attention and, furthermore, stimulants may cause additional constriction of attention irrespective of the clinical group to which a child belongs.

Over the years, investigators have occasionally commented on apparently negative effects of stimulants in ADHD children or related clinical groups. For example, Rie et al. (1976b) remarked anecdotally that their subjects seemed less spontaneous and showed reduced interest, emotional expression, and pleasure or surprise while on methylphenidate. However, empirical support for such impressions has been slow to materialize, perhaps because we lack satisfactory experimental techniques for demonstrating narrowed attentional focus. In a study of playroom behavior, Barkley (1977) found that methylphenidate caused a reduction in the number of toy changes while the amount of time spent per toy remained unchanged, and he interpreted this as showing that the drug may reduce children's interest in their surroundings. Dyme, Sahakian, Golinko, and Rabe (1982) assessed the effect of 1.0 mg/kg of methylphenidate on both repetitive tasks and a flexibility of thinking task (the Wisconsin Card Sorting Test) in hyperactive children. With methylphenidate, the children improved on all of the repetition tasks, but most children also showed perseveration of thinking on the flexibility test, suggesting difficulty in changing mental set from one problem to another.

Thus, it is possible (especially at higher doses) that the stimulants may cause some undesirable changes (variously referred to as reduced flexibility, lessened interest, narrowed focus of attention). Although certainly worthy of replication and further pursuit, the evidence on this issue is sparse and only suggestive at this time. However, if proven to be correct, this reduced flexibility in thinking *may* offset some of the short-term cognitive performance gains typically seen with hyperactive children, and it may help to explain why long-term academic gains have not been documented more often (or more dramatically) with the stimulant drugs.

Discussion and Conclusions

Discussion

Although the studies reviewed here admit to relatively few firm conclusions, the growth in research in recent years does provide indicators for likely directions that may prove profitable in the future. To return to the issue of subject selection and nosology, there continues to be a need for rigorous and clear-cut specification of subject variables if further studies are going to provide additional information. In this respect, Tables 16.1 and 16.2 provide us with some likely leads for achieving this. For example, carefully conducted a priori comparisons between groups selected for learning disability only versus groups having learning disability plus hyperactivity is likely to lead to useful guidelines, especially regarding the stimulants. Indeed, at least one research group (Dykman, Ackerman, & McCray, 1980) has found this division to provide useful theoretical and practical findings. Likewise, the results of previous studies suggest that a distinction between mild to moderate learning problems and severe learning disabilities may be helpful in distinguishing children more likely or not, respectively, to respond to pharmacotherapy. Furthermore, the learning disabilities field is one that is rich in etiological theories (Aman & Singh, 1983), and these etiological distinctions may also prove useful for separating subgroups likely to respond to pharmacotherapy, although few studies have attempted to do so thus far.

One problem that permeates this literature is the failure of investigators explicitly to distinguish between immediate changes, due to the drug prescribed at that time, and long-term drug changes that reflect relatively permanent, consolidated gains in learning. It seems to the writers that both approaches to pharmacological research are legitimate, but that they call for slightly different methodologies and they lead to different conclusions. For example, Aman and Werry (1982) attempted to assess the acute effects of methylphenidate and diazepam on the reading *process*, as determined by a psycholinguistic analysis that reflected qualitative changes in the way that the subjects read. Any significant findings would have reflected likely changes in the children's strategic approach to reading but would not necessarily result in long-term changes in achievement. In contrast, Richardson et al. (1988) followed children treated with methylphenidate over a period of 6 months. All groups, irrespective of treatment condition, were assessed at the end of the study while off medication. An advantage on certain variables could unequivocally be attributed to the intervening drug therapy rather than the possibly immediate and confounding effects of different drugs on the day of testing. Thus, investigators need to be clear about the purpose of their investigations and to design and interpret their findings appropriately. A number of the studies reviewed here failed to do this and have reported short-term effects as though they reflected changes in achievement levels.

Another issue has to do with the interplay between dosage levels, changes in learning performance, and changes in overt behavior. As noted earlier, there is conflicting evidence on this question, with several studies suggesting that changes in behavior and learning may be largely independent. The work of Sprague and Sleator (1975, 1977) suggests that these apparently conflicting data may be accounted for in part by different dose-response curves for learning and behavior. This is obviously an important issue, as it may be counterproductive if dosage is adjusted solely with behavior change in mind, with the consequence that learning and achievement may suffer. Some further efforts have been made of late to disentangle these issues (e.g., Kupietz et al., 1988; Rapport et al., 1988; Richardson et al., 1988), but it is clear that more of this type of dose research is needed.

Finally, there is a need to adopt better measures regarding achievement assessment. A substantial number of studies have employed the Wide Range Achievement Tests (WRAT) (and/or similar types of indices) as their principal or only measure of outcome. Presumably this is due in large part to the popularity, ease of administration, and brevity of such tests. However, there is also a liability in the use of tests like the WRAT, because they tend to have relatively few items per grade level and, therefore, they tend to be insensitive to small but potentially important treatment effects (Aman, 1978). There is a variety of alternatives to this type of test, such as more "refined" instruments that have finer gradations between levels, learning readiness instruments, tests for diagnosing areas of strength and weakness, and psycholinguistic approaches (to reading) (Aman & Werry, 1982; Clay, 1975) as described earlier. It is clear from the preceding reviews that drug effects on learning and academic outcome (when they do occur) usually tend to be rather subtle. This warrants a careful search for the most appropriate instruments in order to employ those capable of detecting such effects.

Conclusions

It appears that large numbers of elementary school age children with learning disabilities do receive medication, either for concomitant behavior problems or for a learning disability. Minimally, at least 6% of such children are so treated at any given time, although the true prevalence in the United States probably exceeds this. Many studies of the effects of pharmacotherapy on learning and achievement have employed large numbers of dependent measures, certainly not a feature confined to this field alone. Nevertheless, this often complicates the process of determining which significant findings are "real" and which are due to be operation of chance.

In an earlier review, one of the authors concluded that drug treatment simply is not a viable approach for treating learning disabilities that are not accompanied by other problems, such as psychiatric disorders (Aman, 1982a). Our current position is basically unchanged, although recent evidence with the cerebral stimulants may permit slightly more optimism and confidence that some secondary academic benefits may occur in children with Attention Deficit Hyperactivity Disorder. However, if this is the case, it is also clear that such secondary benefits are rather fragile, subtle, variable from individual to individual, and difficult to document. Nevertheless, some variables have been identified that may permit a prediction of differential probability regarding spinoffs in academic areas, so that it may be possible to increase the likelihood that children treated for a behavior disorder may show collateral gains in academic areas. In the case of the nootropics, the evidence is weaker, and it remains to be seen whether these drugs have any role to play in children with learning disabilities or in other handicapping conditions. The authors regard the publicity surrounding and interest in the antimotion sickness drugs as a possible treatment for reading disorders to be utterly unwarranted. There currently appears to be no sound research justifying the use of these drugs in children with learning disabilities. There is insufficient evidence with any of the remaining psychotropic drugs to draw conclusions about their effects on academic learning per se, although there is little reason to believe that they have a direct role to play in this regard. However, their use may result in some secondary benefits in appropriately diagnosed children with genuine psychiatric disorders.

The last decade has witnessed the publication of a substantial number of good studies, especially with the cerebral stimulants, in children having learning disabilities. Although these investigations have not resulted in simple answers, they have helped to define the limitations and possible useful applications of these agents.

Acknowledgments. Work on this chapter was supported by grants from the United States Office of Human Development Services (grant 07 DD 0270/16) and the Maternal and Child Health Service (Training Project 922) awarded to The Nisonger Center for Mental Retardation and Developmental Disabilities, Ohio State University. The authors thank Ms. Deb E. McGhee for assistance on library research for this chapter.

References

Aman, M. G. (1978). Drugs, learning, and the psychotherapies. In J. S. Werry (Ed.), *Pediatric psychopharmacology: The use of behavior modifying drugs in children* (pp. 79–108). New York: Brunner/Mazel.

Aman, M. G. (1979). Cognitive, social, and other correlates of specific reading retardation. *Journal of Abnormal Child Psychology, 7*, 153–168.

Aman, M. G. (1980a). [Letter to the editor.] *Journal of Learning Disabilities, 13,* 10–11.

Aman, M. G. (1980b). Psychotropic drugs and learning problems—a selective review. *Journal of Learning Disabilities, 13,* 87–96.

Aman, M. G. (1982a). Psychotropic drugs in the treatment of reading disorders. In R. N. Malatesha & P. G. Aaron (Eds.), *Reading disorders: Varieties and treatments* (pp. 453–471). New York: Academic Press.

Aman, M. G. (1982b). Stimulant drug effects in developmental disorders and hyperactivity: Toward a resolution of disparate findings. *Journal of Autism and Developmental Disorders, 12,* 385–398.

Aman, M. G. (1984a). Drugs and learning in mentally retarded persons. In G. D. Burrows and J. S. Werry (Eds.), *Advances in human psychopharmacology* (Vol. 3, pp. 121–163). Greenwich, CT: JAI Press.

Aman, M. G. (1984b). Hyperactivity: Nature of the syndrome and its natural history. *Journal of Autism and Development Disorders, 14,* 39–56.

Aman, M. G., & Singh, N. N. (1980). The usefulness of thioridazine for treating childhood disorders—fact or folklore? *American Journal of Mental Deficiency, 84,* 331–338.

Aman, M. G., & Singh, N. N. (1983). Specific reading disorders: Concepts of etiology reconsidered. In K. D. Gadow & I. Bialer (Eds.), *Advances in Learning and Behavioral Disabilities* (Vol. 2, pp. 1–47). Greenwich, CT: JAI Press.

Aman, M. G., & Singh, N. N. (1988). Vitamin, mineral, and dietary treatments. In M. G. Aman & N. N. Singh (Eds.), *Psychopharmacology of the developmental disabilities* (pp. 168–196). New York: Springer–Verlag.

Aman, M. G., & Sprague, R. L. (1974). The state-dependent effects of methylphenidate and dextroamphetamine. *Journal of Nervous and Mental Diseases, 158*, 268–279.

Aman, M. G., & Turbott, S. H. (1991). Prediction of clinical response in children taking methylphenidate. *Journal of Autism and Developmental Disorders, 21*, 211–228.

Aman, M. G., & Werry, J. S. (1982). Methylphenidate and diazepam in severe reading retardation. *Journal of the American Academy of Child Psychiatry, 21*, 31–37.

American Psychiatric Association (1987). *Diagnostic and statistical manual of mental disorders, third edition, revised*. Washington, DC: Author.

Arnold, L. E., Christopher, J., Huestis, R. D., & Smeltzer, D. J. (1978). Megavitamins for minimal brain dysfunction. *Journal of the American Medical Association, 240*, 2642–2643.

Ballinger, C. T., Varley, C. K., & Nolen, P. A. (1984). Effects of methylphenidate on reading in children with Attention Deficit Disorder. *American Journal of Psychiatry, 141*, 1590–1593.

Barkley, R. A. (1977). The effects of methylphenidate on various types of activity level and attention in hyperkinetic children. *Journal of Abnormal Child Psychology, 5*, 351–369.

Barkley, R. A., & Cunningham, C. E. (1978). Do stimulant drugs improve the academic performance of hyperkinetic children? A review of outcome research. *Clinical Pediatrics, 17*, 85–92.

Becker-Mattes, A., Mattes, J. A., Abikoff, H., & Brandt, L. (1985). State-dependent learning in hyperactive children receiving methylphenidate. *American Journal of Psychiatry, 142*, 455–459.

Bente, D., Glatthaar, G., Ulrich, G., & Lewinsky, M. (1978). Piracetam and vigilance: Electroencephalographic and clinical results of long term therapy in gerontopsychiatric patients. *Arzneimittelforschung, 28*, 1529–1531.

Bradley, C. (1937). The behavior of children receiving benzedrine. *American Journal of Psychiatry, 94*, 577–585.

Brown, B., Haegerstrom-Portnoy, G., Yingling, C. D., Herron, J. Galin, D., & Marcus, M. (1983). Dyslexic children have normal vestibular responses to rotation. *Archives of Neurology, 40*, 370–373.

Campbell, S. B., & Werry, J. S. (1986). Attention deficit disorder (hyperactivity). In H. C. Quay & J. S. Werry (Eds.), *Psychopathological disorders of childhood* (3rd ed., pp. 111–155). New York: Wiley.

Charles, L., Schain, R., & Zelniker, T. (1981). Optimal dosages of methylphenidate for improving the learning and behavior of hyperactive children. *Developmental and Behavioral Pediatrics, 2*, 78–81.

Chase, C. H., Schmitt, R. L., Russel, G., & Talla, P. (1984). A new chemotherapeutic investigation: Piracetam effects on dyslexia. *Annals of Dyslexia, 34*, 29–48.

Clay, M. M. (1975). *The early detection of reading difficulties. A diagnostic survey*. Auckland: Heinemann Educational Books.

Clements, S. D., & Peters, J. E. (1962). Minimal brain dysfunctions in the school-age child. *Archives of General Psychiatry*, *6*, 185–197.

Cole, S. O. (1986). Effects of benzodiazepines on acquisition and performance: A critical assessment. *Neuroscience and Biobehavioral Reviews*, *10*, 275–272.

Coles, G. (1987). *The learning mystique: A critical look at "learning disabilities"*. New York: Pantheon Books.

Conners, C. K. (1972). Symposium: Behavior modification by drugs. II. Psychological effects of stimulant drugs in children with minimal brain dysfunction. *Pediatrics*, *49*, 702–708.

Conners, C. K., Blouin, A. G., Winglee, M., Lougee, L., O'Donell, D., & Smith, A. (1984). Piracetam and event related potentials in dyslexic children. *Psychopharmacology Bulletin*, *20*, 667–673.

Conners, C. K., Blouin, A. G., Winglee, M., Lougee, L., O'Donell, D., & Smith, A. (1986). Piracetam and event-related potentials in dyslexic males. *International Journal of Psychophysiology*, *4*, 19–27.

Conners, C. K., Reader, M., Reiss, A., Caldwell, J., Cladwell, L., Adesman, A., Mayer, L., Berg, M., Clymer, R., & Erwin, R. (1987). The effects of piracetam upon visual event-related potentials in dyslexic children. *Psychophysiology*, *24*, 513–521.

Conners, C. K., Rothschild, G., Eisenberg, L., Schwartz, L. S., & Robinson, E. (1969). Dextroamphetamine sulfate in children with learning disorders. *Archives of General Psychiatry*, *21*, 182–190.

Conners, C. K., & Taylor, E. (1980). Pemoline, methylphenidate, and placebo in children with minimal brain dysfunction. *Archives of General Psychiatry*, *37*, 922–930.

Conners, C. K., Taylor, E., Meo, G., Kurtz, M. A., & Fournier, M. (1972). Magnesium pemoline and dextroamphetamine: A controlled study in children with minimal brain dysfunction. *Psychopharmacologia*, *26*, 321–336.

Conrad, W., Dworkin, E. S., Shai, A., & Tobiessen, J. E. (1971). Effects of amphetamine therapy and prescriptive tutoring on the behavior and achievement of lower class hyperative children. *Journal of Learning Disabilities*, *4*, 45–53.

Cott, A. (1971). Orthomolecular approach to the treatment of learning disabilities. *Schizophrenia*, *3*, 95–105.

Cott, A. (1972). Megavitamins: The orthomolecular approach to behavioral disorders and learning disabilities. *Academic Therapy*, *7*, 245–258.

Cott, A. (1974). Treatment of learning disabilities. *Journal of Orthomolecular Psychiatry*, *3*, 343–355.

Critchley, M. (1970). *The dyslexic child*. London: Heinemann.

Cullinan, D., Gadow, K. D., & Epstein, M. H. (1987). Psychotropic drug treatment among learning-disabled, educable mentally retarded, and seriously emotionally disturbed students. *Journal of Abnormal Child Psychology*, *15*, 469–477.

Denckla, M. B., & Rudel, R. G. (1976). Rapid automatized naming (R.A.N.) dyslexia differentiated from other learning disabilities. *Neuropsychologia*, *14*, 471–479.

DiIanni, M., Wilsher, C. R., Blank, M. S., Conners, C. K., Chase, C. H., Funkenstein, H. H., Helfgott, E., Holmes, J. M., Lougee, L., Maletta, G. J.,

Milewski, J., Piozzolo, F. J., Rudel, R. G., & Tallal, P. (1985). The effects of piracetam in children with dyslexia. *Journal of Clinical Psychopharmacology*, *5*, 272–278.

Dimond, S. J., & Brouwers, E. Y. M. (1976). Increase in the power of human memory in normal man through the use of drugs. *Psychopharmacology*, *49*, 307–309.

Douglas, V. I., Barr, R. G., O'Neill, M. E., & Britton, B. G. (1986). Short term effects of methylphenidate on the cognitive, learning and academic performance of children with attention deficit disorder in the laboratory and the classroom. *Journal of Child Psychology and Psychiatry*, *27*, 191–211.

Douglas, V. I., & Peters, K. G. (1979). Toward a clearer definition of the attentional deficit of hyperactive children. In G. A. Hale & M. Lewis (Eds.), *Attention and cognitive development*. New York: Plenum.

Dykman, R. A. (1980). [Letter to the editor]. *Journal of Learning Disabilities*, *13*, 298.

Dykman, R. A., Ackerman, P. T., & McCray, D. S. (1980). Effects of methylphenidate on selective and sustained attention in hyperactive, reading-disabled, and presumably attention-disordered boys. *The Journal of Nervous and Mental Disease*, *168*, 745–752.

Dyme, I. Z., Sahakian, B. J., Golinko, B. E., & Rabe, E. F. (1982). Perseveration induced by methylphenidate in children: Preliminary findings. *Progress in Neuro-Psychopharmacology and Biological Psychiatry*, *6*, 269–273.

Ellis, N. S., & Miles, T. R. (1978). Visual information processing in dyslexic children. In M. M. Gruneberg, P. E. Morris, & R. N. Sykes (Eds.), *Practical aspects of memory*. London: Academic Press.

Fagan, J. E., Kaplan, B. J., Raymond, J. E., & Edgington, E. S. (1988). The failure of antimotion sickness medication to improve reading in developmental dyslexia: Results of a randomized trial. *Journal of Developmental and Behavioral Pediatrics*, *9*, 359–366.

Famularo, R., & Fenton, T. (1987). The effect of methylphenidate on school grades in children with Attention Deficit Disorder without hyperactivity: A preliminary report. *Journal Clinical Psychiatry*, *48*, 112–114.

Fenelon, B., Holland, J. T., & Johnson, C. (1972). Spatial organization of the EEG in children with reading disabilities: A study using nitrazepam. *Cortex*, *36*, 444–464.

Fenelon, B., & Wortley, S. (1973). Effect of auxiliary acoustic stimulation on two-flash fusion thresholds of reading disabled children: A study using nitrazepam. *Perceptual and Motor Skills*, *36*, 443–450.

Frank, J., & Levinson, H. N. (1975–1976). Dysmetric dyslexia and dyspraxia. Synopsis of a continuing research project. *Academic Therapy*, *11*, 133–143.

Frank, J., & Levinson, H. N. (1976–1977). Seasickness mechanisms and medications in dysmetric dyslexia and dyspraxia. *Academic Therapy*, *12*, 133–153.

Frank, J., & Levinson, H. N. (1977). Anti-motion sickness medications in dysmetric dyslexia and dyspraxia. *Academic Therapy*, *12*, 411–424.

Freed, H., Abrams, J., & Peifer, C. (1959). Reading disability: A new therapeutic approach and its implications. *Journal of Clinical and Experimental Psychopathology and Quarterly Review of Psychiatry and Neurology*, *20*, 251–259.

Gadow, K. D., (1976). *Psychotropic and anticonvulsant drug usage in early childhood special education programs. I. Phase one: A preliminary report: Prevalence, attitude, training, and problems.* Paper presented at the annual meeting of the Council for Exceptional Children, Chicago, Illinois, April 1976. (ERIC Document Reproduction Service No. E D 125 198.)

Gadow, K. D. (1983). Effect of stimulant drugs on academic performance in hyperactive and learning disabled children. *Journal of Learning Disabilities*, *16*, 290–299.

Gan, J., & Cantwell, D. P. (1982). Dosage effects of methylphenidate on paired associate learning: positive/negative placebo responders. *Journal of the American Academy of Child Psychiatry*, *21*, 327–342.

Gittelman-Klein, R., & Klein, D. F. (1975). Are behavioral and psychometric changes related in methylphenidate-treated, hyperactive children? *International Journal of Mental Health*, *4*, 182–198.

Gittelman-Klein, R., & Klein, D. F. (1976). Methylphenidate effects in learning disabilities. *Archives of General Psychiatry*, *33*, 655–644.

Gittelman, R., Klein, D. F., & Feingold, I. (1983). Children with reading disorders: II. Effects of methylphenidate in combination with reading remediation. *Journal of Child Psychology and Psychiatry*, *24*, 193–212.

Giurgea, C. E. (1973). The nootropic approach to the integrative activity of the brain. *Conditional Reflex*, *8*, 108–115.

Gualtieri, C. T., Golden, R. N., & Fahs, J. J. (1983). New developments in pediatric psychopharmacology. *Journal of Developmental and Behavioral pediatrics*, *4*, 202–209.

Hallsten, E. A. (1970). *State dependent recognition with methylphenidate and thioridazine in retarded children.* Unpublished doctoral dissertation, University of Illinois, Champaign, Illinois.

Hansen, P., & Keogh, B. K. (1971). Medical characteristics of children with educational handicaps. Implications for the pediatrician. *Clinical Pediatrics*, *10*, 726–730.

Harris, A. T., & Sipay, E. R. (1980). *How to increase reading ability* (7th ed.). New York: Longman.

Haslam, R. H. A., Dalby, J. T., & Rademaker, A. W. (1984). Effects of megavitamin therapy on children with attention deficit disorders. *Pediatrics*, *74*, 103–111.

Helfgott, E., Rudel, R. G., & Kairam, R. (1986). The effect of piracetam on short- and long-term retrieval in dyslexic boys. *International Journal of Psychophysiology*, *4*, 53–61.

Helfgott, E., Rudel, R. G., & Krieger, J. (1984). Effects piracetam on the single word and prose reading of dyslexic children. *Psychopharmacology Bulletin*, *20*, 688–690.

Huddleston, W., Staiger, R. C., Frye, R., Musgrave, R. S., & Stritch, T. (1961). Deanol as aid in overcoming reading retardation. *Clinical Medicine*, *68*, 1340–1342.

Hurst, P. M., Radlow, R., Chubb, N. C., & Bagley, S. K. (1969). Effects of d-amphetamine on acquisition, persistence and recall. *American Journal of Psychology*, *82*, 307–319.

Kershner, J., & Hawke, W. (1979). Megavitamins and learning disorders: A controlled double-blind experiment. *Journal of Nutrition*, *109*, 819–826.

522   Michael G. Aman and Johannes Rojahn

Krager, J. M., Safer, D., & Earhart, J. (1979). Follow-up survey results of medication used to treat hyperactive school children. *The Journal of School Health*, *49*, 317–321.

Kupietz, S. S., Winsberg, B. G., Richardson, E., Maitinsky, S., & Mendell, N. (1988). Effects of methylphenidate dosage in hyperactive reading-disabled children: I. Behavior and cognitive performance effects. *Journal of the American Academy of Child and Adolescent Psychiatry*, *27*, 70–77.

Lerer, R. J., Lerer., & Artner, J. (1977). The effects of methylphenidate on the handwriting of children with minimal brain dysfunction. *Journal of Pediatrics*, *91*, 127–132.

Levinson, H. N. (1980). *A solution to the riddle dyslexia*. New York: Springer-Verlag.

Masland, R., & Usprich, C. (1981). [Book review of *A solution to the riddle dyslexia* by Harold N. Levinson.] *Bulletin of the Orton Society*, *31*, 256–261.

McCarthy, J. M., & Paraskevopoulos, J. (1969). Behaviour patterns of learning disabled, emotionally disturbed, and average children. *Exceptional Children*, *36*, 69–74.

McNair, D. M. (1973). Antianxiety drugs and human performance. *Archives of General Psychiatry*, *29*, 611–617.

Millichap, G. J. (1968). Drugs in management of hyperkinetic and perceptually handicapped children. *American Medical Association Journal*, *206*, 1527–1530.

Misurec, J., & Strnad, P. (1980). Piracetam (Nootropil) in posttraumatical neurasthenic syndrome with lowered vigility level in the EEG. *Abstracts of the 12th CINP Congress* (p. 243). New York: Pergamon.

Overton, D. A. (1968). Dissociated learning in drug states (state dependent learning). In D. Efron (Ed.), *Psychopharmacology: a review of progress 1957–1967* (pp. 918–930). Washington, DC: U.S. Government Printing Office, Public Health Service Publication No. 1836.

Page, J. G., Janicki, R. S., Bernstein, M. S., Curran, C. F., & Michelli, F. A. (1974). Pemoline (Cylert) in the treatment of childhood hyperkinesis. *Journal of Learning Disabilities*, *7*, 498–503.

Pelham, W. E., Bender, M. E., Caddell, J., Booth, S., & Moorer, S. H. (1985). Methylphenidate and children with attention deficit disorder. *Archives of General Psychiatry*, *42*, 941–952.

Polatajko, H. J. (1987). Visual-ocular control of normal and learning-disabled children. *Developmental Medicine and Child Neurology*, *29*, 477–485.

Quinn, P. O., & Rapoport, J. L. (1975). One-year follow-up of hyperactive boys treated with imipramine or methylphenidate. *American Journal of Psychiatry*, *132*, 241–245.

Rapoport, J. L., & Mikkelson, E. J. (1978). Antidepressants. In J. S. Werry (Ed.), *Pediatric psychopharmacology: The use of behavior modifying drugs in children* (pp. 208–233). New York: Brunner/Mazel.

Rapoport, J. L., Mikkelson, E. J., & Werry, J. S. (1978). Antimanic, antianxiety, hallucinogenic and miscellaneous drugs. In J. S. Werry (Ed.), *Pediatric psychopharmacology: The use of behavior modifying drugs in children* (pp. 316–365). New York: Brunner/Mazel.

Rapoport, J. L., Quinn, P. O., Bradbard, G., Riddle, D., & Brooks, E. (1974). Imipramine and methylphenidate treatments of hyperactive boys. A double-blind comparison. *Archives of General Psychiatry*, *30*, 789–793.

Rapport, M. D., Stoner, G., DuPaul, G. J., Kelly, K. L., Tucker, S. B., & Schoeler, T. (1988). Attention deficit disorder and methylphenidate: A multilevel analysis of dose-response effects on children's impulsivity across settings. *Journal of the American Academy of Child and Adolescent Psychiatry*, *27*, 60–69.

Reid, J. F. (1972). Dyslexia: A problem of communication. In J. F. Reid (Ed.), *Reading: problems and practices* (pp. 130–141). London: Ward Lock Educational.

Richardson, E., Kupietz, S. S., Winsberg, B. G., Maitinsky, S., & Mendell, N. (1988). Effects of methylphenidate dosage in hyperactive reading-disabled children: II. Reading achievement. *Journal of the American Academy of Child and Adolescent Psychiatry*, *27*, 78–87.

Rie, H. E., Rie, E. D., Stewart, S., & Ambuel, J. P. (1976a). Effects of methylphenidate on underachieving children. *Journal of Consulting and Clinical Psychology*, *44*, 250–260.

Rie, H., Rie, E., Stewart, S., & Ambuel, J. (1976b). Effects of Ritalin on underachieving children: A replication. *American Journal of Orthopsychiatry*, *46*, 313–322.

Rimland, B. (1988). [Letter to the editor]. *Journal of Learning Disabilities*, *21*, 322.

Robbins, T. W., & Sahakian, B. J. (1979). "Paradoxical" effects of psychomotor stimulant drugs in hyperactive children from the standpoint of behavioural pharmacology. *Neuropharmacology*, *18*, 931–950.

Robinson, H. (1946). *Why pupils fail in reading*. Chicago: University of Chicago Press.

Rudel, R. G., & Helfgott, E. (1984). Effect of piracetam on verbal memory of dyslexic boys. *American Academy of Child Psychiatry*, *23*, 695–699.

Rutter, M., Graham, P., & Yule, W. (1970). *A neuropsychiatric study in childhood*. London: Heinemann.

Rutter, M., & Yule, W. (1973). Specific reading retardation. In L. Mann & D. A. Sabatino (Eds.), *The first review of special education* (Vol. 2, pp. 1–50). Philadelphia: JSE Press.

Rutter, M., & Yule, W. (1975). The concept of specific reading retardation. *Journal of Child Psychology and Psychiatry*, *16*, 181–197.

Schain, R. J. (1972). *Neurology of childhood learning disorders*. Baltimore: Williams & Wilkins.

Shea, V. T. (1982). State-dependent learning in children receiving methylphenidate. *Psychopharmacology*, *78*, 266–270.

Shumway-Cook, A., Horak, F., & Black, F. O. (1987). A critical examination of vestibular function in motor-impaired learning-disabled children. *International Journal of Pediatric Otolaryngology*, *14*, 21–30.

Silver, L. B. (1988). [Letter to the editor]. *Journal of Learning Disabilities*, *21*, 324.

Simeon, J. G., Volakva, J., Trites, R., Waters, B., Webster, I., Ferguson, H. B., & Simeon, S. (1983). Electroencephalographic correlation in children with learning disorders treated with piracetam. *Psychopharmacology Bulletin*, *19*, 716–720.

Simeon, J., Waters, B., Resnick, M., Fiedorowicz, C. Trites, R., Volavka, J., & Simeon, S. (1980). Effects of piracetam in children with learning disorders. *Psychopharmacology Bulletin*, *16*, 65–66.

Sprague, R. L., & Sleator, E. K. (1973). Effects of psychopharmacologic agents on learning disorders. *Pediatric Clinics of North America*, *20*, 719–735.

Sprague, R. L., & Sleator, E. K. (1975). What is the proper dose of stimulant drugs in children? *International Journal of Mental Health*, *4*, 75–118.

Sprague, R. L., & Sleator, E. K. (1977). Methylphenidate in hyperkinetic children: Differences in dose effects on learning and social behavior. *Science*, *198*, 1274–1276.

Sprague, R. L., & Werry, J. S. (1971). Methodology of psychopharmacological studies with the retarded. In N. R. Ellis (Ed.), *International review of research in mental retardation* (Vol. 5, pp. 147–219). New York: Academic Press.

Steinhausen, H., & Kreuzer, E. (1981). Learning in hyperactive children: Are there stimulant-related and state-dependent effects? *Psychopharmacology*, *74*, 389–390.

Stephens, R. S., Pelham, W. E., & Skinner, R. (1984). State-dependent and main effects of methylphenidate and pemoline on paired-associate learning and spelling in hyperactive children. *Journal of Consulting and Clinical Psychology*, *52*, 104–113.

Swanson, J. M., & Kinsbourne, M. (1976). Stimulant-related state-dependent learning in hyperactive children. *Science*, *192*, 1354–1357.

Tallal, P., Chase, C., Russell, G., & Schmitt, R. L. (1986). *International Journal of Psychophysiology*, *4*, 41–52.

Tareen, K. I., Bashier, A., Saeed, K., & Hussain, T. (1988). Clinical efficacy of codergocrine mesylate in children with learning difficulties. *The Journal of International Medical Research*, *16*, 204–209.

Thomson, M. E. (1977). Identifying the dyslexic child. *Dyslexia Review*, *18*, 5–12.

Union Chimique Belge (1976). *Piracetam*. Brussels: Author.

Vencovsky, E., Hronek, J., Drahokoupil, L., Fait, V., Hudcova, T., Laciga, Z., & Vankova, H. (1980). Clinical experience with treatment by piracetam in geropsychiatry. *Czechoslovakian Psychiatry*, *76*, 89–99.

Volakva, J., Simeon, J., Simeon, S., Cho D., & Reker, D. (1981). Effect of piracetam on EEG Spectra of boys with learning disorders. *Psychopharmacology*, *72*, 185–188.

Wacker, J. A. (1988). [Letter to the editor]. *Journal of Learning Disabilities*, *21*, 322–232.

Weingartner, H. (1978). Human state dependent learning. In B. T. Ho, D. W. Richards, III, & D. Chute (Eds.), *Drug discrimination and state dependent learning*. New York: Academic Press.

Weingartner, H., Langer, D., Grice, J., & Rapoport, J. L. (1982). Acquisition and retrieval of information in amphetamine-treated hyperactive children. *Psychiatry Research*, *6*, 21–29.

Weiss, G., & Hechtman, L. T. (1986). *Hyperactive children grown up. Empirical findings and theoretical considerations*. New York: the Guilford Press.

Werry, J. S. (1974). Minimal brain dysfunction (neurological impairment) in children. *New Zealsand Medical Journal*, *80*, 94–100.

Werry, J. S. (1980). Anticholinergic sedatives. In G. Burrows & J. S. Werry (Eds.), *Recent advances in human psychopharmacology* (pp. 19–42). Greenwich, CT: JAI Press.

Werry, J. S., & Aman, M. G. (1975). Methylphenidate and haloperidol in children. Effects on attention, memory, and activity. *Archives of General Psychiatry*, *32*, 790–795.

Werry, J. S., & Aman, M. G. (1980). Anxiety in children. In G. D. Burrows & B. M. Davies (Eds.), *Handbook of studies on anxiety* (pp. 165–192). Amsterdam: ASP Biological and Medical Press.

Westman, J., Arthur, B., & Scheidler, E. (1965). Reading retardation: an overview. *American Journal of Diseases in Children*, *109*, 359–369.

Wilsher, C., Atkins, G., & Manfield, P. (1979). Piracetam as an aid to learning in dyslexia. *Psychopharmacology*, *65*, 107–109.

Wilsher, C., Atkins, G., & Manfield, P. (1985). Effects of piracetam on dyslexic's reading ability. *Journal of Learning Disabilities*, *18*, 19–25.

Wilsher, C. R., Bennett, D., Chase, C. H., Conners, C. K., DiIanni, M., Feagans, L., Hanvik, L. J., Helfgott, E., Koplewicz, H., Overby, P., Reader, M. J., Rudel, R. G., & Tallal, P. (1987). Piracetam and dyslexia: Effects on reading tests. *Journal of Clinical Psychopharmacology*, *7*, 230–237.

Wilsher, C. R., & Milewski, J. (1983). Effects of piracetam on dyslexic's conceptualizing ability, *Psychopharmacology Bulletin*, *19*, 3–4.

Winsberg, B. G., & Yepes, L. E. (1978). Antipsychotics (major tranquilizers, neuroleptics). In J. S. Werry (Ed.), *Pediatric psychopharmacology. The use of behavior modifying drugs in children* (pp. 234–273). New York: Brunner/ Mazel.

Yule, W., & Rutter, M. (1970). Selection of children with intellectual or educational retardation. In M. Rutter, J. Tizard, & K. Whitmore (Eds.), *Education, health and behaviour*. London: Longman, 1970.

Zametkin, A. J., Reeves, J. C., Webster, L., & Werry, J. S. (1986). Promethazine treatment of children with attention deficit disorder with hyperactivity—ineffective and unpleasant. *Journal of the American Academy of Child Psychiatry*, *25*, 854–856.

17
Remediation of Psychological Process Deficits in Learning Disabilities

Ivan L. Beale and Lynette J. Tippett

Psychological processes have dubious status in the field of learning disabilities. The concept of process deficits as a basis of learning disorders, once generally accepted and even popular, is now anathemic to many professionals in the field. To these same professionals there is an even more disreputable notion, that learning disabilities may be remediated by the treatment of deficient psychological processes. Yet, despite the increasingly prevalent insistence by educationists that process theory and process remediation are ill-conceived and irrelevant to the treatment of learning disabilities, the issue is far from being resolved.

The field of learning disabilities was founded on the concept that learning disability is the manifestation of anomalous functioning of one or more basic psychological processes. Over the decades different processes have been emphasized as important at different times, according to current wisdom or misapprehension. Various process theories have waxed and waned, and although few have endured to the present as strong contenders, all have retained at least a little support in some quarters. A survey reported by Kirk, Berry, and Senf (1979) showed that at that time many teachers were using process-based remedial procedures.

Theories as to the involvement of processes in learning disabilities have gone hand in hand with remedial practices derived from them, and since the 1920s the learning disabilities field has witnessed the rise (less often, the fall) of a succession of remedial models with their basis in some sort of process theory. Ill-considered enthusiasm in the promotion of some of these models, usually without adequate research as to their efficacy, has led to an almost universal scepticism by responsible professionals, an attitude reinforced by the simplistic or illogical character of some of the underlying theories. On the other hand, newcomers to the learning disabilities field are constantly rediscovering theories and methods already discarded by serious researchers and practitioners, thus adding fuel to a continuing controversy. An unfortunate result of all this has been the development, among special educators in particular, of a general intolerance of a broad class of psychological concepts often used in

526

process theory and many are now inclined to reject on sight any theory or remedial model that seems belong to this class.

In this chapter, the view is taken that there is insufficient evidence to conclude that process approaches are entirely without merit. We believe that there are good arguments for not discarding process theory and remediation as a general class until conclusive evidence comes to hand. This chapter sets out a model for evaluation of process theories and their associated assessment and remedial methods. The model is illustrated by reference to the literature on remediation of the processes of attention and memory, processes that well illustrate the pervasive, multifaceted character of typical processes that makes them so difficult to deal with. Attention and memory play such a fundamental role in learning that a description of learning disabilities that did not incorporate these processes would necessarily be of limited usefulness.

The chapter first sketches the role of processes in the past history of the learning disabilities field. Problems encountered with early conceptualizations of psychological processes are described, and the varied fortunes of past process-based remedial methods are noted. Characteristic deficiencies of process remediation are outlined, and the argument is made that the apparent weakness of the process approach has usually not resulted from bad theory so much as from inadequate models for assessment of the effectiveness of treatment. A different approach is offered, based on the behavioral assessment model, and its advantages are illustrated by reference to the literature on remediation of attentional and memory problems in learning disabilities. The chapter deals with both developmental problems and acquired problems resulting from head injury or cerebral diseases. Finally, relevant literature is reviewed and conclusions reached concerning the effectiveness of process remediation.

What are Psychological Processes?

From the learning disabilities definitions reviewed in chapter 1 it can be seen that psychological processes play a central role in accepted definitions of learning disabilities. An assumed dificiency in the operation of one or more basic processes is the defining characteristic that distinguishes learning disabilities from learning problems having a basis in educational, cultural, or emotional factors. Yet, lack of agreement on the definition and measurement of such processes tends to undermine the usefulness of the learning disabilities definition itself.

In general, psychological processes are theoretical constructs inferred from direct observations of behavior. They take their character from that of the theoretical framework in which the observations were made. Because learning has been approached from several different theoretical frameworks (e.g., cognitive theory, behavioral theory), there are different conceptions of what sort of processes describe adequately what is going on. Different theoretical stances at this basic level themselves impede agreement on how to define and measure processes.

To illustrate this point, consider the idea of a basic process called *attention*. In the context of cognitive theory this is usually dealt with in the framework of information processing theory, and a class of attention processes are identified such as *sustained attention*, *focused attention*, *selective attention*, *divided attention*, and so forth. There is no general agreement on the number or defining characteristics of these processes (see, e.g., Levin, Grafman, & Eisenberg, 1987). Cognitive models generally emphasize intrinsic operating properties of the attention components and the intrinsic interconnections between them. In the learning disabilities field, the appeal of cognitive models seems to lie in their compatibility with a "mental process" type of analysis that many learning disabilities professionals might informally use as an heuristic when attempting to understand their clients' problems. But these models have little to suggest regarding effective procedures for remediating attentional problems.

In the context of behavior theory, on the other hand, attention is synonymous with stimulus control. It is defined by the controlling relation between the stimulus and behavior and refers to the type of behavior controlled by the stimulus, rather than something inferred about the internal state of the organism (see, e.g., Mostofsky, 1970). In contrast to the information processing approach, behavior theory emphasizes the environmental determinants of attention. It is therefore easily applicable to questions about how to address attentional problems, always provided that these can be conceptualized within the behavioral model.

Assumptions of Process Models

Torgesen (1979) identified three assumptions that cause difficulties for process models of learning disabilities: (a) the basic psychological processes necessary for learning can be identified and measured, (b) these processing skills can be trained, and (c) training on a given skill within one task setting will generalize to other academic skills. Torgesen considered that the processes involved varied according to the specific requirements of the task, but allowed that where these requirements were known there was some evidence that appropriate training could improve performance. He was of the view that there was little support for the assumption of generalization, however. He referred specifically to generalization across tasks, but it should be noted that the assumption of generalization might also be taken to apply to other domains, including time, setting, and other salient environmental variables. This important issue will be taken up later in this chapter.

To the assumptions noted by Torgesen might be added one other that has been a major generator of heat in the controversy about the validity of process theory; that is, the assumption that learning disability, or even particular manifestations of it, is caused by problems in just one or another psychological process. Even in the 1970s it was not uncommon to see journal articles in which the assumption was made that a deficit in a single process might account for *all* learning disabilities. More prevalent today is the more realistic assumption that a specific category of learning disability, such as specific reading difficulty of a dysphonetic variety, is associated with a deficit in one or more particular basic processes (e.g., short-term memory; Jorm, 1983). Even this weaker assumption may not be to everyone's satisfaction, given the variety of operational definitions available for a given deficit and the usual validity and reliability problems in establishing "abnormal" performance. Added to this is the difficulty of ruling out other factors such as unmeasured processes, educational shortcomings, and emotional problems.

The identification of "subtypes" of learning disabilities is now a major focus of research that emphasizes the need to distinguish between apparently similar learning disability manifestations that have different origins, that is, where different process deficits are involved (see, e.g., Kavale & Forness, 1987; Rourke, 1985). Better knowledge of this area is necessary before convincing demonstrations will be possible of causal relations between anomalous psychological processes and learning disabilities.

History of Process Theory

The antecedents of the modern learning disabilities field and the general classes of process theory that have played an important role in the field's development have been extensively dealt with elsewhere (Kavale & Forness, 1985; Radencich, 1984). Early conceptualizations emphasized perceptual–motor organization (e.g., Strauss & Lehtinen, 1947), lateralization of visual memory traces (Orton, 1937), and psycholinguistic processes (Kirk, 1962). Elements of these theories may still be found in modern counterparts, even though the original theories, together with the remedial programs based on them, largely have been dropped from the mainstream core of the learning disabilities field.

The persistence of these elements of process theory suggests that there may be some validity in the observations on which they are based. Successive generations of clinicians and researchers are in turn impressed by the very same patterns of aberrant performance in the learning disabled clients they see. The observations may be valid, but there is a difficulty in using them to develop a theory from which can be derived effective remedial programs. The learning disabilities field is driven by the need to provide effective treatment, and this dictates the final criterion that theories will be expected to meet.

By this criterion, process theories have performed equivocally. Reviews of the efficacy of process-oriented treatment have tended to show that such treatments have a poor track record in bringing about improvements in academic performance (Hammill & Larsen, 1978). Worse yet, there is evidence that some may fail even to bring about change in the process targeted as deficient (Hammill & Larsen, 1978), although others may manage to do so (Kavale, 1981; Wade & Kass, 1987). However, the methods used to evaluate process-oriented treatments may themselves be criticized as failing to distinguish between competent and incompetent application of a remedial program, good and bad program design, suitable and unsuitable subjects, sensitive and insensitive dependent variables, and so on. Perhaps it is a general awareness of these problems that has permitted many process approaches to survive in the face of lack of any strong evidence of their effectiveness.

Characteristics of Process Remediation

It is usual to make a fundamental distinction between academic or criterion skills remediation and process remediation. The former focuses on the problem behavior(s) as the object of concern, to which remedial measures are directly applied. Effects of remedial efforts are measured directly by change in the behavior. Behavioral methods (e.g., Koorland, 1986; Singh & Beale, 1986) generally fall into this category. Process remediation, on the other hand, is based on a model that assumes that a criterion skills problem is just one effect of an underlying process problem that may have many other manifestations not necessarily apparent at the time.

As already indicated, process theory assumes that if problems in acquisition of criterion skills are caused by problems with a basic process necessary for the learning of those skills, the problem is best addressed at the process level. One corollary is that a criterion skill cannot improve by direct remediation unless the process problem is also addressed. Of course, it has been argued that process remediation, although possibly necessary, could not by itself be sufficient. To illustrate with a simple example, suppose that a child cannot read because of a visual memory problem, and that this problem can be overcome by an effective process training program. The result does not instantly make the child an adequate reader, but rather makes him now *able* to profit by direct instruction in reading skills.

A distinction must be made between psychological processes and those skills that are once (or twice) removed from the criterion behavior but comprise an essential part of the chain of events leading to a successful performance. Examples of such skills might include rehearsal, "word attack" skills, and conscious directing of attention. Basic processes are typically regarded as more fundamental, unconscious, and automatic than this. Thus, training a child in rehearsal strategies might not be considered process training unless the view is taken that this results in the modification of some automatic process underlying rehearsal mechanisms. On the other hand, training a child in left-to-right scanning of visual material might be considered process training if the aim is to influence lateralization of ocular motor control.

This distinction captures one typical characteristic of process remediation, but there is one other that is probably closer to a defining characteristic. Whereas criterion skills are normally trained in the context of the criterion task, process training usually employs a quite different context. For example, a criterion skills approach to a reading problem might involve the reinforcement of self-correction of errors while reading text, whereas a process approach might involve training in "intersensory integration" of visual and auditory cues outside the reading context.

This remoteness of process training from the criterion task is probably its most criticized aspect, emphasizing as it does both the assumed but unproven causal link and the assumed generalization of training gains. It is paradoxical that the most remote interventions attract the greatest incredulity from sceptical professionals at the same time as they spark the greatest interest and hope among potential recipients and their families. The faith and loyalty engendered among the practitioners of remote process remediation seems unrelated to the amount of effort or expense involved, since it characterizes both resource-intensive approaches such as that advocated by Doman, Spitz, Zucman, Delacato, and Doman (1960) and the "magic-bullet" approaches represented by dietary or pharmacological treatments (see Silver, 1987) and tinted lenses (Irlen, 1983).

This aspect of process approaches may best be understood in terms of our indoctrination in the "medical model," nicely captured by the observation of the physician William Osler that the thing that most distinguishes animals from mankind is the insatiable desire of the latter to take medicine. This is reinforced by a natural contempt for anything as familiar to us as a straightforward educational approach that, on the face of it, seems really no different from the thing that has already failed us.

The acceptability of treatment has to be considered, since the client's motivation to participate is clearly an important determinant of how useful a treatment is. If a remedial program is tedious, too demanding of time or effort, or lacks credibility in the eyes of the client, it is unlikely to be adopted or carried to completion. Resources available for supervising or tutoring a program will also influence its appeal. Programs that are time intensive but can be supervised in a normal classroom may be quite appropriate for a school-aged child, but usually will not suit an adult with an acquired disability who has no access to such a teaching resource. These considerations may explain why process-oriented programs, often computerized, predominantly are advocated for adults with acquired learning disabilities, whereas children's developmental problems increasingly are dealt with in an educational, criterion skills framework.

There is perhaps another reason why a different approach might be taken with acquired, as opposed to developmental, learning disabilities. Children with developmental learning disabilities who have yet to develop certain skills will need eventually to be taught them, using skills training. But this is not necessarily true of acquired learning disabilities, where well learned skills may be lost as a result, say, of head injury. In such cases, process treatment alone theoretically may be sufficient to remove the impediment to performance of any skills lost as a result of the injury (see, e.g., Bracy, 1986).

Varieties of Process Intervention

The aim of remediation in learning disabilities is to overcome, wholly or in part, the client's learning difficulties. When the criterion skills approach is taken, remedial training is based on an analysis of precisely which skills require attention, followed by training of these skills. When a process approach is used, emphasis is placed on identification of problems at the process level that underlie the problems at the criterion skills level.

Process-based interventions have used three basic strategies, built on assessment of the integrity of the client's psychological processes. Chronbach and Snow (1977) distinguished these strategies according to whether they capitalized on existing strengths, compensated for or circumvented areas of weakness, or attempted to strengthen weaknesses. In the field of special education, the efficacy of these different approaches has been extensively argued under the headings of *aptitude-treatment interactions* and *diagnostic-prescriptive teaching* (Arter & Jenkins, 1979; Chronbach & Snow, 1977; Hartlage & Telzrow, 1987; Singh & Beale, 1986). In addition to the problems inherent in any treatment outcome studies, there are additional problems associated with the validity of the neuropsychological diagnostic procedures used to assess the clients' strengths and weaknesses. A review of these is outside the scope of this chapter, which will be confined to a brief description of the first two categories but a much fuller exploration of the third. This is because the third category, *process training*, is the one most identified with process approaches, but does not seem yet to have been subject to much logical analysis.

The first category, *capitalization of strengths*, involves identifying the client's strongest or most intact skill areas and designing a remedial program that maximizes the use of these. For example, a child with poor auditory but good visual skills would be thought to profit more from a remedial reading program that emphasized a visual route than one emphasizing an auditory route. In the second category, *compensatory or circumventive*, the client is taught to find ways around his difficulty, or alternatively to structure the environment so that the difficulty does not impede progress. In either case the desired skills are attained by an unusual route, and there may be marked limitations on what the client will be able to achieve with these methods.

The third category, *process remediation*, is the most controversial, in that it assumes the possibility of modifying a deficient psychological process, a *strengthening of weaknesses*. The attraction here is the promise of a "normal" psychological process that will allow normal learning without circumvention or compensation. It is hardly surprising that it is the process remediation theories that capture the public interest—they simply offer more.

Not all process approaches fit neatly the categories proposed by Chronbach and Snow. As will be seen, some are amalgams of two or more categories. In the next section we turn to a discussion of the nature of process remediation and the evidence necessary to show that process remediation is effective.

The Relation between Psychological Processes and Behavior

The variety of remedial procedures that might be seen as process oriented makes it difficult to define satisfactorily what is and what is not a process approach. There may be an advantage in setting out a clear framework showing functional relations between processes, the criterion skills that depend on them, and how different levels of remediation relate to both of these. This framework might shed light on the theoretical advantages and disadvantages of different remedial approaches and generally help to systematize and clarify the whole remedial endeavor.

Such a framework is presented in Figure 17.1, which encompasses all psychological processes in a general way, for the purpose of demonstrating how such a framework can clarify remediation issues.

The top level in the diagram represents the "innermost" level of function and contains all those basic functions that might be considered "basic psychological processes." Only a few are named here to give the general idea. These could be further subdivided into component subprocesses, of course. At the next level down are represented other processes that are, arguably, less basic, because they involve interactions between basic processes (e.g., sensory integration) or between basic processes and the external environment (e.g., learning). This level is differentiated here because this level of process has been emphasized in

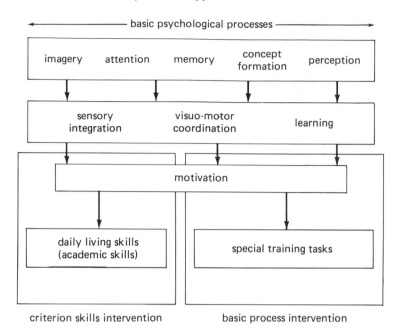

FIGURE 17.1. A diagrammatic representation of the organization of basic psychological processes and learned skills. The square boxes at the bottom indicate the distinction between criterion skills intervention and basic process intervention (see text).

some process theories of learning disabilities (Ayres, 1978; Frostig & Horne, 1964). Again, these are a few examples from a more extensive list.

The next two, outermost, levels represent the involvement of basic processes, together with motivational factors, in the learning and execution of skills. Two classes of skills are differentiated. Criterion skills are those by which the learning disability is identified. In an academic context, these are usually reading, writing, math, or language skills. In a head injury rehabilitation context, they might be daily living skills or work skills. Special skills are those taught in process training. As noted previously, the skills trained and the training context typically are somewhat removed from the criterion skills and context in which learning disability is defined. An example would be visual–perceptual training using nonword material, where a learning disability in reading was identified.

In Figure 17.1, the square boxes indicate the essential difference between process intervention and criterion skills intervention. The only difference is the nature of the skills to which training is directed, together with the context of training. Both involve the training of skills in some motivational framework intended to promote learning. So far, this analysis shows a disadvantage for process intervention, because there is no guarantee that the benefits of process training will generalize to the criterion skills and context. In fact, the relevant literature is usually interpreted as showing that generalization seldom occurs without specific generalization training (Stokes & Baer, 1977). Direct intervention with criterion skills does not require this step, provided that training is given in all affected skills and contexts.

If this analysis were sufficient, no case could be made for process training at all. But other aspects must be considered. First, it can be argued that generalization depends not just on the number of similar elements (stimuli and behaviors) in the trained and untrained tasks, but also on the similarity of the underlying processes required for performance of the task (Mostofsky, 1965). Thus, a case can be made that if a process is influenced by training on one task, other tasks involving that process will be influenced by generalization. The question, then, is whether processes are more influenced as a result of "process training" than as a result of criterion skills training.

Second, advocates of process remediation have argued that there is no point in attempting to train criterion skills unless the required underlying processes are functioning adequately. As already noted, accepted definitions of learning disabilities specify a deficiency in one or more underlying processes. Given these arguments, the critical issue seems to be whether process training really influences the underlying processes in a way that criterion skills training does not. What is special about process training tasks that could confer this ability?

Processes are not behavior, but are inferred from observations of behavior. Attempts to train processes must proceed by training behavior in a way designed to modify not just the behavior, but also the process that gives rise to it. It is assumed that by strengthening skills that require the correct operation of the underlying process, the process in turn will be strengthened. This is familiar to behaviorists as the chaining model (Catania, 1984). Process remediation must also assume that some skills have a sufficiently direct connection with the targeted process, that such training will be effective, even though training on the criterion skills will not be effective. To illustrate, Delacato (1966) adopted a remedial reading program based on an assumed deficiency in lateralization of verbal processing, in which he sought to influence lateralization through perceptual–motor exercises, outside the context of reading. He assumed that reading remediation would be ineffective in modifying lateralization because the connection was too remote.

It is straightforward to show that process training can result in improvement of the *skill* that is trained, but it is more difficult to show that the underlying process is affected. To do this requires showing generalization of training effects to other skills that are quite unlike the trained one in most respects, except that they depend on the same underlying process. It must also be possible to rule out alternative possible causes of improvement, such as increased motivation or expectancy effects. Finally, it should be appreciated that generalized improvement is not to be expected in the performance of untrained skills, but rather in the client's ability to learn these skills. To illustrate with the previous example of perceptual–motor training as process remediation for reading disability, the process training ought not to create sudden improvements in reading scores, but only make it possible for reading skills training to achieve this.

Assessment of Process Deficits and their Remediation

It is one thing to advocate the advantages of process approaches to assessment of learning disability and its remediation, and quite another to demonstrate the effectiveness of these approaches. Adequate research in this area requires a model that incorporates both assessment and treatment considerations. A strong case can be made that the Behavioral Assessment (BA) model is best able to handle this task. When applied as recommended, it permits an evaluation of assessment and treatment that takes account of several issues that have been stumbling blocks to progress (Nelson & Hayes, 1986). Issues addressed include:

1. identification of problem behaviors
2. selection of dependent measures, with appropriate social and ecological validation
3. identification of client characteristics
4. selection of remedial method
5. setting of treatment goals
6. programing and measurement of generalization
7. measurement of treatment integrity.

The model is sufficiently broad to combine criterion-based assessment measures with neuropsychological measures, thereby permitting problems both at the behavioral and the process level to be examined. A frequent criticism of process approaches is that they may address a process deficit that is irrelevant to the problem identified at the behavioral level. A great strength of the model is its emphasis on the use of single-subject research designs to enable the effects of treatment to be measured within a single individual. This is necessary in an area such as learning disabilities, where clients' problems and their underlying causes may be idiosyncratic. This uniqueness both in causation and effect renders traditional group designs ineffective until such time as the important subject characteristics, and the way they operate, are known. Classification research is not sufficiently developed at this time to provide functional subtypes for the purpose of treatment selection (e.g., Rourke, 1985).

The variety and flexibility of single-subject designs makes them particularly suitable for the learning disabilities area, where treatment is often an uncharted journey with many pitfalls and changes in direction dictated by the client's response to treatment components. The need to provide for extensive generalization training and testing is also well served by these designs (Drabman, Hammer, & Rosenbaum, 1979; Stokes & Baer, 1977). Generalization training increases the likelihood that the trained behavior will occur in other settings, at other times, with different reinforcers, and other environmental changes. Generalization testing permits measurement of the extent to which this occurs.

It is regrettable that nearly all studies of process training have used between-groups designs that are insensitive to individual variations in response to the training variables, making it difficult to see whether a subgroup of the whole subject sample might have responded favorably to the training, even though the sample as a whole did not. An even more problematic aspect of process-training research, however, is the neglect of any systematic generalization training or testing such as would be required to produce convincing evidence that training had resulted in more than just improvement on a process-training task. Although these are not the only design problems encountered, they are the ones that hinder most the ability of this literature to support the notion that process training is viable.

Attention Remediation

Attention Deficits in Learning Disabilities

Before proceeding to discuss attention remediation, it is first necessary to ask whether it has been established that learning disabilities can be caused by underlying problems with attention processes. It has generally been asserted that this is so, on several grounds. First, theoretical arguments can be made that any sort of learning requires attention to stimuli, responses, and consequences. These are some arguments against this position in the literature on respondent conditioning and learning without awareness (Catania, 1984), but these have little practical import for the applied field of learning disabilities. Most theories of learning that have been applied to humans involve attention as an essential part of the learning process. The difficulty is that there are many different conceptions of what attention is and now it works. Reviewing these would be a major task outside the scope of this chapter, but a brief synopsis will help make sense of what is to follow.

Varieties of Attention

We have already referred to the basic distinction between cognitive and behavioral approaches to attention. In behavioral models, attention is a property of a stimulus (stimulus control; see Boakes & Halliday, 1972) or a type of response (observing response; see Wyckoff, 1952). In a strict behavioral model, there are no underlying processes to be addressed, only the attentional behaviors and stimulus characteristics. In the strict sense, then, there is no place in the behavioral model for process remediation as we have already defined it. As we shall see, behavioral approaches to attention remediation are usually structured around criterion skills and are not considered to be affecting those skills by influencing some underlying process.

Cognitive psychology has placed heavy emphasis on the role of attention in the cognitive system. Of major interest here are several categories of attention that have been proposed. Useful distinctions have been made between arousal, alertness, vigilance, sustained attention, capacity, and selectivity. *Arousal* refers to the state of general wakefulness that permits the person to receive stimulation from the environment. *Alertness* is the degree of readiness to respond to particular input, that permits a rapid response to be made. *Vigilance* refers to the ability throughout a long interval to respond to stimuli that are infrequently and unpredictably presented. *Sustained attention* differs from vigilance in that stimuli are presented frequently over a prolonged period and must be rapidly processed. *Capacity*, or breadth of attention, refers to the number of stimuli, or dimensions of a stimulus, that can simultaneously be apprehended. *Selective attention*, or focused attention, refers to the focusing of attention on relevant aspects of the environment and the exclusion of irrelevant or distracting stimuli. These categories, and their roles in learning disabilities, are discussed in detail elsewhere (e.g., Samuels & Edwall, 1981).

It should not be thought that this is the only, or best, taxonomy of attention, but only that it is typical. In the head injury area, for example, some more complex attentional constructs are receiving consideration. An example is *divided attention*, where two or more tasks are performed concurrently (van Zomeren & Brouwer, 1987). Others who have offered classifications of attention are Berlyne (1970) and Posner and Rafal (1987).

Attention Deficits in Learning Disabilities

The literature on this topic is so extensive that a comprehensive review is not appropriate here, so we will simply allude to the variety of evidence to show that there can be no doubt that attention is widely considered to play a vital role in learning disabilities. That the issue is still contentious is apparent from recent reviews (e.g., Krupski, 1986).

Among the first to suggest an important role for attention deficits in learning disabilities were Zeaman and House (1963) and later Fisher and Zeaman (1973), who built influential theoretical models around experimental data on discrimination learning by intellectually retarded children. They advanced the view that learning by retarded children was impeded by a too-limited breadth of attention across dimensions of critical stimuli. Other lines of evidence from different attention-testing paradigms seemed consistent with this idea (Hagen & Huntsman, 1971; Ullman, 1974). Lovaas, Schreibman, and their collaborators (e.g., Lovaas, Schreibman, Koegel, & Rehm, 1971) cited *overselective attention* as a key factor limiting the learning ability of autistic children. Later studies showed that the typical attention problems both of retarded and autistic children were modifiable by training (e.g., Allen & Fuqua, 1985; Beale & Singh, 1986).

Ross (1976) has reviewed several studies of children with learning disabilities that indicated a developmental lag in the capacity to employ and sustain selective attention. In the same book, Ross also presents a strong case for regarding "impulse-control" problems of hyperactive children as reflecting an impairment of selective attention. This linking of attentional problems with hyperactivity has become well accepted in the DSM III and DSM III-R definitions of Attention Deficit Disorder and Attention Deficit-Hyperactivity Disorder, respectively (see also Douglas & Peters, 1979).

At the empirical level, there have been many demonstrations of differences between learning disabled children and normal controls in the performance of tasks having strong attentional components of one sort or another. These include sustained attention (Beale, Matthew, Oliver, & Corballis, 1987; Eliason & Richman, 1987; Swanson, 1983), visual search (McIntyre, Murray, & Blackwell, 1981), focused attention (Hallahan, Gajar, Cohen, & Tarver, 1978; Hebben, Whitman, Milberg, Andresko, & Galpin, 1981), and attention span (McIntyre, Murray, Cronin, & Blackwell, 1978).

It might seem from this that there is no aspect of attention that has not been implicated, but it would be unwise to accept too willingly the idea that attentional deficits are the prime basis of learning disabilities. In many studies contrasting learning disabilities with "control" children, the criterion for learning disability has been dubious, and often there has been no attempt to create a group that is homogeneous with respect to learning disability characteristics. Unless more than one control group is used, it can be difficult to decide whether a group difference on some attention measure is a cause, a result, or merely a correlate, of learning disabilities (Jorm, 1983; Koppell, 1979).

Head injury and other types of cerebral trauma seem frequently to result in learning and performance problems in which attentional deficits are implicated (Binder, 1896; Brooks, 1984; Gronwall, 1987). The nature of the attentional problem depends on the type of injury and the neurological pathways affected. For example, the attentional disorder known as hemineglect is typically associated with damage to the right parietal region (Hecaen & Albert, 1978). Closed head injury often has attentional sequelae, although the nature of these is still a matter of debate (van Zomeren & Brouwer, 1987). Research on this topic has identified deficits in sustained attention (Rosvold, Mirsky, Sarason, Bransom, & Beck, 1956; van Zomeren & Deelman, 1978), selective attention (Wood, 1987), arousal, and divided attention (Gronwall, 1987). As is the case with developmental learning disabilities, there are strong indications of attentional deficits of some sort underlying learning problems (Wood, 1987). With acquired disorders, learning is required not only for new skills, but also may be needed for the recovery of skills that have been lost.

Remediation of Attention Deficits

In the following description of the literature on process remediation, it is not intended to cite all the relevant studies, but rather to indicate typical results and illustrate the impediments preventing clear conclusions regarding the efficacy of the process approach. It will be clear from the foregoing that there are various approaches to remediation of basic process deficits, but that this chapter focuses on what Chronbach and Snow (1977) referred to as *process remediation*, or direct modification of the deficiency in the basic process. However, in the following description of research on attention remediation a variety of approaches are considered in order to give a broad appreciation of what has been attempted. Consequently, studies are classified primarily by the type of remedial approach (e.g., circumventive, capitalization on strengths, or process remediation), but it is also noted whether they targeted criterion skills or basic processes.

Circumventive Approaches

Circumventive approaches for overcoming attentional problems have a long history. Early attempts to improve the classroom performance of brain damaged and hyperactive children involved the use of special rooms in which distracting stimuli were minimized and novel (attention grabbing) relevant stimulus materials were used (Cruikshank, Bentzen, Ratzberg, & Tannhauser, 1961). Similarly, the *limited breadth of attention* hypothesis of attention deficit in retarded children led to teaching practices in which stimuli to be differentiated by the clients were artificially made different on many dimensions. Increasing the number of relevant stimulus dimensions theoretically would increase the likelihood that a relevant dimension would be attended to (e.g., Zeaman & House,

1963). A similar approach has been advocated for teaching autistic children, in which the training methods force attention to more than one dimension of the relevant stimuli (Allen & Fuqua, 1985). Rehabilitation programs for victims of head injury sometimes emphasize circumventive or compensatory procedures. One approach involves alerting the client to avoid activities that are demanding of the deficient process. Another is to have the client, or others concerned with the case, so structure the client's environment so that the consequences of the process deficit are minimized (Diller, 1976; Trexler, 1982).

Although there is evidence that circumventive or compensatory procedures are better than nothing, there is no denying that they are restrictive in what they can achieve. In the end, the client may be functional only in a limited and artificial environment, with little prospect of a normal life. Of course, this approach could be combined usefully with other remedial approaches that directly addressed the process deficit. Attentional processes are so pervasive a requirement in most tasks that it is hard to imagine a circumventive strategy at the most basic level. The best that could be achieved would be to minimize tasks that were particularly demanding of those aspects of attention in which the client was deficient.

Capitalization on Strengths

The *capitalization on strengths* approach may have more to recommend it, as it is often seen as an aid to process remediation. Several examples of the application of this approach to developmental learning disabilities have been reviewed by Hartlage and Telzrow (1983) and by Singh and Beale (1986). We are not aware of any studies of this sort dealing specifically with attention deficits, although this would be possible in principle. For example, a child demonstrating reading problems having an underlying auditory attentional deficit but with normal visual and tactile attention processes could be taught using procedures that emphasized visual and tactile stimuli. The value of such an approach would depend on whether it could result in the development of a normal repertoire of reading skills or whether it would assist with the later development of normal auditory attentional processes.

The *capitalization of strengths* approach has been advocated strongly by Luria (1963) for the rehabilitation of those with acquired learning disabilities. In fact, Luria's approach seems a combination of two approaches, *strengths* and *compensation*. The key concept here is the use of an intact mechanism to support an impaired one. According to Luria's "bridging" model, such support can progressively be faded out as the function is gradually acquired by the impaired mechanism (see e.g., Craine, 1982; Horton & Miller, 1985). For this approach to be used with attention deficits, it would be necessary to have such deficits confined to certain sensory modalities or particular classes of motor response. We know of no studies that fit this category.

A model closely related to Luria's is implicit in the rehabilitation procedures used by Ben-Yishay and his collaborators for the remediation of attention deficits resulting from cerebral trauma (Ben-Yishay, Piasetsky, & Rattock, 1987; Piasetsky, Ben-Yishay, Weinberg, & Diller, 1982). In this case the "bridging" is between hierarchically layered levels of attentional skills, training commencing at the most elementary level and proceeding upward through successively more complex stages. The skills training is conducted on specialized equipment, and gains have not been shown to generalize to other classes of task in which attention is an essential ingredient. Thus, the validity of these procedures for addressing deficits in criterion skills such as the activities of daily life is unknown.

Process Remediation

Direct attention remediation includes both process remediation as we have defined it and attention skills modification in which "attention behaviors" are targeted directly. When the behaviors targeted are criterion skills, for example, attending to task in a classroom, it is assumed that process training is not intended. If, on the other hand, training is given on some special task, for example, a computerized reaction time task, it is assumed that process training is intended.

Numerous studies have shown that classroom attention skills are directly modifiable by the manipulation of antecedent stimuli or behavior consequences (e.g., Coleman, 1970; Glynn, Thomas, & Shee, 1973) or by self-recording of attention (Rooney, Hallahan, & Lloyd, 1984). It has been shown that changes in attention behaviors brought about by such methods are not necessarily accompanied by improvements in academic performance, even though targeting academic performance may often result in indirect improvements in (untargeted) attention behavior. This well illustrates that attention behaviors are not usually criterion skills, but rather prerequisite skills to academic performance, one step back in the chain. There has been little investigation of whether such changes generalize across settings (e.g., to untrained classrooms), teachers, or academic materials.

Positive reinforcement and other operant conditioning procedures have been employed successfully for increasing the attentive behavior of head injured persons engaged in rehabilitation programs (Wood, 1987). As in the developmental examples just described, the attention behaviors taught were one step removed from criterion skills, but some (informal) evidence was cited to support the idea that there were generalized improvements in the ability to learn the criterion skills that were the true goal of rehabilitation.

Several studies have used process training to remediate attention problems in learning disabled children. Brown and Alford (1984) studied a group of learning disabled children identified as having pervasive attention problems. Their training program contained a number of component tasks including matching-to-sample, word analysis, visual memory, and picture arrangement. Variants of each task were arranged in order of difficulty to facilitate transfer from easier to harder examples. Self-verbalization of problem-solving strategies was taught in the context of all component tasks, following the procedures of Meichenbaum (1977). Direct effects of training on performance of these tasks was not reported, emphasis being placed instead on changes in performance on a group of untrained tasks considered to reflect attention skills and academic skills. Tests on which the learning disabled children improved, relative to untrained controls, suggested some generalized improvements both in attention skills and academic performance. However, improvements were not found in some skill areas that were closely related to training tasks, and those improvements that were statistically significant did not seem large enough to be of practical importance, in view of the 16 hours of individual training given to each learning disabled child.

Hallahan, Tarver, Kauffman, and Graybeal (1978) compared the effectiveness of reinforcement versus response cost used for training selective attention during a central–incidental learning task. Using developmental learning disabled children, they found that positive reinforcement increased selective attention on the training task, but response cost did not. This result could be taken as evidence of process remediation, since the training task was not directly related to academic skills. However, no evidence was sought of generalization of process gains to performance of criterion skills, so the relevance of the result to the treatment of learning disabilities is unclear.

Other studies have explored the effects of different training variables on performance of developmental learning disabled children on the central–incidental learning task. Dawson, Hallahan, Reeve, and Ball (1980) identified three categories that had been investigated: perceptual aspects of the stimuli, cognitive and verbal mediational strategies, and motivation. This work identifies variables that have a weak or strong influence in procedures used for training selective attention in learning disabled children; however, it has little to say about whether such training has any effect on the performance of academic skills in the classroom.

Several studies have explored the modifiability of attention processes affected by head injury or other cerebral trauma. Since clients in this category are often adults who are no longer in school, the criterion skills by which the problem is detected are usually daily living activities rather than academic performance. Also, those responsible for rehabilitation are likely to have little access to, or control over, the situations in which the normal activities will be performed. This situation raises problems usually not faced by those dealing with developmental problems, where ability to control the normal environment, both home and classroom, is taken for granted. In addition, the provision of professional resources for developmental problems, although inadequate, far exceeds that for acquired disorders, especially where habilitation or rehabilitation is concerned.

One result of this state of affairs has been an effort to develop self-administered training procedures for those suffering acquired learning disabilities. This has resulted in an emphasis on process remediation, especially involving the use of computerized training with minimal direct professional supervision. There is some concern that enthusiasm for this approach, and promotion of it, should be cognizant of the need first to demonstrate that the approach is truly effective. In particular, it must be shown that performance gains are clinically significant and that they are not limited just to process training tasks.

Some attention remediation programs for head injury victims have given training on tasks requiring attention, relying only on practice or intrinsic motivation as sources of improved performance. For example, Miller (1980) used a form-board task from the Minnesota Spatial Relations Test and found both a practice effect and generalized gains on related tasks. The attention training program developed by Ben-Yishay and colleagues, referred to in a previous section of this chapter, also appears not to involve any explicit procedure for shaping improved attentional responses, with practice and, in some cases, feedback apparently being the only agents of change. These studies do not provide evidence that such procedures result in clinically significant change that is generalized to activities of daily living.

In the same vein, Sohlberg and Mateer (1987) trained three head injured clients on a variety of computerized tasks intended to address several aspects of attention. They did not report the degree of improvement on these tasks, but did report results of occasional generalization tests on the Paced Auditory Serial Addition Test, a test requiring intact attention skills. They interpreted the results as showing evidence of generalized improvement in attention reasonably (although not conclusively) attributable to the remedial program.

Wood and Fussey (1987) evaluated the effectiveness of a computerized program for attention rehabilitation of severely brain injured subjects with attention problems. The training task required organized visual scanning, visual discrimination and judgment, and anticipation and timing of a motor response. In terms of attention components, it required selective, sustained, and divided attention. Training components included practice, visual and auditory feedback for correct and incorrect responses, and automatic adjustment of level of task difficulty to suit individual subjects' ability levels. There was substantial improvement in performance on the training task over the 20 days of training, but only limited transfer to other outcome measures. Generalized gains were observed only on direct observations of attending-to-task behavior and on an attention rating scale completed by staff. Performance on untrained psychomotor and vigilance tasks with attentional components did not benefit from the training program. Wood and Fussey have pointed out that their head injured subjects had severe problems and were not typical of the sort of patient normally considered suitable for attention rehabilitation. Elsewhere (Wood, 1987) it has been suggested that generalization of effects of attention training might be fostered by the use of reinforcers that play a more important part in normal life than those that are typically used in computerized training tasks.

Summary of Attention Process Training

In summary, studies of attention process training, both in head injured and developmental learning disabled subjects, show that although gains can be made on the tasks used for training, this is not usually accompanied by generalized improvements in attention. However, it is noted that no studies have addressed the issue of generalization in a systematic way. There is a clear need for remediation research that is based on a generalization model and that systematically explores the effects of generalization training variables. Until this is done, the literature will continue to be ambiguous as to the validity of the process training approach.

Memory Remediation

The Nature of Human Memory

Most researchers who have studied memory would agree that it is not a unitary phenomenon. Rather, memory is a complex psychological ability that has been subdivided into different kinds of memory and also into different memory processes that underpin the formation and functioning of memories and memory systems. Agreement about the nature of memory would probably not extend further, as different researchers emphasize different distinctions that have been drawn between types or organization of memory. Many seek to explain the observation that some information may be stored in consciousness for relatively brief periods of time and then forgotten, whereas other information seems to be stored indefinitely. Others seek to develop theories of memory that can also explain wide-ranging aspects of cognition.

Typical distinctions include primary memory and secondary memory (James, 1890), sensory memory (iconic, echoic), short-term memory, long-term memory (Atkinson & Shiffrin, 1971; Milner, 1966), working memory subdivided into the central executive (an attentional component), an articulatory loop, and a visuospatial sketch pad (Baddeley & Hitch, 1974; Baddeley & Lieberman, 1980), and long-term memory subdivided into episodic and semantic memory (Tulving, 1972). Dual coding theory posits verbal and imaginal systems of long-term memory (Paivio, 1969, 1974), whereas network theories of long-term semantic memory propose sets of nodes that are concepts interconnected by relations, such as the ACT theory of memory. ACT theory distinguishes between declarative knowledge and procedural knowledge (Anderson, 1976).

Some researchers have focused on the processes that allow memory to function, which to some extent are not linked to any particular model of memory. These include processes such as encoding, storage, and retrieval. Distinctions applied to these processes include the levels of processing theory with different kinds of rehearsal (Craik & Lockhart, 1972), encoding specificity principle (Tulving & Thomson, 1973), and encoding operations on an automatic, effortful continuum (Hasher & Zacks, 1979).

There is considerable theoretical overlap and interaction among different sets of distinctions drawn between memory types and processes, although for practical reasons, researchers tend to focus on one or two of these dimensions. This chapter adopts the idea of working memory proposed by Baddeley, which emphasizes short-term or transient memory as a working storage system of more than one modality that is involved in everyday cognitive tasks. Reference to the organization of long-term memory uses the concept of semantic knowledge.

For the reader who wishes to evaluate the effectiveness of memory training in individuals with a memory deficit, this diverse compendium of memory can be confusing. It is important that researchers and therapists working in applied settings with individuals who have memory problems understand that "the beast" they are dealing with is complex and not a single entity and that there are many ways of viewing it. As a result, the description of the memory deficit suffered by a client depends both on the kind of questions that have been asked and the methods used to measure memory performance in the individual.

Memory Deficits in Learning Disabilities

The issue of whether developmental learning disability is caused by underlying problems with memory processes is complex. Research findings are blurred by methodological difficulties of a diverse nature which all too frequently are overlooked. Of particular concern are the problems inherent in the interpretation of differences between nonhomogeneous groups of subjects.

Another factor that contributes to the muddle in the literature is a consequence of the diverse theoretical views on memory. As a result, different researchers interpret the same performances on tasks in different ways depending on which theory or aspect of a theory they have adopted. Although this is inevitable to some degree, it is important to acknowledge this difficulty and search for ways to minimize its effects. Thorough assessment of a wide range of abilities and performance as well as of environmental and interaction factors for each individual can minimize these effects. This is because it forces an evaluation of information in a broader context than the narrow window through which questions are sometimes posed. It is desirable that individuals labeled as learning disabled be properly assessed not only to determine the nature of any impairment correctly, but also because this will guide the choice of remedial method.

Another difficulty in the investigation of causal relationships between memory deficits and learning disability has been pointed out by Deutsch (1978). Many learning disabled readers have little practice on a range of cognitive skills that are connected to reading and this affects the level of proficiency of those skills. In addition, they may suffer a restricted development of their knowledge base, which will likely affect the efficiency of encoding and retrieval processes in memory performance (see Torgesen [1985] for a discussion of this). Thus, defective memory performance might be as often the result of reading difficulty as the cause of it.

Although there is agreement that many learning disabled individuals perform poorly on certain memory-related tasks, the issue of the nature of any memory deficit is controversial. A reliable finding in the literature is that learning disabled readers frequently perform poorly on tasks of memory span that require brief but verbatim retention of strings of verbal items. Jorm (1983) and Torgesen (1985) both review these findings, which they interpret as involving phonological coding in working memory, or, what Baddeley has called the articulatory loop.

Torgesen and Houck (1980), for example, conducted a series of experiments using the digit span task, comparing groups of retarded readers with consistent digit span deficit, retarded readers with no such deficit, and normal readers. Their results led them to conclude that the poor performance of the retarded readers with a digit span deficit could not be explained just by lack of use of efficient strategies but implied some deficiency of a structural nature in the memory system. However, the explanation of the deficit as one of phonological coding has been challenged (see Hulme & Snowling in this volume for a discussion of this).

There is little conclusive evidence that learning disabled readers have deficits in the visuospatial component of working memory, partly because it is difficult to find memory tasks that involve just visuospatial coding.

Even on tasks that are thought to measure this, such as the Visual Sequential Memory test of the Illinois Test of Psycholinguistic Abilities, there is evidence that individuals often code the material verbally as well as visually (Hicks, 1980). Consequently, findings that were initially thought to indicate problems with the visuospatial code could be explained in some cases by inferior verbal coding.

The issue of whether learning disabled individuals have deficits in aspects of long-term memory has been investigated much less often than short-term memory. One task that has been used frequently is paired-associate learning, where associations have to be learned between two items. This can take various forms, for example, two verbal items, two visual items, or visual–verbal pairing. Learning disabled children seem to have difficulty when the task involves a verbal component (Hulme, 1981). It has been argued that learning arbitrary associations is an important element of learning to read, whether using a visual route or a phonic route.

Deficits in long-term memory are frequently discussed in relation to encoding, storage, and retrieval processes. Findings that learning disabled children have reduced primacy effects in serial learning (Bauer, 1979) and that their performance can be differentially increased by the provision of cues to facilitate rehearsal (Bauer, 1977; Rose, Cundick, & Higbee, 1983; Torgesen & Goldman, 1977) have been interpreted as evidence that learning disabled children are less skilled in the use of rehearsal strategies than their peers, which in turn affects storage. Deficits in rote rehearsal and elaborative rehearsal strategies have been claimed. However, this interpretation of the diminished primacy effect is based on the assumption that it is due to deficient elaborative encoding. It is possible to posit plausible alternative explanations that do not focus on this assumption. Jorm (1983) has also pointed out that the inadequate use of strategies and rehearsal may be due to the unavailability of appropriate information in long-term memory. Such studies may simply be reporting the lack of an adequate knowledge base to facilitate encoding and retrieval processes.

The term *acquired learning disabilities* can be interpreted in several ways. As the vast majority of research has been conducted on adults with acquired deficits, the acquisition of skills such as reading is seldom addressed. Although there is an extensive body of literature on *acquired dyslexias* in adults (e.g., Coltheart, Patterson & Marshall, 1980), this deals with the disruption of reading as a well learned skill. Thus, the involvement of memory processes is likely to differ extensively from that in developmental learning disabilities. The following discussion of acquired learning disabilities mainly deals with cases where individuals have deficits in learning new material (information, skills).

Discussion of memory deficits in acquired learning disabilities is free from some of the problems inherent in developmental disorders, where the interaction of cognitive abilities during development makes delineation of the primary processes underpinning the deficits so difficult. When the learning disability is acquired, typically the individual (child or adult) has had normal cognitive development until the onset of the difficulty, for example, head injury or cerebrovascular accident. Of course, interpretation of poor performance is still complicated by the interaction between attention processes and memory processes in normal cognition. However, it is usually possible to assume (and indeed check from premorbid information) that learning strategies and stores of knowledge and skills have developed normally.

Difficulties with memory processes can result from localized damage to memory circuits in the brain or from diffuse processes that also affect areas important in memory processes. The complex nature of memory is reflected in the variety of memory deficits that exist. The most common description of memory problems refers to storage; that is, putting things into long-term memory or certain aspects of long-term memory. Sometimes a distinction is made between deficits in storage and retrieval processes, although there are few methods for reliably separating these. The distinction most commonly made is between material specific storage deficits; that is, difficulty storing verbal or nonverbal material. Less common are reports of reduced working memory, as poor scores on tasks such as digit span are frequently associated with advanced widespread intellectual decline and depressed scores on all tasks. However, exceptions to this have been published (e.g., Shallice & Warrington, 1970; Warrington, Logue, & Pratt, 1971) describing individuals who had very low scores on tests of auditory span with performance on other functions relatively normal. Failure to remember events that occurred before the brain injury is termed *retrograde amnesia*. There are detailed reports in the literature of deficits in memory processes after a variety of cerebral insults (Benson, Segarra, & Albert, 1974; Butters & Cermak, 1980; Gronwall & Wrightson, 1980; Levin, 1989; Milner, 1965, 1966, 1972; Rose & Symonds, 1960; Zangwill, 1966). Precisely what form the deficit takes for any individual depends on subject variables such as age, history, individual development of the brain, and site and size of the lesion.

With advances in medical technology, many individuals who would previously have died are now surviving traumatic brain injuries, particularly head injuries following motor vehicle accidents. Severe memory deficits are a common outcome of head injury (Levin, 1989). As many head injured individuals are young, with 30 to 40 years of their lives remaining, this presents a tremendous challenge to rehabilitation services, both in terms of clinical demands and costs. The need to determine the effectiveness of memory rehabilitation procedures is urgent for clinical, practical, and economic reasons.

To determine the nature of an acquired memory deficit, careful assessment is required to identify cognitive deficits and abilities. A broad assessment is critical, as a low score on a memory test is not sufficient to identify the underlying functional deficit. Frequently, more than one type of cognitive deficit can result in low scores on a particular test. For example, the effects of slowness, concentration, or attention deficits can cause lowered performance on some memory tests, independent of any memory problem.

A thorough neuropsychological assessment, combined with information from behavioral observations of the client in daily life, is critical to delineating the nature of the memory problem. The client's goal, inevitably, is to improve memory functioning in daily life, and obvious point that highlights the need to incorporate generalization measures in the design of remediation procedures.

In summary, there can be little doubt that memory deficits can be a factor in both developmental and acquired learning disability. However, they can be difficult to isolate from other factors, such as attention, and may be secondary rather than primary factors in developmental learning disability.

Remediation of Memory Deficits

Systematic studies of the effectiveness of remediation of memory processes in learning disabled are extremely rare. More usual are studies that measure only changes in performance on the memory task used for training. Sometimes measures are also taken on other memory tests (generalization across tasks) or in other settings (generalization across settings). This constitutes a major problem for evaluation of process remediation in developmental learning disabilities. Even if some forms of generalization are demonstrated, this often does not provide evidence of whether the training has resulted in a reduction of the criterion learning problem. Certainly, if the deficits in memory processes are a consequence of learning disability rather than a cause, this outcome would not be expected, despite the instatement of improved memory skills.

It has already been stated as a general principle that the effectiveness of process remediation should be judged, in the case of a developmental problem, by change in the ability to acquire a skill, rather than by the ability to perform it without training. As many skills are acquired over an extensive period rather than just one or two training sessions, an adequate study would presumably have to look at development of skills over time.

Bauer (1987) has discussed this point in the context of improving control processes (e.g., amount of time spent in elaborative encoding of material to be remembered) in memory and learning. He observed that manipulations in the use of control processes did not result in equivalent performance by learning disabled children and non–learning disabled children, leading some researchers to conclude that deficient control processes were not responsible for performance differences. His view was that the efficient use of control processes normally develops over a few years rather than just a short instruction period. (Bauer, incidentally, felt that change came about not from an alteration in the nature of the control process but from change in the usage of the process, that is, increased metaknowledge about benefits of its use.)

Basic processes have frequently been targeted in attempts at remediation of acquired deficiencies in memory processes. As mentioned earlier in the chapter, this may reflect the fact that most of the work in the remediation of acquired deficits has involved adults, for whom supervision of criterion skill learning in the normal environment may not be seen as feasible or appropriate, and would be very time and labor intensive.

Within the area of acquired learning disability, published work is again plagued by inadequate designs and neglect of generalization across task, setting, and time. Unlike developmental learning disability, however, provided there is sufficient information about the premorbid level of functioning of the individual, a thorough assessment can establish which processes are dysfunctional and contributing to learning problems. This is because the knowledge of normal development allows predictions to be made about process and skill performance. As already pointed out, individuals with acquired learning disability typically have developed adequate learning skills, but are now prevented from performing these by the disturbance of a particular psychological process. Therefore, process treatment alone may be sufficient to remove the impediment and restore normal function.

Circumventive Approaches

The literature on developmental learning disability provides several illustrations of compensation, or, circumvention of weakness of a process. At a general level this involves accurately delineating the deficient process, finding successful aids or strategies that compensate for the deficiency, and establishing the use of these in the areas of learning disability. Much of this is still at the "suggestion" stage rather than the remediation stage.

Rose et al. (1983) compared the effectiveness of three types of instruction on the performance of groups of learning disabled children on recall of a written passage. In two of the instruction conditions, red dots were placed in the written prose and children were required either to rehearse verbally the material between the dots or make mental pictures of the material. The third instruction was based on concentration and effort. The verbal rehearsal and visual imagery strategy both significantly improved recall, although it was unclear whether the size of this difference was clinically significant. The children preferred using the verbal rehearsal strategy. The authors did not address generalization issues although they suggested that this kind of training would help learning disabled children become more competent learners. Bauer (1987) used these findings as a basis for the suggestion that providing learning disabled children with cues for rehearsal of material might result in improved memory for what is learned. The provision of cues (say, marking written text) could compensate for the process deficit and facilitate the use of strategies for learning the cued material. However, there is no indication that these individuals would eventually apply the principles of rehearsal in contexts where no cues were provided.

In the area of acquired learning disability, many researchers and remediators use strategies that are essentially *compensation* or *circumvention of weakness*. This category includes many approaches that involve the teaching of mnemonic strategies (which need to be consciously learned and used) to individuals or groups with undifferentiated memory deficits.

For example, a group study by Lewinsohn, Danaher, and Kikel (1977) looked at the effects of training of visual imagery on long-term recall. Included were measures of the persistence of the retained material (i.e., long-term recall of up to a week) and generalizability of training effects across two tasks, paired-associate learning and a face–name task thought to resemble everyday interactions. The findings were that the facilitatory effect of imagery on the paired associates task was not evident after a 1-week delay and not significant on any of the delays on the face–name task. As the face–name task had been viewed as the one most likely to relate to normal situations, these findings implied that this form of compensation does not result in amelioration of acquired learning disability. However, the subjects used in the study were "brain damaged individuals" who had lesions at a variety of unknown locations. Combining their data prevented the possible identification of any individuals with deficits of particular processes who may have benefited from the training. This illustrates a major limitation of traditional group methodology in research on the efficacy of remediation procedures.

Another strategy that has been used to circumvent memory difficulties is the PQRST (Preview, Question, Read, State, Test) method. PQRST is an acronym for a series of steps designed to organize, elaborate, and rehearse written material to be remembered (Robinson, 1970). Whereas this appears to be directly addressing memory processes (rehearsal, elaboration), it is viewed as a strategy that replaces deficient processes rather than directly remediates the processes. A good illustration of this method is provided by Glasgow, Zeiss, Barrera, and Lewinsohn (1977), who worked with a young woman (Mrs J) who had difficulty with long-term recall of meaningful material (verbal or written). Two strategies (simple rehearsal and the PQRST method) were compared to her own preintervention strategy in a laboratory context, with the finding that the PQRST strategy was superior to the rehearsal strategy, which was superior to the control condition. Generalizability across settings was measured by applying the PQRST technique to the reading of newspaper articles, conducted in Mrs J's daily life context. Self-rating measures indicated that PQRST training improved performance in her daily life context, although no direct measure of memory performance were taken. Whether this technique could generalize to a wider range of memory tasks (other than written material) has not been established.

This PQRST approach has also been investigated by Wilson (1987). She found that the PQRST technique was more effective than rote rehearsal, particularly when answers were invoked by direct questioning, perhaps because this made the test situation more like the learning situation (the encoding specificity principle). Less severely impaired subjects were also more successful, which Wilson argued may have been a result of the deeper thinking and hence deeper level of processing than occurred with use of the PQRST technique.

The other general approach that falls into the class of *circumvention of weakness* is the use of external aids and ways of cuing individuals to use these external aids (Harris, 1984; Moffat, 1984). Several reasons have encouraged remediators to use this approach. One is the apparently poor generalization of internal strategies and the negative impact on clients of training in methods that fail to generalize; another is the clinician's drive to facilitate significant or noticeable change in the lives of their clients. Circumvention of weakness also includes the general approach advocated by Prigatano (1987) of teaching the patient and therapist to be realistic about the severity of deficits and guiding realistic life choices that take this into account. Users of this approach do not exclude attempts at the remediation of memory processes, but advocate that they must be viewed in the context of a realistic appraisal of generalization. The effectiveness of this approach is judged not from whether or not the client continues to have acquired learning disabilities, but from a more holistic evaluation of the quality of life attained.

Capitalization on Strengths

Remediation processes of this type, by definition, require an assessment of the learning disabled individual that can determine areas of strength. For example, do deficits of memory processes involve impairment of learning that is specific to modality or type of material? Is there more impairment in learning verbal than nonverbal material, or in learning information that is presented in the auditory modality rather than the visual modality?

Within studies of remediation of developmental learning disabilities, this kind of assessment is rarely thorough. One method used classifies children according to discrepancy between the Verbal IQ and the Performance IQ on the WISC–R (i.e., Cermak, Goldberg, Cermak, &

Drake, 1980; Rose et al., 1983). Exactly what this method achieves is disputable. Although it is true that a high Verbal IQ frequently reflects well developed verbal skills, scores on the Performance scale subtests can be lower for a number of reasons other than poor visual or visuospatial skills. For example, all Performance subtests are timed, so a child who performs slowly will score less well than on the predominantly untimed Verbal subtests. Summary scores, such as the Verbal and Performance IQs, result in a loss of information from individual subtest scores, because any variation between subtests within the two scales is immediately obscured. A decision beforehand about which subtests of the WISC–R and/or which other tests will allow separation of learning disabled individuals into the desired groups, will result in more precise separation of individuals with differential impairments of learning disabilities.

Another method classifies learning disabled children on the basis of their preference for visual or auditory stimulus modality. For example, Lily and Kelleher (1973) identified subjects' modality preference by pretesting their visual and auditory memory for words. There is some evidence that this type of preference can be altered by encouraging the use of the weaker modality by contingent reinforcement (Koorland & Wolking, 1982).

There is some evidence that strengths and weaknesses, as identified by stimulus-modality preference, may be equalized to a large extent by appropriate reinforcement contingencies. [This indicates that such preferences may not represent a fundamental difference in basic visual processes so much as a learning history that has favored the use of one modality over another (Koorland & Wolking, 1982).]

Although remediation of developmental learning disabilities, based on capitalization on strengths, has been reported to be effective (e.g., Curley & Reilly, 1983), reviews of studies using this approach have not been encouraging (e.g., Tarver & Dawson, 1978).

The capitalization on strengths approach has often been used with individuals identified as having acquired deficits of memory processes, particularly for those individuals whose deficit is more severe for specific kinds of material and thus a particular kind of memory, (e.g., verbal or nonverbal memory). Most commonly, an appropriate mnemonic strategy has been taught that is based on the more intact form of memory. Individuals with problems mainly of verbal memory would be taught some form of visual imagery procedure, such as peg-type mnemonics based on the formation of strong visual interacting images, or a technique such as the method of loci where items to be learned are linked with a visual image to familiar locations. Alternatively, someone who had difficulty mainly with visual memory would be taught strategies that facilitated verbal coding.

A classic group study using this approach was reported by Jones (1974). She compared the effectiveness of imagery in facilitating verbal memory in groups of left temporal lobectomy subjects, bilateral temporal lobectomies, right temporal lobectomies, and normal controls. It increased the verbal memory performance of the left temporal group but was ineffective with subjects in the bilateral temporal group. Ceiling levels of performance before training prevented any real measurement of improvement in the control group and the right temporal group. However, there were no attempts to assess generalization across time or setting. Thus, there was no information about whether the improved recall persisted or whether training in this area of strength generalized to other memory tasks and situations or across time.

There are several descriptive case studies that claim to show positive effects of teaching mnemonics to increase the effectiveness of intact memory systems (Crovitz, 1979; Patten, 1972). Patten described four single cases of individuals with verbal memory deficits who benefited from training in visual imagery methods. These case studies lacked design and active measurement of generalization across settings and tasks. Crovitz also provided an essentially descriptive case approach in describing the effects of a chaining mnemonic that involved semantic links and visual imagery. This style of report has encouraged further research in this area but has added little to the knowledge about the effectiveness of process training.

Another common approach has been to teach the client several strategies (often this will include at least one mnemonic focusing on a strength and one mnemonic strategy focusing on weakness) and compare the relative effectiveness of these. Crosson and Buenning (1984) have reported a study of memory retraining in a 32-year-old man who had suffered a closed head injury and complained of severe memory difficulties. Testing revealed a severe memory deficit that was most pronounced with verbal material. This study compared the relative effectiveness of feedback and concentration, use of visual imagery (use of a strength), and a strategy to increase the client's interaction with the material and thus deepen the processing. The client believed that the visual imagery was the most helpful to him. The results confirmed this but showed that there was also significant improvement with the deeper processing strategy. (However, an inadequate design meant that it was not possible to eliminate order effects as an explanation for these results.) This study attempted to address issues of generalization across settings, tasks, and time by doing some of the training at home with the aid of a friend, measuring performance on other tasks, and doing follow-up measures. There was impressive generalization to the stories subtest of the Wechsler Memory scale although at the 9-month follow-up this had declined a little.

Although this implies the occurrence of generalization from the training task to memory performance on other tasks, measures were not taken of whether it assisted the client's memory in daily life. However, because of doubts about poor generalization from other studies, when the client finished training it was suggested that he supplement his verbal memory with a note pad, which he did. It is clinically and ethically sound to provide the client with the best information available; however, this unfortunately limited adequate evaluation of generalization of the training strategies to learning disabilities experienced in his normal activities.

Prigatano (1987) sounded a caution to therapists who trained clients in memory mnemonics with the assumption that such training results in improved day-to-day memory. He cited an example of a client who he and others had trained in visual imagery to improve his verbal memory. This procedure improved performance on paired-associate learning, an improvement that was sustained over several years. However, in his day-to-day life the client was frequently unable to apply visual imagery. The "success" of the remediation program restrained the client from becoming aware of the true extent of his difficulties and made him attribute his inability to remember to personal failure. These experiences led him to contemplate suicide. Individuals with previously normal levels of functioning who have acquired deficits will have high self-expectations and be vulnerable to failure because of this background. Certainly this case vividly illustrates a possible negative outcome of remediation that is not accompanied by a commitment to investigating generalization thoroughly from process teaching to the client's regular activities and providing assistance with the outcome. Despite the demands of research, ethical issues concerning the total impact on a client of remediation attempts and the question of responsibility of the therapist for this impact must be considered.

Direct Process Remediation

Much of the literature on direct memory process remediation in developmental learning disabilities is focused on showing change in the performance of learning disabled groups after training in a particular memory process. It is rare for studies to address both change as a result of training and issues of generalization to different tasks and contexts.

Torgesen and Goldman (1977) found that on a delayed recall task many poor readers did not spontaneously use verbal rehearsal as a strategy to the same extent as good readers and they were unaware that any strategy would assist them. Furthermore, as a group the poor readers showed differential improvement on recall on a task where both groups were cued to rehearse verbally. They suggested that their general performance might improve if learning disabled children were offered environmental supports in the use of proper strategies. If improved performance remained contingent on cues supplied by external sources, then this must be viewed as a compensation approach. If, however, these cues are supplied then faded at an appropriate point, this methodology would address the issue of training memory processes to produce enduring changes. The same argument could be made for placing red dots as signals for rehearsal in written material, as suggested by Rose et al. (1983).

Ceci (1984) reported that learning disabled children had difficulty with memory processes that involved semantic linking of information, elaborative encoding, chunking, and elaborative rehearsal. These processes, called *purposive semantic processing*, were differentiated from the automatic semantic processing demonstrated by priming effects. It was suggested that training should be focused on these purposive semantic processes, although once again there is little evidence available to demonstrate this is effective and that there is generalization beyond the task used in training.

Gelzheiser (1984) looked particularly at issues of generalization and the transfer of newly learned skills to novel but appropriate tasks. Using groups of learning disabled adolescents (control, plus two different instructional groups) and non–learning disabled adolescents, she found that several learning disabled adolescents transferred the use of several instructed strategies to a prose recall task. She found that four validated instructional components of a direct instruction package were influential in skill generalization, and also that teaching the subjects to recognize the problem isomorph (conducting specific generalization training) was related to whether increase in recall was significant or not. This study implied that generalization across tasks is possible and isolated some of the factors important in this. This work provides an indication that generalization is attainable; however, it cannot be assumed that generalization across tasks will follow training in any skill or process. A more extensive analysis of this particular issue in cognitive strategy training is provided in another chapter.

Direct memory process remediation in cases of acquired deficits has not been addressed in a systematic way. The most common approach is the method of repeated practice on memory games or tasks (often computerized). Rather than being based on any recent theory of memory, it appears to be based on the assumption that memory is like a mental muscle, which will respond with exercise. However, it appears that memory is not like a muscle and more exercise does not make it stronger or bigger (Brooks & Baddeley, 1976; Glisky & Schacter, 1986). The specific material presented in practice is learned but there is little or no generalization from the task practiced even to apparently similar tasks. Although it appears to fail to remediate memory processes, Harris and Sunderland (1981) noted that repetitive practice may be good for the patients' morale because they believe something is being done to help their difficulties. (It is not clear how these same patients feel farther down the road when their memory for everyday tasks has not improved.) The approach has illustrated, however, that particular tasks can be taught even to those individuals with very severe memory impairments. Glisky and Schacter (1988) have subsequently used this finding to teach an individual with a severe memory disorder different kinds of complex domain-specific knowledge that enabled her to learn and perform a job. The aim of this approach was to have the client learn specific material and procedures, rather than retrain her memory processes, so it most closely resembles criterion skill learning.

The other type of process remediation has been to train clients on the processes involved in storage and retrieval of material. How this should occur depends on the theory of memory subscribed to by the researchers. Gianutsos and Gianutsos (1979) provide an illustration of the thinking behind this approach. They attempted to improve elaborative rehearsal by training four subjects on a form of memonic where they learned to say something meaningful and memorable about words to be remembered. In contrast to simple repetition, this was thought to constitute elaborative rehearsal, which would in turn yield a more permanent representation of the information. In fact, the subjects were encouraged to achieve this by forming a story that linked the words to be remembered. It could be argued that this procedure is a circumventive strategy, but certainly the philosophy was one of training memory processes. It was tested on a task where three words to be remembered were presented, followed by a varying number of other words to be read but not recalled, then recall of the earlier words. Outcome was variable over the four subjects, not surprisingly, since two had damage to the hemisphere that was probably nondominant for speech and two to their hemisphere dominant for speech. Testing before training did not clearly demonstrate a difficulty with forming verbal memories although three had markedly impaired scores on Visual Reproduction. There was improved performance on some aspect of the task for all subjects, although whether this amounted to clinical improvement is unclear. Despite the use of the Wechsler Memory Scale as a generalization measure, there was inadequate measurement of memory performance in other contexts, a point acknowledged by the authors.

Other Methods

Not all studies fall neatly within the classes of criterion skill training and process remediation, nor within the three categories illustrated above.

Scruggs, Mastropieri, and Levin (1987) discussed a criterion skill training that involved teaching a mnemonic strategy that they claimed had good generalization properties. Using instruction in the mnemonic keyword method (based on recoding, relating, and retrieving strategies), they cited studies with learning disabled students that showed its effectiveness in teaching single attributes of educational material, such as

North American minerals and the learning of multiple attributes of similar material and low frequency vocabulary words. This is criterion skill training because it involves direct training on a learning task to be achieved by the students.

From a process point of view, such training does not target the presumed cause of the learning disability and therefore would not be expected to result in changes that would generalize to other tasks and contexts. However, these authors also cited work that demonstrated that students trained with this mnemonic on vocabulary learning were able to use it independently and successfully on untrained vocabulary lists. This demonstrates generalization across settings but not across task or time, factors that should also be addressed.

The authors claimed that these findings demonstrate that learning disabled students' learning can be increased in an important area of school functioning. This type of approach seeks to increase the learning disabled students' knowledge, rather than redress the difficulties presumed to underlie the learning disability. If process-based approaches were successful, this would result in the learning disabled individual being able to learn the normal range of material in the normal range of settings. However, the combination of criterion skills and memory strategies may yet prove to be the best that can be achieved in remediation of learning disabilities.

Summary of Memory Process Training

The literature on effectiveness of memory remediation is at a similar stage of development to that on attention remediation. First of all, the nature of memory deficits in learning disabilities and their suitability as targets for remedial efforts are both contentious matters. Second, memory assessment is problematic, especially in the area of developmental learning disabilities. Of particular concern in that context is the possibility that performance on many tasks used to measure memory may be affected by limited reading skills.

Studies attempting to evaluate memory remediation procedures have been designed with insufficient regard to generalization training and testing, echoing the situation previously outlined with respect to attention remediation.

Conclusions and Recommendations

The term *psychological process* has been used in a variety of ways, and historically, process remediation refers to a broad group of procedures. We have attempted to identify a subset of these on the basis of a set of characteristics that we consider to typify a common type of process approach, and we have described a set of assumptions that seem implicit in this approach.

According to these assumptions:

1. The deficits of criterion skills that define learning disabilities may reflect a problem in one or more underlying psychological processes.
2. The underlying processes, rather than the criterion skills, are a valid target for remediation.
3. Remediation of processes may result in the elimination of impediments to the learning of criterion skills.
4. Without process remediation, impediments will remain to other efforts to teach related criterion skills.

It appears that all these assumptions are, at least, questionable. We have focused on 3 because we consider that the validity of process training depends critically on whether there are demonstrable gains in criterion skills that can be shown to result from such training. There is at present little evidence that is consistent with this assumption. When the Behavioral Assessment model is used as a yardstick for evaluating the adequacy of studies of the effectiveness of attention and memory process remediation, several deficiencies and found that are typical of most studies.

In the area of developmental learning disabilities, particularly, there is an overreliance on between-groups designs to demonstrate treatment effects, coupled with unjustifiable assumptions about the homogeneity within groups on subject variables that could well have important effects on treatment outcome. Identification of a process deficit is rarely based on an adequate neuropsychological assessment. In addition, there is usually little consideration of the question of whether a suspected deficit could be shown to be at the root of the manifest learning difficulty.

Of particular concern is the frequent failure to measure generalization of the effects of process training either to similar, untrained tasks or to those criterion skills by which the learning disability was identified in the first place.

Our appraisal of process approaches to remediation of attention and memory problems in learning disabilities has indicated some fundamental shortcomings that make it impossible to make general conclusions at this time about the viability of process remediation. It is not that the results are equivocal so much as that design strategies and methodologies used have not permitted some vital questions to be answered.

Our recommendations for future research are as follows. It needs to be recognized that there are probably subject characteristics that are unique to every learning disability case, and in many instances these may bear importantly on the outcome of a particular treatment approach. This indicates the need for a thorough neuropsychological assessment. In every case there should be a clear indication of a relation between the learning disability problem of concern and the process deficit to be targeted for remediation. Remediation should be carried out within the framework of a single-subject design so that changes in performance can be reasonably attributed to treatment variables. An added advantage is that treatment can be varied according to the subject's response without compromising the treatment evaluation. Strenuous efforts should be made to introduce generalization training and testing procedures, with the goal of establishing just what training is necessary to promote adequate generalization to whatever skill deficits are of greatest concern in the subject's normal environment.

Treatment evaluation studies along these lines, systematically replicated with many subjects, eventually will provide a sound basis for conclusions about the validity of process remediation. The resulting treatment literature will surely provide better guidance to practitioners than what is currently available.

References

Atkinson, R. C., & Shiffrin, R. M. (1971). The control of short-term memory. *Scientific American*, *225*, 82–90.

Allen, K. D., & Fuqua, R. W. (1985). Eliminating selective stimulus control: A comparison of two procedures for teaching mentally retarded children to respond to compound stimuli. *Journal of Experimental Child Psychology*, *39*, 55–71.

Anderson, J. R. (1976). *Language, memory and thought*. Hillsdale, NJ: Erlbaum.

Arter, J. A., & Jenkins, J. R. (1979). Differential diagnosis-prescriptive teaching: A critical appraisal. *Review of Educational Research*, *49*, 517–555.

Ayres, A. J. (1978). Learning disabilities and the vestibular system. *Journal of Learning Disabilities*, *11*, 18–29.

Baddeley, A. D., & Hitch, G. J. (1974). Working memory. In G. A. Bower (Ed.), *The psychology of learning and motivation* (Vol. 8, pp. 47–89). Orlando, FL: Academic Press.

Baddeley, A. D., & Lieberman, E. K. (1980). Spatial working memory. In R. Nickerson (Ed.), *Attention and performance* (Vol. V111). Hillsdale, NJ: Erlbaum.

Bauer, R. H. (1977). Memory processes in children with learning disabilities: Evidence for deficient rehearsal. *Journal of Experimental Child Psychology*, *24*, 415–430.

Bauer, R. H. (1979). Memory, acquisition, and category clustering in learning-disabled children. *Journal of Experimental Child Psychology*, *27*, 365–383.

Bauer, R. H. (1987). Control processes as a way of understanding, diagnosing, and remediating learning disabilities. In H. Lee Swanson (Ed.), *Advances in Learning and Behavioral Disabilities* (Suppl. 2, pp. 41–79). Greenwich, CT: JAI Press Ltd.

Beale, I. L., Matthew, P. J., Oliver, S., & Corballis, M. C. (1987). Performance of disabled and normal readers on the continuous performance test. *Journal of Abnormal Child Psychology*, *15*, 229–238.

Beale, I. L., & Singh, N. N. (1986). Observing responses during discrimination learning by mentally retarded children. In S. E. Breuning & R. A. Gable (Eds.), *Advances in Mental Retardation and Developmental Disability* (Vol. 3, pp. 23–47). CT: JAI Press.

Ben-Yishay, Y., Piasetsky, E. B., & Rattock, J (1987). A systematic method for ameliorating disorders in basic attention. In M. Manfred, A. Lester, & D. Leonard (Eds.), *Neuropsychological rehabilitation.* New York: Guilford Press.

Benson, D. F., Segarra, J., & Albert, M. L. (1974). Visual agnosia-prosopagnosia. *Archives of Neurology, 30,* 307–310.

Berlyne, D. E. (1970). Attention as a problem in behavior theory. In D. I. Mostofsky (Ed.), *Attention Contemporary theory and analysis* (pp. 25–50). New York: Appleton-Century-Crofts.

Binder, L. M. (1986). Persisting symptoms after mild head injury: A review of the postconcussive syndrome. *Journal of Clinical and Experimental Neuropsychology, 8,* 323–346.

Boakes, R. A., & Halliday, P (1972). *Inhibition in learning.* London: Academic Press.

Bracy, O. L. (1986). Cognitive rehabilitation: A process approach. *Cognitive Rehabilitation, 4,* 10–17.

Brooks, D. N., & Baddeley, A. (1976). What can amnesics learn? *Neuropsychologia, 14,* 111–122.

Brooks, N, (1984). *Closed head injury: Psychological, social, and family consequences.* Oxford: Oxford University Press.

Brown, R. T., & Alford, N. (1984). Ameliorating attentional deficits and concomitant academic deficiencies in learning disabled children through cognitive training. *Journal of Learning Disabilities, 17,* 20–26.

Butters, N., & Cermak, L. S. (1980). *Alcoholic Korsakoff's syndrome.* New York: Academic Press.

Catania, A. C. (1984). *Learning.* Englewood Cliffs, NJ: Prentice-Hall.

Ceci, S. J. (1984). A developmental study of learning disabilities and memory. *Journal of Experimental Child Psychology, 38,* 352–371.

Cermak, L. S., Goldberg, J., Cermak, S., & Drake, C. (1980). The short-term memory ability of children with learning disabilities. *Journal of Learning Disabilities, 13,* 25–29.

Chronbach, L. J., & Snow, R. E. (1977). *Aptitudes and instruction methods.* New York: Irvington.

Coleman, R. A. (1970). A conditioning technique applicable to elementary school classrooms. *Journal of Applied Behavior Analysis, 3,* 293–297.

Coltheart, M. C., Patterson, K. E., & Marshall, J. C. (1980). *Deep dyslexia.* London: Routledge.

Craik, F. I. M., & Lockhart. R. S. (1972). Levels of processing: A framework for memory research. *Journal of Verbal Learning and Verbal Behavior, 11,* 671–684.

Craine, J. F. (1982). Principles of cognitive rehabilitation. In L. E. Trexler (Ed.), *Cognitive rehabilitation* (pp. 83–98). New York: Plenum Press.

Crosson, B., & Buenning, W. (1984). An individualized memory retraining program after closed-head injury: A single-case study. *Journal of Clinical Neuropsychology, 6,* 287–301.

Crovitz, H. F. (1979). Memory retraining in brain-damaged patients: The airplane list. *Cortex, 15,* 131–134.

Cruickshank, W. M., Bentzen, F. A., Ratzberg, F. H., & Tannhauser, M. T. (1961). *A teaching method for brain damaged and hyperactive children.* Syracuse: Syracuse University Press.

Curley, J. F., & Reilly, L. J. (1983). Sensory process instruction with learning disabled children. *Perceptual and Motor Skills, 57,* 1219–1226.

Dawson, M. M., Hallahan, D. P., Reeve, R. E., & Ball, D. W. (1980). The effect of reinforcement and verbal rehearsal on selective attention in learning-disabled children. *Journal of Abnormal Child Psychology, 8,* 133–144.

Delacato, C. H. (1966). *The treatment and prevention of reading problems.* Springfield, IL: Charles C. Thomas.

Deutsch, J. A. (1978). Reading disability: Methodological problems in information-processing analysis. *Science, 200,* 802.

Diller, L. (1976). A model for cognitive retraining in rehabilitation. *Clinical Psychologist, 29,* 13–19.

Doman, R. J., Spitz, E. B., Zucman, E., Delacato, C. H., & Doman, G. (1960). Children with severe brain injuries: Neurological organizations in terms of mobility. *Journal of the American Medical Association, 174,* 257–262.

Douglas, V., & Peters, K. (1979). Towards a clearer definition of the attentional deficit of hyperactive children. In C. Hale & M. Lewis (Eds.), *Attention and cognitive development* (pp. 173–247). New York: Plenum Press.

Drabman, R. S., Hammer, D., & Rosenbaum, M. S. (1979). Assessing generalization in behavior modification with children: The generalization map. *Behavioral Assessment, 1,* 203–219.

Eliason, M. J., & Richman, L. C. (1987). The continuous performance test in learning disabled and nondisabled children. *Journal of Learning Disabilities, 20,* 614–618.

Fisher, M. A., & Zeaman, D. (1973). An attention-retention theory of retardate discrimination learning. In N. R. Ellis (Ed.), *International Review of Research in Mental Retardation* (Vol. 6, pp. 169–256). New York: Academic Press.

Frostig, M., & Horne, D. (1964). *The Frostig program for the development of visual perception.* Chicago: Follett.

Gelzheiser, L. M. (1984). Generalization from categorical memory tasks to proce by learning disabled adolescents. *Journal of Educational Psychology, 76,* 1128–1138.

Gianutsos R., & Gianutsos, J. (1979). Rehabilitating the verbal recall of brain-injured patients by mnemonic training: An experimental demonstration using single-case methodology. *Journal of Clinical Neuropsychology, 1,* 117–135.

Glasgow, R. E., Zeiss, R. A., Barrera, M., & Lewinsohn, P. M. (1977). Case studies on remediating memory deficits in brain-damaged individuals. *Journal of Clinical Psychology, 33,* 1049–1054.

Glisky, E. L., & Schacter, D. L. (1986). Remediation of organic memory disorders: Current status and future prospects. *Journal of Head Trauma Rehabilitation, 1,* 54–63.

Glisky, E. L., & Schacter, D. L. (1988). Acquisition of domain-specific knowledge in patients with organic memory disorders. *Journal of Learning Disabilities, 21,* 333–339.

Glynn, E. L., Thomas, J. D., & Shee, S. M. (1973). Behavioral self-control of on-task behavior in an elementary classroom. *Journal of Applied Behavior Analysis, 6,* 105–113.

Gronwall, D. (1987). Advances in the assessment of attention and information processing after head injury. In H. S. Levin, J. Grafman, & H. M. Eisenberg

(Eds.), *Neurobehavioral recovery from head injury* (pp. 355–371). New York: Oxford University Press.

Gronwall, D., & Wrightson, P. (1980). Memory and information processing capacity after closed head injury. *Journal of Neurology, Neurosurgery and Psychiatry*, *44*, 889–895.

Hagen, J. W., & Huntsman, N. J. (1971). Selective attention in mental retardates. *Developmental Psychology*, *5*, 151–160.

Hallahan, D. P., Gajar, A. H., Cohen, S. B., Tarver, S. G. (1978). Selective attention and locus of control in learning disabled and normal children. *Journal of Learning Disabilities*, *11*, 231–236.

Hallahan, D. P., Tarver, S. G., Kauffman, J, M., & Graybeal, N. L. (1978). A comparison of the effects of reinforcement and response cost on the selective attention of learning disabled children. *Journal of Learning Disabilities*, *11*, 39–47.

Hammill, D. D., & Larsen, S. C. (1978). The effectiveness of psycholinguistic training: A reaffirmation of position. *Exceptional Children*, *44*, 402–414.

Harris, J. (1984). Methods of improving memory. In B. A. Wilson & N. Moffat (Eds.), *Clinical management of memory problems* (pp. 46–62). London & Sydney: Croom Helm.

Harris, J. E., & Sunderland, A. (1981). A brief survey of the management of memory disorders in rehabilitation units in Britain. *International Rehabilitation Medicine*, *3*, 206–209.

Hartlage, L. C., & Telzrow, C. F. (1983). The neuropsychological basis of educational intervention. *Journal of Learning Disabilities*, *16*, 521–528.

Hasher, L., & Zacks, R. T. (1979). Automatic and effortful processes in memory. *Journal of Experimental Psychology (General)*, *108*, 356–388.

Hebben, N. A., Whitman, R. D., Milberg, W. P., Andresko, M., & Galpin, R (1981). Attentional dysfunction in poor readers. *Journal of Learning Disabilities*, *14*, 287–290.

Hecaen, H., & Albert, M. L. (1978). *Human neuropsychology*. New York: Wiley.

Hicks, C. (1980). The ITPA Visual Sequential Memory task: An alternative interpretation and the implications for good and poor readers. *British Journal of Educational Psychology*, *50*, 16–25.

Horton, A. M., & Miller, W. G. (1985). Neuropsychology and behavior therapy. In M. Hersen, R. M. Eisler, & P. M. Miller (Eds.), *Progress in behavior modification* (Vol. 19, pp. 1–55). Orlando, FL: Academic Press.

Hulme, C. (1981). *Reading retardation and multi-sensory teaching*. London: Routledge & Kegan Paul.

Irlen, H. (1983). *Successful treatment of learning disabilities*. Paper presented at 91st annual conference of American Psychological Association.

James, W. (1980). *The principles of psychology*. New York: Henry Holt.

Jones, M. K. (1974). Imagery as a mnemonic aid after left temporal lobectomy: Contrast between material-specific and generalized memory disorders. *Neuropsychologia*, *12*, 21–30.

Jorm, A. F. (1983). Specific reading retardation and working memory: A review. *British Journal of Psychology*, *74*, 311–342.

Kavale, K. A. (1981). Functions of the Illinois Test of Psycholinguistic Abilities (ITPA): Are they trainable? *Exceptional Children*, *47*, 496–510.

Kavale, K. A., & Forness, S. R. (1985). Learning disability and the history of science: Paradigm or paradox? *RASE*, *6*, 12–23.

Kavale, K. A., & Forness, S. R. (1987). The far side of heterogeneity: A critical analysis of empirical subtyping research in learning disabilities. *Journal of Learning Disabilities*, *20*, 374–382.

Kirk, S. A. (1962). *Educating exceptional children*. Boston: Houghton Mifflin.

Kirk, S. A., Berry, P. B., & Senf, G. M. (1979). A survey of attitudes concerning learning disabilities. *Journal of Learning Disabilities*, *12*, 238–245.

Koorland, M. A. (1986). *Applied behavior analysis and the correction of learning disabilities*. In J. K. Torgesen & B. Y. L. Wong (Eds.), Orlando, FL: Academic Press.

Koorland, M. A., & Wolking, W. D. (1982). Effect of reinforcement on modality of stimulus control in learning disabled students. *Learning Disabilities Quarterly*, *5*, 264–273.

Koppell, S. (1979). Testing the attentional deficit notion. *Journal of Learning Disabilities*, *12*, 43–48.

Krupski, A. (1986). Attention problems in youngsters with learning handicaps. In J. K. Torgesen & B. Y. L. Wong (Eds.), *Psychological and educational perspectives on learning disabilities* (pp. 161–192). Orlando. FL: Academic Press.

Levin, H. S. (1989). Memory deficit after closed-head injury. *Journal of Clinical and Experimental Neuropsychology*, *12*, 129–153.

Levin, H. S., Grafman, J., & Eisenberg, H. M. (1987). *Neurobehavioral recovery from head injury*. New York: Oxford University Press.

Lewinsohn, P. M., Danaher, B. G., & Kikel, S. (1977). Visual imagery as a mnemonic aid for brain-injured persons. *Journal of Consulting and Clinical Psychology*, *45*, 717–723.

Lilly, S. M., & Kellcher, J. (1973). Modality strengths and aptitude-treatment interaction. *Journal of Special Education*, *7*, 5–13.

Lovaas, O. I., Schreibman, L., Koegel, R., & Rehm, R. (1971). Selective responding by autistic children to multiple stimulus imput. *Journal of Abnormal Psychology*, *77*, 211–222.

Luria, A. R. (1963). *Restoration of function after brain injury*. New York: Macmillan.

McIntyre, C. W., Murray, F. E., Cronin, C. M., & Blackwell, S. L. (1978). Span of apprehension in learning disabled boys. *Journal of Learning Disabilities*, *11*, 468–476.

McIntyre, C. W., Murray, M. E., & Blackwell, S. L. (1981). Visual search in learning disabled and hyperactive boys. *Journal of Learning Disabilities*, *14*, 156–158.

Meichenbaum, D. (1977). *Cognitive behavior modification*. New York: Plenum Press.

Miller, E. (1980). Psychological intervention in the management and rehabilitation of neuropsychological impairments. *Behaviour Research and Therapy*, *18*, 527–535.

Milner, B. (1965). Visually-guided maze learning in man: Effects of bilateral hippocampal, bilateral frontal and unilateral cerebral lesions. *Neuropsychologia*, *3*, 317–338.

Milner, B. (1966). Amnesia following operation on the temporal lobes. In C. W. M. Whitty & O. L. Zangwill (Eds.), *Amnesia*. London: Butterworths.

Milner, B. (1972). Disorders of learning and memory after temporal lobel lesions in man. *Clinical Neurosurgery*, *19*, 421–446.

Moffat, N. (1984). Strategies of memory therapy. In B. A. Wilson & N. Moffat (Eds.), *Clinical management of memory problems* (pp. 63–88). London & Sydney: Croom Helm.

Mostofsky, D. I. (1965). *Stimulus generalization*. Stanford: Stanford University Press.

Mostofsky, D. I. (1970). *Attention: Contemporary theory and analysis*. New York: Appleton-Century-Crofts.

Nelson, R. O., & Hayes, S. C. (1986). *Conceptual foundations of behavioral assessment*. New York: Guilford Press.

Orton, S. T. (1937). *Reading, writing and speech problems in children*. New York: Norton.

Paivio, A. (1969). Mental imagery in associative learning and memory. *Psychological Review*, *76*, 241–263.

Paivio, A. (1974). Language and knowledge of the world. *Educational Researcher*, *3*, 5–12.

Patten, B. M. (1972). The ancient art of memory. *Archives of Neurology*, *26*, 25–32.

Piasetsky, E. B., Ben-Yishay, Y., Weinberg, J., & Diller, L. (1982). The systematic remediation of specific disorders: Selective application of methods derived in a clinical research setting. In L. E. Trexler (Ed.), *Cognitive rehabilitation* (pp. 205–222). New York: Plenum Press.

Posner, N. I., & Rafal, R. D. (1987). Cognitive theories of attention and the rehabilitation of attention deficits. In M. Meier, A. Benton, & L. Diller (Eds.), *Neuropsychological rehabilitation*. New York: Churchill Livingston.

Prigatano, G. P. (1987). Recovery and cognitive retraining after craniocerebral trauma. *Journal of Learning Disabilities*, *20*, 603–613.

Radencich, M. C. (1984). The status of learning disabilities: The emergence of a paradigm or a paradigm shift? *Learning Disabilities*, *3*, 79–89.

Robinson, F. P. (1970). *Effective study*. New York: Harper.

Rooney, K. J., Hallahan, D. P., & Lloyd, J. W. (1984). Self-recording of attention by learning disabled students in the regular classroom. *Journal of Learning Disabilities*, *17*, 360–364.

Rose, F. C., & Symonds, C P. (1960). Persistent memory defect following encephalitis. *Brain*, *83*, 195–212.

Rose, M. C., Cundick, B. P., & Higbee, K. L. (1983). Verbal rehearsal and visual imagery: Mnemonic aids for learning-disabled children. *Journal of Learning Disabilities*, *16*, 352–354.

Ross, A. O. (1976). *Psychological aspects of learning disabilities and reading disorders*. New York: McGraw-Hill.

Rosvold, H. E., Mirsky, A. F., Sarason, I., Bransom, E. D., & Beck, L, H. (1956). The continuous performance test of brain damage. *Journal of Consulting Psychialtry*, *20*, 343–350.

Rourke, B. P. (1985). *Neuropsychology of learning disabilities: Essentials of subtype analysis*. New York: Guilford Press.

Samuels, S. J., & Edwall, G. (1981). The role of attention in reading with implications for the learning disabled student. *Journal of Learning Disabilities*, *14*, 353–368.

Scruggs, T. E., Mastropieri, M., & Levin, J. R. (1987). Implications of mnemonic-strategy for theories of learning disabilities. In H. Lee Swanson (Ed.), *Advances in learning and behavioral disabilities* (Suppl. 2, pp. 225–244). Greenwich, CT: JAI Press.

Shallice, T., & Warrington, E. K. (1970). Independent functioning of the verbal memory stores: A neuropsychological study. *Quarterly Journal of Experimental Psychology*, *22*, 261–273.

Silver, L. B. (1987). The "magic cure": A review of the current controversisl approaches for treating learning disabilities. *Journal of Learning Disabilities*, *20*, 498–512.

Singh, N. N., & Beale, I. L. (1986). Learning disabilities: psychological therapies. In J. L. Matson (Ed.), *Treating childhood and adolescent psychopathology*. New York: Plenum.

Sohlberg, M. M., & Mateer, C. A. (1987). Effectiveness of an attention-training program. *Journal of Clinical and Experimental Neuropsychology*, *9*, 117–130.

Stokes, T. F., & Baer, D. M. (1977). An implicit technology of generalization. *Journal of Applied Behavior Analysis*, *10*, 349–367.

Strauss, A. A., & Lehtinen, L. E. (1947). *Psychopathology and education of the brain-injured child*. New York: Grune & Stratton.

Swanson, H. L. (1983). A developmental study of vigilance in learning disabled and nondisabled children. *Journal of Abnormal Child Psychology*, *11*, 415–429.

Tarver, S. G., & Dawson, M. M. (1978). Modality preference and the teaching of reading: A review. *Journal of Learning Disabilities*, *11*, 17–29.

Torgesen, J. K. (1979). What shall we do with psychological processes? *Journal of Learning Disabilities*, *12*, 16–23.

Torgesen, J. K. (1985). Memory processes in reading disabled children. *Journal of Learning Disabilities*, *18*, 350–357.

Torgesen, J. K., & Goldman, T. (1977). Verbal rehearsal and short-term memory in reading-disabled children. *Child Development*, *48*, 56–60.

Torgesen, J. K., & Houck, D. G. (1980). Processing deficiencies of learning-disabled children who perform poorly on the digit span test. *Journal of Educational Psychology*, *72*, 141–160.

Trexler, L. E. (1982). *Cognitive rehabilitation*. New York: Plenum Press.

Tulving, E. (1972). Episodic and semantic memory. In E. Tulving & W. Donaldson (Ed.), *Organization of memory*. New York: Academic Press.

Tulving, E., & Thomson, D. M. (1973). Encoding specificity and retrieval processes in episodic memory. *Psychological Review*, *80*, 352–373.

Ullman, D. G. (1974). Breadth of attention and retention in mentally retarded and intellectually average children. *American Journal of Mental Deficiency*, *78*, 640–648.

van Zomeren, A. H., & Brouwer, W. H. (1987). Head injury and concepts of attention. In H. S. Levin, J. Grafman, & H. M. Eisenberg (Eds.), *Neurobehavioral recovery from head injury* (pp. 398–415). New York: Oxford University Press.

van Zomeren, A. H., & Deelman, B. G. (1978). Long term recovery of visual reaction time after closed head injury. *Journal of Neurology, Neurosurgery and Psychiatry*, *41*, 452–457.

Wade, J., & Kass, C. E. (1987). Component deficit and academic remediation of learning disabilities. *Journal of Learning Disabilities*, *20*, 441–447.

Warrington, E. K., Logue, V., & Pratt, R. T. C. (1971). The anatomical localisation of selective impairment of auditory verbal short-term memory. *Neuropsychologia*, *9*, 377–387.

Wilson, B. A. (1987). *Rehabilitation of memory*. New York & London: The Guilford Press.

Wood, R. L. (1987). *Brain injury rehabilitation*. London: Croon Helm.

Wood, R. L., & Fussey, I. (1987). Computer-based cognitive training: A controlled study. *International Disabilities Studies*, *9*, 149–153.

Wyckoff, L. B., Jr. (1952). The role of observing responses in discrimination learning: Part 1. *Psychological Review*, *59*, 431–442.

Zangwill, O. L. (1966). The amnesic syndrome. In C. W. M. Whitty & O. L. Zangwill (Eds.), *Amnesia*. London: Butterworths.

Zeaman, D., & House, B. J. (1963). The role of attention in retardate discrimination learning. In N. R. Ellis (Ed.), *Handbook of mental deficiency* (pp. 159–223). New York: McGraw-Hill.

18
A Commentary on
Learning Disabilities

JOHN WILLS LLOYD

My colleagues and I sometimes quip that if one does not know the literature in an area, one must "go to school." We use the phrase as a euphemism for studying a topic intensively. Consistent with that use, I can say that this book *took* me to school.

In reading this volume, I have studied the work of an international group of scholars who have addressed questions about the nature, causes, assessment, and treatment of learning disabilities. I have read chapters that drew on educational, medical, psychological, and sociological perspectives. I have studied everything from beginning reading to adult social status, from curriculum-based assessment to positron emission tomography, from visual- and verbal-deficit hypotheses to multiple-allele theories, from metacognition to brain organization, from phonological mediation to shaping and chaining. After reading this book, I feel as if I am prepared for a doctoral examination in learning disabilities.

I first began working with children who would now be considered to have learning disabilities in 1966.[1] Since then I have devoted a great deal of my time and effort to teaching such children and youth, studying learning disabilities, and teaching about learning disabilities. Over the course of this time, I became familiar with many of the concepts presented by the authors of these chapters and feel conversant with most, if not all of them. But, after I finished reading this book, I had a new respect for the importance of learning disabilities, the knowledge that has been generated on topics relevant to learning disabilities, and the problems that face the field of learning disabilities.

---

[1] I correspond with one of the individuals whom I taught in the 1960s. Although she did not express much when I knew her then, she now recounts her life to me in terms that make the chapter about adult status by Reiff and P. Gerber (1992) even more poignant. I encourage people interested in the field of learning disabilities to seek out and talk with adults, with learning disabilities; the exercise is quite enlightening.

Not the least of these problems is the nebulous nature of the term *learning disabilities*.[2] Learning disabilities has different meanings to many, including the authors of chapters in this text. Depending on with whom one talks, the term learning disabilities may be any of the following:

a synonym for dyslexia
a label for students who have extremely low levels of achievement
a generic term for difficulties in acquiring or using new academic skills
a generic term for difficulties in acquiring or using any new knowledge or skill
a legal term used in the United States to refer to certain pupils with special education needs
a concept referring to extreme intraindividual differences.

Of course, no one of these phrases—nor others that have been offered—is absolutely correct. They each describe some facet of the phenomenon that we have come to call learning disabilities. And they also reflect the difficulty we have in defining this phenomenon.

In the remainder of this chapter, I take up several topics that were raised in the previous chapters. I have structured my discussion along slightly different lines than the organization of the text, focusing on selected issues that, in some cases, have been addressed by authors of chapters in different sections of the book. In my subsequent discussion, I consider the following topics: (a) defining learning disabilities, (b) identifying the causes of learning disabilities, (c) characterizing learning disabilities, (d) assessing learning disabilities, and (e) treating learning disabilities. Admittedly, the commentary that follows reflects personal biases. It omits some important topics and overemphasizes others. I regret these errors of omission and comission. I beg readers' indulgence, however, in considering the topics I discuss as the most important issues that the present volume elicited from me. Because it is central to many of the problems in learning disabilities, I address definition first.

Definition

My colleagues and I began an introductory text about learning disabilities with these words:

---

[2] In passing, I want to note that although Sam Kirk is rightfully given credit for popularizing the concept and the term *learning disabilities*, his use of it in 1963 was not its first use. H. E. Thelander, J. K. Phelps, and E. W. Kirk published a paper in 1958 entitled "Learning Disabilities Associated with Lessor Brain Damage."

Today people from nearly every walk of life recognize the term *learning disability*. Teachers, students, and parents use it frequently and with apparent understanding. . . . Although the term has gained almost universal acceptance among educators and the general public in the United States and many foreign countries since its inception in the early 1960s, the precise definition of learning disability is still being debated. Ironically, though even the illiterate student of education is likely to know the term, even the most literate scholar is likely to have difficulty explaining exactly what a learning disability is. (Hallahan, Kauffman, & Lloyd, 1985, p. 2)

As Kavale and Forness (1992) and Short, Schatschneider, and Friebert (1992) recount, there have been many alternative definitions proposed over the years. Nevertheless, in the United States, we still have an administrative and legal definition of learning disabilities that is open to interpretation and criticism. I suspect that we shall not have a more precise definition of this concept until we have approached resolution of issues about (a) performance characteristics of individuals with learning disabilities, (b) subtypes of these individuals, and (c) causes of learning disabilities.

Certainly, one of the central notions of learning disabilities is the idea that these individuals display a discrepancy between ability and achievement. Kavale and Forness (1992) and Siegel and Metsala (1992) doubt the utility of including the concept of discrepancy in definitions of learning disabilities. As presented here and elsewhere (e.g., Siegel, 1989), this argument rests in large part on problems with tests—particularly the measurement aspects of intelligence and achievement tests, and their relationship to reading—especially to phonological processing.

Kavale and Forness (1992) contend that the problem with discrepancy is not just psychometric but also conceptual. They say that discrepancy is tied too closely to underachievement and, although underachievement is a necessary condition for identification as having learning disabilities, it is not sufficient. Kavale and Forness suggest that other factors are necessary for an appropriate diagnosis of learning disabilities.

I, too, have reservations about the utility of IQ, standardized tests, and discrepancy formulae (Lloyd, Sabatino, Miller, & Miller, 1978), but I hesitate to discard the *concept* of a discrepancy between ability and achievement. I think that the difficulties with the concept of discrepancy identified by Kavale and Forness (1992) lie in the application of the concept, not the concept itself.

The concept of discrepancy does not have to refer solely to intelligence and achievement; it may also be applicable to intraindividual differences between aspects of linguistic performance, social behavior, and other domains relevant to learning disabilities. Bateman (1989) contended that discrepancy was, after all, a phrase she and others originally used as a means of conveying the concept that these pupils did not perform at the level of which they seemed capable. Her comments suggest that our predecessors' use of the term was much more informal and flexible than our recent use of it.

Researchers, however, have substantial need for precision in definition, as pointed out by many of the authors in this volume. This holds regardless of whether they are concerned with psychological (e.g, Solman & Stanovich, 1992), psychosocial (e.g., Pearl, 1992), pharmacological (Aman & Rojahn, 1992), genetic (Stevenson, 1992), or other aspects of learning disabilities. Among their myriad effects, inadequately defined samples (a) obfuscate differences between groups, (b) mitigate the chances of replications, (c) cloud interpretation of results, and (d) impede generalization of results. These sorts of problems have been well documented in learning disabilities and in the mid- and late 1970s they led to discussions of a system of marker variables (Keogh, Major, Reid, Gandara, & Omari, 1978; Keogh, Major-Kingsley, Omari-Gordon, & Reid, 1982).

Keogh reminded us that we must discriminate between classification and identification. "The development of a comprehensive and useful classification system is a long-range goal. Meanwhile, pupils with problems in schools need to be identified, as they require and deserve appropriate services" (1987, p. 7). Increased precision in definition probably would be of greater benefit to researchers and school administrators than to practitioners and almost certainly would be of greater benefit to these groups than to individuals with learning disabilities. Despite the outcry about increases in the proportion of pupils served in United States learning disabilities programs (some of which Kavale & Forness, 1992, recount), I am as convinced now as I was a decade ago (Lloyd, Hallahan, & Kauffman, 1980) that we need a loose, flexible educational administrative definition of learning disabilities so that we can make case-by-case decisions and ensure that pupils who need services receive those services.

Researchers, in contrast, must take it upon themselves to obviate difficulties such as those alluded to previously. The task here is one of using classifications that facilitate the accretion of integrated knowledge. Probably the best means to accomplish this is to establish a grass-roots movement among researchers that requires us to provide extensive and substantive information about participants in studies.[3] Given such information, we will be able to compare samples on empirical bases rather than bemoaning the incomparability of administratively classified individuals.

---

[3] We can only hope that financial supporters of research will agree to the additional expense such efforts (and other efforts I discuss later) will require.

One of the most divisive aspects of the definition of learning disabilities has been the matter of causes, particularly presumed neurological causes. In the next section, I turn to this topic.

Causes

In the educational arena, authorities have offered diverse causes for learning disabilities. Although some of their champions may have contended that the proposed factors were correlates rather than causes, psychological factors such as perceptual problems and biological factors such as minimal brain dysfunction occupied the center of the stage in dramas about causes of learning disabilities.

The psychological deficits that were thought to be central to learning disabilities in the earlier history of the field—generally known as process deficits—included problems with visual perception, auditory perception, the processing of information (before the current use of the phrase *information processing*), and so forth. Kavale and Forness (1992) recounted the influence of these ideas on the field.

Few would likely recommend a revival of the visual–perceptual hypotheses of the 1960s and 1970s, but Lovegrove (1992) challenged the widely held idea that a visual-deficit hypothesis was mistaken (Vellutino, 1979, 1987). Lovegrove (1992) recounts data showing differences between children with and without reading disabilities on visual processing tasks and thereby questions complete rejection of the possibility that visual deficits contribute to reading problems. And Beale and Tippett (1992) consider such processes as attention and memory that are more consonant with contemporary views of information processing than the perceptual processes and modalities that dominated our thinking in the 1960s and 1970s.

Some authors (Hulme & Snowling, 1992; Larson & M. Gerber, 1992; Solman & Stanovich, 1992), however, discuss more currently popular information processing problems in a manner that suggests a causal role for these variables. I am not moved to draw detailed comparisons between these variables and those that were popular during the 1960s and 1970s, although Kauffman and Hallahan (1979) presciently identified the potential pitfall of elevating such variables to a status similar to that occupied by visual perception and psycholinguistic processes. But, I want to identify what seems to me to be an essential conflict between this view and the perspective offered by authorities with a more biological orientation (e.g., Willis, Hooper, & Stone, 1992). If the source of the performance deficits that we call learning disabilities is in the psychological domain (viz., metacognition), then it is essentially a matter of learning. To the extent that a computer science analogy is informative, consider this: Would one reasonably search for the source of a software problem (e.g., metacognition deficit) by examining hardware (e.g., neurology)? If the answer is no, then I suppose psychologists should ignore biologists and vice versa. If the answer is yes, then we must postulate an anatomical seat for the executive. On its face, I find each of these possibilities untenable.

Of course, there is another possibility, one that I find much more viable. It is that we must begin to consider the cause of learning disabilities from a multifactoral perspective. Perhaps no one variable in and of itself is powerful enough to cause learning disabilities, but each of a host of variables is related to learning disabilities. The effects of several variables can combine to produce the decrements in performance that we observe in some individuals. The probability of an individual having learning disabilities is the joint probability of several of these variables. This idea—essentially based on conditional probabilities or Bayseian statistics—is illustrated in Table 18.1.

In their highly informative chapters on neuropsychology and genetics, Willis et al. (1992) and Stevenson (1992) remind us that we are unlikely to identify a unitary cause of learning disabilities. Indeed, this appropriately circumspect view is consistent with the heterogeneity of the population of individuals with learning disabilities (discussed in a subsequent section) and with earlier commentaries that have advocated searching for multifaceted syndromes in related areas such as dyslexia (e.g., Doehring, 1978). Even if we located a single allele or identified a specific neurological subsystem that was the source of some certain deficit in mathematics, for example, we would not have discovered the cause of learning disabilities. We would still need to identify presumably different causes for different phenotypes.

Furthermore, we might reasonably wonder about the relationship between such physical causes and educational treatments, as did Bateman

TABLE 18.1. Thinking about causes of learning disabilities as problems in conditional probability.

Given:
  Probability of learning disability = $P(LD) = X$
We can ask, what is:
  $P(LD/NI)$? i.e., what is the $P(LD)$ given that there are neurological impairments?
  $P(LD/MM)$? i.e., what is the $P(LD)$ given maladaptive metacognition?
  $P(LD/NI \text{ and } IT)$? i.e., what is the $P(LD)$ given neurological impairment and inadequate teaching?
  etc.
Then we can ask whether there are significant increments in prediction based on the conditional probabilities:
  Is $P(LD/NI) > P(LD)$?
  Is $P(LD/IT \text{ and } MM) > P(LD)$?
  etc.

(1973) and Bryan, Bay, Lopez-Reyna, and Donahue (1991). In a presentation to the New York Academy of Sciences, Bateman contended that medical classifications are irrelevant for educators. She noted that asking which educational procedures were most appropriate for individuals with minimal brain dysfunction was about as sensible as asking which antibiotics were most appropriate for pupils in the lowest reading group.

Almost certainly, we shall ultimately discover the causes of learning disabilities. At first, these probably will be based on subgroups of individuals with learning disabilities. Only much later, I suspect, will we be able to identify the causes of the learning disabilities of any one individual. While work on such fundamental questions continues, however, we must contend with the clinical need for appropriate treatment. At present, this must be based on the characteristics of individuals.

Characteristics

Along the path to establishing their theses, most chapters in this book provide extensive information about the characteristics of individuals with learning disabilities. Although there are many more topics that merit discussion, I shall comment on only two issues: heterogeneity and subtyping.

Heterogeneity

Chapter authors who did not mention the heterogeneity of the learning disabilities population were in the minority in this text. The diversity of characteristics of learning disabilities and, particularly, the inconsistency of characteristics across individuals with learning disabilities has clouded research and practice. As amply illustrated in this volume, some individuals have greater facility with, for example, understanding spoken language than they do with producing oral equivalents for written words. Others may share difficulties with understanding what they have read, but differ in how they approach social interactions. Still others may share a lack of success in social interactions but differ in arithmetic and reading performance.

Despite this diversity, I think it is safe to say that individuals with learning disabilities are no more diverse than other individuals. Surely, were we to measure the performance of a large sample of students not identified as having handicaps, we would find diverse levels of performance among them. Similarly, were we to measure a large sample of individuals identified as having mental retardation, we would find great diversity. Individuals with learning disabilities are no more wondrously unique than other people. What animates this field is a concept that can be traced back through Kirk's work on the Illinois Test of Psycholinguistic Abilities (Kirk, 1968) to Marion Monroe's work on diagnosis of reading problems (Kirk, 1976): *Individuals with learning disabilities have marked intraindividual differences.*

The approach to this diversity by learning disabilities clinicians has been to treat each individual as a unique case, an approach that has the benefit of permitting clinical flexibility but has the drawback of inhibiting the chances of finding subject-by-treatment interactions. For the present, we shall be well served if we continue to take advantage of this approach, however, even in fields as diverse as pharmacology (Aman & Rojahn, 1992) and education (Harris, Graham, & Pressley, 1992; Singh, Deitz, & Singh, 1992). In the absence of definitive nomothetic information, an idiographic approach that makes in-roads on individuals' learning disabilities is desirable. When we are able to identify subtypes of individuals with learning disabilities (Siegel & Metsala, 1992), then we shall have more choice in the matter. As a practical matter, we must treat students as individuals; as a conceptual matter, we need to understand subgroups of students with learning (or other) disabilities.

Subtypes

Research on subtypes seeks to identify homogeneous groups within the population of individuals who have learning disabilities. This area of research has developed rapidly since the 1960s (see Feagans, Short, & Meltzer, 1991; Hooper & Willis, 1989), basically following two divergent approaches, one using conceptually derived subtypes and the other using empirically derived subtypes (McKinney, 1988).

Siegel and Metsala (1992) advocate adopting a conceptually driven approach to subtyping research. Following this perspective, researchers who are interested in reading, as are Siegel and Metsala, might identify pupils with phonological deficits and compare them to pupils without such deficits. The results of such comparisons should tell us something about those students as well as something about the role of phonological processing in relation to the dependent variables assessed.

Torgesen, Rashotte, and Greenstein (1988) made valuable use of this approach in a series of studies of language comprehension skills among children who had extreme difficulty in memory. They compared pupils identified as having learning disabilities and deficits on a digit-span task to various other groups including, most importantly, other children with learning disabilities who did not have atypical scores on the digit-span task.

This deductive or top-down approach has the advantage of permitting researchers to focus closely on the characteristics of pupils who are believed to share specific deficits. But, the approach has at least one drawback, too. It can lead to subgroupings such as those of Boder (1971), which are based on questionable theory and classification schemes of unestablished trustworthiness. Extensive research on spelling performance (e.g., M. Gerber & Hall, 1987) indicates that such error patterns may simply reflect relatively greater or lesser competence in developing spelling skills.

The alternative approach—a more inductive, bottom-up tactic—is to assess the performance of a "heterogenous sample of individuals who vary both across and within a given set of attributes" (McKinney, 1988, p. 261) and submit the data to cluster analysis (either via Q-factor or cluster-analytic procedures). Despite the fact that such an approach may lack an explicit theoretical perspective, the literature resulting from this approach is yielding subgroups that show some consistency (see Lyon & Flynn, 1991; Willis & Hooper, 1989).

These two approaches to subtyping remind me of alternatives in the classification of behavior disorders. On one hand, behavior disorders (Cullinan, Epstein, & Lloyd, 1983) traditionally were classified according to psychoanalytic theory or what might be called *clinical-inductive* systems. On the other hand, such disorders might be classified "by measuring the behavior and occasionally other characteristics of many children in order to determine which characteristics *covary*" (Cullinan, Epstein, & Lloyd, 1983, p. 128; emphasis in original) or a *statistical-inductive* approach. The two main approaches to subtyping in learning disabilities seem congruent with these two approaches in classification of behavior disorders. What I find instructive is not so much that one may be preferred over another but that over time the categories identified by the two approaches to classifying behavior disorders have gradually become more similar. For example, broad-band classifications such as externalizing and internalizing (e.g., Achenbach & Edelbrock, 1978) are sufficiently like some traditional psychiatric nosologies, as reflected in DSM-III-R. Perhaps our approaches to classification of subtypes of learning disabilities will follow a similar pattern.

Assessment

Many of the problems in definition are probably related to difficulties in assessment (Swanson, 1991). Surely, learning disabilities have contributed greatly to the rise and growth of the testing industy. In earlier days and still today there is a tremendous emphasis on assessment in learning disabilities.

We need to think about the utility of some cherished measures such as IQ and achievement, as Kavale and Forness (1992) and Siegel and Metsala (1992) indicated. Of course, we cannot tolerate the use of instruments with inadequate psychometric characteristics. But, of greater importance, to what extent are these measures useful for either research or practice?

Elsewhere, I have contended that practice, at least, would be far better served by focusing assessment on matters that are directly related to instruction (Lloyd & Blandford, 1991). In that regard, the present volume offers Cipani and Morrow's (1992) discussion of assessment that is tied directly to intervention; their recommendations about assessment are eminently sensible. Clearly, practitioners should heed the recommendations of these authors and others (e.g., Howell & Moorehead, 1987) who have advocated that assessment for instruction move away from identifying types of learners according to patterns of scores on intelligence or personality tests and toward assessment of what individuals can and cannot do. From there it is only a short step to providing individualized programs based on the idiographic methods that have been developed to date.

In addition, we still need to think about diagnosing instruction. According to this notion, advanced by Engelmann, Granzin, and Severson (1979), we can best identify learners with atypical learning characteristics by systematically varying learning tasks so that learners cannot make correct responses without knowing the central concept or operation being assessed. If variations of tasks can be answered correctly by responding to other, noncentral aspects of presentations, then we only know that learners *might* fail the task if it was presented more cleanly. To design a clean assessment item, we must insure that there is only one reason that individuals might respond erroneously. Assessment for the purposes of identifying research samples and for the purposes of designing instruction would both benefit mightily from such diagnoses.

An important corollary of this notion was implicit in Larson and M. Gerber's (1992) summary for their chapter. They contended that by considering individuals with learning disabilities without also considering the individuals—teachers, researchers—with whom they interact, we ignore important parameters in the study of learning disabilities. Both our research and clinical understanding of learning disabilities would be enhanced by an ecological analysis of the phenomenon, an analysis that incorporates not only teachers and physical settings but includes other important variables, particularly peers (Pearl, 1992). When, where, and under what circumstances do problems or successes obtain?

In regard to assessment, I am again reminded of Keogh's (1987) advice that we must discriminate between classification and identification. In the area of assessment, however, we must neither let assessment slip into classification of individuals into groups (until research has shown us that we can identify subtypes reliably and that these subtypes are systematically related to interventions) nor confuse assessment for the purposes of identification with assessment for the purpose of program planning.

Treatments

Given the diverse and sometimes contradictory characteristics of individuals as having learning disabilities and the wide range of backgrounds among professionals with interest in the field, it is little wonder that treatments for learning disabilities have been controversial. None of the treatments discussed in this volume are narrow, faddish, or ill-conceived as were some earlier treatments proposed in the field.[4] Instead, we have thoughtful analyses of (a) the usefulness of the inactive learner hypothesis (Short et al., 1992), (b) issues in pharmacology (Aman & Rojahn, 1992), (c) behavioral interventions (Cipani & Morrow, 1992; Singh et al., 1991), (d) cognitive–behavioral approaches (Harris et al., 1992), (e) psychological processes such as attention and memory (Beale & Tippett, 1992), and (f) potential applications of computer technology (Karsh & Repp, 1992).

Important aspects of schooling have been addressed in different chapters. Although they come from separate sections of the text and have different foci, chapters have brought together perspectives on common topics. For example, several chapters have considered matters related to mathematics (Karsh & Repp, 1992; Singh et al., 1992). Others have addressed concerns about learning disabilities and social relations (Pearl, 1992; Reiff & P. Gerber, 1992). Of course, the largest number have addressed aspects of written language (Aman & Rojahn, 1992; Harris et al., 1992; Hulme & Snowling, 1992; Karsh & Repp, 1992; Lovegrove, 1992; Short et al., 1992; Siegel & Metsala, 1992; Singh et al., 1992; Solman & Stanovich, 1992).

As I am particularly fond of studies about interventions (e.g., Lloyd, 1988), I was especially concerned about the aspects of chapters that addressed treatments. The recommendations for remediation in the various chapters of this book are reasonable and they raise many interesting questions. However, I shall limit my comments here to only one topic, the need for research on coordinated, comprehensive treatments.

The learning disabilities field has developed a substantial literature about effective educational practices (see, e.g., Scruggs & Wong, 1990). But, as I think most of the investigators involved in such research would readily admit, we do not have a comprehensive model for treatment of learning disabilities. Instead, we have a host of interventions—many of which arise from perspectives also reflected in the chapters of this text—

---

[4] We are currently witnessing the onset of what appears to be a new intervention with characteristics similar to many of those that have preceded it. The December 1990 issue of the *Journal of Learning Disabilities* includes a special series of articles on the ideas about scoptopic sensitivity advanced by Helen Irlen and applications of these ideas (primarily use of colored lenses and colored plastic overlays for printed material).

that address specific aspects of the problems of individuals with learning disabilities. We have a mixed bag with only minimal information about how the contents of the bag may function together.

We need to begin developing an approach that reflects a broader conceptualization of the problems of individuals with learning disabilities. Such a conceptualization would necessarily draw from the broad range of disciplines and perspectives presented in this text. Instead of playing, educational interventions against medical treatments, for example, we need to analyze comprehensive therapy packages.

I am not calling for an atheoretical eclecticism. Instead, I suggest that we now have or are soon to develop therapies that address specific aspects of the problems individuals with learning disabilities experience. For example, the detailed work on using mnemonics with learning disabilities provided by Mastropieri, Scruggs, and their colleagues (e.g., Mastropieri & Fulk, 1990) illuminates a potent means for obviating the difficulties students with learning disabilities have with remembering factual information. We need to entertain the view that combinations of these therapies may be appropriate for some of these individuals.

In extreme cases, the package that I see being needed may be a megatherapy composed of, for example, Direct Instruction (Engelman, Becker, Carnine, & Gersten, 1988) in basic academic skills such as decoding, cognitive–behavioral training in self-management of attention (e.g., Lloyd & Landrum, 1990) and production and comprehension of written materials (e.g., Harris et al., 1992), psychostimulant therapy for enhancement of teachability as seen by educators and parents (Aman & Rojahn, 1992), adoption of computer-assisted instructional presentation formats to facilitate needed practice (Karsh & Repp, 1992), and so on. In addition to variations on this idea depending on the individual needs of learners, we may need to explore some other potential components (e.g., crisis counseling for both children and parents).

In less extreme cases, only one or two certain components of a package may be needed. In either case, it is clear that we must develop a way to determine which set of interventions is appropriate for whom. This is no simple task. It will require careful and broadly conceived research.

As developed in greater detail elsewhere with regard to emotional or behavioral disorders (Hill, in press), to evaluate such interventions, we must expand our perspective. Research in learning disabilities will stagnate without emphasis on (a) early identification, (b) longitudinal outcomes, (c) individualization, (d) multidisciplinary collaboration, and (e) broad-based analysis of effects.

Conclusions

Consistent with the nature of most science, the discovery and understanding of new information usually raises more questions than it provides answers. The authors of these diverse chapters have contributed the basis for a much more thorough and trustworthy understanding of learning disabilities. Here we have information that has been interpreted by authorities in biological, psychological, and educational fields. And, with the enhanced understanding of learning disabilities that these experts have provided come additional or new questions.

Not the least of these questions is one about how we might integrate our knowledge into a functioning guide for further research and more beneficial practice. I think that this problem suggests the need for development of comprehensive theories of learning disabilities, theories that contrast with and encourage refinement of each other.

A working theory of learning disabilities must take into account the heterogeneity of the population, the diversity of interventions, and the potentially conditional nature of any relationships between individuals or groups of individuals and treatments or classes of treatments. We still assume that there are features of some learners that predispose them to benefiting from some different kinds of instruction. (Why else identify them as have learning disabilities? Why not simply provide them with the same instruction they would receive otherwise?) But such a theory must also account for the observation that the behavior (academic, social, or both; the phenotype) of individuals we identify as have learning disabilities is inconsistent with their expected performance.

In his delightful opening paragraph for an article, Stanovich (1989) noted the field of learning disabilities has been beset with problems:

The field of learning disabilities (LD) has a checkered history that is littered with contention, false starts, fads, dead ends, pseudoscience, and just a little bit of hard-won progress. It seems as though the field is constantly getting into scrapes, is always on probation, is never really secure. Why is this? Surely one of the reasons is that, when borrowing ideas from allied fields such as developmental psychology, neuropsychology, and cognitive psychology, the LD field has displayed a remarkable propensity to latch on to concepts that are tenuous and controversial. Examples of this tendency are legion, ranging from visual process training to the concept of minimal brain damage. The LD field seems addicted to living dangerously. (p. 487)

On the whole, the authors of these chapters do not live dangerously; they are appropriately circumspect. They eschew excessive advocacy and assault; instead they offer informed and enlightening discussion of the status of disciplines contributing to our understanding of learning disabilities. From it, I can take hope that we shall solve some of the particularly intriguing puzzles in learning disabilities and that we shall develop the kinds of comprehensive and effective interventions that will serve those who have learning disabilities.

Acknowledgments. Acknowledging people to whom I owe a debt for my thinking about this chapter would make for wearisome reading, so I limit myself here to only a few of the deserving. Obviously, I owe a great obligation to Barb Bateman, from whom I learned a great deal about learning disabilities as a graduate student and by whom I continue to be influenced. I also want to acknowledge the more recent influences of my colleague, Dan Hallahan, whose quips, comments, and questions have encouraged what I hope can pass for growth in my understanding of learning disabilities. Also, I want to acknowledge the benefits of conversations about many of these topics with Mel Tankersley and Bets Talbott. Of course, the usual disclaimer applies: Barb, Dan, Mel, and Bets get the credit for any perspicacious tidbits and I alone get responsibility for each and every mistake. Woe is me.

References

Achenbach, T. M., & Edelbrock, C. S. (1978). The classification of child psychopathology: A review and analysis of empirical efforts. *Psychological Bulletin, 85*, 1275–1301.

Aman, M. G., & Rojahn, J. (1992). Pharmacological intervention. In N. N. Singh & I. L. Beale (Eds.), *Learning disabilities: Nature, theory, and treatment* (pp. 478–525). New York: Springer-Verlag.

Bateman, B. (1973). Educational implications of minimal brain dysfunction. In F. F. de la Cruz, B. H. Box, & R. H. Roberts (Eds.), *Minimal brain dysfunction* (Vol. 205). New York: Annals of the New York Academy of Sciences.

Bateman, B. (1989). *Hot spots in special education law*. Presentation at the University of Virginia Curry School of Education, Charlottesville, VA.

Beale, I. L., & Tippett, L. J. (1992). Remediation of phonological process deficits in learning disabilities. In N. N. Singh & I. L. Beale (Eds.), *Learning disabilities: Nature, theory, and treatment* (pp. 526–568). New York: Springer-Verlag.

Boder, E. (1971). Developmental dyslexia: A diagnostic screening procedure based on three characteristics patters of reading and spelling. In B. Bateman (Ed.), *Learning disorders: Reading* (Vol. 4, pp. 297–342). Seattle: Special Child Publications.

Bryan, T., Bay, M., Lopez-Reyna, N., & Donahue, M. (1991). Characteristics of students with learning disabilities: A summary of the extant data base and its implications for educational programs. In J. W. Lloyd, N. N. Singh, & A. C. Repp (Eds.), *The regular education initiative: Alternative perspectives on concepts, issues, and models* (pp. 113–131). Sycamore, IL: Sycamore Press.

Cipani, E., & Morrow, R. D. (1992). Educational assessment. In N. N. Singh & I. L. Beale (Eds.), *Learning disabilities: Nature, theory, and treatment* (pp. 61–95). New York: Springer-Verlag.

Cullinan, D., Epstein, M. H., & Lloyd, J. W. (1983). *Behavior disorders of children and adolescents*. Englewood Cliffs, NJ: Prentice-Hall.

Doehring, F. H. (1978). The tangled web of behavioral research on developmental dyslexia. In A. L. Benton & D. Pearl (Eds.), *Dyslexia: An appraisal of current knowledge* (pp. 123–135). New York: Oxford.

Engelmann, S., Becker, W. C., Carnine, D., & Gersten, R. (1988). The Direct Instruction Follow Through Model: Design and outcomes. *Education and Treatment of Children, 11*, 303–317.

Engelmann, S., Granzin, A., & Severson, H. (1979). Diagnosing instruction. *Journal of Special Education*, *13*, 355–363.

Feagans, L. V., Short, E. J., & Meltzer, L. N. (Eds.), (1991). *Subtypes of learning disabilities: Theoretical perspectives and research*. Hillsdale, NJ: Erlbaum.

Gerber, M. M., & Hall, R. J. (1987). Information processing approaches to studying spelling deficiencies. *Journal of Learning Disabilities*, *20*, 34–42.

Hallahan, D. P., & Cruickshank, W. M. (1973). *Psychoeducational foundations of learning disabilities*. Englewood Cilffs, NJ: Prentice-Hall.

Hallahan, D. P., Kauffman, J. M., & Lloyd, J. W. (1985). *Introduction to learning disabilities* (2nd ed.). Englewood Cliffs, NJ: Prentice–Hall.

Harris, K. R., Graham, S., & Pressley, M. (1992). Cognitive-behavioral approaches in reading and written language: Developing self-regulated learners. In N. N. Singh & I. L. Beale (Eds.) *Learning disabilities: Nature, theory, and treatment* (pp. 415–451). New York: Springer-Verlag.

Hill, P. C. (in press). Problems and promises in special education and related services for children and youth with emotional or behavioral disorders. *Behavioral Disorders*.

Hooper, S. R., & Willis, W. G. (1989). *Learning disability subtyping: Neuropsychological foundations, conceptual models, and issues in clinical differentiation*. New York: Springer-Verlag.

Howell, K. W., & Moorehead, M. K. (1987). *Curriculum-based evaluation for special and remedial education: A handbook for deciding what to teach*. Columbus, OH: Merrill.

Hulme, C., & Snowling, M. (1992). Phonolgical deficits in dyslexia: A "sound" reappraisal of the verbal deficit hypothesis. In N. N. Singh & I. L. Beale (Eds.), *Learning disabilities: Nature, theory, and treatment* (pp. 270–301). New York: Springer-Verlag.

Karsh, K. G., & Repp, A. C. (1992). Computer-assisted instruction: Potential and reality. In N. N. Singh & I. L. Beale (Eds.), *Learning disabilities: Nature, theory, and treatment* (pp. 452–477). New York: Springer-Verlag.

Kauffman, J. M., & Hallahan, D. P. (1979). Learning disability and hyperactivity (with comments on minimal brain dysfunction). In B. B. Lahey & A. E. Kazdin (Eds.), *Advances in clinical child psychology* (Vol. 2, pp. 71–105). New York: Plenum.

Kavale, K., & Forness, S. (1992). History, definition, and diagnosis. In N. N. Singh & I. L. Beale (Eds.), *Learning disabilities: Nature, theory, and treatment* (pp. 3–43). New York: Springer-Verlag.

Keogh, B. K. (1987). Learning disabilities: In defense of a construct. *Learning Disability Research*, *3*(1), 4–9.

Keogh, B. K., Major, S. M., Reid, H. P., Gandara, P., & Omari, H. (1978). Marker variables: A search for comparability and generalizability in the field of learning disabilities. *Learning Disability Quarterly*, *1*(3), 5–11.

Keogh, B. K., Major-Kingsley, S., Omari-Gordon, H., & Reid, H. (1982). *A System of marker variables for the field of learning disabilities*. Syracuse, NY: Syracuse University Press.

Kirk, S. A. (1968). Illinois Test of Psycholinguistic Abilities: Its origin and implications. In J. Hellmuth (Ed.), *Learning disorders* (Vol. 3, pp. 395–427). Seattle: Special Child Press.

Kirk, S. A. (1976). Samuel A. Kirk. In J. M. Kauffman & D. P. Hallahan (Eds.), *Teaching children with learning disabilities: Personal perspectives* (pp. 239–269). Columbus, OH: Merrill.

Larson, K. A., & Gerber, M. M. (1992). Metacognition and learning disabilities. In N. N. Singh & I. L. Beale (Eds.), *Learning disabilities: Nature, theory, and treatment* (pp. 126–169). New York: Springer-Verlag.

Lloyd, J. W. (1988). Direct academic interventions in learning disabilities. In M. C. Wang, M. C. Reynolds, & H. J. Walberg (Eds.), *Handbook of special education: Research and practice. Vol. 2. Mildly handicapped conditions* (pp. 345–366). London: Pergamon.

Lloyd, J. W., & Blandford, B. J. (1991). Assessment for instruction. In H. L. Swanson (Ed.), *Handbook on the assessment of learning disabilities: Theory, research, and practice* (pp. 45–58). Austin, TX: Pro-Ed.

Lloyd, J., Hallahan, D. P., & Kauffman, J. M. (1980). Learning disabilities: A review of selected topics. In L. Mann & D. A. Sabatino (Eds.), *Fourth review of special education* (pp. 35–60). New York: Grune & Stratton.

Lloyd, J. W., & Landrum, T. J. (1990). Self-recording of attending to task: Treatment components and generalization of effects. In T. E. Scruggs & B. Y. L. Wong (Eds.), *Intervention research in learning disabilities* (pp. 235–262). New York: Springer-Verlag.

Lloyd, J., Sabatino, D., Miller, T., & Miller, S. (1978). Proposed federal guidelines: Some open questions. *Journal of Learning Disabilities, 11*, 655–657.

Lovegrove, W. (1992). The visual deficit hypothesis. In N. N. Singh & I. L. Beale (Eds.), *Learning disabilities: Nature, theory, and treatment* (pp. 246–269). New York: Springer-Verlag.

Lyon, G. R., & Flynn, J. M. (1991). Assessing subtypes of learning abilities. In H. L. Swanson (Ed.), *Handbook on the assessment of learning disabilities: Theory, research, and practice.* (pp. 59–74). Austin, TX: Pro-Ed.

Mastropieri, M., & Fulk, B. J. M. (1990). Enhancing academic performance with mnemonic instruction. In T. E. Scruggs & B. Y. L. Wong (Eds.), *Intervention research in learning disabilities* (pp. 102–121). New York: Springer-Verlag.

McKinney, J. D. (1988). Research on conceptually and empirically derived subtypes of special learning disabilities. In M. C. Wang, M. C. Reynolds, & H. J. Walberg (Eds.), *Handbook of special education: Research and practice. Vol. 2. Mildly handicapped conditions* (pp. 253–281). London: Pergamon.

Pearl, R. (1992). Psychosocial characteristics of learning disabled students. In N. N. Singh & I. L. Beale (Eds.), *Learning disabilities: Nature, theory, and treatment* (pp. 96–125). New York: Springer-Verlag.

Reiff, H. B., & Gerber, P. J. (1992). Adults with learning disabilities. In N. N. Singh & I. L. Beale (Eds.), *Learning disabilities: Nature, theory, and treatment* (pp. 170–198). New York: Springer-Verlag.

Scruggs, T. E., & Wong, B. Y. L. (Eds.). (1990). *Intervention research in learning disabilities.* New York: Springer-Verlag.

Short, E. J., Schatschneider, C. W., & Friebert, S. E. (1992). The inactive learner hypothesis: Myth or reality? In N. N. Singh & I. L. Beale (Eds.), *Learning disabilities: Nature, theory, and treatment* (pp. 302–351). New York: Springer-Verlag.

Siegel, L. S. (1989). IQ is irrelevant to the definition of learning disabilities. *Journal of Learning Disabilities, 22*, 469–478, 486.

Siegel, L. S., & Metsala, J. (1992). An alternative to the food processor approach to subtypes of learning disabilities. In N. N. Singh & I. L. Beale (Eds.), *Learning disabilities: Nature, theory, and treatment* (pp. 44–60). New York: Springer-Verlag.

Singh, N. N., Deitz, D. E. D., & Singh, J. (1992). Behavioral approaches. In N. N. Singh & I. L. Beale (Eds.), *Learning disabilities: Nature, theory, and treatment* (pp. 375–414). New York: Springer-Verlag.

Solman, R. T., & Stanovich, K. E. (1992). Information processing models. In N. N. Singh & I. L. Beale (Eds.), *Learning disabilities: Nature, theory, and treatment* (pp. 352–371). New York: Springer-Verlag.

Stanovich, K. E. (1989). Has the learning disabilities field lost its intelligence? *Journal of Learning disabilities, 22*, 487–492.

Stevenson, J. (1992). Genetics. In N. N. Singh & I. L. Beale (Eds.), *Learning disabilities: Nature, theory, and treatment* (pp. 327–351). New York: Springer-Verlag.

Swanson, H. L. (1991). Introduction: Issues in the assessment of learning disabilities. In H. L. Swanson (Ed.), *Handbook on the assessment of learning disabilities: Theory, research, and practice* (pp. 1–19). Austin, TX: Pro-Ed.

Thelander, H. E., Phelps, J. K., & Kirk, E. W. (1958). Learning disabilities associated with lesser brain damage. *Journal of Pediatrics, 53*, 405–409.

Torgesen, J. K., Rashotte, C. A., & Greenstein, J. (1988). Language comprehension in learning disabled children who perform poorly on memory span tasks. *Journal of Educational Psychology, 80*, 480–487.

Willis, W. G., Hooper, S. R., & Stone, B. H. (1992). Neuropsychological theories of learning disabilities. In N. N. Singh & I. L. Beale (Eds.), *Learning disabilities: Nature, theory, and treatment* (pp. 201–245). New York: Springer-Verlag.

Author Index

Subject Index